Hentsch / Rodenhausen / MacGreevy

EU Video Games Law

EU Video Games Law

A Handbook

by

Christian-Henner Hentsch
Anselm Rodenhausen
Dara MacGreevy

2026

BECK • HART • NOMOS

Published by
Nomos Verlagsgesellschaft mbH & Co. KG, Waldseestraße 3-5, 76530 Baden-Baden, Germany,
email: service@nomos.de

Co-published by
Verlag C.H.Beck GmbH & Co. KG, Wilhelmstraße 9, 80801 München, Germany,
email: bestellung@beck.de

and

Hart Publishing, Kemp House, Chawley Park, Cumnor Hill, Oxford, OX2 9PH, United Kingdom,
online at: www.hartpub.co.uk

Published in North America by Hart Publishing,
An Imprint of Bloomsbury Publishing 1385 Broadway, New York, NY 10018, USA
email: mail@hartpub.co.uk

ISBN 978 3 7560 0130 9 (NOMOS Print)
ISBN 978 3 7489 4737 0 (NOMOS ePDF)
ISBN 978 3 406 83323 6 (C.H.BECK)
ISBN 978 1 048 00304 8 (HART)

First Edition 2026

Foreword

For years, the games industry has been the most dynamically growing media industry. Games are now enjoyed by all age groups worldwide, and the social, cultural, and economic significance of computer and video games is increasing accordingly. This is accompanied by growing interest in the innovative business models, investment opportunities, and legal peculiarities of this international and originally digital industry. Regulation is also increasing in line with the importance of the industry, particularly in the areas of youth protection, data protection, and, above all, consumer protection. With the aim of completing the digital single market, the EU has already issued numerous directives and regulations that have largely harmonized the legal framework for games across Europe. To date, there is no scientific work that presents all European directives and regulations and there is eeven no handbook which provides compact and practical assistance for those working in games companies. This handbook is intended to fill this gap, following the example of the German handbook "Games und Recht" from 2023, while at the same time making it clear that games are already comprehensively regulated at EU level.

The handbook is a project of the diverse European games industry, which is represented in this work by the three editors via the European Federation Video Games Europe in collaboration with the Cologne Research Center for Media Law at the University of Applied Sciences in Cologne. Numerous leading managers and in-house lawyers from renowned European and international publishers and developers have contributed to the handbook, as have the most prominent games lawyers with European and international mandates and years of experience in this specific area of law, as well as association specialists and academics from relevant games studies in Europe. This means that not only legal and regulatory issues, but also many practical and economic aspects can be included in this handbook.

In terms of content, the handbook is divided into 41 chapters covering the exploitation cycle of a video game, starting with founding a games company, game development, then publishing and distribution, and finally the special frameworks for platforms and marketing. At the beginning of each main chapter, the economic fundamentals and prerequisites are explained and classified in a first subchapter. The following chapters comprehensively cover all legal areas of the respective exploitation stage. The handbook is written in a practical and solution-oriented manner so that it is suitable for use in the everyday work of companies and law firms. It is aimed at managing directors, in-house lawyers, youth protection officers, data protection officers, and other employees in the games industry, as well as anyone with a general interest in the fields of investment, law, science, and, above all, politics and regulation.

The work takes into account the law in force until February 2026. The upcoming new regulations on consumer protection and guidelines on youth protection are partly reflected, even if they are not yet applicable in practice. The many new EU legal acts on platform regulation and liability on the internet and in data protection, as well as the consultation on a Digital Fairness Act, have also been addressed and discussed in part. In addition, there are numerous other regulatory issues that may be addressed in the future. This shows how dynamic not only the games industry is, but also the legal framework for it. The handbook can therefore only provide a snapshot, but it has been deliberately written in a practical legal style so that it also offers solutions for the new regulations and will therefore remain sufficiently up to date in the coming years. In any case, a new edition will not be published until the end of the current legislative period at EU level.

We would like to thank the three publishers C.H.Beck, Nomos, and Hart and their prudent and always helpful staff, especially Dr. Marco Ganzhorn and Dr. Josef Herbasch (both from Nomos). We are very pleased that this publishing cooperation has made this EU project possible and has thus created a permanent scientific standard work for the international games industry. We are delighted with the outcome of this project and are, of course, always grateful for criticism and suggestions for the next edition.

In March 2026 *The Editors*

CONTENTS

Foreword V
Authors IX
Abbreviations XIII

CHAPTER 1
INTRODUCTION TO VIDEO GAMES

§ 1 The Importance of the Video Games Industry to Europe's economy 3
§ 2 The European Video Game Market, Industry and Players 4
§ 3 The Cultural Impact of Video Games 10
§ 4 EU Video Game Law 16

CHAPTER 2
FOUNDING A VIDEO GAME COMPANY

§ 5 Building a Game Studio in 2025: Purpose, Grit and the Founder's Reality 31
§ 6 Private Funding 37
§ 7 EU State Aid Law 50
§ 8 Public Funding 62
§ 9 Corporate Law Aspects in the Computer Games Industry in Europe 72
§ 10 Mergers and Acquisitions in the Video Game Industry: A Buyer's Guide 90
§ 11 Taxes in Video Games 105

CHAPTER 3
DEVELOPING A VIDEO GAME

§ 12 Video Games Development 119
§ 13 Copyright in and for Video Games 134
§ 14 EU Copyright Exceptions and Limitations 150
§ 15 EU Copyright Contract Law 163
§ 16 Music in Games 182
§ 17 EU Trademark Protection in and for Games 200

CHAPTER 4
LICENSING A VIDEO GAME

§ 18 Unpacking the European Video Game Publishing Landscape 215
§ 19 Publishing Contracts 227
§ 20 Game Localisation and Culturalisation: Navigating Creative Challenges on a Global Scale 243
§ 21 Greener Play: EU Environmental Law and Games 252
§ 22 Protection of Minors – PEGI 263
§ 23 Protection of Minors – USK 275

CHAPTER 5
RETAILING A VIDEO GAME

§ 24 Business Models of the Games Industry 293
§ 25 Consumer Contracts 305
§ 26 Digital Items – Consumer Protection 323
§ 27 Digital Items – Intellectual Property 337
§ 28 Enforcement 347
§ 29 Data Protection and Privacy in the Video Games Industry 362
§ 30 Value Added Tax 375

CHAPTER 6
DISTRIBUTING A VIDEO GAME

§ 31 Consoles and Platforms 393
§ 32 Platform Obligations 403
§ 33 Illegal Content and Activity on Game Platforms 419
§ 34 Technical Youth Protection on Platforms 437
§ 35 Antitrust Law and Related Regulation 451

CHAPTER 7
MARKETING A VIDEO GAME

§ 36 Gaming Marketing Law, Tools and Partnerships 465
§ 37 Advertisement Law in Games Marketing 483
§ 38 In-Game Advertising 495
§ 39 Influencer Marketing 508
§ 40 Guidelines and Licences for Let's-Plays 520
§ 41 Esports 530

Index 545

Authors

Jürgen Bänsch, Senior Director Policy & Public Affairs Video Games Europe, Brussels
Paragraph 29

Kai Bodensiek, Lawyer, Berlin
Paragraph 40

Florent Boisneault, Ubisoft, Director Legal
Paragraph 16

Dirk Bosmans, Pan-European Game Information (PEGI), Brussels
Paragraph 22

Guillaume Croisant, Lawyer and ESG Lecturer, Brussels
Paragraph 21

Isabel Davies, Lawyer, London
Paragraphs 26, 27

Gaetano Dimita, Dr., Queen Mary University of London
Paragraph 24

Andrea Dufaure, Lawyer, Paris
Paragraph 17

Willy Duhen, Dr., Senior Director Legal Activision Blizzard King, London
Paragraph 38

Kate Edwards, CEO and Principal Consultant, Geogrify, Seattle
Paragraph 20

Konstantin Ewald, Lawyer, Cologne
Paragraph 25

Jan-Peter Ewert, Dr., Lawyer, General Counsel Valve GmbH, Hamburg
Paragraphs 26, 27

Felix Falk, CEO German Games Industry Association (game), Berlin
Paragraph 3

Thomas Fischer, MBA (Columbia), Associate General Counsel, PLAION, Munich
Paragraph 10

Emanuele Fava, In-house Lawyer, Activision Blizzard King, London
Paragraph 39

Julia Foguel, Pan-European Game Information (PEGI), Brussels
Paragraph 22

Manuel Fragoso Mendes, Senior Manager Legal and Policy Video Games Europe, Brussels
Paragraph 21

Laura Godfrin, Lawyer, Paris
Paragraph 39

Hans-Martin Grambeck, Dr., Tax consultant, Norderstedt
Paragraph 30

Virginie Gringarten, Ubisoft, Vice President Legal
Paragraph 12

Christian-Henner Hentsch, Prof. Dr., Cologne Research Center for Media Law, TH Köln; Director Legal & Regulatory Affiars, game; MD VHG – Verwertungsgesellschaft für die Hersteller von Games, Cologne/Berlin
Paragraphs 4, 40

Felix Hilgert, Lawyer, San Francisco
Paragraph 34

Jari-Pekka Kaleva, Managing Director European Games Developer Federation (EGDF), Helsinki
Paragraph 8

Jakub Kubalski, Partner at SSW Law & Beyond, Video Games Association Poland (SPiDOR), Warsaw
Paragraph 37

Hendrik Lesser, President European Games Developer Federation (EGDF), CEO remote control productions GmbH, Munich
Paragraph 5

Peter Lewin, Lawyer, London
Paragraph 19

Simon Little, CEO Video Games Europe, Brussels
Paragraph 2

Andreas Lober, Dr., Lawyer, Frankfurt
Paragraph 32

Michaela MacDonald, Queen Mary University of London
Paragraph 24

Dara MacGreevy, Legal Consultant, Video Games Europe, Dublin
Paragraph 13

Jean-Sébastien Mariez, Lawyer, Paris
Paragraph 39

Clemens Mayer-Wegelin, LL.M., Lawyer, Specialist Lawyer for Information Technology Law, European General Counsel – Senior Director, Nintendo of Europe SE, Frankfurt a. M.
Paragraph 31

Sergi Mesonero, Head of Esports Video Games Europe, Brussels
Paragraph 41

Jean-Baptiste Morguet, Ubisoft, Director Legal
Paragraph 12

Ulf Morys, Ubisoft, Senior Director Accounting
Paragraph 11

Philippe Mouron, Professor, University Aix-Marseille, Aix-en-Provence
Paragraph 38

Claas Oehler, Dr., Lawyer and Notary, Berlin
Paragraph 9

Pieter Paepe, Lawyer, Brussels
Paragraph 7

Vikram J. Pandit, Lawyer, Brussels
Paragraph 35

Dan Penfold, Vice President Legal Affairs Warner Bros. Games, London
Paragraph 19

Lorenzo von Petersdorff, Legal Counsel & Deputy Managing Director Entertainment Software Self-Regulation Body (USK), Berlin
Paragraph 23

Anna Piechówka, Deputy General Counsel, CD PROJEKT RED, Warsaw
Paragraph 17

Christoph De Preter, Lawyer, Brussels
Paragraph 33

Andy Ramos Gil de la Haza, Partner at Pérez-Llorca, Madrid
Paragraph 41

Christian Rauda, Prof. Dr., Lawyer, Hamburg
Paragraphs 26, 27

Anselm Rodenhausen, Dr., MJur. (Oxford), Vice President Legal & Policy Video Games Europe, Brussels
Paragraphs 4, 35

Zoran Roso, ZR Consulting, Munich
Paragraph 18

Alexandre Rudoni, Lawyer, Paris
Paragraph 28

Emmanuelle Sarlangue, Lawyer, Paris
Paragraph 28

Elisabeth Secker, Managing Director Entertainment Software Self-Regulation Body (USK), Berlin
Paragraph 23

Ted Shapiro, Lawyer, Brussels
Paragraph 14

Martin Soppe, Dr., Lawyer, Hamburg
Paragraph 15

Per Strömbäck, Managing Director Dataspelsbranschen Swedish Games Industry, Stockholm
Paragraph 6

Daniel Trunk, LL.M., Lawyer, Frankfurt
Paragraph 32

Ingrid Vandenborre, Lawyer, Brussels
Paragraph 35

Tim Varney, Senior Corporate Counsel, Microsoft, London
Paragraph 36

David Verbruggen, General Manager Video Games Federation Belgium, Brussels
Paragraph 7

Hester Woodliffe, Senior Vice President Publishing International, Warner Bros. Games, London and Chair Video Games Europe
Paragraph 1

Cordula Zimmer, VP Legal Affairs Wooga, Berlin
Paragraph 25

Abbreviations

2FA	Two-factor authentication
AG	Advocate General
AG	Amtsgericht (German District Court)
AI	Artificial Intelligence
AI Act	Regulation (EU) 2024/1689 of the European Parliament and of the Council of 13.6.2024 laying down harmonised rules on artificial intelligence and amending Regulations (EC) No. 300/2008, (EU) No 167/2013, (EU) No. 168/2013, (EU) 2018/858, (EU) 2018/1139 and (EU) 2019/2144 and Directives 2014/90/EU, (EU) 2016/797 and (EU) 2020/1828 (Artificial Intelligence Act)
alt.	Alternative
API	Application Programming Interface
Art.	Article(s)
AVMSD	Audiovisual Media Services Directive
B2C	Business to customer
BeckRS	beck-online.RECHTSPRECHUNG (database)
BEREC	Body of European Regulators for Electronic Communications
BGB	Bürgerliches Gesetzbuch (German Civil Code)
BGBl	Bundesgesetzblatt (German Law Gazette)
BGH	Bundesgerichtshof (German Federal Court)
BMWK	Bundesministerium für Wirtschaft und Klimaschutz (German Federal Ministry for Economic Affairs and Climate Action)
BoR	Board of Regulators
BT	Bundestag (German Federal Parliament)
BT-Drs.	Bundestags-Drucksache (German Federal Parliament Document)
BVerfG	Bundesverfassungsgericht (German Federal Constitutional Court)
CC	Código Civil (Spanish Civil Code)
CCiv	Código Civil (Portuguese Civil Code)
CCPC	Irish Competition and Consumer Protection Commission
cf.	see, compare
CFR	Charter of Fundamental Rights of the European Union
Ch.	Chapter
CJEU	Court of Justice of the European Union
CMA	Competition and Markets Authority
CMLR	Common Market Law Review
CMO(s)	Collective Management Organisation(s)
Consumer rights directive	Directive 2011/83/EU of the European Parliament and of the Council of 25.10.2011 on consumer rights, amending Council Directive 93/13/EEC and Directive 1999/44/EC of the European Parliament and of the Council and repealing Council Directive 85/577/EEC and Directive 97/7/EC of the European Parliament and of the Council Text with EEA relevance
Copyight Directive	Directive 2001/29/EC of the European Parliament and of the Council of 22.5.2001 on the harmonisation of certain aspects of copyright and related rights in the information society (Infosoc)

CPI	Código da Propriedade Industrial (Portuguese Industrial Property Code)
CPS	core platform service
CR	Computer und Recht (journal)
Data Act	Regulation (EU) 2023/2854 of the European Parliament and of the Council of 13.12.2023 on harmonised rules on fair access to and use of data and amending Regulation
DCC	Dutch Civil Code
DCD	Directive (EU) 2019/770 of the European Parliament and of the Council of 20.5.2019 on certain aspects concerning contracts for the supply of digital content and digital services
DCCP	Dutch Code of Civil Procedure
DDG	Digitale Dienste Gesetz (German Digital Services Act)
DG CNECT	Directorate-General for Communications Networks, Content and Technology (European Commission)
DG COMP	Directorate-General for Competition (European Commission)
Dir.	Directive
DMA	Regulation (EU) 2022/1925 of the European Parliament and of the Council of 14.9.2022 on contestable and fair markets in the digital sector and amending Directives (EU) 2019/1937 and (EU) 2020/1828 (Digital Markets Act)
DSA	Regulation (EU) 2022/2065 of the European Parliament and of the Council of 19.10.2022 on a Single Market For Digital Services and amending Directive 2000/31/EC (Digital Services Act)
DSC	Digital Services Coordinator
DSM	Digital Single Market
DSM copyright directive	Directive (EU) 2019/790 of the European Parliament and of the Council of 17.4.2019 on copyright and related rights in the Digital Single Market and amending Directives 96/9/EC and 2001/29/EC
e.g.	for example
EBDS	European Board for Digital Services
EBIT	Earnings before interest and taxes
EC	European Commission
ECB	European Central Bank
EC Directive	Directive 2000/31/EC of the European Parliament and of the Council of 8.6.2000 on certain legal aspects of information society services, in particular electronic commerce, in the Internal Market
ECJ	European Court of Justice
ECLI	European Case Law Identifier
ECN	European Competition Network
EEA	European Economic Area which extends the EU's single market (free movement of goods, services, capital, people) to Iceland, Liechtenstein and Norway
EECCD	Directive (EU) 2018/1972 of the European Parliament and of the Council of 11 December 2018 establishing the European Electronic Communications Code
ed(s)	editor(s)
edn	Edition

EEC	European Economic Community
EGC	European General Court
ELR	European Law Review
ELSPA	UK Entertainment and Leisure Software Publishers Association
Enforcement Directive	Corrigendum to Directive 2004/48/EC of the European Parliament and of the Council of 29.4.2004 on the enforcement of intellectual property rights
EnWZ	Zeitschrift für das gesamte Recht der Energiewirtschaft (journal)
EP	European Parliament
ePrivacy Directive	Directive 2009/136/EC of the European Parliament and of the Council of 25.11.2009 amending Directive 2002/22/EC on universal service and users' rights relating to electronic communications networks and services, Directive 2002/58/EC concerning the processing of personal data and the protection of privacy in the electronic communications sector and Regulation (EC) No 2006/2004 on cooperation between national authorities responsible for the enforcement of consumer protection laws
ESRB	US Entertainment Software Rating Board
et al.	and others
et seq./et seqq.	Following
etc.	and so forth
EU	European Union
EUCO	European Council
EULA	End-User License Agreement
EUR	Euro(s)
FCJ	Federal Court of Justice
FCO	Federal Cartel Office (Bundeskartellamt)
fn.	Footnote
FordhamLRev	Fordham Law Review
FS	Festschrift (Liber Amicorum)
GAFMA/GAFAM	Google, Apple, Facebook, Microsoft and Amazon
GBER	Commission Regulation (EU) No 651/2014 of 17.6.2014 declaring certain categories of aid compatible with the internal market in application of Articles 107 and 108 of the Treaty Text with EEA relevance (General Block Exemption Regulation)
GC	General Court
GCVA	Games Consoles Voluntary Agreement
GDPR	Regulation (EU) 2016/679 of the European Parliament and of the Council of 27.4.2016 on the protection of natural persons with regard to the processing of personal data and on the free movement of such data, and repealing Directive 95/46/EC
Geo-blocking regulation	Regulation (EU) 2018/302 of the European Parliament and of the Council of 28.2.2018 on addressing unjustified geo-blocking and other forms of discrimination based on customers' nationality, place of residence or place of establishment within the internal market and amending Regulations (EC) No 2006/2004 and (EU) 2017/2394 and Directive 2009/22/EC
GG	Grundgesetz (German Constitution)
GLTR	Georgetown Law Technology Review
GRA	UK Games Rating Authority

GRUR	Gewerblicher Rechtsschutz und Urheberrecht (journal)
GRUR-Int	Gewerblicher Rechtsschutz und Urheberrecht – International (journal)
GRUR-Prax	Gewerblicher Rechtsschutz und Urheberrecht – Praxis im Immaterialgüter- und Wettbewerbsrecht (journal)
GSD	Game Sales Data (data platform)
GWB	Gesetz gegen Wettbewerbsbeschränkungen (German Competition Act)
GWR	Gesellschafts- und Wirtschaftsrecht (journal)
HdB	Handbuch (handbook)
i.e.	that is
IARC	International Age Rating Coalition (age rating body)
ibid.	ibidem – in the same place
ICC	Italian Civil Code
IIC	International Review of Intellectual Property and Competition Law
IMCO	Committee on Internal Market and Consumer Protection (European Parliament)
Infra	Below
IoT	Internet of Things
IP	Intellectual Property
IT	Information Technology
ITS	Implementing Technical Standards
IWRZ	Zeitschrift für Internationales Wirtschaftsrecht (journal)
JBL	Journal of Business Law
JECLAP	Journal of European Competition Law & Practice
JIPITEC	Journal of Intellectual Property, Information Technology and Electronic Commerce Law
JIPLP	Journal of Intellectual Property Law and Practice
JLE	Journal of Law and Economics
JLS	Journal of Legal Studies
JREG	Yale Journal on Regulation
K&R	Kommunikation & Recht (journal)
KidD	Stelle zur Durchsetzung von Kinderrechten in digitalen Diensten (German Centre for the enforcement of children's rights in digital services)
LEC	Ley de Enjuiciamiento Civil (Spanish Civil Procedural Act)
LG	Landgericht (German Regional Court)
LIBE	Committee on Civil Liberties, Justice and Home Affairs (European Parliament)
lit.	Littera
M&A	Mergers and acquisitions
MFN	Most Favored Nation (clause)
MIS	Management Information System
MLR	Modern Law Review
MMR	Multimedia und Recht (journal)
mn.	margin number(s)
MStV	Medienstaatsvertrag (German Interstate Media Treaty)
NetzDG	Netzwerkdurchsetzungsgesetz (German Network Enforcement Act)

NFT	Non fungible token
no.	number(s)
NYUJLL	NYU Journal of Law & Liberty
OECD	Organisation for Economic Co-operation and Development
OJ	Official Journal of the European Union
OLG	Oberlandesgericht (German Higher Regional Court)
Omnibus Directive	Directive (EU) 2019/2161 of the European Parliament and of the Council of 27.11.2019 amending Council Directive 93/13/EEC and Directives 98/6/EC, 2005/29/EC and 2011/83/EU of the European Parliament and of the Council as regards the better enforcement and modernisation of Union consumer protection rules
p./pp.	page(s)
para.	paragraph(s)
PEGI	Pan European Game Information (age-rating body)
PHi	Produkthaftpflicht international (journal)
PIMS	personal information management system
PRC	pratiques restrictives de concurrence (restrictive practices)
rec.	recital(s)
Reg.	Regulation(s)
RFI	request for information
SACEM	Société des Auteurs, Compositeurs et Éditeurs de Musique
Sec.	Section
sent.	sentence(s)
SME	Small and Medium-sized Enterprise, referring to independent businesses with <250 employees and specific revenue/asset limits, crucial to the EU economy
Software Directive	Directive 2009/24/EC of the European Parliament and of the Council of 23.4.2009 on the legal protection of computer programs
subpara.	subparagraph(s)
TCO	Regulation (EU) 2021/784 of the European Parliament and of the Council of 29.4.2021 on addressing the dissemination of terrorist content online
T&Cs	Terms and Conditions
TEU	Treaty on European Union
TFEU	Treaty on the Functioning of the European Union
TTBER	Commission Regulation (EU) No. 316/2014 of 21.3.2014 on the application of Art. 101(3) of the Treaty on the Functioning of the European Union to categories of technology transfer agreements (Technology Transfer Block Exemption Regulation)
UCPD	Directive 2005/29/EC of the European Parliament and of the Council of 11.5.2005 concerning unfair business-to-consumer commercial practices in the internal market and amending Council Directive 84/450/EEC, Directives 97/7/EC, 98/27/EC and 2002/65/EC of the European Parliament and of the Council and Regulation (EC) No. 2006/2004 of the European Parliament and of the Council ('Unfair Commercial Practices Directive')
UGC	User-generated content
UK	United Kingdom

UrhDaG	Urheberrechts-Diensteanbieter-Gesetz (German Copyright Service Provider Act)
UrhG	Urheberrechtsgesetz (German Act on Copyright and Related Rights)
US	United States of America
USD	US Dollar
USK	Unterhaltungssoftware Selbstkontrolle (age-rating body)
UWG	Gesetz gegen den unlauteren Wettbewerb (German Act Against Unfair Competition)
V	Versus
VBER	Commission Regulation (EU) 2022/720 of 10.5.2022 on the application of Article 101(3) of the Treaty on the Functioning of the European Union to categories of vertical agreements and concerted practices (Vertical Block Exemption Regulation)
VC	Venture Capital
VGE	Video Games Europe
VHG	Verwertungsgesellschaft für die Hersteller von Games (collecting society)
VLOP	Very Large Online Platform
VLOSE	Very Large Online Search Engine
Vol.	Volume
VR	Virtual reality
vs.	versus
WEEED	Waste Electronic and Electric Equipment Directive
YaleLJ	Yale Law Journal
ZD	Zeitschrift für Datenschutz (journal)
ZUM	Zeitschrift für Urheber- und Medienrecht (journal)

CHAPTER 1
INTRODUCTION TO VIDEO GAMES

§ 1
The Importance of the Video Games Industry to Europe's economy

I've had the pleasure of working in the video game industry for over 15 years and never has it been a more **vibrant, dynamic and growth sector** than right now, especially in Europe. Whether it's playing a mobile game on the morning commute, competing online with friends, or playing cooperatively with your family in your living room, video games have become an integral part of our daily lives and cultural experience. 1

Video games are a **significant contributor to Europe's economy**, generating substantial revenue and employment opportunities. In 2024, the industry generated 26.7 billion EUR across five key markets in Europe,[1] marking a steady 4 % growth from the previous year. This growth is powered by the skills and creativity of the 114,400 people[2] employed in the sector across Europe, stretching across the continent, with developers known for their rich storytelling, immersive world creation and technological innovation. 2

It's worth highlighting that the video game sector has many **unique characteristics and dynamics** compared to other entertainment sectors, bringing together the best in technology with incredible artistic creativity and talent. Leveraging advancements in digital technology and at the forefront of transferable technology like AR and VR, the European video games industry is important in driving innovation, skills and economic value that also act as enablers and growth drivers for many other European sectors such as education. 3

The industry is not only a major economic player but also **a cultural force**, with Europe being home to some of the most successful game studios globally, such as those behind *Minecraft*, *Assassin's Creed*, and *The Witcher*. These worlds, stories and characters combine to create immersive entertainment experiences that are enjoyed by millions of consumers across the globe. 4

The sector's continued growth, resilience and innovation make it a **vital part of Europe's economy**, driving technological advancements and cultural influence worldwide, and reinforcing its position as a major player on the world stage of video games. 5

This handbook will be a must read for video game companies that create, publish and/or distribute games in Europe. It will help to navigate the **raft of legislation that applies to video games companies**, ranging from intellectual property laws that underpin the creative work, its subsequent licencing, distribution and innovation, to consumer protection, competition law, data protection and much more. 6

---

[1] GameTrack data provided by IPSOS Mori published in Video Games Europe Key Facts Report 2024.
[2] EGDF & VGE 2022 European Video Games Industry Insight Report.

Hester Woodliffe

§ 2
The European Video Game Market, Industry and Players

A. What is the European industry? 4
The industry value chain 4
B. What is the market – methodology? 14
C. What is the market? 18
D. Who are the players? 28
I. Age demographics 31
II. Male/female split and average player age 33
III. Time spent playing 36

1 At the turn of the millennia when creative industries such as music and film were struggling with the 'digital transition' it used to be said that the video games industry was better positioned because it was 'born digital'. As the noughties came to a close, the industry started to fully **embrace its 'digital origin'**. In particular, digital distribution in the form of full game downloads started to take on an ever more important role. Together with digital distribution came other business evolutions, such as episodic games (which evolved into ongoing content updates rather than as TV-like 'episodes'), live service games, digital payments, freemium games and in-game purchases or micro transactions as well as advertising funded games.

2 This short chapter aims to give a condensed introduction to the European video game industry, **exploring the market as it currently stands** and the players that drive the market. Where possible, longer-term trends are presented rather than just a snapshot in time, with the aim of giving the reader some background to help put the rest of this handbook in context.

3 Unfortunately, there is **no standard industrial classification** for the video game industry which means government statistics are not available directly in a meaningful form. As a result, we generally rely on commercial data sources.

A. What is the European industry?

The industry value chain

4 Before looking at the numbers behind Europe's video games industry, it is worth briefly clarifying **the industry value chain**.

5 **Developers**: developers are the creative and technical talent who create the games. A developer may be owned by a publisher or be independent. Developers can range in size from a single person (who may subcontract elements) to several thousand staff.

6 **Publishers**: publishers finance, market and distribute games. Publishers may commission or publish games from internal studios or third-party developers. It is rare to have a pure developer or pure publisher; most are hybrids, doing a mix of both.

7 **Distributors**: distributors historically acted as a sales and logistics intermediary between publishers and retailers. Now that physical sales represent only 10 % of total revenue, the importance of distributors has diminished and is being replaced by digital storefronts and platform holders who perform the function of distributor/retailer in the digital space.

8 **Retailers**: traditionally, these were brick-and-mortar shops selling packaged games. Now, they includes digital storefronts, some of which are also platform holders.

Platform Holders: platform holders include companies that produce the hardware on which games are played but also the software ecosystem in which games exist. 9

Service Providers: the list of service providers to the industry is extensive and includes game technology-focused companies that produce games engines, middleware, cloud infrastructure and online services or specialise in elements of game production such as art, animation, modelling, audio production, localisation, translation and Q&A. There are also ecosystem support companies that focus on payment processing, advertising networks, analytics platforms or customer support. 10

Whilst it can be argued that the European video games industry lacks a high number of big-name platforms or publishers, it is very well represented in the mid-size publishers and development sector. The 2022 EDEF/Video Games Europe study counted **5,300 companies developing games in the EU.**[1] In terms of headcount, 114,400 people are directly employed in Europe (90,000 in the EU). 11

The top 5 video game development countries by headcount are UK, Poland, France, Germany, and Sweden. 12

Across Europe there is **no discernable preferred platform** for development, though some countries favour certain platforms such as mobile in Finland or VR in Belgium. Many developers create their game for multiple platforms which spreads development risk and reduces the average development cost per platform. 13

B. What is the market – methodology?

GameTrack[2] was the primary source used for market size and video game player behaviours. It is operated by Ipsos on behalf of Video Games Europe. It includes all devices that might be used for playing video games – from PCs and laptops, games consoles and portable games devices through smartphones and tablets as well as currently niche devices such as smart TVs. Similarly, this includes all games formats – from packaged (new, pre-owned/rental) to apps (paid and free) to online games (including downloads, subscriptions to multiplayer games, browser games, games on social network sites and on-demand/streaming subscriptions). 14

Central to GameTrack are the key metrics of **Reach** (who play games and how they play), **Game time** (how long they play for each week), **Volume** (the number of games being acquired (both paid and free)) and **Value** (the amount of money being spent on games). 15

Although GameTrack covers only the largest five European markets in UK, Germany, France, Spain and Italy, these represent around 78 % of the estimated total European market. Therefore, these five markets can be seen as a reasonable proxy for Europe as a whole. 16

To supplement GameTrack, data from **GSD (Games Sales Data)**[3] was sourced. GSD is another project of Video Games Europe operated by Sparkers S.A. which captures paid for, full games, sales data for both European retailers and digital platforms covering PC, PlayStation, Xbox and Nintendo platforms (so not smart devices). The GSD data referred to here focuses on the following 16 European countries: Austria, Belgium, Denmark, Finland, France, Germany, Ireland, Italy, the Netherlands, Norway, Poland, 17

---

[1] European Game Developers Federation (EGDF). 2022 European Video Games Industry. Available at: https://www.egdf.eu/2022-european-video-games-industry-insight-report/.

[2] GameTrack. Available at: https://www.videogameseurope.eu/data-key-facts/gametrack-info/.

[3] Games Sales Data (GSD). Available at: https://www.videogameseurope.eu/data-key-facts/games-sales-data/.

Portugal, Spain, Sweden, Switzerland, and the United Kingdom for which both retail and digital sales data exits.

C. What is the market?

18 In terms of the way games are sold, whilst app games for smart devices are only sold digitally, games for consoles and PCs are **sold in two main formats**: physical (or packaged) and digital. There are several key differences between packaged and digital games. Packaged games can, in practice, be resold on the second-hand market, whereas digital games typically cannot. Additionally, packaged games do not require (as much) storage space on the console or PC but do need physical storage space, while digital games are stored digitally, consuming limited hardware capacity, especially on consoles. Furthermore, digital games are downloaded to one device, restricting play to that specific device, whereas packaged games can be easily transported and used on different devices. An emerging third way for consumers to enjoy games is via on demand/streaming/subscription services. This has not yet met its initial promise but may yet gain traction as internet speeds continue to improve and connection latency drops.

19 Digitalisation has significantly impacted the games industry in several ways. Firstly, the **shift from physical to digital distribution** for both PCs and consoles has led to cost efficiencies in production and distribution, as digital copies eliminate the need for packaging, stock management, and distributors. Secondly, developers now have the **ability to self-publish** their games, allowing independent developers to access consumers directly through various platforms. Consequently, publishers can sell their games directly to consumers via their own retail platforms for PCs, bypassing third-party retailers.

20 As of 2024 the market for video games in the five markets covered by GameTrack was worth some 20.2 billion EUR. Since 2014 this represents a compound annual growth rate of over 9.5 %.

21 **MARKET VALUE SUMMARY BY DEVICE TYPES**

YEAR TO DATE (MILLIONS)

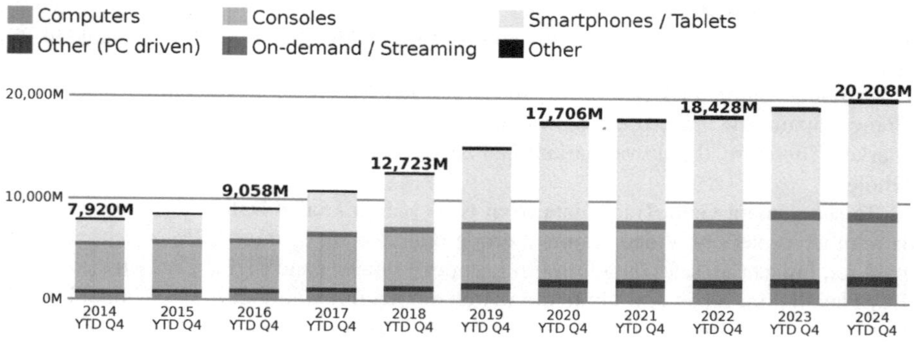

Figure 2.1

22 One can see within the chart that the majority of the growth since 2014 has come from apps on smart devices with secondary growth coming from consoles.

23 As far as game sales are concerned, the digitisation of games sold on the PC, PlayStation and Xbox formats have been steadily increasing with PC leading the way.

Share of digital and packaged unit sales by platform (16 European countries), 2019–2023, GSD. 24

25

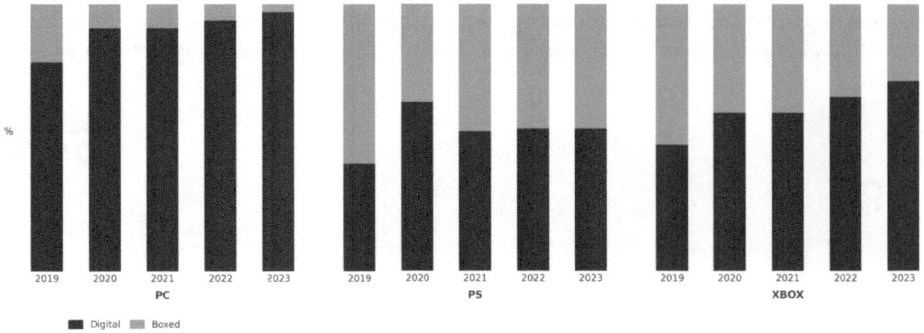

Figure 2.2

Looking more broadly at total software revenue (per GameTrack), one can see in the next chart that 90 % of the total software revenue is now digital with packaged games steadily dropping in relevance to represent only 10 % in 2024. App revenue represents 43 % of the total, with online (covering full game downloads, in-game purchases and digital subscriptions) accounting for 47 %. 26

27

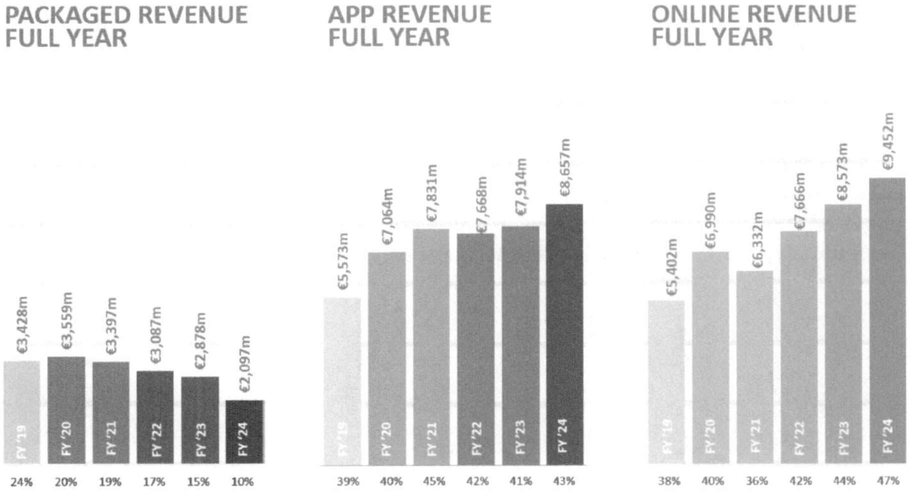

Figure 2.3

D. Who are the players?

28 Thanks to GameTrack we have a very detailed picture of game players.

29 Starting with the **Reach of Gaming**[4] we see that the percentage of the 6–64 population that play games (even occasionally) is slowly but steadily increasing to reach 54 % in 2024.

30

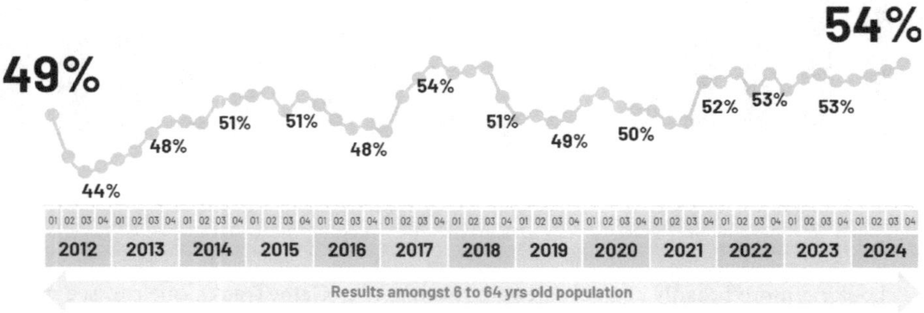

Figure 2.4

I. Age demographics

31 Although the majority of children play video games, the majority of game players are not children. 85 % of 11–14 year olds play which totals 11.8 million players whereas the 33 % of 45–64 year-olds totals 29.7 million players. In total 75 % of players are over the age of 18. This is important when discussing child protection issues around the use of video games (see Chapter 01 Europe's Video Game Players[5]). It is also important to remember that the visual language of video games often differs from 'classic' media, so one cannot assume that just because a game uses bright colours and a cartoon style that its target or main audience is children. If it is a puzzle or hidden object game, the most common player may be a female over the age of 45.

32

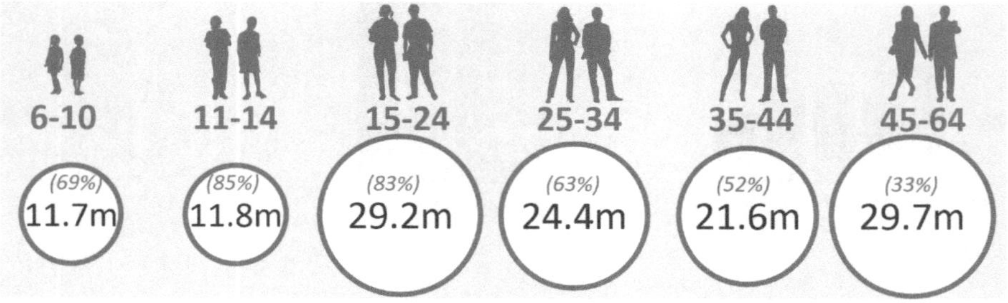

Figure 2.5 Age Breakdown of Players[6] across the GameTrack countries.

[4] Video Games Europe. All About Video Games – European Key Facts 2024. Available at: https://www.videogameseurope.eu/publication/2024-video-games-european-key-facts/.

[5] Ibid.

[6] Ibid.

II. Male/female split and average player age[7]

In aggregate, **male players slightly outnumber female players** (55 % vs. 45 %) but the detail shows this split varies by device type with smart devices being the closest to an equal split at 52 % male to 48 % female and PCs being the most male-dominated device with 63 % male vs. 36 % female. 33

34

Device Type	Male vs. Female	Mean Age
Smart Devices	52 % vs. 48 %	29.1
Console	58 % vs. 41 %	26.3
PC	63 % vs. 36 %	29.9
Total	55 % vs. 45 %	31.3

Table 2.1

Digging deeper into the demographics shows that it is the **45–64 age group that drives the female population higher** – 66 % of smart devices players are female in that age group. 35

III. Time spent playing[8]

The average time spent on games has, for the last 10 years, **remained fairly constant at around 9 hours per week**, a spike that occurred during the Covid lockdowns returned to the baseline once we regained our freedom. 36

37

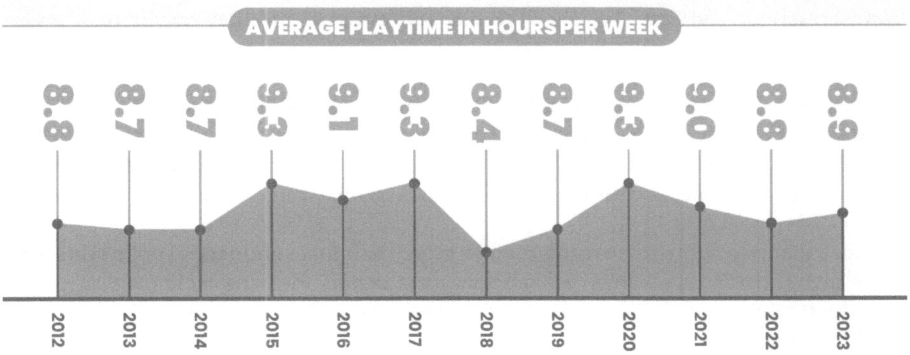

Figure 2.6

To put these 9 hours into context, the Thinkbox TV Viewing Report 2024[9] reports that the average time spent watching TV (of all kinds) is 23 hours per week and the average time spent on social media according to GlobalWebIndex GWI Report is just over 16.75 hours per week.[10] 38

[7] Video Games Europe, (no. 4).

[8] Ibid.

[9] ThinkBox. TV Viewing Report. Available at: https://www.thinkbox.tv/research/nickable-charts/viewing-and-audiences/tv-viewing-report.

[10] GWI. Social Media Trends: 2024 Global Report. Available at: https://www.gwi.com/reports/social.

§ 3
The Cultural Impact of Video Games

Bibliography: Bosman/van Wieringen/Archibald (eds), 'Video Games as Art. A Communication-Oriented Perspective on the Relationship between Gaming and the Art', 2023; Crückeberg/Heinicke/Kalbhenn/Lohbeck/Mohr/Landau-Donnelly (eds), 'Handbuch Kulturpolitik', 2024; Gibbons/Grimshaw-Aagaard (eds), 'The Oxford Handbook of Video Game Music and Sound', 2024; Köhler, 'A Short History of Modding', Klagenfurter Beiträge zur visuellen Kultur, vol. 5, 2017, 193-219; Rauscher, 'Spielerische Fiktionen. Transmediale Genrekonzepte in Videospielen', 2012; Robson/Tavinor (eds), 'The Aesthetics of Videogames', 2018; Schwingeler, 'Kunstwerk Computerspiel – Digitale Spiele als künstlerisches Material. Eine medientheoretische und bildwissenschaftliche Analyse', 2014; Schwingeler, 'Unspielbare Spiele – Künstlerische Computerspielmodifikationen im medientheoretischen Schwebezustand', Freyermuth/Gotto/Beil (eds), New Game Plus – Perspektiven der Game Studies, 2014, 219–245; Sharp, 'Works of Game: On the Aesthetics of Games and Art', MIT Press 2015; Spöhrer, (ed), 'Augenblick 87/88. Cinegames: Filmspiele und Spielfilme', 2023; Zimmermann/Falk, 'Handbuch Gameskultur', 2025.

A. Introduction 1
B. Cultural impact 4
C. The power of video games 7
D. The heartbeat of the cultural world 10
E. A unique culture 17

A. Introduction

1 Video games, which once met with scepticism and were regarded as a frivolous or even harmful pastime, have grown into a widely **accepted and respected part of the cultural family**. They are now played and enjoyed by people of all ages, genders and backgrounds. Like film, music or literature, video games span a wide range of forms, from the serious and educational to the silly and escapist, and they inspire both praise and criticism.

2 Engagement with video games is as **diverse** as the medium itself. Some players are passionate enthusiasts constantly seeking innovation and novelty, while others are casual players or prefer to watch professionals or streamers rather than playing themselves. And as with any other art form – be it abstract painting, avant-garde theatre or jazz – not everyone connects with the same works. Art, including video games, is always a matter of personal taste.

3 Video games deserve to be recognised as **more than just commercial entertainment**. Their digital nature gives them a head start in a rapidly evolving technological world, and their international production and appeal make them a truly global medium. Furthermore, video games increasingly interact with other art forms. Their music is performed in concert halls, their stories are adapted into blockbuster movies and their technology is used in cinema, theatre and media art. These cultural connections further affirm video games' rightful place in the broader artistic landscape.

B. Cultural impact

4 Video games are still a comparatively **young medium**, with origins dating back to the 1950s. In that era, young people interested in technology were able to experiment with the first computers at US universities. Video games only became accessible to a larger target group in the 1970s, thanks in large part to the release of the first video game console for home use, the 'Magnavox Odyssey', along with one of the most iconic video

game titles of all time: *'Pong'*. This marked the birth of video games as a mass medium. In the years that followed, more and more new platforms on which to play video games were added. Alongside video game consoles and computers, the smartphone developed into one of the most important gaming platforms. Today, almost every third person[1] on the planet plays computer and video games. The industry's annual sales revenue has long since surpassed 150 billion USD, overtaking all other areas of the cultural and creative industries. The success story of video games is unique and, given the constant innovations in the sector, far from over.

However, computer and video games have not just undergone remarkable technical 5
and economic development, but have also been **culturally influential** for many years. Characters like *Super Mario* and *Lara Croft* are familiar even to people who have never played video games themselves. Football stars celebrate their most important goals with dances from *'Fortnite'*[2] and Hollywood stars name their children after video game characters such as *Zelda*.[3] Major video game brands such as 'Assassin's Creed' and 'The Witcher' are just as much at home on the big screen or in the concert hall as they are on a PC or a game console. Various subcultures have also grown up around video games. Esports already reach millions of people worldwide. The best players in digital competition enjoy a level of fame among younger generations previously only attained by international sports icons. Not only are European teams such as Fnatic, Team Vitality and G2 Esports worth several hundred million euros,[4] they are also on a par with the world's largest sports organisations in terms of popularity.

These examples show how **dynamically** the video game industry has developed in 6
recent years. A medium that was initially only available to a small target group – namely technically interested students at individual US universities – has become the most influential cultural and mass medium of our time within just a few decades. How influential? A look at economic developments over the past few years provides a good overview.

C. The power of video games

'FarmVille' beats 'James Bond' – that could serve to summarise the takeovers in the 7
international entertainment industry in the early 2020s. While IT giant Amazon paid around 8.45 billion USD[5] for the film studio Metro-Goldwyn-Mayer – including the rights to 'James Bond', one of the biggest brands in the film world – this would have been far too little to acquire Zynga, the maker of the social and mobile game *'FarmVille'*. The studio was bought shortly afterwards by video game publisher Take-Two Interactive for around 12 billion USD.[6] When this takeover was announced, it generated excitement

---

1 Wijman, 'The World's 2.7 Billion Gamers Will Spend $159.3 Billion on Games in 2020; The Market Will Surpass $200 Billion by 2023', 2020, https://newzoo.com/resources/blog/newzoo-games-market-numbers-revenues-and-audience-2020-2023.

2 Kramer, 'Freude aus der Konsole', 2019, available at: https://www.zeit.de/2019/08/fussball-fortnite-torjubel-sergio-ramos-antoine-griezmann.

3 Shanley, 'Zelda Williams Recalls Growing Up Playing the Video Game Her Father Named Her After', 2017, https://www.hollywoodreporter.com/movies/movie-news/zelda-williams-recalls-growing-up-playing-video-game-her-father-named-her-984891/.

4 Settimi, 'The Most Valuable Esports Companies 2020', 2020, https://www.forbes.com/sites/christinasettimi/2020/12/05/the-most-valuable-esports-companies-2020/?sh=e1610ec73d0c.

5 Lang/Spangler, 'Amazon Buys MGM, Studio Behind James Bond, for $8.45 Billion', 2021, https://variety.com/2021/digital/news/amazon-buys-mgm-studio-behind-james-bond-for-8-45-billion-1234980526/.

6 Takahashi, 'Take-Two buys Zynga for $12.7B enterprise value', 2022, https://venturebeat.com/2022/01/10/take-two-buys-zynga-for-12-7b-enterprise-value/.

as the largest sum ever paid for a video game company. It was overshadowed, however, by news of a far more lucrative deal just a few days later, when Microsoft, operator of the Xbox platform and already the owner of numerous video game studios, announced its intention to acquire Activision Blizzard – the largest pure-play video game publisher by market capitalisation – for just under 70 billion USD.[7] This followed Microsoft's purchase a year and a half earlier of the video game publisher ZeniMax for around 7.5 billion USD.[8] But what is most noteworthy about these takeovers is that, although they are certainly outstanding in terms of their size, they aren't isolated cases. Rather, they are part of a larger trend that shows the enormous increase in the **economic importance** of the video game industry. A medium that was once pursued by only a select target group has long since become the largest entertainment medium of our time – and has done so in a comparatively short period.

8 While the high takeover price tags may come as a surprise to some, they can be understood in terms of market development. The **global video game market** has been developing very dynamically for several years now, with an anticipated volume of 177.9 billion USD in 2024.[9] By contrast, global sales of music totalled around 29.4 USD billion in 2024[10] and the global cinema market is expected to have generated about 33.9 billion USD[11] in 2023. This comparison alone shows that the video game market has already overtaken certain traditional entertainment industries and is now in a league of its own. And there is still plenty of room for growth in the future: While around 3.3 billion[12] played computer and video games in 2024, the global population stands at almost 7.8 billion.

9 However, it isn't just new players that are fuelling the dynamic growth of the video game market. A key aspect of the economic success story of video games is their role as a **driver of innovation**, as no other cultural and media industry is so quick to try out new technologies and approaches and turn them into products. From free-to-play games to virtual reality, the video game industry has long been a front runner in digital innovation. At the same time, video game players are often particularly open to new technologies that promise a better gaming experience. As a result, the video game industry and video game players have often helped technical innovations achieve a breakthrough on the mass market. In addition to completely new devices such as virtual reality headsets, the video game sector is also driving the demand for ever faster processors, graphics cards and internet connections, and thus technological progress as a whole. And this development is far from over. The biggest visions of the digital economy today include central pillars of the video game industry – artificial intelligence, virtual or augmented reality and the so-called metaverse all draw on innovations in video games – an indication that the relevance of the video game sector will continue to grow significantly in the coming years and decades. This will also increase the economic importance of the video game industry, which will become a key industry of digitalisation. Viewed

---

[7] Sinclair, 'Microsoft acquires Activision Blizzard', 2022, https://www.gamesindustry.biz/report-microsoft-to-acquire-activision-blizzard.

[8] Batchelor, 'Xbox buys Bethesda parent ZeniMax for $7.5bn', 2020, https://www.gamesindustry.biz/articles/2020-09-21-xbox-buys-bethesda-parent-zenimax.

[9] Buijsman, 'Global games market outlook: Key growth drivers and challenges for 2025–2027', 2025, https://newzoo.com/resources/blog/global-games-market-update-q1-2025.

[10] IFPI: 'Global Music Report', 2025, https://ifpi-website-cms.s3.eu-west-2.amazonaws.com/GMR_2025_State_of_the_Industry_Final_83665b84be.pdf.

[11] Gower Street Analytics: 'Gower Street Analytics estimates 2023 Global box office hit $33.9 billion', 2024, https://gower.st/articles/gower-street-analytics-estimates-2023-global-box-office-hit-33-9-billion.

[12] Genius: 'How many gamers are out there?', 2025, https://joingenius.com/statistics/number-of-gamers.

from this perspective, the large sums paid for takeovers of video game companies are understandable.

D. The heartbeat of the cultural world

But assessing the importance of video games solely on the basis of their sales development is clearly not enough. Video games are more than just a cultural asset. And they are more than just a driver of innovation. They must also be seen as an **integral part of the cultural family**. This has increasingly been demonstrated in recent years as, for example, German Chancellor Angela Merkel opened the world's largest games event gamescom in 2017, Danish Prime Minister Lars Løkke Rasmussen played a round of *'Counter-Strike'* with the professionals from the Astralis esports team in 2019 and French President Emmanuel Macron congratulated the game developers from Sandfall Interactive on their great success with the title *'Clair Obscur: Expedition 33'*. However, video games haven't always received such positive political recognition. Debates around the allegedly negative influence of video games on society, some of them very heated in Germany, paralysed this cultural medium for many years. 10

For a long time, the negative political debate also obscured the uniqueness of video games as a cultural medium: They are the only medium that is **originally digital**. This characteristic also makes video games an important source of inspiration in many areas far removed from cultural production, in the overall context of the digitalisation of society and the economy. What's more, no other cultural medium is so social and international. Video games are almost always developed for the global market – because gaming is a language that is understood all over the world. In addition, computer and video games are often experienced together. Unlike other media, the experience of multiplayer video games is based on the interaction of participants with and against each other. This gives rise to different and completely new narrative forms that no other medium can offer. 11

In the short period that video games have existed as an independent medium – at least compared to other media – an incredibly diverse and international video **game culture** has emerged. There have long been connections and overlaps with almost every other area of cultural production. Not only are video games themselves in part an art form, but they have also long influenced artists. This is particularly evident in literature, which has entered into a symbiotic relationship with video games. Many video games are based on literary models. The sources range from classic stories like the Argonauts' search for the golden fleece; to folklore, as in the successful video games in 'The Witcher' series, which are based on Polish legends and fairy tales; to contemporary fantasy literature such as the cosmos of 'The Lord of the Rings' or the German fantasy novel series 'The Dwarves'. Furthermore, there is an established history of well-known authors working on the stories of successful video games, most prominently George R.R. Martin on *'Elden Ring'*. At the same time, more and more novels and stories are being published that are based on well-known video games. If you visit your favourite bookshop today, you can't help but notice shelves of books about *'Minecraft'* or the numerous comics that continue stories from the game worlds. 12

A similarly intensive exchange also takes place between **film and video games**. The rise of computer and video games and the rapidly growing community that accompanies them didn't go unnoticed by Hollywood for long. Early on, video games were perceived as a mere extension of film universes. The example of *'E.T. the Extra-Terrestrial'*, which was developed for the Atari 2600 in 1982 to copy the success of the movie in the same 13 year and of which several thousand unsaleable game copies were buried in the New Mexico desert due to the poor reception of the video game, shows that this approach didn't always meet with success. Due to the different production time frames of the two forms, the 'game for film' is only rarely produced today. Instead, the universes of films are used to develop video games that often complement and expand on the stories from the big screen. From 'The Lord of the Rings' to 'The Avengers' to 'Avatar', there is hardly an international cinema blockbuster that can do without a high-quality game adaptation. But successful video games have also been used as a source material for films. While video game IPs were initially of particular interest to film makers because they were comparatively cheap and were followed by large communities comprising an exciting target group, a lot has changed here too in recent years. Films based on video games are typically now high-quality, big-budget productions with Hollywood stars – 'The Super Mario Bros. Movie' and 'Uncharted' being just two examples from recent years. A comparable development can be observed in the triumphant advance of TV series. In times when streaming portals are fighting for the most attractive content possible, they have long been aware of successful game IPs, including for instance 'The Last of Us', 'Fallout' and 'The Witcher'.

14 Books, films and TV series are examples of the mutual influence of video games and other areas of cultural production. There are similar developments in **music** as well. Not only has music itself become the subject of video games – in such titles as 'Garage Band', 'Just Dance' and 'Beat Saber' – but the music from well-known game series such as 'Final Fantasy' and 'Assassin's Creed' is played by full orchestras. The cultural areas with which video games have entered into a symbiotic relationship are seemingly limitless. Video games based on **board and card games** are another example of this. The many digital versions of classic board video games, which have been around almost as long as digital media itself, have increasingly been joined by board game adaptations of well-known video games in recent years. Whether *'Stardew Valley'*, *'Doom'* or *'Dark Souls'* – across all genres, there is hardly a major game brand that doesn't have a corresponding board game today.

15 And these are but a few examples of the **reciprocal influence** between video games and other parts of the cultural and creative industries. The list could go on and on, including how museums now use video games, how the special aesthetic of video games is spreading into ever more areas of life and how theatre and video games influence each other. As a cultural medium, video games have long been firmly established in education. Whether it be a serious game developed for a specific purpose or the use of a classic video game, there are numerous instances in all areas of teaching of the tremendous positive influence of video games in the educational field. The Foundation for Digital Games Culture in Germany continually offers excellent examples of this, working with a wide range of partners to demonstrate the unique power of video games in this sphere.[13]

16 As with other cultural assets, the important task now arises as to how to preserve these unique treasures. Video games raise their own specific questions. More and more video games evolve dynamically over time. The current version of *'World of Warcraft'* or *'Fortnite'* is very different from that of the original release date. This makes it all the more important to find a means of preserving video games. In Germany, we have embarked on a major undertaking in this area with the International Computer Game Collection. Still in its early stages, this could, with the right (political) support, become

---

[13] https://www.stiftung-digitale-spielekultur.de/en/.

the world's largest collection of video games within just a few years, making a significant contribution to the **preservation of video games** as a cultural asset.

E. A unique culture

However, game-specific cultural characteristics have also emerged. One of these is the paramount importance of the **community**. In no other medium do the recipients themselves become producers. In particular, live streams of players on platforms such as Twitch, YouTube and TikTok have firmly established themselves as independent formats. Interactivity has in turn contributed to their success. Instead of passively watching others play, audiences engage in live chats during a stream, introducing an interactive component that characterises the format and clearly sets it apart from linear television. It is no wonder that this combination of live broadcasting and interactivity is being used more and more outside of gaming streams. 17

Yet the influence of the community goes even further. In some cases, it even extends to the development of new titles, with close involvement from an early stage, or to the independent development of new content. Some of the biggest and most successful video games are based on these 'mods'. Some of these have even become elite disciplines of esports, as exemplified by *'Counter-Strike'*, *'Dota 2'* or *'League of Legends'*. And esports as a whole is another specific form of video game culture.[14] Although competition in digital video games has many similarities with traditional sport, it is an entity unto itself, from its disciplines to its organisation. Esports' deep roots in video game culture feed its great success: esports is international, can be followed digitally in many different ways – both live and on demand – and in many cases is community-driven and interactive. This makes **esports** a great fit for the media reality of the digital generation, surpassing many traditional sports and event formats. At the same time, esports, long a global phenomenon recognised far beyond gaming communities, is a means of communicating the video game culture itself. Spectator numbers, prize money and team ratings all continue to rise. The resulting visibility of esports has made it synonymous with the global success of gaming culture overall. 18

The profound influence of video games as a medium on contemporary culture is particularly evident at **gamescom**, the world's largest event dedicated to computer and video games. Taking place in Cologne every year at the end of August, gamescom not only inspires hundreds of thousands of people on-site, but millions worldwide as well. Whether it's esports, content creators from the world of video games or cosplayers – people who dress up as video game characters – the event makes clear how comprehensively and with what great diversity video games influence people's lives. Video games have long since become the heart of popular culture – in Europe and worldwide. 19

[14] See § 41.

§ 4
EU Video Game Law

Bibliography: Dimita et al., '"The ultimate unboxing": in search of the right questions to ask about loot boxes', Interactive Entertainment Law Review 2021, Vol. 4, Issue 1; Dimita/Lee/MacDonald, 'Copyright infringement in the video game industry', WIPO 2022; Dimita/Rizzi/Serao, 'Image rights, Creativity and Video Games, Journal of Intellectual Property Law and Practice', Vol. 15, Issue 3, 185; Duisberg/Picot, 'Recht der Computer- und Videospiele', Berlin 2014; Ewald/Haar, 'Gaming meets Law: Rechtsfragen der Entwicklung und Vermarktung von digitalem Content', K&R, Supplement 1 to Issue 7/8/2017, 12; Franz, 'Ist "Virtual Reality" eine neue Nutzungsart? – Zur zukünftigen Verwertung von Computerspielen', ZUM 2017, 207; Greenspan/Dimita, 'Mastering the Game', 2nd edn, WIPO 2022; Haar, 'Lizenz- und Plattformverträge im Bereich der Onlinespiele', DSRITB 2010, 359; Hentsch in Hoeren/Sieber/Holznagel, Handbuch Multimedia-Recht Teil 22 Games, 62. EL Juni 2024; Hentsch, 'The very first collecting society for games', Interactive Entertainment Law Review 2023, Vol. 6, Issue 2, 66; Hentsch/Ewald/Schwartmann (eds), 'eSport – Praktikerperspektiven aus der Games-Branche', MMR Supplement 8/2018; Hentsch/Ewald/Schwartmann (eds), 'Neue Wege der Rechtsdurchsetzung für Games', MMR Supplement 8/2019; Hentsch/Ewald/Schwartmann (eds), 'Herausforderungen auf dem Weg zu einem modernen, konvergenten und international anschlussfähigen Jugendschutz für Games', MMR Supplement 8/2020; Hentsch/Ewald/Schwartmann (eds), 'Datenschutz in der Games-Branche', MMR Supplement 8/2021; Hentsch/Ewald/Schwartmann (eds), 'Digitaler Verbraucherschutz in Games', MMR Supplement 8/2022; Hentsch/Ewald/Schwartmann (eds), 'Urheberrecht und Games', MMR Supplement 8/2023; Hentsch/Ewald/Schwartmann (eds), 'KI und Games', MMR Supplement 8/2024; Hentsch/Ewald/Schwartmann (eds), 'DSA und Games', MMR Supplement 8/2025; Hentsch/Falk, 'Handbuch Games und Recht', 2023; Hentsch/Rodenhausen, 'Einsatzfelder von KI in Games', Supplement MMR 8/2024, 714; Hentsch/v. Petersdorff, 'Statutory Protection of Minors in the Games Industry', Supplement MMR 8/2020, 33; Hilgert/Sümmermann, 'Youth Protection Compliance by Technical Means', Supplement MMR 8/2020, 56; Lee et al., 'On the value of human labour and creativity in the video game industry', Interactive Entertainment Law Review, Vol. 7, Issue 1, 1; Liesching, 'Hakenkreuze in Film, Fernsehen und Computerspielen – Verwendung verfassungsfeindlicher Kennzeichen in Unterhaltungsmedien', MMR 2010, 309; Liesching, 'Das Herkunftslandprinzip nach E-Commerce- und AVMD-Richtlinie', MMR 2020, 3; Lober/Jäkel-Gottmann, 'Anti-Constitutional Symbols, Green Blood, Zombies and Poses', Supplement MMR 8/2020, 38; Longan et al., 'Cloud Gaming Demystified: An Introduction to the Legal Implications of Cloud-Based Videogames', Michigan Technology Law Review Vol. 29, 2022, Issue 1; Nickel/Feuerhake/Schelinski, 'Lootboxen in Computerspielen', MMR 2018, 586; Oehler, 'Komplexe Werke im System des Urheberrechtsgesetzes am Beispiel von Computerspielen', Baden-Baden 2016; Ramos et al., 'The Legal Status of Video Games: Comparative Analysis in National Approaches',WIPO 2013; Rauda, Recht der Computerspiele, München 2013; Rauda, 'Government Protection for Minors Using Apps and Parallel App-Stores Rules', Supplement MMR 8/2020, 43.

A. Introduction 1

B. Legal categorisation of games 3
- I. Diversity of games 4
- II. Games in the EU single market 5
- III. Games in distinction to other media 8
- IV. Games as digital services 13

C. Legal framework for games in the EU 14
- I. EU video game law 15
- II. Horizontal games regulation 19
- III. Games-specific regulation 21
- IV. ECJ case law and other landmark cases on games 22

D. Trends in games law 24
- I. Cloud gaming 25
- II. Metaverse 27
- III. Games and AI 29

A. Introduction

1 With the growing social and economic significance of the video games industry (as described by Hester Woodliffe, Simon Little and Felix Falk in the first three chapters),

the legal issues around video games are increasingly coming into focus. The video games industry has been growing dynamically for many years, even though the industry is currently in a consolidation phase following the boom during the coronavirus pandemic. The growing popularity and increasing sales of video games have been accompanied by a growing interest in innovative business models, investment opportunities and the legal particularities of the industry. Although video games are also the product of a creative media industry, they differ considerably from traditional media such as books, films or music. Video games are a native digital industry, with content that can be distributed on physical media, but that is now largely digitalised. As an international medium that always has the global market in mind, video games are **distributed across borders worldwide**. They are, therefore, particularly impacted by the rules of the EU digital single market, but – at the same time – can also benefit greatly from such a market. So far, the EU has adopted numerous directives and regulations that aim to create the EU digital single market, which has already largely harmonised the legal framework for video games. Even in the presence of multiple solo national efforts to regulate games, especially for the protection of minors, video games law in Europe today can only be really understood in EU terms. For this reason, it is high time for the publication of a comprehensive handbook on EU video games law with contributions from some of the most prominent games lawyers in Europe.

This **handbook provides a comprehensive overview of EU video games law** and 2
is aimed at managing directors, in-house lawyers, youth protection officers, data protection officers and other employees in the games industry, as well as legislators and regulators, lawyers and academics, investors and other interested parties outside the industry. The handbook is written in a practical and solution-oriented manner so that it is suitable for everyday use by companies and law firms. The 41 short chapters are intended to provide an overview of the main legal issues relevant for the video games industry. The handbook is structured along the value chain, starting with the foundation of a video games company, then followed by the development, publishing and distribution of video games, and finally focusing on the special features of platform regulation and marketing for and with video games. In the introduction section to this handbook, Hester Woodliffe, Chair of the European industry association *Video Games Europe*, highlights the general importance of the video games industry. *Simon Little*, Managing Director of *Video Games Europe* and Managing Director of the *Game Sales Data* (GSD) platform, outlines the key economic numbers for Europe as a video games location. In addition, *Felix Falk*, Managing Director of *game*, the German industry association and publisher of the games culture handbook, sheds some light on the cultural impact of games in and for Europe. On that basis, this **introductory legal chapter** now provides a legal classification and an explanation of the different concepts relevant for EU video games law. To this end, we first provide an overview of the fundamental legal issues that the video games industry is facing today. This starts with a brief discussion of the diversity of video games, while also highlighting the differences from other creative sectors. Even if there is still no uniform definition of video games on an EU level, as a digital medium, video games are already comprehensively regulated by the various laws of the EU's digital single market and other EU laws that have been in force for a long time such as consumer protection or competition law. The overview of the legal issues, which is at the core of this chapter, also presents the legal framework for video games in the EU and thus serves as a bridge to the following chapters. This not only includes an overview of the most important directives and regulations, but also a discussion of the different approaches to video games regulation. The most important CJEU rulings on games are presented as well. Finally, as a foretaste of things to come, three current

trends are addressed: i) cloud gaming, ii) metaverse and iii) AI, for which no established legal frameworks yet exist (and therefore for which there is no separate chapter in this handbook), but which deserve attention in this introductory chapter as they may well define the future of video games.

B. Legal categorisation of games

3 Video games and their underlying business models vary to a wide extent, and are therefore difficult to categorise legally. Looking at video games from the EU law perspective, games are already regulated to a large extent by the rules of the EU digital single market. The **video games sector has its own business models and specificities**, which must be taken into account by legislators. While video games are not defined under EU law, they are covered by numerous EU provisions, and notably by the term 'digital services'.

I. Diversity of games

4 The business models underlying video games are as diverse as the games themselves. Depending on the offer and the concept of the individual game, very **different and tailor-made business models** have been developed which, despite their diversity, are often based on proven principles for monetisation and are adapted to the respective needs of individual games. Depending on their concept and scope, video games rely on different business models such as free-to-play, one-time purchases or subscriptions. Titles with higher production costs often integrate several models to refinance these costs. Even if the business models of many video games appear to be based on similar principles and concepts that are applied in different variations depending on the game and target market, there is no standard business model in the video games industry. The choice of model depends not only on the level of production costs and the target market, but also on the long-term goals of the game, such as its planned longevity or the retention of an active community. For the purpose of a schematic overview, however, five categories of financing models may be distinguished, some of which can also be found in combination with each other: i) sales, ii) subscription, iii) free-to-play (F2P), iv) in-game transactions and v) advertising financing.

II. Games in the EU single market

5 The main objective and thus also the most important basis for EU directives and regulations relating to games is the realisation and funtioning of the internal market (Art. 26 (1) TFEU). The EU's powers to adopt laws for other reasons, such as the promotion of culture (Art. 167 TFEU), are quite limited. Therefore, the focus of EU regulation for video games has to date clearly been on **harmonising the legal framework of the internal market**. Accordingly, video games companies and their business models may invoke the fundamental freedoms of the EU just like those in all other creative media sectors. In this respect, video games law is always caught between the poles of harmonisation and subsidiary regulation by the Member States.

6 When creating new EU rules and national regulations or when reviewing them, it must always be determined which of the four **fundamental freedoms** referred to in Art. 26 (2) TFEU is implicated. As regards the physical distribution of video games, the

free movement of goods pursuant to Art. 28 et seq. TFEU is relevant. Purely digital offers are qualified as services (Art. 56 et seq. TFEU) due to their non-physical nature.[1] The free movement of persons and in particular the free movement of workers under Art. 45 TFEU may also be relevant, particularly in the case of cross-border co-productions or remote working. The free movement of capital (Art. 63 TFEU) has played a role in the regulations imposed on payment providers of online games in reaction to the debt crisis in Greece. In all cases, restrictions on these freedoms are prohibited, unless there is a legal justification and provided such restrictions are proportionate. According to Art. 36 TFEU, restrictions on the freedoms may be justified on grounds of public morality (e.g., protection of minors), order and security (e.g., offenses and hate speech, as well as terrorism), the protection of health (e.g., gambling) and human, animal or plant life, national treasures (e.g., public broadcasting) or industrial and commercial property (e.g., copyright). According to the case law of the CJEU, there must be an overriding requirement of such importance that justifies the impairment of the internal market.[2]

Now that the EU digital single market is advanced, video games as a digital medium are to a high degree subject to EU regulations. While some of these rules are implemented or enforced by national authorities, they are largely harmonised. Regulation is carried out in the so-called 'country of origin', i.e., the country in which the video games company has its headquarters in the EU. Any national regulation therefore potentially represents a breach of the **country of origin principle** and must have a legal justification. On this point, the CJEU applies very strict standards and recently ruled that 'general and abstract measures which relate to a generally defined category of certain information society services and apply without distinction to all providers of that category of services' are contrary to EU law.[3] Particularly in view of the implementation of the DSA and numerous Member State initiatives for the protection of minors[4] and against hate speech on the Internet,[5] it is clear that the vast majority of competences to regulate video games now lies with the EU.[6] 7

III. Games in distinction to other media

Video games are of course part of the creative media and entertainment industries. 8
However, in some respects, **video games differ from other creative industries** such as film, books or music. One special feature is that video games are complex works and also have software components. Although video games sometimes include certain audiovisual elements such as cut-scenes, unlike films, players can control the plot and experience a new story in every game session. This is why games might be considered similar to films, but are not an audiovisual medium such as a film. Consequently, games are also not covered by the Audiovisual Media Services Directive (AVMSD), which originally regulated television. Video games are not social media either; even if some games allow users to upload their own information or content, including their own modified games (mods), these are only ancillary features of a game. Ultimately, the

[1] See CJEU, 4.10.2011 – case C-403/08 and case C-429/08 – Murphy.
[2] CJEU, 20.2.1979 – case C-120/78 – Cassis de Dijon.
[3] CJEU, 9.11.2023 – case C-376/22 – Google Ireland.
[4] See recently an Italian draft bill on the use of digital devices and video games by children under 12, a Spanish Draft Bill of Minor Protection in Digital Environments, and a draft of the 6th Media Amendment State Treaty to amend the Youth Media State Treaty in Germany.
[5] Network Enforcement Act in Germany, Communication Platforms Act in Austria.
[6] On the DSA and the country-of-origin principle, see → Lober/Trunk in § 32; on the technical protection of minors, see → Hilgert in § 34.

video games industry is now an industry in its own, so existing regulations for similar industries need to be assessed on a case-by-case to determine to what extent certain parts of those regulations also apply to the video games sector.

9 Unlike other creative industry works, games are so-called **complex works**[7] because their various elements such as story, design, sound and software are generally subject to their own particular IP protection regimes. This differentiation is particularly relevant with regard to the special provisions for computer programs under Directive 2009/24/EC on the legal protection of computer programs. This concerns, for example, the requirements for the level of creativity (Art. 1). In addition, the rights for the economic exploitation of computer programs according to Art. 2(3) usually lie with the employer. Private copies may only be made of works within the meaning of the Copyright Directive; according to Art. 5, only backup copies are permitted for computer programs. It has been disputed whether the technical and artistic parts of the overall work should be treated separately for video games (separation theory) or whether the game should be considered as a whole according to the character of the overall work (focus theory). In the *Nintendo v. PC Box* judgment, the CJEU answered the question of classification by granting video games protection as **'hybrid works'** under the Copyright Directive.[8] A video game must therefore be differentiated according to its components, such as the software that controls the game, graphics, music, texts and film sequences. These components may be protected by copyright 'or may contribute to the originality of the entire work and, together with the latter, enjoy copyright protection' under the Copyright Directive.[9] According to a majority of opinions, video games enjoy copyright protection both as a whole and in relation to their individual components. In this respect, the classic copyright protection applies to parts of a video game and thus, for example, also the related rights for film producers.[10]

10 Video games are also fundamentally different from audiovisual media. Although audiovisual works are a component of video games, they are only one part of them. Video games are much more like mixed works of cultural audiovisual products and services, and software elements. Video games are both similar to and very different from film and audiovisual media and should be acknowledged as a **separate entertainment sector on equal terms with film**. Considering this, games need a specific approach for a custom-fit funding framework. Accordingly, games do not fall within the scope of the AVMSD, according to the majority of opinions, with specific reference to the explicit exception for online games in rec. 22 of the AVMSD. This respects the different interests involved, as, on the one hand, games – unlike television and even many media libraries – are designed from the outset to cross borders, and the cultural policy considerations for national implementation leeway of the directive are neither necessary nor beneficial in the context of games. Furthermore, the AVMSD would take precedence over the DSA, which, with its fully harmonised, graduated catalogue of obligations, is much better suited to the diversity of games business models.

11 Video games could be – at least partly – considered as platforms if user-generated content may be shared via them. However, video games are generally **different from social networks**. Social networks are online platforms whose main purpose or essential function is to enable users to communicate and interact with each other by sharing con-

[7] On this in more detail, see MacGreevy in § 13.

[8] CJEU 23.1.2014 – case C-355/12, GRUR 2014, 255, mn. 23 – *Nintendo v PC Box.*

[9] See BGH, GRUR 2017, 266 – World of Warcraft I, with reference to CJEU, GRUR 2014, 255 – *Nintendo v PC Box*, and BGH, GRUR 2013, 1035 – Videospiel-Konsolen I.

[10] On the basis of the German Ancillary Copyright Law, the collecting society VHG administers the private copying levy for games companies, → Bodensiek/Hentsch in § 40.

tent with other users or making it accessible to the public. When it comes to the worlds created within video games, their content and dialogue, as well as the rules and possible actions, are all predetermined by the video game providers. Players can only interact within this framework and usually cannot upload their own user-generated content. This is fundamentally different from social networks, which thrive primarily on the mass uploading of content by their users. While some games do allow the creation and sharing of user-generated content, this generally happens to a much lesser extent than on social networks. In general, providers of video games have a great interest in ensuring that their games remain safe spaces, so that players return. For this reason, possibilities for uploading content and thereby violating personal rights are often restricted and specially moderated as a prophylactic measure. Therefore, in video games, the risk of rights violations is considerably lower than on social networks. With regard to the distribution platforms for video games, it can be stated that their main purpose is the sale and purchase of video games and the clear presentation of the individual game titles. Rating and commenting on games are also possible, as generally known from e-commerce shops. Distribution platforms offer potential buyers of video games a consumer-friendly way to inform themselves about the different titles offered and to exchange information about them. Art. 17 of the DSM copyright directive does not apply to games or gaming platforms either, because in this case they are not service providers for sharing online content, especially since it is not the main purpose of the game company to provide the public with access to user-uploaded copyrighted content.

Games are also **not a communication service**. In addition to the game itself, many games or consoles and other platforms offer the option of networking with other players to play together. Usually, contact can be established on gaming platforms via the user ID or separately from the gaming platform in the game itself. The communication options are quite rudimentary compared to specialised message services such as Discord or voice-over IP services such as Teamspeak. In addition, the communication function may be restricted or completely deactivated. Because communication in games usually cannot be used without the main service and is therefore incidental ('ancillary service'), games are explicitly excluded in the Electronic Communications Code Directive (Rec. 17 Directive (EU) 2018/1972) and are in most cases not to be classified as online platforms under the DSA.[11] In any event, in the large majority of cases, video games cannot be qualified as communication services. 12

IV. Games as digital services

In light of the above, it can be concluded that video games in their wide diversity are fully covered by EU law, and that the rules of the EU's internal market for games are largely harmonised. It is clear that any regulation of video games, in contrast to other media, would need to be based on a tailored and proportionate approach, taking into account the specifics of this industry. However, there is currently still **no explicit definition of video games** in EU law or in the national law of the Member States. Nevertheless, all digital games are to be understood as digital service according to Art. 3 (a) of the DSA, in conjunction with Art. 1 (1) (b) of Directive (EU) 2015/1535, on condition that they are provided electronically at a distance and at the individual request of a recipient of the service, usually in return for payment. In addition to the criterion i) of remuneration, which is already given when paying with data, the criterion ii) 'service provided at a distance' for the purpose of trading goods or for the provision of electronic games in an 13

[11] On this in more detail, see → Lober/Trunk in § 32.

amusement arcade in the presence of the user (Art. 1 (1) (b)) is initially distinguished. In addition, the criterion iii) of a service provided at the individual request of a recipient excludes, in particular, point-to-multipoint transmissions such as television and radio. According to (2), video games that fall within the scope of digital services cannot also be audiovisual media services or telecommunications services. This is consistent in that otherwise video games would be regulated twice.

C. Legal framework for games in the EU

14 In view of the diversity of business models, the distinction between the free movement of goods and services, and the differences from other media industries, a legally **independent perspective on video games** and a differentiated approach that depends on the design and is in line with the associated possible legal challenges is required even without a separate definition of games. There are already numerous EU directives and regulations that cover video games and that address almost all the challenges. In view of the high dynamic and high level of innovation in the design of games, a specific regulation of video games in many cases would not be very meaningful and also not future-proof. Instead, it becomes clear that the horizontal regulatory approach, which addresses challenges and dangers in the abstract, has proven itself in principle. Case law, and in particular that of the CJEU, contributes significantly to the fact that existing law and its evaluation may be applied to video games also in the light of further technological developments. This established legal framework for video games law will be discussed in more detail below.

I. EU video game law

15 As in other creative industries, the law of video games is not an explicit area of law on its own, but is basically **IP law with references from many other areas of law**. For developers and publishers of video games, copyright law is the decisive basis upon which a complex work is created, sometimes with several thousand creatives from almost all copyright fields, and then exploited on different platforms and using differentiated monetisation models. However, there are many special features in copyright law with regard to computer programs, copyright contract law and law enforcement. For this reason, but also because games are often created collaboratively and internationally and encompass almost all copyright-related works and many other services, publishing contracts are quite complex and sometimes differ considerably from other 'publishing contracts'. This requires not only a special understanding of the technical context, but also of the underlying game-specific business models and revenue streams. Of particular importance are the numerous new EU consumer protection laws, being part of the digital single market. Marketing tools such as Let's Plays, live streaming and communities, as well as esports tournaments, also require knowledge of competition law, media law and even sports law. Due to technical innovations and new trends such as Games as a Service, cloud gaming and the metaverse, there is always a lot of new territory to discover, so that 'creative law'[12] must be practiced constantly. In addition to EU directives and regulation, there is also an increasing amount of soft law in the area of youth and consumer protection, which is partly set by self-regulation but also partly by voluntary commitments and codes. It thus becomes obvious that a special new field of law and research – 'video

[12] Haar, 'Kreatives Jura für eine kreative Branche', MMR Supplement 8/2021, 1.

games law' – has emerged, which requires not only legal expertise but also in-depth technical knowledge and, in view of the different monetisation models, a special sense of the underlying economics. These topics raise many legal questions for which the industry has often found practical and globally functioning solutions. In this respect, it is imperative that the law of video games is conceived in European and international terms, because changes in the individual jurisdictions usually have to be implemented in other countries and because video games are distributed worldwide.

Video games are produced for the world market. As almost all video games are **16** released digitally and can be used anywhere via the relevant platforms (consoles, app stores and other internet distribution platforms such as Steam), there is usually only one version, which is then partially localised by local publishers.[13] Therefore, in most cases, the exploitation is not territorial, as in the case of films or books, but rather is usually non-exclusive and unrestricted in terms of time and location. Accordingly, the **license agreements** (EULA – End-User License Agreement) are also designed as uniformly as possible, at least for the EU internal market. In view of the, at times, quite specific national digital consumer protection laws, many publishers are faced with the challenge of either aligning the EULA uniformly and therefore along the lines of the most far-reaching consumer protection regime, or implementing individual provisions only in the respective country and thus designing different contracts. In principle, the economic success of the video game and the importance of the market are the main factors in determining how best to address this challenge. The higher the potential additional revenue, the more it makes sense to have specific terms and conditions for a national market, for example for Germany. However, with the creation of the European digital single market, EU-wide EULAs are the norm in the games industry, with the numerous solo German regulatory efforts[14] then often being implemented as a 'gold standard' throughout Europe. In terms of regulation, therefore, German law plays a major role in international games law.

As regards copyright law and other IP rights such as trademarks and patents, a **17** predominance of Anglo-Saxon law may be discerned. The work-made-for-hire doctrine makes it more attractive for game developers to conclude development contracts under common law. EU copyright law, with its many legal exceptions and the mandatory requirements of copyright contract law, grants fewer rights to developers and publishers of games and is therefore at somewhat of a **disadvantage from an investment perspective compared to Anglo-Saxon law**. The new DSM Copyright Directive, with its harmonisation of copyright contract law, has at least led to a level playing field in Europe. However, in the future, this may also be a reason for investment decisions against a production in the EU. Nevertheless, copyright contract law must always be taken into account in the international context due to its territoriality and indirect application. The statutory exceptions, the copyright limitations, are also reflected in the guidelines for the permitted use of video games in Let's Plays or other user-generated content. Ultimately, European copyright law is generally circumvented as much as possible internationally, but it must always be taken into account.

Media law is still not that harmonised on an international level and therefore is of **18** great relevance with its provisions for the protection of minors, on hate speech and on toxic behaviour. In general, the country-of-origin principle applies to video games as digital services in Europe, so that publishers are regulated only according to the legal requirements of their country of establishment. However, there can be partial exceptions

[13] On publishing, → §§ 18–23; on localisation, in particular → Edwards in § 20.

[14] Most recently, the Act for Fair Consumer Contracts, which, in addition to the new EU directives, also provides for a mandatory 'cancel' button in Section 312k of the German Civil Code.

to this principle, particularly for the protection of minors and to combat hate crime, so that the national provisions of the member states must be considered. With the DSA, the liability regime is largely harmonised by a regulation and uniform due diligence requirements have also been introduced. It remains to be seen to what extent Member States will use the possibility for exceptions and to create more far-reaching regulations. In the area of youth protection, *PEGI*[15] is a Europe-wide system for the protection of minors. Only Germany has its own self-regulatory system with *USK*.[16] Overall, both internationalisation tendencies and national exceptionalism may be observed in international media law for video games, with large Member States such as Germany often setting new standards.[17]

II. Horizontal games regulation

19 Video games, like all other media, are subject to the general legal provisions that can be applied to them as **horizontal regulation in each individual case**. Indeterminate legal concepts need to be and are accordingly interpreted in the individual case, thus enabling a precise and future-proof legal framework. In disputed cases, the CJEU ensures an EU-wide uniform interpretation of the law. EU law already contains numerous directives and regulations that set horizontal rules for video games and that are presented and discussed in this Handbook. In the area of copyright law, the Copyright Directive (Directive 2001/29/EC), the Software Directive (Directive 2009/24/EC), the Enforcement Directive (Directive 2004/48/EC) and, most recently, the DSM Copyright Directive (Directive 2019/790) are particularly relevant. In data law, in addition to the General Data Protection Regulation (GDPR) (Regulation 2016/679), there is the ePrivacy Directive (Directive 2009/136/EC) and the Data Act (Regulation 2023/2854). In the area of platform regulation, the provisions of the DSA (Regulation 2022/2065) and the Digital Markets Act (Regulation 2022/1925), but also of the e-commerce Directive (Directive 2000/31/EC) and the Terrorist Content Online Regulation (Regulation 2021/784) may also apply. There are not yet many EU laws on the protection of minors, but with Art. 28 DSA and the proposal for a regulation to prevent and combat child sexual abuse, harmonisation is also progressing in this area. In addition, EU laws on labour law, company law, competition law, tax law and sustainability reporting, as well as many other duties and obligations, naturally also apply to video games.

20 Video games and their business models are already extensively regulated, particularly in the area of **consumer protection**. With regard to the B2C relationship, primarily contract law applies, which includes the general provisions for the protection of minors when concluding a contract. EU harmonised consumer protection law also applies, in particular the Consumer Rights Directive (Directive 2011/83/EU) on consumer rights of withdrawal and the Digital Content Directive (Directive 2019/770/EU) on warranty rights. The Unfair Commercial Practices Directive (Directive 2005/29/EC) may also be applied to video games in many cases, as can the Omnibus Directive (Directive 2019/2161/EU) and its revision as part of the 'New Deal for Consumers'. This overview is not by any means exhaustive, as new directives and regulations are constantly being

---

[15] Pan European Game Information <www.pegi.info>, on this in more detail, → Bosmans/Foguel in § 22.

[16] Unterhaltungssoftware Selbstkontrolle <www.usk.de>, on this in more detail, → Secker/v. Petersdorff in § 23, mn. 15.

[17] See, for example, Germany's Network Enforcement Act, which, however, does not apply to video games, according to its explanatory memorandum.

added and as courts are applying the existing general rules to new practical cases. It can therefore be stated that video games are largely regulated at the European level.

III. Games-specific regulation

Sector-specific regulation addressed solely at video games does not exist at the EU level, although soft law is clearly emerging. For example, since 2021, the UCP Directive (Directive 2005/29/EC) has included Guidance on its interpretation and application with specific case studies on video games and in particular on loot boxes. A Commission Communication has been published on the Geo-Blocking Regulation (Regulation 2018/302), which explicitly excludes video games. The Commission Communication on the General Block Exemption (GBER) so far only refers to audiovisual media, although it could and should be applied to video games as well. However, a separate communication on the GBER to explicitly include video games would be useful and desirable in view of the many differences and special features of games compared to films. For the current EU legislative mandate, the Commission has announced a Digital Fairness Act, which could possibly introduce for the first time sector-specific rules for video games and their business models. This raises the question of how future-proof such rules can be in view of the dynamics of the video games industry and constant technological developments. Of course, this question not only arises for video games, as specific regulation in general has the advantage of clarity but also the disadvantage that, due to a lack of flexibility, some cases or future developments may not be covered by it. It can be stated that the video games industry has so far developed along with consumer desires even without sector-specific regulation. 21

IV. ECJ case law and other landmark cases on games

Due to the extensive EU harmonisation of rules that are also relevant for video games, it can be stated that the CJEU now **uniformly interprets** video games law at the European level. It has already handed down some landmark judgments in this area that have ensured legal clarity in copyright law. The most important judgment is likely to be that in the *Nintendo v PC Box* case. The dispute underlying that case was whether in the case of video games the technical and artistic parts of the overall work should be treated separately (separation theory) or whether the video game should be considered as a whole according to the character of the overall work (focus theory). In the *Nintendo* judgment, the CJEU answered the question of classification by recognising video games as 'hybrid works'.[18] Therefore, according to the prevailing opinion today, video games enjoy copyright protection both as a whole and in relation to their individual components. Most recently, the CJEU confirmed this approach in the *Sony v Datel* case and ruled that cheats which do not modify the source or object code of a video game do not infringe the copyright of the game under Art. 1 (1)-(3) of the Software Directive. However, such a scenario likely only occurs in single-player games; in the case of multiplayer games, which are predominant today, there is likely to be such modification and infringement. Furthermore, it is important to note that protection under the Copyright Directive was not considered by the CJEU in the *Sony v Datel* case on procedural grounds, although raised by the European Commission in its observations. As regards the question of digital exhaustion, the French Supreme Court ruled in the *Que Choisir v* 22

[18] CJEU 23.1.2014 – case C-355/12, GRUR 2014, 255 mn. 23 – Nintendo v PC Box.

Valve case that the terms in Steam's Subscriber Agreement that say that accounts and games must not be transferred to others are valid and comply with EU law. This is in line with an older decision by Germany's highest court (the so-called *Half-Life 2* decision), but there had been debate over this since the CJEU's *Oracle v Usedsoft* decision.

23 In consumer protection law, there has not yet been an explicit video games case before the CJEU. However, there have already been **landmark cases** at the national Supreme Court level regarding EU rules and loot boxes in particular. In Germany, for example, the Federal Court of Justice (BGH) ruled that promotional statements in the game '*Runes of Magic*' constituted an impermissible invitation to purchase for children because of the language used to address the players (predominantly in the second person singular and characterised by terms that are supposedly typical for children).[19] Regarding the question of whether loot boxes constitute illegal gambling, the highest general administrative court in the Netherlands has overturned a ban by the Dutch gambling authority and ruled that the loot box at issue was not gambling because only a random element had been added to the overall game. It also ruled that exploitation on a separate black market does not constitute normal use and is therefore irrelevant. The Supreme Court of Justice in Austria has also ruled that the loot boxes in the football simulation *FIFA 23* do not constitute gambling. According to the court, there is no intention of making a profit when acquiring the loot boxes, which is why they cannot be classified as gambling. So there is a clear trend to not classify loot boxes as gambling. However, there has been a discussion whether to regulate loot boxes under EU consumer protection law.

D. Trends in games law

24 Due to the many technical innovations in video games and the rapid adaptation of new business models, **many copyright and media law issues arise first in video games law**. For example, video games have been using artificial intelligence (AI) or machine learning for some time now to 'bugfix' or to adjust the level of difficulty. Virtual reality (VR) was also used for videos games very early on, so that the question of VR as an unknown type of use under copyright law arose here first.[20] The same applies to augmented reality, which was first made accessible to a broad user base via the game *Pokémon Go*. Blockchain technology and cryptocurrencies have also been used for micropayments for virtual goods in video games for some time. Non-fungible tokens (NFTs) are also already used in games and in particular in esports, where smart contracts are also used that allow the issuer of such a token to participate in the subsequent value creation. In addition, the first mass phenomena of the so-called metaverse took place as live concerts by *Trevor Scott* and *Ariana Grande* in the online game *Fortnite*. The following paragraphs address selected trends and areas of law which have not yet warranted their own chapters in this handbook.

[19] BGH, MMR 2015, 328 mn. 27 – Runes of Magic II, in particular on Section 3 (3) UWG in conjunction with No. 28 of Annex I of Directive 2005/29/EC; cf. also ÖOGH, 9.7.2013, GRUR Int. 2014, p. 181 – Videospiel D-Universe.

[20] For more details, see Franz, ZUM 2017, 207, which comes to the conclusion that VR uses have so far lacked economic independence and therefore do not (yet) constitute a new use that is subject to remuneration.

I. Cloud gaming

25 Demand for cloud gaming is increasing worldwide, with several million users now taking advantage of offers such as *GeForce Now*, *PlayStation Now* and *Xbox Game Pass*. *Microsoft's* acquisition of *Activision Blizzard King* for 69 billion EUR underscores the importance of attractive portfolios. With cloud gaming, games can be played independently of the user's device Users do not need any special gaming hardware and can play titles from anywhere. All the computation takes place on external servers, so that even technically demanding blockbuster titles can be played on simple laptops, smartphones or tablets.

26 Cloud gaming is not a use in terms of copyright law, as the video game is not installed on the hardware of the user and thus no computer program is (permanently) duplicated. On the one hand, this weakens the legal position of publishers vis-à-vis users and no further copyright claims may be asserted. On the other hand, the provider retains maximum control because the game can only be played with an account and the data is hosted on the provider's servers. In this scenario, classic piracy is almost impossible. Instead, the service is provided on a contractual basis (**games as a service**), which is, however, determined by the new sales and warranty laws for digital content. Here, too, there is a right of withdrawal and, quite recently, an obligation to update, which would otherwise lead to a defect and corresponding warranty claims. If a contract is terminated, user data must also be handed over, but game data itself probably does not have to be handed over. It is also highly questionable whether the GDPR gives users the right to portability, i.e., to be able to take scores and characters with them when they change providers. For telecommunications providers, this is applicable and probably intended by the legislator. For video games, however, this cannot be applied due to the very different operating systems involved.

II. Metaverse

27 Future technical innovations may also enable disruptive changes in the virtual gaming world. Based on blockchain, which is already used for microtransactions for virtual items in video games, digital content could be traded and passed on between users not only in the game but even across platforms via **non-fungible tokens**. An NFT is a certificate of authenticity for digital data stored on the blockchain, which can therefore be identified as an original and traded exclusively. As such, an NFT is not protected by copyright law as a computer-generated string, but the associated work usually is. NFTs thus enable the subsequent value creation of the linked work or content to be tracked and, through stored smart contracts, also evaluated and assigned. Without NFTs, this value creation could be reproduced at will. However, this would change the nature of a video game from a pure entertainment offering to a general trading platform including cryptocurrencies. Due to the numerous new regulatory and practical issues involved, and also because video games are primarily about the game and the story, there is still no popular video game that uses NFTs and cryptocurrencies, despite numerous announcements.

28 Some video games, however, already provide a glimpse of the vision of the so-called **metaverse**. The notion of the metaverse refers to the convergence of physical, augmented and virtual reality, in which users can interact with other users in a computer-generated environment. Such a metaverse again thrives on user-generated content, which makes such an environment vulnerable to cheats and inappropriate content, which in

turn requires content management and legal measures for the protection of minors. This is why platforms like *Epic* have recently made considerable efforts in this area. Also advertising should be possible in the metaverse. For example, advertising was shown at the *Travis Scott* concert, which attracted more than 45 million virtual visitors. This raises the question of whether the general advertising regulations of the UCP Directive apply to such metaverse scenarios and, if so, which jurisdiction is applicable. In sum, the metaverse raises fundamental challenges in copyright and media law.[21]

III. Games and AI

29 Already for some time now, AI has been used extensively in the video games industry. Games companies use AI applications primarily to increase efficiency in the production process, but also to improve the gaming experience, to comply with other laws, and for quality assurance.[22] However, a game engine generally does not have its own AI because it rather functions in a rule-based manner within a predefined field. As a result, video games are usually only deployers of AI and rarely providers in terms of the EU AI Act.

30 Accordingly, the new **AI Act** will apply to video games only to a limited extent. To comply with the new transparency requirement of Art. 50(4) of the AI Act, which is intended to prevent deep fakes, a simple mention in the credits should suffice as a rule, since video games are obviously artistic, creative or fictional works. For this reason, it is also questionable if the transparency requirements of Art. 50 of the AI Act should apply to video games in the first place, as it is obvious to the average user that this is part of a fictional experience.

31 The AI Act does not mention video games at all. There was a reference to video games during the legislative process: For example, when presenting the first draft, the European Commission mentioned 'AI-based video games' as an example of applications with minimal risk, the free use of which the AI Act was intended to enable. When the Commission then presented a risk pyramid to visualise the risk groups, AI-supported games were also placed in the fourth, i.e., **lowest risk group**. This classification makes sense, as video games do not pose any dangers comparable to those associated with the applications of the other groups (e.g., the use of AI in critical infrastructures, robot-assisted surgery or the automated processing of visa applications).

---

[21] For a detailed account, see Konni Ewald/Tom Harding, 'The Metaverse Report'. < https://www.osborneclarke.com/insights/metaverse-report>.

[22] Hentsch/Rodenhausen, 'Einsatzfelder von KI in Games', Supplement MMR 8/2024, 714.

CHAPTER 2
FOUNDING A VIDEO GAME COMPANY

§ 5
Building a Game Studio in 2025: Purpose, Grit and the Founder's Reality

Bibliography: Ball, *"The State of Video Gaming 2025"*, https://www.matthewball.co/all/stateofvideogaming2025; Blanchard/Johnson, "The New One Minute Manager", Delivers simple but highly effective systems for delegation, coaching, and management – critical as founders move beyond personal execution into organisational leadership. I learned to pat myself on the back with this, https://www.amazon.com/New-One-Minute-Manager/dp/0062367544; Dalio, "Principles: Life and Work", Provides founders with a systematic, principles-based approach for making high-stakes decisions while balancing transparency, learning, and control, https://www.amazon.com/Principles-Life-Work-Ray-Dalio/dp/1501124021; EGDF – European Game Developer Federation. Official Policy Positions and Annual Industry Reports, https://www.egdf.eu; Goleman "Primal Leadership", Helps founders understand emotional leadership beyond charisma. It helped me to understand that not all is coaching and democracy (and that I am the not wrong person), https://www.amazon.com/Primal-Leadership-Realizing-Emotional-Intelligence/dp/1422168034; Horowitz, "The Hard Thing About Hard Things", Candid, brutal, and probably the most honest startup book out there, https://www.amazon.com/Hard-Thing-About-Things-Building/dp/0062273205; Laloux, "Reinventing Organizations", Challenges traditional leadership structures and offers alternative models for self-managing creative teams – highly relevant as indie studios experiment with governance models, https://www.amazon.com/Reinventing-Organizations-Frederic-Laloux/dp/2960133501; Newzoo, *"The PC & Console Gaming Report 2024"*, https://newzoo.com/resources/trend-reports/newzoos-global-games-market-report-2024-free-version; Scott "Radical Candor", Provides a framework for leading creative teams with honest feedback while maintaining personal care. Startups often fail due to unresolved communication failures; this book directly addresses that leadership challenge. https://www.amazon.com/Radical-Candor-Kim-Scott/dp/1250103509; Sinek, "Start With Why", Demonstrates how defining purpose early drives alignment, resilience, and long-term success – fully in sync with the core message of this chapter, https://www.amazon.com/Start-Why-Leaders-Inspire-Everyone/dp/1591846447; Taleb, "The Black Swan", A must-read for founders who want to understand foresight and risk management. It frames unpredictability not as a bug in your plan, but the system you operate in, https://www.amazon.com/Black-Swan-Improbable-Robustness-Fragility/dp/081297381X; Wasserman "The Founder's Dilemmas", A detailed breakdown of early-stage founder traps – from equity splits to hiring decisions. It's the most data-driven map to understanding what drives a founder. https://www.amazon.com/Founders-Dilemmas-Anticipating-Challenges-Startup/dp/0691158304; Wickman/Winters, "Rocket Fuel", Essential for one or two-person founding teams. This is an essential read before agreeing on the ownership structure, https://www.amazon.com/Rocket-Fuel-Essential-Combination-Business/dp/1942952317.

A. Introduction – this is for founders 1
I. The industry you're entering 7
II. Studio identity and leadership alignment 10
III. Business foundations 17
IV. Funding realities 22
V. Product development and community building 26
VI. Today's European political landscape 31
VII. Founders' principles for building in 2025 37
B. Conclusion – profits are the fuel, but purpose drives us 42

A. Introduction – this is for founders

This chapter is for anyone who's serious about not just making a game, but **building a company – a business with long-term ambition**. Whether you're starting fresh or transitioning from years inside the industry, this isn't about freelance projects or short-term experiments. It's for those who want to lead teams, take responsibility for their future, and build companies capable of enduring hard markets. 1

One of the first and most important choices any founder faces: **Are you really a Creator?** 2

Creators invest in their own ideas, building original IP, accepting high risk for the potential of significant creative and financial reward. But that also means committing to 3 long timelines, fierce competition, and the constant uncertainty of whether the market will care about your vision when it finally lands. Are you willing to take that bet – and lead a team through the ups and downs, creatively and commercially? Can you pitch, market, and defend that vision early and often? Can you handle the emotional and financial strain if things don't work out quickly?

4 These are hard questions – but they're crucial. If you don't see yourself in this, fear not. **There is a stable, equally valuable path: becoming a Contributor studio.** Contributor studios focus on delivering paid production services to others, optimising processes, and maintaining stable, EBIT-driven businesses. They play an essential role in our ecosystem, building reliable teams, honing craft, and growing strong foundations that can pivot when the time is right.

5 The most dangerous path is trying **to do both without clear alignment** – hybrid studios often face conflicting demands and stretched leadership.

6 This distinction isn't about ego. It's about being clear from day one who you are, what you're building, and how your business decisions will follow. At its core, building a studio today is about discipline, resilience, and clarity of purpose.

I. The industry you're entering

7 The market in 2025 is mature, complex, and increasingly challenging. While total revenue across PC and console remains substantial, the easy growth phases are long gone. Established IPs dominate player attention – according to recent data, a small number of companies account for the vast majority of global playtime, and much of that time is spent on *old games* or well-established franchises.[1] This 'old games problem' makes it even harder for new titles to break in and find an audience, no matter how strong the idea.

8 Yet opportunity remains. Teams with **sharp creative focus, business discipline, and strong execution** still find success. Recent breakout cases like *Clair Obscure: Expedition 33* demonstrate that even in a crowded market, a focussed idea, executed smartly with colleagues who are massively intrinsically motivated, can create standout titles that punch far above their weight. Sandfall Interactive's work stood out with bold aesthetics, clear narrative vision, and a team aligned behind every decision – proving that precision, not size, is what breaks through.

9 But it's important to be realistic: Making games is not a startup-like scaling game. You're not building an SaaS platform. You're building **a creative enterprise**, which is an even bigger challenge. Your ability to sustain a studio depends less on one great idea and more on your capacity to lead a functioning business through multiple product cycles.

II. Studio identity and leadership alignment

10 The identity of your studio defines every strategic choice that follows. The earlier you make this decision consciously, the better your long-term chances.

11 If you want to build original IP, be prepared for years of risk and delayed payoff. Owning your own creative destiny is hard – but deeply rewarding if you're ready for the long game.

[1] Ball, 'The State of Video Gaming 2025', p. 100 et seqq.

If you prefer to build stability early, delivering services to publishers or other partners may offer more immediate cash flow, but comes with operational demands, client dependency, and limited upside. 12

Many founders attempt to balance both – developing original IP while delivering work-for-hire services. This hybrid approach sounds appealing, but in practice, it's the hardest path to sustain. Divided focus often leads to **misaligned priorities, resource conflicts, and leadership exhaustion**. 13

Equally important is how you structure your founding team. Aligning equity splits is only one piece. Decision-making rights, voting structures, and governance discipline matter even more as the company evolves. Leadership isn't about consensus. Teams need clarity on who makes final decisions and under what conditions. 14

And you must plan for life events. Founders leave. Personal circumstances change. Having structured agreements **that anticipate exits or shifts in roles** can prevent epic fails later. 15

Culture forms early. An accountable, anti-bottleneck mindset – where responsibilities are clear and nobody blocks the team – builds long-term stability. In my opinion, making games is a privilege. Leading or co-leading teams through that journey is a responsibility that demands a drive for maturity from day one. 16

III. Business foundations

Before you think about business models, you must define your purpose. Purpose can be discussed as a team, with colleagues and partners, and should be – but often, it's the CEO who has to make the final call. 17

- Why does your studio exist?
- What kind of success do you want to build – creatively and financially?
- Are you optimising for creative control, financial stability, long-term growth – or an eventual exit?

Without clarity, decisions become guesswork, and priorities blur. Your **purpose determines your business pillars and goals** – not the other way around. 18

Founders also need to think carefully about ownership structures. The legal jurisdiction you incorporate in affects taxation, funding eligibility, and complexity of international operations. Cap table design is strategic: Be aware of dilution early. Publishing deals, debt instruments, or certain financing structures may involve IP pledges or co-ownership risks, which may mean sharing or losing partial control over your IP – particularly if it's pledged as security or becomes part of a rights package. Always **understand and challenge** what you sign. 19

In the beginning, your most valuable assets are often your team, your learning curve, and your ability to adapt – not the first prototype or pitch deck. After some time you might look back and realise that except for your core team, you threw overboard everything that you started with – and that was probably the right thing to do. 20

Success in game development often hinges on your ability to defend and leverage these people over time. 21

IV. Funding realities

22 The funding landscape for game studios remains fragmented and inconsistent – especially for smaller studios without proven IP.

23 In practical terms, most early-stage founders will sequence their funding roughly like this:

- **Bootstrapping** – Self-funding, side work, savings, sweat equity and the famous FFF – family, friends, fools.
- **Regional and national public funding** – Highly dependent on country-specific programmes, with widely varying eligibility and focus areas.
- **Work-for-hire contracts** – Delivering external projects to generate steady revenue with work-for-hire can also mean that you sometimes work on your own ideas – here you must have clarity where IP ownership truly is.
- **Publishing funding** – Typically structured around production milestones nowadays, rather than traditional advances against royalties.
- **Private capital** – Venture capital rarely fits early-stage content studios. Expectations around scale and return are often misaligned with the reality of game development – especially in this market cycle. VC interest usually skews towards tools, platforms, or highly scalable technology plays rather than content studios.

24 Publisher funding has become more volatile, with many publishers re-evaluating portfolios and internal structures. Private capital remains highly selective. Public funding is often essential – but navigating fragmented programmes requires patience and professional guidance.

25 Fortunately, **support structures exist**. In Europe, organisations like remote control productions (disclaimer: rcp – my company) have helped many studios balance creative independence with business infrastructure support, providing operational, production, and strategic guidance without forcing founders to give up control. There are also companies like Kepler Interactive, who combine infrastructure support with publishing capability.

V. Product development and community building

26 Beyond building a great game, founders must recognise that early community engagement is one of the strongest forms of market validation available.

27 Active communities aren't just about generating buzz. They create feedback loops that help refine your product, build loyalty, and establish a network of early advocates who amplify your visibility long before formal marketing budgets come into play. Streamers, influencers, and active Discord servers can drive meaningful momentum even before full release.

28 At the same time, founders need to be their own most critical customers. Too many new teams fall in love with a single idea and never truly market-test it. You must **be ready to throw out or pivot ideas** quickly if the data and player response show they aren't resonating. This is not about losing passion – it's about protecting your time, resources, and ultimately your team's future.

29 While you don't need to finalise detailed monetisation mechanics on day one, you do need a viable business logic. Who will pay for your game? What is your realistic price point? What revenue models align with your genre, audience, and production capacity?

Community engagement and commercial logic are not opposing forces. Done right, early community-building helps you refine your monetisation approach and core product decisions through real-world feedback rather than abstract business modelling. **30**

VI. Today's European political landscape

Europe remains fragmented in its approach to supporting independent game development. **31**

Public funding structures often remain stuck in outdated cultural, R&D, or SME silos, making it difficult for founders to access consistent, scalable support that reflects the hybrid nature of modern game studios – blending technology, art, business, and culture. **32**

At the same time, global volatility adds uncertainty far beyond what founders can control: Trade wars, data flow restrictions, hybrid conflicts, and shifting regulatory landscapes all pose unpredictable risks for international operations. **33**

The EGDF continues to advocate for reform, fighting for stronger SME support, better growth funding, and more coherent frameworks that recognise the economic, cultural, and technological contribution game development makes across Europe.[2] **34**

While founders cannot directly solve these systemic gaps, awareness of this reality helps manage expectations and emphasises the importance of diversified funding sources and strong partner networks from the start. **35**

This is also **a call to action**: Staying informed on funding and policy shifts can mean access to niche support programmes tailored to your studio's unique focus. **36**

VII. Founders' principles for building in 2025

You must lead. **37**

Running a studio is not democratic. Listening matters. But someone has to make final decisions. Strong leadership culture forms early – one that balances accountability with creative ambition.

Your assets go far beyond your product. **38**

People, IP, technology, networks, and platform visibility all matter as strategic assets. Protecting and leveraging these assets makes the difference between surviving one project and building a sustainable company.

Community is more than marketing. **39**

Early community-building gives you validation, feedback, and long-term retention leverage. Your first players are your first investors – long before funding rounds begin.

Growth requires leadership depth. **40**

As your studio grows, you cannot lead every function personally. Building trusted second-line leaders is one of the hardest transitions – but essential for any studio that wants to expand responsibly.

Mental resilience is part of the job. **41**

Grit doesn't mean burnout. The industry is hard – emotionally and financially. Founders who survive prioritise both team health and personal sustainability.

---

[2] EGDF – European Game Developer Federation. Official Policy Positions and Annual Industry Reports: https://www.egdf.eu.

B. Conclusion – profits are the fuel, but purpose drives us

42 You don't need a massive AAA budget, you don't even want that. You need focus, endurance, and a vision worth following. This industry is tough – emotionally, financially, and creatively. But for those who really want it, it's one of the most rewarding places to build. **Building games is a privilege** – and it demands commitment. If you're not all-in, you'll feel it fast.

43 Support is out there. From gaming associations, peer developers, founder circles, friends, competitors – you're not alone, there are people to help you.

44 And if, in the end, you've built a few meaningful games that mattered to someone – that's success. That's worth it.

45 What it takes? Grit, foresight, curiosity, moral clarity, passion, empathy, and a healthy obsession with data and doing the work.

§ 6
Private Funding

A. Risk and reward 1
B. How games are made 2
C. Waterfall vs. iterative development 7
D. Making money 10
E. Marketing – community-building vs. buying users 13
F. Marketing case: Minecraft 16
G. Invest in games 17
H. Co-investment and fund-raising rounds 19
I. Pre-seed funding: 10,000–300,000 EUR 21
II. Seed funding: 50,000 to 3 million EUR 25
III. Series A, B, C 26
I. Fundraising model problems 27
J. Debt financing 28
K. Publisher funding 30
L. IPO 34
M. Other kinds of game companies 36

A. Risk and reward

Private investment is by far the biggest source of funding for video games. It comes 1
in many different flavours, which will be explored in this chapter. For an outside investor, there are many reasons to look at games: **consistent industry growth, promising exit opportunities** and **revenue potential** almost without limit for hit games. At the same time, investment in video games is difficult for many reasons: games are born digital, born global and hit-driven. They are a creative expression by the game developers, the value is intangible and assessing risk is challenging. In order to explore private investment into games, we must first look at how the games business works. And in order to do that, we must first find out how games are made. Some of these processes are examined in greater detail in other chapters of this book; here I will try to restrict myself to what is relevant only to the context of investment.

B. How games are made

Video game companies may have different roots, but all game developers started 2
the same way: somebody wanted to make a game. Video game developers are **creators** first. Those who are successful become **entrepreneurs** on the way or find someone who manages the business. I have yet to see anyone succeed as an entrepreneur first and creator second.

Making games is exceptionally unforgiving. I know this from experience. It is difficult 3
in design, in technology, in business, in management… almost all activities (perhaps things like phone bills and coffee machines are the same for everybody). Starting a game project means making decisions about technology, scope, budget, team, timeline and contracts with very limited visibility of the next steps. Game development is often more a **process of exploration** than executing a plan. The ideas and features you have in mind may not work as you thought when put into the game. Game developers must

constantly re-evaluate their direction and decisions. Now, imagine this process with the same people in the same room for several years and it is obvious how also the human dimensions and group dynamics come into play.

4 And then there are the players. Josef Fares – a very successful Swedish game developer and founder of the game studio Hazelight with award-winning hits *A Way Out*, *It Takes Two* and most recently *Split Fiction* – was a feature film director before making games. He describes the **interaction with the players** as 'it's like I was on set and invited the audience to join, touch the actors, take the camera, pull at the cables... In games you make something for others to take part in and that's what makes it difficult.'[1]

5 It used to be that games were products. Game developers made the game, worked hard toward a deadline, sent the 'gold master' off to be printed on discs (usually in November) and enjoyed their Christmas break – back then also known as 'post-shipping season'. Players bought the discs from their local retailer and if it sold a lot, the game developers could get a contract to make a sequel. Not so today. In the last two decades, games have transformed into **digital services**. They can start small and grow as more players join. Game developers can change the game and add to it, based on their vision and expression but also in reaction to player preferences. Working on the game does not stop, they keep adding content, features, levels, balancing, etc. This process has many different flavours: DLC (downloadable content), add-ons, live services and so on.

6 How big is a **game project**? The answer is: it depends. Some of the biggest games in the so-called AAA ('triple-A') category are released to several different game platforms such as Playstation, Xbox, Steam, Nintendo Switch, PC and in rare cases even Macintosh ('multi-platform release'). Those games can have hundreds of people on the team, hundreds more working as contractors, in co-development or outsourcing studios or in sister companies in the same corporate structure. Some games take five, six, seven years or more to reach release quality. The production budgets for those games are hundreds of millions of dollars (at the time of writing, *GTA6* is rumoured to be the most expensive game of all time with a two billion dollar budget). Such big investment is almost without exception tied to a strong IP (brand): a film or sports license, or a sequel to a famous game. On the opposite end of the scale, there are hundreds of thousands of games made by solo developers or very small teams on a shoestring budget, some with very short development times (months or even days). So it depends, and between these opposites, there is a spectrum of game sizes. In the last half-decade, the middle of the spectrum has been more populated with the rise of so-called AA games (console titles with almost AAA quality but at a fraction of the budget) and mid-core mobile games (more advanced than the casual games that dominated the first decade of mass market mobile games).

C. Waterfall vs. iterative development

7 In this way, today a game is more like an artist than an album (or a song). This process is called **iterative development**, as opposed to traditional software development regimes such as **waterfall development**. In a waterfall project, the end result is defined before development begins, typically in a detailed file called 'design document'. This fits well with publisher contracts where the deliverables are broken down into milestones which on approval by the publisher's executive producer triggers payments to the developer in the form of production cost coverage or royalty advances. However, while the waterfall model may work for the formalities of contracts and payments, it is not

---

[1] Josef Fares, svt.se: https://www.svt.se/kultur/spelutvecklaren-josef-fares-sex-langfilmer-var-ingenting.

well-suited for explorative design – what if you find out half-way that the game is no fun? This problem is better addressed with iterative development, where a small part of the game is made first to verify the game mechanic concept and other key ingredients (for example characters, controllers or special software features), then tested, tweaked or discarded before moving forward. These iterations can be numerous and increase the chance of a good outcome in terms of gameplay quality. The final result can be very different from the original idea. This is a strength of the method. By exploring through iterations, the developers find out about the game they are making. Key features may be discovered on the way. (I had a conversation with one of the original developers of *Angry Birds* and he told me the famous slingshot was added very late in the process.)

Of course, in contrast to the milestone/waterfall model, this model makes timelines, **8** deliverables, contract payments and release planning (including marketing, more on that below) more difficult. However, some argue that applying the waterfall model to game development is much like trying to push a round peg into a square hole – it won't fit! The waterfall model may look good on paper, but it is no help for the game development. The **iterative model** is most accessible to development where the budget is provided **in-house**, for example from a mother company, investors or other strategies (more below).

The move away from the waterfall model, design documents and package goods/ **9** premium consumer offers coincided with the rise of **digital distribution, online and mobile games**, self-publishing and new business models such as **subscriptions** and **in-game purchases**. These have the added benefit of being less vulnerable to copyright infringement in the form of download piracy, as payments are collected via services that the game company controls or at least have contractual influence over.

D. Making money

In digital distribution, games can be sold directly by the game company, for example **10** via **download** from its own website. More often, an intermediary is used such as a marketplace: Steam for PC, App Store and Google Play for mobile are some of the more well-known. They provide a virtual window display for the game and convenience for the players, but of course take a cut of the sales (typically 12–30 %). The power balance in the marketplace economy is the topic of much discussion, but this chapter will not focus on those aspects. Some games are included in **subscription services**, such as Apple Arcade or Xbox Game Pass, which give the player access to a library of games for a monthly fee.

A prominent business model in digital distribution is **free-to-play**, where the game **11** can be played at zero cost and the monetisation is done via offers inside the game ('in-game purchases'). Typically very small amounts ('micro-transactions') buy items in the game. In a single-player game, such items can help the player in the game, but in multi-player games that is in most cases considered unethical so those games tend to have cosmetic items for sale: a tag that can be painted on a wall or a 'skin' that makes the player's game character or weapon look different. (I sometimes make the joke that we are actually in the fashion business.) In most games, the vast majority of players (95 % or more[2]) don't buy anything inside the game, choosing to play for free. The free-to-play-model relies on large amounts of players, some of which 'convert' to paying customers. **Purchases** inside the games are typically made using **in-game currency**, which is bought

[2] Duncan, Tooxclusive.com, https://tooxclusive.com/editorial/the-free-to-play-goldmine-mobile-games-monetization-secrets/.

with **real-world money** outside the game. This is important in order to separate the real world from the realm of imagination inside the game and not break the illusion. At the time of writing, there is an initiative from EU consumer authorities to change this norm[3] (which is established with case law and earlier interpretations by authorities) which may impact this economic model.

12 Games that are paid up-front are called 'premium' games; this is the norm for example for PC games sold on Steam. A rare few very strong game brands can combine premium and in-game purchases. It is likely not possible to make an exhaustive list of **monetisation models in games**; much innovation happens and new business models are born as others fade away. I hope this brief account gives the reader some idea of the digital business models and how an investor can understand a game company's economy.

E. Marketing – community-building vs. buying users

13 The specific characteristics of games of course also sets them apart in terms of marketing. There are certainly many different ways to get a game noticed. For big titles **traditional methods** such as advertising, media interviews, launch campaigns, etc., are par for the course. Mobile games and smaller titles, however, tend to apply complete different strategies. Mobile games today tend to take a **quantitative approach** with terms like 'player acquisition' and 'cost per mille' – where the marketing budget is invested in online advertising that brings new potential players who can try the game, and if they enjoy it, continue to play and later 'convert' to paying players (as described above about the free-to-play-model). This approach requires significant budget resources and good data analytics. Mobile games companies with hit games can also use **cross-promotion** to market games inside their own games – a variant of player acquisition which saves the cost of paying third parties but of course means forfeiting third-party revenue if the same ad space could have been sold to paying customers.

14 Some will say it is difficult to break new mobile games as the cost of player acquisition creates a **barrier of entry to the market**. While that point has some merit, there is no shortage of examples of game titles which have found completely different ways to the players hearts. Let's take a look at a different part of the games market.

15 The 'indie' scene prides itself on being less concerned about commercial success and more about artistic appreciation. However, one does not exclude the other. **Indie** is a term that escapes definition, perhaps the best is the sentence you just read**: the definition of success**. Another candidate is that indie game creators keep the rights to their works. Except that does not explain the phenomenon of 'indie publishers'. While that debate may never be settled, today the indie games community revolves around PC games primarily distributed on the marketplace Steam with a premium business model but with low price point, typically starting from 4.99 USD but rarely exceeding 39.99 USD. **Indie games** are not advertised in traditional channels and indie developers don't talk about player acquisition. Instead, the keyword is **community-building**. Keeping the players involved is key. Discord is an important social media platform for building community around indie games, each game or game company with its own server on Discord where updates, content, videos and such are shared. Steam also provides community-building tools, most importantly the 'wishlist' feature. Investors look at this as a way

---

[3] The Consumer Protection Cooperation Network's Key Principles on In-game Virtual Currencies, commission.europa.eu/document/download/8af13e88-6540-436c-b137-9853e7fe866a_en?filename=Key+principles+on+in-game+virtual+currencies.pdf.

to assess sales potential. Wishlisting means that a player signs up to receive notice when a game is available for purchase. The conversion rate from wishlists to actual sales varies of course; some estimates put the median around 10 % but there is a power law distribution dynamic at play where some titles outperform the wishlist with double-digit multiples, whereas the long tail of titles convert fewer than 1–2 % of the wishlists to actual purchases. Event participation, live streams, social media activities, influencer collaborations, in-game videos and development updates are some examples of activities used to build community.

F. Marketing case: Minecraft

A case in point is *Minecraft*. Beginning as the stereotypical bedroom project, it was a single person's passion project. Creator Markus 'Notch' Persson had a career as a professional game developer. In *Minecraft*, he invited the players to participate very early. On his Twitter account, Notch shared his design considerations and conundrums, receiving advice and sympathy from the budding player community – much like indie game developers use Discord servers today. Others had tried before, but Notch may have been the first to successfully use the 'early access' business model, which is now standard and integrated in many sales platforms. This allowed players to pay for the game and get access to it, despite it not being anywhere near finished. Notch got not only paying customers at an early stage, the **players** also became **ambassadors** helping spread the word and market *Minecraft*. It provided revenue that made possible the further development of the game. Another fascinating aspect is the psychology of bugs in early access: when the players found a problem with the game, they reported it to Notch to be fixed – and were happy that they could contribute to the development of the game. Normally, paying customers are unhappy when they find flaws, but Notch turned that into the complete opposite. The rest is history: 2011 *Minecraft* won more than half of all prizes at the Independent Games Festival/Game Developers Choice Awards in San Francisco. In 2014 Notch sold his company (Mojang) to Microsoft for two billion USD. In 2023, *Minecraft* sales surpassed 300 million copies, making it the best-selling game in history[4]. And the funding and marketing methods it championed continue to be the template for indie games fifteen years later. **16**

G. Invest in games

Having explored what drives game developers and how games are made, marketed and sold today, we are ready to look at **investment**. Private investment into games can be made in many different ways. The three main forms are **investment into the company** (such as equity), **investment into the game** (such as games publishing) and **credits** (bank loans for example). In addition, there are **crowdfunding, not-for-profit funding, bootstrapping** and other variants, which will be discussed too. **17**

From an investment point of view, games are difficult in many dimensions. Games must be fun – if not, nobody will play them and no money will be made (there is no point in releasing a game that is no fun, which is one of the reasons games are often delayed). Assessing risk is difficult and so is valuation. Exit options are not always clear, the market changes, macro-economic factors are at play, there are regulatory risk and **18**

[4] Minecraft becomes first video game to hit 300m sales – BBC News (https://www.bbc.co.uk/news/technology-67105983).

so-called 'black swans'. Player preference changes, other games may steal the attention, sometimes game developers fall out during projects... there are many different ways investing in games can go wrong. In fact, most games fail. Many are never finished, others never reach more than just a few players, plenty of games struggle to make money. Most games fail. That is important to keep in mind for any games investor. Let's break down these difficulties.

a. **Fun**. How can an investor be sure that the game is fun? I've met investors who said they can tell which games will be successful. Great for them, but most people don't have such gifts. Rather, I would advise to trust the team. Let them use the iterative design model as described, let players try the game early via focus groups, early access, soft launch or some other method. Protect the teams creative integrity and give them time so they can change the game until it works. Or kill the project early if there is no progress.
b. **Risk**. How can an investor assess risk in a game company? There are many types of risk, let's start with production risk or creative risk (will the game be finished and fun?). If I may interpret this as mitigating risk, the most popular way is to invest in an experienced team. If they have delivered one or more good games before, that is the strongest card. Sometimes more experienced team members need to be added to the team. This is very difficult for the investor to push for, however. Team dynamics are sensitive and there is no guarantee that somebody who has experience from one team will be successful in a new group. Sometimes the team members fall out and won't work together anymore. These are human factors beyond money and contracts and investors may find themselves as diplomats or counsellors rather than bankrollers. A very popular way for investors to mitigate production (and other forms of) risk is to shift it onto the developer. The more finished the game is when the investor enters, the lower the risk. Many investors delay their decision, asking the developer to provide more content, more features, more data points around player community or something else. This is often frustrating for the developer and as the investor is in most cases the stronger party in the negotiation there is an ethical aspect to not abuse that power-position. In very practical terms, the investor also risks that the developer finds a different solution or cancels their project or company if the process is too slow. That said, the timing of the contract is a normal part of any negotiation and the contract parties often have different interests.
   Next type of risk is **market risk**. Many pitches compare sales figures from similar games, but of course it is near impossible to this in a strict and relevant way, as some many factors apply (look and feel, timing, marketing, trends, sentiment, coincidence). Investors can look at metrics such as wishlists, Discord-server memberships, trailer views and such as described above. But there are no guarantees. However, time can work in favour of a game. If it is not a hit at launch, developers can keep working on it and try again and again. Many games have failed to meet expectations but given second chances by players (*No Man's Sky* and *Cyberpunk 2077*'s older console versions are often mentioned as examples of this). If an investor can afford to let the team work together with the player community, the market risk can be managed. Another way investors mitigate market risk is by licensing a well-known brand ('IP' in industry-lingo) for the game. This helps bring attention but also may increase the expectation in the player community. Plus of course there is a cost involved, up-front and/or as some form of revenue share. In rare cases, games can discuss controversial topics and some marketplaces may refuse to distribute them.

Competition risk is a separate flavour of market risk. Imagine starting work on an innovative game format, let's say a knitting game, delivered with novel hardware knitting needles. Production is complicated and manufacturing solutions difficult and costly, but that's not all – what if a bigger company releases a knitting game first? Your knitting game may have nothing to do with theirs, but you still look like a copycat.

Legal risks. Is there a chance that the game may be infringing on somebody else's intellectual property? Are there any contracts in place that limit the freedom for the company or game title? Is the development software licensed and does that come with any restrictions or liabilities? Do the online portions of a game rely on third-party cloud services? What are the terms of those? Is there a shareholder agreement in place regulating the relationships between the founders/developers/co-owners? Investors are well-advised to hire specialised lawyers to carry out proper due diligence so risks like these can be made visible and the investor can make an informed decision. However, lawyers are trained to be risk-averse, whereas creators and entrepreneurs need to be the complete opposite. The balance is for the investor to strike.

Culture risk. Games are entertainment. Some say art. Creative expressions of the human mind. Whichever term you prefer, this means they are open to interpretation – different people will take away different things from the same game experience. Some may be offended, they may find the game content interfering with their identity or politics. Sometimes real-world politics touch the games, for example when games talk about real-world countries, names and borders. Or when games are hijacked for propaganda purposes. The answer here is not to avoid any potential culture sensitivities. Some games want to make a statement. Some want the attention. Some want to bring change. But for the investor, it is important to know about these risks and, again, make informed decisions. There are specialists who advise on these topics, but a good place to start is to discuss them with the team. If books are translated, the next step for games is 'localisation' – where also art, audio and sometimes gameplay are tailored for the local audience. The gold standard is 'culturalisation', where culture risks are recognised and addressed.

Regulatory risk is a close cousin of culture risk. Governments have an appetite to regulate games for various reasons. In the West, it tends to be driven by concerns for the well-being of the youth – screen-time, violent content, stranger-danger in online games – whereas in authoritarian countries it may be more about information control. Regulatory initiatives can come unexpectedly and be quite draconic, sometimes outright banning certain games or offers. The best way to deal with these issues is together with others. Game industry associations (such as the one this writer works for) are put in place to deal with these types of problems and have ambitious self-regulatory programs to address the concerns that oftentimes are behind regulatory initiatives. Make sure your game developers are members of their local association!

Macro-economic risk and **black swans**. Games are not removed from the rest of the world. Global events influence games companies in various ways, but are difficult to influence and sometimes predict for obvious reasons. The lockdown in the Covid-pandemic increased sales of many games: as half the world's population was more or less confined to their homes, games offered some social connection, fun and distraction. Global sales grew. Development was difficult and many new games were delayed. In the same timeframe, the macro-economy was dominated by very low interest rates and much investment capital was looking for risk and growth. The games market had many years of consistent strong growth prior to the pandemic. Publicly traded games companies shares were valued at very high multiples. New game companies could easily find investors. Post-pandemic, global game sales slowed, geopolitical tensions (and war) made international investors more cautious, interest rates increased dramatically, companies struggled to pay their creditors, share prices dropped. This period was a roller-coaster ride for investors, but the factors had little or nothing to do with the games or the teams. Investors are advised to analyse which factors can be influenced and which cannot as they make and adjust their plans. An important observation, however, is that the foundational market forces remain: more people want to play games and game developers keep making more and better games. This will not change in the foreseeable future.

c. **Valuation**. How much is a game company worth? For publicly traded companies, this question is easy: the value is defined every day by the market capitalisation. For any other games company, it is incredibly difficult to say. Microsoft paid 2,5 billion USD to acquire Mojang (*Minecraft*) in 2014, many industry profiles say it was a bargain but very few outside the industry would have believed such money was possible before it happened. Traditionally, company valuation looks at metrics such as revenue, profit and balance sheet. But for a game company, revenue and profit often depend on the next release and the assets on the balance sheet are typically the IP of their own games, the value of which depends on the sales. There is no simple answer to valuation of non-listed game companies. The best way to assess value is via transaction: when a buyer negotiates an acquisition with the owners/founders. This explains why strategic acquisitions are much more common than other forms of M&A in games. An industry actor can much better assess the value of a company and its games than a third party could. Also, industry actors have more tools to secure successful progress: marketing, development support, knowledge, network and such.

d. **Exit**. How does the investor leave with a profit? In the tech startup fundraising model (discussed in more detail below), the investors have many opportunities to exit: in later fundraising rounds or ultimately when the tech startup is acquired by an incumbent. In games, it is not as clear-cut. Some exits happen like that, when the company is acquired by a bigger industry actor. In other cases, investors can exit to new owners from outside the industry who want to invest but at lower risk. In the last decade, initial public offerings (IPO) on the stock exchange have been a very popular way to exit (Sweden has more than 20 publicly traded games companies, Poland over 90). This is when the good folks at the stock market step in to say that going public is not an exit but a new chapter for the company. True (more on that below), but for some investors it's an exit. And some investors don't want to exit but rather stay on for the long haul, making their money back through dividends or otherwise. The point here is that investors are well-advised to have nuanced expectation of how the exit can happen and to discuss this with the owners/founders to pre-empt misunderstandings.

H. Co-investment and fund-raising rounds

19 **Co-investment**. I said in the beginning of this chapter that private funding is the main source of funding for games. That is not to say that it is singular. Private funding is often combined with various forms of **public funding**. More importantly for this chapter, various forms of private funding are often combined. Perhaps an investor

provides equity funding in an early phase, which brings the company to where it could get publisher-funding for their project. Or two or more private investors share an equity investment in a game company.

Private equity investors often want to apply the principles of investment to tech startups to games. This method has some merits: it is well understood among investors and established. Its downsides are because it is not tailored to games but tech. I will discuss the differences below. 20

I. Pre-seed funding: 10,000–300,000 EUR

In tech startups, there are different steps of investment called 'rounds'. The first steps are called **'pre-seed'** and involve things like **'bootstrapping'** and 'friends, fools, family'. This means they are informal, bootstrapping is when the founders pay for business costs from their savings or a day job and no one gets a salary, there may not be a formal legally registered company at this point. Borrowing money or taking investment from the closest circle is a next step. Such investment is typically emotionally motived rather than financially. This is where somebody takes a second mortgage on their house, for example. Both of these are viable for game companies. This is also the phase where the company may choose to join a **business incubator** to get help with the business basics (and sometimes domain-specific services such as access to advice or international events). Pre-seed investment can be from 10,000 EUR to 250,000–300,000 EUR. 21

Crowdfunding such as Kickstarter or GoFundMe is sometimes considered at this stage, but over the years crowdfunding for games has developed into more of a strategy for community-building than raising money. (A problem with crowdfunding is that it means making promises to a large amount of people and those promises may prove difficult to keep.) It is also common for game startups to take on consultancy work to get some revenue, fund their game project budget or extend the runway of whatever budget they have. If so, game startups are well-advised to consult for other game companies if possible. That way they get experience from other game projects, the team members work on real games, they get credited and build a portfolio. If the consultancy is outside of games, it can create tensions in the team, where some team members bring in the money when others work on the game. This is also a phase where the founders would be well-advised to make a shareholder agreement. This document describes how decisions are made in the business, who can sell shares to whom, what happens if a shareholder wants out, how investment can be taken on, etc. Conventional wisdom says the shareholder agreement ought to be written as if 'the founders are in disagreement', but in reality it is very difficult to predict how the founders may disagree in the future and likely impossible to cover all such scenarios. 22

There is a specific type of pre-seed investment in games that may be less prominent in tech startups. I like to call it **not-for-profit-investment**. By this I mean funding from foundations/charities, communities, scholarships and such. They have completely different terms than commercial investors, rarely ask for a return on their investment but rather look at completely different criteria. A few years ago, our office did a stock-taking of not-for-profit-investors in Sweden and found close to 100 (we may have found more if we hadn't run out of project budget… the irony!). These were local patrons of the arts, culture heritage funds, family charities and many others. Some were open to applicants with roots in a certain part of the country, others demanded that the business set up in a specific location, some measured the success in artistic terms. There were almost as many different types of terms as there were investors. Not-for-profit investors form a 23 separate category besides public and private funding. They tend to invest small amounts, making it most relevant for the pre-seed funding stage. My understanding is that games may have more access to this type of funding than tech startups as games are not only technology but also art (or complex works[5] to be very specific!).

24 **'Angel investment'** can be part of a pre-seed or seed (the next round). Business angels are typically private investors who invest their own money. They want to invest small amounts early when risk is high for a shot at big wins. Often the investment is paired with personal interest in the company or sector. Business angels often have long experience and good networks and thus can help the startup with more than money. Angel investment can work for game startups, however these investors rarely have domain knowledge about games and may overstate the relevance of insights and contacts from other sectors. Perhaps as a measure of maturity in the games industry, many successful game companies put some of their money into investing in new companies, creating a virtuous circle of pay it-forward culture.

II. Seed funding: 50,000 to 3 million EUR

25 **Seed funding** is the next phase and the first formal round. This means that institutional investors such as funds, venture capital firms and banks can join. Valuation is calculated based on what investors pay for a share, for example if the founders sell 20 % of the shares for 50,000 EUR, that puts the valuation of the company at 250,000 EUR. There is no strict formula for valuation at this stage; the company likely has no revenue so it's not possible to use traditional multipliers. Rather, it's a negotiation where the game company tries to get the necessary funding for their project and the investor wants to get a good deal while keeping an eye on the valuation for future rounds (a high valuation may send a strong message to other investors but also make the next round more difficult). This is where the shareholders need to think about the 'cap table' – who owns how much of the company? In theory, there should be room for selling (or issuing) more shares in upcoming rounds, but also making sure the founders' shares are big enough to keep them committed to the company. Too many owners may make future steps more difficult and founders losing control of the majority of votes may impact their enthusiasm. However, all this is investor psychology – in real life, game developers tend to think much more about how to finish their game and often sacrifice long-term benefits for the current project. Investors tend to think about what happens after the first game, sometimes also after the second game. Game developers would be well-advised to have good answers for those questions when talking to investors. (Easier said than done, though: as discussed, making games is very demanding and any deviation from the focus of the game project may jeopardise it.)

III. Series A, B, C

26 After the seed round, a company can continue to fundraise in rounds called **Series A, B, C** etc. In tech, this is meant to be funding to 'scale' (=grow) when the company's business is proven to work but may need investment to reach a size where profit is possible. As the reader has guessed, this does not necessarily work well for game

[5] ECJ case C-355/12 § 29: 'Videogames (...) constitute complex matter comprising not only a computer program but also graphic and sound elements, which, although encrypted in computer language, have a unique creative value which cannot be reduced to that encryption. (...)'.

companies. If the company has started to make money, it is very likely that it can grow on its own ('organically'). If it has yet to make money – perhaps because the game is not ready for release – it does not fit the mould for the investors. Some can make this work of course, perhaps some funding is needed for marketing volume. Or some more work on the game in order to get a publishing contract. But this is only one example of how the tech startup fundraising model is not ideal for games.

I. Fundraising model problems

Tech startups tend to try to fix a very specific problem (investors sometimes call them 'painkillers') – for example 'how can I get my dry cleaning more quickly?' Games just want to be fun to play. Tech entrepreneurs typically want to make money but game developers want to make games. Tech startups follow the logic of scaling fast, with less interest in revenue and more in growing number of users in most cases. Game companies tend to make money from players, tech startups tend to make money via exit to an incumbent which integrates the startup into its existing business. For these and other reasons, the **tech startup fundraising model** is not ideal for games and game entrepreneurs will often tell you that they spend more time explaining the games industry to investors than pitching their project. 27

J. Debt financing

Loans are unusual in games funding. In a way, they are an under-utilised source of capital. The benefits are that the developer keeps its shares and IP, and the only cost is the interest rate. In practice, however, game entrepreneurs are very reluctant to take on debt, as risk assessment is difficult and nobody wants to be stranded with loans they have to pay out of their own pocket. Also for the creditors, debt funding is difficult. In addition to risk assessment, it is also the question of collateral: what can be held as security for the loan? Typically, the asset on the balance sheet of the game company is the game IP, which won't work for the bank. And what if the bank would take game IP as collateral, and the company defaults on its payments? Should the bank claim the IP and try to finish work on the game? Also, in the long term, much debt can limit the freedom for management and owners to evolve the business in the direction it wants. 28

However, debt financing has proven useful for one type of company: **publicly traded companies.** The problems described do not apply to them, the valuation is always up-to-date from the market and the company's shares are good collateral. As a consequence, many of the publicly traded companies have used credits to make investments. This is perfectly normal practice but with the rapid change in the macro-economy following the end of the pandemic and the geopolitical tensions, some have struggled with rapidly increasing interest cost. 29

K. Publisher funding

In addition to equity investment, games can be funded by publishers. **Game publishers** are companies which specialise in marketing, intellectual property and investment in games. They have good market understanding and established procedures for distributing and selling games. Publishers do not take equity, but instead look for good games to add to their release catalogue. In principle, the publisher is responsible for marketing, 30 customer support, distribution, managing revenue, legal issues such as rights clearance for music, etc. – anything that is outside of making the game itself. In real-life, of course, those lines blur as the publisher will require the developer to make marketing assets such as in-game videos, screenshots and cover art (games with no package goods distribution still have cover art) – plus developers in most cases won't trust any third party to create material that is so closely connected to the game. And for customer support, in many cases the publisher will need the developer's help with difficult queries. When it works well, publishers and developers have a symbiotic relationship. However, many developers complain that their publisher interferes with their creative decisions, whereas publishers complain that developers never finish their projects.[6]

31 The heart of the publisher agreement is the **transfer of intellectual property rights**. Keep in mind that this includes the trademark (game title) and the rights to potential sequels for example. These points are subject to negotiation of course, but publishers tend to prefer to have control over the IP and sometimes a sequel is made by a different developer than the original.

32 A traditional games publishing contract is built as a **copyright license by the creator** (the game developer) to the publisher, against which payment is made as a royalty advance – the royalty advance is the game developer's production budget. Once the game is released, the publisher collects the revenue, deducts its relevant costs and pays a royalty as a percentage toward paying back the advance – once the advance is repaid, developers receive royalty payouts. However, this model is rarely seen in the wild. Advances are rarely covered in the end; many developers negotiate a different deal (smaller advance in exchange for higher royalty for example), sometimes the production budget is bigger than the value of the developer so the publisher ends up buying the developer making it an in-house production unit instead (this is called 'strategic investment'). There are many different ways games publishing plays out, which brings us to self-publishing.

33 **Self-publishing** is when the game developer retains the copyright to their game and takes care of marketing, PR, distribution, sales and other traditional publisher duties themselves. Revenue is collected by the developer, minus cuts taken by online marketplaces, payment service providers and others. The developer controls the IP (=copyright) and can license it for merchandise, other media (film adaptations, cartoons) and also controls the rights to sequels. This means that the game developer needs to develop commercial competencies around marketing and publishing. Much of this can be bought from specialist consultancies, but the management must know what its buying. It is a common pattern that a successful self-publishing developer builds a department for marketing and publishing, only to find out that their own games are not enough to fill the capacity of this department. The next logical step is to provide marketing and publishing services to other game developers. In that way, one can say that self-publishing begets publishing.

L. IPO

34 The financial markets have a growing interest in games in the last decade. From my vantage point in Sweden, the spectacular acquisitions of Mojang (*Minecraft*) by

[6] I once worked on a rock star simulation game and wanted to put drugs in it. The executive producer refused, to my frustration. I saw it as a cool game for rock fans, the publisher saw it more as family entertainment. In the end, it was the latter.

Microsoft in 2014 at 2,5 billion USD[7] and King (*Candy Crush Saga*) by Activision the year after at 5.9 billion[8] very much opened the eyes of some traditional finance actors: stock exchange, investment bankers, fund managers. It was obvious to them that there is a lot of **value** being created which was not accessible to most **investors**. The answer was to take companies to the stock exchange and make them available for anyone to invest in. In Sweden, this trend started around 2017 and was very successful for several years, until the shift in the macro-economy changed the sentiment of investors from risk to profit and the rise in interest rates meant increased cost for many companies. Since then, share prices have dropped (some would say normalised) and most companies are trading at less optimistic multipliers.

From the point of view of the company, there are many benefits of being listed on the stock exchange. Access to credit (also for owners who can use shares for collateral), opportunity of new share issues to finance investments or acquisitions, exit opportunity for investors and founders, incentive programs for staff… even community-building as fans often like to own shares in the company that makes their favourite games (this can be a mixed blessing as fans are sometimes disappointed in the games too). **35**

M. Other kinds of game companies

This chapter has looked at **investing in companies that make games**. Within the games industry, there are many other kinds of companies: software tools developers, service providers, outsourcing and co-development studios, publishers, communications agencies and many more which too are parts of the eco-system. While these companies certainly deserve attention in their own right, they are typically business-to-business actors, whereas those I've discussed in this chapter can better be understood as **business-to-consumer**. The peculiarities of the games market are the same backdrop for both, but in my opinion, the business-to-business model is better understood in most parts of than financial sector: banks, auditors, investors, analysts etc. There is no shortage of knowledge in other places on how to assess risk and make valuation in the business-to-business model. With this, I hope the reader will accept my choice of focus for this chapter. **36**

[7] Microsoft pays $2.5bn for Minecraft maker Mojang – BBC News (https://www.bbc.com/news/technology-29204518).

[8] 'Candy Crush' owner King sold to Activision Blizzard for $5.9bn (https://www.ft.com/content/680ccbd2-81d4-11e5-8095-ed1a37d1e096).

§ 7
EU State Aid Law

A. State aid ... 3
I. Undertakings ... 6
II. Advantage – State aid can take various forms ... 9
III. State resources and imputability to the state ... 14
IV. Selective advantage ... 15
V. Distortion of competition and effect on trade between Member States .. 16
B. Notification obligation ... 17
C. Compatibility of aid measures to video games ... 19
I. General Block Exemption Regulation (GBER) ... 21
II. No specific guidelines for video games ... 26
D. Decisional practice in relation to state aid for video games ... 29
I. General legality principle ... 31
II. Promotion of culture: requirement of 'verifiable national criteria' ... 37
III. Appropriateness, necessity and proportionality test ... 43
IV. Limited distortion of competition and effect on trade ... 55
E. Conclusion ... 57

1 This chapter explores various aspects of the application of EU state aid law to national aid measures in the video game industry. It provides a high-level overview of how the European Commission has assessed the compatibility of Member State measures aimed at supporting this sector under EU state aid rules.

2 The **structure** of this chapter is as follows. Section A outlines which national measures qualify as state aid. All proposed state aid measures must in principle be notified to the European Commission – this process is discussed in Section B. While state aid is in principle prohibited, there are important exceptions. Section C discusses the main grounds on which aid measures may be considered compatible with the internal market. Finally, Section D offers a more detailed analysis of the Commission's decision-making practice in relation to state aid for the video game industry.

A. State aid

3 Art. 107(1) of the Treaty on the Functioning of the European Union (TFEU) provides, in essence, that state aid is, in principle, prohibited. The first question to address, therefore, is whether a particular national measure **qualifies as state aid** within the meaning of this provision.

4 As confirmed by established EU case law, a measure can be classified as state aid within the meaning of Art. 107(1) TFEU only if a **number of conditions** are met.[1] Below, we explain how these conditions have been applied by the European Commission in its assessment of national measures aimed at supporting undertakings in the video game industry.

5 It is **often relatively straightforward** to conclude that certain state measures aimed at supporting the video game industry qualify as state aid. These measures typically confer a selective advantage, as they are available exclusively to undertakings in the video game sector. Moreover, given the existence of an international market for the production and

[1] See, for example, judgment of 13.32025, Cividale, case C-746/23 and case C-747/23, EU:C:2025:171, point 33.

distribution of video games, such measures are, in principle, capable of affecting trade between Member States and potentially distorting competition.

I. Undertakings

6 Recipients of state aid must qualify as **'undertakings'**, a term that, according to established EU case law, refers to entities engaged in an economic activity, regardless of their legal status and the way in which they are financed.[2] In the context of state aid for video games, the beneficiaries are typically companies involved in the production and development of video games, known in the sector as studios. These companies are considered undertakings, and the Commission's decisions indicate that this classification is often so self-evident that it is not explicitly stated in most cases.

7 While most aid schemes are designed to support undertakings involved in the creation and development of video games, there are also measures that focus on the **promotion and distribution of games**. One such example is the aid scheme in Flanders (Belgium), where support can be granted to undertakings for the purpose of 'developing talent' in the video game industry, as well as for the 'promotion' of games.[3]

8 In rare instances, the European Commission has expressed **doubts as to whether an aid measure would benefit undertakings**. One such example is found in the Commission's decision on the Danish scheme for the development, production and promotion of cultural and educational digital games. The scheme offered four types of aid, including 'game development support', which involved direct grants intended 'for the general promotion of games and to promote the international advancement of Danish game development and culture'. While some activities were excluded, the Danish authorities clarified that the aid targeted non-commercial activities relevant to the video game sector, such as organising seminars and courses, or publishing and sharing knowledge related to Danish game development. The Commission noted that such activities are 'unlikely to be economic activities' and therefore support for them would not constitute state aid.[4]

II. Advantage – State aid can take various forms

9 For a measure to qualify as state aid, it must confer an 'advantage' on its beneficiaries. The term 'advantage' is **interpreted broadly** and encompasses any economic benefit which an undertaking could not have obtained under normal market conditions, that is to say in the absence of state intervention.[5]

10 Where a national measure **relieves an undertaking of costs** it would normally have to bear under normal market conditions, it will be considered to confer such an advantage.

11 The form that the advantage takes is irrelevant, provided it confers an economic benefit on the undertaking. As illustrated by the Commission's state aid decisions concerning the video game sector, an advantage **can take various forms**. Such an advantage

[2] Judgment of 10.1.2006, Cassa di Risparmio di Firenze SpA and Others, case C-222/04, EU:C:2006:8, point 107.

[3] SA.101526 (2022/N) – Belgium – VAF Gamefonds, decision of 28.4.2022, point 14.

[4] SA.45735 – Denmark – Scheme for the development, production and promotion of cultural and educational digital games, decision of 12.5.2017, points 16 and 39.

[5] See, for example, judgment of 13.3.2025, Cividale, case C-746/23 and case C-747/23, EU:C:2025:171, point 40.

may take the form of conditionally repayable loans provided by national authorities that serve to reduce the production costs of undertakings active in games development and production. Such loans relieve these undertakings of costs that they would have to bear under normal market conditions.[6] More generally, measures that reduce the production costs of such companies will be considered as an advantage.[7]

12 Importantly, **tax benefits** may also qualify as an advantage. Such benefits reduce the costs that undertakings should bear under normal market conditions. The Commission's decisional practice includes several examples of tax incentives that have been assessed under EU state aid rules. Most commonly known are tax credit mechanisms. Examples are the Italian tax credit of 25 % of the eligible costs of the production budget of undertakings producing certain video games[8] and the Irish tax credit aid scheme for digital games.[9]

13 Another example worth mentioning is the **Belgian tax shelter**. Under this mechanism, if a company invests a certain amount of money in the production or development of a game, that investment is offset by a 'tax shelter certificate', which grants the investor a tax benefit in the form of a reduction in its taxable profit. The Commission explained that the support provided to the game producer originates from the investor's contribution, which is made possible by the tax deductibility triggered by the investment. Essentially, the advantage derived from the tax deduction is transferred from the investor to the game producer.[10]

III. State resources and imputability to the state

14 If the advantage is **financed from the state budget**, the condition of state resources is met. It is immaterial whether that is the budget of the federal state, or from federated entities, such as for example the Länder in Germany,[11] or the Communities in Belgium.[12]

IV. Selective advantage

15 If a state measure is limited to a particular sector, such as the video game industry, it will in principle satisfy the criterion of a 'selective' advantage. The European Commission's decisional practice confirms that state measures **aimed specifically at benefiting undertakings in the video game industry** are considered selective. An example is the Commission's decision concerning Germany's 'video games support by the federal government'. The measure was deemed selective because the aid is granted only to

[6] SA.101124 (2022/N) – Germany – Berlin-Brandenburg video games support measure, decision of 14.6.2022, point 27.

[7] SA.101526 (2022/N) – Belgium – VAF Gamefonds, decision of 28.4.2022, point 29.

[8] SA.63373 (2021/N) – Italy – Tax credit for the production of video games of 'Italian nationality' with cultural value, decision of 26.10.2021.

[9] SA.102047 (2022/N) – Ireland – Tax credit for digital games, decision of 27.9.2022.

[10] SA.54817 (2020/C) (ex 2019/N) – Belgium – Tax shelter aid scheme for videogame production, decision of 25.7.2022, points 15 and 37–39.

[11] See, for example, SA.114290 (2024/N) – Germany Promotion of digital games and interactive media content in central Germany (aid is financed from the budget of the Länder of central Germany) and SA.101124 (2022/N) – Germany – Berlin-Brandenburg video games support measure, decision of 14.6.2022, point 26 (aid financed from the budget of the states of Berlin and Brandenburg).

[12] SA.101526 (2022/N) – Belgium – VAF Gamefonds, decision of 28.4.2022, point 28 (state financed from the budget of the Flemish Community); SA.55046 – Belgium – Soutien aux jeux vidéo culturels, artistiques et éducatifs (Wallimage), decision of 24.1.2020, point 38 (state aid financed from the Walloon Region).

certain undertakings, specifically to undertakings that develop and produce high-quality video games or interactive content that meet certain requirements. As a result, 'other undertakings in a comparable legal and factual situation within that sector or other sectors' are excluded from benefiting from the measure.[13]

V. Distortion of competition and effect on trade between Member States

16 The European Commission will typically hold that the measure distorts competition and affects trade between Member States as the **video game sector has an 'international character'**[14] or because of the 'international dimension of trade in videogames'.[15]

B. Notification obligation

17 Under Art. 108 (3) TFEU, a **prior notification** of aid measures to the European Commission is required. Member States must notify draft state aid measures beforehand to the European Commission. The aid cannot be implemented until it has been approved by the European Commission (stand-still obligation). If a Member State does not notify the draft measure beforehand to the European Commission, there is a breach of Art. 108 (3) TFEU and that measure is unlawful.[16]

18 After it has been notified, the Commission will examine whether the draft state aid measure is **compatible** with the internal market. A prior notification is not required if the envisaged state aid measure can benefit from a **'block exemption'**.

C. Compatibility of aid measures to video games

19 Art. 107(1) TFEU establishes the general rule that state aid is prohibited, but this prohibition is not absolute, as there are significant exceptions. Art. 107(3) TFEU outlines specific types of aid that the Commission **may consider compatible with the internal market**. Under this provision, the Commission can grant exemptions for certain state aid measures from the general prohibition set forth in Art. 107(1) TFEU.

20 As discussed in greater detail in Section D, the Commission has so far approved state aid measures for video games under Art. 107(3)(d) TFEU. This provision states that '**aid to promote culture** and heritage conservation where such aid does not affect trading conditions and competition in the Union to an extent that is contrary to the common interest' is compatible with the internal market.

[13] SA.116220 (2024/N) – Germany – Video games support by the federal government, decision of 13.12.2024, point 30.

[14] SA.102047 (2022/N) – Ireland – Tax credit for digital games, decision of 27.9.2022, point 36.

[15] SA.49947 (2017/N) – Belgium – VAF Gamefonds, decision of 28.4.2022, point 32; SA.101124 (2022/N) – Germany – Berlin-Brandenburg video games support measure, decision of 14.6.2022, point 29.

[16] SA.64615 (2021/NN) – Germany – Prolongation of the Bavarian games support measure SA.46572, decision of 23.9.2021, point 5 (the original aid scheme was extended without notifying beforehand the European Commission).

I. General Block Exemption Regulation (GBER)

21 Commission Regulation (EU) No. 651/2014 of 17.6.2014 defines specific categories of aid that are deemed compatible with the internal market. Commonly referred to as the General Block Exemption Regulation (GBER), this regulation **outlines the types of aid measures that are exempt from the requirement of prior notification** to the European Commission.

22 In essence, the GBER sets out the **conditions under which Member States are permitted to grant state aid without submitting** the proposed measures **to the Commission for approval**. The application of the GBER first requires that the aid complies with the 'common provisions' set out in Chapter I, as well as the monitoring requirements in Chapter II. Additionally, the aid must meet the specific conditions for the 'different categories of aid' outlined in Chapter III of the GBER. That Chapter III identifies thirteen different categories of aid, including 'aid for culture and heritage conservation' (Section 11). Other examples are 'aid for research and development and innovation' (Section 4) and 'aid for sport and multifunctional recreational infrastructures' (Section 12).

23 Regarding 'aid for culture and heritage conservation', the relevant conditions for applying the block exemption are outlined in Art. 53 of the GBER. Under this provision, aid must support a 'cultural purpose or activity' as listed in Art. 53(2). These include 'art or cultural events and performances', 'cultural and artistic education activities' or 'writing, editing, production, distribution, digitisation and publishing of music and literature'. Notably, **video games are not included in the list of eligible cultural activities**. This exclusion is confirmed by point 72 of the GBER preamble, which explicitly states that cultural purposes 'should not include commercial sectors such as fashion, design or video games'. Consequently, aid schemes aimed at supporting video games do not qualify for the exemption under Art. 53.

24 Additionally, Art. 54 of the GBER provides for aid in support of **audiovisual works**. According to Art. 54, the exemption applies to aid schemes 'to support the scriptwriting, development, production, distribution and promotion of audiovisual works'. Subject to the conditions set out in the GBER, such schemes may receive aid of up to 55 million EUR per year. The aid must be directed toward supporting a 'cultural product'.

25 It follows that aid measures for video games do not qualify for the exemption of both Art. 53 and 54 of the GBER. In light of this, just like the European Games Developer Federation (EGDF), **Video Games Europe has advocated for a revision of the GBER to include video games**, as outlined in its 2024–2029 Manifesto.

II. No specific guidelines for video games

26 In some areas, the European Commission has published guidelines outlining the policies and principles for various categories of aid under Art. 107(3) TFEU. However, **no specific guidelines have been issued for aid to the video games sector**. In 2013, the Commission published its 'Communication on state aid for films and other audiovisual works' (also known as the Cinema Communication).[17] This Communication not only covers state aid for film production, but also extends to related activities such as scriptwriting, development, distribution and promotion of films. Furthermore, the Cinema Communication includes provisions for aid to 'cinemas' and aid to 'transmedia

[17] OJ 2013 C 332, 1.

storytelling', which is described as the technique of telling stories across multiple platforms and formats using digital technologies, like films and games. The compatibility of aid measures for activities addressed in the Cinema Communication will be based on the specific assessment criteria set out in that document.

27 The Commission explains in its Cinema Communication that the rules designed for **film production** do not automatically extend to video games and explicitly stated that the Communication 'does not cover aid granted to games'. The exclusion of games was further justified by the fact that, at the time, the Commission lacked a 'critical mass' of state aid decisions concerning the video game sector.[18]

28 Consequently, as there is **no specific guidelines** of the European Commission in relation to state aid measures specifically to the video game industry, the compatibility of these measures will be assessed on a case-by-case basis. Section D will describe how the European Commission has conducted such assessments with respect to aid measures supporting undertakings in the video game sector during the period from 2007 to 2025. The Cinema Communication is relevant also to that assessment, as it indicates that the 'aid intensity criteria' will be applied 'by analogy' to aid schemes targeted at games which serve a cultural or educational purpose.

D. Decisional practice in relation to state aid for video games

29 Given the absence of Commission guidelines on state aid for video games and the fact that aid for video games does not fall under the scope of application of the GBER, the compatibility of state aid measures supporting video games has been assessed by the European Commission on a **case-by-case** basis. To date, the Commission has approved state aid measures for video games under Art. 107(3)(d) TFEU. This provision states that 'aid to promote culture and heritage conservation where such aid does not affect trading conditions and competition in the Union to an extent that is contrary to the common interest' is compatible with the internal market.

30 As illustrated by Commission decisions on state aid in relation to video games,[19] an aid measure will only be compatible with the internal market **if all of the following conditions are satisfied**:

- it adheres to the 'general legality principle';
- it 'promotes culture' within the meaning of Art. 107(3)(d) TFEU;
- it is at the same time an 'appropriate', a 'necessary' and a 'proportional' instrument;
- there is a limited distortion of competition and effect on trade;
- it is 'transparent', meaning that detailed information about the aid measure will be made publicly available.

I. General legality principle

31 Before approving state aid measures, the European Commission must first ensure that the aid complies with the 'general legality' principle. This involves verifying that the **eligibility conditions and award criteria** do not include provisions that would be incompatible with provisions or general principles of EU law. An illustration can be found in the Commission's decision regarding the German 'video game support by

[18] Point 24 of the Cinema Communication.

[19] See SA.116220 (2024/N) – Germany – Video games support by the federal government, decision of 13.12.2024.

the federal government', where the Commission examined that the aid is granted 'in a manner consistent with the principles of transparency, non-discrimination and proportionality'.[20] The Commission will in particular verify that the aid measure **complies with internal market freedoms** (free movement of goods, free movement of persons, freedom to provide services and free movement of capital).[21]

32 According to the Commission's decisional practice, aid measures that require the **beneficiary to be an undertaking established in the Member State concerned** would not be accepted. However, the Commission does allow aid measures that impose the condition that the beneficiary must have a registered office, permanent establishment, or branch office in the Member State 'at the time the advantage under the measure is used'.[22] The Commission's decisional practice also establishes that a Member State cannot require that the team members involved in the development of a video game must have the nationality of the Member State granting the aid or be resident in that Member State.[23]

33 As part of this assessment, the Commission will examine whether the measure includes so-called **'territorial spending conditions'**. A Member State may not require beneficiaries to spend a certain amount of the aid within its national territory as a condition for receiving the aid.[24] In certain cases, the Commission was unwilling to issue a decision not to raise objections at the preliminary investigation phase and instead chose to open a formal investigation procedure. In those instances, the Member State has subsequently amended the aid measure in such a way that the Commission has concluded the formal investigation procedure with a positive decision.

34 A first example of how the Commission deals with territorial spending obligation concerns the **Belgian tax shelter mechanism**. The notified aid measure initially specified that the value of the tax shelter certificate issued to the investor was set at nine-tenths of the video game production costs 'made in Belgium'. The Commission observed that such a territorial spending condition could conflict with the free movement of goods and the freedom to provide services, as protected by Art. 34 and 56 of the TFEU. Moreover, the Commission argued that, unlike films, the production of video games is mobile and relatively flexible in terms of location and video games are developed and often produced by people working continuously on computers in a relatively stable environment. On this basis, the Commission decided to open a formal investigation procedure, rather than issuing a decision not to raise objections.[25] Following the Commission's comments, the Belgian legislature decided to revise the draft state aid scheme, notably by removing the territorial spending condition. The amended measure stipulated that eligible exploitation and production costs must be incurred 'within the European

[20] SA.116220 (2024/N) – Germany – Video games support by the federal government, decision of 13.12.2024, point 35.

[21] See, for example, State Aid SA.102047 (2022/N) – Ireland – Tax credit for digital games, decision of 27.9.2022, point 39.

[22] State Aid SA.102047 (2022/N) – Ireland – Tax credit for digital games, decision of 27.9.2022, point 40. See also State Aid SA.114290 (2024/N) – Germany – Promotion of digital games and interactive media content in central Germany, decision of 10.10.2024, point 43.

[23] State Aid SA.114290 (2024/N) – Germany – Promotion of digital games and interactive media content in central Germany, decision of 10.10.2024, point 44; SA.63373 (2021/N) – Italy – Tax credit for the production of video games of 'Italian nationality' with cultural value, decision of 26.10.2021, point 25.

[24] See, for example, SA.116220 (2024/N) – Germany – Video games support by the federal government, decision of 13.12.2024, point 39.

[25] SA.54817 – Belgium – Tax shelter aid scheme for videogame production, decision to initiate the formal investigation procedure of 30.4.2020, points 31–34.

Economic Area'. As a result, the European Commission no longer raised objections to the Belgian tax shelter mechanism and issued a positive decision.[26]

35 A second example concerning territorial spending obligations can be found in the Commission's decisions concerning the **UK video games tax relief**. The notified aid scheme stipulated that relief would only apply to expenditure on goods or services used or consumed 'within the United Kingdom'. The Commission expressed concerns about the compatibility of this condition with EU law, again emphasizing that video games can, and often are, developed by individuals working on computers across multiple countries.[27] Following the Commission's comments, the United Kingdom decided to remove the territorial spending obligation from the aid scheme and also agreed to cap the subcontracting costs eligible for aid at 1 million GBP. Based on these changes, the Commission confirmed that the tax relief mechanism complied with the general principle of legality.[28]

36 Under the general legality principle, the Commission also had to consider whether it is lawful to include a selection criterion that a (substantial) part of the work to **develop games** should be done **in the Member State** concerned. As will be explained later, as part of the cultural test, certain Member States have included such a requirement. For example, one of the selection criteria under the central Germany scheme for supporting the development and production of digital games was that a substantial part of the creative work was carried out in central Germany. This circumstance allowed potential beneficiaries to demonstrate their connection to the region's cultural and creative hub. The European Commission did not view this as an unjustified restriction, notably because it is also possible to establish a connection to central Germany in other ways, such as by including team members who can demonstrate a link to the region's culture.[29]

II. Promotion of culture: requirement of 'verifiable national criteria'

37 The Commission will assess whether an aid measure or scheme is effectively **'promoting culture'** within the meaning of Art. 107(3)(d) TFEU. This requirement is sometimes phrased differently in the Commission decisions, stating that the aid must be 'directed towards a cultural objective'[30] or must 'serve the promotion of culture'.[31]

38 As far as we are aware, France was the first Member State to notify a draft aid measure for the video game industry, asserting its compatibility under Art. 87(3)(c) of the EC Treaty (now Art. 107(3)(d) TFEU). Whilst acknowledging that the 'main objective' of video games is 'interactive entertainment', the Commission noted in its decision of 11.12.2007 that certain video games can nonetheless have a 'cultural dimension'. In the same decision, the Commission further observed that, although video games may be

26 SA.54817 (2019/N) – Belgium – Tax shelter for the production of video games, decision of 25.7.2022, points 27–28, 33 and 49.

27 SA.36139 (2013/C) (ex 2013/N) – United Kingdom – UK video games tax relief, decision to initiate the formal investigation procedure of 16.4.2013, points 18–21.

28 SA.36139 (2013/C) (ex 2013/N) – United Kingdom – UK video games tax relief, decision of 17.3.2014, points 37–38.

29 State Aid SA.114290 (2024/N) – Germany – Promotion of digital games and interactive media content in central Germany, decision of 10.10.2024, point 47. See also SA.63373 (2021/N) – Italy – Tax credit for the production of video games of 'Italian nationality' with cultural value, decision of 26.10.2021, point 26 (although carrying out 25 % of development work in Italy earns 20 points (out of 100), applicants can qualify their work as one of 'Italian nationality' without any territorial spending).

30 SA.22668, Ciudad de la Luz, decision of 8.5.2012, point 111.

31 SA.36139 (2013/C) (ex 2013/N) – United Kingdom – UK video games tax relief, positive decision of 27.3.2014, point 41.

regarded more as computer programs than as audiovisual products, this does not preclude some of them from qualifying as cultural products within the meaning of Art. 87(3)(c) of the EC Treaty.[32] Noting that the exception of Art. 87(3)(c) of the EC Treaty must be interpreted strictly, the Commission stated that it would apply the principle whereby 'each Member State must ensure that the content of the aided production is cultural according to verifiable national criteria (in compliance with the application of the subsidiarity principle)'.[33]

39 Since this decision, the Commission has taken the approach of verifying whether an aid measure for video games – where the Member State invokes the exemption under Art. 107(3)(d) TFEU – includes **verifiable national criteria** that ensure the eligible video games qualify as cultural products and that the aid measure can be considered as pursuing a cultural objective. Within this framework, reference is also sometimes made to a 'cultural test'. Furthermore, the Commission indicates that there must be a 'truly selective cultural test'.[34]

40 The Commission will examine the criteria set out in the **cultural test** established by the Member State to ensure that the video games eligible for aid genuinely qualify as cultural products. If the Member State claims to have put in place criteria or a test that limits eligibility to games with cultural or educational content, the Commission will verify that this will indeed be the case in practice. There have been instances where the Commission has expressed doubts regarding the cultural test and, as a result, has declined to issue a decision not to raise objections at the preliminary investigation stage, opting instead to open a formal investigation procedure. For example, in its decision of 16.4.2013 concerning the UK video games tax relief, the Commission explained that the cultural test was not sufficiently restrictive to guarantee that the aid would support only games with cultural content. In particular, the Commission emphasised that the test should place greater weight on the cultural quality and aspects of the game and not merely require a territorial link to the UK or the EEA.[35]

41 If a **selection process** is in place, the fact that the selection is made by a panel of experts to determine the eligible games does not prevent the Commission from concluding that the cultural test, with sufficiently detailed criteria, is being met.[36]

42 The Commission may also take into account the **estimations provided by the Member State** indicating that only a certain percentage of video games are expected to pass the cultural test. In its 2007 decision to open the formal investigation procedure concerning the French tax credit scheme, the Commission argued that the fact that 49 % of video games produced in France were eligible for aid, suggested that the measure was not genuinely aimed at promoting culture.[37] By contrast, following modifications to the cultural test, that percentage dropped to 31 %, which, according to the Commission, indicates that the measure 'does not simply have an industrial objective'. In the case of the Danish aid scheme, the Commission took into account the fact that the estimated pass

[32] C 47/2006 (ex N 648/2005) – France – Tax credit for the creation of video games, decision of 11.12.2007, point 64.

[33] C 47/2006 (ex N 648/2005) – France – Tax credit for the creation of video games, decision of 11.12.2007, points 66–67. The Commission referred on this point to its Communication 'on certain legal aspects relating to cinematographic and other audiovisual works', COM (2001) 534 final.

[34] SA.45735 – Denmark – Scheme for the development, production and promotion of cultural and educational digital games, decision of 12.5.2017, point 48.

[35] SA.36139 (2013/C) (ex 2013/N) – United Kingdom – UK video games tax relief, decision of 16.4.2013, points 32 and 34.

[36] See, for example, SA.101526 (2022/N) – Belgium – VAF Gamefonds, decision of 28.4.2022, point 38.

[37] C 47/2006 (ex N 648/2005) – France – Tax credit for the creation of video games, decision of 11.12.2007, point 83.

rate was very low, representing only 6 to 8 % of the total video game production output.[38]

III. Appropriateness, necessity and proportionality test

As part of its assessment of the compatibility of a draft state aid measure, the Commission examines whether the measure is an 'appropriate', 'necessary' and 'proportional' instrument. When Member States notify aid for video games under the objective of 'promoting culture' within the meaning of Art. 107(3)(d) TFEU, the Commission must determine, based on the information provided, whether the aid measure effectively meets these **three criteria** in pursuing that cultural objective. 43

First and foremost, the aid measure must be ***appropriate*** for achieving the cultural objectives it seeks to pursue. In one of its decisions, the Commission clarified that appropriateness implies 'that without this support there would not be sufficient incentive for market actors to produce the desired kind of games'.[39] 44

In most cases, Member State authorities present arguments concerning the market conditions under which 'cultural' video games must be developed, distributed and commercialised. They commonly contend that **financing the production of culturally valuable video games** is both challenging and entails significant financial risk. As part of its assessment of the appropriateness test, the European Commission must verify that such arguments are credible and well-substantiated. 45

For example, in the context of an aid scheme aimed at promoting digital games and interactive media content in central Germany, the German authorities argued that video game companies face **high production costs and considerable risks**. To ensure their survival, these companies, according to the German authorities, 'often produce games with universally or globally appealing content, keep expenditures deliberately low and avoid experimenting with innovative gameplay'. In this context, they claimed that aid in the form of development grants or conditionally repayable loans could help mitigate the financial risks faced by such companies. The Commission accepted these arguments, noting that 'culturally important games may have comparable production costs to global games, but significantly smaller markets' and that their production involves a higher economic risk. The Commission further emphasised that 'many culturally valuable games cannot be designed, developed and produced without funding'.[40] In such circumstances, the aid measure is deemed an appropriate tool, as it provides a necessary economic incentive to support the development of culturally significant games. 46

In the second place, under the ***necessity*** test, the Commission must assess, on a case-by-case basis,[41] whether the aid is necessary to support and incentivise the production of video games. The aid must have an **'incentive effect'** – that is, it should encourage recipient undertakings to adopt conduct likely to achieve one of the objectives referred to Art. 107(3) TFEU,[42] in this case, the promotion of culture. 47

---

[38] SA.45735 – Denmark – Scheme for the development, production and promotion of cultural and educational digital games, decision of 12.5.2017, point 47.

[39] SA.36139 (2013/C) (ex 2013/N) – United Kingdom – UK video games tax relief, decision of 27.3.2014, point 40.

[40] SA.114290 (2024/N) – Germany – Promotion of digital games and interactive media content in central Germany, decision of 10.102024, point 56.

[41] SA.36139 (2013/C) (ex 2013/N) – United Kingdom – UK video games tax relief, decision of 16.4.2013, point 27.

[42] Judgment of 13.6.2013, HGA, case C-630/11 P to case C-633/11 P, EU:C:2013:387, point 103.

48 The burden of proof rests with the Member State. It follows from a review of the Commission's decisions that Member States' authorities argue in general that the **development and production of 'cultural' video games** incur production costs similar to those of globally popular games, but these games face a significantly **smaller market**.

49 For instance, the German authorities highlighted the following points regarding the federal government's aid scheme for video game support: video games with cultural ties to Germany or the EU are often developed by **SMEs and start-ups that struggle to secure private financing**. The aid, according to the German authorities, is necessary 'to foster the production of culturally relevant video games, as commercial market pressures would otherwise lead to fewer video games'. Without the aid, there would be a reduction in video games with German and European cultural elements, which would, in turn, harm the industry's competitiveness. The German authorities also stated that the aid would 'help to mitigate or even compensate for the existing locational disadvantages, making investments more attractive for multinational companies and creating a healthy game-based ecosystem of SMEs and large undertakings', and will 'allow projects to be more ambitious'.[43]

50 When evaluating the 'necessity' for aid to undertakings producing and developing video games, the Commission's decisions, despite some differences, generally acknowledge that educational, cultural and artistic games often incur production costs comparable to those of globally popular games but face a significantly **smaller market**. As a result, their production carries a **higher economic risk**.[44] On this basis, the Commission has accepted in all published decisions that the Member State has demonstrated that it is necessary to incentivise the production of 'cultural' games.

51 In the third place, the state aid measure must be ***'proportional'***. The aid amount must be limited to the minimum needed to induce the additional investment or activity.

52 A key element assessed by the Commission under the proportionality test is the **'aid intensity'**. As previously discussed, while the Cinema Communication does not apply to state aid measures for video games, the European Commission has indicated that the maximum aid intensities set out therein may be applied by analogy to such measures. This approach is also clearly reflected in the Commission's decisional practice.

53 Point 52 (2) of the Cinema Communication states that the aid intensity must **in principle be limited to 50 % of the *production* budget**. On this basis, the European Commission will consider that aid which provides support amounting to less than 50 % of the game's production budget meets the proportionality test. For example, under the Irish tax credit scheme, the support represented 26 % of the game's budget.[45] Under the Italian tax credit scheme, aid was capped at 25 % of eligible costs, and when combined with other funding sources, the total aid could not exceed 50 % of eligible production costs.[46]

54 The Cinema Communication also specifies that aid for the production of 'difficult audiovisual works' is excluded from the general aid intensity limits. On this basis, the Commission has accepted the application of **higher aid intensities for the production of 'difficult' video games**. In this context, the Commission refers to the Cinema Com-

---

[43] SA.116220 (2024/N) – Germany – Video games support by the federal government, decision of 13.12.2024, points 56–59.

[44] See, for example, SA.101526 (2022/N) – Belgium – VAF Gamefonds, point 43; SA.45735 – Denmark – Scheme for the development, production and promotion of cultural and educational digital games, point 52.

[45] SA.102047 (2022/N) – Ireland – Tax credit for digital games, decision of 27.9.2022, point 52.

[46] SA.63373 (2021/N) – Italy – Tax credit for the production of video games of 'Italian nationality' with cultural value, decision of 26.10.2021, point 37.

munication and considers factors such as the limited territory of the original language in which the work is produced, as well as the generally commercially challenging nature of the supported works, as possible indicators that a work may be classified as 'difficult'.[47]

IV. Limited distortion of competition and effect on trade

The Commission must also assess whether **the negative effects of the state aid measure are sufficiently limited**, such that the overall balance of the measure remains positive. In its published state aid decisions concerning video games, the Commission has confirmed that this condition is effectively met. 55

Within this framework, the Commission has taken into account **various factors**, including: the relatively low number of titles published by local publishers compared to the rest of Europe;[48] limited aid intensities; small aid budgets; or the requirement that aid be granted only to projects possessing 'a truly cultural character'.[49] Regarding the Italian tax credit scheme, the European Commission noted that Italian production companies accounted for about 1.5 % of console game production relative to the domestic market and only 0.5 % for PC games. According to the Commission, this created a 'serious competitive imbalance between domestic and foreign production', while the overall volume of the aid was considered very limited in relation to the total turnover of the Italian market. Based on this, the Commission concluded that the aid scheme would have a minimal impact on competition and trade between Member States.[50] 56

E. Conclusion

While EU Member States aim to support companies in the video game sector across development, promotion and distribution, **EU state aid rules impose certain limitations** on how such support can be granted. Draft state aid measures must be notified to the European Commission, unless they fall within the scope of an exemption under the General Block Exemption Regulation (GBER). 57

The European video game **trade federations have advocated for an amendment to the GBER** to exempt specific state aid measures for video games from the notification requirement. As demonstrated by the Commission's decisional practice, however, all existing state aid measures in this sector have so far been assessed on a case-by-case basis. 58

This article has also shown that **the legal basis for all such decisions remains Art. 107(3)(d) TFEU**. Consequently, these measures must demonstrate that they serve the objective of promoting culture, which is why Member States include a cultural test in their support schemes for video games. 59

---

[47] SA.45735 – Denmark – Scheme for the development, production and promotion of cultural and educational digital games, decision of 12.5.2017, point 61.

[48] State Aid SA.102047 (2022/N) – Ireland – Tax credit for digital games, decision of 27.9.2022, point 54.

[49] SA.114290 (2024/N) – Germany – Promotion of digital games and interactive media content in central Germany, decision of 10.10.2024, point 66.

[50] SA.63373 (2021/N) – Italy – Tax credit for the production of video games of 'Italian nationality' with cultural value, decision of 26.10.2021, point 38.

§ 8
Public Funding

A. Introduction ... 1
I. The foundations of the EU state aid framework ... 2
II. The impact of the EU state aid framework ... 5
B. Different types of public support ... 10
I. Cultural aid ... 11
II. R&D aid ... 17
III. SME aid ... 20
C. Different aid instruments and their target groups in the video game industry ecosystem ... 24
D. Conclusion ... 28

A. Introduction

1

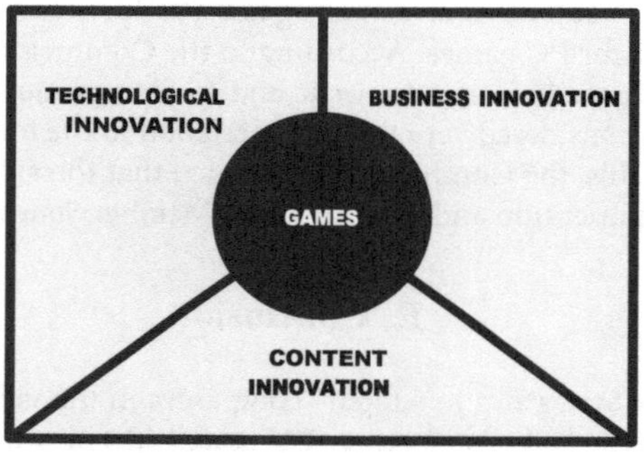

Figure 8.1: Games are at the crossroads of technological, business and content innovation

I. The foundations of the EU state aid framework

2 The foundations of the **EU state aid framework** discussed in the previous chapter were developed in the industrial era. In the times before digital distribution and production, the distinction between R&D activities and cultural production made perfect sense. Developing a new TV camera was an R&D activity, and using it to film a TV series was a cultural production. This increasingly obsolete separation of state aid for the development of economic activities (including R&D and SME aid) and state aid to promote culture is even cemented in the founding treaty of the European Union. Article 107(3)(c) of the **Treaty on the Functioning of the European Union (TFEU)** covers state aid for economic activities, and Article 107(3)(d) of TFEU covers state aid to promote culture.

3 Similarly, in the industrial era, it was clear when a prototype of a new tool was finalised, when it entered trial production and when it moved to production and distribution. This industrial era R&D process is still present in the **OECD Frascati Manual** for the classification of R&D activities. This manual is often used to separate activities

eligible for R&D state aid (prototypes), partly eligible for R&D aid (trial production) and business activities that are not eligible for R&D aid.[1]

In the digital era, especially in the video games industry, the aforementioned artificial **barriers** between cultural and R&D activities under the EU state aid framework are becoming increasingly artificial. Game prototypes (demos), for example, are funded through both cultural and R&D funding instruments. 4

II. The impact of the EU state aid framework

The importance of the public support framework for the national and local game industry ecosystems in Europe should not be underestimated. If there is a single policy document that shapes the national video game industry ecosystem, it is the **public funding application form**. As almost every game developer studio in the country applies for public funding at some point, the **questions** it asks and its **eligibility criteria** heavily influence the whole mindset of the local industry ecosystems. 5

Furthermore, EGDF highlights that public support plays a crucial role in ensuring **the artistic and technological sovereignty** of European game developer studios. The public support has enabled European game developer studios to realise their artistic visions, strengthen their position in the video game industry value chain by enabling self-publishing, and sustain the rights of their IPs and the shares of their companies in their own hands much longer.[2] 6

EGDF reminds that, as video game markets are by their nature global, public support is rarely able to disturb price **competition** in the markets. However, EGDF notes that subsidies can play a crucial role in the game developer studios' ability to compete for top global talent or investment for their games.[3] 7

EGDF sees video games at the crossroads of new technologies, groundbreaking business models, and artistic content (See figure 8.1). Consequently, video games are also at the crossroads of **cultural state aid, R&D aid and SME aid.**[4] On the one hand, this makes video games eligible for a wide range of different public support instruments. On the other hand, navigating the complex European state aid framework, and especially combining different support instruments, requires outstanding holistic support from public funding authorities, as well as excellent project administration and reporting skills from game developer studios. 8

Most importantly, the fact that video games, as digital products, are far from a perfect fit for the European state aid framework means that the European game industry has been and continues to be forced to fight for being eligible for different state aid instruments. For the European game industry, the cultural nature of video games has always been also a question about the **eligibility** of video games for cultural state aid. European Games Developer Federation (EGDF) itself, representing European trade associations, 9

---

1 EGDF, 'EGDF white paper on public funding for video games industry' <https://www.egdf.eu/wp-content/uploads/2025/06/202505-EGDF-WHITE-PAPER-ON-PUBLIC-FUNDING-FOR-GAME-INDUSTRY-V1-5.pdf> (last accessed: 10.6.2025), p.61.

2 EGDF, 'EGDF white paper on public funding for video games industry' <https://www.egdf.eu/wp-content/uploads/2025/06/202505-EGDF-WHITE-PAPER-ON-PUBLIC-FUNDING-FOR-GAME-INDUSTRY-V1-5.pdf> (last accessed: 10.6.2025), p. 7, 14.

3 EGDF, 'EGDF white paper on public funding for video games industry' <https://www.egdf.eu/wp-content/uploads/2025/06/202505-EGDF-WHITE-PAPER-ON-PUBLIC-FUNDING-FOR-GAME-INDUSTRY-V1-5.pdf> (last accessed: 10.6.2025), p. 14.

4 EGDF, 'EGDF white paper on public funding for video games industry' <https://www.egdf.eu/wp-content/uploads/2025/06/202505-EGDF-WHITE-PAPER-ON-PUBLIC-FUNDING-FOR-GAME-INDUSTRY-V1-5.pdf> (last accessed: 10.6.2025), p. 1.

was founded in 2007 to defend French cultural state aid for video games against International Software Federation (ISFE) which represented international publishers[5] and lobbied heavily against video games being cultural products and thus eligible for cultural state aid[6].

B. Different types of public support

10 As discussed in the previous chapter, the European state aid framework divides the state aid for video games into **cultural aid** and **R&D aid**. Furthermore, it is meaningful to discuss **SME aid** as its own category, as its focus goes beyond R&D activities.[7]

I. Cultural aid

11 **Table 8.1: Cultural funding for video game productions**[8]

Commonly used forms of cultural support	**The role of cultural funding for game production in the video game industry**	**The impact of the cultural funding for game production on the video game industry**	**Usually used legal basis**	**Best examples**
Cultural grants for video game prototypes and/or production **Cultural tax breaks**	Cultural state aid is the key enabler of **artistic risk-taking and experimentation** for the industry pioneers pushing the boundaries of the games as a cultural medium.	Cultural funding for video game productions encourages game developer studios to focus on creating **artistically ambitious games**.	**Notification process** (video games are not currently included in the General Block Exemption Regulation)	**French tax breaks for games** (Crédit d'Impôt Jeu Vidéo)[9] **The Federal German Games Funding Programme** (Computerspieleförderung des Bundes)[10]

12 Traditionally, video games have been considered to be part of the **audiovisual sector.** Consequently, according to EGDF, most of the cultural funding instruments for the games industry have their roots in film funding[11]: Screen Brussel Fund, Flanders Audiovisual Fund (VAF), Wallonia Wallimage Enterprises, Croatian Audiovisual Centre Fund-

[5] EGDF, 'About EGDF' <https://www.egdf.eu/about/> (last accessed: 10.6.2025).

[6] 2008/354/EC: Commission Decision of 11 December 2007 on State Aid C 47/06 (ex N 648/05) Tax credit introduced by France for the creation of video games <https://eur-lex.europa.eu/legal-content/EN/TXT/PDF/?uri=OJ:L:2008:118:FULL> (last accessed: 10.6.2025).

[7] EGDF 'European Video video games Industry Insights Report', <https://www.egdf.eu/wp-content/uploads/2024/06/2022-European-video-video games-industry-insight-report.pdf> (last accessed: 10.6.2025), p. 20 et seqq.

[8] EGDF, 'EGDF white paper on public funding for video games industry' <https://www.egdf.eu/wp-content/uploads/2025/06/202505-EGDF-WHITE-PAPER-ON-PUBLIC-FUNDING-FOR-GAME-INDUSTRY-V1-5.pdf> (last accessed: 10.6.2025), p. 6, 17.

[9] CNC <https://www.cnc.fr/professionnels/aides-et-financements/jeu-video/credit-dimpot-jeu-video_121078> (last accessed: 10.6.2025).

[10] BMWK <https://www.bmwk.de/Redaktion/DE/Dossier/ s.html> (last accessed: 10.6.2025).

[11] EGDF, 'EGDF white paper on public funding for video games industry'

ing (HAVC), Finnish Audiovisual Center (AVEK), French Centre National du Cinéma et de l'Image Animée (CNC), Bavarian Film and Television Fund (FFF), Norwegian Film Institute (NFI) and Irish Western Region Audiovisual Producers (WRAP) just to name a few national and regional cultural audiovisual funding bodies providing cultural funding for video games.[12]

However, year by year, these cultural video game funding instruments are slowly becoming instruments in their own right, separate from film funding, as they are becoming more and more tailored to the specific needs of the video game industry. Danish Danmaks Institut for Spiludvikling (NIMBI) is the first cultural funding institution dedicated solely to video game development[13]. 13

EGDF notes that often, **cultural funding instruments** are as successful as the **cultural test** used to ensure that funding fulfils the cultural **state aid criteria**. A too strict focus on, for example, **narrative storytelling** games means that the scope of an instrument becomes overly narrow and the instrument misses other cultural aspects of video games (such as location of the story, subject matter, lead characters, reflection of local culture, etc.)[14]. The wider the cultural scope of the instrument, the better it can cover the full **cultural diversity** of video games. 14

According to the European Games Funding Guide, cultural funding instruments are often focused on the creation of **video game prototypes** (pre-production) or supporting **video game production**.[15] Cultural funding could also be used for **audience building**, but so far, launching a video game or video game marketing activities are poorly covered by public video game support instruments. 15

The role and impact of cultural funding are discussed in more detail in the table 8.1. EGDF reminds that cultural funding instruments are particularly important for European SME developers, as they enable the development of **artistically risk-taking video game prototypes (demos)** and strengthen their negotiating position with publishers and risk investors by covering part of the production costs.[16] However, the cultural funding instruments also carry a risk of guiding game developer studios to become overly focused on the artistic nature of video games and forgetting the crucial role of building a technologically solid game that is based on a profitable business model. 16

<https://www.egdf.eu/wp-content/uploads/2025/06/202505-EGDF-WHITE-PAPER-ON-PUBLIC-FUNDING-FOR-GAME-INDUSTRY-V1-5.pdf> (last accessed: 10.6.2025), p. 19.

12 Baujard et al, 'European games funding guide 2021' <https://www.creativeeuropedesk.nl/sites/default/files/2021-12/GFG2021_HighRes_12.11.21.pdf> (last accessed: 10.6.2025).

13 Nimbi <https://nimbi.dk/> (last accessed: 10.6.2025).

14 EGDF, 'EGDF white paper on public funding for video games industry' <https://www.egdf.eu/wp-content/uploads/2025/06/202505-EGDF-WHITE-PAPER-ON-PUBLIC-FUNDING-FOR-GAME-INDUSTRY-V1-5.pdf> (last accessed: 10.6.2025), p. 19.

15 Baujard et al, 'European games funding guide 2021' <https://www.creativeeuropedesk.nl/sites/default/files/2021-12/GFG2021_HighRes_12.11.21.pdf> (last accessed: 10.6.2025).

16 EGDF, 'EGDF white paper on public funding for video games industry' <https://www.egdf.eu/wp-content/uploads/2025/06/202505-EGDF-WHITE-PAPER-ON-PUBLIC-FUNDING-FOR-GAME-INDUSTRY-V1-5.pdf> (last accessed: 10.6.2025), p. 19.

II. R&D aid

17 **Table 8.2: R&D funding for technological and business innovation in video games**[17]

Commonly used forms of R&D support	The role of the R&D funding for technological innovation in the video game industry	The impact of the R&D&I funding for technological innovation in the video game industry	Usually used legal basis	Best examples
R&D grants **R&D loans** **R&D tax breaks**	State aid for research, development, and innovation enables industry forerunners to exploit the **possibilities of new technologies and business models** fully in game development.	R&D funding guides game developer studios to focus on improving the **tools and methods they use in game** production. Furthermore, it encourages them to pay attention to the **business models and monetisation strategies** of their video games.	**De minimis** **General Block Exemption Regulation**	**Business Finland** funding for game development[18]

18 The EGDF approach to the role and impact of R&D funding is summarised in more detail in the table 8.2. Traditionally, **R&D support instruments** have been targeted at **technological innovation** (e.g., the development of video game production processes, game engines, game production, marketing or analytic tools). However, EGDF observes that during the 2010s, we have seen more and more R&D funding for **business innovation** (e.g., the development of new business and monetisation models or marketing models) and **game design innovations** (e.g., new game genres, concepts, game mechanics, user interfaces or narrative techniques)[19]. Successful R&D instruments targeted for the game industry can combine all of these approaches to innovation.

19 According to EGDF, one of the biggest challenges for the video game industry is that under the **Frascati guidelines** guiding the implementation of the EU state aid rules, R&D support instruments are limited strictly to the development of **game prototypes** (demos), **trial production** (early access or soft launch) and **redevelopment** (introduction of novel features in an existing game).[20] **Video game production** itself and **game marketing** are therefore limited out of the scope of the R&D instruments. This demonstrates how the

---

[17] EGDF, 'EGDF white paper on public funding for video games industry' <https://www.egdf.eu/wp-content/uploads/2025/06/202505-EGDF-WHITE-PAPER-ON-PUBLIC-FUNDING-FOR-GAME-INDUSTRY-V1-5.pdf> (last accessed: 10.6.2025), p. 4 et seqq., 19.

[18] Business Finland <https://www.businessfinland.fi/en/for-finnish-customers/services/funding/tempo-funding/game-business-funding> (last accessed: 10.6.2025).

[19] EGDF, 'EGDF white paper on public funding for video games industry' <https://www.egdf.eu/wp-content/uploads/2025/06/202505-EGDF-WHITE-PAPER-ON-PUBLIC-FUNDING-FOR-GAME-INDUSTRY-V1-5.pdf> (last accessed: 10.6.2025), p. 6, 17.

[20] OECD, 'Frascati manual 2015'

European state aid framework developed for R&D in traditional retail industries fails to capture the realities of innovative emerging digital industries. In an ideal case, while waiting for the state aid framework to be updated, the national state aid framework would always include cultural funding instruments to cover the limitations of R&D support.

III. SME aid

Table 8.3: SME funding supporting entrepreneurship[21] 20

Commonly used forms of SME support	The role of SME funding in the video game industry	The impact of the SME funding on the video game industry	Usually used legal basis	Best examples
SME and start-up grants, including aid for accessing training, consultancy or trade fairs **SME and start-up loans** **SME and start-up tax breaks**	SME aid mainstream **entrepreneurial skills** in the game industry ecosystem	SME support instruments build **a route to entrepreneurship** by enabling industry newcomers and veterans to take entrepreneurial risk and launch and run a new game business (e.g., business skills and business ethics)	**De minimis General Block Exemption Regulation**	**Regional SME cluster funding in Sweden**

The EGDF observations on the role and impact of SME funding are summarised in more detail in the table 8.3. EGDF underlines that there is no one-size-fits-all solution for SME support that can be transferred as such from one location to another. SME support instruments must always be tailored to a **local context and needs.** Most of the European game developer studios are microcompanies or SMEs. Risk-taking SMEs play a crucial role in pushing the technological, business and artistic boundaries of the game industry. Furthermore, as most of the game industry SMEs fail, they play a crucial role in growing talent with tested entrepreneurial skills for the more established game developer studios in the local game industry ecosystem.[22] 21

SME and start-up support instruments are often run through local or regional incubators, accelerators or cluster organisations. According to the EGDF, this makes SME funding particularly vulnerable to changes in **policy priorities.** Often, SME support instruments for specific industry sectors are the first to be cut when policy priorities move from one industry sector to another. The unpredictable nature of SME support instruments creates a significant structural risk for local and regional video game industry 22

<https://www.oecd.org/content/dam/oecd/en/publications/reports/2015/10/frascati-manual-2015_g1g57dcb/9789264239012-en.pdf>, p. 61;

EGDF, 'EGDF white paper on public funding for video games industry' <https://docs.google.com/document/d/1YNHPD74avk4-_e8-4icwE2cxVsaYjGTgY22aU63-_Fs/edit?tab=t.0#heading=h.frm9rovi21t5> (last accessed: 10.6.2025), p. 17 et seq.

21 EGDF, 'EGDF white paper on public funding for video games industry' <https://docs.google.com/document/d/1YNHPD74avk4-_e8-4icwE2cxVsaYjGTgY22aU63-_Fs/edit?tab=t.0#heading=h.frm9rovi21t5> (last accessed: 10.6.2025), p. 9 et seq., 33.

22 EGDF, 'EGDF white paper on public funding for video games industry' <https://www.egdf.eu/wp-content/uploads/2025/06/202505-EGDF-WHITE-PAPER-ON-PUBLIC-FUNDING-FOR-GAME-INDUSTRY-V1-5.pdf> (last accessed: 10.6.2025), p 16.

ecosystems. Without a long-term commitment to SME support, there is a significant risk that the growth of the local industry ecosystem stagnates.[23]

23 From the EGDF perspective, it is crucial to note that **general SME support instruments** are rarely successful in supporting the local or regional game industry ecosystems. The video game industry is a global **digital B2C business** that requires a highly specific skill set. For this reason, it also needs incubators, accelerators, and cluster organisations that are specifically targeted at the industry. In particular, it needs trade promotion programs that allow local studios to attend international conferences and seminars that play a vital role in mapping emerging industry trends.[24]

C. Different aid instruments and their target groups in the video game industry ecosystem

24 Cultural, R&D and SME aid can take many forms. Each of them has its unique **advantages** and **disadvantages**.

25 **Table 8.4: EGDF approach on the pros and cons of different forms of public support instruments**[25]

	Grants	Tax breaks	Loans	Equity
Pros	Grants are the best way to encourage developers to **take risks** and **test and develop innovative technologies, business models and storytelling methods**, as those projects are often too risky to be funded with any other funding instrument.	Tax support schemes allow **budgets that are bigger** than grant-based models, they are a particularly effective way to secure that big productions are still being realised in Europe by attracting major international productions to Europe and improving the attractiveness of the industry to private investors. This, in turn, will enable more studios to innovate and develop their own IP.	Loan-based funding allows public institutions to fund **bigger projects with more limited financial constraints** on how money can be used than with grant-based models.	The public support for European **venture capital investors** ensures that European game developer studios do not depend on overseas investors to access venture capital to launch or scale up their companies. Equity funding allows European video game industry angel investors to build venture capital funds and to scale up small video game industry funds to proper venture capital funds.

[23] EGDF, 'EGDF white paper on public funding for video games industry' <https://www.egdf.eu/wp-content/uploads/2025/06/202505-EGDF-WHITE-PAPER-ON-PUBLIC-FUNDING-FOR-GAME-INDUSTRY-V1-5.pdf> (last accessed: 10.6.2025), p. 33.

[24] EGDF, 'EGDF white paper on public funding for video games industry' <https://www.egdf.eu/wp-content/uploads/2025/06/202505-EGDF-WHITE-PAPER-ON-PUBLIC-FUNDING-FOR-GAME-INDUSTRY-V1-5.pdf> (last accessed: 10.6.2025), p. 39.

[25] EGDF, 'EGDF white paper on public funding for video games industry' <https://www.egdf.eu/wp-content/uploads/2025/06/202505-EGDF-WHITE-PAPER-ON-PUBLIC-FUNDING-FOR-GAME-INDUSTRY-V1-5.pdf> (last accessed: 10.6.2025), p. 7, 12 et seqq., 26 et seq.

	Grants	Tax breaks	Loans	Equity
Cons	Unfortunately, grants are often limited to **project-based funding** with limited budgets and significant constraints on how money can be used.	**Reimbursement rates** with tax breaks are often much smaller than with grants.	Unless **soft-loan models** are used where the unpaid part of the loan can be transformed into a grant if needed, the **risks** related to loan-based funding, especially when combined with personal guarantees, can be huge for risk-taking entrepreneurs. When loan funding is provided as loan guarantees to banks, it is important to note that in many European countries, they fail to lead in taking increased risk-taking in granting loans because banks have been hesitant to increase their risk taking.	The resources of national support instruments for equity financing are currently limited. It is often difficult for small angel-based venture capital funds to meet the high **threshold** for fund sizes required by public funding for funds.

Often, public support for the video game industry is discussed in the context of game developer studios. However, it is crucial to recall that support for a local video game industry ecosystem should be based on a strategic approach that identifies all key actors in the ecosystem that enable the success of individual video game developer studios. 26

Table 8.5: EGDF mapping of the role of different actors in the video game industry ecosystem and the most common support instruments for them[26] 27

	Role in the ecosystem	Common types of public support
Game developer studios	Game developer studios make the video games	Grants and loans through cultural, R&D and SME aid speeding the growth of the company and enabling risk taking and innovation

[26] EGDF, 'EGDF white paper on public funding for video games industry' <https://www.egdf.eu/wp-content/uploads/2025/06/202505-EGDF-WHITE-PAPER-ON-PUBLIC-FUNDING-FOR-GAME-INDUSTRY-V1-5.pdf> (last accessed: 10.6.2025), p. 9 et seqq.

	Role in the ecosystem	Common types of public support
Video game publishers and distributors	Publishers and distributors are often needed for successful market access. It is essential to support the creation and consolidation of European companies responsible for publishing and distributing video games in the Digital Single Market area and abroad.	Grants and loans through cultural, R&D and SME aid speeding the growth of the company and enabling risk taking and innovation
Investors	Investors make the success of the studio financially possible	Equity funding through cultural, R&D and SME aid enabling the growth of the local VC funds
Service providers	Service providers like middleware developers, legal experts and analytics services are needed to secure that European game developers can focus on creating video games instead of services enabling the creation of video games.	Grants and loans through R&D and SME aid speeding the growth of the company and enabling risk taking and innovation
Incubators and accelerators	Incubators and accelerators help growth-oriented video game industry start-ups to succeed.	Grants trough regional development funding and SME aid enabling local ecosystem development
Cluster organisations	Cluster organisations ensure access to talent and investment through location marketing and enable access to trade missions, public funding, and other public services targeted at entrepreneurs.	Grants trough regional development funding and SME aid enabling local ecosystem development
Game education institutions and non-formal game education	Game education institutions and non-formal game education (e.g. youth clubs) enabling game development as a hobby are needed to secure access to skilled employees and local super talents for the studios.	Grants trough public funding for education and youth work nurturing local talent and R&D funding for universities

D. Conclusion

28 Ideally, as demonstrated by EGDF, the video game industry's public support frameworks should be based on a **national game industry strategy** that overcomes artificial barriers created by the European state aid framework and builds a support system that combines cultural, R&D and SME funding to a **consistent structure** that is able to support to growth of the local game developer studios from a start-up to an established SME and eventually a large corporation. Public funding structures should be able to tackle **all the challenges** the industry is facing, from ensuring artistic excellence and creation of its own IPs, technological and business excellence, entrepreneurial excellence, to ensuring operational autonomy of the local companies. They should not support just prototype building and game production, but also audience building and marketing. They should enable **risk-taking** and **strengthen** the position of European game developer studios in the global game industry value chain. And, most importantly, all public support instruments must be constantly developed further in close collaboration with industry stakeholders.[27]

29 EGDF underlines that **competitive and successful public support instruments** are well-resourced, meaning that they are able to make investments of hundreds of thousands of euros in a single project with over 50 % financing rates. They are **tailored** for game industry practices instead of being based on funding instruments from other sectors or general business support instruments. They are **SME friendly,** meaning that they are unbureaucratic, predictable, transparent, and automated as far as possible. They must not be drastically cut down when policy priorities change, and they are run by **competent public officials** with industry experience and the means to join the main international industry events.[28]

30 As EGDF concludes, all this requires that the EU moves the focus of its state aid regulation from minimising competition between member countries to improving the global competitiveness of the Union and European companies operating in global markets.[29] It is clear that the EU needs 'game communication' that does not just set clear rules for public support targeting video games, but also brings the whole EU state aid framework from the industrial to the digital era.

[27] EGDF, 'EGDF white paper on public funding for video games industry' <https://www.egdf.eu/wp-content/uploads/2025/06/202505-EGDF-WHITE-PAPER-ON-PUBLIC-FUNDING-FOR-GAME-INDUSTRY-V1-5.pdf> (last accessed: 10.6.2025), p. 42.

[28] EGDF, 'EGDF white paper on public funding for video games industry' <https://www.egdf.eu/wp-content/uploads/2025/06/202505-EGDF-WHITE-PAPER-ON-PUBLIC-FUNDING-FOR-GAME-INDUSTRY-V1-5.pdf> (last accessed: 10.6.2025), p. 12, 19, 42.

[29] EGDF, 'EGDF white paper on public funding for video games industry' <https://www.egdf.eu/wp-content/uploads/2025/06/202505-EGDF-WHITE-PAPER-ON-PUBLIC-FUNDING-FOR-GAME-INDUSTRY-V1-5.pdf> (last accessed: 10.6.2025), p. 15 et seq.

§ 9
Corporate Law Aspects in the Computer Games Industry in Europe

Bibliography: Altmeppen, GmbHG, 10th edn, Munich, C.H. Beck, 2021; Bank/Möllmann, Venture Capital Agreements in Germany, 1st edn, Munich, C.H. Beck, 2017; Bartlett, Venture Capital: Law, Business Strategies, and Investment Planning, 4th edn, New York 2019; Bertoni/Colombo/Grilli, 'Venture Capital Investor Type and the Growth Mode of New Technology-Based Firms', Small Business Economics 2013, Vol. 40, 527–552; Bussgang, Mastering the VC Game: A Venture Capital Insider Reveals How to Get from Start-up to IPO on Your Terms, New York 2020; Calacanis, How to Invest in Technology Startups, New York 2017; Courtney, The Law of Private Companies, 4th edn, Dublin 2022; Cozian/Viandier/Deboissy, Droit des sociétés, 35e éd., Paris 2022; Cumming/Johan, Venture Capital and Private Equity Contracting: An International Perspective, 2nd edn, London 2019; Fleischer (ed), Rechtsformneuschöpfungen im in- und ausländischen Gesellschaftsrecht, Tübingen 2024; Grilli/Murtinu, 'Venture Capital and High-tech Start-ups in Europe: A Systematic Review of the Empirical Evidence', Small Business Economics 2024, 1–42; Grundmann, Europäisches Gesellschaftsrecht: Systematische Darstellung unter Einbeziehung des Europäischen Kapitalmarktrechts, Berlin 2025; Herler, Gesellschaftsrecht in der Notar- und Gestaltungspraxis, 3rd edn 2025; Hentsch/Falk, Praxishandbuch Games und Recht, Baden-Baden: Nomos 2022; Kalss/Deutsch (eds), Europäisches Gesellschaftsrecht, 2nd edn, Munich 2025; Kraakman et al., The Anatomy of Corporate Law: A Comparative and Functional Approach, 3rd edn, Oxford 2017; Lutter/Hommelhoff/Teichmann (eds), SE-Kommentar zur Europäischen Gesellschaft, 3rd edn, Cologne 2025; Mallaby, The Power Law: Venture Capital and the Making of the New Future, London 2022; Michalski et al., GmbH-Gesetz, 3. Aufl. 2017; Möslein/Omlor (eds), Gesellschaftsrecht im digitalen Zeitalter, Heidelberg 2020; Royse, 10,000 Startups: Legal Strategies for Startup Success, Berkeley 2021; Weitnauer, Handbuch Venture Capital, 6th edn 2019; Wegen/Spahlinger/Barth, Gesellschaftsrecht des Auslands, Munich C.H. Beck 2025.

A. Introduction 1

B. Status of the harmonisation of company law in Europe 4
- I. Company law 4
- II. Register law and procedure in company law 10

C. Foundation 19
- I. Choosing the right legal form 19
  - 1. Typology and supranational legal forms 23
    - *a) Hobby and leisure projects* 23
    - *b) Developer studio/small publisher* 25
      - *aa) No supranational legal form* 27
      - *bb) Legal issues arise from national law* 28
    - *c) Exit-driven (venture capital-financed studios)* 29
    - *d) Project companies* 32
  - 2. European (supranational) legal forms 34
    - *a) Societas Europaea (SE)* 34
    - *b) European Economic Interest Grouping (EEIG)* 40
- II. Formation of a limited liability company 41
  - 1. Regular Formation Procedure 41
    - *a) Preparation of the foundation* 42
    - *b) Notarisation (if required)* 43
    - *c) Payment of the share capital* 44
    - *d) Entry in the commercial register* 45
  - 2. Online justification 46
  - 3. Articles of association content 54
  - 4. Cross-border aspects (Proof of existence and representation) 59
    - *a) Authorisations* 63
    - *b) Registered office abroad* 64

D. Organisation of financing 65
- I. CLA and SAFE Agreements 65
  - 1. CLA 65
    - *Typical CLAs* 66
  - 2. SAFE 68
- II. VC financing and 'Series A round' 69
- III. Other aspects 73

E. Exit 76

A. Introduction

This chapter examines company law aspects throughout the lifecycle of a games company. Given their complexity and this handbook's scope, we can only provide an overview of the key topics. Our focus is on industry practices and how different legal aspects fit into the broader context. 1

The games industry is inherently international, with cross-border cooperation, international investors, and global distribution. However, most company law matters remain governed by national legislation. While EU directives provide some harmonisation, this remains partial and selective. At best, we can offer guidance on the key principles. 2

Supranational European legal forms such as the SE (Societas Europaea) generally suit only larger games companies, though they greatly simplify internationalisation and Europe-wide cooperation. Smaller and medium-sized companies still lack a suitable European legal form. Most games companies therefore initially rely on national legal forms, which this chapter can only outline. However, the freedom of establishment and European reorganisation law create new strategic options for smaller companies. 3

B. Status of the harmonisation of company law in Europe

I. Company law

European company law is experiencing progressive but selective harmonisation. The EU achieves harmonisation primarily through directives, which function as framework legislation and only take direct effect when transposed into national law. Today, the legal basis for adopting such directives is primarily Artt. 50(1) and (2)(g) TFEU (formerly Art. 44 TEC). The Council may adopt measures coordinating national laws relating to companies within the meaning of Art. 54(2) TFEU, particularly for protecting shareholders and third parties. 4

Coordination aims not only to remove obstacles to freedom of establishment but also to create equivalent protection levels for market participants across all Member States. European regulation has focused on corporations due to their limited liability and economic importance. Consequently, most directives relate exclusively to stock corporations (AG), partnerships limited by shares (KGaA), and limited liability companies (GmbH), while partnerships have rarely been subject to EU regulation. 5

The EU has introduced 14 company law directives since the 1960s, though implementation has been mixed. Key directives include: the Publicity Directive (68/151/EEC); the Capital Directive (77/91/EEC); the Single Member Company Directive (89/667/EEC); the Cross-Border Mergers Directive (2005/56/EC); the Shareholders' Rights Directive (2007/36/EC); and Directive (EU) 2017/1132 which codified most of these regulations into a standardised structure. The recently enacted Digitalisation Directive II (EU) 2025/25 has modernised this framework (see II). Directive (EU) 2019/2121 further harmonises conversion law. 6

European company law development occurred in three phases. The first phase emphasised comprehensive harmonisation, primarily for creditor protection. The second phase, beginning in the 1990s, saw stagnation with no new directives. ECJ case law broke this stagnation -particularly the *Centros* decision (case C-212/97) – strengthening freedom of establishment and cross-border conversion. The current third phase takes a more flexible approach, pursuing selective harmonisation to strengthen the internal market functionally while allowing Member States regulatory discretion. 7

8 Beyond harmonising directives, the EU has created supranational company forms. The most important is the Societas Europaea (SE), introduced by Regulation (EC) No. 2157/2001. Other projects like the Societas Privata Europaea (SPE) or Societas Unius Personae (SUP) failed due to Member State resistance, particularly disputes over co-determination and minimum capital. New models such as the Société Européenne Simplifiée (SES), which aims to create a simplified European corporation for SMEs, are under discussion but have not yet become legislation.

8a On 18 March 2026, after submission of this chapter, the European Commission published its proposal for an EU-wide optional 28th regime in company law ('EU Inc.'). The creation of a harmonised European company form suitable for startups and growth companies is, in principle, a welcome objective that could reduce transaction costs and facilitate cross-border operations within the Single Market. However, the specific proposal raises concerns.

8b The legal basis may merit closer scrutiny. The Commission relies on Article 114 TFEU (qualified majority voting) rather than Article 352 TFEU (unanimity requirement), although the proposal creates an entirely new company form rather than approximating existing national provisions.

8c The proposal appears to move away from some established features of Continental European preventive legal supervision in favour of a more digitalised and partly privatised model with reduced ex ante control in certain areas. Digitalisation and procedural efficiency are legitimate and important objectives. At the same time, it is open to question whether the safeguards envisaged by the proposal are fully equivalent, in functional terms, to those currently provided in some Member States by notarial or other independent public oversight. In particular, the 48-hour incorporation procedure (Article 16), although not entirely devoid of preventive control, reflects a model in which rapid digital formation plays a central role. Likewise, share transfers are recorded in company-maintained private registers (Articles 53-54) and may be carried out digitally without mandatory notarial involvement (Article 59(5)). In many jurisdictions, notaries currently verify identities reliably, notify tax authorities of taxable events, examine beneficial ownership structures, and conduct sanctions screening—mechanisms that prevent disputes and maintain reliable public registers.[1] To the extent that such mechanisms are reduced or displaced, the proposal may create legal and practical risks for money laundering, tax evasion, and "corporate hijacking" through identity fraud. Tax authorities and social security systems would become dependent on self-reporting, risking substantial revenue losses particularly concerning real estate transfer tax and profit allocation.

8d The registered-office rule gives founders considerable flexibility in choosing the applicable company-law framework, which could, depending on future practice, encourage regulatory competition between Member States. Whether this would lead to a problematic 'race to the bottom' cannot be predicted with certainty, but the risk is not purely theoretical, particularly in areas closely linked to company law such as employee participation and aspects of corporate governance. Moreover, the proposal imposes substantial implementation costs on Member States while capping incorporation fees at €100, requiring entirely new digital infrastructure and increased judicial capacity.

---

[1] Historical experience demonstrates the practical consequences of such systems: in Germany before 2008, share transfers were subject to notarial certification, but shareholder lists were prepared by the company itself without notarial or judicial verification of their accuracy, resulting in a substantial number of incorrect shareholder lists and defective documentation that significantly increased subsequent litigation and transaction costs (particularly in due diligence processes).

These concerns do not reflect opposition to a European company form as such, but highlight that the specific implementation is fundamentally flawed. A successful EU Inc. must preserve registry reliability, maintain effective anti-fraud safeguards, respect proven institutional arrangements for preventive legal supervision, and rest on a sound legal basis. Due to the timing of its publication, this proposal could only be addressed cursorily in this contribution. While the objective remains valuable, the current proposal requires fundamental revision before it can be supported. **8e**

European company law currently represents a system of selective harmonisation that coordinates core corporate areas while remaining strongly characterised by national features. Future developments will likely depend on political agreement on further harmonisation. **9**

II. Register law and procedure in company law

Directive (EU) 2025/25 ('**Digitalisation Directive II**')[2] brought the second phase of EU digitalisation in company law into force on 30.1.2025. Member States must implement it by 31.7.2027 and apply it from 31.7.2028 at the latest. The directive aims to remove obstacles to cross-border register information use and strengthen confidence in this information's reliability across all Member States.[3] The practical necessity arises because company data in national company registers has often been inaccessible or unusable at the Union level. Divergent requirements persist across the Union regarding apostilles, translation, or public certification, causing unnecessary delays, higher costs, and limited trust in other Member States' register contents. The directive therefore extends existing register structures -particularly the Business Registers Interconnection System (BRIS) – and technically links them with BORIS (beneficial owners register) and IRI (insolvency register). **10**

The Directive introduces the so-called **once-only principle** in company law. Under this principle, authorities may not request information already in the register from companies again (Art. 16e Directive (EU) 2017/1132 as amended). For example, when establishing a subsidiary in another Member State, existing parent company data is accessed electronically without requiring repeated submission.[4] **11**

Two new instruments will be introduced to improve cross-border legal binding force: **12**

The EU company certificate pursuant to Art. 16b of Directive (EU) 2017/1132 as amended is a standardised, multilingual and electronically signed document with essential register data that is recognised as proof throughout the EU without legalisation or translation. **13**

This document is intended to enable authorities, courts and contractual partners to rely on the authenticity and currency of the information it contains. **14**

The digital EU power of attorney pursuant to Art. 16c Directive (EU) 2017/1132 as amended provides a standardised, multilingual model form for proof of representation throughout the EU, compatible with the EU Digital Identity Wallet in accordance with the eIDAS Regulation.[5] In particular, it can be submitted via the *EU Digital Identity Wallet*. In contrast to the company certificate, it does not have a constitutive effect but **15**

[2] Directive (EU) 2025/25 of the European Parliament and of the Council of 19.12.2024 amending Directives 2009/102/EC and (EU) 2017/1132 to extend and optimise the use of digital tools and processes in company law (Text with EEA relevance).

[3] Directive (EU) 2025/25, rec. 1–4, 11–15.

[4] DIRiL II, rec. 14–15.

[5] (EU) No. 910/2014 amended by the digital eID regulation (EU) 2024/1183.

does represent a rebuttable substantiation of the power of representation. Its validity is still dependent on the substantive legal examination and registration in the respective national law; an entry in the register can but does not have to be made.

16 Furthermore, the **legalisation requirement** (apostille) for register documents will be abolished (cf. Art. 16d of the new Company Law Directive),[6] which further facilitates cross-border recognition and partially solves the problems described below regarding the formation and investment of companies from different Member States.

17 The directive also provides **mandatory preventive review** of all formation documents by notaries, registration authorities, or courts in all Member States (Art. 13 Directive (EU) 2017/1132 as amended). This particularly applies to legal review of articles of association, statutes, and their amendments. This control serves not only to clarify the register and increase transparency but also to combat abusive practices such as circumventing tax, labour, or money laundering laws (see recitals 8–10, 16–18).

18 The directive also harmonises the preventive control of the content of company formations. In future, notaries, courts and authorities will also have to check contributions, company purpose and the legality of articles of association throughout the EU.

C. Foundation

I. Choosing the right legal form

19 Even when tax optimisation drives legal form and structure choices, these are closely interlinked with company law. Company law aspects can control company parameters (liability, co-determination, flexibility, etc.). Legal form choice depends largely on project size, financing, economic objectives, and planned studio development.

20 European legal developments since the landmark decisions *Centros*,[7] *Inspire Art*,[8] and *Polbud*,[9] have considerably liberalised practical legal form choice, enabling companies to move freely within Europe. Member States must accept other European legal forms. Theoretically, all conceivable European company types are available to founders, but in practice, established legal forms in the founding state are used.

21 In addition to national company forms, cross-border and in some cases supranational forms are also available in the EU.

22 In most countries a limited liability company is the frequently chosen standard such as the German GmbH, the SARL in France, the SRL in Italy or the BV in the Netherlands.

1. Typology and supranational legal forms

a) Hobby and leisure projects

23 Games developed part-time or by students rarely have active company law structures. Game projects often begin with loose agreements and are usually legally categorised under respective national simple civil law partnership forms at the registered office. Examples include the French *Société en nom collectif (SNC)*, Dutch *Vennootschap onder*

---

[6] Where copies and extracts of documents and information provided and certified by a register, including certified translations, are to be presented in another Member State, Member States shall ensure that they are exempt from any form of legalisation and similar formality.

[7] ECJ 9.3.1999, case C-212/97, *Centros*, ECR 1999, I-1459.

[8] ECJ 30.9.2003, case C-167/01, *Inspire Art*, ECR 2003, I-10155.

[9] ECJ 25.10.2017, case C-106/16, Polbud, EU:C:2017:804.

firma (vof), German *Gesellschaft bürgerlichen Rechts* (GbR), or Spanish *Sociedad Civil*. These company forms are uncomplicated, require no minimum capital, and are legally based on informal partnership agreements. However, partners have unlimited liability with their private assets. Depending on applicable law, problems may arise if minors are involved.

When individual players finance projects and assume the main responsibility, silent partnerships or in-house companies are sometimes created – depending on applicable law. Game rights then belong only to this person, with compensation and participation based on contractual rules or respective national 'silent partnership' or internal company rules. Without further rules, the extent to which game rights are contributed may be disputed. This depends on copyright law principles and company purpose. As a rule, therefore, only simple usage rights necessary for game commercialisation to the intended extent are granted. 24

b) *Developer studio/small publisher*

With increasing professionalisation or serious market entry intention, most developers opt for limited liability companies. Most European game developers fall into this category. 25

No standardised European legal form currently exists for small and medium-sized enterprises (SMEs); respective established national legal forms serve as the legal entity. Typical legal forms in this category include the **Société à responsabilité limitée (SARL) or the SAS** in France,[10] the **Società a responsabilità limitata (SRL)** in Italy, the **Besloten vennootschap (BV)** in the Netherlands,[11] the **GmbH** or the **UG**[12] **(haftungsbeschränkt)** in Germany, the **Private Company Limited by Shares (LTD)** in Ireland[13] and the **Osaühing (OÜ)** in Estonia.[14] For reasons of space, it is not possible to provide a detailed description of the respective national forms; however, a **tabular overview** of 26

---

[10] France offers two attractive options with SARL and SAS. The SARL is functionally equivalent to the German GmbH and only requires a minimum capital of 1 EUR. The SARL must have at least two and no more than 100 shareholders. An SARL with a sole shareholder is called an 'Entreprise Unipersonnelle à Responsabilité Limitée' (EURL) and is subject to the same rules as the SARL. The Société par Actions Simplifiée (SAS) (Artt. L. 227-1 to L. 227-20 CCOM) has become the gold standard for French start-ups. It allows different share classes, flexible voting rights regulations and is ideal for VC financing. In addition, BSPCE (Bons de Souscription de Parts de Créateur d'Entreprise) can be used for tax-privileged employee shareholdings.

[11] Since the 2012 reform, the Besloten Vennootschap (BV) can be established without minimum capital and has developed into one of the most flexible European legal forms. The BV is particularly attractive for international IP structures and holding structures. The Dutch innovation box regime taxes profits from self-developed intellectual property at only 9 %. This can bring considerable tax advantages for game studios that develop their own IP.

[12] The GmbH remains the standard for German game studios. With a minimum capital of 25,000 EUR, it is solid and the articles of association can be flexibly structured. The Unternehmergesellschaft (haftungsbeschränkt), or UG for short, is a special form of GmbH; a share capital of just 1 EUR is sufficient. In contrast to a normal GmbH, contributions in kind are excluded, the share capital must be paid in full and a quarter of the annual surplus must be saved as a reserve by law until the minimum capital of a GmbH is reached. In this way, the UG is intended to make it easier for small start-ups to become limited liability companies, while at the same time ensuring a gradual build-up of capital.

[13] The Private Company Limited by Shares (Ltd.) is particularly accessible with a minimum capital of 1 EUR and fully digital formation via the Companies Registration Office. Ireland is attractive for international studios due to its low corporation tax (currently 12.5 %) and English-speaking legal system. The Ltd. is comparable to the English Ltd. and follows the common structure in Anglo-American law. As registration law is less developed in Ireland than in most continental European countries, this legal form requires a company secretary. In addition, at least one director must be an EU resident or provide security.

[14] Osaühing (OÜ) was a pioneer in digital online incorporation. The official portal (https://ariregister.rik.ee/eng/application/start) allows companies to be founded entirely online. With e-residency, even

the most important legal forms of this category in the Member States is included in this chapter for better orientation.

aa) No supranational legal form

27 Although the European Union has made several attempts to create a supranational legal form suitable for small and medium-sized enterprises, these have not yet prevailed in the political process.[15] New momentum currently exists: A draft for a **Société Européenne Simplifiée (SES)** has been presented, based on the French SAS and integrates elements of the German GmbH. An alternative model with a similar objective, the **Societas Europaea Simplicior**, was presented by the Haute Comité Juridique de la Place Financière de Paris and is intended to better meet the legal needs of growth-orientated SMEs at European level.

bb) Legal issues arise from national law

28 When projects have already started before company incorporation, questions often arise about **contributing already-created rights** from preliminary work to the company to be founded, depending on applicable tax and company law. When **transferring rights** and **significant preparatory work**, provisions are sometimes forgotten that grant the company rights to use preparatory work. If preliminary work is transferred, **tax advice** must be urgently obtained beforehand (associated questions and problems cannot be dealt with in depth here). Some Member States have rules on **concealed formation in kind** or similar abuse control, which intervenes if **cash formation** is initially carried out and registered, but **cash** is then **used to acquire corresponding items/rights** from a shareholder based on **preliminary agreements** with **temporal and factual connection**.

c) Exit-driven (venture capital-financed studios)

29 In exit-oriented studio start-ups aiming to sell the established company in the near future (with development financed via venture capital) – founders often want to use holding structures found in the start-up sector. Individual natural persons do not themselves become shareholders in a corporation, but instead initially establish holding companies (companies that hold and manage shares in other companies), again as corporations.

30 It is not the natural persons themselves, but the companies they previously founded as asset-managing (holding) companies that then act as founders of the company operating the studio.

31 The **holding structure**, which is motivated by tax law, is intended to ensure that subsequent profits from the sale of shares in the operating company holding the studio are taxed at a lower rate.[16] Although the profits are taxed later when they are distributed to the shareholders of the holding company, they can have a considerable leverage effect if they are reinvested rather than consumed. Given the current market conditions, it

non-Estonians can set up and manage companies digitally. Profits are not taxed until they are distributed, which favours reinvestment. This can bring liquidity advantages for growing studios.

[15] The proposal for a regulation on the Societas Privata Europaea (SPE) in 2008 was the first serious attempt to create a standardised legal form for small and medium-sized enterprises (SMEs) across Europe. However, the proposal failed due to political differences over co-determination, minimum capital and the principle of the country of domicile and was later officially withdrawn. Another attempt was the proposed directive on Societas Unius Personae (SUP) from 2014, which was also not implemented.

[16] In Germany, for example, only 5 % (Section 8b (2), (3) KStG).

is not uncommon for even smaller German studio companies to realise double-digit million amounts as proceeds from sales.

d) Project companies

Project companies are common in the games industry. **Independent subsidiaries or sister companies** are founded, usually as limited liability companies, serving as **legal entities for individual projects** (*single-purpose vehicles*). They become contractual partners of publishers, middleware providers, and sponsors where applicable. The aim is to isolate production risk in a corporation. This usually creates a **group of companies**. This raises questions particularly when using employees from other affiliated companies (employee leasing) – only for tax law reasons, (intra-group) service/facility agreements must then be concluded between individual group companies, also to avoid hidden distributions or hidden contributions through service exchanges, which can lead to liability. These agreements regulate shared IT infrastructure use, administration, legal advice, and employees in other group companies. **Remuneration** for service exchanges between affiliated companies should be carefully checked with tax advisors for transfer pricing tax requirements. If SPV character – risk encapsulation – is in the foreground, liability-extending interventions or profit transfer or control agreements should be avoided. Protection concepts under group law vary considerably between countries.[17] 32

If establishing corporations solely to 'decouple' existing intellectual property risks, note that in some Member States, executive bodies may be *personally* liable. This aspect is occasionally overlooked in structural advice. In Germany, a managing director tends to be liable to IP rights owners alongside the company due to intent, breach of organisational duties, or the guarantor position established under general tort law principles.[18] Therefore, in the case of computer games, a corporation provides only limited protection in the event of virulent or known risks. 33

2. European (supranational) legal forms

a) Societas Europaea (SE)

The European Company under Regulation (EC) No. 2157/2001[19] is the 'flagship of European company law' and is generally also a choice for larger game studios or publish- 34

[17] In Italy, Art. 2497 Codice Civile stipulates that a parent company is liable for damages resulting from unlawful influence on a dependent company in the context of de facto management ('direzione e coordinamento') – a form of group liability that intervenes in the event of improper management. In France, case law only allows the parent company to intervene in the context of an overriding group interest and requires that neither an existential threat nor a structural imbalance arises at the subsidiary. In the Netherlands, a parent company can be held liable on the basis of 'doorkijk' case law if it undermines the independent management of a subsidiary in an unauthorised manner; this applies in particular in the event of unlawful interference or in the event of de facto interference. In Germany, group law is comprehensively codified and provides for the possibility of a comprehensive profit transfer as well as a mandatory obligation to assume losses (Section 303 AktG) by the controlling company, particularly within the framework of corporate contract law (Sections 291 et seq. AktG), which establishes far-reaching legal responsibility within group-affiliated structures. In Austria, the controlling company is liable according to general civil law principles for immoral influence on the dependent company, in the case of interventions that threaten the existence of the company or jeopardise creditors (see OGH 6 Ob 123/99b).

[18] In Germany BGH, judgement of 18.6.2014 – Ref. I ZR 242/12, BGHZ 201, 344 = GRUR 2014, 883 – Geschäftsführerhaftung; for infringements of Section 95 (3) UrhG BGH, judgement of 27.11.2014 – Ref. I ZR 124/11, GRUR 2015, 672 (80) – Videospiel-Konsolen II; BGH, judgement of 6.10.2016 – Ref. ZR 25/15 GRUR 2017, 266 (68) – World of Warcraft I.

[19] Regulation (EC) No. 2157/2001 of 8 October 2001, OJ L 294/10.11.2001 *pp.* 1–21 (hereinafter 'SE Regulation').

ers. However, due to its minimum capital of 120,000 EUR[20] and the complex formation requirements,[21] the SE is practically unsuitable for start-ups and smaller studios. Formation is restricted by a **numerus clausus** of formation forms and **requires founders to have multiple nationalities**, often excluding small and medium-sized companies. The SE becomes relevant for **cross-border mergers** of established studios or when **creating holding structures**. Nintendo of Europe, for example, is now organised as an SE.[22]

35 **Formation requirements:** An SE can be formed by merging public limited companies from at least two Member States, by founding a holding SE or by converting a public limited company with a subsidiary of at least two years' standing in another Member State.[23] The SE is therefore ruled out for purely new foundations. In practice, however, it is possible to use shelf companies that are offered on the market as empty shells.

36 **SE Advantages:** One advantage is **reducing psychological barriers** to cross-border mergers, as choosing a supranational legal form like the SE overcomes national labelling and counteracts possible reservations about foreign legal forms. The SE also offers **cross-border registered office relocation** possibilities. Companies enjoy **management structure choice freedom** by choosing between monistic and dualistic management systems. There is also **greater flexibility** regarding supervisory body or administrative board member numbers and **one-off co-determination structure definition**. Of practical importance is **customising co-determination** through negotiation procedures under the Employee Involvement Directive. Companies without co-determination expecting future growth or companies subject to **one-third parity** can 'freeze' this structure by choosing the SE early, thus avoiding transition to parity co-determination, often seen as advantageous by companies with strict co-determination regimes (e.g., Germany). **Reducing supervisory board seats** can reduce national employee representative influence but requires greater coordination between international employee representatives. The SE makes **cross-border restructuring** and reorganisation considerably easier, enabling **cost reduction** for administration and Europe-wide structural measures. It has **standardised management and reporting systems** in all Member States and **uniform financial supervision** in its base country. Finally, a **six-year term** can be specified for management or administrative body members, contributing to company management continuity.

37 **Disadvantages:** However, the SE suffers from not being **a standardised legal form** in the true sense, as the SE Regulation contains only fragmentary regulations and largely refers to **national stock corporation law**. In practice, it is primarily **a legal form for large companies**, as both **minimum capital** is required and **direct formation** is only possible for legal entities. Beyond the SE Regulation, **national regulations** must also be applied, leading to increased complexity. **Articles of association strictness** under Art. 9 (b) SE Regulation also restrict company legal structure flexibility. **Legal uncertainties** arise from **differing implementations** in Member States, particularly regarding central aspects like corporate co-determination and board structure. Finally, the **'before and after' principle** in **employee involvement** regulation means there is **little room to manoeuvre** for entrepreneurial solutions, particularly in countries with extensive co-determination – such as Germany.

[20] Art. 4 (2) SE Regulation.
[21] Art. 2 SE Regulation.
[22] Nintendo of Europe SE, registered office Frankfurt, Germany, HRB 135709, Local Court Frankfurt a.M.
[23] Art. 2 (1–4) SE Regulation.

Experience shows that ambitious founders' tendency to opt for national **stock corporations** or **SE** for marketing reasons leads to **problems**. Unless financing issues and experienced shareholders can justify such legal form choice, an SE is rather **unsuitable** for studio setup, as experience shows founders are unfamiliar with **rigid formal stock corporation law rules**. 38

If an SE is to be managed error-free, **considerable structural costs** are incurred that can be better utilised for start-ups. The legal form is therefore **only recommended for experienced founders** familiar with stock corporation law or studios wanting capital market refinancing and able to provide corresponding structural costs. 39

b) *European Economic Interest Grouping (EEIG)*

The EEIG in accordance with Regulation (EEC) No. 2137/85[11] has a shadowy existence. Theoretically, **cooperative development projects** between studios from different EU countries could be organised through it. As the EEIG is not designed to make a profit but to promote the economic activity of its members, it can be considered for **joint research projects**, **technology transfer** or **coordinated market entry strategies**, for example, but is hardly ever used in practice. The unlimited liability of the members[13] makes the EEIG problematic for most participants. 40

II. Formation of a limited liability company

1. Regular Formation Procedure

The formation of small limited liability companies follows a structurally comparable process in almost all European countries. These phases can be categorised as follows: 41

a) *Preparation of the foundation*

Once legal form choice is made, founders need to consider details that bring the legal form to life in practice. These include company name choice, articles of association drafting, or at least varying regulations. Before incorporating, founders should consider the following points, even if not all must or should be regulated in the articles of association (see → § 3): 42

- Company Object: Must be clearly defined whether the studio will focus solely on development or also on publishing, platform operation, IP exploitation, or consulting.
- Capital Structure: Determining share capital, shareholder distribution, and provisions for subsequent capital increases where applicable.
- Transfer Restrictions: Regulations on share transfers (transfer restrictions, consent requirements), especially for future investments.
- Management and Representation: Number and powers of managing directors, majority decisions or individual representation, and veto rights for certain shareholder groups. Having several founders all appoint themselves as managing directors for equal treatment reasons is an organisational error. This is not only criticised in later financing rounds but also entails several disadvantages (liability, business area delimitation, usage rights granting). Additional agreements on rights granting are required for founders who are not only managing directors but generally also programme or contribute to the computer game.
- Profit Distribution: Regulations deviating from statutory distribution can be useful, e.g., for investors or vesting structures or to protect minority shareholders.

- Shareholder Resignation: Resignation regulations, notice periods, compensation modalities, possibly good leaver/bad leaver clauses or comparable rules.
- Non-Compete Clauses: Useful for specific industries to protect against parallel start-ups or poaching.
- IP Regulations: Clear regulation whether all copyrights and exploitation rights to game content, code, assets, etc., are transferred to the company – even for work contracts or freelance developer participation.

This preparation is usually carried out by founders themselves or through counselling, often involving notaries or lawyers. Additionally, share capital provision must be planned.

Founders should also consider which issues should be regulated in the articles of association and which should be regulated outside the articles of association.

b) Notarisation (if required)

43 Many Member States require mandatory notarisation of articles of association or partnership agreements, such as Germany (§ 2 GmbHG),[24] Italy (Art. 2463 Codice Civile), Austria (§ 4 GmbHG), Spain (Art. 20 LSC) or Poland (Art. 157 KSH). The notary not only undertakes the notarisation, but often also the structuring and legal advice, which can make the involvement of a lawyer unnecessary.

c) Payment of the share capital

44 Almost all corporations require minimum share capital, with amounts regulated by law. This capital must be paid into a company account either before or immediately after company incorporation. Immediately after notarisation, the managing director takes a copy of the deed to the bank with which **account opening** was agreed, preferably before notarisation, and deposits money after account opening. **When foreign companies are involved**, opening an account can be difficult due to **time-consuming money laundering checks**. Coordinating with the bank before notarisation is therefore advisable.

d) Entry in the commercial register

45 The company acquires its legal capacity through entry in the national commercial register. This requires the submission of various documents, in particular the articles of association, the list of shareholders and, if applicable, proof of payment of the share capital. In some countries, registration is carried out electronically (e.g., Estonia, Denmark, France).

---

[24] In Germany, for example (if there is no online notarisation), this is done by the parties involved appearing in person at the notary's office or being represented by a *notarised* or certified **power of attorney** (Section 2 (2) GmbHG). The notary then reads out the formation protocol and the annex (articles of association) in a notarisation procedure in accordance with §§ 8 ff. BeurkG and answers questions and explains typical pitfalls. The minutes of incorporation are then signed by all parties involved (and the notary). In practice, the **commercial register application** (formation, appointment of managing directors, etc.) is then signed by the managing directors together with the corresponding insurance policies and submitted to the notary with a **fiduciary mandate**. The notary only submits the commercial register application to the commercial register electronically (§ 12 HGB) once the **necessary evidence** has been provided and the managing directors have notified the commercial register that **the capital to be raised** is finally at the free disposal of the management (cf. § 8 GmbHG).

2. Online justification

The **online start-up** options created in the Member States are particularly suitable for decentralised teams that develop at different locations or even internationally.[25] 46

Directive (EU) 2019/1151 (Digitalisation Directive I) of the European Parliament and Council of 20.6.2019 on digital tools and processes use in company law created an EU legal framework to facilitate and harmonise online limited liability company formation throughout the EU. The transposition deadline expired on 1.8.2021 (Art. 28 Directive 2019/1151/EU). Since then, many Member States have taken legislative steps to enable digital incorporation procedures – at least for certain company types. Nevertheless, the picture is heterogeneous regarding implementation degree, procedure depth, and access requirements.

Estonia is regarded as a pioneer in digital company formation. Since 2007, corporations can be set up completely online via the e-Business Register. The prerequisite is a qualified electronic signature issued by Estonian e-residency cards or recognised eIDs from other EU countries. Companies are founded via a central state online portal[26] digitalising all steps – from name choice and articles of association drafting to commercial register registration. Estonia even allows e-residents (foreigners with digital identity) to set up companies entirely online, which has had considerable innovative effects on other Member States. 47

Denmark also enabled complete online corporation formation via the 'Virk.dk' portal even before implementing Directive 2019/1151. Since 2018, companies can be founded fully electronically, provided all founders have NemID or MitID. The platform enables registration, name verification, capital payment, and company document submission in a standardised process. Germany introduced online incorporation[27] on 1.8.2022 as part of the 'Act Implementing the Digitalisation Directive' (DiRUG). Notarial authentication will be replaced by a video conferencing procedure, which will be handled via the notary portal (Section 16a et seq. BeurkG new version). The prerequisite is qualified electronic identification via the new ID card or an equivalent EU eID procedure. The procedure is considered to be particularly secure and reliable. 48

Italy already enabled online S.r.l.s. (*Società a responsabilità limitata semplificata*) formation in 2016, expanding procedures in 2021 by implementing the EU directive. The digital procedure includes articles of association creation using standardised templates, electronic identification via SPID (*Sistema Pubblico di Identità Digitale*), and submission via commercial register portals (*Registro delle Imprese*). 49

The Netherlands already enabled online registrations via the 'KVK' (*Kamer van Koophandel*) before the directive, but complete incorporation digitalisation (including notarisation) has only been gradually available since 2022. Qualified signature use (eHerkenning, iDIN) is mandatory. Online incorporation initially applies to the *besloten vennootschap* (BV). 50

Other Member States such as Belgium, Luxembourg, Portugal, Spain, and Finland have established digital procedures, albeit to varying degrees and sometimes still with analogue notarisation components. In Spain, for example, the CIRCE portal (https://www.circe.es) has allowed digital company founding since 2010, although notarisation is 51

[25] Art. 13g I of the Accounting Directive; Art. 20 No. 2b DiRUG (3) – new.

[26] https://ariregister.rik.ee/eng/application/start.

[27] The minutes of incorporation and the articles of association can be notarised purely electronically by a notary in accordance with Sections 16a to 16e BeurkG via a **video communication system** operated by the **Federal Chamber of Notaries** (Section 78b BnotO).

still required in certain cases. Portugal has had a standardised procedure since 2006 with the 'Empresa na Hora' model, now being successively digitalised.

52 Poland has enabled online *spółka z ograniczoną odpowiedzialnością* (Sp. z o.o.) establishment via the S24 system (https://ekrs.ms.gov.pl) since 2021, also requiring qualified electronic signatures or ePUAP.

53 Cyprus, Greece, Croatia, and Bulgaria offer online incorporation in standardised forms, but EU directive implementation is still being developed in some of these countries.

3. Articles of association content

54 Space constraints require reference to extensive existing specialist literature for partnership agreement drafting details.[28] At this point, we note that 'sophisticated', 'complicated' considerations regarding articles of association (which technology-affinity founders often like to do themselves) are often less effective than **established standards and abstract models** from notaries or lawyers experienced in company law.

55 To maintain flexibility and avoid frequent notarisation needs, many European company regulations recommend that provisions not mandatory under articles of association should be set out in separate civil law agreements between shareholders. These so-called shareholder agreements (also: *pactes d'associés, contratto parasociale*) functionally supplement articles of association and create legal clarity in areas needing dynamic adaptation to individual companies.

56 What these agreements have in common in European practice is that – subject to national content controls – they are not subject to register publicity and can be concluded and amended in any form (including in writing or digitally). They are particularly suitable for the following regulatory matters:

- **Approval Requirements and Catalogue Management:** Regulating transactions for which managing directors or management require prior shareholder meeting or individual shareholder approval. This applies, for example, to investments, borrowing, personnel decisions, or major expenditure. In France (SAS), such approval requirements are often reflected in articles of association or *pacte d'associés*; in Anglo-American Ltds., shareholder agreements contain typical 'reserved matters'.
- **Management Distribution:** Specific internal task distribution among managing directors, operational competences and responsibility areas, ideally with investor feedback. Particularly relevant in practice for international studios with labour division management.
- **Vesting and Leaver Clauses:** In growth companies, shareholders commonly receive shares only successively and linked to continued cooperation ('vesting') – in premature departure cases under certain conditions, retransfer takes place ('good/bad leaver'). Such clauses are established in British, Dutch, and Estonian contracts, for example.
- **Exit Regulations:** Sale obligations in exit cases (drag along, tag along), IPO clauses, co-sale rights, sale mechanisms, and valuation parameters.
- **Investor Rights:** Minority shareholder special rights, e.g., information rights, veto rights, consent reservations, or special delegation rights for committees.

---

[28] Concise presentation, e.g., at Haines/Herrler, Gesellschaftsrecht in der Notar- und Gestaltungspraxis, 2nd edn 2021, § 6, extensive samples.

- **Voting Commitments:** Agreements on voting behaviour in certain shareholder resolutions – permitted under civil law in Spain or Italy, but often cannot be registered in commercial registers.
- **Confidentiality and Non-Competition Clauses**: More detailed provisions than are possible under the articles of association, for example on the confidentiality of IP, corporate strategy or mandates.

The specific structure varies depending on national law – for example, in the French SAS, many provisions that are typically anchored in shareholders' agreements elsewhere can be included directly in the articles of association. In the limited company, on the other hand, the articles of association are formally concise and functionally supplemented by a detailed shareholder agreement. **57**

Particularly in the case of **newly founded companies**, it is advisable to **use model articles of association** (not the model protocol). The parties involved should rely on the experience of a lawyer or notary specialising in corporate law. **Bilingual articles of association** can be useful in international contexts, but also increase **notarisation costs** and are usually only required at a later stage of the company's development or if the founding shareholders are from several language areas. **58**

4. Cross-border aspects (Proof of existence and representation)

Given the games industry's international orientation, foreign corporation involvement is common (whether as investors, as founder vehicles, or as German subsidiaries of existing foreign companies). When incorporating in another country, proof of existence and representation must often be provided, sometimes requiring preparation time and potentially delaying the incorporation process. **59**

For most European companies, proof of existence and representation is usually relatively easy to provide as commercial register extracts from the country where the company is domiciled. Commercial registers in Switzerland, Liechtenstein, Japan, China, and South Korea are also considered reliable. **60**

The situation differs for some frequently involved English-speaking countries (e.g., UK, USA, Singapore, the Cayman Islands). Their registers are often not considered comparable to continental European registers. **61**

For Anglo-American legal system companies, you can usually provide Certificate of Incorporation, Certificate of Good Standing, and Company Secretary certificates regarding representation relationships, which must then be publicly notarised. Alternatively, legal opinions from respective regions can be submitted. Documents usually must be provided with apostilles. Considerable lead-time must be allowed for this. **62**

a) Authorisations

When **investors or international shareholders are involved**, not all parties are usually present, but are represented. In principle, no special **power of attorney** is required for this, however, **notarisation** is required for certain transactions in many countries when a new company is founded. In the case of **foreign companies**, the power of attorney notarised abroad often has to be provided with an **'apostille, stamp'** or even **'legalisation'**. The time required for this should be planned in good time. **63**

b) Registered office abroad

64 In the case of **purely virtual teams** that work on a product in different countries via the internet and wish to use a corporation as a joint vehicle, care must be taken when **choosing the law** to ensure that the **actual place of administration** – i.e., the place of management – is compatible with this company and the tax domicile. Although all European companies are to be recognised in the other Member States, this does not apply in all Member States to all non-European companies (e.g., public limited companies under Swiss law or limited liability companies from Liechtenstein or the English limited company). In some Member States, the domicile theory applies to these, with the result that the limited liability legal forms are reinterpreted as partnerships under national law, with undesirable consequences for taxation and at the cost of losing the limitation of liability.[29]

D. Organisation of financing

I. CLA and SAFE Agreements

1. CLA

65 **Convertible loans** are now very **established forms of financing** (in addition to pure project financing) for start-ups and companies in the games industry and are practically mandatory in many member states.[30] These are loan agreements where repayment can (sometimes must) be made **by converting loan receivables** (plus interest) into shares in the respective company (developer studio). As a financing form, convertible loans are more likely found in **companies' early stages** when concrete studio (company) valuation cannot yet be made, is too low, or financing is necessary for time reasons before **Series A financing rounds** can be carried out. The latter is also often the case when investor existence and proof of representation or decision-making processes take time due to large numbers of international investors, but companies urgently need financing. In the games industry, such convertible loans are sometimes combined with **project contracts.** For larger game projects, loans can also be offset against project contracts or otherwise converted. CLA models are used in various EU countries. Such structures are generally recognised in France, Italy, the Netherlands, Estonia, and Ireland, but there may be different tax and company law implications depending on country. In France, for example, certain convertible loans (*obligations convertibles*) may be subject to prospectus publication obligations. In Italy, the instrument is usually embedded via '*finanziamento soci*' or mezzanine structures.

Typical CLAs

66 Because a limited liability company can rarely undertake to issue shares to itself in many jurisdictions, convertible loans are structured in such a way that, in addition to the loan, the shareholders decide to carry out a **capital increase** at a later date, in which they then create the corresponding shares of the lender/investor or join the convertible loan in such a way that they undertake to exercise their voting rights in this way at a later date. The **subsequent conversion** takes place via a **capital increase** in which the **loan**

[29] BGH 27.10.2008 – Ref. II ZR 158/06, BGHZ 178, 192 = NJW 2009, 289 (291).

[30] The Netherlands, Art. 2:206 BW; Companies Act 2014 Part 17; in France, *obligations convertibles* may be subject to a prospectus requirement.

receivable is **converted** into the **premium to be paid**. The loan claim is either waived or assigned to the company subject to the condition precedent of the entry of the capital increase in the commercial register. When **implementing this,** care must be taken to ensure that the company still has **sufficient capital to repay** the loan, as otherwise **extraordinary income** may be generated which can trigger an unnecessary tax burden.

Usually, subordination clauses are included in CLAs to ensure that the company is **67** not over-indebted on its balance sheet due to the loan. This is also a weakness of CLAs, as it is practically impossible to enforce repayment of the loans if the companies are not yet generating profits. Investors typically price this risk by negotiating discounts and valuation caps for the conversion of their loans. An enforceable conversion mechanic as well as various guarantees are common additional safeguards to mitigate the risk.

2. SAFE

Similar to CLAs, **SAFE agreements** (*Simple Agreement for Future Equity*)[31] are also **68** geared towards **early corporate financing phases.** Here too, investors are granted **rights to future company shares** without conversion prices already being fixed. Unlike CLAs, however, SAFEs **are not loans** but rather types of **warrants.** No interest is paid and there are no maturity dates, which is probably regarded as **interest-free loans** under German law and therefore differs little from CLAs. This is intended to **prevent company over-indebtedness**, which could of course also be realised with **subordination agreements.** In some EU Member States (e.g., Ireland, Estonia), SAFEs are easier to implement as company law allows greater capital raising flexibility. In traditional continental European systems (e.g., France, Spain, Italy, Germany), SAFEs are more difficult to categorise legally, particularly due to potential conflicts with capital raising regulations. Hybrid models or locally customised SAFE variants are recommended here. In any case, careful examination is required, particularly regarding subsequent capital measures and shareholder rights.

II. VC financing and 'Series A round'

A 'Series A' financing round is the first **significant investment** by one or more **69** **venture capital investors.** This involves a comprehensive set of contracts, which usually consists of an investment agreement[31] and **shareholder agreements (SHA)** or combinations of **investment and shareholder agreements (ISA).** This is almost always accompanied by existing articles of association amendments/revisions (attached to ISAs) or even legal form changes from GmbH to AG (SE).

Before the financing round, the **legal and financial risks of an investment are** **70** analysed (in varying degrees of detail) **(due diligence).** The resulting risks are either priced in or mapped in the subsequent contract negotiations (e.g. in the guarantees or so-called covenants).[32]

Employee participation: Programmatic bases for virtual shareholdings (VSOPs), **71** options or genuine company shareholdings. The instruments vary in the individual

---

[31] For an overview, sample contracts and more detailed information: Bank/Möllmann VCA/Möllmann/Bank 2nd Series A Financing Round para. 24 et seq.; Weitnauer Venture Capital-HdB/Weitnauer Beteiligungsvertrag/Investment and Shareholders Agreement, Annex VII; Jesch/Striegel/Boxberger Private Equity-HdB/Stengel/Muhs § 31 para. 24 et seq.

[32] Bank/Möllmann VCA/Ullrich/Bank 8. Company Guarantees para. 102; Weitnauer Venture Capital-HdB/Weitnauer Teil D. VC-ergänzende Finanzierungsmittel para. 24 ; Risse NZG 2020, 856 (862).

member states due to tax law and national structuring options.[33] *The Stichting Administratiekantoor* (STAK) in the Netherlands offers a particularly flexible model for employee share ownership.[34] France also uses 'BSPCE' (*bons de souscription de parts de créateur d'entreprise*) instruments, allowing tax-privileged employee participation, but also used in VC financing contexts. However, using these instruments is subject to certain conditions (e.g., SME qualification, activity type). Investors often utilise SAS as flexible legal forms enabling individual participation rights. Germany has traditionally favoured virtual stock options (VSOPs), attempting to map something similar. In the Netherlands, so-called 'Stichting Administratiekantoor' (STAK) is often used for VC financing, separating economic ownership from legal ownership. This structure allows voting rights to be held centrally while investors still participate in profits. It also serves to protect against hostile takeovers and facilitates succession planning.

72 In all Member States, careful consideration must be given to which company law instruments – such as option rights, liquidation preferences, or conversion rights – are recognised and enforceable locally. Investors increasingly pay attention to international standards compatibility, which is why 'Anglo-American standards' have also become established in European VC markets in practice.

III. Other aspects

73 Beyond the financing forms described above – capital increases, traditional loans (without conversion rights), state funding, and the like – there are other capital-raising ways for games companies in establishment processes. One phenomenon also found in the games industry is crowdfunding. This is often organised so large numbers of people participate in game development costs or company financial equipment by paying small contributions. As a rule, they do not acquire company rights and are therefore unable to effectively monitor contributed money use. In return for contributions, they often receive rights to use games at reduced prices or free of charge. Details are regulated by crowdfunding terms and conditions. However, Small Investor Protection Act limits must be observed. For example, start-ups must publish investment information sheets and, if financing targets exceed 2.5 million EUR, prospectuses. Additionally, investment amounts for private investors are limited.

74 Beyond SAFE Agreements, KISS Agreements are frequently used, particularly for financing US (parent) companies. KISS stands for 'Keep It Simple Security'. There are both debt KISS agreements, where loan interest and final maturity are agreed, and equity KISS agreements, structured similarly to SAFEs without interest rate agreements and final maturity.

---

[33] Germany traditionally relies on virtual stock options (VSOPs), which, however, are less favoured for tax purposes than the instruments in other EU countries. VSOPs are generally taxed as wages when they are paid out, which can lead to considerable tax burdens. The Federal Labour Court's ruling of 19.3.2025 on vesting clauses has further restricted the structuring options. The Federal Labour Court ruled that virtual options that have already been 'vested' may not automatically expire upon termination of the employment relationship if the employee himself gives notice. As a result, German studios will have to revise their employee participation programmes and develop more complex structures in order to adequately reflect bad leaver scenarios.

[34] In this structure, a foundation holds the shares of the operating company and issues certificates to the employees. These certificates grant economic participation in the company's success without the certificate holders receiving voting rights or qualifying as shareholders under company law. This enables the founders to retain control of the company, while employees still participate in the company's economic success.

Regardless of chosen financing forms, respective national laws must be checked in advance. Attention must also be paid to money laundering regulation and sanctions regime compliance. 75

E. Exit

There are several ways for founders to exit companies. The easiest to implement is sale, i.e., company share transfer. The decisive factor for companies is often whether it involves strategic investors and not just financial investors. Transfer forms depend on chosen legal forms. If founders are also managing directors or board members, they often divest these positions by selling shares or undertake to remain active in companies for transitional periods or be available as advisors. Sometimes first-phase start-up investors also sell shares to other investors later (so-called secondary transactions or secondaries), without leading to financial but ideally strategic company advantages. Admissibility and timing of such transactions, as well as any approval requirements, are often determined by corresponding shareholder agreement agreements. 76

Many founders dream of taking 'their' companies public one day. However, 'IPO readiness' processes and subsequent stock market listings can be very expensive and time-consuming. A major challenge is that companies must align processes, regulations, functions, and decision-makers with stock market practices and requirements. In many cases, this leads to major cultural changes and carries risks of overburdening organisations. Additionally, questions must be answered about which stock exchanges companies ultimately want listing on. 77

Some time ago, so-called 'De-SPAC transactions' were promoted as elegant, time- and resource-saving ways to go public. SPAC refers to 'Special Purpose Acquisition Company'. Investors join forces to form companies, which they provide with funds and float on stock exchanges. Listed company purposes are to search for suitable acquisition targets. Once such targets are found, they are merged into SPACs and thus become listed companies without their own prospectus diversions and other challenges. Going public processes have been shortened, so to speak. Recently, however, such transaction numbers have decreased again. On one hand, supervisory authorities in various countries, such as the US SEC, have taken critical views of this IPO form from investor protection perspectives. On the other hand, so-called PIPE investor willingness to invest has somewhat waned. PIPE stands for 'Private Investment in Public Equity'. In many De-SPAC transactions, PIPE investors are needed to raise total capital required for IPOs. 78

§ 10
Mergers and Acquisitions in the Video Game Industry: A Buyer's Guide

A. Who this chapter is for and what it is about 1
B. From why you buy to what you buy: Follow the value 7
C. Preparing for a deal 10
D. Due diligence: Value meets risk 22
E. Deal structuring 23
F. Regulatory and compliance (merger control and beyond) 34
G. Post-merger integration (PMI) 35
H. Final thoughts 38

A. Who this chapter is for and what it is about

1 This chapter provides **practical guidance** for in-house legal counsel and company executives or CEOs leading and supervising mergers and acquisitions (M&A) transactions within the video game industry. The emphasis is on the **buyer's perspective**, particularly in the context of acquisitions of small to mid-sized, private video game development companies (studios) where a controlling majority stake or full ownership is sought. Given that intellectual property (IP) and related contracts are often at the core of such companies, this chapter is IP-centric and therefore broadly applicable to IP purchases as standalone assets, and may so be useful beyond the video game industry in any field where intellectual property takes centre stage, such as IT, software, or linear filmed entertainment.

2 While major transactions, such as Microsoft's 2023 acquisition[1] of Activision/Blizzard Group for around 70 billion USD – the largest in video game M&A history as of this writing – attract significant attention for their scale and the considerable political and antitrust dimensions involved[2], this chapter deliberately avoids providing a historical overview of M&A activity or outlooks and forecasts of any kind. Instead, it offers a **hands-on guide**, tailored to the **mid-market segment**. Here, the buyer's legal department frequently takes the lead role, coordinating the deal team, managing legal due diligence, negotiating contracts, and handling regulatory filings. External advisers may also be brought in as needed, but core project management remains internal, requiring a deep understanding of both legal, business and gaming industry specifics. For larger targets, with transaction values in the multiple hundreds of millions of EUR and beyond, highly specialised outside teams are typically engaged to manage the transaction in its entirety. In such instances, the in-house legal counsel focuses primarily on high-level topics and on selecting the right experts.

3 This chapter also aims to offer important insights for **sellers** that enable them to better understand a buyer's perspectives and priorities, as these can significantly influence the value of a company for sale. Sellers should consider these aspects as early as possible, even before founding a company, so as to be better placed to take advantage, say, of potential tax structuring opportunities. The guiding principle should be to build the company with a **future sale in mind**, ideally ensuring absolute clarity in IP ownership contracts and avoiding clauses (e.g. Change of Control clauses) that could impair com-

[1] https://en.wikipedia.org/wiki/Acquisition_of_Activision_Blizzard_by_Microsoft.
[2] 'Microsoft Beats the Antitrust Odds on Its Activision Deal', 13.10.2023: The New York Times.

pany value. Buyers scrutinise certain specific elements during due diligence precisely because they represent either significant value or substantial risk. Focusing on these elements helps safeguard a company's survival and ability to create value while maintaining focus on true value drivers that might otherwise be overlooked in day-to-day business. In essence, concentrating on keeping the company consistently saleable helps to ensure that urgent daily tasks will not preclude thinking about long-term strategic imperatives. This approach is even useful in case a sale is not intended or never happens.

This chapter does **not address** the **acquisition of publicly listed companies** due to the highly formalized and strategic nature of such transactions, which involve adding another layer of specialist expertise (squeeze outs, irrevocable undertakings, etc.)[3]. When buying a publicly traded company, there is limited scope for negotiation of the kind discussed here in this chapter because shares are fungible, meaning the scope of rights is both predefined and identical for every shareholder class. In addition, because of insider trading regulations, due diligence on publicly listed companies is confined to publicly available documents and information. 4

Moreover, this chapter does **not discuss** the **acquisition of minority stakes**. While due diligence in such instances may be similar, a minority stake acquisition concentrates primarily on the limitations imposed on the new minority shareholder and the existing rights (veto rights, for instance) of other shareholders. Creating value in such a scenario often involves thinking like a venture capitalist and relying on the rules, rights, and contractual mechanisms that characterise the world of start-up financing[4], such as drag-along rights, tag-along rights and veto rights. 5

Besides game industry-specific aspects, this chapter also addresses general M&A topics. For lawyers, it is essential that they familiarise themselves with such basic economic terms and concepts as **enterprise value**, **equity value**, **goodwill**, and **net working capital**. An understanding of finance and accounting fundamentals, including the structure of a balance-sheet, assets and liabilities, profit and loss statements, the valuation concept of discounted cash flows, and an equity bridge, is important. When representing a game company buyer, a firm grasp of the fundamentals of video games – including the technical development process, different business and monetisation models (advertisement driven, Free-to-Play, Premium, Freemium, etc.), and the distribution and release processes – is essential. 6

B. From why you buy to what you buy: Follow the value

The question at the core of any M&A transaction in the game sector is the commercial rationale for acquiring a video game company. Strategic motivations range widely, but typically[5] include the acquisition of valuable IP; consolidation and addition of talent through **'acqui-hiring'**[6] to strengthen development capabilities; access to proprietary technology stacks or game engines; increasing market share; expanding into new platforms or geographical markets; or diversifying content portfolios. The main asset in many video game studio deals is IP, encompassing game code, trademarks, and brands. Beyond these core IP assets, acquirers may also target thriving online player communi- 7

---

[3] See 'Glossary' of LexisNexis published under www.lexisnexis.co.uk/legal/glossary/.

[4] Mendelson/Feld, Venture Deals, 4th edn.

[5] 'M&A Considerations across the Technology Sector', 7.5.2025, published by Morgan Lewis & Bockius LLP (www.morganlewis.com).

[6] 'Acqui-hiring is an M&A strategy in which a company acquires another not for its product, service, or specific assets, but primarily for its human talent.' (https://pipeline.capital/acqui-hiring-the-ma-of-people/).

ties or access to established live-service operations, which often represent significant user engagement and ongoing revenue streams. Due to the intangible nature of many of these key assets, valuations and deal structures in the video game industry often differ sharply from those in traditional industries.

8 Understanding the commercial 'why' behind management's decision to buy a target company directly leads to the **'what' to acquire**, which in turn governs the legal tasks. This is especially true during the **due diligence process**, where it is critical to verify that the perceived value is actually present, and in the drafting of acquisition documents (whether a share purchase agreement or an asset purchase agreement), where contractual protections for the desired acquisitions must be crafted meticulously. It is also beneficial to comprehend management's post-acquisition plans for unlocking value – the so-called equity story – which might involve expansion or staff reductions, divestiture of company parts, or closure of specific units. Such plans must be legally permissible and economically viable, necessitating a 'forward due diligence' approach. Due diligence efforts should be prioritised based on the amount of value and risk at stake; commercially unimportant legal tasks that will not significantly impact the deal, even if they go wrong, should not be overly focused upon. The depth of due diligence naturally depends on the acquirer's risk appetite, available budget for deep dives, and the time allotted to close a deal.

9 **Collaboration** with your own internal departments is highly recommended to gain both advice on potential problems and their support during due diligence or interviews with the seller's management team. If internal teams are unavailable, it is worth considering hiring external consultants or leveraging professional networks. The specific areas of expertise required will depend on the target; however, departmental insights are typically sought from HR, business development, IT, development/coding, finance/tax, and marketing/product release teams. These internal professionals possess crucial knowledge of real-life operational risks and value drivers, and can possibly provide potential risk mitigation solutions. In a game industry acquisition, heavy reliance on heads of development and IT is typically necessary to understand the technical capabilities and risks of the target company, such as the status of games in development and the quality of source-code and documentation, the program architecture, backups, and protection mechanisms.

C. Preparing for a deal

10 Once a **non-disclosure agreement (NDA)** has been signed and subsequent high-level management discussions between both parties have led to serious interest in exploring a deal, the preparation phase can commence.

11 When dealing with smaller owner-operators who have very often built their company with significant personal investment, it is crucial to ascertain early on if they are genuinely **ready to sell** and their **price expectations** are realistic. Although a cautious approach that respects the emotional bond sellers have with their 'baby' is important, it may be necessary to bring them back down to earth if their perceived valuations are sky-high. Understanding whether they wish to continue working in the business to the extent their ongoing involvement is essential for the buyer is likewise key, as transitioning from being **company masters to employees**, subject to new corporate policies, can be challenging. While covenants, warranties, and post-closing obligations, coupled with attractive stay-on bonuses, can encourage management's continuation, their sustained interest may depend on previously unavailable factors, such as access to

higher funding or high-profile IPs. Without such incentives, friction or early departures may occur once stay-on bonuses have been earned.

a) Letter of intent[7] **(LOI)**: The M&A process typically begins with the letter of intent. The LOI serves to avoid misunderstandings about major deal points already discussed and to outline rules (negotiation exclusivity, for instance), and deal closing timing expectations. It usually also includes a **price** or price range for the target, subject to due diligence. However, caution is advised, as amounts communicated, especially in writing, can establish expectations that are difficult to reverse. The purchase price can be partially paid contingent on a future outcome or event, known as an 'earn-out'. The LOI is typically not binding and therefore not legally enforceable (except for parts specifically agreed to be binding such as confidentiality clauses), but it remains a useful psychological instrument. It can also serve to lay out valuation concepts, underlying assumptions, and the conditions upon which an earn-out depends. Ensuring exclusivity along with a break-up fee is less usual and legally challenging to enforce; such clauses typically stipulate a period during which the seller cannot sell to, or even speak with, other parties, after which the seller is free. 12

Press release: It is prudent to include a clause that obligates the parties to agree on a joint press release, to be issued shortly after the transaction is completed. This allows both parties to collaboratively 'own the narrative' of the rationale for the deal. Our industry's goal is to sell video games (a consumer product), so a press release is a good, free opportunity to position your brand and product in a positive light – and a missed opportunity if done poorly. 13

b) High-level LOI deal points (game-specific): In video game acquisitions, the LOI may specify the required development stage and **quality of a game** at the time of purchase, along with **benchmarks** for such quality. For instance, video game quality or reception could be tied to its rating on Metacritic[8], which aggregates and scores reviews from game experts (the Metascore) on a scale from 0 to 100. While not a guarantee of commercial success (there have been instances where perceived quality and actual financial performance diverge), there is generally a correlation. Another option is to tie part of the purchase price to future sales success, measured in units sold or revenue/profits. It is crucial to clarify that the buyer, as the new owner, reserves the right, at their sole discretion, to make any commercial decision (including stopping game development or reducing marketing spend), even if it negatively impacts sales and, consequently, the earn-out. The more detail in which the accounting terms for earn-outs are defined, the lower the likelihood of future conflict. If revenue is the driver, parties could define the minimum marketing budget to be applied or the budget for, and number of post-release downloadable content (DLCs) to be developed, released and financed. If profit is employed as a driver, the deductible costs must be defined. This includes specifying whether just external out-of-pocket costs or internal costs, too – for the internal marketing team, for instance – are deductible, and what proportion of overheads (capped or uncapped) can be applied. In general, using profit (EBIT or EBITDA) as a driver is dispute-prone because of the range of elements that can trigger arguments, including accounting methods and principles, and the allocation of joint corporate costs. Furthermore, integrating an acquired entity into another corporate unit or dissolving and merging it diminishes earn out accounting transparency drastically to the point such actions are too risky to take for the new owners. 14

---

[7] 'The Letter of Intent in M&A Transactions' by Roedl&Partner, published 23.2.2024 (roedl.com/insights/ma-dialog/2024–02/letter-intent-ma-transactions).

[8] www.metacritic.com.

15 **c) AI tools**: The use of AI tools by outside investors, particularly for due diligence, is on the increase; in-house adoption, by contrast, remains niche unless M&A is a recurring activity. If companies regularly buy other companies, it may be beneficial to evaluate or trial potentially useful applications, especially in the target screening, valuation, and due diligence spaces.

16 **d) Advisers**: The choice of advisers depends on the deal size, the buyer's experience, risk appetite, budget, and company policy. Besides valuation analysts and tax experts, the key question is whether outside legal counsel is needed. The entire deal can be handed over to an international law firm, which, while providing excellent service, will, however, charge substantial fees. This is particularly true with international transactions to buy a game company with IP and contracts spanning multiple territories, as law firms will involve their network of country teams as soon as a question touches a foreign jurisdiction. While ensuring state-of-the-art legal work, high fees should be anticipated, which may be too high for some transaction values or budgets. To mitigate this, negotiating a flat fee upfront can be considered. However, any such fee might need to be increased subsequently if the scope proves to be greater than initially expected. External legal costs vary significantly. US firms can charge up to 1,400 USD per hour, and for mid-size transactions (10 million-100 million EUR), external counsel costs can range from 200,000 EUR to 2 million EUR, depending on the depth of due diligence, the problems to be solved, and the length of the negotiation process.

17 **e) Seller's lawyer**: It is important to insist that the seller engages a lawyer experienced in M&A, as this can streamline the process for all parties significantly or even prevent a deal from falling apart due to an inexperienced lawyer's wrong advice that the seller falsely is listening to. However, for impartiality reasons, it is advisable to avoid making specific recommendations. Having an M&A-experienced lawyer on-board when it comes to handling a once-in-a-lifetime deal for the seller should be obvious to the seller. Furthermore, given that the target is a video game company, the M&A lawyer should have specific knowledge of entertainment law, video games, and IP; ideally, they should have worked previously with the target and be thoroughly familiar with it. If an M&A lawyer lacks specific entertainment law expertise, they can collaborate with such an expert, either within their own law firm or by engaging outside counsel.

18 **f) Deal process**: Once the LOI is signed, an introductory meeting or video call should be scheduled in which all members of the parties are introduced to one another, their respective roles established, and their contact details shared. The legal lead should set up a recurring, fixed meeting schedule that continues until the acquisition is completed or terminated. Weekly one-hour calls with the core team (lawyers and M&A advisers) and bi-weekly all-hands meetings, for instance, are often effective, depending on the deal size and timeline.

19 **g)** The next step involves sending the seller a formal **information request list**[9] (IRL), which includes all documents required from such areas as tax, finance, HR, and legal. This list is crucial as it serves to ensure that no important information is overlooked. IRLs can be extensive, so they should be shortened as needed and customised for each project – ideally using a company template that reflects standard departmental requirements. Game-specific items to include in the IRL are vital and encompass:

- A comprehensive list of owned game IPs, including supporting documents, chain of title, and associated contracts.
- Details of all inbound and outbound licences.

[9] Example on https://files.klgates.com.

- Information on trademarks, copyright registrations, and websites pertaining to game titles, characters, logos, fonts, and the company name itself.
- Status of games in development.
- Studio architecture, security protocols (including source code storage, backups, and escrow storage agreements).
- Technology used for coding, such as studio tools, software, engines, and any open-source resources employed.

The IRL documents should be uploaded to a **virtual data room (VDR)** agreed upon by both parties. There are many VDR providers, some of whom guarantee compliance with EU law and have server locations within the EU. It is crucial that the VDR includes a Q&A section for submitting questions to the seller. The answers provided and the documents uploaded to the data room constitute relevant legal information upon which the acquisition is based, potentially leading to claims if found to be inaccurate or incomplete. The negotiation of the long-form purchase agreement (a share purchase agreement or asset purchase agreement – see further details in the section on deal structuring) occurs concurrently with the due diligence process. Negotiating parallel to due diligence is mutually beneficial. Due diligence essentially involves verifying that all expectations and promises made regarding the company's value are accurate, and identifying any risks that might need to be resolved, mitigated, or accepted. Ideally, someone from the buyer's team should conduct a physical visit to the premises and meet staff of the target company. This may be 'old-school' but it provides a qualitative feel for a business that no document, data room, or video call can match. Speaking with talkative employees and engaging with management informally over dinner can sometimes yield the most valuable due diligence insights. In creative industries, where collaboration is both intensive and intense, a feel for companies' styles and cultures is arguably more important than in other industries. 20

h) Purchase agreement: Typical long-form purchase agreements, which are drafted later on in the process, will include detailed representations and warranties regarding the originality of game assets, the absence of infringement claims, and robust assurances concerning IP ownership. It is also wise to have a 'subject to board approval' clause in the purchase agreement until finally signed, allowing always an exit from otherwise binding statements. 21

D. Due diligence: Value meets risk

Legal due diligence[10] (DD) can be enormously detailed and time-consuming. For in-house counsel, it requires making a judgement call on the scale and depth of DD that takes into account the company's resources, time and budget constraints, overall culture, and appetite for risk. The focus here should be on the target's primary value drivers and on any major risks that the buyer may be acquiring. Findings should be summarised for management in a concise, solution-focused red flag report[11], prioritised by risk. **DD topics** should be **categorised** into green flags (no issues), orange/yellow flags (material or ancillary issues), and red flags (critical legal issues or risks that could severely impact either the valuation or the buyer's ability to conduct business as intended, and require resolution before signing). To ensure that a due diligence report 22

[10] For further explanation see: https://en.m.wikipedia.org/wiki/Due_diligence.
[11] "M&A Due Diligence Issues Reporting Template" by Bloomberg Law, published August 9th, 2023 (https://pro.bloomberglaw.com/insights/contracts/ma-due-diligence-issues-reporting-template-2/).

is precise and to-the-point, it is crucial to work with department heads to obtain their assessments of which topics are of key importance within their remit or area of expertise. The report should be unencumbered by needless ancillary information and offer clear solutions for managing and mitigating identified risks.

- Important game-specific due diligence points: Legal DD must thoroughly cover **IP ownership, chain of title, copyright originality, clean licensing of middleware and game engines**, and **publishing agreements**. It is also essential to check for any liens or pledges of IP as collateral and ensure creditor releases are obtained. The absence of such encumbrances is a major representation and warranty that the seller will have to provide in the purchase agreement. Examination of union affiliations (e.g., SAG-AFTRA) for (voice) acting employed by the target is important, as these can entail lifelong union membership and adherence to union rules, and many games involve actual filming for cut-scenes or intensive motion capture using union actors. A new area of concern is AI-generated assets, given the uncertain copyright implications. **AI law is evolving rapidly**, and understanding its impact on ownership once the company is acquired is crucial. Ensure that no black-box or un-auditable code is used, particularly where ownership or licensing cannot be verified, and confirm that key IP rights, licences, and service agreements will remain valid and enforceable after the acquisition. Examine the target's data protection compliance, especially if the target's value lies in an accumulated player base or player information – something not uncommon with free-to-play mobile games reliant on advertisement revenues.
- IP and other **intellectual property rights**: Often, an acquisition involves the IP rights of a game franchise, publishing rights, and accompanying necessary rights for source code ownership and game assets (video, picture, or audio creations). The chain of title, tracing rights from source to end product, must be clearly documented, ensuring that all contributors to the IP or game have signed contracts granting exclusive, worldwide, perpetual rights for exploitation on all platforms without restrictions. With more recent games or games in development, it is important to review and **verify all and any relevant conditions** – to ensure, for instance, that contributors have been paid in full – because the IP or ownership position must be free from any challenge. A critical area here is ensuring that each signed employment contract (not just the seller's template) includes sufficient clauses for the transfer of any IP created by employees, especially those involved in coding, creative work, or otherwise contributing to the video game IP. This also applies to managing directors and executives influencing IP creation. Ideally, such clauses are standard in all contracts of a creative company. If the target is in a foreign jurisdiction, a local IP lawyer must review these clauses to address country-specific rules. For example, French law[12] may demand an author's proportional participation in revenue (not profit), making it difficult to determine what percentage is considered 'proportional/meaningful' by a judge.
  - If the IP/game is **based on a story from a book** or other underlying rights, **verify that these rights have been acquired**. Check for any associated veto rights of original creators or change-of-control clauses. Ascertain if any pre-emptive acquisition rights or last matching rights in the event of a change of control or IP sale exist. Determine if other rights stemming from distribution contracts need to be adhered to, if the game is bound to release by a certain time (and what the consequences of missing the deadline are), or if a release window or motion

[12] Art. L.131 – 4 of the CPI (Code de la Propriété Intellectuelle).

picture release based on the same IP might block a video game launch. Verify whether any story elements (e.g., a second universe, time period or character) are blocked from use.

- Be **wary of one-sided termination clauses** in key contracts, especially with powerful IP rights licensors, who often dictate terms allowing termination for minor reasons. General warranty language should confirm the completeness and correctness of owned IP, associated licences (inbound and outbound), and full payment of all fees related to registered IP, and that the target holds sole, registered legal and beneficial ownership of the IP, free from encumbrances. The seller should represent that the IP has not been subject to challenges, claims, or proceedings in recent years, and that there are no known circumstances that might give rise to such disputes. The IP owned by the company should not be subject to undisclosed outbound licences, and the company must own or have the right to use all necessary IP to continue business operations post-completion, consistent with past conduct. No **third-party claims** alleging infringement, misuse, or potential infringement/misuse of third-party IP should have been made, nor should there be circumstances that might reasonably give rise to such claims.
- With the US at the centre of the entertainment industry, many target contracts may involve **US counterparties**. Be vigilant regarding contracts that provide for the application of US law and any potential disputes arising from said contracts. Such lawsuits can be costly (especially if the contractual clause for reimbursement of reasonable attorney costs is missing), and rulings may result in, say, high punitive damages that seem excessive or unfair from a European legal perspective. In the international entertainment industry, the US American legal concept of 'work made for hire' is applied widely. In jurisdictions where this is not known or recognised, contracts typically use the 'royalty-free assignment of rights in scope as far as permissible' alternative, which generally functions well. However, many **European countries** value the **author** as the **creative centrepiece** of a work, protecting them as a valuable societal contributor, sometimes in a weaker position vis-à-vis a producer with deep pockets. Germany's Copyright Law, for instance, includes a 'bestseller paragraph'[13] that allows a creative contributor to claim additional monies if the financial success of their work proves extraordinary in comparison to their initial remuneration.

– **Game engines**: Almost all games utilise so-called engines. Prominent examples include Unity, Unreal Engine 5 and CryEngine. These provide a generic tool kit for functionalities like movement and camera angles, and facilitate faster, better, and more efficient programming by eliminating the need to write code from scratch. Unless open-source, these engines have remuneration models that usually depend on sales, platform distribution, etc. To ensure continued ownership of the necessary licence to run the game, it must be verified that no atypical deals are in place. While engine providers generally understand that buyers expect to exploit games without prohibitive or unfair licensing models, the costs can be significant, and legal due diligence should highlight the cost structure for correct valuation. Some developers use their own specialised mini-engines in specific contexts. One such mini-engine might be a fighting tool used in conjunction with the main game engine. It is crucial to check that fully paid-up licences for such mini-engines are included when buying a game that utilises them.

[13] §§ 32a, 36 UrhG.

- **Open-source software (OSS)**: The use of open-source software in its entirety is sometimes prohibited in game development contracts. If it is partially used by the target to code a game, this must be flagged to management, and potential problems assessed. The primary concern with open source is a lack of documentation and 'copyleft' provisions in the licence agreements[14] that require any software incorporating that code to be released under the same licence, including making the source code public. This could severely undermines the value of a game IP in an acquisition as it is non-exclusive at least in parts.
- **Community-generated content (CGC/mods)**: Studios using community-generated content require special legal scrutiny. Many games (especially sandbox[15] and mod-friendly titles[16]) allow players to create their own content, such as levels, characters, mods, and artwork. If the studio has not properly structured its terms of service (ToS) or end-user licence agreements (EULAs) to assign or license those player creations, the studio may not fully own parts of its game IP. This creates a risk for the acquirer, as players may assert ownership or IP claims. User-created content can also contain infringing, defamatory, hateful, or illegal materials. The studio's agreements with users, modders, and community contributors may lack clear clauses on liability, IP transfer, and permitted use, and an acquiring company inherits these contractual risks. Modding or creator communities are often highly active and vocal, and changes in IP ownership (say, after an M&A transaction) can lead to legal or reputational disputes if CGC rights are restricted post-acquisition.
- **Digital distributors**: The legal team must also assess contracts with digital distributors (e.g., Steam, PlayStation Store) and ensure compliance.
- **Source code**: The source code is the fundamental computer program of the game. As a buyer of a video game (not merely the publisher or distributor), ownership of the source code is crucial. If a game is at the development stage, permanent access to the source code should be granted – possibly through an escrow solution provider. For work-in-progress source code to have any value (in case of a takeover or change of developer, for instance), it must be reviewed by your developers and steps taken to ensure that documentation is available that accurately describes how the code is structured. To understand the source code and to be able to accurately assess its quality and development progress, it has to be monitored closely. Without proper documentation, source code inherited from another developer has barely any value, even if a decent manual exists, as it remains someone else's creation.
- **Assets**: Assets are essentially everything that can be seen or heard in a video game, such as characters, graphics, and sounds. These are typically protected by various forms of intellectual property law; some assets (superheroes, for instance) are even protected by trademarks/design and possess considerable standalone value. Technically, there are different levels of originality, from simple visual scribbles to actual end products, such as playable characters. In between, there are layers of data: character files containing different resolutions, render variants, 3D formats, and locomotion data. Whether all of this is included in a purchase (in an asset deal)

[14] For example: GNU General Public License originally written by Richard Stallman: https://copyleft.org/guide/.

[15] Very common examples of sandbox games are ones where the player has the ability to create, modify, or destroy their environment, i.e., a game that includes some form of a game creation system. (https://en.wikipedia.org/wiki/Glossary_of_video_game_terms#M).

[16] A third-party addition or alteration to a game. Mods may take the form of new character skins, altered game mechanics or the creation of a new story or an entirely new game-world. Some games (such as Fallout 4 and Skyrim) provide tools to create game mods. (https://en.wikipedia.org/wiki/Glossary_of_video_game_terms#M).

can significantly impact the cost of reproducing an asset in a usable form. This is less of a concern in a share deal, where the entire company is acquired; however, if just selected IP or a company is purchased through an asset deal, it should be clearly stated that all technical files relating to the IP and assets are included.

- **Contractual obligations**: Many contracts contain easily overlooked clauses, such as those that commit a buyer to spending a certain amount of money on marketing a game. If a game performs poorly, the marketing department's natural inclination might be to cease further expenditure. While commercially sound, such a move could violate contractual obligations with a co-publisher, potentially leading to damages claims or loss of rights. Legal and marketing departments are often unaware of such cross-departmental implications.
- **Change of control clauses**: These clauses are always a significant issue in M&A activities. Check for such clauses and their consequences, which can range from termination rights to payment obligations.
- **AI use in creation**: When buying entire games or creative works, buyers should be wary of any use of AI in their creation. Human authorship is currently a condition for copyright to arise, and copyright may not exist if AI – being non-human – is considered the sole author. While AI can support artists, human contribution should be dominant. The ongoing discussion on AI and copyright ownership requires continuous monitoring.
- **In-game purchases and children**: Video games featuring in-game purchases should be scrutinised with an eye to current legal requirements that could adversely affect the target company's value, especially if its portfolio relies heavily on such revenues (as with Free-to-Play or Freemium games). The same applies generally when activities and revenues stem from children; the protection of minors is an increasing focus for politicians on account of its social relevance. Business models that rely on so called loot boxes[17] (banned in Belgium[18]) or gambling, for instance, need careful evaluation, particularly with an eye to possible regulatory changes.
- **Worlds of IP/franchises**: If the target owns IP that qualifies as a franchise (multiple video games or other media outlets like comic books, films, novels, for instance), extra scrutiny must be applied to the actual rights acquired. Such IPs usually encompass a whole universe of stories, backstories, and main and side characters. The following considerations are key:
  - Ensure that all contributors, including sub-service providers, have **clearly handed over any rights contractually**, particularly if they have worked on or created new stories, characters, or places, or have developed an existing story in a new direction, thereby expanding the universe.
  - Determine whether **all rights are being acquired**, or just part of a story, such as a specific setting or period of time (e.g., Warhammer Fantasy, Warhammer 40,000, and Warhammer Age of Sigmar) or there are touchpoints between stories and universes that need to be clarified (e.g., J.R.R. Tolkien's 'Lord of the Rings' vs. 'The Silmarillion'). Clarify whether all characters can be used for new spin-offs, in which a side character becomes a main character. It is helpful to have the support of someone familiar with a given universe, who can explain its intricacies. The legal description in the contract must be sufficiently detailed for a judge (not just a fan) to understand the scope of rights being acquired, as a too narrow or loose definition can lead to significant financial losses.

[17] For a definition of loot boxes see: https://en.wikipedia.org/wiki/Loot_box.

[18] In 2018, the Belgian Gambling Commission ruled that paid loot boxes fall under Belgian gambling law (Video Games Federation Belgium: https://vgfb.be/loot-boxes-in-belgium/).

• Beware of **creative veto rights** that may exist in contracts with powerful creators or their heirs. At best, such rights could prove costly if conflicts arise and need to be resolved with financial compensation; at worst, they could lead to a financially disastrous creative stalemate of the kind often exacerbated by emotional, irrational, and personal factors. A recent example is Amazon's acquisition of MGM, which at first only included the James Bond movie and TV series rights, but went on – after severe creative differences – to encompass the six decades of creative control rights held by the Broccoli family's EON company[19].

– **Last matching rights**: These clauses, part of the acquired package, are triggered by certain events, such as a planned IP sale or new game development. In practice, an actual last matching right is highly cumbersome to manage, as the holder retains the right to interfere with a deal painstakingly negotiated with a third-party buyer. Legal matching rights can devalue a property, as potential buyers may refuse to even enter negotiations until said rights are waived.
– **Regulatory changes**: Keep an eye on the latest regulations. The video game industry is affected by numerous laws, including the GDPR, the Data Act, the Digital Services Act, the Supply Chain Act, the Digital Market Act, the Digital Fairness Act, and the AI Act, as well as for example stricter age-rating systems imposed by the Pan European Game Information (PEGI) and Entertainment Software Self-Regulation (*Unterhaltungssoftware Selbstkontrolle* – USK) bodies[20].
– **Subsidies**: A video game development company may enjoy subsidies (cultural, innovation, etc.) granted by governmental institutions for cultural or economic reasons. Such subsidies may cease or become repayable if the company is taken over by a larger or foreign entity. Conversely, a buyer with a footprint in another geography may gain access to previously unavailable subsidies.
– **Key people**: A game development executive needs to assess the key people within the target along with the attendant risks if these individuals were to decide to leave the company. Review their contracts for termination timelines and, if necessary, implement an incentive plan to make the departure of key employees less likely.

E. Deal structuring

23 The deal structure can have a huge impact on the actual price paid. Therefore, the buyer must seek tax advice early to leverage any available tax advantages.

24 **a) Share deal vs. asset deal**: The primary structural choice is between a share deal and an asset deal. In a share deal, the buyer acquires the shares of the target company (via a share purchase agreement), thereby gaining everything within the company, including physical assets (furniture, computers, etc.), owned IP, accounts receivable, and all concluded contracts (e.g., licence agreements and office rental agreements). The advantage of a share deal is its simplicity: The buyer acquires all the assets and contracts needed for profitable operation without having to list thousands of individual items where important elements of the deal could be overlooked. However, the buyer also inherits all claims against the company, risks arising from past negligence, and potential (unknown) claims for damages.

25 In an **asset deal**, the buyer cherry-picks and acquires only the specific assets desired, which must then be explicitly identified and listed in the asset purchase agreement. This

[19] Available at: www.manager-magazin.de (Manager Magazin 21.2.2025).

[20] Others for example are: ESRB (Entertainment Software Rating Board) for the United States and Canada, CERO (Computer Entertainment Rating Organization) for Japan.

can be particularly intricate when purchasing IP rights, as the buyer must also acquire the underlying contracts that grant the target company the IP. For instance, a contract with a third-party licensor who licenced a superhero IP to the target must be assigned to the buyer, requiring the licensor to sign an assignment agreement with the buyer. The target company is then left with the unsold assets, which are typically of little value, and the sellers usually close the company.

Goodwill[21]: Companies built from scratch and never previously sold do not typically have goodwill on their balance sheet. While they possess goodwill in reality, it is usually a hidden reserve. If the goodwill largely consists of a company's owned brands (e.g., a game IP), the brand must be valued yearly with an impairment test. While a famous superhero IP could retain or increase its market value for decades, any increase will only be capitalised when the IP or company is sold. From a cash-flow perspective, structuring the acquisition as an asset deal is often more favourable tax-wise for the buyer, as all purchased assets, including the real goodwill (or at least parts of it), can be written off over time. In a share deal, goodwill is created but cannot be written off unless an impairment test reveals a loss of value. However, a publicly listed company may choose to capitalise the target's goodwill as it remains on its balance sheet, not diminishing profits by showing depreciation as costs. **26**

b) Earn-outs: Earn-outs must align incentives without triggering disputes over game greenlighting, budgeting or marketing decisions. This is a challenging task, and the clearer, more detailed, and thoroughly thought-out the earn-out mechanism, the better. Earn-outs can be tied to various triggers: **27**

- Company growth by headcount.
- Adherence to timelines and/or budgets for specific milestones.
- Release of game(s) or development milestones reached (e.g., first playable, vertical slice, alpha, beta, gold master, or receipt of first-party certification).
- Results of a silent review or playtest.
- Financial metrics such as EBITDA, EBIT, revenues, or units sold.
- Awards received.
- Subsidies received.

An earn-out might be classified as an **expense for employment services** (cash flow enhancing as there are costs to reduce profits instead of capitalised firm value) or capitalised as **part of the purchase price** (balance sheet enhancing). While there is no free choice, classification depends on the consideration provided by the counterparty: If merely time as an employed manager is given for money (a stay-on bonus), it is typically accounted for as an expense. However, if the earn-out payment is triggered by certain results – mostly, independent of labour services, such as reaching EBIT or sales numbers – it can be argued that it is part of the purchase price. **28**

c) Paying with shares: For publicly traded companies, partially paying the purchase price in shares (usually between 25 % and 50 % of the purchase price) offers advantages: It is easy on the cash position of the buyer and aligns the seller's interests (at least emotionally) with the buyer's. If the share payment is substantial, lock-up periods and structured sale provisions are necessary, with an investment bank assisting in phased sales to avoid negatively impacting the buyer's share price. When offering shares as part of the purchase price, explain to the seller that they can use hedging mechanisms (e.g., put op- **29**

---

[21] 'It's the portion of the purchase price that's higher than the sum of the net fair value of all of the assets purchased in the acquisition and the liabilities assumed in the process'. (www.investopedia.com/terms/g/goodwill.asp).

tions) to avoid the excessive exposure of having much of their net worth in a single company in the often volatile video game market. This helps mitigate disappointment if the stock value should fall drastically.

30 **d) Locked box vs. closing accounts**: There are two mechanisms for determining the final purchase price and accounting for operations that occur during negotiation, signing, and closing: locked box and closing accounts. Ideally, the choice of mechanism should be made at the LOI stage or, at the very latest, when long-form agreements are drafted. While it typically does not dramatically alter the final purchase price and can favour either party, opting for locked box often simplifies the process for both legal and finance departments, saving accounting headaches.

31 **e) Withholding tax**: As the games industry operates globally, transactions frequently involve international payments. Understanding the effective amount of money received is crucial for target valuation. Withholding tax is a levy imposed by a country on income (e.g., royalties) paid to foreign entities. In international licensing, when a European game developer licences its IP or publishing rights to a non-European company, the licensee's country may withhold a portion of the royalty payments as tax. However, under mutual tax treaties, some or all of the withheld tax may be able to be reclaimed, depending on the jurisdictions in question. It is important to check contracts involving cross-border payment flows to clarify who shall bear the tax burden if it is not reimbursable.

32 **f) Accounting standards and the capitalisation of development costs**: The target company may apply different accounting standards (US GAAP or IFRS, for instance) than the buyer. When assessing financial statements, it is crucial to understand whether development costs have been capitalised and appear as a depreciable asset or not, as this impacts cash flow and valuation and the buyer's fundamental understanding of the target's financial state. Depending on the standards applied, development costs sometimes must be capitalised; or they may be capitalised; or they may require certain criteria (say, the establishment of technological feasibility) in order to be capitalised. The period over which a capitalised asset is depreciable is another important fact to verify.

33 **g) Miscellaneous**:

- **Covenants**: Covenants may include obligations for the buyer, such as retaining key staff. On the seller's side, there should be a non-solicitation clause regarding employees as well as a non-compete clause, applicable both to the formation of new businesses by the seller and to the seller personally. These clauses should be valid for a reasonable time, typically not longer than four years after parting ways. A financial consideration may be exchanged to ensure the validity of these provisions.
- **Warranties and damages**: It is highly advisable to hold back a certain amount (ideally 20 % for three years – maybe releasing half after two years) of the purchase price, either in the buyer's account or in an escrow account, to have recourse for potential damages. Warranty and indemnity (W&I) insurance can be purchased to guard against damages resulting from indemnifications and violations of representations and warranties. W&I insurance typically makes sense in deals involving an enterprise value in excess of 20 million EUR, and costs around 1–2 % of that. Policies for game industry M&A activity are not underwritten by all insurance providers, and if they are, they can be on the costly side.
- Previous management that is not staying on shall sign **letters of resignation**. Management that stays on shall sign new management agreements conditional on the transaction closing.

F. Regulatory and compliance (merger control and beyond)

It is important to have at least a rough understanding of **merger control triggers**, such as financial revenue thresholds in various jurisdictions (EU, US, UK, China), and to involve expert, international legal counsel if there is any doubt. It is also advisable to think about these regulatory aspects early in the process, so that they do not turn into show-stoppers. Filing timelines can significantly delay closings, and management needs to be made aware of this. The M&A approach to this is to have two phases of completion: (1) signing, which establishes the obligation to sell if conditions are fulfilled, and (2) closing, when all conditions are fulfilled. The recent Microsoft-Activision/Blizzard acquisition serves as a notable transaction that was almost blocked by governments due to merger control concerns. In video game acquisitions, awareness of cultural merger control rules is also important, as the target may fall into the category of a sensitive national cultural organisation in its home country's jurisdiction (e.g., in Canada). For more detailed information, refer to the dedicated sub-chapter on merger control in this book (see → Ch. 35, C.). **34**

G. Post-merger integration (PMI)

Post-merger integration – the process of 'digesting' the acquisition – is a less glamorous yet crucial part of deal-making that can take years to complete. To streamline the process and keep it on track, it is advisable to set up a weekly or bi-weekly integration meeting with key players to assign responsibilities for, and follow up on, **specific integration tasks**. PMI should ideally commence even before signing the deal. Proponents of the deal should appoint a 'synergy captain' – a person outside daily operations who is responsible for ensuring that projected synergies on paper translate into real-world results. New teams should be welcomed with a handbook detailing practical aspects such as travel policies, signature authorisation, and expense rules. It is essential that they understand clearly what changes apply and where they retain independence. Reducing bureaucracy, offering backend support, and highlighting new opportunities (access to more interesting IP, partners or more game development budgets, for instance) can ensure lasting integration. Creative companies like game studios have their own unique cultures and can react sensitively to integration efforts, which they may find stifling. Team events, consistent information flow, and open communication can help soften the transition. Also be aware that culture clashes are common, arising from differences in company size, hierarchy levels, management styles, dress codes, and countless other factors. Expect some individuals to leave immediately after or even before the acquisition. Ensure robust backup solutions are in place, and avoid reliance on single individuals so as to not be in a position of weakness or vulnerability. **35**

It is important to check what categories of insurance the target company needs according to the buyer's corporate standards and how these can be included in the group coverage. This also serves as a due diligence item, particularly if the target engages in risky activities or has pending claims. In such cases, be aware of liability caps, incident limits, and USA exclusions. A specialised broker should advise on **common financial losses** for companies in the information and communications technology, advertising, and media industries. While highly specific types of cover, such as key person loss insurance, advertising insurance, or lottery/raffles insurance exist, generally required classes of cover include general/operation liability (including contractual), product liability, errors and omissions, advertisement, cyber/IT, and infringements. **36**

37 **Post-acquisition**, amend the target's governance and articles of association to reflect the buyer's governance needs, fiscal year changes, and consent rights. File with company register new ownership and new management information.

H. Final thoughts

38 Most acquirers experience a loss in share value, post-announcement, due to a tendency to overpay. This is often attributed to the **winner's curse**: The highest bidder secures the deal, but they have also paid the most – a price that everyone else deemed too high. While only time will tell, probability suggests that the highest bidder is often incorrect in their valuation. In addition, implementing an acquisition is a challenging and lengthy process. More often than not, future increases in profits have already been priced into the acquisition, meaning these gains must materialise just to break even with the purchase price. Furthermore, as is common knowledge, things usually take longer, are harder, and do not progress nearly as smoothly as presented on a PowerPoint slide.

39 If you are a CEO overseeing the deal rather than the lawyer leading it, make sure you remain closely involved and in touch with what is being negotiated or discussed. Make executive decisions when you think 'over-lawyering' is happening or when lawyers' egos threaten the successful close of your transaction. **Alternative dispute resolution (ADR)** can be particularly beneficial in the rapidly changing and highly specialised game industry as it can avoid having to argue cases before unknowledgeable judges in national courts. Organisations such as WIPO and JAMS[22] offer ADR services with specific game industry expertise. ADR typically mandates the naming of legal experts by the parties – one per party and one jointly – which allows for the appointment of industry insiders.

40 Beyond hard knowledge, soft negotiation skills are crucial. Many books[23] address this subject; familiarise yourself with the key concepts. In high-stakes deals or complex situations, employing a shadow negotiator to advise on the optimal next move can be advantageous. Valuation is not an exact science, but it requires the application of logic and rationale grounded in reality. Avoid calculations based on overoptimistic future developments or unattainable synergies, especially where **revenue synergy** is concerned (the notion that 1+1=3). In reality, most synergies are cost synergies, which often translate into saving on better scale than before regarding necessary services such as accounting or legal, having better purchasing negotiation power due to bulk buying and cutting duplicate cost, especially by staff reductions despite public statements before acquisitions to the press and unions. Acquiring insolvent or distressed companies in need of a turnaround presents even greater difficulties than regular M&A projects. Do not be intrigued by a low price; start with a cash flow positive company (or wait until IP as standalone can be bought as part of the insolvency sale), and only after gaining positive experience in normal M&A should you consider moving to the next level. Otherwise, in the M&A arena, it could be 'game over'.

---

[22] www.jamsadr.com.

[23] Deal!, 1st edn, Goldmann Verlag (2015), 2nd edn by Prof Dr. Jack Nasher announced for 2025.

§ 11
Taxes in Video Games

A. Tax types and tax aspects 3
  I. Tax types 7
  II. Tax aspects 10
    1. Location 13
    2. Legal form of incorporation 20
    3. Business model 21

B. CIT: the big picture 25
  I. Tax determination basics 27
    1. Reliable accounting 28
    2. The miracle of different results (and deferred taxes) 30
  II. Tax deductibility and add-backs 37
  III. Transfer Pricing 40
  IV. Tax breaks and other funding sources 42

C. Tax notes & tax instalments 47

D. Tax audits and litigations 51

This chapter on **taxes** will try to provide a 30-mile high view on the subject. That is the best that can be done in the context of the present handbook. Taxes are a very fragmented subject for various reasons. The most important ones are: 1

1. The high number of tax types with their different tax bases and ways to calculate them.
2. The inherently national nature of taxes, which leads to a high variety of rules and to overlaps with other legislations, either on the national or supranational level, if a company engages in international activity – which is likely to be the case for games companies.
3. The Janus-faced role of taxes to serve both as a source for public finances and as a way to stimulate economic activity through tax brakes or other advantages.

So this chapter can only help to develop a **general understanding** for the nature and mechanics of taxes and how they impact your games business. For all concrete questions, the devil is in the detail and will require either own research and/or the consultation of an external tax expert, considering the concrete situation at hand that needs to be evaluated from a tax perspective. 2

A. Tax types and tax aspects

Due to the polymorph nature of the subject, there is **not ONE standard** tax book definition for taxes – so I'll try to wrap up the essentials that recur in most definitions one can find on the subject: 3

Taxes are **mandatory**, **unrequited payments** imposed by a government on individuals or entities to fund public expenditures and services. They are typically levied at local, regional, or national levels and can take various forms, such as income taxes, sales taxes, property taxes, or tariffs. Unlike voluntary payments, taxes do not provide a direct benefit proportional to the amount paid by the taxpayer. 4

Or, in other words: taxes are a **black box** where your money enters on the one hand side – and less money comes out at the other end. But in return you receive, in a best case scenario, security, infrastructure, education and other public services that enable you to do your work. 5

6 If you are running a (games) company, you will likely want to **minimise taxes** because you can think of 1,000 other ways you could use the money for. But to be able to do this kind of tax optimisation, you must be aware of two things:

- The kinds of taxes your activity exposes you to. The above definition already gave you some hints.
- The aspects of your own activity that are interdependent with the different tax types.

I. Tax types

7 Point 1 can be boiled down to a few major tax types one will encounter in the games industry:

- **Corporate Income Tax (CIT)**: a tax levied on the (usually annual) profit resulting from the business activity.[1]
- **Consumption Taxes**: in Europe, mostly the Value Added Tax (VAT), but in the US rather referred to as Sales Tax. Companies do not ultimately pay this tax themselves. Instead, they are obliged to collect it from consumers and pay it to the tax authorities. As the name suggests, this tax is mostly based on direct consumption and thus, mostly, the sales revenue the company generates with consumers.[2]
- **Payroll Tax**: The taxes levied on the employees' salaries. Similarly to the VAT, companies do not ultimately pay this tax themselves, but are (in most jurisdictions) obliged to pay their employees' share of taxes to the tax authorities.

8 Payroll taxes are out of scope for the further chapter. Nevertheless, they constitute an important factor for the work of HR and accounting. So, two points related to payroll taxes merit a brief focus before leaving the subject alone:

- The fact of not being the actual **tax subject**, but still being obliged to do the collection and payment, is referred to **tax withholding**[3]
- because, in the case of payroll taxes, the company withholds money that the employees owe to the state from these employees and pays it directly to the tax authorities. There are other withholding taxes you may encounter in your journey (e.g. on licence fees or dividends), so it's good if you understand the basic concept of **withholding taxes.**[4]
- Payroll taxes are not to be confused with social security contributions.[5] In most countries, these show also up on the individual payroll and the companies must also pay them to the relevant bodies. However, there are two details that make them fundamentally different from taxes:
  - Normally, the employer has to pay a certain share of the social security contributions out of his own pocket. So this truly comes on top of the gross salaries and thus adds to the overall staff costs of the company.
  - These charges do provide a direct benefit in return, as they are paid to receive (under specific circumstances) coverages for health, unemployment and pensions. This list is not exhaustive, but names the most important risks usually

---

[1] https://www.britannica.com/money/income-tax/Corporate-income-tax.

[2] https://ec.europa.eu/eurostat/statistics-explained/index.php?title=Glossary%3AValue_added_tax_%28VAT%29.

[3] https://www.law.cornell.edu/wex/tax_withholding.

[4] https://en.wikipedia.org/wiki/Tax_withholding.

[5] https://ec.europa.eu/eurostat/statistics-explained/index.php/Glossary:Social_contributions.

covered by most social security schemes. Details may vary, though, depending on local legislation.

Consumption taxes are also out of scope for this chapter – but not for this book. Please refer for details to → Chapter 29 which is entirely devoted to this subject of VAT as most important consumption tax in the EU. The reason for this is simple – and builds a perfect bridge to the next subject, the relevant tax aspects for your company. Because if or if not consumption taxes become a matter of preoccupation for your company depends primarily on your business model. 9

II. Tax aspects

Three major aspects determine which precise taxes will impact a company – and to what extent. This is shown in Figure 11.1. 10

11

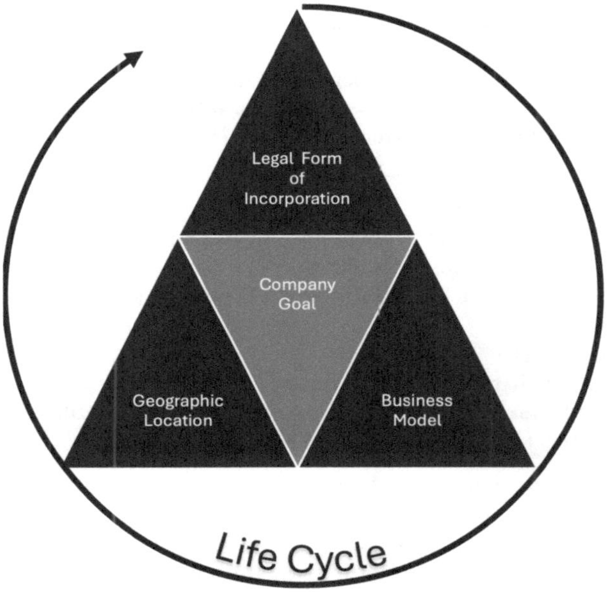

Figure 11.1: The interdependencies between fundamental setup choices

1. The geographic location.
2. The legal form of incorporation chosen.
3. The business model.

The graphic shows these 3 major aspects to define when setting up a (games) company. It also shows how these aspects are interwoven with the fundamental question of what the company stands for (its core purpose) and how both the aspects and the company's focus may evolve over time throughout its life cycle. 12

1. Location

13 As most tax law is national, the **geographic location** comes first. If you don't want to be subject to the overcomplicated tax rules or high rates of country XYZ, don't set up shop there. It's (almost) as simple as that.

14 However, especially in the EU, a lot of aspects are already regulated on the higher EU level. The most impactful EU-wide tax harmonisations regard consumption taxes (VAT), whereas **Corporate Income Tax** (CIT and thus the focus of this article) is still widely seen and treated as a national affair, either to replenish state coffers or to give the local economic policy a boost, depending on the taste of the day of national party politics. VAT, on the other hand, requires a better coordination between Member States because loopholes in regulations on the intra-community delivery of goods and services have led to material tax income losses for Member States in the past, often through fraud.[6, 7] Expect more on this in → Chapter 29 to see how this problem is tackled.

15 Accordingly, there is still a rather wide range of CIT tax rates in the EU, going from 9 % in Hungary to 32 % in Portugal in 2022.[8] In broad lines, the larger Member States tend to impose higher rates whereas smaller Member States use a lower tax rate as incentive to attract more activity.

16 It is also important to know that, depending on the chosen location, there may not be just ONE CIT, but several components that constitute jointly what is internationally regarded as CIT. Just to give the example of the two largest Member States, we have:

- In France[9]
  - Standard CIT (25 %)
  - Social Contribution on Corporate Income (3.3 %; but only beyond a threshold of 763,000 EUR corporate tax liabilities)
  - Local Business Tax (CET – Contribution Économique Territoriale)
- In Germany[10]
  - Standard CIT (15 %)
  - Solidarity Surcharge (5.5 % on Standard CIT)
  - Local Trade Tax (the so-called "Gewerbesteuer" with locally defined leverages; generally this tax is also in the 14–15 % range)

17 The tax rate competition within the EU is currently at risk to a certain extent. Over the last years, political initiative to impose a global minimum taxation have made good progress. And new rules (drafted mainly by the OECD under the acronym GloBE, standing for "Global Anti-Base Erosion") to impose a minimum corporate taxation of at least 15 % are on their way to be translated into national tax law in many countries worldwide and will be mandatory to adopt by EU Member States.[11] The focus word here is **minimum corporate taxation**: these initiatives aim particularly at globally active corporations that have, in the past, often optimised their tax position through "tax treaty shopping" and smart setups of internal flows to a point that the result was de facto equivalent to tax evasion.

18 Because these new rules aim at larger corporations, the associated thresholds are accordingly high: as of 2024, only companies with a global revenue of more than 750

---

6 https://www.europarl.europa.eu/cmsdata/156408/VAT%20Fraud%20Study%20publication.pdf.

7 https://taxation-customs.ec.europa.eu/taxation/vat/fight-against-vat-fraud/vat-gap_en.

8 https://en.wikipedia.org/wiki/Tax_rates_in_Europe.

9 https://www.impots.gouv.fr/international-professionnel/tax4busines.

10 https://en.wikipedia.org/wiki/Taxation_in_Germany.

11 https://www.oecd.org/content/dam/oecd/en/topics/policy-sub-issues/global-minimum-tax/minimum-tax-implementation-handbook-pillar-two.pdf.

million EUR will fall under these new rules.[12] Which means that a vast majority of games companies can ignore them for the time being.

As latest development, the global consensus on **minimum tax rules** has eroded thru the changed positions of the US on this subject under its new administration. As in many other aspects: the volatility of the US administration's position on important points of international trade, tax and finance has created an unprecedented level of uncertainty on the final outcome of globally applicable rules. But expect the EU to stay the course of imposing minimum corporate taxation within its sphere.[13] 19

2. Legal form of incorporation

In most countries, different taxation rules apply depending on the legal form of the company. It matters a lot, not only for liability purposes, if a company is set up as private partnership company, as limited liability company or directly as a share company. 20

From a founder perspective, choosing the legal form of a company has other important aspects which quickly let tax considerations take second seat: how many founders are there? Is the defined goal already a later potential buy-out? Is the company intended to realise a single (games) project? Or are all in there for building and running a games company in the long run?

At this point, the importance to be able to clearly formulate the company's goal becomes apparent. And, as shown in the in Figure 11.1: both the goals and the legal form can change over time!

In terms of total tax burden, the choice does usually not make a huge difference, but taxation rules and reporting duties to the tax office can vary substantially.

Some jurisdictions now also offer **option models**: these give e.g. now in Germany partnerships the possibility to be treated in tax matters like a limited liability company. It's basically diversity taken to the corporate level: there can now be partnerships that identify as corporations in tax terms.[14]

3. Business model

This is certainly the most complex aspect impacting taxation issues – and the one most related to the company goal: what is the company built for and what is its operating model? 21

And since every company does not only have one goal, but several and because every company is different and since there are so many roles a single company can take within the video games eco system, there is a combinatorial explosion of potential configurations. 22

A non-exhaustive list of important questions to answer against the planned business model is: 23

- Developer or (self-)publisher?
- Creating own IP or making work for hire?
- Selling on which platforms with or without an intermediary ("merchant of record")?
- Selling via which platform in which country?

---

[12] https://oecdpillars.com/pillar-tab/pillar-two-750-million-euros-threshold/.

[13] https://kluwertaxblog.com/2025/03/17/global-minimum-taxation-and-eu-competitiveness-what-now/.

[14] https://www.goerg.de/en/insights/publications/15-02-2022/taxing-partnerships-like-corporations-under-the-modernized-german-corporate-income-tax-act-a-new-taxation-model-neutral-to-legal-form.

- Operating an online game with in-game-monetisation or base revenue on full game sales? Or combine both?
- Based in only one location – or potentially several locations; eventually in different jurisdictions?

24 Probably the most important business model decision impacting taxes relates to VAT and not CIT: will the company sell directly to consumers?

Direct B2C sales immediately trigger the long tail of VAT compliance requirements in multiple countries, well beyond the EU. The dedicated → Chapter 29 will explain in more details what this means. Suffice it to say that, for a starter, staying clear of B2C sales or selling instead via platforms that function as "merchant of record" vis-a-vis the end user is probably a better choice than going down the rabbit hole of international value added and sales taxes too early.

B. CIT: the big picture

25 From the big picture on taxes in general now to the CIT in particular. According to the Encyclopedia Britannica, a corporate tax is "a type of direct tax levied on the income or capital of corporations and other similar legal entities".[15]

26 In the EU, we can thus be more specific and call the tax Corporate Income Tax because the tax base (aka: the amount that the tax rate is applied to determine the tax amount the company owes) is generally based on the income. And to clean up right away with one frequent misconception: the income is the result (aka: profit or loss) of the period, not the revenue!

I. Tax determination basics

27 From here, it's easy to understand that the P&L (profit & loss statement, aptly also often referred to as income statement)[16] is usually the most important document for the tax determination. And there are two questions one must be able to answer before determining the resulting CIT:

1. Can I trust the figures?
2. Which P&L statement?

1. Reliable accounting

28 The answer to point 1. above is an easy "Yes" if you have implemented a professional accounting from the start.

The accounting serves to record all relevant economic transactions in the company. It gives an overview about products created and revenue generated and the costs associated with this process. If the revenue generated is higher than the associated costs, the period closes with a profit and the profit serves as tax base for the CIT. If the costs are higher, the period closes with a loss. This results usually in no taxes to be paid... but potential future tax savings through a so-called **loss carry forward** on the balance sheet. This loss carry forward can usually be used to compensate profits in future periods, resulting in lower taxes to be paid compared to the profit of the then current period alone.

---

[15] https://www.britannica.com/money/income-tax/Corporate-income-tax.

[16] https://www.investopedia.com/terms/p/plstatement.asp.

One aspect cannot be overstated in this context: without a reliable and trustworthy accounting, it is not possible to correctly calculate and declare taxes. Or simply put: the famous *Shit in, shit out*-rule fully applies to accounting. And if the figures of your P&L are not reliable, the tax calculation (and declaration) will not be reliable either.[17] 29

2. The miracle of different results (and deferred taxes)

Now to the second question. And you may wonder: if the accounting is reliable, why should there be different statements? Also here, the basic answer is simple: different accounting standards lead to different results. And companies usually do not have one but several accounting standards to follow. 30

The base accounting is done according to **local GAAP**, the local generally accepted accounting principles. But as far as the treatment of specific transactions or processes are concerned, these local GAAP rules may differ from what local tax legislation allows. 31

Two good examples with relevance for the games industry are: 32

- Treatment of self-developed software: consider that local GAAP does not allow the capitalisation of self-developed software. In this case, all costs related to develop this software in-house immediately hit the P&L and lower the result. However, local tax rules may allow (partial) capitalisation of self-developed software. This means that the costs associated with the development of the software do not fully enter the cost base in this case. Instead, parts of these costs are capitalised. Or to put it in more understandable terms: the costs are moved from the P&L statement (where they would lower the result of the current period) to the balance sheet (which does not immediately lower the result) for depreciation in later periods. Even though both accounting standards recorded the very same transaction, the local GAAP result will look comparably worse in the described case than the tax result.
- Depreciation of assets: if larger assets are used over a longer period of time, they are first capitalised and then depreciated over a longer period of time. Take an expensive workstation as an example: if the workstation costs 9,000 EUR and can be used for a period of 3 years, this would impact (in the case of linear depreciation) the P&L statement in local GAAP not with 9,000 EUR in the year of the purchase, but with 3,000 EUR each year for 3 consecutive years. Now consider that the local government wanted to push the digitalisation of companies and allows the immediate depreciation of IT equipment for tax purposes. This will lead, as described above, to 9,000 EUR costs in the year of the purchase (aka: full depreciation in year 1) and zero costs in the following years. So here, the outcome is the other way around: the local GAAP result in year 1 is 6,000 EUR better than the tax result because different rules lead to different results.

This means: you may have different results, depending on the standards applied. Which gives rise to another tax phenomenon that you should be aware of: **deferred taxes.**[18, 19] They are an item on the balance sheet that records differences between local GAAP results and the results used of tax purposes – and the resulting different taxation. To take up the previous example of an expensive workstation: the company saved taxes on 6,000 EUR in year 1, due to the immediate full depreciation vs. its local GAAP account. Now consider a CIT rate of 25 %: a tax result that is 6,000 EUR lower means that 33

[17] https://onlinelibrary.wiley.com/doi/full/10.1111/1475-5890.12320.

[18] https://www.grantthornton.com.au/globalassets/1.-member-firms/australian-website/technical-publications/ifrs/gtal-2013-deferred-tax-a-chief-financial-officers-guide-to-avoiding-the-pitfalls.pdf.

[19] https://www.accountingtools.com/articles/accounting-for-deferred-taxes.html.

the company has to pay 1,500 EUR less CIT in year 1 compared to being taxed based on its local GAAP accounts. However, this also means that the tax result in year 2 and year 3 for this example will be correspondingly higher (because, unlike in local GAAP, there is nothing left to depreciate). And the tax office loves to remember! The company must hence record this tax saving and book a liability of 1,500 EUR with the tax office, representing the future taxes to be paid in year 2 and year 3. This represents the tax statement catching up with local GAAP over time – and the entire process is called **tax deferral**.

34 The deferred tax position on the balance sheet can be an asset or a liability, depending on whether the difference produces more taxes to be paid in the future (and thus a liability, as in the example above) or less taxes to be paid in the future (creating a **deferred tax asset**).

35 Finally, to make matters even more complicated, you may need to adhere to yet more standards. As said above (mn. 25): if e.g. the objective for the company is a later buy-out through an international player, you should consider also reporting under **IFRS** (International Financial Reporting Standard)[20]. The aim of this standard is to bridge the gap between the many local GAAP details and to make financial statements easier to compare between companies operating in different jurisdictions.

36 And because it is so important, I come back to the insistence on reliable bookkeeping: a good quality measure for your accounting is if they are able, at all times, to produce a seamless transition calculation that explains the why and how of the differences between the different account representations. Normally at least between the local GAAP and the tax representation – or between even more standards, if you decide that you also want to be able to provide e.g. an IFRS representation of your accounts, due to the goals you have set for the company.

II. Tax deductibility and add-backs

37 It's in the best interest of the tax office that you make a good profit – because higher profits mean higher CIT. However, there are different ways that can lead to higher profits, aka the delta between revenue and costs: either the company truly widens this gap by increasing revenues and/or reducing costs... or the tax rules do not allow the company to recognise all expenses as tax deductible expenses.

38 Local tax rules can define so-called **tax add-backs**[21]: they are based on specific local rules that define certain kinds of expenses as non-tax-deductible (in parts or in whole). A good example would be the refill for the management champagne fountain: this is the typical kind of expense you will find difficult to get accepted as a tax-deductible expense by tax offices in most countries due to excessive luxury.

39 The inventiveness of local tax legislators is boundless on this subject: depending on the country (and the tax type) you may have add-backs for excessive luxury (as in the example above), company car expenses, rent and leasing expenses, interests on loans and many other cost items. To get things right in this matter, you will always depend both on good tax consultants and, again, a solid accounting that is able to isolate these kinds of expenses in the company books to properly quantify the amount of these add-backs in the due cause of the tax base determination.

[20] https://en.wikipedia.org/wiki/International_Financial_Reporting_Standards.
[21] https://www.viabeacon.com/blog/what-is-an-add-back.

III. Transfer Pricing

40 One tax aspect you will likely only encounter if you get involved with larger corporations, e.g. in the due process of having been acquired by one, is **transfer pricing.**[22, 23] This describes the process of defining rules for the reasonable pricing of the intercompany flows of goods and services within a globally operating corporation. At its core, the aim of the transfer pricing rules is to prevent the profit shifting to low tax countries.

41 This approach was only mildly successful in the past, leading to the new minimum taxation rules mentioned above [mn. 17-19]. Nevertheless, complex **Transfer Pricing Rules** are still the norm to define the conditions that rule the pricing of cross-border internal flows in corporations – and are often designed to determine a local tax base within clearly defined bandwidths.

IV. Tax breaks and other funding sources

42 Due to its importance for a lot of games companies, the subject of funding has received several chapters [→ Chapters 6, 7 and 8] in this handbook which explain various funding aspects in more detail. However, the subject has important overlaps with the tax subject:[24]

1) Direct impact: The funding may come in form of outright tax breaks.
2) Indirect impact: received funding must be accounted for correctly, impacting on the tax result of the current period.
3) Indirect impact: the company's financial (tax) statements serve as assessment basis for funding eligibility.

43 In case 1, the CIT owed by the company is directly lowered by amounts defined in the funding rules. If e.g. the tax break is intended to fund staff costs related to certain R&D activities, these staff costs are directly deducted from the CIT liability resulting from the normal process of tax determination.

44 To give again a concrete example: let's consider a period tax profit of 500 KEUR and a CIT rate of 30 %, resulting in a "normal" CIT liability of 150 KEUR. If the tax break is linked to the mentioned staff costs related to specific R&D activities and the staff costs attributable to this R&D activity are 80 KEUR, the final tax liability is reduced to 70 KEUR.

45 In case 2, received funding must be recorded properly (mostly as "other operating income", but sometimes also as lower acquisition costs, e.g. in the case of direct investment funding) and it must be clear if or if not the received funding directly increases the period result or not (in case it is defined as a tax-free funding).[25] These are detailed points that must be cleared on a case-by-case basis with funding and tax experts.

46 The case 3 is indirect in the sense that the financial (tax) statements are often seen as a reliable data source for other funding-relevant assessments, e.g. the amount of staff costs incurred for certain activities, like in the example, above or the investments done

---

22 https://www.oecd.org/en/topics/transfer-pricing.html.

23 https://taxation-customs.ec.europa.eu/taxation/business-taxation/transfer-pricing-eu_en.

24 https://www.europarl.europa.eu/RegData/etudes/STUD/2025/772636/ECTI_STU(2025)772636_EN.pdf.

25 https://www.etuc.org/sites/default/files/page/file/2021-09/Annex%204%20%20-%20European%20Commission%20Financial%20Guidelines%202019.pdf.

to acquire certain kinds of equipment or machinery which are eligible for investment funding.

C. Tax notes & tax instalments

47 Turning in the tax declaration based on the above-mentioned tax determination should be left to an expert. Filling out endless and complicated forms is no fun (but potentially offers ample opportunity for playful gamification). In case you want to find out about the great lines of the tax process in your specific country, internet sites of the European Union offer a great entry point.[26]

48 In most countries, you should receive a **tax note** after a while, once the tax office was able to process your input. In a best case scenario, there is no or very little difference compared to your own tax determination calculation.

49 However, this tax note is usually preliminary and under reservation of a subsequent **tax audit**. The tax note also often triggers a reassessment of the **tax instalments**[27] that the company needs to pay during the year: these are prepayments on the expected next year's profit. After all: the state consumes money continuously and does not want to wait too long before receiving cash from its tax subjects.

50 This may be important if you encounter singular situations with your company that lead e.g. to unusually high profits in one period without hardly any chance for a repetition in the next period (e.g. a major game launch). In this case, it may make sense to get in touch with the tax office beforehand to avoid that their wishful thinking lets them fix unreasonably high instalments for the next period, based on a singular peak profit figure.

D. Tax audits and litigations

51 As said, the tax note is virtually always under reservation of a subsequent audit. The **audit culture** of the tax authorities varies considerably from one EU Member State to the other. Some countries have installed continuous audits, others truly take their time (waiting to audit a 3–4 years period every 3–4 years). In case an audit is called, you are well advised to familiarise yourself with the current rules and schedules governing such audits[28] and also seek external advice. And make no mistake: an audit will come.

52 The more immediate the audit, the better. Especially the long audit intervals can become problematic very quickly in the exciting life cycle of a young video games company because a lot can happen in 3–4 years: rapid growth, changes in ownership structure, quick staff turnover or changes of the legal form etc.

53 And, as mentioned above [→ mn. 39]: the tax office loves to remember! They assume that you can conclusively answer any question pertaining to transactions that easily date back 4–5 years at the time of the audit.

54 Yet again, the importance of a solid and professional accounting becomes clear. This time not only in terms of recording all transactions, but also in terms of performing the seamless archiving of older transactions. Details ranging back this far have often been removed from operational systems or systems have changed. But for tax audits, you better make sure that you can still access all relevant documentation. This is not limited

---

26 https://europa.eu/youreurope/business/taxation/business-tax/company-tax-eu/index_en.htm.

27 https://service.consultinghouse.eu/en/knowledge/income-tax-advance-payments.

28 https://scholar.smu.edu/cgi/viewcontent.cgi?article=2247&context=til.

to the accounting transactions recorded in your (ERP-)software, but also covers the underlying contracts, e.g. on ownership changes or with suppliers, partners, banks etc... So, in this case, you should also have a good relationship and understanding between the accounting and either your own legal department or your legal counsel that has accompanied you in your growth journey.

In a best case scenario, you are able to answer all questions and the tax audit ends **55** with no findings. However, this is rarely the case. After all: the auditor's objective is to find more money for the tax office. For this reason, they often have **focus subjects**. These are mostly related to issues that exist in all companies (they do not only audit games companies) and where either the experience from the past or recent rulings or clarifications have led to a situation where the auditors can reasonably assume that the tax base was wrongly calculated in the past.

Your tax council will usually be aware of the current **focus subjects** and can assess **56** if or if not you are at risk with your company – and what to do to counter or limit any resulting claims. But be prepared to not escape completely unscathed: the auditor comes for your money, not for your games.

And in case the auditor claims are, in your perception and in the perception of your **57** tax council, either exaggerated or unfounded, a **litigation** is the way to go. But be aware that litigations with the tax office take effort and even more time – so the amounts in question better be worth it.

The positive part of the story: once you have received the final audit findings and **58** the according adjustments, the tax notes for the audited period become final. Which means: these years are closed also from a tax perspective (unless the tax office can prove intentional tax evasion, that is; but let us assume that this was never the plan).

Now you are left only with the current fiscal year and the new set of still open years **59** for the next audit cycle... and so the eternal cycle begins again. Because only two things are certain in life: death and taxes.

CHAPTER 3
DEVELOPING A VIDEO GAME

§ 12
Video Games Development

A. Understanding the context and challenges of video game development 5
I. The variety of video games 5
1. The different video game genres 5
2. The different scopes of video game development: from indie studios to AAA developers 8
a) Video game development categories and their characteristics 10
b) Deciding to stay indie vs. going big 19
II. Selected strategic choices in video game development 22
1. Defining your video game: balancing creative vision and market potential 23
a) Selecting a video game concept: original IP, licensed properties and revivals 23
b) Choosing game features and business models 26
2. Establishing your development process and contractual approach 30
a) In-house development vs. external collaboration 30
b) Self-publishing vs. partnering with a publisher? 32
c) Game engine choice: developing a proprietary engine vs. licensing a third-party engine 34

B. The different phases of game development 38
I. Conception phase 39
1. Ideation and prototyping 40
2. Key stakeholders and roles 44
3. Selected legal and business considerations during conception 48
a) Licensing and technology use 49
b) Intellectual property (IP) protection 53
c) Funding and publishing agreements 56
II. Production phase 57
1. Preproduction, Alpha and Beta milestones 57
2. Key stakeholders and roles 61
3. Outsourcing 66
4. Involving the players in the development 70
5. Legal and business considerations during production 73
III. Live phase 80
1. Game's release and post-launch lifecycle 81
2. Key stakeholders and roles in live phase 86
3. Legal and business considerations during live phase 90

Video games have transcended entertainment to become a **global cultural and economic powerhouse**. Once the domain of passionate hobbyists crafting video games in their garages, the industry has evolved into a highly complex, multi-billion-euro sector where large-scale productions can surpass the budgets of blockbuster films. This transformation is inherent to the industry's foundation as a technology-driven sector, where evolution is both a necessity and a natural progression. The video game industry has long been a pioneer in innovation, with the growing capabilities of consoles and platforms pushing developers to create increasingly ambitious and immersive experiences for players' communities with ever-evolving expectations. Tools and technologies, such as video game engines and artificial intelligence, continue to advance, reshaping production workflows and expanding creative possibilities. Moreover, the industry needs to adapt to generational shifts, with new audiences and creators redefining expectations and innovation. 1

To understand the video game industry, it is essential to explore the diverse approaches to video game creation, from the ambitious projects of AAA studios to the bold experimentation of independent developers. As player expectations rise, so does the **complexity** of video **game creation**. Massive development teams, extensive budgets, 2 cutting-edge technology and intricate production pipelines have become standard for AAA studios seeking to deliver the next immersive, expansive worlds, high-fidelity and cinematic experience, whilst independent developers continue to grow by exploring niche and bold ideas. Regardless of studio size, one constant remains: passion, paired with the crucial trait of agility to navigate the ever-evolving gaming industry.

3 Video game development is a unique fusion of artistry and engineering, requiring a deep understanding of storytelling, design, technology, and business strategy.

4 This chapter examines the vast landscape of video game development, exploring the variety of video games being created, the impact of team structures and production scales, and the phases of development and key stakeholders shaping the industry's future.

A. Understanding the context and challenges of video game development

I. The variety of video games

1. The different video game genres

5 Video games encompass a wide range of genres, each offering distinct gameplay and player experiences. Understanding these genres is essential for recognising market opportunities and addressing the legal and business considerations in video game development. Below is a non-exhaustive overview of key genres and notable European-developed titles:

a) **Adventure and role-playing games (RPGs)** focus on narrative exploration, player choices, and character progression, immersing players in detailed worlds and deep storytelling.
   - *Syberia* series (Microids, France) – graphic adventure
   - *Detroit: Become Human* (Quantic Dream, France) – interactive storytelling
   - *The Witcher 3: Wild Hunt* (CD Projekt Red, Poland) – open-world action RPG
   - *Divinity: Original Sin 2* (Larian Studios, Belgium) – tactical RPG
   - *Fable series* (Lionhead Studios, UK) – action RPG with a focus on player's choice
   - *Dying Light* (Techland, Poland) – a mix of action adventure and shooter in a survival horror setting
   - *Dishonored* (Arkane Studios, France) – action RPG stealth video game/immersive simulation
   - *Control* (Remedy Entertainment, Finland) – action RPG in a "X-files" setting
   - *Disco Elysium* (ZA/UM, Estonia) – heavy text RPG
   - *The Grand Theft Auto (GTA) series* (Rockstar, Scotland) – the currently most successful franchise in gaming
   - *Kingdom Come Deliverance* (Warhorse studios, Czech Republic) – action adventure in medieval times
   - *Clair Obscur: Expedition 33* (Sandfall Interactive, France) – turn-based RPG in a dark fantasy Belle Epoque setting

b) **Action video games** focus on physical challenges like reflexes, precision, and hand-eye coordination, often featuring fast-paced gameplay that requires mastery of combat or platforming mechanics.

- *Rayman* (Ubisoft Montpellier, France) – platformer
- *Hellblade: Senua's Sacrifice* (Ninja Theory, UK) – action-adventure video game with psychological themes
- *Ori and the blind forest* (Moon studios, Austria) – platformer
- *Streets of Rage 4* (Dotemu, France) – beat them up
- *Mordhau* (Triternion, Slovenia) – massively online medieval fighting video game
- *Fall Guys: Ultimate Knockout* (Mediatonic, UK) – party battle royale video game

c) **Shooter video games** focus on shooting enemies, whether controlled by AI or other players, requiring skills like precision, anticipation, and environmental awareness. With numerous subgenres, shooters are often regarded as the most lucrative genre in the HD industry.
- *Battlefield* series (DICE, Sweden) – competitive first-person shooter
- *S.T.A.L.K.E.R. series* (GSC Game World, Ukraine) – first-person survival shooter
- *Helldivers 2* (Arrowhead Game Studios, Sweden) – third-person cooperative shooter
- *Sniper Elite series* (Rebellion developments, UK) – third-person stealth shooter
- *The Finals* (Embark, Sweden) – competitive first-person shooter
- *Tom Clancy's Ghost Recon series* (Ubisoft Entertainment, France) – cooperative military third-person shooter
- *ARMA III* (Bohemia Interactive, Czech Republic) – military simulation
- *Hunt Showdown* (Crytek, Germany) – competitive extraction first-person shooter

d) **Simulation and strategy video games** range from recreating real-world experiences to tactical decision-making and resource management, appealing to players who enjoy planning, problem-solving, and creativity.
- *Farming Simulator* (Giants Software, Switzerland) – agricultural simulation
- *Anno series* (Ubisoft Blue Byte, Germany) – city-building and strategy
- *Football Manager series* (Sports Interactive, UK) – sports management simulation
- *Total War series* (Creative Assembly, UK) – real-time strategy video game in historical or fantasy settings
- *Crusader Kings III* (Paradox Interactive, Sweden) – grand strategy
- *Planet Zoo* (Frontier Developments, UK) – zoo management simulation
- *Flight Simulator* (Asobo Studios, France) – flight simulation
- *Top Eleven Football Manager* (Nordeus, Serbia) – football management simulation
- *Eve Online* (CCP Games, Iceland) – massively multiplayer online in space

e) **Sports and racing video games** focus on competitive gameplay in real-world or fantasy settings, emphasising realism, skill, and multiplayer competition.
- *Forza Horizon* series (Playground Games, UK) – open-world racing
- *Tour de France series* (Cyanide Studio, France) – cycling simulation
- *TrackMania series* (Nadeo, France) – arcade-style racing
- *Assetto Corsa* (Kunos Simulazioni, Italy) – racing simulation
- *Riders Republic* (Ubisoft Annecy, France) – skiing and mountain sports simulation

6 In addition to the above, **mobile games** feature specific genres and subgenres tailored to broad audiences, with accessible mechanics designed for ease of play:

f) **Hypercasual games**
- *2048* (Ketchapp, France) – puzzle game
- *Crowd city* (Voodoo, France) – puzzle game
- *Stack Ball* (Azur Games, Cyprus) – platforming

g) **Casual games and midcore games**
- *Candy Crush Saga* (King, Sweden) – match3 puzzle game
- *Toon Blast* (Peak Games, Turkey) – match3 puzzle game
- *Angry Birds* (Rovio Entertainment, Finland) – physics-based puzzle game
- *Clash of Clans* (Supercell, Finland) – strategy-based mobile game
- *Rise of Cultures* (Innogames, Germany) – civilization management game

7 The diversity of genres reflects the breadth and dynamism of the **European gaming industry**, which also includes other notable genres such as survival, horror, puzzle, party, rhythm, sandbox, roguelike, massively multiplayer online (MMO), and idle/incremental games. From indie developers to AAA studios, European video game creators continue to shape and innovate the global gaming landscape.

2. The different scopes of video game development: from indie studios to AAA developers

8 The European video game industry is home to a **diverse ecosystem** of developers, from small independent studios to major AAA publishers. Understanding the differences in scale, funding models, development practices, and legal considerations is key to appreciating the sector's creative and economic landscape.

9 This section outlines the **defining features** of indie, AA, and AAA studios; the factors shaping their growth or independence; and the business and legal challenges each category faces. It also considers typical growth paths and why some studios choose to remain small within the European market.

a) Video game development categories and their characteristics

10 **From garage projects to blockbusters: a historical perspective.** Over the past twenty years, the video games industry has shifted from being dominated by major publishers to a more diverse and accessible landscape. Advances in tools such as Unity and Unreal Engine, along with digital platforms like Steam, the Epic Games Store, and console (i.e., First Parties) initiatives, have enabled small teams to develop and release video games independently.

11 While artificial intelligence has long played a role in development, the **rise of generative AI** brings both opportunities and challenges, particularly for larger studios. It can streamline workflows and boost creativity, but also raises legal and ethical questions around confidentiality, intellectual property, authorship, and responsible use, as well as the need to adapt to evolving AI regulations.

12 These innovations have driven the growth of Europe's vibrant indie scene and a new wave of **mid-sized AA studios**. However, the increased accessibility of tools and platforms has also led to market saturation, making discoverability an ongoing challenge despite greater creative and commercial freedom.

13 **Indie studios: where creativity meets constraints.** Indie studios are small, agile teams – often fewer than 50 people, sometimes just one – operating without the financial support of major publishers. With modest budgets (ranging from a few thousand to one million

euros), they depend on word-of-mouth and social media for promotion and typically choose self-publishing or crowdfunding over traditional publishing (→ Ch. 6 to 8). Their focus is on innovative gameplay and unique storytelling rather than high-end graphics, allowing them to explore niche ideas and experiment with design.

This smaller scale enables **rapid adaptation to player feedback and emerging trends**. Franchising is rare, though successful indie games may lead to sequels or expanded universes post-launch. Digital platforms such as Steam, Epic Games Store, and GOG.com, along with console initiatives, provide access to wide audiences, but market saturation and discoverability remain significant challenges. Success often relies on **iterative development** and **early player involvement**. *Dead Cells* by Motion Twin (France) is a prime example, achieving critical and commercial success through bold design and ongoing updates, and selling over 10 million copies worldwide. **14**

AA studios: the business of mid-tier video games. AA studios sit between indie and AAA developers, producing high-quality video games with moderate budgets – typically between one and fifty million euros. Teams usually range from 50 to 300 staff, balancing creative ambition with financial discipline. Their marketing efforts are more substantial than those of indie studios yet remain smaller than AAA campaigns. Often supported by publishers, AA studios benefit from **greater financial security** while retaining some creative independence. **15**

Distinct legal challenges include managing multi-title publishing agreements, potentially co-owned intellectual property, and ensuring compliance with consumer protection and cross-border regulations. **16**

AAA studios: scaling up infrastructure and investment. AAA studios represent the highest tier of video game development, with budgets ranging from fifty to more than two hundred million euros and teams of hundreds or even thousands. Their video games feature cutting-edge graphics, immersive sound, complex mechanics, expansive worlds, and advanced animation, typically aiming to launch major franchises. Many AAA developers, such as Ubisoft and CD Projekt Red, also act as **publishers**, managing global distribution and marketing for their titles, which allows greater control over production and business strategy. **17**

A key challenge for AAA studios is to **create sustainable IP franchises** and **business models** in an increasingly competitive market of blockbuster games and advanced game engines, all while responding to evolving player expectations and growing regulatory scrutiny. Despite their scale, AAA studios remain highly creative, often pioneering new gameplay experiences, storytelling techniques, and technological innovations. While they pursue mass-market appeal and push the boundaries of what games can achieve, they must also **manage significant financial risks** and the complexities of research and development in the continual search for the next disruption that will drive appeal, sales, and profitability. **18**

b) Deciding to stay indie vs. going big

The decision to remain an indie studio or scale up to AA or AAA production is a pivotal one for video game developers, shaping both the creative direction and business strategy of the studio's future. This choice requires careful consideration of factors such as creative freedom, financial risk and exposure, market reach, operational complexity, and legal and regulatory requirements. **19**

Indie developers, working with small teams and limited budgets, often rely on personal savings, investors, or crowdfunding, and promote their video games through word-of-mouth and social media. However, standing out in a **crowded marketplace**, where platforms like Steam release over 1,000 new video games each week, remains a **20** significant challenge. Scaling up to AA or AAA enables access to greater resources, talent, and global distribution, supporting more ambitious projects with higher production values. Yet, this also brings increased financial risk, greater operational and regulatory complexity, and sometimes a reduction in creative autonomy.

21 Regardless of scale, studios face **intense competition** and must differentiate themselves, connect with players, and deliver compelling experiences to succeed. Ultimately, the decision depends on the studio's goals, risk appetite, and vision, requiring a careful balance between creative ambition and business realities, while remaining true to its identity and long-term aspirations.

II. Selected strategic choices in video game development

22 Making informed strategic choices in video game development requires a **thorough understanding** of market trends, technological advancements, and industry benchmarks to identify gaps and opportunities. Developers must determine which type of video game makes sense to create, select the business model that aligns with their objectives, and assess the technological landscape that will shape their project. The following section explores the key considerations and emerging disruptions influencing strategic direction in video game development.

1. Defining your video game: balancing creative vision and market potential

a) Selecting a video game concept: original IP, licensed properties and revivals

23 One of the first decisions developers face is whether to **create a new IP** or work with existing ones. Developing a new IP or brand allows studios to craft unique worlds, characters, and gameplay mechanics, with the potential to establish enduring franchises. However, this approach carries greater risk, as there is no guaranteed audience.

24 Alternatively, **licensed video games** leverage established IPs from films, books, or other franchises, offering immediate recognition and a built-in fan base. While this can reduce market risk, success still depends on effective adaptation, creative execution, and the ability to attract both existing and new audiences. Working with licensed IP also requires navigating complex licensing agreements, creative restrictions, and the expectations of rights holders, all while ensuring the final product stands out in a competitive market and complies with contractual and regulatory obligations.

25 **Ports, remakes, and remasters** present further opportunities to expand a studio's reach. **Ports** adapt video games to new platforms, opening additional markets (such as bringing a console video game to PC or mobile) but requiring technical optimisation for hardware differences and user experience. **Remakes** modernise classic titles with updated graphics and mechanics, appealing to nostalgia and new players alike. **Remasters** enhance the visual and technical aspects of existing video games, offering refreshed experiences for both loyal fans and newcomers. In all cases, developers must balance fidelity to the original with innovation to capture contemporary audiences' interest.

b) Choosing game features and business models

26 The choice of business model is fundamental to a video game's development, shaping both revenue generation and long-term appeal to users. The traditional model of one-off sales at launch has largely given way to **subscription** services such as Xbox Game Pass and PlayStation Plus, where players access a variety of video games for a monthly fee. This shift places greater emphasis on video game longevity, replayability, and ongoing

content updates to maintain interest in a competitive market. As subscription models become more prevalent, it dilutes the perceived value of individual video games in the minds of consumers. At the same time, development costs are skyrocketing, and players increasingly expect regular updates, expansions, and new in-game items, adding further pressure to studios navigating this shifting landscape.

Today, a video game's release marks the start of an extended lifecycle, often lasting 27 months or even years. So-called '**live service**' or '**games as a service**' titles require amongst other things, scalable infrastructure, regular content updates, and effective community management. Features such as esports readiness and user-generated content can further extend a game's appeal and help build vibrant player communities – whether by supporting competitive multiplayer experiences or enabling players to create and share their own content. However, these features also introduce specific challenges: For example, **esports** requires balanced mechanics and robust multiplayer functionality, while **user-generated content** raises legal considerations around intellectual property and the need for careful moderation. The video games industry is built on innovation, with its dynamic nature and rapid technological advancements continually opening up fresh opportunities for creative development and growth. Seizing these opportunities is an integral part of the industry's DNA.

Technologies such as **blockchain** are enabling new forms of user interaction, support- 28 ing concepts like the metaverse, where players become co-creators of digital worlds. In addition, blockchain technology can enable **revenue-sharing mechanisms** with player-creators through simple, transparent, and secure processes, supporting sustainable **co-creation models**. Traditional legal frameworks, especially regarding intellectual property, may become outdated and must evolve towards more innovative, value-sharing models. Both developers and legal professionals are constantly reassessing their practices to keep pace with industry changes.

Similarly, advances in **cloud gaming** and 5G networks are beginning to influence 29 development priorities. While these technologies are still maturing and their commercial potential continues to develop, they offer the possibility of lowering hardware barriers and reducing latency, enabling users to stream video games directly to their devices.

2. Establishing your development process and contractual approach

a) In-house development vs. external collaboration

A key decision is whether to manage all aspects of development internally or to 30 outsource or co-develop with external partners. **Outsourcing** (as further detailed in → Ch.12 mn. 66) can provide specialised skills, technology, and resources, potentially reducing costs and speeding up production. However, it demands careful contract negotiation, clear timelines, and stringent quality control. It is essential, for example, that agreements clearly define intellectual property ownership, warranties, approval processes, payment terms, data management and closing kit delivery, to ensure smooth collaboration and protect the interests of both parties. Good organisation on both sides of the partnership is also crucial to guarantee transparency, responsiveness, and effective communication.

Co-development with another studio brings additional expertise and capacity but 31 requires alignment on creative vision and shared responsibilities. Successful co-development often hinges on regular communication, well-defined milestones, and mutual trust between partners. The size and experience of your team will influence the need for, and success of, external collaboration.

b) Self-publishing vs. partnering with a publisher?

32 Another important choice is whether to self-publish or partner with a publisher. **Self-publishing** gives developers full control over intellectual property, creative direction, and revenue, but requires significant investment in marketing and distribution. It also means taking on all legal, regulatory, and customer support responsibilities. **Working with a publisher** offers access to funding, established networks, and promotional support, but often involves sharing revenue, creative input, or IP rights. Publishers may also fund development, making this decision integral to the overall process. When negotiating with publishers, developers should pay close attention to contract terms regarding IP ownership, revenue shares, and creative control.

33 **Crowdfunding** platforms like Kickstarter can offer alternative funding for self-publishers, enabling direct support from players and early community building. However, success depends on transparency, clear communication, and careful planning. It is important to set realistic goals and keep backers regularly updated to maintain trust. Team size and cultural differences can also affect crowdfunding outcomes.

c) Game engine choice: developing a proprietary engine vs. licensing a third-party engine

34 Choosing the right game engine is a critical decision that impacts the development process, costs, and creative flexibility not only for the lifetime of the video game but most importantly for the studio direction and organisation. Developers need to decide whether to build their own proprietary engine or license a third-party engine.

35 **Developing a proprietary engine** gives studios full control over features, optimisation, and scalability, and can reduce long-term costs by eliminating licensing fees. However, building an engine demands substantial upfront investment, technical expertise, and ongoing maintenance, which can divert resources from core game development and increase operational complexity.

36 **Licensing a third-party engine** gives studios immediate access to advanced tools, regular updates, and industry-standard support, enabling quicker development and lowering technical barriers. Widely used engines like Unity and Unreal offer reliability and scalability, but involve costs such as revenue sharing or subscription fees, which can affect profitability. Studios may also encounter limits on customisation and risk dependency on the provider's business decisions, including pricing changes or discontinued features.

37 Ultimately, the decision to develop a proprietary engine or license a third-party solution depends on the studio's resources, technical expertise, and long-term objectives. For smaller teams or projects with tight deadlines, established engines typically offer the best balance of cost and efficiency. Larger studios with specialised requirements may benefit from investing in their own technology, despite the greater initial investment and ongoing maintenance demands.

B. The different phases of game development

38 Video games development is a **multi-stage process** that transforms an initial idea into a fully realised interactive experience. Each phase, conception, production, and live operations, requires collaboration across disciplines, and adaptability to technological and market trends. Understanding these phases provides insight into the industry's stakeholders, workflows, and key decision points.

I. Conception phase

The **conception phase** is where the vision for a game is born. Developers explore different concepts, evaluate technical feasibility, and build early prototypes to validate ideas before full-scale production begins. This phase is crucial for defining the video game's core identity, ensuring market viability, as well as identifying technical challenges to set up a realistic roadmap for development. **39**

1. Ideation and prototyping

The **ideation process** is the creative engine that powers video game development, beginning with brainstorming sessions to imagine innovative gameplay mechanics, compelling narratives, and immersive experiences (and hopefully all three!). Successful video games balance creative ambition with market viability, ensuring that their core concepts resonate with players while remaining technically and commercially feasible long term. **40**

Genre selection is a critical first step, as genre dictates core mechanics, storytelling style, and market positioning. Identifying the right audience ensures that design choices, from gameplay complexity to monetisation models, resonate with the intended player base. **41**

Competitor analysis and **market research** further refine the concept, offering insight into successful trends, player demands, and market gaps. Studying both hits and failures in the industry helps developers position their video game uniquely, avoiding common pitfalls while innovating where opportunities arise. **42**

With a solid concept in place, **prototyping** becomes essential. Early versions allow developers to test mechanics, identify technical constraints, and secure stakeholder confidence before committing full resources. **43**

2. Key stakeholders and roles

At the heart of early development is the **Core Team**, a multidisciplinary group responsible for shaping the video game's vision and laying its technical foundation. This team brings together game designers, who define mechanics, level structure, and player experience, alongside creatives who establish the artistic identity and overall narrative direction. The technical director assesses feasibility, selects the appropriate game engine, and develops an early prototype with developers. **44**

On the business side, marketing and business strategists conduct **market research**, define target audiences, and evaluate commercial viability. Following industry trends could prove risky, as players' interest in a trend are likely to change during the production timeline (often lasting years) of the video game. Aiming to create a new experience is a better bet, but one easier said than done. **45**

Overseeing it all, a **producer** manages timelines, budgets, and team coordination, keeping development on track. **46**

The composition of the **Core Team** varies depending on the scale of the developer. AAA studios typically assign specialised roles to individual experts. In contrast, indie teams often work within smaller groups, with developers wearing multiple hats to cover design, programming, and production tasks. Regardless of team size, maintaining alignment across disciplines is critical to a streamlined and effective development process. **47**

3. Selected legal and business considerations during conception

48 **Legal and business** considerations at the conception stage are essential for foreseeing opportunities, mitigating risks, securing funding, and ensuring the long-term viability of a project. Addressing these issues early helps developers protect their creative assets, avoid disputes, and establish a strong foundation for production and commercialisation.

a) Licensing and technology use

49 Most video game projects rely on third-party tools, software, and even assets, making proper **licensing agreements** necessary to develop and operate the video game.

50 Third party video game engines like Unity and Unreal Engine, but also other software and digital content creation tools, come with specific **licensing terms**, including revenue-sharing clauses or subscription-based pricing models. Developers must carefully consider these agreements to ensure their own compliance and assess the long-term financial implications for their video games.

51 Beyond traditional software, emerging technologies are reshaping game development in profound ways. AI-driven tools help streamline production pipelines, enabling developers to facilitate, and sometimes fully automate, certain tasks. **Generative AI tools** may help democratise game creation by reducing the workload for specific tasks, allowing for optimisation of resource allocation on more creative areas of the development.

52 But while AI offers vast potential for improving production efficiency, it also triggers debates regarding **creative autonomy and job displacement**. Automation of artistic and technical tasks may alter traditional roles within development teams, prompting necessary discussions about balancing technological advancements with human creativity.

b) Intellectual property (IP) protection

53 Securing intellectual property rights early in development ensures long-term control over a video game's creative assets. One of the first steps is **trademarking** the video game's title, which involves conducting a thorough search to verify its uniqueness and registering it to prevent disputes with existing trademarks (→ Ch. 17 mn. 32).

54 Beyond the title, the legal framework governing **copyright** in the EU is explored later in this book, providing insights into how developers can secure protections for their work and understand the limitations of copyright in the gaming industry.

55 For teams working collaboratively, whether in-house or through external partnerships, drafting clear intellectual property agreements to define **ownership** of assets and ensure that rights remain with the developer rather than individual contributors or third-party vendors. Without proper contractual clarity on the grant of rights, disputes over ownership can arise, particularly if a video game is a commercial success.

c) Funding and publishing agreements

56 Securing financial stability early in development is essential, whether a project is self-funded or backed by external investors. Developers must assess their **funding** options, which may include private investors, crowdfunding campaigns, publisher deals, or government grants. Each financing route comes with different expectations regarding revenue distribution, creative control, and long-term commitments, hence clearly defining how revenues will be shared among stakeholders helps prevent conflicts as the video game progresses toward launch.

II. Production phase

1. Preproduction, Alpha and Beta milestones

Once the conception phase has established a clear vision for the video game, the market analysis has been done and the funding has been secured, the **production phase** can begin, turning concepts into a playable product. This phase is often divided into multiple key milestones to track progress and ensure alignment with development goals. We will only focus here on three critical gates, out of many more. 57

Preproduction: This stage refines the video game's design, technology stack, business model and project structure. Teams need to settle on development tools such as video game engines, digital content creation software, audio design tools, etc. 58

Alpha: At this milestone, the video game is in an early playable state, with core mechanics implemented but assets and features still in development. Testing focuses on functional gameplay, verifying that systems interact correctly, and identifying major design flaws. 59

Beta: By this stage, the video game is feature-complete, meaning all gameplay systems, mechanics, and assets have been integrated. However, fine-tuning and optimisation remain ongoing. Beta testing conducted either through closed sessions (with selected testers) or open betas (available to a broader audience) to identify balancing issues, and usability problems (bugs). This stage provides critical insights into technical performance, player behaviour and overall interest, ensuring the video game is polished before launch. 60

2. Key stakeholders and roles

As production ramps up, the core team expands to accommodate the **full development** pipeline, sometimes involving hundreds of specialists working across multiple locations. 61

Game designers refine gameplay mechanics, balance progression, and finalize level design, ensuring a cohesive and engaging player experience. Meanwhile, **artists** and **animators** focus on creating detailed 2D or 3D assets, character models, textures, and environmental elements, while **programmers** implement core mechanics, physics, AI behaviour, and user interface functionality. **Writers** and **narrative designers** continue shaping the video game's story, refining dialogue, and deepening in-game lore to enhance immersion. 62

The **audio team**, including sound designers and composers, develops sound effects, voice-over assets, and musical scores, ensuring that the video game's audio enhances its atmosphere and emotional impact. 63

Producers and **project managers** play a critical role in overseeing deadlines, budget constraints, and cross-team coordination, keeping production aligned with milestones. 64

As the video game nears completion, **QA testers** conduct extensive testing to identify bugs, performance issues, and inconsistencies, ensuring that the final product meets quality expectations. Additionally, **localization teams** work to translate and adapt in-game text, voiceovers, and interface elements for international markets, ensuring accessibility and cultural relevance across different regions. 65

3. Outsourcing

While larger studios often have dedicated in-house specialists, many developers rely on external vendors to supplement their production efforts. **Outsourcing** allows studios to access specialised talent for tasks such as art asset creation, animation, voice acting, 66 and technical development, but it also introduces additional complexities that require coordination and structured agreements to ensure smooth collaboration.

67 To mitigate risks such as incomplete or untimely delivery, developers must define deliverables and **milestones** upfront through structured contracts that outline the scope of work, expected quality standards, and deadlines. Establishing milestone-based deliverables enables developers to monitor progress at multiple stages, ensuring that outsourced work aligns with project expectations and providing opportunities to request refinements before final submission.

68 A **payment schedule** tied to milestone completion helps maintain accountability and incentivises timely delivery. Instead of lump-sum payments, larger projects benefit from staggered payments, reducing financial risks for both parties and ensuring that vendors remain committed to delivering high-quality work.

69 Contracts should explicitly state whether the outsourced work is **exclusive** to the video game, preventing vendors from repurposing or reselling assets. Developers must also secure full **ownership rights** over outsourced content to avoid legal disputes over asset usage, ensuring that all external contributions seamlessly integrate into the final product without restrictions.

4. Involving the players in the development

70 Modern video game development is no longer a one-way process where developers create a product and release it to the market. Instead, players have become active participants, shaping development both before and after a video game's release (→ III.).

71 Community-driven development is an increasingly common approach, where studios engage directly with their audience to gauge sentiment, test new ideas, and refine features in response to real player feedback. This iterative approach is particularly effective for **live-service** video games, where frequent updates and balance patches are essential to maintaining players' interest.

72 The rise of early access programmes and **crowdfunding** platforms has further strengthened player involvement in development, providing smaller developers with an opportunity to secure funding while simultaneously building a dedicated player base before launch by fostering a sense of ownership and loyalty within the player community.

5. Legal and business considerations during production

73 Video game development is an intricate and resource-intensive process, often facing challenges that can derail even the best-planned projects.

74 One of the most persistent challenges is when projects expand beyond their initial vision, straining resources and extending development timelines. While new ideas naturally emerge during production, unchecked scope growth can lead to bloated development cycles, financial overruns, and ultimately, an unfinished or compromised product. Loose planning could also lead to '**crunch**', where excessive overtime and intense pressure increases to meet deadlines. Sustainable development practices, such as realistic scheduling, regular playtesting phases, and efficient resource allocation, help studios maintain productivity without overburdening their teams. Finally, many projects underestimate the time required for debugging, optimisation, and final polishing, causing cascading delays that affect marketing campaigns.

75 Regarding legal challenges, the production phase is where the video game starts taking shape, meaning that legal topics become more pressing than ever. While this section highlights key areas requiring attention, it is by no means exhaustive; other

chapters in this book provide deeper insights into legal frameworks and best practices that developers and their legal counsel should evaluate closely.

Intellectual Property. Whether working with in-house developers, freelancers, or outsourcing vendors, a key topic in video game development is ownership of assets. Contracts should explicitly state that all work created belongs exclusively to the developer (or publisher) upon completion, as retaining full and transferable rights over assets is crucial for long-term flexibility, allowing modifications, updates, or sequels without legal uncertainty. 76

Also, if external intellectual properties (such as characters, vehicles, narrative elements from pre-existing works, etc.) are incorporated into the video game, **licensing** arrangements must specify usage rights, exclusivity, duration, and compensation structures. 77

Distribution agreements. As the video game approaches its final stages, developers must secure agreements that will govern how their video game is distributed. Digital stores such as PlayStation Store, Xbox, Nintendo eShop, Steam or the Epic Games Store, determine revenue-sharing models, marketing responsibilities, and technical compliance. 78

Marketing and **localisation** responsibilities must also be clearly defined. Whether a publisher or the developer covers costs for advertising, regional adaptation, and translation can significantly impact the video game's visibility and success across different markets. Localisation is more than just translating text; it requires cultural adaptation, sometimes voice-over work, and adjusting user-interface elements to suit different languages and regional preferences. 79

III. Live phase

The **launch** of a video game is a defining moment, representing the culmination of years of development. However, in today's industry, a video game's release is not its endpoint but rather the beginning of an ongoing relationship with players. A successful launch requires strategic planning, technical polish, and post-release support to ensure a smooth experience for players and maintain the interest for the title in the long run. 80

1. Game's release and post-launch lifecycle

Launch: the final sprint. As the release date approaches, developers enter a crucial phase of final polish, refining both technical and artistic elements to ensure the video game meets quality expectations. The priority during these last weeks is to address outstanding bugs, beginning with those that threaten stability and performance, while also fine-tuning minor details that enhance the overall player experience. Balancing gameplay mechanics, optimising frame rates, and preparing Day 1 updates become essential tasks, ensuring the video game runs smoothly across platforms. Yet, despite rigorous testing, no launch is ever entirely flawless. Developers must be ready to monitor the game in real time, swiftly respond to unexpected technical issues, and deploy immediate hotfixes when necessary. A well-optimised and stable release not only safeguards a developer's reputation but also sets the foundation for long-term player engagement and success. 81

Post-launch phase: Sustaining interest. Once a video game is released, developers must shift their focus from production to maintenance and growth to keep the player base interested in the game and expand the video game's lifespan. 82

83 Addressing player-reported issues through **patches** is a priority. Developers closely analyse player data and community feedback to identify areas needing improvement, particularly in competitive multiplayer titles, where balance adjustments prevent any single weapon, character, or strategy from becoming overpowered. A well-maintained video game meta keeps gameplay fresh, fair, and engaging, reducing player frustration and enhancing long-term retention.

84 Beyond technical fixes, many developers adopt a **game-as-a-service** model, continuously introducing new content to sustain interest. Regular updates, whether free expansions, paid downloadable content, or limited-time events, add fresh missions, characters, challenges, and cosmetic items, extending the video game's lifespan.

85 A strong **post-launch strategy** can transform a game into a long-term success. Titles like *Rainbow Six: Siege* and *The Witcher 3* thrived post-release due to well-executed patches, expansions, and consistent developer engagement. Conversely, neglecting post-launch support can result in rapid player drop-off and reputational damage.

2. Key stakeholders and roles in live phase

86 At the heart of post-launch support is the **Live Operations** (LiveOps) team, which continuously monitors performance, analyses player behaviour, and implements updates to maintain a balanced and enjoyable experience.

87 Artists, writers, and designers collaborate with monetisation experts to introduce new storylines, missions, characters, and customisation options, ensuring that fresh content keeps the video game dynamic.

88 A video game's success post-launch is also deeply tied to its **community management** and **customer support**. Community managers act as a link between players and developers, gathering feedback, addressing concerns, and relaying insights that inform future updates. Their role extends beyond communication, fostering an active and engaged player base through social media, forums, and in-game events. Customer support teams work alongside them to troubleshoot technical issues, resolve account-related problems, and ensure a smooth experience for players.

89 For highly competitive or multiplayer-driven games, **esports coordinators** may also play a role in organizing tournaments and competitive events, further strengthening community engagement.

3. Legal and business considerations during live phase

90 As a video game enters the **live phase**, the legal and business landscape shifts from development-focused concerns to those related to player interactions. Maintaining good practices in consumer protection, intellectual property management, and clear player behaviour policies helps support a sustainable and responsible post-launch ecosystem.

91 **End User License Agreement** (EULA) or **Terms of Service** (TOS) serve as the foundation of a video game's legal framework, defining the conditions under which players access and interact with the product. These agreements clarify that purchasing a video game grants a license to use the software rather than ownership of the video game itself. They also establish behavioural guidelines, prohibiting actions such as cheating, harassment, and unauthorised modifications, while setting liability limitations in cases of unintended technical failures. To remain effective, these agreements should be clear, enforceable, and adaptable to evolving legal standards and player expectations.

92 **Monetisation and microtransactions** have become common in the modern video gaming economy, but they have also attracted regulatory scrutiny, particularly concerning loot boxes, in-game currencies, and pay-to-win mechanics. Developers must ensure

that monetisation models are transparent, providing players with a clear understanding of what they are purchasing, whether it be cosmetic items, gameplay enhancements, or randomised content. Consumer protection laws (→ Ch. 26 mn. 8) require transparency regarding in-game purchases that must avoid manipulative or predatory practices, particularly when targeting younger audiences. Monetisation strategies that fail to adhere to these principles can lead to player backlash, regulatory intervention, or legal disputes.

User generated content (UGC) and modding have significantly extended the lifespan of many modern video games, fostering vibrant communities where players create and share levels, skins, mods, or entirely new game modes. Titles like Minecraft and The Elder Scrolls series have demonstrated the power of UGC in sustaining players 'interest for the title long after launch. However, allowing player-created content introduces intellectual property hazards that must be carefully managed. Developers must establish clear terms regarding ownership, whether players retain full rights to their creations, grant the developer a license, or relinquish ownership entirely. Additionally, moderation policies should be in place to prevent the distribution of infringing, offensive, or unauthorised content, ensuring compliance with platform policies. 93

Intellectual property disputes, plagiarism claims and copyright infringement become more prominent as a video game gains visibility. Increased exposure can invite claims of plagiarism or copyright violations, requiring developers to protect their original content while ensuring they do not infringe upon existing IPs. Some studios may face accusations of copying mechanics, storylines, or artistic elements from competitors, necessitating a legal defence strategy. Conversely, unauthorised distribution of game assets, modifications, or pirated copies may require developers to issue takedown notices to remove infringing content. 94

Navigating new consumer regulations can be challenging, as the industry may be impacted by regulations not drafted specifically with video games as targeted products. GDPR adoption has led to scrutiny of video games collecting player data, gambling-related mechanics have faced class-action lawsuits and misleading in-game promotions have also led to consumer lawsuits. By proactively addressing these legal and business risks, developers can minimise exposure to litigation and regulatory penalties while maintaining a trustworthy and transparent relationship with their player base. 95

The live phase of a video game is an exciting yet legally intricate period, requiring careful management of player interactions, **monetisation**, **content ownership**, and regulatory **compliance**. A well-structured legal framework not only protects developers from lawsuits and disputes but also fosters a trustworthy and player-friendly gaming ecosystem. 96

§ 13
Copyright in and for Video Games

Bibliography: Dimita/Lee/MacDonald, Copyright infringement in the video game industry, Geneva 2022; Lindner/Shapiro, Copyright in the Information Society: A Guide to National Implementation of the European Directive, 2nd edn, Cheltenham 2019; Ramos et al., The Legal Status of Video Games: Comparative Analysis in National Approaches', WIPO Geneva 2013; Rosati, Copyright and the Court of Justice of the European Union, 2nd edn, Oxford 2023; The Brehon Academy, Nature's Copyright? The Early Irish Legal Principle of "To Every Cow Its Calf", (2024) The Brehon Academy; Boyd, Pyne and Kane, Video Game Law: Everything You Need to Know About Legal and Business Issues in the Game Industry, (2019) CRC Press; Greenspan/Dimita, Mastering the Game, 2nd edn, WIPO 2022; Ekin Gürünlü I., 'Video Games and Copyright Protection Under International, European, and U.S. Law' (https://law.stanford.edu/wp-content/uploads/2020/06/gu%CC%88ru%CC%88nlu%CC%88_wp59.pdf), Stanford-Vienna TTLF Working Paper No. 59, 2020; Cappello (ed), Legal challenges and market dynamics in the video games sector, IRIS, European Audiovisual Observatory, Strasbourg, November 2024; Grenzner, 'Copyright Issues Concerning Cheat Software: A Comparative Analysis of EU and US Law', Stanford-Vienna TTLF Working Paper No. 126 (https://law.stanford.edu/wp-content/uploads/2024/12/TTLF-WP-126-Grenzner.pdf); Schmidt/Großekettler, 'Is cheating copyright infringement? CJEU clarifies specific protection of computer programs' (https://www.hoganlovells.com/en/publications/is-cheating-copyright-infringement-cjeu-clarifies-specific-protection-computer-programs); Belcheva, 'Sony v Datel – a 'cheat code' for copyright infringement?' (https://thelens.slaughterandmay.com/post/102jsev/sony-v-datel-a-cheat-code-for-copyright-infringement#:~:text=On%2017%20October%2C%20the%20Court,transfers%20to%20the%20device%27s%20RAM); Brown/Ibbetson/Purdie, 'Blizzard v Bossland: An account of profits judgment for licensing video game 'cheats and bots' software', (https://www.bristows.com/news/blizzard-v-bossland-an-account-of-profits-judgment-for-licensing-video-game-cheats-and-bots-software/); Gardner, 'High Court rules on account of profits in relation to copyright infringement by seller of software allowing users to cheat when playing certain well known online video games' (https://www.wiggin.co.uk/insight/high-court-rules-on-account-of-profits-in-relation-to-copyright-infringement-by-seller-of-software-allowing-users-to-cheat-when-playing-certain-well-known-online-video-games/); Harper/Maloney, UK High Court Confirms That Grand Theft Auto Cheat Software Infringes Copyright (https://www.irwinmitchell.com/news-and-insights/newsandmedia/2020/february/uk-high-court-confirms-that-grand-theft-auto-cheat-software-infringes-copyright#:~:text=%22This%20case%20constitutes%20a%20clear,to%20combat%20cheating%20tool%20websites.%22); Kahlor-Witzel, https://www.insidetechlaw.com/blog/2025/08/german-federal-court-refers-ad-blocker-case-back-to-hamburg-higher-regional-court#:~:text=On%2031%20July%202025%2C%20the,to%20support%20such%20a%20conclusion. (August 2025); Gardner, 'High Court grants summary judgement for breach of contract and copyright infringement in relation to 'cheat' software designed for Grand Theft Auto V', (https://www.wiggin.co.uk/insight/high-court-grants-summary-judgement-for-breach-of-contract-and-copyright-infringement-in-relation-to-cheat-software-designed-for-grand-theft-auto-v/#:~:text=(Take%2DTwo%20Interactive%20Software%20Inc%20v%20Nathan%20James,the%20judgment%20in%20full%2C%20click%20here).%20Expertise).

A. Introduction ... 1

B. The importance of copyright for video games ... 5

C. The classification of video games ... 11

D. The importance of understanding copyright law for game developers ... 21
- I. The originality test ... 22
- II. The expression vs. ideas divide ... 23
- III. What copyright protects in video games ... 24
  - 1. Source code and software ... 24
  - 2. Visual elements and artwork ... 25
  - 3. Audio components ... 26
  - 4. Written content ... 27
  - 5. What copyright does not protect ... 28
    - *a) Game mechanics and rules* ... 29
    - *b) Functional elements* ... 30
    - *c) Short phrases and titles* ... 31
    - *d) Scenes à faire* ... 32
- IV. Building your copyright strategy ... 33
  - 1. Documentation ... 33
  - 2. Joint ownership ... 34

3. Work-for-hire ... 35
4. Common misconceptions ... 36
a) 'I cannot copyright gameplay' ... 36
b) 'Open-source means no copyright' ... 37
c) 'Copyright requires registration' ... 38
5. Key takeaways ... 39
E. Cheating in video games ... 43
I. The Court of Justice ruling in Sony v Datel (case C-159/23) ... 44
II. Why the ruling in Sony v Datel is not a game changer ... 52
III. Conclusions from case analysis ... 59
IV. A parallel to Lewis Galoob Toys, Inc. v Nintendo of America, Inc. ... 60
V. UK cases ... 61
VI. *Springer v Eyeo* and ad-blocking software ... 62
F. The principle of exhaustion ... 63

A. Introduction

Many readers of this handbook probably think that **copyright** or **droit d'auteur** (author's right) began with the English Statute of Anne in 1710 or with the French Decrees of 1791 and 1793. However, as a proud Irishman, I am duty bound to relate to you the story[1] of St. Colmcille (or Columba), a 6th century monk who studied under St. Finian in the northwest of Ireland. These were the days of religious manuscripts that were beautifully illuminated by monks toiling away in monasteries across the land. The story goes that St. Colmcille secretly copied a psalter (a book of Old Testament Psalms) belonging to St. Finian and refused to return either the psalter or its copy to St. Finian. The dispute between the two monks was brought before the High King of Ireland, Diarmait MacCerbaill who, it is reported, ruled as follows: *'To every cow her calf and to every book its copy'*. The High King's ruling led to the battle of Cúl Dreimhne in 561 AD (in which some 3,000 people reportedly died) and eventually to the self-imposed exile of St. Colmcille to the island of Iona in Scotland, where he established another important and influential monastic settlement. 1

Of course, copyright as we might begin to recognise it today only started to emerge after **Gutenberg's invention of the printing press** in the 15th century, and its roots lie in the regulation of printing and authorial rights in key European countries such as England, France and Germany. In the 19th century, many European countries began to adopt national copyright laws based on author-centric models. The French concept of **droit d'auteur** was rooted in the idea that a creative work is an expression of the author's personality and emphasises the inalienable **moral rights** of authors (such as the rights of attribution and integrity) alongside exclusive economic rights to copy, distribute, adapt and perform a work. Copyright in the **common law tradition** found in the UK, the U.S., Ireland and some other countries (including Malta and Cyprus in the EU) is more focused on the economic exploitation of creative works and generally provides weaker or waivable moral rights. 2

Led by France and other European nations, the **1886 Berne Convention** for the Protection of Literary and Artistic Works[2] created a framework for international copyright, recognised authors' rights and introduced the principle of automatic protection (without a need for registration). In recent decades, the EU began to partially harmonise 3

[1] See https://brehonacademy.org/natures-copyright-the-early-irish-legal-principle-of-to-every-cow-its-calf/#:~:text=Final%20Thoughts,over%20reproductions%20of%20their%20work (18 May 2024).

[2] World Intellectual Property Organization (WIPO), *'Berne Convention for the Protection of Literary and Artistic Works'*,. https://www.wipo.int/treaties/en/ip/berne/.

copyright law through various directives to ensure greater consistency across its Member States.[3] The 2001 Copyright Directive[4] (Directive 2001/29/EC) (also referred to as the **InfoSoc Directive**) harmonised many aspects of copyright and related rights across the EU. In 2006, the Copyright Term Directive[5] (Directive 2006/116/EC) harmonised the term of copyright protection, extending it to 70 years after the death of the last surviving author for literary and artistic works. In 2019, the DSM Copyright Directive[6] (Directive (EU) 2019/790) sought to address copyright in the digital age and introduced a number of **new exceptions** to exclusive rights (including for **text and data mining**, which is relevant today in the context of the training of AI models). It also regulated the use of copyright works in digital and cross-border teaching activities, permitted the use of out-of-commerce works by cultural heritage institutions, established a protection for press publications concerning online uses and regulated the use of protected content by **online content-sharing service providers** (which is important for video game companies as gameplays are some of the most popular videos on platforms like YouTube and Twitch). Copyright in Europe today reflects **a blend of economic and moral rights** that have been shaped by centuries of legal, philosophical and technological change. While it is possible to talk in general terms about EU copyright law, it is important to note that there are often important differences among Member States.

4 This chapter, of course, is specifically about copyright in video games. It seeks only to provide **general information about EU copyright law** and should not be considered as legal advice. This entire handbook could easily be entirely given over to the topic of copyright in video games, so it is simply not possible to cover in a single chapter all of the issues and topics that arise in this area. I must, therefore, confine myself to a broad overview and focus in more detail on just a few topics that I think might of interest to readers today, such as **cheating** in video games and the **principle of exhaustion**. It is important to remember, too, that **copyright law can vary in important details** between EU Member States, and that specific situations always require professional legal advice. One should always consult with qualified legal counsel for advice on particular copyright matters.

B. The importance of copyright for video games

5 There is little doubt that copyright is by far the most important **intellectual property (IP)** right for game developers and publishers.[7] As David Greenspan and Gaetano Dimita put it in the WIPO publication *Mastering the Game*, *'As houses are made from wood and stone, video games are made almost exclusively from IP.*'[8] IP law, and copyright law in particular, enables game developers **to commercialise their works** and **to protect them** from infringers and competitors.

[3] EU copyright legislation consists of 11 Directives and 2 Regulations, harmonising the exclusive rights of authors, performers, producers and broadcasters.

[4] Directive 2001/29/EC of the European Parliament and of the Council of 22.5.2001 on the harmonisation of certain aspects of copyright and related rights in the information society, OJ 2001 L 167, 10 (Copyright Directive).

[5] Directive 2006/116/EC of the European Parliament and of the Council of 12.12.2006 on the term of protection of copyright and certain related rights (codified version), OJ 2006 L 372, 12 (Term Directive).

[6] Directive (EU) 2019/790 of the European Parliament and of the Council of 17.4.2019 on copyright and related rights in the Digital Single Market and amending Directives 96/9/EC and 2001/29/EC, OJ 2019 L 130, 92 (DSM Copyright Directive).

[7] See Boyd G., Pyne B. and Kane S-F., Video Game Law: Everything You Need to Know About Legal and Business Issues in the Game Industry, (2019) CRC Press, 20.

[8] See Greenspan/Dimita, Mastering the Game, 2nd edn, WIPO 2022.

As far as games are concerned, copyright covers the stories, characters, imagined environments and geographical locations, music, art, graphics and even the software source code itself. Moreover, it also protects **the game as a whole**. However, it is important to remember that **copyright only protects the expression of ideas** and not the ideas themselves. Copyright protects original works of authorship by granting to the rightsholder **certain exclusive rights**, including the right to copy or distribute the work concerned. Copyright **protection arises automatically**, upon (depending on the jurisdiction) creation or fixation, without any formalities. Copyright now lasts for the duration of the author's lifetime plus 70 years. 6

Over the years, the **Court of Justice** has developed an extensive jurisprudence underpinning copyright law principles that determine, among other things, when copyright protection arises. 7

The Court of Justice has clarified in a number of decisions[9] that to achieve copyright protection, **a work must fulfil two criteria**: 1) it must be **original** (in the sense that it must be the author's own intellectual creation) and 2) it must be expressed in a manner which makes it **identifiable with sufficient precision and objectivity**, even though that expression is not necessarily in permanent form. 8

It is now undisputed that the individual elements of a video game (including its story, characters, music, art, graphics and software) enjoy **independent copyright protection** if they meet the above criteria.[10] The software in a video game is protected by copyright under the Software Directive. For games this means that the source and object codes that constitute the game engine, plug-ins, and scripts are covered by the Software Directive. This was confirmed by the Court of Justice in the *BSA* case,[11] but the court excluded the graphic user interface from such protection, while in the *SAS Institute* case[12] the Court also excluded their functionality, programming languages and the format of data files. In both cases, however, the court indicated that **works that cannot be protected under the Software Directive might nevertheless find protection under the Copyright Directive**. This approach was, of course, later consolidated in the *Nintendo v PC Box* case. 9

So, the only real remaining issue in the copyright protection of video games is the legal protection of video games as **single, unique works of authorship**. 10

C. The classification of video games

Video games are often referred to as **complex digital works** comprised of multiple works of authorship, and while they are undoubtedly protected by copyright, there is **a lack of international consensus** on the precise nature of this protection. However, as correctly stated by David Greenspan and Gaetano Dimita on page 63 of *Mastering the Game*: '*It is safe to assume that all modern video games are protected by copyright in the EU, at least in some of their elements, even in the strictest of jurisdictions.*' 11

The question of how video games should be classified for the purposes of copyright law has presented **a challenge for many jurisdictions** around the world. A 2013 12

---

[9] Infopaq International, C-5/08, EU:C:2009:465, Levola Hengelo, C-310/17, EU:C:2018:899, and Cofemel, C-683/17, EU:C:2019:721.

[10] See Dimita/Lee/MacDonald, 'Copyright Infringement in the video game industry' (https://www.wipo.int/meetings/en/doc_details.jsp?doc_id=576652), WIPO 2022.

[11] Bezpečnostní softwarová asociace, C-393/09, EU:C:2010:816.

[12] SAS Institute, C-406/10, EU:C:2012:259.

WIPO-commissioned study[13] found that different jurisdictions have adopted different approaches: some have classified video games as computer programs, others have classified them as 'complex subject matter'; some jurisdictions treat each protectable element of a game as a separate work, and a small number of others treat games as predominantly audiovisual works or software. While the different approaches to the classification of video games as copyright subject matter can have implications for enforcement, and may also have a bearing on who the author or rightsholder is, on which exclusive rights are applicable and on who is entitled to sue for infringement of those rights, this has had, in my experience, **little effect on the protection afforded** to video games.[14]

13 There are two main approaches to the **legal nature** of video games for copyright protection purposes:

1. **the 'unitary' approach**, where a game is considered predominantly as a computer program, an audiovisual work or a complex subject matter, or
2. **the 'distributive' approach**, where each protectable subject matter within a video game is considered as a separate work.

14 While the classification of video games as a whole as either audiovisual works or computer programs does throw up some unique legal issues, it has never, to my knowledge, resulted in a video game being **denied copyright protection**. Courts do, nevertheless, tend to embrace the more conservative distributive approach and to find legal protection of the different elements of a video game separately, due to the obvious complexities involved[15].

15 In the **seminal** *Nintendo v PC Box* case,[16] the Court of Justice declared that video games

> *constitute complex matter comprising not only a computer program but also graphic and sound elements, which, although encrypted in computer language, have a unique creative value which cannot be reduced to that encryption. In so far as the parts of a videogame, in this case, the graphic and sound elements, are part of its originality, they are protected, together with the entire work, by copyright in the context of the system established by Directive 2001/29 [InfoSoc Directive].*

16 In *Grund v Nintendo,*[17] the Court was also asked to deal with the hybrid legal nature of video games **in the context of technological protection measures (TPMs).** But the referring court (Germany's BGH) withdrew the case after the ruling in *Nintendo v PC Box.*

17 In *UsedSoft*[18] (case C-128/11), the Court of Justice had stated that the Software Directive (Directive 2009/24) constituted **a lex specialis** in relation to the provisions of the Copyright Directive (Directive 2001/29). In *Nintendo v PC Box*, Advocate General Sharpston stated in her Opinion that **this statement must be read as meaning** that the provisions of the Software Directive take precedence over those of Directive 2001/29, *'but only where the protected material falls entirely within the scope of the former'.* Video games, she wrote, *'cannot be reduced to the status of computer programs alone. They in-*

---

[13] Ramos et al., The Legal Status of Video Games: Comparative Analysis in National Approaches (https://www.wipo.int/publications/en/details.jsp?id=4130), WIPO 2013.

[14] For a deeper analysis see Ekin Gürünlü I., 'Video Games and Copyright Protection Under International, European, and U.S. Law' (https://law.stanford.edu/wp-content/uploads/2020/06/gu%CC%88ru%CC%88nlu%CC%88_wp59.pdf), Stanford-Vienna TTLF Working Paper No. 59, 2020.

[15] As noted by Gaetano Dimita on page 47 of Cappello (ed), Legal challenges and market dynamics in the video games sector, IRIS, European Audiovisual Observatory, Strasbourg, November 2024.

[16] *Nintendo and Others*, case C-355/12, EU:C:2014:25.

[17] *Grund*, case C-458/13, EU:C:2014:589.

[18] *UsedSoft*, case C-128/11, EU:C:2012:407.

clude also intellectual works in narrative and graphic form, which appear to be inextricable from the programs themselves'.

The ruling of the Court of Justice in *Nintendo v PC Box* is **sometimes interpreted** as meaning that, for video games, only the Copyright Directive applies, but others (including some national courts and the European Parliament) read it as meaning that games are **regulated by both the Copyright and Software Directives**: 18

> *... the Court of Justice of the EU has recognised that video games are complex creative works with a unique and creative value, protected both by Directive 2009/24/EC on the legal protection of computer programs and Directive 2001/29/EC on copyright;*[19]

It would be wrong for me to leave this discussion of the *Nintendo v PC Box* case without mentioning the importance of the Court's ruling for the protection of **technological protection measures (TPMs)**. The ruling was in line with the international obligations of the EU and its Member States under the **WIPO Copyright Treaty**, and furthermore supported national courts in various Member States that had already considered and applied the same provisions of EU law resulting in positive decisions against the sellers of circumvention devices. The outcome of the case was **crucial for the industry** as it used (and still uses) a wide variety of TPMs to not only protect its products from piracy, but to ensure the development of new means of delivery, so creating more product development, growth and jobs. 19

Piracy still constitutes a threat to the game industry today and **causes widespread economic damage** to game developers, publishers, distributors and retailers. It also hurts national tax revenues and undermines the prospects for economic growth, employment and technological innovation. The industry incurs particular damage due to the availability of devices and software designed to circumvent the TPMs that are used to protect the industry's games. **TPM circumvention devices fuel piracy levels** because each one functions as a gateway to multiple future infringements and inflicts serious damage on legitimate game sales. The industry, therefore, regards the enforcement of effective provisions against the manufacture, distribution and use of circumvention devices (including software) as an essential factor in preventing or limiting the download and sale of pirate games. 20

D. The importance of understanding copyright law for game developers

For video game developers in the EU, understanding **the basics of copyright law** isn't just about legal compliance. It's about maximising the value of their creative work and protecting their business interests in an increasingly competitive market. 21

I. The originality test

As stated above, a work must demonstrate **sufficient originality** to qualify for copyright protection. This does not mean groundbreaking innovation, but simply that it **must reflect the authors' creative choices and bear their personal stamp**. As we have seen above, the Court of Justice has consistently held that originality requires a work to be the author's **'own intellectual creation'**. For video game developers, this 22

[19] European Parliament resolution of 10.11.2022 on esports and video games (2022/2027(INI)), paragraph [D] (https://www.europarl.europa.eu/doceo/document/TA-9-2022-0388_EN.html).

means that even common gaming elements can receive copyright protection if they are implemented **with sufficient creative expression**.

II. The expression vs. ideas divide

23 This is an area where many game developers get confused. **Ideas cannot be protected** under copyright law, **but the specific expression of those ideas can be**. The distinction protects innovation while preventing anyone from monopolising broad game concepts.

III. What copyright protects in video games

1. Source code and software

24 As we have seen, the software behind a video game, i.e., the program (source and object code) and the preparatory design materials are protected by copyright under the EU Software Directive (Directive 2009/24/EC). **Computer programs** receive strong protection as literary works, meaning that game code is protected from unauthorised copying, distribution, or modification.

2. Visual elements and artwork

25 The most obvious copyrightable elements in video games are their **visual components**:

- **Character designs**: Original character models, from simple 2D sprites to complex 3D avatars, are protected by copyright. This includes the final rendered versions and also concept art, texture maps, and animation rigs.
- **Environmental art**: Game worlds are protected as artistic works, including both the overall aesthetic vision and individual asset designs.
- **User interface elements**: While functional UI components are not copyrightable, creative interface designs that go beyond pure utility are protected.
- **Cinematics and cutscenes**: These generally receive copyright protection similar to traditional films, covering both the visual sequences and any accompanying dialogue or music.

3. Audio components

26 Sound plays a crucial role in video games, and most **audio elements** are also copyright protected:

- **Musical compositions**: Both the underlying musical compositions and their specific recordings are protected.
- **Sound effects**: Original sound effects are copyright protected.
- **Voice acting and dialogue**: Recorded performances and written dialogue scripts are protected, although the protection for dialogue may be limited if it only consists of very short, functional phrases.

4. Written content

Video games frequently include substantial **written content**, all of which may be copyright protected: 27

- **Narrative scripts**: Quest dialogue, cutscene scripts, and story elements receive the same protection as other literary works.
- **Flavour text**: Item descriptions, loading screen tips, and world-building text are protected if they demonstrate sufficient creativity.
- **Instructional materials**: Manuals, tutorials, and help documentation will also be protected as literary works.

5. What copyright does not protect

It is important to understand the **limits** of copyright protection. 28

a) *Game mechanics and rules*

Gameplay mechanics and ideas are not copyright protected. This fundamental limitation means that the basic systems that make a video game work – the rules, the win conditions, the core mechanic – cannot be monopolised using copyright. So, the idea of jumping on enemies to defeat them is not copyright protected. Nor is the concept of levelling up characters through experience points. 29

b) *Functional elements*

Functional elements like health bars are not copyright protected. This includes: 30

- **Interface necessities**: Health bars, mini-maps, and inventory screens that follow standard conventions typically lack the creativity needed for copyright protection.
- **Standard control schemes**: Common control mappings are considered as functional rather than creative expressions.
- **System requirements**: Technical specifications and compatibility requirements are also functional information.

c) *Short phrases and titles*

Short phrases and titles **lack sufficient originality** for copyright protection. 31

d) *Scenes à faire*

EU copyright law recognises the concept of **'scenes à faire'** – elements that are so common or necessary to a particular game genre that they cannot be owned by any single creator. These might include: 32

- Standard fantasy character archetypes (e.g., wizards and warriors)
- Common sci-fi tropes (e.g., spaceships and alien invasions)
- Typical horror elements (e.g., dark corridors and creepy music)

IV. Building your copyright strategy

1. Documentation

Documentation can be crucial when establishing ownership, especially in collaborative game development environments. Game developers should **maintain detailed** 33

records of their creative processes, including concept art and iteration histories, code comments and development logs, design documents and decision rationales, and asset creation timelines and authorship records.

2. Joint ownership

34 Video games are frequently made by hundreds, if not thousands, of creative contributors. When multiple creators contribute to copyrightable elements, **complex ownership situations may arise**. EU copyright law generally recognises joint ownership, but the specific rights and obligations of co-owners will vary by Member State.

3. Work-for-hire

35 It is important to remember that **many EU Member States do not have broad work-for-hire doctrines**. This means that employees will retain certain rights in their creative contributions, making the terms of employment contracts and copyright assignments particularly important.

4. Common misconceptions

a) 'I cannot copyright gameplay'

36 While one cannot copyright the abstract idea of **gameplay mechanics**, their specific implementation may be copyright protected. The key is to understand the difference between the underlying system and its particular expression.

b) 'Open-source means no copyright'

37 **Open-source games** are still copyright protected. Their owners have simply chosen to license their rights very broadly. It is crucial, therefore, to understand open-source licenses when incorporating third-party code or assets in a video game.

c) 'Copyright requires registration'

38 In the EU, **copyright protection is automatic** upon the creation of an original work. While registration systems do exist in some Member States, they are not required for protection.

5. Key takeaways

39 **For indie developers:**

- Focus on protecting your **unique implementations** rather than worrying about others using similar concepts
- **Document** your creative process to establish clear ownership and timing
- Understand that **sharing gameplay concepts** is normal and legally permissible

40 **For studios and publishers:**

- Develop clear **copyright assignment policies** for all contributors
- **Create systems** for tracking and managing copyrighted assets
- Consider **the full scope of protectable elements**, from code to audio to visual design

For legal teams: 41

- Remember the **fundamental expression vs. ideas distinction** when evaluating potential infringement
- Consider **both copyright and other IP protections** (trademarks, trade secrets) in your strategy
- **Stay current** with evolving EU jurisprudence on digital media and software protection

Understanding copyright basics provides the foundation for all other intellectual property decisions in video game development. These principles shape how one's creative efforts are created, protected, and monetised. 42

E. Cheating in video games

There has been cheating in video games for almost as long as they have been around. In the early days, though, developers would intentionally put cheats into their games to speed up their development and testing, and would then leave them in for clever users to find. Third-party cheats started in 1990 with the release of **the Game Genie** for the Nintendo Entertainment System (NES), which sat between the NES and the game cartridge, altering the data exchanged between them to provide users with additional features such as infinite lives and enhanced abilities. That same year, Nintendo sued Galoob Toys, Inc., the US distributor of the Game Genie. But because the game did not copy any game code and did not permanently alter the game, the courts sided with Galoob Toys.[20] **Fast forward some forty years** to a very different video game and legal environment, and a similar case found itself before the Court of Justice of the European Union.[21] 43

I. The Court of Justice ruling in *Sony v Datel* (case C-159/23)

In its judgment of 17.10.2024 in *Sony v Datel*[22] (case C-159/23), the Court of Justice ruled on the copyright protection of **computer programs** under the EU Software Directive (Directive 2009/24/EC). In a preliminary ruling on a reference from Germany's Bundesgerichtshof (BGH – Federal Court of Justice) in **a long-running dispute** between Sony Computer Entertainment Europe Ltd and the British peripherals and 'cheat software' maker, Datel Design and Development Ltd, the Court of Justice found that while such software can substantially impact gameplay, it **does not infringe copyright under the Software Directive**, as long as the modifications it makes are limited to variables stored in the computer's RAM (random access memory) and do not alter the game's underlying program code. The ruling confirmed that, as long as the source code and 44

[20] See *Lewis Galoob Toys, Inc. v Nintendo of America, Inc.* (964 F.2d 965) (https://law.resource.org/pub/us/case/reporter/F2/964/964.F2d.965.91-16205.html).

[21] See Grenzner, 'Copyright Issues Concerning Cheat Software: A Comparative Analysis of EU and US Law', Stanford-Vienna TTLF Working Paper No. 126 (https://law.stanford.edu/wp-content/uploads/2024/12/TTLF-WP-126-Grenzner.pdf).

[22] *Sony v Datel*, case C-159/23, EU:C:2024:887.

object code are untouched, rightsholders would have no claim under the Software Directive to ensure that their programs were run as they had originally intended.[23]

45 At first sight, this judgment might appear to be a **'game changer'** for video game developers and publishers, and indeed it has been widely presented as such in various online articles. One comes across references to the judgment 'dealing a blow to Sony' and to other console makers, to it being called a 'cheat code' for copyright infringement,[24] and to it 'significantly narrowing down the window to challenge cheating software'. Some claim that the ruling will have significant implications for the video game modding community which is now a multi-million euro industry. But is the ruling in this case really such a game changer? Let's take a closer look at it to see.

46 So, what did Datel actually do in this case? It developed and distributed what the Court of Justice rather euphemistically called **'complementary' products** for Sony's video game consoles, including a program called 'Action Replay PSP', which worked exclusively with Sony's original games, and in this particular case, with the car racing game, 'Motorstorm: Arctic Edge'. Datel's software allowed users to modify gameplay, by removing restrictions on the use of the 'turbo' (or 'booster') function or on the selection of drivers. The software basically enabled users to bypass the need to progress in the game through regular gameplay. Sony, as one might expect, took a poor view of this and initiated a legal action against Datel in Germany back in 2010 seeking **an injunction, information disclosure and confirmation of liability for damages**. Sony claimed that users, by using Datel's software, altered the game software and infringed their copyrights. They claimed that the modifications made by Datel's software were akin to a 'parasite' latching on to its game. They also asserted **alternative claims** under competition and tort law, alleging interference with Sony's right to establish and operate an undertaking. Sony further claimed that Datel should be enjoined from making it possible or easy to circumvent technological protection measures (TPMs). It is important to note, however, that these various alternative claims were not dealt with by the Court of Justice.

47 At first instance in January 2012, the Hamburg Regional Court largely upheld Sony's claims. Both sides appealed that decision, but the appeal was not heard by the Higher Regional Court until 2021. Apparently, the appeal court's docket has been heavily backlogged for years. The Higher Regional Court completely dismissed Sony's appeal, finding that the use of Datel's software did not lead to an alteration of the programs underpinning Sony's games. Sony then **appealed on a point of law** to the BGH which confirmed that only data in the working memory that were generated from the game in play were changed, and that the variable contents of that data were not in themselves the expression of a self-styled creation unique to the author. Sony argued that the game program's objective – of providing a particular gaming experience – presupposed that certain variable data could be retrieved from the console's working memory.

48 In early 2023, the BGH decided to **refer two questions** to the Court of Justice **for a preliminary ruling**, asking (1) if the modification of the content variables in the console system's RAM could be a copyright infringement under the Software Directive and (2) if that modification could be an 'alteration' of the game software under Art. 4(1)(b) of that

[23] See Schmidt/Großekettler, 'Is cheating copyright infringement? CJEU clarifies specific protection of computer programs' (24.10.2024) (https://www.hoganlovells.com/en/publications/is-cheating-copyright-infringement-cjeu-clarifies-specific-protection-computer-programs).

[24] See Belcheva, 'Sony v Datel – a 'cheat code' for copyright infringement?' (6.1.2025) (https://thelens.slaughterandmay.com/post/102jsev/sony-v-datel-a-cheat-code-for-copyright-infringement#:~:text=On%2017%20October%2C%20the%20Court,transfers%20to%20the%20device%27s%20RAM).

Directive (which grants to the author of a computer program the exclusive right to all kinds of alterations of that program and to reproductions of such alterations).

The Court of Justice **confined itself to the first question** and confirmed that, when assessed solely within the framework of the Software Directive, the use of cheat software that temporarily alters variables in RAM is permissible under copyright law. In its final judgment (I ZR 157/21)[25] of 31.7.25, the BGH duly followed the Court of Justice's interpretation and held that the modification of the content of the variables at issue did not infringe Sony's copyright. 49

Before the Court of Justice, Sony argued that a game should be taken as a whole and that what values the variables have in any given moment reflect the author's original plan. So, if you change the variables, you essentially change the game itself and create an **unauthorised derivative work**. However, both Advocate General Szpunar and the Court of Justice rejected Sony's argument as amounting to protecting the ideas and principles underlying the program (expressly excluded from such protection by Art. 1(2) of the Software Directive), rather than the program itself. Advocate General Szpunar likened the case to someone skipping to the end of a book to reveal the ending.[26] 50

Interestingly, the European Commission in its observations to the Court suggested that the case should be analysed from the point of view of the Copyright Directive (Directive 2001/29/EC) due to the 'complex nature' of video games as confirmed by the Court in the *Nintendo v PC Box* case.[27] However, because Sony had not claimed infringement of its rights to the non-software elements of the game at issue in the main proceedings (and the BGH had not mentioned the Copyright Directive in its referral), both Advocate General Szpunar and the Court considered the issue (i.e., of the Copyright Directive) to be **purely hypothetical**. 51

II. Why the ruling in *Sony v Datel* is not a game changer

Despite the ultimately disappointing outcome of this case for Sony, there are a number of things that I believe demonstrate quite clearly that **the ruling in the case is not the game changer** that some have claimed it to be. 52

In the first place, the ruling only applies to cheat **software that temporarily modifies variables** in the system's memory and it does not take account, as explained above, of the Copyright Directive or, for that matter, of any other directive other than the Software Directive. The ruling simply confirms that, when assessed solely within the framework of the Software Directive, the use of 'cheat software' that temporarily alters variables in RAM is permissible under copyright law. 53

Secondly, **the ruling does not extend to other types of cheat software**, particularly those that do actually modify the underlying program code of a video game. The distribution of such software will still constitute a copyright infringement under the Software Directive. This was confirmed by the Higher Regional Court of Dresden in 2015 (Oberlandesgericht, OLG) in the *Bossland v Blizzard* case.[28] The so-called 'buddy bots' at issue in that case altered the code of the 'World of Warcraft' game and also bypassed TPMs. The BGH upheld the Dresden Court's decision in October 2016 in 54

---

[25] https://www.bundesgerichtshof.de/SharedDocs/Pressemitteilungen/DE/2025/2025149.html?nn=19778950.

[26] See paragraph 57 of Advocate General Szpunar's Opinion of 25.4.2024 (https://curia.europa.eu/juris/document/document.jsf?text=&docid=285207&pageIndex=0&doclang=EN&mode=lst&dir=&occ=first&part=1&cid=4782738).

[27] *Nintendo and Others*, case C-355/12, EU:C:2014:25.

[28] OLG Dresden, 20.1.2015 – case 14 U 1127/14 – *Bossland v Blizzard.*

what is now called the *World of Warcraft I* case[29] (judgment of 6.10.2016, case I ZR 25/15), finding that the commercial downloading and copying by Bossland of the client software to develop its cheat software constituted copyright infringement. In the *World of Warcraft II* case (judgment of 12.1.2017, case I ZR 253/14), the BGH also found that the bots constituted both **anticompetitive interference** and copyright infringement through unauthorised modification and circumvention of TPMs. Germany is, I believe, the only country in the world where the highest civil court in the land has rendered **not one but two decisions** on the inadmissibility of cheat software.

55 Thirdly, it must be remembered that the *Sony v Datel* case dates back to 2010 and that it was **about a long-discontinued game console** (the PlayStation Portable or PSP was discontinued in 2014) **and a single-player video game**, 'Motorstorm: Arctic Edge'. The law has developed considerably since the action was first initiated and there are very different considerations to be taken into account with online multi-player games. I am confident that if a similar case were to be launched today, it would not be solely founded upon a claim of copyright infringement under the Software Directive. Cases today are far more likely to be about multiplayer games and based on violations of the developers' EULAs and competition law.

56 Fourthly, the ruling of the Court of Justice is **entirely consistent with its previous caselaw**. The Court has consistently sought to limit the protection of a 'computer program' to its source code and object code, and has held that elements such as the graphic user interface, the functionality of a program, its programming language, and specific data file formats do not constitute 'expressions' of a computer program (See the judgments of 22.12.2010, case C-393/09 – *BSA*,[30] and 2.5.2012, case C-406/10 – *SAS Institute*).[31]

57 Fifthly, the **unfair competition aspects** of the case were not discussed by either the BGH or by the Court of Justice.

58 Sixthly and finally, neither were **aiding and abetting infringement** by users in violation of the EULA (end-user license agreement), the **circumvention of TPMs** or claims of **trademark infringement**. Cheat software makers frequently infringe the trademarks of game publishers when advertising their cheat software.

III. Conclusions from case analysis

59 So, from my perspective, the bottom line here is that developers and publishers of multiplayer online games can still rely on **established case law** in Europe when acting against cheat software, and they can turn to what has been termed 'standard' copyright law harmonised under the Copyright Directive, to unfair competition law, to national provisions implementing the TPM anti-circumvention provisions in Art. 6 of the Copyright Directive, and also to possible trademark infringement claims.

IV. A parallel to *Lewis Galoob Toys, Inc. v Nintendo of America, Inc.*

60 The *Sony v Datel* ruling is, I think, **a strong parallel** to the 1992 U.S. judgment in *Lewis Galoob Toys, Inc. v Nintendo of America, Inc.* (964 F.2d 965), although that case

[29] Ruling of the BGH of 6.10.2016 (case no. I ZR 25/15) – *Bossland v Blizzard – World of Warcraft I* (https://juris.bundesgerichtshof.de/cgi-bin/rechtsprechung/document.py?Gericht=bgh&Art=en&sid=44fe996a5c9a69a90990c5884e00a74b&nr=77132&pos=3&anz=4).

[30] Bezpečnostní softwarová asociace, case C-393/09, EU:C:2010:816.

[31] SAS Institute, case C-406/10, EU:C:2012:259.

involved hardware (i.e., the pass-through Game Genie device) rather than software. The U.S. Court of Appeals for the Ninth Circuit ruled in the *Galoob Toys* case that temporary modifications to a game's data during gameplay that do not result in a permanent derivative work do not constitute copyright infringement.[32]

V. UK cases

It would be remiss of me not to mention here **two cases from the UK** that dealt with cheat software when the UK was still a member of the EU. These were *Blizzard v Bossland* [2019] EWHC 1665 (Ch)[33] and *Take-Two v James* [2020] 179 (Pat).[34] The first case did not proceed to a liability trial or hearing, but Bossland admitted all wrongdoing and the case demonstrated that there was **a clear legal pathway** in the UK to prevent companies selling cheats. In the second case, the High Court of England and Wales granted summary judgment to Take-Two Interactive Software Inc and Rockstar Games Inc for breach of contract, inducing breach of contract and authorising copyright infringement against a number of individuals who had developed and distributed the 'Epsilon' cheat software for users of the game, *Grand Theft Auto V*. This case was, in the words of one of the claimants' lawyers, 'a clear victory for developers, publishers and the global fight against cheating in games'.[35] 61

VI. *Springer v Eyeo* and ad-blocking software

To conclude this section on cheating in video games, I would simply offer the opinion that the *Sony v Datel* **ruling will have far less impact** on the video game sector than on the IT and software sectors more generally, where it could encourage more innovation and investment in software 'enhancements'. In Germany, on 31.7.25 the BGH issued its decision (in case I ZR 131/23) in a long-running dispute concerning ad-blocking software between Axel Springer and Eyeo (Adblock Plus), and referred the case back 62

[32] *Nintendo of America, Inc., Plaintiff-appellant, v Lewis Galoob Toys, Inc., Defendant-appellee*, 16 F.3d 1032 (9th Cir. 1994): Justia.

[33] *Blizzard Entertainment SAS & Anor v Bossland GmbH & Ors* [2019] EWHC 1665 (Ch) (https://www.bailii.org/ew/cases/EWHC/Ch/2019/1665.html). See also Brown/Ibbetson/Purdie, 'Blizzard v Bossland: An account of profits judgment for licensing video game 'cheats and bots' software', (https://www.bristows.com/news/blizzard-v-bossland-an-account-of-profits-judgment-for-licensing-video-game-cheats-and-bots-software/) and Gardner, 'High Court rules on account of profits in relation to copyright infringement by seller of software allowing users to cheat when playing certain well known online video games' (https://www.wiggin.co.uk/insight/high-court-rules-on-account-of-profits-in-relation-to-copyright-infringement-by-seller-of-software-allowing-users-to-cheat-when-playing-certain-well-known-online-video-games/).

[34] *Take-Two Interactive Software Inc v Nathan James* [2020] EWHC 179 (Pat) (29.1.2020) (https://www.bailii.org/ew/cases/EWHC/Patents/2020/179.html).

[35] See Harper/Maloney, UK High Court Confirms That Grand Theft Auto Cheat Software Infringes Copyright (https://www.irwinmitchell.com/news-and-insights/newsandmedia/2020/february/uk-high-court-confirms-that-grand-theft-auto-cheat-software-infringes-copyright#:~:text=%22This%20case%20constitutes%20a%20clear,to%20combat%20cheating%20tool%20websites.%22). See also Gardner, 'High Court grants summary judgement for breach of contract and copyright infringement in relation to 'cheat' software designed for Grand Theft Auto V', (https://www.wiggin.co.uk/insight/high-court-grants-summary-judgement-for-breach-of-contract-and-copyright-infringement-in-relation-to-cheat-software-designed-for-grand-theft-auto-v/#:~:text=(Take%2DTwo%20Interactive%20Software%20Inc%20v%20Nathan%20James,the%20judgment%20in%20full%2C%20click%20here).%20Expertise).

to the Higher Regional Court of Hamburg for further examination.[36] The BGH had temporarily stayed the case pending the *Sony v Datel* ruling.

F. The principle of exhaustion

63 There is one principle regarding rightsholders' exclusive rights to which I would like to give a little further attention. Authors have an exclusive right to authorise or prohibit the distribution of their works by sale or otherwise. In the EU, this is subject to **the principle of exhaustion**[37] which essentially provides that a copyright owner's right to control copies of their work 'exhausts' on its first sale by the copyright owner or with their consent in the EU/EEA (**in the U.S., this is known as the first-sale doctrine**). For many years, there was a doubt about whether this principle applied to digital works as well as analogue ones. This would be highly relevant to any assessment of key selling, account transfers and the sale of second-hand video games. The application of the exhaustion principle hinges on the difference between the distribution right (which is exhaustible) and the right of making available (which is not exhaustible). The *UsedSoft* case[38] (case C-128/11) was the first to explore the application of the exhaustion principle in the digital context. UsedSoft sold 'second-hand' licenses to Oracle's software which was made available to customers for download. Use of the software was governed by a licence agreement which provided that, in return for a one-off fee, the customer received a non-exclusive, non-transferable right to use the software for an unlimited period. The Court of Justice was asked to **consider what constitutes the sale of a copy**, which, in turn, would result in the exhaustion of the distribution right. The Court chose to focus on the transaction's substance rather than on its form and concluded that while the terminology used was of little consequence, it was the economic circumstances of the transaction that mattered. The Court ruled that digital exhaustion would not be available under the 2001 Copyright Directive considering that the right of communication to the public under Art. 3(1) of that directive would be relevant to the offering for sale of copyright works on the internet.

64 The last decision of the Court of Justice on this subject was in the *Tom Kabinet* case[39] (case C-263/18) where in December 2019 the Court further confirmed the distinctive nature of the 2001 Copyright Directive in relation to the Software Directive (which is *lex specialis* and **applies only when it concerns computer programs**). The Court of Justice concluded that the supply by downloading, for permanent use, of an e-book was not covered by the right of 'distribution to the public' provided for by Art. 4(1) of the 2001 Copyright Directive, but by the right of 'communication to the public' provided for in Art. 3(1) of that directive, in which case exhaustion was excluded under paragraph 3 of that Article. In support of this finding, the Court concluded in particular from the WIPO Copyright Treaty underlying the 2001 Copyright Directive, and from the *travaux préparatoires* for that Directive, that the EU legislature had intended the principle of exhaustion to be reserved for the distribution of tangible objects, such as books on a material medium. The Court found that the application of the exhaustion principle to e-books would be likely to affect the interests of rightsholders in obtaining appropriate re-

[36] See Kahlor-Witzel, https://www.insidetechlaw.com/blog/2025/08/german-federal-court-refers-ad-blocker-case-back-to-hamburg-higher-regional-court#:~:text=On%2031%20July%202025%2C%20the,to%20support%20such%20a%20conclusion (August 2025).

[37] See Rosati in *Copyright and the Court of Justice of the European Union*, 2nd edn, Oxford, 2023, pp. 193–210.

[38] UsedSoft, case C-128/11, EU:C:2012:407.

[39] Tom Kabinet, case C-263/18, EU:C:2019:697S.

ward much more than in the case of books on a material medium, since dematerialised digital copies of e-books do not deteriorate with use and are, therefore, perfect substitutes for new copies on any second-hand market. Furthermore, rec. 29 of the Copyright Directive states that '*exhaustion does not arise in the case of services and on-line services in particular*'. This results in a situation where whenever a work is distributed through digital means, this distribution necessarily corresponds to the provision of a service and not the sale of goods. The Court's position made it clear that **the distribution right** is based on an understanding of the exhaustion principle that only covers the circulation of physical copies.

The **proposition** that exhaustion does not apply to digital copies of video games has **65**
been **tested in both Germany and France** in cases brought by consumer organisations against Valve, which operates the PC digital distribution platform, Steam. In Germany, the consumer watchdog group Verbraucherzentrale Bundesverband ('VZBV') brought an action against Valve over terms in its EULA, disallowing the sale and transfer of Steam gaming accounts. The court ruled in Valve's favour, holding that even if the principle of exhaustion applied, it did not require Valve to design its business in such a way that it facilitated the sale of 'used' games. The case was decided following *UsedSoft* but before *Nintendo v PC Box* and *Tom Kabinet*. In the *World of Warcraft I* case,[40] Germany's Federal Court of Justice (BGH) **ruled in 2016 that the principle of digital exhaustion did not apply to video games**. This was because *UsedSoft* was decided under the Software Directive, while **video games were more than just software**. They also contain audiovisual elements and therefore fall under the regime established by the 2001 Copyright Directive, which, unlike the Software Directive, does not contain provisions enabling digital exhaustion.

On 23.10.2024, the **French Supreme Court** rejected an appeal by consumer group **66**
UFC-Que Choisir against a decision of the Court of Appeal of Paris on 21.10.2022 ruling that the protection of video games is, like that for e-books, subject to the application of the 2001 Copyright Directive, as it cannot be reduced to that provided for computer programs under the 2009 Software Directive. In so doing, the Supreme Court ruled that the judgment of the Court of Justice in the *Tom Kabinet* case had to be extended to video games.

Ever since the ruling of the Court of Justice in the *Nintendo v PC Box* case (case **67**
C-355/12) to the effect that video games constitute '*complex matter comprising not only a computer program but also graphic and sound elements, which although encrypted in computer language, have a unique creative value which cannot be reduced to that encryption*', and must be protected by copyright under the 2001 Copyright Directive, **the game industry has been quietly confident** that digital video games would not be subject to any form of exhaustion and that purchasers of digital games would have no right to sell them on second-hand without the copyright owner's permission.

---

[40] Ruling of the BGH of 6.10.2016 (case no. I ZR 25/15) – *Bossland v Blizzard – World of Warcraft I* (https://juris.bundesgerichtshof.de/cgi-bin/rechtsprechung/document.py?Gericht=bgh&Art=en&sid=44fe996a5c9a69a90990c5884e00a74b&nr=77132&pos=3&anz=4).

§ 14
EU Copyright Exceptions and Limitations

Bibliography: Ficsor, Guide to the Copyright And Related Rights Treaties Administered By WIPO and Glossary of Copyright and Related Rights Terms, Geneva 2004; Geiger, 'Copyright and Free Access to Information: For a Fair Balance of Interests in the Digital Age', EIPR 2022, 123; Lindner/Shapiro, Copyright in the Information Society: A Guide to National Implementation of the European Directive, 2nd edn, Cheltenham 2019; Rosati, Copyright in the Digital Single Market, Oxford 2021; Stamatoudi/Torremans, EU Copyright Law: A Commentary, Cheltenham (UK) 2014.

A. Introduction 1

B. Some relevant exceptions at EU level 5
I. Copyright Directive 5
Exceptions and limitations 6
Art. 5(3)(a): Exception/limitation for illustration for teaching 14
II. DSM Copyright Directive 17
Art. 5: Exception/limitation for digital use of works for illustration for teaching 18
III. Application to the use of video games for teaching purposes in classrooms 26
1. Conditions set out in Art. 5 of the DSM Copyright Directive 27
2. Limitations to the Art. 5 DSM Copyright Directive exemption 34
a) Limitations imposed by the wording of Art. 5 and respective Recitals 34
b) Limitations imposed by the three-step test 40
c) Let's Play 45
IV. Artificial intelligence, text and data mining (TDM) and rights reservation 46
1. TDM exceptions 47
2. Rights reservation – is Art. 4 like the Hotel California? 53
3. Rights reservations as applied to video game distribution 58
4. Examples from rights reservation practices 59
5. Emerging rights reservation techniques 60

A. Introduction

1 The **copyright system** is an intricately designed *Montesquieuan* edifice of checks and balances. The principal aim of which is to incentivise the creation and production of, as well as investment in, original works of authorship[1] to the benefit of not only rightholders, but also users, consumers and indeed society at large.[2] In the interactive entertainment sector, the existence of copyright protection for a work comprising the creative contributions of game designers, coders, artists and composers underpins and

[1] The questions of what type of copyright work (or other protected subject matter) is a 'video game' and whether a particular video game qualifies for copyright protection or not is beyond the scope of this chapter. In the Nintendo case, the CJEU recognised that although a video game is partly software code, it is more than a computer programme; and that individual elements of video games may constitute copyright works, in particular the graphic and sound elements, protected under the system established by Directive 2001/29/EC of the European Parliament and of the Council of 22.52001 on the harmonisation of certain aspects of copyright and related rights in the information society, OJ 2001 L 167, 10 (Copyright Directive), ECJ 23.12.2014 – case C-355/12, ECLI:EU:C:2014:25 mn. 23 – *Nintendo v PC Box*. See also, → § 4 mn. 9.

[2] In the EU, the system also provides protection for so-called related or neighbouring rights which are in essence the poor cousins of copyright. This somewhat lesser form of protection, which attaches without regard to originality, extends to producers, press publishers, broadcasters and performers. For the sake of brevity, and because in the EU there are far too many categories of rightholders (including within the category of author), this chapter will refer only to copyright.

incentivises the investment that games studios and publishers make in the creation of new video games.

The copyright system operates by granting authors a series of **exclusive rights** to authorise or prohibit certain uses of protected works for a proscribed period.[3] Unauthorised use of those protected works is treated as **copyright infringement** and authors have recourse to a range of civil, administrative and/or criminal remedies to counter such activity. However, in return for this enforceable monopoly, authors must tolerate certain so-called exceptions and limitations, which operate to restrict the scope of their exclusive rights for different types of uses, often only for certain beneficiaries, and under certain defined conditions.[4] Copyright exceptions therefore function as defences to what would otherwise be considered as infringement. Most exceptions are designed to advance certain public interests[5] subject to the outer limits imposed by the three-step test.[6] 2

The importance of **exceptions as a means** of promoting the public interest was baked into the copyright system from the very beginning: 3

> Consideration also has to be given to the fact that limitations on absolute protection are dictated, rightly in my opinion, by the public interest. The ever-growing need for mass instruction could never be met if there were no reservation of certain reproduction facilities, which at the same time should not degenerate into abuses.[7]

This chapter provides a **brief overview** of the **legal framework for exceptions** in the **EU** with some specific considerations on the relevance of that framework to the video games sector. The subject of exceptions and its application to video games is potentially quite broad (like so many others). This contribution to the handbook is focused on the exceptions pertaining to educational use of video games and to text and data mining in the context of artificial intelligence (AI). 4

---

[3] At international level, the basic rule is that term of protection runs 50 years after the death of the author (Art. 7 Berne Convention for the Protection of Literary and Artistic Works (as amended on 28.9.1979). In the EU, Directive 2006/116/EC of the European Parliament and of the Council of 12.12.2006 on the term of protection of copyright and certain related rights (codified version), OJ 2006 L 372, 12 (Term Directive), the basic rule is that copyright protection runs for 70 years after the death of the last surviving author (Art. 1–2).

[4] For a detailed definition, see Ficsor, Guide to the Copyright And Related Rights Treaties Administered By WIPO and Glossary of Copyright and Related Rights Terms, Geneva 2004, p. 287: '… the expression 'limitations and exceptions' covers all kinds of free uses, non-voluntary licenses, as well as other possible limitations (such as subjecting the right to obligatory collective management) …' In this chapter, we use the term 'exception'.

[5] The principal derogation from this point is the so-called private copy exception. While some argue that this exception serves a public interest, its very title suggests otherwise. In this regard, EU copyright law treats it somewhat differently than other 'public interest' exceptions – see, e.g., the Copyright Directive as it pertains the relationship between exceptions and technological measures in Art. 6(4)(1), on public interest exceptions and Art. 6(4)(2) on private copy, respectively. On private copy levies for games companies in Germany.

[6] See, e.g., Art. 9 Berne Convention, Art. 13 TRIPs Agreement Art. 10 WIPO Copyright Treaty (WCT), Art. 16 WIPO Performances and Phonograms Treaty (WPPT).

[7] Droz, President of the Preparatory Diplomatic Conferences of the Berne Convention – Reports of Various Diplomatic Conferences, Appendix 2, Records of the International Conference for the Protection of Authors' Rights, Convened in Berne, September 8–19, 1884, Minutes of the Sixth Meeting, 18.9.1884, p. 99, http://global.oup.com/booksites/content/9780198259466/15550022.

B. Some relevant exceptions at EU level

I. Copyright Directive

5 While the Copyright Directive (also often referred to as the InfoSoc Directive) was recently amended by the DSM Copyright Directive[8] (see below), the former remains the 'cornerstone' of the EU copyright framework.[9]

Exceptions and limitations

6 As noted above, copyright exceptions operate to leave 'certain uses' of copyright protected works 'outside the sphere of control of the right holder'.[10] While exceptions play a critically important role in the system, there is perennial debate over how to balance exclusive rights with exceptions to copyright which are designed to further public interests and/or flow from certain fundamental rights. Most everyone agrees that the **system needs to be balanced** but almost no one agrees on how. While from the outset exceptions operated as defences to what would otherwise be copyright infringements, many stakeholders have come to see them as 'user rights'. Although the Court of Justice has used the term 'user rights'[11] and a variety of other labels, it seems clear that in practice it considers exceptions to be derogations from exclusive rights, and as such, defences to infringements.

7 Art. 5 of the Copyright Directive establishes an exhaustive list of specific,[12] but optional (except Art. 5(1) on temporary copies), exceptions and limitations to the exclusive rights of rightholders, subject to subsequent amendments to EU law (e.g., the Orphan Works[13] or DSM Copyright Directives). No other exceptions may be applied by Member States or be permitted under national law.[14]

8 The Court of Justice has reiterated, the objective of the Copyright Directive '*is to harmonise only certain aspects of the law on copyright and related rights, of which a number of provisions also disclose the intention of the EU legislature to grant a degree of discretion to the Member States in the implementation of the directive*'.[15] The Copyright Directive thus ensures a degree of legal certainty throughout the EU, insofar as to the exceptions which *may* be applied. Although these exceptions are optional, they do

[8] Directive (EU) 2019/790 of the European Parliament and of the Council of 17.4.2019 on copyright and related rights in the Digital Single Market and amending Directives 96/9/EC and 2001/29/EC, OJ 2019 L 130, 92 (DSM Copyright Directive).

[9] Reinbothe in Lindner/Shapiro, Copyright in the Information Society: A Guide to National Implementation of the European Directive, 2nd edn (Cheltenham: Edward Elgar, 2019), p. xl. The Copyright Directive entered into force on 22.6.2001 and the deadline for implementation by EU Member States was 22.12.2002.

[10] Stamatoudi/Torremans, EU Copyright Law: A Commentary, Cheltenham (UK) 1.7.2014, p. 437.

[11] ECJ 11.9.2014 – case C-117/13, ECLI:EU:C:2014:2196 mn. 43–49 – *Technische Universität Darmstadt v Eugen Ulmer KG*; ECJ 29.7.2019 – case C-469/17, ECLI:EU:C:2019:623 mn. 70 – Funke Medien NRW; ECJ 29.7.2019 – case C-516/17, ECLI:EU:C:2019:625 mn. 54 – *Spiegel Online v Beck*. Some commentators consider that exceptions are (or at least should be) treated as rights, see Geiger, 'Copyright and Free Access to Information: For a Fair Balance of Interests in the Digital Age', EIPR 2022, 123 (see especially 130–135).

[12] The EU approach of specific exceptions linked to particular activities/beneficiaries contrasts with the prevailing approach in the US which is generally based on the so-called fair use defence (see, 17 U.S. Code § 107).

[13] Directive 2012/28/EU of the European Parliament and of the Council of 25.10.2012 on certain permitted uses of orphan works, OJ 2012 L 299, 5 (Orphan Works Directive).

[14] But see Art. 5(3)(o) of the Copyright Directive, which 'grandfathers' minor exceptions in the analogue realm.

[15] See *Spiegel* at mn. 23.

constitute measures of full harmonisation, since where they are applied, they must be applied in compliance with EU law – Member States may not go further and establish broader exceptions and as noted above no other exceptions are allowed.[16]

In addition to the criteria set out in each exception itself, Art. 5(5) requires that all the exceptions and limitations provided for under Art. 5 be applied in accordance with the **'three-step test'**. In essence, the three-step test sets the outer limits of permissible exceptions and limitations in the national laws of the EU Member States. The test requires that, to be permissible at all, any exception or limitation to an exclusive right: (1) applies only to certain special cases, (2) does not conflict with normal exploitation of the work, and (3) does not unreasonably prejudice the legitimate interests of the rightholder. These conditions are cumulative.[17] **9**

The Court of Justice's approach to the application of the three-step test has not always been consistent. Moreover, although the Court has recognised the principle of restrictive interpretation of exceptions as a derogation from the general rule of protection,[18] it has sometimes departed from that rule and has demonstrated a tendency to cumulate[19] exceptions as part of its development of the *'effectiveness of the exception'*[20] doctrine. **10**

More recently, the Court referred to the effectiveness of exceptions in the following terms: **11**

> It follows that the interpretation of the exceptions and limitations provided for in Article 5 of Directive 2001/29 must allow, … their effectiveness to be to [sic] safeguarded and their purpose to be observed, since such a requirement is of particular importance where those exceptions and limitations aim, ... to ensure observance of fundamental freedoms.[21]

That said, the Court was clear (as noted above) that this does not permit going beyond the terms of current exceptions under EU law.[22] In other words, while specific exceptions may advance the goals of a number of important fundamental rights, such as the **freedom of expression**, those fundamental rights do not give rise to additional **12**

---

[16] See, e.g., *Spiegel Online; Funke Medien NRW;* ECJ 29.7.2019 – case C-476/17, ECLI:EU:C:2019:624 – *Pelham GmbH and Others v Hütter and Others.*

[17] See also rec. 44: When applying the exceptions and limitations provided for in this Directive, they should be exercised in accordance with international obligations. Such exceptions and limitations may not be applied in a way which prejudices the legitimate interests of the rightholder or which conflicts with the normal exploitation of his work or other subject-matter. The provision of such exceptions or limitations by Member States should, in particular, duly reflect the increased economic impact that such exceptions or limitations may have in the context of the new electronic environment. Therefore, the scope of certain exceptions or limitations may have to be even more limited when it comes to certain new uses of copyright works and other subject-matter.

[18] ECJ 5.6.2014 – case C-360/13, ECLI:EU:C:2014:1195 mn. 23 – *Public Relations Consultants Association Ltd v Newspaper Licensing Agency Ltd. and Others (Meltwater)*; ECJ 16.7.2009 – case C-5/08, ECLI: EU:C:2009:465 mn. 56–57 – *Infopaq International A/S v Danske Dagblades Forening*; ECJ 4.10.2011 – joined cases C-403/08 and C-429/08, ECLI:EU:C:2011:631 mn. 162 – *Football Association Premier League Ltd and Others v QC Leisure and Others (FAPL).*

[19] See *Darmstadt*, at mn. 43.

[20] *FAPL* at mn. 163; ECJ 1.12.2011 – case C-145/10, ECLI:EU:C:2011:798 mn. 133 – *Eva-Maria Painer v Standard VerlagsGmbH and Others*; ECJ 3.9.2014 – case C-201/13, ECLI:EU:C:2014:2132 mn. 23 – *Johan Deckmyn and Vrijheidsfonds VZW v Helena Vandersteen and Others; Darmstadt*, at mn. 32 and 43 as well as mn. 53–57.

[21] See *Funke Medien*, at mn. 71.

[22] *Funke Medien*, mn, 70; *Spiegel Online*, mn. 54. Indeed, the rights and interests of rightholders must be interpreted broadly.

restrictions on exclusive rights outside the existing framework of exceptions in the EU. There is no 'EU fair use doctrine'.[23]

13 The **Copyright Directive** thus provides Member States with a menu from which they can select a number of delicious optional exceptions apart, as noted above, from Art. 5(1) on temporary copies, which is mandatory and thus comes with every order like it or not. The exceptions apply either to the exclusive right of reproduction[24] (including for private copy or copying by libraries, educational establishments, museums or archives) or the exclusive rights of reproduction and communication to the public[25] (including for the sole purpose of illustration for teaching or scientific research; benefit of the disabled; for press reporting, quotation for criticism or review; for caricature, parody or pastiche; or, research or private study at education establishments, and more). The exceptions in the Copyright Directive can also be applied to exclusive right of distribution in Art. 4. Finally, as noted above, all exceptions are subject to the three-step test in Art. 5(5).

Art. 5(3)(a): Exception/limitation for illustration for teaching

14 Regarding the use of video games for teaching purposes in classrooms, the relevant EU-level exception is found in Art. 5(3)(a) of the Copyright Directive. This Article permits Member States to provide for an **exception or limitation to the exclusive rights of reproduction and communication to the public** (including making available to the public) for 'use for the sole purpose of illustration for teaching … as long as the source, including the author's name, is indicated, unless this turns out to be impossible and to the extent justified by the non-commercial purpose to be achieved'.[26]

15 Rec. 14 explains the rationale behind the Art. 5(3)(a) exception, noting that the Copyright Directive seeks to 'promote learning and culture by protecting works … while permitting exceptions or limitations in the public interest for the purposes of education and teaching'. Rec. 31 adds that 'a fair balance of rights and interests … between the different categories of rightholders and users of protected subject-matter must be safeguarded'.

16 As noted above, this exception is an optional provision.[27] Although the legal basis for the exception exists at the EU level, it remains a matter of discretion for each Member State whether they choose to implement this exception into their national law – subject of course to the conditions therein. As will be seen below, this optional paradigm has changed with the adoption of the DSM Copyright Directive.

II. DSM Copyright Directive

17 The **DSM Copyright Directive**, which was to be implemented by 7.6.2021 (most Member States did not make the deadline), has led to a greater degree harmonisation and legal certainty with the introduction of a mandatory exception for the digital use of

[23] Cf. the approach in the US which operates largely on the basis of the fair use doctrine, 17 U.S. Code § 107. That said, obviously the application of the fair use test must yield results that are consistent with the three-step test under international copyright norms in order for the US to comply with its treaty obligations.

[24] Art. 5(2) of the Copyright Directive.

[25] Art. 5(3) of the Copyright Directive.

[26] See Art. 2 and 3 of the Copyright Directive on the respective rights of reproduction and communication to the public.

[27] Rec. 34 of the Copyright Directive reiterates that '*Member States should be given the* ***option*** *of providing for certain exceptions or limitations for cases such as educational … purposes*' (our emphasis).

works for the purpose of illustration in teaching. Indeed, the two **text and data mining exceptions** in Art. 3 and 4 (see below) as well as the exception for preservation of cultural heritage are also mandatory, i.e., must be implemented by the Member States. In addition to rendering exceptions mandatory,[28] the DSM Copyright Directive applies further gold-plating in that the new exceptions are generally immune from contractual override (except in a couple of cases subject to certain conditions) and the derogation in Art. 6(4)(4) of the Copyright Directive concerning technological measures and content made available on agreed contractual terms is ***disapplied*** (see Art. 7(2) of the DSM Copyright Directive). As a result of the latter, video game companies could in relatively narrow circumstances find themselves required to accommodate the new exceptions (i.e., ensure that beneficiaries of the exception can benefit) or potentially face Member State action or even self- help measures (i.e., users making their own circumvention utilities).

Art. 5: Exception/limitation for digital use of works for illustration for teaching

The DSM Copyright Directive expands upon the teaching exception provided for in **18**
the Copyright Directive by introducing, in Art. 5, a new mandatory exception to the exclusive rights of reproduction and communication to the public (including making available to the public) 'in order to allow the digital use of works and other subject matter for the sole purpose of illustration for teaching'. Member States are therefore obliged to introduce into their national laws an **exception or limitation for educational establishments** to use copyright protected works for the sole purpose of illustration for teaching, subject to the conditions imposed by the DSM Copyright Directive.[29]

This new exception was intended to complement the existing optional exceptions in **19**
relation to illustration **for teaching purposes** and to clarify the scope to which the existing optional exceptions in the Copyright Directive, including Art. 5(3)(a), apply to digital uses, online and distance learning, as well as to provide expressly for the cross-border effect of the exception. According to rec. 19, the rationale behind the introduction of this mandatory exception was to 'ensure that educational establishments benefit from full legal certainty when using works or other subject matter in digital teaching activities, including online and across borders'. Rec. 20 acknowledges that 'digital tools and resources are increasingly used at all education levels … to improve and enrich the learning experience'.

Rec. 20 further clarifies that the Art. 5 exception 'should … benefit all educational es- **20**
tablishments recognised by a Member State', and that this includes 'those involved in primary, secondary, vocational and higher education'.

Art. 5(1)(a) and (b) impose certain conditions on the application of this exception, **21**
namely, that

(a) the use 'takes place under the responsibility of an educational establishment', and **22**
(b) that the use 'is accompanied by an indication of the source, including the author's name, unless this turns out to be impossible'.

Further, rec. 6 notes that the exceptions and limitations set out in the DSM Copyright **23**
Directive 'can be applied only in certain special cases that do not conflict with the normal exploitation of the works or other subject matter and do not unreasonably prejudice

[28] See also Art. 17(7) of the DSM Copyright Directive, which renders the exceptions for quotation, criticism, review and use for the purpose of caricature, parody or pastiche (Art. 5(3)(d) and 5(3)(k) of the Copyright Directive respectively) mandatory at least in the context of use of protected content by online content-sharing service providers.

[29] Rosati, Copyright in the Digital Single Market, Oxford 2021, p. 252.

the legitimate interests of the rightholders', i.e., in compliance with the three-step test. Art. 7(2) of the DSM Copyright Directive also expressly states that 'Art. 5(5) [three-step test] of [the Copyright Directive] shall apply to the exceptions and limitations provided for under this Title' including the exception set out in Art. 5.

24 Regarding the scope of this exception, rec. 21 notes that the 'exception or limitation ... for the sole purpose of illustration for teaching should be understood as covering digital uses of works or other subject matter to support, enrich or complement the teaching, including learning activities'. However, rec. 21 includes the limitation that 'in most cases, the concept of illustration would ... imply the use only of parts or extracts of works'. Further, rec. 22 indicates that 'the use of works ... under the exception ... should be limited to what is necessary for the purpose of such activities', indicating that the exemption should be interpreted narrowly. Thus, while it would be possible to use parts of video games, it seems unlikely that the exception extends to the wholesale use of entire video games. If the scope of a national exception did extend this far, it would arguably fall afoul of the three-step test.

25 Art. 5(2) provides that **licences** (if available) can take **priority over the exception** for education set out in Art. 5(1). As in rec. 31 of the Copyright Directive, rec. 6 of the DSM Copyright Directive notes that 'the exceptions and limitations provided for in this Directive seek to achieve a fair balance between the rights and interests of authors and other rightholders ... and of users'.

III. Application to the use of video games for teaching purposes in classrooms

26 The DSM Copyright Directive's objective of using digital tools 'to improve and enrich the learning experience' aligns somewhat with the goal of promoting video games as educational tools.[30] The Art. 5 exception has a role to play here but licensing is also a critical component in supporting educational use of video games in this context.

1. Conditions set out in Art. 5 of the DSM Copyright Directive

27 Art. 5 of the DSM Copyright Directive sets out certain conditions for the application of the exception.

28 Firstly, the exception may only be applied 'to the extent justified by the non-commercial purpose to be achieved'.[31] In this use case, the 'non-commercial purpose' is of course education. Rec. 20 notes that 'the organisational structure and the means of funding of an educational establishment should not be the decisive factors in determining whether the activity is non-commercial in nature', thus indicating that even **private educational establishments may benefit** from the exception, insofar as the specific use made of a protected work is for a non-commercial purpose. However, there must be a direct and objective link between the use for a non-commercial purpose and the teaching activity.[32] The use of video games by teachers 'as pedagogical support in the classroom', i.e., for 'educational purposes'[33] appears likely to comply with this requirement.

29 Art. 5(1)(a) imposes the condition that use of works pursuant to the exception 'takes place under the responsibility of an educational establishment'. This includes 'on its

[30] See, e.g., https://www.videogameseurope.eu/news/unicef-and-video-games-industry-highlight-benefits-of-using-video-games-as-educational-tool-in-the-eu-and-around-the-world/.

[31] DSM Copyright Directive, Art. 5(1).

[32] Rosati, p. 258.

[33] https://www.videogameseurope.eu/games-in-society/education/about-games-in-schools/.

premises or at other venues, or through a secure electronic environment'. The use of **video games in the classroom** would therefore take place on the physical premises of educational establishments. The Directive also provides scope to enable access to digital teaching resources via a 'secure electronic environment' if required.

Art. 5(1)(b) dictates that such use 'is accompanied by an indication of the source, including the author's name, unless this turns out to be impossible'. This acknowledgement requirement presumably should not present a significant hurdle as it is a relatively simple step for teachers/schools to comply with in practice. 30

Art. 5(2) states that 'Member States may provide that the exception or limitation ... does not apply as regards specific uses or types of works or other subject matter, such as material that is primarily intended for the educational market ... to the extent that suitable licences ... are easily available on the market'. This is a matter of discretion for each Member State. The rationale for this provision is to encourage licensing solutions, particularly for materials which depend on educational markets[34] – but much will depend on specific national implementations of the Directive. Where the exception is considered applicable to a particular use case in a Member State which has availed itself of this option, it would make sense to develop a licensing solution. It should be noted that in such a scenario the exception would apply to games not covered by the license (to the extent permitted by the exception of course – see below). In such a case, the concerns about commercial impact should be less of a factor as the alternative would be application of the exception. 31

If a **suitable licensing mechanism** were to be established, Member States are obliged to 'take the necessary measures to ensure that the licences ... are available and visible in an appropriate manner for educational establishments'.[35] 32

Art. 5(4) sets out a further discretionary provision, that 'Member States may provide for fair compensation for rightholders for the use of their works or other subject matter pursuant to [Art. 5(1)]'. If Member States do avail themselves of this option, the payment of 'fair compensation' could operate as a further requirement to enable application of the exception. 33

2. Limitations to the Art. 5 DSM Copyright Directive exemption

a) Limitations imposed by the wording of Art. 5 and respective Recitals

Although the DSM Copyright Directive does not define the key element of the exception 'use ... for the sole purpose of illustration for teaching' and the CJEU has not rendered any judgments on the corresponding language in the Copyright Directive, the rec. provide some guidance. 34

As noted above, rec. 21 indicates that the notion of 'use' pursuant to the exception concerns uses of copyright protected works 'to support, enrich or complement the teaching, including learning activities'. The use of video games for educational purposes would conceivably fall within this scope as a general matter. Of course, one might question whether that works for all games, or only specific types of games, or indeed only specific games – such that a case-by-case analysis may be required. 35

Moreover, rec. 21 raises a further limitation that 'in most cases, the concept of illustration would ... imply the use only of parts or extracts of works'. Although Member States remain free to set their own specifications as to the proportion of a work that 36

[34] It seems likely that a broad educational exception applied to materials specifically developed for education markets might encounter difficulties with the three-step test, particularly the second step – indeed the language in Art. 5(2) seems to have been drafted with that in mind. See below.

[35] DSM Copyright Directive, Art. 5(2).

can be used,[36] rec. 22 states that 'the use of works … under the exception … should be limited to what is necessary for the purpose of such activities'. This indicates that the exception should be interpreted narrowly, in line with EU and international norms. Furthermore, settled CJEU case law requires that terms be interpreted in their ordinary meaning, 'considering the usual meaning in everyday language of a term'.[37] Ordinarily, 'illustration' would be understood as a narrower concept than enabling teachers/students to play an entire video game, or substantial parts thereof, in the name of illustrating a concept in teaching.

37 Whether the intended use of video games in the classroom comes within the scope of the exception may therefore turn upon how much of the relevant games individual schools/teachers intend to use. Making use of a short part of a game for the purposes of teaching 'illustration' is more likely to be permitted under the Art. 5 exception. On the contrary, it is much more difficult to argue that the use of a substantial part, or the whole of a game would be permissible, particularly as a general proposition.

38 This said, it is acknowledged that 'there might be instances in which the entirety of a work … (e.g., a photograph) will need to be used for the purpose of illustration for teaching without that necessarily precluding the possibility for educational establishments to invoke successfully the exception or limitation under Article 5'.[38] However, the example given here of a photograph is a substantially different case to that of using an entire video game as a means of illustration for teaching. It is understandable that a photograph (or similarly any visual artwork) would need to be seen in its entirety in order to be used for the purposes of teaching illustration. A 'part' of such a work could conceivably be of little use when removed from the whole work. By contrast, even though using the whole or a substantial part of a video game may give a broader illustration for the teaching point it is used for, it seems a stretch of the intended scope of the exception under Art. 5 to argue that such use would be permissible.

39 Both rec. 31 of the Copyright Directive and rec. 6 of the DSM Copyright Directive note that 'the exceptions and limitations provided for in this Directive seek to achieve a fair balance between the rights and interests of authors and other rightholders … and of users'. The potential benefits of the use of video games in education must therefore be balanced against the copyright and commercial position of video game companies. Furthermore, rec. 6 and Art. 7(2) of the DSM Copyright Directive state that the exception 'can be applied only in certain special cases that do not conflict with the normal exploitation of the works or other subject matter and do not unreasonably prejudice the legitimate interests of the rightholders', i.e., in compliance with the three-step test.

b) Limitations imposed by the three-step test

40 In addition, all exceptions and limitations must be applied in accordance with the three-step test pursuant to Art. 5(5) of the Copyright Directive and Art. 7(2) of the DSM Copyright Directive.[39] In essence, the three-step test sets the outer limits of permissible exceptions and limitations in the national laws of the EU Member States. The test requires that, in order to be permissible at all, any exception or limitation to an exclusive right: (1) applies only to certain special cases, (2) does not conflict with normal exploita-

---

[36] DSM Copyright Directive, rec. 21.

[37] *Pelham*, mn. 28.

[38] Rosati, p. 257.

[39] Rec. 44 of the Copyright Directive further notes that 'when applying the exceptions and limitations provided for in this Directive, they should be exercised in accordance with international obligations. Such exceptions and limitations may not be applied in a way which prejudices the legitimate interests of the rightholder or which conflicts with the normal exploitation of his work or other subject-matter'.

tion of the work, and (3) does not unreasonably prejudice the legitimate interests of the rightholder. These conditions are cumulative, so implemented exceptions or limitations must comply with each step in turn.[40]

To pass the first step of the test, the intended use under the exception may only cover 'certain special cases'. Thus, it must be **limited in scope** – it must not be a carveout with a general impact; and, it also has to be special – there needs to a specific and sound justification. The use of video games for educational purposes in classrooms seems likely to pass the first step though there might be might some difficulty if it were to apply to any and all video games without distinction. 41

The second step prevents exceptions from **conflicting** with the 'normal exploitation of the work'. If the exception were to extend to the use of entire video games, it might be said to effectively enter into economic competition with the way in which rightholders normally derive value from their works, i.e., video publishers licensing the use of their works – this would be particularly the case with regard to video games developed specifically for educational purposes. 42

If the second step is satisfied, it then falls to determine whether application of the exception to the use of video games in class would 'unreasonably prejudice the legitimate interests of the rightholder'. This wording indicates that rightholders can be expected to tolerate some degree of **prejudice** to their **legitimate interests as owners of rights**, but it must be reasonable based on considering the relevant norms and public policies. In some cases, exceptions are accompanied with remuneration components (as noted above, under Art. 5(4) Member States have this option) which may operate to cure the unreasonable prejudice. 43

Some video game publishers may take the view that direct licensing is more lucrative. However, they may have to tolerate some prejudice and be content with **statutory remuneration** ***if*** the second step is satisfied, and if a remuneration component is included in the national exception. 44

c) Let's Play

Finally, Let's Play[41] may have both general and specific relevance. The creation and dissemination of videos from the content in video games will likely implicate the exclusive rights of reproduction and communication to the public, including making available. As such, a license would normally be necessary unless an exception is applicable. Moreover, guidelines issued by video games publishers will often **support the use of production materials for education purposes** subject to certain restrictions including that usage is generally limited to non-commercial purposes. This is consistent with the exception itself. The question of whether such videos might so be considered an adaptation (or derivative work) will be a matter of national law – one of the few remaining areas left to Member States. That said, successive CJEU decisions may be encroaching. 45

[40] Lindner/Shapiro, p. 71.

[41] Presumably, video game handbook readers know this, but just in case: Let's Play is a fan video genre documenting the playing of a video game with commentary and camera shots of the player.

IV. Artificial intelligence, text and data mining (TDM) and rights reservation

46 As noted above, in addition to the exception for digital use of works for illustration for teaching analysed in the previous section and a revamped exception for preservation of cultural heritage in Art. 6, the DSM Copyright Directive **has two exceptions for text and data mining** which we described briefly here with a nod to artificial intelligence.

1. TDM exceptions

47 Art. 3 and 4 of DSM Copyright Directive set out two mandatory exceptions to the right of reproduction in Art. 2 of the Copyright Directive[42] which permit text and data mining ('TDM') of copyright works and other subject-matter. These exceptions apply only where the beneficiary has lawful access to the content.

48 The beneficiaries are research organisations and cultural heritage institutions (Art. 3); and everyone, including commercial companies (Art. 4), who invoke the exceptions for **sourcing input data for AI model training.** TDM encompasses any automated analytical technique used to analyse text and data in digital form to generate information, including but not limited to patterns, trends, and correlations.[43] The exact scope of these two exceptions is subject to ongoing debate. However, the relevance of TDM to at least certain types of AI training is reinforced by Art. 53(1)(c) of Regulation (EU) 2024/1689 ('AI Act'), which explicitly references the Art. 4 TDM exception in the context of training data requirements for general-purpose AI models.

49 While the two exceptions differ in terms of beneficiaries and the extent to which they apply in the commercial realm, the key distinction concerns the question of rights reservation ('opt-out'). The ability for affected rightholders to nix the exception by opting back into protection.

50 Art. 3 permits text and data mining for non-commercial scientific research by research organisations and cultural heritage institutions. Notably, this exception does **not include** an **opt-out clause for rightholders**, meaning that if these organisations meet all the requirements set out in the DSM Copyright Directive – chief among them having lawful access to content – rightholders cannot oppose the text and data mining of their content.

51 Art. 4, on the other hand, allows anyone to conduct TDM for any purposes, with the crucial distinction that rightholders can reserve their rights, thereby preventing TDM from being applied to their works. Additionally, the three-step test and other potential obligations arising from international copyright treaties may impose further constraints on the application of the exception. However, the extent to which these additional constraints will affect the exception remains to be clarified by the courts and practice.

52 This part of this chapter briefly considers the question of opt-out and how it might apply in the context of video games. Are AI developers using video games to train AI models? What happens when AI eats its own data?

---

[42] The text and data mining exception also operates as limitation on reproduction type of rights on other subject matter. It also limits the extraction and re-utilization rights of *sui generis* database (Art. 7(1) of Directive 96/9/EC), the reproduction right over a copyright protected database (Art. 5(a) of Directive 96/9/EC), the press publishers' rights (Art. 15(1) of the DSM Copyright Directive) and the reproduction and adaptation/alteration rights (Art. 4(1)(a) and (b) of Directive 2009/24/EC).

[43] Art. 2(2).

2. Rights reservation – is Art. 4 like the Hotel California?

The rules on how to implement rights reservation (or opt-out) are set out in Art. 4(3) and rec. 18 of the DSM Copyright Directive. The rights reservation should be expressed in 'an appropriate manner'. For content 'made publicly available online', the rights reservation should be done *by machine readable means*, which includes metadata and terms and conditions of a website or a service. While for content not made available publicly online, other means, such as contractual agreements or a unilateral declaration should suffice. **53**

The Directive contains no definition of content made publicly available online, but it should encompass any openly accessible website with or without paywalls, such as a video game service streaming platform. **54**

Where paywalls are in place, the would-be beneficiary of the exception would need to have a valid subscription. The question then arises whether opting out via the terms of service or use would be sufficient to constitute a valid reservation of rights vis-à-vis subscribers. Some content owner/distributors have included rights reservation in their terms of service or use. **55**

Some uncertainty remains concerning **the application of machine readability standard.** Contradictory judgments have been rendered in different Member States on what amounts to 'machine readable'. The leading German case[44] found that a declaration in natural language on the subpage of a website meets the standard. However, this approach was not upheld at the next level.[45] A recent Dutch case,[46] also seems to have taken a more restrictive approach, whereby the exclusion of search bots through robot.txt was deemed necessary to meet the standard. By implication, the mere use of natural language on a subpage may not suffice. This issue should ultimately be resolved by higher level courts, including perhaps the Court of Justice of the EU – but this will play out slowly over the next few years. **56**

In the context of the implementation of the EU's AI Act, the **General-Purpose AI Code of Practice** was finalised in summer of 2025. The Code is meant to assist AI model providers with compliance with the AI Act. The machine-readable requirement was one of the stumbling blocks. This voluntary code could only identify one right reservation protocol (the age-old robots.txt), while describing future opt-out standards that AI providers should identify and comply with once they are widely adopted. **57**

3. Rights reservations as applied to video game distribution

The appropriate form of rights reservation depends on the type of content and how it is distributed. Given the multiple modes of video games distribution, the relevant rightholders may want to apply all available means to express the reservation of rights under Art. 4(3) of the DSM Copyright Directive. That said, for online gaming, subscription-based services, and app-based gaming, users need to accept 'terms and conditions of a website or a service'. Based on rec. 18 of the DSM Copyright Directive, one might argue that the opt-out is machine readable if it is done in the terms and conditions of a website or a service. **58**

---

[44] *Kneschke v LAION*, LG Hamburg, 27.9.2024, *310 O 227/23*.

[45] On appeal, while the Higher Regional Court of Hamburg upheld the lower court's dismissal of the claimant's action for injunctive relief, it did not agree with the court of first instance on the matter of natural language opt-out, *Kneschke v. LAION*, OLG Hamburg, 10.12.2025, *5 U 104/24*.

[46] *DPG Media et al. v HowardsHome, Rechtbank Amsterdam*, 30.10.2024, C/13/737170 /HA ZA 23-690.

4. Examples from rights reservation practices

59 The standard practice emerging from the European rightholder community is to issue **unilateral public declarations**, usually in the form of public statements to express their rights reservation against unauthorised TDM regarding their whole repertoire. For example, in the music sector, ICMP (music publishers' trade body) launched a dedicated portal that industry participants may sign up to: www.rightsandai.com. It provides a means by which music rightholders may make a statement to opt-out formally from the TDM exception. A number of collective management organisations (CMOs) representing rightholders from the music, audiovisual and literary sectors have also issued similar declarations such as the SABAM[47] or SACEM.[48]

5. Emerging rights reservation techniques

60 Some private initiatives for implementing rights reservation have recently emerged. However, these solutions were primarily developed by other creative sectors and are not tailored to the video game sector. Desk research has not revealed any sector specific initiatives for video games, at the time of this writing. Two types of rights reservations are being developed: source-based and asset-based. Obviously, a rightholder can and may very well want to rely on as many techniques to express rights reservation as suitable for their content – subject of course to economic and resource considerations.

[47] 'Sabam safeguards rights of its authors for AI use | Sabam' https://www.sabam.be/en/press/sabam-safeguards-rights-its-authors-ai-use (last accessed: 15.1.2026).

[48] Sacem, in favour of virtuous, transparent, and fair AI, exercises its right to opt-out – SACEM https://societe.sacem.fr/en/news/our-society/sacem-favour-virtuous-transparent-and-fair-ai-exercises-its-right-opt-out (last accessed: 15.1.2026).

§ 15
EU Copyright Contract Law

Bibliography: Brauner/Brauneck (ed), Angemessene Vergütung von Urhebern und Künstlern, Munich 2022; Götting/Lauber-Rönsberg/Rauer (ed), Beck'scher Onlinekommentar zum Urheberrecht, 46th edn, 2025; Hentsch, Die Umsetzung der Urheberrechts-Richtlinie aus Sicht der Games-Branche, MMR 2019, 351; Jacobs, 'Die Karlsruher Übersetzertarife – zugleich Anmerkung zu BGH "Destructive Emotions"', GRUR 2011, 306; Kübler/Billinger, 'Europäisches Urheber- und Verlagsrecht', in Ulmer-Eilfort/Obergfell, Verlagsrecht, 2nd edn 2021; McGuire/Bernzen, Geistiges Eigentum, in Gebauer/Wiedmann, Europäisches Zivilrecht, 3rd edn Munich 2021; Oehler 'Computerspiele und Multimediale Werke' in Berger/Wündisch (ed), Handbuch zum Urhebervertragsrecht, 3rd edn, Baden-Baden 2021; Oehler 'Angemessene Vergütung' in Hentsch/Falk, Games und Recht, Baden-Baden 2023; Peifer, 'Die urhebervertragsrechtlichen Normen in der DSM-Richtlinie', ZUM 2019, 648; Soppe/Fuchs, 'Inhalt und Grenzen der neuen Auskunftspflicht nach § 32d Abs. 1 UrhG für Presseverlage', AfP 2021, 487; Wandtke/Bullinger (ed), Urheberrecht, 6th edn 2022; Zimmer/Soppe, 'Urhebervertragsrecht im Games-Bereich – spezifische urhebervertragsrechtliche Analyse bei einer Vielfalt von Beteiligten, Beiträgen und Nutzungen', MMR 2023, 633.

A. Introduction: What is EU copyright contract law? 1

B. Copyright contract law in the DSM-Directive 7
- I. Preliminary remarks 7
- II. Appropriate and proportionate remuneration 12
- III. Transparency obligation 18
- IV. Contract adjustment mechanism 28
- V. Alternative dispute resolution procedure 34
- VI. Right of revocation 37
- VII. Mandatory nature of Artt. 19, 20 and 21 DSMD 40
- VIII. Conclusion 42

C. Challenges in applying these rules on games 43
- I. Peculiarities in the games industry 46
- II. Rules on copyright contract law shaped by traditional use cases 50
- III. Applying copyright contract law on games – a cautious look into the future 55
  1. Art. 18 DSMD 56
  2. Art. 19 DSMD 61
  3. Art. 20 DSMD 71
  4. Art. 21 DSMD 75
  5. Art. 22 DSMD 76
  6. Conclusion 78

A. Introduction: What is EU copyright contract law?

1 Until the present day, there is **no fully harmonised European Union** (EU) **copyright law.**[1] This is in contrast to other areas of intellectual property (IP) law like, e.g., trademark law and design law, where respective EU Regulations[2] provide for EU-wide harmonised legislation. The underlying reason for this lack of full harmonisation is the fact that the EU Member States have not been able to agree on a common copyright law concept, probably due to their different legal traditions. Whereas on the continent, many Member States share the tradition of the so-called droit d'auteur-system,[3] the

[1] Wandtke, in Wandtke/Bullinger, Introduction, mn. 29.

[2] Cf. the EU Trademark Regulation (Regulation (EU) 2017/1001 of 14.6.2017) and the EU Design Regulation (Regulation (EU) 2024/2822 of 23.10.2024) respectively. In the patent area cf. Regulation (EU) 1257/2012 of 17.12.2012 and in relation to trade secrets see Directive (EU) 2016/943 of 8.6.2016.

[3] Literally 'Right of the author' system; cf, e.g., for France Art. L121–1 Code de la proprieté intellectuelle (French IP Act): 'L'auteur jouit du droit au respect de son nom, de sa qualité et de son oeuvre. Ce droit est attaché à sa personne. Il est perpétuel, inaliénable et imprescriptible.'; for Germany Sec. 11 German Copyright Act (Urheberrechtsgesetz – UrhG).

Anglo-Saxon concept is based on the copyright approach.[4] One of the most important differences is that the Anglo-Saxon concept acknowledges the possibility of fully transferring copyright ownership to another person, in this regard comparable to other IP laws, as, e.g., a trademark owner may entirely transfer their legal position to the trademark to another person. In contrast, under the droit d'auteur system, the author of a copyrighted work always keeps a certain relation to their work. These so-called moral rights ('droit morals') of the author include, inter alia, that an author has an interminable right to be named as the author of the work (acknowledgement of authorship) or to object to any derogatory action in relation to their works by third parties.[5] Up to now, the European Union therefore focussed on harmonising specific aspects of copyright in a number of Directives.[6] And although the EU legislator understands the importance of copyright in a single European market,[7] a full harmonisation of Copyright on a Union level is not in sight.

2 More specifically, there is also **no fully harmonised EU copyright contract law regime**, at least not with such a name. Generally, copyright contract law, under national law, deals with all aspects of copyright related contracts, for example rules on setting up license agreements (grant of rights, form requirements etc.), contractual rights and obligations of the parties, term and termination of such licenses, performance of such contracts and possible remedies in case of problems. In this regard, often general principles of contract law apply (e.g., the principle of offer and acceptance) which also include the principle of contractual freedom, i.e., that, as a rule, there is no obligatory typology of copyright contracts and the parties are free to formulate their agreements as they deem reasonable.

3 However, national copyright contract law regimes often contain provisions that **limit this general contractual freedom** in order to **protect the authors** and their **rights to their works**. Although this obviously has not been researched empirically, there seems to be consensus among many national regulators that authors are the weaker parts in comparison to professional exploiters of their works, e.g., an author in relation to their publisher, a director in relation to the producer of the movie or a graphic designer in relation to their principal. Whereas it seems widely accepted that employed authors are sufficiently protected by the rules of employment law, in the last two decades national regulators have set up guardrails for agreements between freelance authors and exploiters which aim at ensuring negotiation balance between these parties and protect the author as the allegedly weaker party against unfair contractual arrangements with their work-exploiting counterparts. It is the set of these rules – which sometimes remind one to a certain extent of the set of consumer protection laws – that are often referred to as copyright contract law *stricto sensu* under national law regimes.

---

[4] For the UK see Art. 1 (1) Copyright, Designs and Patents Act 1988: 'Copyright is a property right…', similarly for Ireland in Art. 17 (1) Copyright and Related Rights Act.

[5] Cf. Sec. 13 and 14 German Copyright Act (Urheberrechtsgesetz – UrhG) respectively.

[6] Cf., e.g., the Directive 2001/29/EC of 22.5.2001 on the harmonisation of certain aspects of copyright and related rights in the information society (also called InfoSoc-Directive); the Directive 2014/26/EU of 26.2.2014 on collective management of copyright and related rights, or the Directive (EU) 2019/789 of 17.4.2019 laying down rules on the exercise of copyright and related rights applicable to certain online transmissions of broadcasting organisations and retransmissions of television and radio programmes (also called Online-Sat-Cab-Directive).

[7] See Rec. (2) of the Directive (EU) 2019/790 of 17.4.2019 on copyright and related rights in the Digital Single Market, hereinafter referred to as 'DSM-Directive' or 'DSMD'. The term 'EU Copyright Directive' or 'EUCD', that is also often used in practice, is not entirely clear because of other copyright-related EU-Directives (see previous note).

In the absence of an overarching EU copyright law regime (cf. above), there are **provisions** on the **European Union level** that go in this very direction: Title IV Chapter 3 (Art. 18 et seqq.) DSMD contains provisions that aim specifically at securing '[f]air remuneration in exploitation contracts of authors and performers'.[8] 4

In this context, '**authors**' means all creators of copyrighted works, not only of texts, but also of graphical works, music, films etc. However, Title IV Chapter 3 shall explicitly not apply to creators of computer programs (coders).[9] '**Performers**', in contrast, do not create a copyrighted work, but perform the works (of others), e.g., as musicians, singers, actors or dancers. In the present context, they will not be dealt with in detail.[10] 5

According to its Art. 31, the DSM-Directive entered into force on 7.6.2019 and Art. 29 (1) DSMD required the Member States to 'bring into force the laws, regulations and administrative provisions necessary to comply with this Directive by 7.6.2021'. This is also the relevant date for the Directive's application in time.[11] However, it must be noted that transposition did not happen in a timely manner throughout the Union. So, in 2023, the EU Commission decided to take action against six Member States for failing to implement the Directive: Bulgaria, Denmark, Finland, Latvia, Poland and Portugal.[12] It seems that more current data on the implementation status is not available, therefore, the case given, it should be checked carefully if implementation has taken place in the jurisdiction concerned;[13] if not, provisions of the Directive might be directly applicable according to CJEU jurisprudence.[14] 6

B. Copyright contract law in the DSM-Directive

I. Preliminary remarks

The legislative blueprint of the rules in Artt. 18–23 DSMD can be found in **German copyright contract law**.[15] Already in 2002, the German legislator introduced the following mandatory claims in the German Copyright Act (Urheberrechtsgesetz – UrhG): equitable remuneration for the author (Sec. 32 UrhG); author's further participation (Sec. 32a UrhG); and right of revocation for non-exercise (Sec. 41 UrhG). Moreover, German law contains both claims for information for the substantiation of IP-related claims and voluntary alternative dispute resolution mechanisms. Altogether, this is conceptually very similar to Art. 18–23 DSMD. Furthermore, the German legislator introduced a number of provisions fostering certain collective bargaining agreements (so-called Joint Remuneration Agreements, Sec. 36 et seqq. UrhG), which are referenced also in Title IV 7

---

[8] Cf. the heading of Title IV Chapter 3 DSM-Directive.

[9] See Art. 23 (2) DSMD: 'Members States shall provide that Artt. 18 to 22 of this Directive do not apply to authors of a computer program within the meaning of Art. 2 of Directive 2009/24/EC'.

[10] When citing from the DSM-Directive, a blank ('…') will be used when references to performers or their subject matter are omitted for easier legibility.

[11] Art. 26 DSMD; for applicability in time in regard to national laws see CJEU, 6.3.2025 – case C-575/23 – ONB et al., ECLI:EU:C:2024:141.

[12] See Press Release of 15.2.2023: https://ec.europa.eu/commission/presscorner/detail/en/ip_23_704.

[13] For the respective general national transposition laws see, e.g., for France Ordonnance no. 2021-580 of 12.5.2021, for Germany Urheberrechtsanpassungsgesetz of 31.5.2021; for Italy Legislative Decree No. 177 of 8.11.2021; for the Netherlands Wet van 16.12.2020; for Poland Ustawa z dnia 11 sierpnia 2021 r. o zmianie ustawy o prawie autorskim i prawach pokrewnych oraz niektórych innych ustaw.

[14] CJEU 4.12.1974 – 41/74 – van Duyn, ECLI:EU:C:1974:133, for cases of belated transposition of an EU Directive into national law.

[15] See Kübler/Billinger, mn. 1209: Art. 18 et seqq. DSMD 'modelled on German law'; Hentsch, MMR 2019, 351 et seqq.; Peifer, ZUM 2019, 648, 650; McGuire/Bernzen, mn. 509.

Chapter 3 of the DSM-Directive. Finally, also the idea that authors have only limited negotiation power vis-à-vis the exploiters can be found in German legislative materials already in the year 2002.[16]

8 According to rec. (72) DSMD:

Authors … tend to be in the weaker contractual position when they grant a licence or transfer their rights, including through their own companies, for the purposes of exploitation in return for remuneration, and those natural persons need the protection provided for by this Directive to be able to fully benefit from the rights harmonised under Union law. That need for protection does not arise where the contractual counterpart acts as an end user and does not exploit the work … itself, which could, for instance, be the case in some employment contracts.

9 Although the premise of the 'weaker contractual position' seems to **lack empirical evidence,**[17] it is the basis for the rules on copyright contract law in Art. 18 et seqq. DSMD. Obviously, the EU legislator had in mind the constellation of an author, being an individual natural person, who needs to contract with a financially and organisationally superior exploiter, probably a company that is able to dictate the terms of a license contract unilaterally unless it was contained by respective legislation. This is in line with Member States' approaches to this issue.[18] However, it must not be overlooked that the relationship between authors and their contractual partners is often different: it may be that the author is well-placed in the market themselves and thus able to conclude contracts with the exploiter at arms' length; or that (also) the exploiter is financially and organisationally not as strong as assumed by the legislator; or that authors are acting jointly in relation to their counterpart and therefore enjoy strong bargaining power. Nevertheless, this premise is the foundation for the following safeguards for 'fair remuneration in exploitation contracts of authors' in the DSM-Directive.

10 As always, also this Directive is addressed to the EU Member States (cf. Art. 32 DSMD) and obliges them to transpose its content into their national laws. In doing so, the Member States shall be bound, as to the result to be achieved, but shall have the choice of form and methods how to do this (cf. Art. 288 (3) TFEU). This legislative approach leads to a **certain flexibility for the national lawmakers** and a certain variety of legislation in the Member States. What is more, Art. 25 DSMD allows Member States to adopt or maintain in force broader provisions for uses or fields covered by the exceptions or limitations provided for in this Directive. Thus, the DSM-Directive does not fully harmonise the law of copyright contract law[19] and it is possible that Member States have even stricter rules to ensure fair remuneration in the present context.[20] To this ex-

---

[16] BT-Drs. 14/8058, 1.

[17] There seems hardly any objective empirical survey available on this topic.

Existing studies like IVIR, Remuneration of authors and performers for the use of their works and the fixations of their performances, (European Commission, 2015) do not seem to generally support this premise, but their key findings sound rather more differentiated, when they state, for example, that 'certain groups of authors and performers, such as those new to the industry, are in a weaker bargaining position than others' (op.cit. p. 8). Moreover, a 'lack of transparency of the remuneration arrangements in the contracts of the authors in relation to the rights transferred' is not described as a lack of negotiation power, but rather as an obstacle to intra-Union mobility, because it 'undermines their freedom of movement across jurisdictions (non-tariff trade barrier) and has an adverse effect on the functioning of the Internal Market' (op.cit. p. 8).

In contrast, e.g., the 2014 publication of the European Parliament, 'Contractual arrangements applicable to creators: Law and practice of selected Member States' also seems to work on the assumption of a weaker contractual position of authors when it mainly assesses selected Member States' 'legal provisions protecting the author in copyright contracts' without empirical economic research.

[18] For Germany see BT-Drs. 14/8058, 1, again.

[19] Cf. Rec. 1 DSMD.

[20] Art. 25 DSMD.

tent it is necessary to keep in mind that, generally, the Directive is not directly applicable as such and the rights and obligations therein require transposition in the Member States. It is therefore essential to check national laws first as the Directive will apply directly only to the extent that national laws conflict with it.[21]

In the present context, it will not be possible to assess the respective implementation laws in all 27 Member States, but the focus will necessarily be on the DSM-Directive itself. However, in the absence of jurisprudence from the European Court of Justice or the General Court and due to the blueprint character of the German law in this regard,[22] a certain emphasis will be placed on decisions of the German Federal Court (Bundesgerichtshof – BGH). 11

II. Appropriate and proportionate remuneration

Art. 18 DSMD contains a 'Principle of appropriate and proportionate remuneration': 12

1. **Member States shall ensure that where authors … license or transfer their exclusive rights for the exploitation of their works …, they are entitled to receive appropriate and proportionate remuneration.**
2. **In the implementation in national law of the principle set out in paragraph 1, Member States shall be free to use different mechanisms and take into account the principle of contractual freedom and a fair balance of rights and interests.**

Subject to Member States' respective transformation progress, Art. 18 DSMD forms the basis of possible individual authors' legal claims for appropriate and proportionate remuneration.[23] In (1), a general principle of **'appropriate and proportionate remuneration'** is laid down. On a first layer, it can be understood as an obligation for the parties to conclude only agreements that respect this principle by agreeing on respective remuneration terms. However, this principle not only serves as a general guideline as to how copyright contracts 'should' (or even just 'might') be formulated, it also shall have legal implications if contracts do not comply with this principle. This becomes clear in (2) where the **'principle of contractual freedom'** is mentioned: Although it is possible that parties to a copyright contract agreed freely on a certain remuneration (e.g.. in the amount of '100'), it could turn out that this is not 'appropriate and proportionate'. In this case, Member States shall provide for a possibility to adjust the remuneration to an 'appropriate and proportionate' level, be it in the given example that a remuneration of '150' or '180' is required, be it that a different remuneration scheme is necessary, for example an ongoing percentage of revenues generated from the exploited works instead of a lump sum payment. 13

In this respect, the underlying Rec. (73) DSMD reads: 14

The remuneration of authors … should be appropriate and proportionate to the actual or potential economic value of the licensed or transferred rights, taking into account the author's … contribution to the overall work … and all other circumstances of the case, such as market practices or the actual exploitation of the work. A lump sum payment can also constitute proportionate remuneration but it should not be the rule. Member States should have the freedom to define specific cases for the application of lump sums, taking into account the specificities of each sector. Member States should be free to imple-

[21] See CJEU, 15.7.1964 – 6/64 – Costa./.E.N.E.L, ECLI:EU:C:1964:66, on the precedence of Community (now Union) law of Member States' legislation.

[22] And because the author of this chapter is a German law-trained lawyer.

[23] See, e.g., for France Art. L. 131–4 Code de la proprieté intellectuelle (French IP Act); for Germany Sec. 32 Urheberrechtsgesetz (German Copyright Act); for Italy Art. 46bis Legge 633/1941 sul diritto d'autore (Italian Copyright Act); for the Netherlands Art. 25c Auteurswet (Dutch Copyright Act); for Poland Art. 43 Ustawa o prawie autorskim i prawach pokrewnych (Polish Copyright Act); for Spain Art. 46 Real Decreto Legislativo (RDL) 1/1996.

ment the principle of appropriate and proportionate remuneration through different existing or newly introduced mechanisms, which could include collective bargaining and other mechanisms, provided that such mechanisms are in conformity with applicable Union law.

15 Although Recitals of an EU Directive are not legally binding, they are relevant for the interpretation of the Directive's provisions.[24] Thus, Rec. (73) makes clear that Member States have a certain freedom how they implement the **'fair balance of rights and interests'** mentioned, and it also acknowledges that 'the specificities of each sector' should be taken into account. But the Member States' obligation to ensure the principle of appropriate and proportionate remuneration follows from Art. 18 DSMD.

16 In this regard, Art. 18 (1) DSMD is applicable to cases, where (i) authors (ii) license or transfer (iii) their exclusive rights (iv) for the exploitation of their works. The provision is accordingly not applicable for cases further down the license chain, e.g., between a licensee (which licensed the rights from an author) and a sublicensee, where no author is involved.[25] It is limited to cases where 'exclusive' rights are involved, thus not in cases with non-exclusive licenses. And it refers only to contracts about the exploitation of the authors' works. However, it must be noted that certain Member States' laws go beyond the requirements of Art. 18 (1) DSMD.[26] For example, Sec. 32 (1) of the German Copyright Act (UrhG) traditionally is not limited to 'exclusive' rights but covers all 'grants of usage rights'.[27]

17 As a consequence, Art. 18 (1) DSMD contains the **right of authors to receive appropriate and proportionate remuneration**. Although this seems clear on an abstract level, it is obvious that the devil is in the details when it comes to applying this principle to a specific case. This is because there are only a few cases where a neutral and objective remuneration can be found. And when the contractual parties have to agree on what actually is 'appropriate and proportionate' in the specific case, there will generally be good arguments for both sides to increase or decrease a certain remuneration. The EU legislator refers this problem to the Member States when both Art. 18 (2) and Rec. (73) underline the latters' freedom of how to implement this principle. It therefore does not come as a surprise that on a national level there are sometimes much more detailed provisions on how to establish appropriateness and proportionality of a remuneration,[28] for example rules on collective bargaining mechanisms.[29] In the end, however, it will often be a matter for the courts to decide what was appropriate and proportionate as remuneration in a specific case. In the absence of detailed jurisprudence on this question, both Art. 18 DSMD and its national implementations leave a large degree of uncertainty and ambiguity for the parties in terms of how an appropriate and proportionate remuneration have to look like in a specific case.[30] And in practice, this problem is even greater because the parties only learn the answer to this question subsequently, after a litigation has taken place and a court has rendered a binding decision.

---

[24] Cf. CJEU, 24.1.2005 – case C-136/04 – *Deutsches Milch-Kontor*, ECLI:EU:C:2005:716, mn. 32.

[25] For the German transposition norm see BeckOK UrhR/Soppe, § 32 UrhG Rn. 15.

[26] Cf. Art. 25 DSMD.

[27] Cf. the broader German wording: 'für die Einräumung von Nutzungsrechten und die Erlaubnis zur Werknutzung'.

[28] See, for example, in Germany Sec. 32 (2) UrhG.

[29] Cf. the last sentence of Rec. (73) DSMD.

[30] Cf. the criticism among legal scholars in Germany, e.g. Jacobs GRUR 2011, 306 ('Pandora's box full of indeterminate legal terms').

III. Transparency obligation

Supplementary to the principle of appropriate and proportionate remuneration in Art. 18 DSMD, Art. 19 DSMD stipulates a detailed transparency obligation. To the extent relevant in the present context, it reads as follows: 18

1. **Member States shall ensure that authors … receive on a regular basis, at least once a year, and taking into account the specificities of each sector, up to date, relevant and comprehensive information on the exploitation of their works … from the parties to whom they have licensed or transferred their rights, or their successors in title, in particular as regards modes of exploitation, all revenues generated and remuneration due.**
2. **Member States shall ensure that, where the rights referred to in paragraph 1 have subsequently been licensed, authors … or their representatives shall, at their request, receive from sub-licensees additional information, in the event that their first contractual counterpart does not hold all the information that would be necessary for the purposes of paragraph 1.**
   Where that additional information is requested, the first contractual counterpart of authors … shall provide information on the identity of those sub-licensees.
   Member States may provide that any request to sub-licensees pursuant to the first subparagraph is made directly or indirectly through the contractual counterpart of the author …
3. **The obligation set out in paragraph 1 shall be proportionate and effective in ensuring a high level of transparency in every sector. Member States may provide that in duly justified cases where the administrative burden resulting from the obligation set out in paragraph 1 would become disproportionate in the light of the revenues generated by the exploitation of the work …, the obligation is limited to the types and level of information that can reasonably be expected in such cases.**
4. **Member States may decide that the obligation set out in paragraph 1 of this Article does not apply when the contribution of the author … is not significant having regard to the overall work …, unless the author … demonstrates that he or she requires the information for the exercise of his or her rights under Art. 20(1) and requests the information for that purpose.**
5. **Member States may provide that, for agreements subject to or based on collective bargaining agreements, the transparency rules of the relevant collective bargaining agreement are applicable, on condition that those rules meet the criteria provided for in paragraphs 1 to 4.**

[6. Exception for agreements with collecting societies].

The reason for this detailed transparency obligation is to give authors the information necessary to understand the economic value of the rights granted in regard to their works and thereby have the relevant information to determine appropriateness and proportionality of their remuneration. The EU legislator puts this as follows. 19

Rec. (74) DSMD: 20

Authors … need information to assess the economic value of rights of theirs that are harmonised under Union law. This is especially the case where natural persons grant a licence or a transfer of rights for the purposes of exploitation in return for remuneration. That need does not arise where the exploitation has ceased, or where the author … has granted a licence to the general public without remuneration.

Rec. (75) DSMD: 21

As authors … tend to be in the weaker contractual position when they grant licences or transfer their rights, they need information to assess the continued economic value of their rights, compared to the remuneration received for their licence or transfer, but they often face a lack of transparency. Therefore, the sharing of adequate and accurate information by their contractual counterparts or their successors in title is important for the transparency and balance in the system governing the remuneration of authors … That information should be up-to-date to allow access to recent data, relevant to the exploitation of the work …, and comprehensive in a way that it covers all sources of revenues relevant to the case, including, where applicable, merchandising revenues. As long as exploitation is ongoing, contractual counterparts of authors … should provide information available to them on all modes of exploitation and on all relevant revenues worldwide with a regularity that is appropriate in the relevant sector, but at least annually. The information should be provided in a manner that is comprehensible to the author … and it should allow the effective assessment of the economic value of the rights in question. The transparency obligation should nevertheless apply only where copyright relevant rights are concerned. The processing of personal data, such as contact details and information on remuneration, that are necessary to keep authors … informed in relation to the exploitation of their works …, should be carried out in accordance with Art. 6(1)(c) [GDPR].

22 To this end, Art. 19 (1) DSMD[31] provides for an **obligation of the exploiters to provide information to the authors proactively**. This goes beyond a claim for information that needs to be raised by the authors but shall ensure authors' access to information without claiming them. Moreover, the information shall be provided on a regular basis, at least once a year. Also, the content of the information is regulated: On a formal level, the information shall be (i) up to date, (ii) relevant and (iii) comprehensive. Materially, the information to be given shall (a) take into account the specificities of each sector and (b) be on the exploitation of (c) the authors' works (d) from the parties to whom they have licensed or transferred their rights, or their successors in title, in particular as regards (e) modes of exploitation, (f) all revenues generated and (g) remuneration due.

23 The EU legislator also acknowledges that the relevant information may come from a sub-licensee further down the license chain. This is dealt with in Art. 19 (2) DSMD and also in its Rec. (76):

In order to ensure that exploitation-related information is duly provided to authors ... also in cases where the rights have been sub-licensed to other parties who exploit the rights, this Directive entitles authors ... to request additional relevant information on the exploitation of the rights, in cases where the first contractual counterpart has provided the information available to them, but that information is not sufficient to assess the economic value of their rights. That request should be made either directly to sub-licensees or through the contractual counterparts of authors ... Authors ..., and their contractual counterparts, should be able to agree to keep the shared information confidential, but authors ... should always be able to use the shared information for the purpose of exercising their rights under this Directive. Member States should have the option, in compliance with Union law, to provide for further measures to ensure transparency for authors ...

24 Whereas such kind (and scope) of information as set out in Art. 19 (1) DSMD may have been good practice for decades in the book publishing industry, where publishers are often sending a statement of copies sold to the author of the respective book every year, this **information obligation can be extremely challenging** in sectors where there is neither just one author per work nor are the exploitation channels as one-dimensional as in the book publishing industry. This is especially true for the games industry with its – often – hundreds or even thousands of **creative staff** involved in the production of a game and its multitude of exploitation channels. The legislator has accepted in Art. 19 (3) DSMD the idea that there are cases where this information leads to a disproportionate administrative burden in the light of the revenues generated by the exploitation of the works. Moreover, (4) gives Member States the possibility to implement a certain *de minimis* threshold in the information obligation for cases of merely insignificant contributions. These limitations to the information obligation are also dealt with in the first part of Rec. (77):

When implementing the transparency obligation provided for in this Directive, Member States should take into account the specificities of different content sectors, such as those of the music sector, the audiovisual sector and the publishing sector, and all relevant stakeholders should be involved when deciding on such sector-specific obligations. Where relevant, the significance of the contribution of authors ... to the overall work ... should also be considered. [...]

---

[31] For the respective national transposition laws see, e.g., for France Art. L. 131–5.1 Code de la proprieté intellectuelle (French IP Act); for Germany Sec. 32d Urheberrechtsgesetz (German Copyright Act); for Italy Art. 110quater Legge 633/1941 sul diritto d'autore (Italian Copyright Act); for the Netherlands Art. 25ca Auteurswet (Dutch Copyright Act); for Poland Art. 47[1] Ustawa o prawie autorskim i prawach pokrewnych (Polish Copyright Act).

Furthermore, the EU legislator is of the opinion that **collective bargaining** may strengthen the authors' allegedly weaker position sufficiently to reach negotiation balance.[32] For this reason, it is accepted in Art. 19 (5) DSMD that deviating transparency rules may be established in collective bargaining agreements and prevail over the statutory requirement. This concept is also mentioned in Rec. 77: 25

[...] Collective bargaining should be considered as an option for the relevant stakeholders to reach an agreement regarding transparency. Such agreements should ensure that authors ... have the same level of transparency as or a higher level of transparency than the minimum requirements provided for in this Directive. To enable the adaptation of existing reporting practices to the transparency obligation, a transitional period should be provided for. [...]

Finally, Art. 19 (6) DSMD contains specific exceptions for agreements with collecting societies which are not relevant in the present context. 26

Art. 27 DSMD contains a transitional provision for the transparency obligation: 'Agreements for the licence or transfer of rights of authors ... shall be subject to the transparency obligation set out in Art. 19 as from 7.6.2022.' This is one year later than the Directive's applicability as of 7.6.2021[33] and was intended to give the contractual partners of the authors time to prepare the respective information. 27

IV. Contract adjustment mechanism

Art. 20 DSMD contains a contract adjustment mechanism: 28

1. **Member States shall ensure that, in the absence of an applicable collective bargaining agreement providing for a mechanism comparable to that set out in this Article, authors ... or their representatives are entitled to claim additional, appropriate and fair remuneration from the party with whom they entered into a contract for the exploitation of their rights, or from the successors in title of such party, when the remuneration originally agreed turns out to be disproportionately low compared to all the subsequent relevant revenues derived from the exploitation of the works ...**

[2. **Exception for agreements with collecting societies].**

Art. 20 (1) DSMD is the basis for Member States laws granting claims to authors for 'additional, appropriate and fair remuneration' from their contractual partners 'when the remuneration originally agreed turns out to be disproportionately low compared to all the subsequent relevant revenues' made with the exploitation of the works concerned.[34] Under German law, which served as a blueprint for EU copyright contract law,[35] the idea of the respective provision was the constellation of a literature bestseller, i.e., the case where a book, for which a 'regular remuneration' was agreed, sold extremely well, leading to (originally unexpected) high revenues for the publisher, but without consequence for the author's remuneration. For such cases the legislator wanted to adjust the original **remuneration** to an appropriate and **fair level** from an *ex post* perspective. This concept has found its way also into the DSM-Directive in its Art. 20 (1) and is elaborated in more detail in its Rec. (78): 29

[32] This concept is also pursued by national legislators, cf, e.g., Sec. 36 et seqq. German Copyright Act (UrhG).

[33] Cf. Art. 26 DSMD.

[34] For the respective national transposition laws see, e.g., for France Art. L. 131–5 II Code de la propriété intellectuelle (French IP Act), for Germany Sec. 32a Urheberrechtsgesetz (German Copyright Act), for Italy Art. 110quinquies Legge 633/1941 sul diritto d'autore (Italian Copyright Act); for the Netherlands Art. 25d Auteurswet (Dutch Copyright Act); for Poland Art. 44 Ustawa o prawie autorskim i prawach pokrewnych (Polish Copyright Act); for Spain 47 Real Decreto Legislativo (RDL) 1/1996.

[35] Cf. above mn. 7.

Certain contracts for the exploitation of rights harmonised at Union level are of long duration, offering few opportunities for authors ... to renegotiate them with their contractual counterparts or their successors in title in the event that the economic value of the rights turns out to be significantly higher than initially estimated. Accordingly, without prejudice to the law applicable to contracts in Member States, a remuneration adjustment mechanism should be provided for as regards cases where the remuneration originally agreed under a licence or a transfer of rights clearly becomes disproportionately low compared to the relevant revenues derived from the subsequent exploitation of the work ... by the contractual counterpart of the author ... All revenues relevant to the case in question, including, where applicable, merchandising revenues, should be taken into account for the assessment of whether the remuneration is disproportionately low. The assessment of the situation should take account of the specific circumstances of each case, including the contribution of the author ..., as well as of the specificities and remuneration practices in the different content sectors, and whether the contract is based on a collective bargaining agreement. Representatives of authors ... duly mandated in accordance with national law in compliance with Union law, should be able to provide assistance to one or more authors ... in relation to requests for the adjustment of the contracts, also taking into account the interests of other authors ... where relevant. Those representatives should protect the identity of the represented authors ... for as long as that is possible. Where the parties do not agree on the adjustment of the remuneration, the author ... should be entitled to bring a claim before a court or other competent authority. [...]

30 Although the general concept of this provision sounds fair and reasonable at first sight, it must be noted from a dogmatic perspective that it breaks up an existing contract that the parties originally have agreed. This, again,[36] is a certain collision with the principle of contractual freedom. The provision also makes it difficult to calculate costs for the exploiters of copyrighted works when they need to be prepared that an additional remuneration may become due, although the legislator may expect this to be no problem on the basis of the high revenues derived from the works. Moreover, when actually applying this concept (respectively its Member States' transposition laws) to a specific case, again the devil is in the details. This is because the term of a 'disproportionately low' remuneration originally agreed compared to the subsequent pertinent revenues does not appear very clear. And it is also not clear, what (additional) 'appropriate and fair remuneration' means – which is very similar to the equally unclear (and presumably materially similar)[37] term 'appropriate and proportionate remuneration' in Art. 18 (1) DSMD. To fill these terms with meaning will again need a number of court decisions in individual cases.

31 German jurisprudence – which may be useful to consider in the absence of decisions from the European Courts for the time being – has found a remuneration to be 'disproportionately low' at least in cases where the **'appropriate and fair remuneration'** should have been twice as high as the remuneration originally agreed (and actually received). To this end, the German Federal Court (BGH) applies a four-step-mechanism in the context of Sec. 32a German Copyright Act (UrhG) as the German equivalent to Art. 20 (1) DSMD: determination of (1) the remuneration agreed with the author, (2) the income and benefits obtained by the exploiter, (3) the remuneration which – in retrospect – is appropriate, and finally (4) examination if the agreed remuneration (1) is disproportionately low compared to the income and benefits (2) in view of this appropriate remuneration (3).[38]

32 Furthermore, as in Art. 19 (5) DSMD, the EU legislator also in this context accepts the idea that collective bargaining agreements may reach similar suitable mechanisms as set out in Art. 20 (1) DSMD and may prevail. However, conceptually it seems difficult to

[36] Cf. the similar conflict re 'appropriate and proportionate remuneration' in Art. 18 DSMD above mn. 13.

[37] We have found no evidence that 'appropriate and proportionate' (Art. 18) and 'appropriate and fair' (Art. 20) would materially differ from each other.

[38] BGH, 22.9.2011 – I ZR 127/10 – Das Boot, mn. 40; BGH, 20.2.2020 – I ZR 176/18 – Das Boot II, mn. 25; BGH, 1.4.021 – I ZR 9/18 – Das Boot III, mn. 32.

imagine an agreement that gives general (*ex ante*) guidance on how the '*ex-post*-scenario' of Art. 20 (1) DSMD – remuneration originally agreed turning out to be disproportionately low – could be resolved, especially with a collective approach for an entire sector.

Finally, Art. 20 (2) DSMD contains specific exceptions for agreements with collecting societies which are not relevant in the present context. 33

V. Alternative dispute resolution procedure

From a procedural perspective, Art. 21 DSMD calls for an alternative dispute resolution procedure in the Member States: 34

Member States shall provide that disputes concerning the transparency obligation under Art. 19 and the contract adjustment mechanism under Art. 20 may be submitted to a voluntary, alternative dispute resolution procedure. Member States shall ensure that representative organisations of authors … may initiate such procedures at the specific request of one or more authors ...

The legislator's reasoning is set out in Rec. (79): 35

Authors … are often reluctant to enforce their rights against their contractual partners before a court or tribunal. Member States should therefore provide for an alternative dispute resolution procedure that addresses claims by authors …, or by their representatives on their behalf, related to obligations of transparency and the contract adjustment mechanism. For that purpose, Member States should be able to either establish a new body or mechanism, or rely on an existing one that fulfils the conditions established by this Directive, irrespective of whether those bodies or mechanisms are industry-led or public, including when part of the national judiciary system. Member States should have flexibility in deciding how the costs of the dispute resolution procedure are to be allocated. Such alternative dispute resolution procedure should be without prejudice to the right of parties to assert and defend their rights by bringing an action before a court.

It is not clear from the legislative materials why the legislator found it specifically necessary to introduce this requirement of alternative dispute resolution (ADR) offers in the DSM-Directive, because it seems that voluntary ADR procedures may be available in all Member States and the EU itself has also been promoting ADR in different contexts.[39] However, from a market participants' perspective suffice it to say that voluntary ADR mechanisms should be available in each Member State to deal with disputes in the context of Artt. 19 and 20 DSMD.[40] 36

VI. Right of revocation

In the case that an author has granted exclusive rights to their contractual partner and the latter does not exploit these rights, the author may have a right of revocation in accordance with Art. 22 DSMD: 37

1. **Member States shall ensure that where an author … has licensed or transferred his or her rights in a work … on an exclusive basis, the author … may revoke in whole or in part the licence or the transfer of rights where there is a lack of exploitation of that work ...**
2. **Specific provisions for the revocation mechanism provided for in paragraph 1 may be provided for in national law, taking into account the following:**

---

[39] See, inter alia, Directive 2013/11/EU of 21.5.2013 on alternative dispute resolution for consumer disputes and Regulation (EU) No. 524/2013 of 21.5.2013 on online dispute resolution for consumer disputes.

[40] There has been no specific national transposition as the pre-existing legislation on ADR-mechanisms has been considered sufficient, e.g., in France and Germany. However, see for Italy Art. 110sexies Legge 633/1941 sul diritto d'autore (Italian Copyright Act); for the Netherlands Art. 25e Auteurswet (Dutch Copyright Act).

(a) the specificities of the different sectors and the different types of works ...; and
(b) where a work ... contains the contribution of more than one author ..., the relative importance of the individual contributions, and the legitimate interests of all authors ... affected by the application of the revocation mechanism by an individual author ...

Member States may exclude works from the application of the revocation mechanism if such works usually contain contributions of a plurality of authors ...

Member States may provide that the revocation mechanism can only apply within a specific time frame, where such restriction is duly justified by the specificities of the sector or of the type of work ... concerned.

Member States may provide that authors ... can choose to terminate the exclusivity of the contract instead of revoking the licence or transfer of the rights.

3. Member States shall provide that the revocation provided for in paragraph 1 may only be exercised after a reasonable time following the conclusion of the licence or the transfer of the rights. The author ... shall notify the person to whom the rights have been licensed or transferred and set an appropriate deadline by which the exploitation of the licensed or transferred rights is to take place. After the expiry of that deadline, the author ... may choose to terminate the exclusivity of the contract instead of revoking the licence or the transfer of the rights.
4. Paragraph 1 shall not apply if the lack of exploitation is predominantly due to circumstances that the author ... can reasonably be expected to remedy.
5. Member States may provide that any contractual provision derogating from the revocation mechanism provided for in paragraph 1 is enforceable only if it is based on a collective bargaining agreement.

38 The legislator has given the background for this right in Rec. (80) DMSD:

When authors ... license or transfer their rights, they expect their work ... to be exploited. However, it could be the case that works ... that have been licensed or transferred are not exploited at all. Where those rights have been transferred on an exclusive basis, authors ... cannot turn to another partner to exploit their works ... In such a case, and after a reasonable period of time has elapsed, authors ... should be able to benefit from a mechanism for the revocation of rights allowing them to transfer or license their rights to another person. As exploitation of works ... can vary depending on the sectors, specific provisions could be laid down at national level in order to take into account the specificities of the sectors, such as the audiovisual sector, or of the works ..., in particular providing for time frames for the right of revocation. In order to protect the legitimate interests of licensees and transferees of rights and to prevent abuses, and taking into account that a certain amount of time is needed before a work ... is actually exploited, authors ... should be able to exercise the right of revocation in accordance with certain procedural requirements and only after a certain period of time following the conclusion of the licence or of the transfer agreement. Member States should be allowed to regulate the exercise of the right of revocation in the case of works ... involving more than one author ..., taking into account the relative importance of the individual contributions.

39 The **right of revocation** is granted in cases of an exclusive license (grant of rights) where the author is bound to the exclusive rightsowner to exploit the work. The interest in the exploitation can be based on immaterial grounds (e.g., the author's interest to publish their ideas) or on material reasons (e.g., earning a percentage of revenues to be generated with the exploitation). Thus, if exploitation does not take place, Art. 22 DSMD[41] gives the author the right, under the conditions contained therein, to either revoke the grant of rights in total or in part (1) or terminate the exclusivity of the contract (3) sent. 3. According to (3) sent. 1 and 2, the expiry of a certain time period after the contract was made plus the expiry of an appropriate deadline to be set by the author is necessary for the exertion of these rights. Moreover, according to (4), (1) shall not apply if the author themselves can remedy the reasons for the non-exploitation; for systematic reasons, the same should be said for the right to terminate the exclusivity of the contract.

---

[41] For the respective national transposition laws see, e.g., for France Art. L. 131-5-2 Code de la propriété intellectuelle (French IP Act), for Germany Sec. 41 Urheberrechtsgesetz (German Copyright Act), for Italy Art. 110septies Legge 633/1941 sul diritto d'autore (Italian Copyright Act).

VII. Mandatory nature of Artt. 19, 20 and 21 DSMD

According to Art. 23 (1) DSMD, 'Member States shall ensure that any contractual provision that prevents compliance with Artt. 19, 20 and 21 shall be unenforceable in relation to authors. Thereby, these copyright contract law provisions to the benefit of the authors cannot be circumvented. As Rec. (81) DSMD underlines, this does not only apply to contractual derogations from said rights but also to cases where the parties try to escape the respective national law as such: 40

The provisions regarding transparency, contract adjustment mechanisms and alternative dispute resolution procedures laid down in this Directive should be of a mandatory nature, and parties should not be able to derogate from those provisions, whether in contracts between authors ... and their contractual counterparts, or in agreements between those counterparts and third parties, such as non-disclosure agreements. As a consequence, Art. 3(4) of [the Rome I] Regulation ... should apply to the effect that, where all other elements relevant to the situation at the time of the choice of applicable law are located in one or more Member States, the parties' choice of applicable law other than that of a Member State does not prejudice the application of the provisions regarding transparency, contract adjustment mechanisms and alternative dispute resolution procedures laid down in this Directive, as implemented in the Member State of the forum.

Interestingly, Artt. 18 (principle of appropriate and proportionate remuneration) and 22 (right of revocation) DSMD are not mentioned in this catalogue in Art. 23 DSMD. This means that they could be derogated from under EU copyright contract law. However, it should be checked if Member States have extended this mandatory nature also to the national transposition norms of Artt. 18 and 22.[42] Moreover, it seems likely that if Art. 18 DSMD was not observed in a license contract with an author, the contract adjustment mechanism of Art. 20 DSMD is even more likely to apply, as the original remuneration will even more likely turn out to be 'disproportionately low' – in this case the author will have a claim to an increase of their remuneration to an 'appropriate and fair' level nevertheless. 41

VIII. Conclusion

In Art. 18 et seqq. DSMD, the EU legislator has established a number of rules in favour of authors vis-à-vis their contractual partners which shall serve to improve the legal and economic situation of authors who are considered as the structurally weaker parts in copyright contracts. It has been upon the Member States to transpose these rules into their respective domestic legislation and it will be upon the national courts to clarify the number of indeterminate legal terms used. Finally, clarification may need to come from the European Court of Justice as these rules will need to be interpreted autonomously under EU law. 42

C. Challenges in applying these rules on games

In the last years, games have played an ever greater role in the concert of the different media, both with regards to numbers of users and economically. However, it seems that the games industry has not had much contact with the rules of copyright contract law so far: There are neither major court decisions to report, nor have the different legislators 43

[42] For the respective national transposition laws see, e.g., for France Art. L. 131-5-3 Code de la propriété intellectuelle (French IP Act), for Germany Sec. 32 (3), 32a (3), 32d (3) and 41 (4) Urheberrechtsgesetz (German Copyright Act) respectively; for the Netherlands Art. 25h Auteurswet (Dutch Copyright Act).

on the Union or the Member States level paid much attention to games nor is there much legal literature to be found dealing with this topic.

44 At first sight, this comes as a surprise, as already in 2014, in its *Nintendo* decision, the European Court of Justice (CJEU) found that (video) games

> constitute complex matter comprising not only a computer program but also graphic and sound elements, which, although encrypted in computer language, have a unique creative value which cannot be reduced to that encryption. In so far as the parts of a videogame, in this case, the graphic and sound elements, are part of its originality, they are protected, together with the entire work, by copyright.[43]

45 In the present context, this means that games – despite their technical nature as a computer program (code) – do not fall under the exception of Art. 23 (2) DSMD, but Title IV Chapter 3 of the DSM-Directive is generally applicable to them, at least as far as not specifically their code elements are concerned.[44]

I. Peculiarities in the games industry

46 At a second glance, however, it becomes clear that there are some peculiarities in the games industry that make the actual application of Artt. 18–23 DSMD to games difficult. As these peculiarities and their impact on copyright are described in this handbook in more detail elsewhere,[45] suffice it to point out the following key points:

47 Compared to other media, the **production of games** is characterised by a number of special features, e.g., with regard to the number and the location of the participants, which can go into the hundreds or even thousands of contributors, often working remotely from other countries and sometimes literally from all over the world. The characteristics of their respective contributions differ from other media due to the different parts to be combined for the production of a game. The complexity of the contributors' interaction is often extremely high, e.g., in constellations where different partworks of a game need to be aligned, which often requires intensive cooperation and iterative works steps from the contributors involved. These special features often make it difficult to assess who is technically speaking a creator of which part of a game and whether this leads to authorship in the legal sense. When it comes to '**games as a service**', which are never 'complete', but are permanently developed further and further on an ongoing basis, the situation becomes even less clear, as existing works are constantly changed, amended or even overwritten, and it is hard to 'freeze' a specific 'state of play' where labels of authorship can be attached to the different bits and pieces.

48 The same applies to the **use of games**, in which the player is always involved interactively, albeit to varying degrees. In contrast to more traditional media where the 'user' is rather a 'consumer', who takes in a piece of content unilaterally presented to them, in the games context, the user is rather a 'player', who interacts with the content. The span of such interaction can reach from the player merely making a couple of simple moves from a predefined set of moves to numerous players interacting independently in a game environment to constellations where players even contribute to the content by creating new 'worlds' or at least new items themselves. Obviously, in the last two scenarios, it is also the players who have an impact on the game and how it looks like (for a given player) at a given moment.

---

[43] CJEU, 23.1.2014 – case C-355/12 – *Nintendo*, ECLI:EU:C:2014:25, mn. 23.

[44] Art. 23 (2) DSMD refers to Art. 2 of the Directive 2009/24/EC.

[45] See §§ 12 - 14.

Another topic to consider is the variety of existing **monetisation models** with their different focuses on distribution and/or marketing revenues in one or more specific countries, the European Union or even globally. All of this can also have an impact on how the works are utilised and which revenues are generated. 49

II. Rules on copyright contract law shaped by traditional use cases

An assessment of the rules on copyright contract law in the DSM-Directive shows that they have obviously been drafted in the light of traditional use cases. It is noteworthy that the word 'game' is not mentioned in the Directive and its Recitals.[46] 50

It can also be seen that the Articles are basically based on a scenario where one author creates one work and licenses this to one other person who afterwards exploits this work commercially and derives revenues from this. Such is the case, for example, in the book publishing industry, where (often) one author writes a book, 'sells' it to a publisher which publishes it and generates sales revenues. Here, **licensee fees at a certain percentage** of the net copy price of the book are due to the author, and the publisher generally is in a position to provide information about the number of book copies sold and revenues generated for any given period. From the legal concept, it is accordingly relatively simple to base claims for participatory remuneration on these revenues generated from one exploiter with the exploitation of one work from one author. 51

Things are a little **more complex** where the number of authors and works increases and the revenue channels do as well. Think, e.g., of a five-person (A, B, C, D and E) music band which records a song that has been composed jointly by three band members (A, B and C) and texted by C and D, whereas in the video A has been replaced by guest musician F. It is clear that these musicians will have different claims against their publisher and the label, according to the involvement in the creation of the respective works. However, it should still be possible to apply Art. 18 et seqq. DSMD to such a scenario. 52

Even more complex could be a movie with a handful of main character actors, some supporting actors and a large number of statists plus the staff behind the camera (script writer, director, camera people, cutters, sound engineers, light technicians, make-up artists, designers etc.). It is obvious that assessing the appropriate remuneration for each of these people is difficult and will certainly lead to discussions not only with the movie producer as exploiter but also among the creative staff involved themselves. 53

Considering the specificities of the games industry mentioned above, it is clear that the rules on **copyright contract law** are hardly fit for **possible claims of creative staff** involved in the development and production of a large game: There are generally too many people involved with too many different roles interacting too closely to sort out who did what, etc. 54

III. Applying copyright contract law on games – a cautious look into the future

Despite the difficulties sketched out above and although there is apparently no case law, claims under copyright contract will certainly be raised also in the games industry one day or the other. Moreover, the transparency obligation in Art. 19 DSMD is applicable even without authors asking for information. It is therefore necessary to have a closer 55

---

[46] Whereas 'audio' is mentioned 16 times, 'video' 9 times, 'film' twice and 'book' once.

look at the possible implications of Art. 18 et seqq. DSMD in the games industry. Taking into account experiences from other industries and from national jurisprudence, one might expect the following.

1. Art. 18 DSMD

56 The principle of appropriate and proportionate remuneration applies whenever authors grant exclusive rights for the exploitation of their works. This is also the case in contracts between publishers and creative people in the games industry.

57 In order to have a reliable basis to argue which remuneration may be appropriate and proportionate in the specific case, it certainly makes sense, from a general perspective, to have a true and realistic description of the agreed work in the underlying contract. In this respect, the scope of the work to be delivered, the level of cooperation and interaction of the author with other creative personnel, and the publisher's right, if any, to alter or amend the works should be defined. The same can be said for the scope of rights to be granted: If (exceptionally) no exclusivity of rights needs to be granted, the contract will be out of the scope of Art. 18 DSMD anyway. But it can also make a difference for the remuneration if a total buyout of rights is agreed or just a small catalogue of specific rights, depending on the publisher's use case.

58 Although lump sum payments are viewed critically by the EU legislator,[47] it seems indispensable that most people involved in the production of a game are paid a fixed amount of money without a revenue share. While such revenue shares may make sense with regard to certain prominent contributors to the entire game as such, they will not be manageable for the sheer mass of hundreds or thousands of creators in the 'engine room' of the game production. It is advisable to document internally why certain levels of creative staff may receive a revenue share and why – and which – others do not.

59 There is data available, at least for the German market in earlier years, that remuneration in the games industry was significantly higher than in other creative industries.[48] To the extent that this is (still) the case (throughout the European Union), such data will also help to establish appropriateness of a given remuneration. Parties should therefore research for respective data in the market.

60 Under German law, on the basis of a specific provision in the Copyright Act,[49] there is a tendency to **treat employed authors differently from freelance authors**. This is because an employment relationship offers social security to the author and generally puts more obligations on the publisher as an employer, which, in turn, makes it acceptable that the wages seem appropriate per se as a remuneration (also) for the rights granted for works created in the course of the employment.[50] In contrast, the publisher's relation to a freelance author is considered to be different with less security and a different understanding of the remuneration paid for the grant of rights in the works. It is not clear if this concept could also be argued under EU law,[51] but it seems possible that employment relationships with the core team for a game production may offer more stability and thus by nature fewer risks of copyright contract litigation.

---

[47] Cf. Rec. (73) Sentence 2 DSMD.

[48] See details from Oehler, in Brauner/Brauneck, Chapter 6 mn. 180 et seqq.

[49] Sec. 43 UrhG.

[50] BT-Drs. IV/270, 62.

[51] Especially as Rec. (72) DSMD also mentions 'employment contracts' but obviously in a different context.

2. Art. 19 DSMD

The obligation contained in Art. 19 (1) DSMD to provide up-to-date, relevant and comprehensive information on the exploitation of the authors' works at least once a year is generally also applicable in the games industry. As to the scope of the information to be provided proactively, i.e., even without authors having asked for it, the legislator has given some guidance in Rec. (74) et seqq. DSMD, which makes it generally advisable to align the practice with the specifications contained therein. **61**

Due to the specific complexities of this sector, however, it seems to be especially challenging for exploiters and their (sub-)licensees to fulfil the obligations properly. But from a general perspective, the legislator has accepted a specified sector approach in Rec. (77) S. 1 DSMD, although no explicit reference to the games sector was made: **62**

When implementing the transparency obligation provided for in this Directive, Member States should take into account the specificities of different content sectors, such as those of the music sector, the audiovisual sector and the publishing sector, and all relevant stakeholders should be involved when deciding on such sector-specific obligations.

Accordingly, the exceptions stated in Art. 19 DSMD may play an important role in properly fulfilling the information obligation in practice. **63**

According to Art. 19 (4) DSMD: **64**

Member States may decide that the obligation set out in paragraph 1 of this Article does not apply when the contribution of the author or performer is not significant having regard to the overall work …

This exception to the rule, which is supported by the second sentence of Rec. (77) ('Where relevant, the significance of the contribution of authors … to the overall work … should also be considered.'), covers cases of insignificant contributions to an overall work. The authors of these do not need to receive said regular information. In the game production this exception may apply to authors whose contribution is limited to pieces which are either very small or a commodity or lack significance for other reasons. As the legislator has not defined (in-)significance here in more detail, it seems fair to assume that it can be argued on all relevant levels, e.g., content-wise ('contribution is not important for the game') or commercially ('contribution is not important for exploitation of the game'). Although it may not always be easy to draw an exact line here, it seems also reasonable to apply this exception to the majority of 'background content' of a game.[52] **65**

The counter-exception is contained in the last half-sentence of (4) which deals with authors' requests for information in order to exercise their rights under Art. 20 (1) DSMD. But this is a counter-exception that requires a claim raised by an author and does not affect the (non-) obligation to grant information without request. **66**

In addition to (4), a more general exception to the information obligation may be derived from (3): **67**

The obligation set out in paragraph 1 shall be proportionate and effective in ensuring a high level of transparency in every sector. Member States may provide that in duly justified cases where the administrative burden resulting from the obligation set out in paragraph 1 would become disproportionate in the light of the revenues generated by the exploitation of the work or performance, the obligation is limited to the types and level of information that can reasonably be expected in such cases.

According to the first sentence, the obligation to inform shall ensure a high level of transparency, which underlines the need for a certain level of information provided. But **68**

---

[52] For a similar discussion re press publications under the German transposition law (Sec. 32d UrhG) see Soppe/Fuchs AfP 2021, 487 mn. 47 et seqq.

on the other hand, the legislator recognises the principle of proportionality also in the present context, which means that information that is not proportionate does not have to be granted.

69 More specifically, the second sentence accepts that Member States may take the 'administrative burden' from the information obligation into account and limit the 'types and level of information' to a reasonable scope. From the wording and its reference (again) to the principle of proportionality, it seems that even a 'reduction to zero' regarding the types and level of information is possible, i.e., to entirely refrain from providing information in the respective cases, but it is necessary to refer to the respective Member States' national laws anyway in this context as this exception requires a respective provision in their internal legislation.[53] In contrast to (4), though, such exception seems to require an economic assessment as disproportionality is referred to here only 'in the light of the revenues generated by the exploitation'.

70 Paragraph (5), finally, contains a further possible deviation from the information obligation in (1) in cases where collective bargaining agreements exist that contain transparency rules. However, no such agreements are apparent for the time being.

3. Art. 20 DSMD

71 The contract adjustment mechanism of Art. 20 (1) DSMD may also apply to the games industry. The mechanism's general concept of an author's remuneration turning out to be 'disproportionately low' in the light of the revenues generated from the exploitation of the works can meet respective cases also in the games industry.

72 From a practical perspective, as with regards to Art. 18 (1) DSMD,[54] also in the context of Art. 20 (1) DSMD it is advisable that the contractual basis between author and exploiter is set out diligently in order to have clarity of the respective contributions. This basis should also be monitored over time and amended appropriately, if necessary. This may help reduce the risk of discussions about the scope of the author's work.

73 If the exploiter's revenues appear to be so high that a possible contract adjustment appears to come into view, specific attention should be paid to the question of causality between the author's work and the exploiter's revenues. This is because the contractual adjustment, if any, shall cover a disproportion between the original remuneration and the revenues 'derived from the exploitation of the works'. Accordingly, **causality** must be established between the **works** on the one hand and the **revenues** on the other hand. This may be a complex task in the games industry, where the exploitation of works is much more differentiated than, e.g., in the book publishing business.[55] And certainly not all contributions from authors will play a role for the possible success of a game, especially not insignificant ones in the sense of Art. 19 (4) DSMD.[56] Therefore, causality between works and revenues is crucial for a contract adjustment.

74 Another important topic to consider in practice is the **timeline**: As the contract adjustment under Art. 20 (1) DSMD requires a claim to be raised from the author, the general prerequisites for claims apply. This also includes the statute of limitations which follows general rules in the absence of specific laws. It is therefore advisable that an author keeps an eye on the information provided by their contractual partner in accordance with Art. 19 (1) DSMD and on the market generally and acts without delay in case of possible claims for adjustment. Otherwise, it might happen that claims, if any, have been

[53] Germany has made use of this exception in Sec. 32d (2) No. 2 UrhG.
[54] Cf. above mn. 54 et seqq.
[55] See above mn. 49 et seqq.
[56] See above mn. 22.

time-barred at least for certain periods in the past and may no longer be raised successfully. In contrast, exploiters that are confronted with claims for contract adjustment should assess if these claims might fall under the statute of limitations. In German court cases under Sec. 32a UrhG, the national equivalent to Art. 20 (1) DSMD, related questions have played, and are playing, a significant role.[57]

4. Art. 21 DSMD

Art. 21 DSMD with its obligation for the Member States to provide for the possibility to submit disputes in the context of Artt. 19 and 20 DSMD to a voluntary, alternative dispute resolution procedure generally does not seem to entail specific obligations for the parties to copyright contracts as such but may provide them with additional possibilities to resolve their disputes. This is also true for the games industry, where legal subjects may make use of such a possibility, however without any obligation to do so. 75

5. Art. 22 DSMD

Finally, also the revocation right in Art. 22 DSMD generally is applicable in the games industry. However, it seems that there are not many specificities in this respect: If exclusive rights in their work have been granted by an author and the work is not exploited properly in the next years, the author may revoke their rights or the exclusivity of these rights. On the basis of the fast-moving games industry it already seems hard to see that there may often be a time-lag of several years between the acquisition of certain exclusive rights and their probably exploitation. In other words: If exclusive rights have been acquired, they will mostly be exploited rather quickly – and if they will not, it seems rather improbable that they might be exploited only in later years. 76

Against this background, it seems necessary to be aware of this revocation right. And it seems advisable for exploiters to internally document the reasons why certain exclusive rights, if any, have not been exploited to counter any possible revocation claims in the future. 77

6. Conclusion

Although the European legislator obviously did not have the games industry on its mind when adopting Art. 18 et seqq. DMSD, these rules on copyright contract law generally also apply to games. Some specificities of games, however, lead to difficulties in their application and leave room for argumentation. Nevertheless, the games industry should also be prepared for **possible claims** under the Member States' respective transposition laws. 78

[57] Cf. inter alia, BGH.5.2012 (I ZR 145/11), WRP 2013, 65, mn. 28 et seqq. – Fluch der Karibik.

§ 16
Music in Games

Bibliography: Bouvery, Les contrats de la musique, 8th edn, Paris, 2022; Chabaud et al., Droit de la Musique, Issy-les-Moulineaux, 2016; Chabaud, La musique à l'image, Paris, 2023; Ficsor, Collective Management of Copyright and Related Rights, 3rd edn, Geneva, 2022; Koskinen-Olsson/Lowe, Management of Copyright and Related Rights in the Field of Music, Geneva, 2012; Uchtenhagen, Copyright Collective Management in Music, Geneva, 2005.

A. Introduction 1

B. Foundations of music rights 3
- I. Historical foundations of musical rights in Europe 3
- II. Key stakeholders and ecosystem 6

C. Legal frameworks and core rights 8
- I. Authors' rights 9
- II. Related rights 14
- III. A practical application 19

D. Original music vs. licensed music 20
- I. Original music 21
  - 1. Essential contractual provisions 23
  - 2. European and American systems comparison 30
- II. Licensed music 33

E. Emerging issues and contemporary challenges 34
- I. CMOs, direct licensing and territories 34
  - 1. Purpose of CMOs and role in the gaming industry 35
  - 2. Enforceability of direct licences 40
  - 3. Potential approaches 44
- II. Impact of new technologies and business models 47
- III. AI-generated music 50

F. Frequently asked questions 55
- I. Short excerpts and modifications 56
- II. Split ownership and licensing complexities 59
- III. Music and video streaming 63
- IV. Music and UGC 66

A. Introduction

1 Music rights have a **long-standing history**, deeply rooted in both cultural and legal traditions. However, as new technologies have emerged, the way these rights are applied and understood has undergone significant transformation. Video games, as an innovative medium, present **unique challenges** to the established frameworks of music rights. Unlike traditional audiovisual works, video games demand interactive and adaptive soundtracks, blurring the lines between pre-recorded compositions and real-time generation. The relationship between music and gaming is **multifaceted**: soundtracks serve not just as background elements but as key components of storytelling, emotional engagement, and player immersion. From the early days of 8-bit MIDI recordings of public domain compositions to today's fully orchestrated scores and licensed pop hits, music in games has evolved alongside the industry, becoming a cornerstone of its creative expression, to the point that there is now a Grammy Award for 'Best Score Soundtrack for Video Games and Other Interactive Media'. In this context, the monetary value of music in video games has significantly increased, the business around it has immensely densified, and the legal challenges have become extremely **complex**.

The **global nature** of video game development adds another layer of complexity to music rights. A single video game might be developed in Japan, feature music composed in France, and the game be distributed globally. This interconnectedness brings multiple legal systems into play, each with its own copyright laws, licensing practices, and enforcement mechanisms. Navigating these **diverse systems** requires not only legal expertise but also practical strategies to harmonise **conflicting rules**. 2

B. Foundations of music rights

I. Historical foundations of musical rights in Europe

The legal **recognition of musical authorship** in Europe can be traced to the broader emergence of authors' rights in the late 18th and early 19th centuries. The Enlightenment's emphasis on individual creativity and expression, alongside the rise of a commercial music industry, prompted new legal frameworks that aimed to protect the moral and economic interests of composers. In France, the revolutionary period laid crucial groundwork: The decree of 19.7.1793 marked early legislative efforts to secure composers' rights to their works, recognising music as a form of intellectual creation deserving of exclusive rights. During the 19th century, the protection of musical rights in Europe began to institutionalise. One landmark development was the founding of the Société des Auteurs, Compositeurs et Éditeurs de Musique (SACEM) in France in 1851. SACEM introduced a collective management model that enabled authors to licence performances and collect royalties more effectively.[1] This approach soon influenced other jurisdictions, with comparable societies emerging across Europe, including PRS in the United Kingdom (1914) and GEMA in Germany (1933). These organisations became essential intermediaries in the licensing and enforcement of rights, especially in an era of rapid technological change marked by the proliferation of public concerts and phonographic reproduction. 3

A major milestone in the **cross-border recognition** of musical rights was the Berne Convention for the Protection of Literary and Artistic Works, adopted in 1886, which gradually formed the cornerstone of international copyright law. Over subsequent decades, European countries implemented the Berne standards through national legislation, fostering greater legal uniformity across the continent. The second half of the 20th century witnessed a shift from national to supranational governance of musical rights: the establishment of the European Economic Community and, later, the **European Union facilitated** the emergence of **a harmonised body** of copyright law. Key directives such as Council Directive 92/100/EEC (on rental and lending rights and on certain rights related to copyright), Directive 2001/29/EC (the InfoSoc Directive), and more recently, Directive 2014/26/EU (on collective rights management) and Directive 2019/790/EU (on copyright and related rights in the digital single market) have aimed to build a coherent digital copyright regime across Member States. 4

While composers' rights were established relatively early, the recognition of **rights for performers and phonogram producers** developed more slowly. Throughout much of the 19th and early 20th centuries, performers lacked formal legal protection for their artistic contributions. However, the rise of sound recording technology and the commercial exploitation of recorded performances highlighted the need for a legal framework. The turning point came with the Rome Convention of 1961, which extend- 5

[1] Ficsor, pp. 15–18.

ed international protection to performers and phonogram producers. This is the first multilateral treaty to recognise so-called neighbouring rights (or related rights), distinguishing them from traditional authors' rights. European countries began adapting their national laws to implement these provisions, although the scope and strength of protection varied widely across jurisdictions. Subsequent developments at the EU level helped harmonise performers' and producers' rights. Directive 2001/29/EC reinforced the rights of communication to the public and making available, while Directive 2006/115/EC codified rental and lending rights in connection with related rights. Finally, Directive 2011/77/EU extended the term of protection for performers and producers to 70 years, while Directive 2019/790/EU was a major milestone in harmonising authors' and related rights' legal status.

II. Key stakeholders and ecosystem

6 The key aspect of the complexity surrounding music rights is the multiplicity of rights at stake, and hence of rightsholders. While incorporating a car in a video game generally takes one licensing agreement, doing the same with what is usually referred to as a 'song' can – literally – involve a dozen agreements. This is because, **legally speaking, a 'song' does not exist**. What you hear when listening to music, especially contemporary music, is a combination of different rights, owned or administered by different rightsholders and stakeholders. They collaborate and sometimes compete, especially when dealing with high-profile soundtracks. It can be roughly summarised as follows and will be developed later:

1. **Authors' Rights** are protecting composers, lyricists, and publishers. The ground for these rights is the *creation* of music. Whether one writes down lyrics in a booklet or whistles a melody in a voice recorder: this is the birth of authors' rights.
2. **Related Rights** cover performers and producers. This is all about *performing*. If I record myself singing a very rough version of my national anthem, and publish it on an obscure website, I am already protected by related rights.

7 It is essential to bear in mind that even **where one party fulfils multiple roles** – for example, an individual acting as composer, lyricist and performer, or a company serving both as producer and publisher of a musical work – the **underlying rights remain distinct**.

C. Legal frameworks and core rights

8 The fragmentation of musical rights does not stop here. Within each of these two main types of rights (authors and related), **several types of 'acts' are at stake**. And each jurisdiction has its own sensibility when it comes to qualifying such acts in terms of legal application. We will try to find a jurisdiction-agnostic description of the key underlying rights within each category.

I. Authors' rights

Authors' rights originate from an **act of creation** such as the writing of lyrics or of a melody.[2] In the European Union they exist from the moment of said creation (*ab initio*) and last for the duration of copyright protection, which is **70 years from the death of the author** (or the last surviving author if applicable) in regard to economic rights – and not subject to prescription when it comes to moral rights.[3] They protect the ones that are involved in the act of creation of a musical **composition** (which itself is defined by the combination of a melody, a rhythm and a harmony) and of **lyrics** (whether original lyrics or adapted lyrics) but also to some extent (depending on the level of creative activity) **arrangements**. 9

These **creators generally delegate** the management of their rights to third parties. 10

The first category of these administering entities are the music **publishers**: Creators and publishers enter individual contracts whereby the creators grant the publishers a (generally exclusive) mandate to administer the commercial life of the musical composition or lyrics. Each has obligations towards the other, and the revenue generated is split according to one or more distribution key(s).[4] 11

The other category is composed of **collective management organisations** (CMOs) which serve the purpose of mutualising the resources to protect these rights, such as SACEM (France), GEMA (Germany) PRS-MCPS (United Kingdom) or ASCAP and BMI (USA). These entities' purpose is to utilise mutualised resources to grant licences and collect royalties at a large scale where individual collection would be practically impossible (radio broadcasts, concerts, music streaming or downloads, etc.) and redistribute the same to the rightsholders (publishers and authors).[5] 12

Authors' rights are, from a European point of view, **split between *economic rights*** (the right to benefit from the exploitation of your creation) **and *moral rights*** (the right to approve or disapprove the use of your creation). We will not focus on this distinction (as this split easily gets blurry in practice) but will rather describe the **categories of rights at stake** when using music for video games: 13

1. **Reproduction rights**. Ensuring music cannot be duplicated without permission. This is historically the most important economical right in terms of music as it was the one prohibiting the printing of musical scores, transcriptions and lyrics without a proper licence. Nowadays, this is the right that obliges you to obtain a licence in order to: incorporate a musical track within your video game build, print a physical medium of this game, but also to make a digital reproduction of this game, i.e., a download (a reproduction can be both tangible and intangible, as long as it is permanently available to the recipient).[6]
2. Communication to the public (or **representation or public performance) rights** are treated as synonymous in this chapter. This type of rights is a little less explicit and is more subject to interpretation but could be explained *negatively* as any act of distribution that is not a reproduction. Traditionally, it covers the interpretation of music to a public, such as concerts. With the rise of technology, it has covered radio, television and movie theatre broadcasts. It is now broadly admitted that music streaming services are *mainly* representing or publicly performing music (while mu-

[2] Chabaud et al., pp. 22–31.
[3] Chabaud et al., pp. 35–37.
[4] For a detailed overview of these agreements under the prism of French law, see Bouvery, pp. 20–80.
[5] See → mn. 34–46.
[6] Chabaud et al., pp. 56–59.

sic downloading services are doing acts of reproduction).[7] While there are debates, *streaming video games* (being understood as a simultaneity between the sending and receiving of the game content, with no permanent availability for the recipient) is generally analysed as an act of public performance or communication to the public, depending on the technical configuration.

3. **Making available to the public** is defined in the InfoSoc Directive as acts whereby works are made available 'in such a way that members of the public may access them from a place and at a time individually chosen by them' (Art. 3(1) InfoSoc Directive) and thus cover on-demand online offering. Its practical impact often overlaps with other rights (such as public performance) in day-to-day licensing practice and will thus not be detailed here.
4. **Synchronisation rights** are governing the use of music *in timed relation* to visual elements, which makes them a cornerstone of video game licensing. The legal basis of what is called 'synchronisation' can vary depending on the jurisdiction and there have been debates, for example in France, as to whether this is a moral right (allowing the creator to refuse the association between the music and an audiovisual work for any given reason),[8] a right to make derivative works, or an economical right (e.g., a dismemberment of the reproduction right, which is currently the dominant approach).[9] Regardless of the legal basis, it is commonly accepted that incorporating a musical work in a video game requires a synchronisation licence. Generally, it comes with a payment, reinforcing the impression that nowadays synchronisation is seen as an economical right. It is broadly admitted that it is up to the entity deciding to incorporate a musical track into a game (usually the developer) to obtain the synchronisation licence.
5. **Adaptation rights**. Covering derivative works, such as remixes or adaptations of music for gameplay (including making sure that the score can be adaptive depending on the player's behaviour). This is not the most challenging right at stake when it comes to using music in a video game, but it is to be considered, especially when drafting and negotiating contracts.

II. Related rights

14 **Related rights** originate from an **act of performance**, such as singing or playing instruments, hence the fact that they are often **referred to as performers**' rights.[10] Performance is the act of interpretation of a musical work, meaning that there cannot be a performance without a work (while there can be a work without interpretation). That does not mean that the musical work must be pre-existing, simply that someone *improvising* is both creating and performing at the same time. In the European Union (subject, for phonogram producers, to fixation) related rights exist from the moment of the performance and last for **70 years from the date of its recording** (or communication to the public).[11]

15 Aside from performers, related rights also cover a key category of rightsholders: the **producers** (or record labels). Producers are the ones that arrange, fund and take the re-

[7] Chabaud et al., pp. 66–67.
[8] Bouvery, pp. 279–281.
[9] Bouvery, pp. 277–278 ; Chabaud et al., pp. 73–74 ; Chabaud, pp. 161–166.
[10] Chabaud et al., pp. 39–43.
[11] Directive 2011/77/EU of the European Parliament and of the Council of 27.9.2011 amending Directive 2006/116/EC on the term of protection of copyright and certain related rights, Article 1(2)(a), OJ 2011 L 265, pp. 3.

sponsibility of the recording sessions, and through these acts obtain distinct rights from the ones of the performers. Like the relationship between the authors and publishers, performers and producers enter into individual agreements, setting forth the roles and responsibilities of both parties.[12] Generally, the producer funds the recording process, potentially grants an advance to the front artist(s), arranges practical aspects and – in exchange – will be the entity exclusively responsible for the commercial exploitation of the outcome (excluding in relation to authors' rights, which remain administered by the applicable publisher). Revenue generated is generally split according to one or more distribution key(s).

It is worth mentioning that, depending on their size and network, producers sometimes enter into agreements with **distributors**:[13] Their responsibility is to use their local or international networks to make sure that the recordings will be widely available to the public, in exchange for a cut of the revenue generated. 16

As for **collective management**, it does exist in the context of related rights,[14] but this section will not develop this aspect as it is not a current challenge for the video game industry yet. 17

Producers are indeed, in most cases, the stakeholders capable of granting all necessary licences to incorporate (i.e., synchronise) the recording itself into video games and to distribute (i.e., reproduce and represent) them. 18

III. A practical application

A practical illustration of the above-mentioned principles can be found in the following scenario: A video game **developer intends to incorporate** into its game a **musical recording that is a duet cover**, performed by two artists. The licensing requirements in such a case are multifaceted and span several rightsholders and categories of rights: 19

1. **Synchronisation of the original composition**: The developer must obtain synchronisation licences to pair it with the video game. This entails securing rights from: **Publisher A**, representing the lyricist; and **Publisher B**, representing the melodist.
2. **Synchronisation of the new arrangement**: The cover artists have substantially rearranged the original song. As such, they are entitled to authors' rights arising from their creative input. Accordingly, the developer must also obtain synchronisation licences from: **Publisher C** and **Publisher D**, representing each one of the cover artists.
3. **Master recording rights**: To integrate the actual sound recording of the duet into the video game, the developer must secure master use licences from: **Producer A** and **Producer B**, the record labels of the two cover artists (this time, as performers).
4. **Reproduction and public performance rights**: While the synchronisation rights are necessary, using a musical work in a video game for commercial distribution may also trigger reproduction and representation rights, depending on the distribution technology (physical, downloading or streaming). Consequently, the developer (or the video game publisher) may also be required to obtain a licence from **the relevant CMO** in every country where the game is distributed.[15]
5. The use of a single musical track requires, in this example, licences from at least 6 rightsholders (Publishers A–D and Producers A–B) and potentially more (CMOs).

---

[12] For a detailed overview of these agreements under the prism of French law, see Bouvery, pp. 109–186.
[13] For a detailed overview of these agreements under the prism of French law, see Bouvery, pp. 209–220.
[14] Koskinen-Olsson/Lowe, pp. 48–64.
[15] This specific issue of licensing through CMOs will be discussed in greater detail in → mn. 34–46.

D. Original music vs. licensed music

20 There are two main ways to ensure that a video game incorporates the appropriate musical soundtrack: **commissioning** the creation of original music and **licensing** pre-existing musical tracks. A video game soundtrack can consist of a mix of these. Both options address specific needs and come with unique stakes and challenges.

I. Original music

21 The commissioning of original music – or modern adaptations of public domain works (such as *Korobeiniki* in *Tetris*) – has been a longstanding practice in the video game industry. In contrast, the licensing of pre-existing commercial music is a relatively recent development. Commissioning typically involves defining the terms under which a completely **new musical soundtrack** will be composed and recorded **specifically for a particular video game**. The resulting work is usually tailored to match the game's narrative, aesthetic universe and gameplay mechanics.

22 While such compositions may at times be created internally by employees under employment agreements, this section focuses on scenarios where **the task is outsourced to an independent contractor**. This external contributor is generally referred to as a *composer* – a term that will be used here for convenience, though the individual may simultaneously fulfil several roles, including lyricist, performer, executive producer or even conductor.

1. Essential contractual provisions

23 The creation of original music for video games is typically governed by an **outsourcing agreement**, which revolves around **certain key legal and operational stakes**.

24 **Creative process**: First, the agreement sets out the framework for the creative process. The composer undertakes to follow the creative direction provided by the video game developer. This may include compliance with editorial guidelines, adherence to musical references provided by a music supervisor (usually an employee acting as an artistic director), iterative revisions based on feedback, and adherence to formal or informal approval procedures.

25 **Delivery obligations**: Second, the agreement also addresses delivery obligations. The composer must conform to the stringent production and technical standards required for game development. These may include committing to delivering a specific duration of music by certain production milestones, providing audio files in agreed formats (e.g., stems, multitrack, high-resolution masters), and ensuring that all materials are usable within the game engine. A distinctive requirement in this context is that the music must be compatible with adaptive and interactive audio systems. This entails designing music in a way that allows the in-game soundtrack to respond dynamically to the player's actions and the gameplay environment.

26 **Use of third-party contributors**: Third, the agreement typically regulates the involvement of additional contributors. Composers rarely work in isolation and may rely on teams or subcontractors, such as orchestrators, session musicians, vocalists, studio technicians or mastering engineers. Game developers usually require the main contractor (i.e., the composer) to secure appropriate agreements with all such contributors. This includes ensuring they are compensated and that all rights – particularly copyright and related rights – are transferred or licensed in favour of the video game company to the extent permitted by applicable law.

Flexibility and modifications: The contract also provides mechanisms for modifying the scope of work. Given the inherent unpredictability of video game development, both parties often wish to stipulate the consequences of increasing or reducing the volume of music requested, or of early termination. These provisions aim to ensure commercial flexibility while preserving legal certainty. 27

Payment terms: Payment provisions are typically structured around production milestones. It is common practice to include an advance payment upon signature, followed by instalments tied to interim deliveries, and a final payment upon satisfactory completion of all contractual obligations by the composer. 28

Ownership and rights: Finally, the contract defines the ownership of intellectual property rights. It is standard industry practice for the video game developer to seek the broadest possible acquisition of rights, including all rights arising from the creative process. This ensures seamless commercial exploitation of the game and its soundtrack. Composers generally accept these terms, provided they are appropriately compensated. Such rights arrangements differ significantly between EU and US legal systems (→ mn. 30-32). 29

2. European and American systems comparison

In the United States, the principle of *work-made-for-hire* plays a central role. Under § 101 of the US Copyright Act, if a composer is employed directly or contractually as part of a work-for-hire agreement, the employer or **commissioning party is deemed** the legal author and **initial copyright holder**. This allows developers to immediately secure full control over the musical score, including both economic and moral rights (to the extent they exist under US law). 30

By contrast, **in most European jurisdictions**, particularly under the framework of continental European civil law, the concept of *work-made-for-hire* does not apply. Instead, the **composer is deemed** to be the original author and **initial rightsholder**, even when the work is created under commission. Moreover, moral rights – such as the right to attribution and the right to object to derogatory treatment – are inalienable. As a result, even where economic rights can be contractually transferred, the creator retains enduring personal rights over the work. 31

Due to these structural differences, **the licensing strategy** for original music in video games **diverges significantly across jurisdictions**. In the United States, commissioning parties typically acquire all relevant rights through a single agreement, ideally classifying the work as a '*work-made-for-hire*', often including an assignment of rights as a fallback. This ensures comprehensive control over synchronisation, reproduction, public performance, and adaptation. In Europe, the transfer of rights must generally be explicit, detailed, and limited to specific modes of exploitation. Broad or blanket assignments may be deemed invalid or ineffective. For example, under French law (Art. L. 131–3 of the Code de la propriété intellectuelle), each mode of exploitation must be individually mentioned, including territory, duration, and nature of the rights transferred. This requires a more granular and jurisdiction-sensitive approach when drafting outsourcing agreements for video game soundtracks. 32

II. Licensed music

Music licensing refers to the process of securing all necessary rights to incorporate **pre-existing musical recordings and compositions** into a video game, and to comply with the contractual obligations associated with these rights. This typically involves 33 obtaining licences from all relevant music publishers, record producers, and, sometimes, CMOs (see → mn. 8-19) taking into account the following:

1. **Licensing process**: The process generally begins with the development team compiling a 'wish list' – a selection of existing musical tracks that would ideally suit the video game's aesthetic and narrative – along with potential substitutes, should the preferred titles appear to be unavailable. The next step involves formulating the proposed licensing conditions, including the financial terms, scope of usage (e.g., in-game use only, promotional materials, specific activations), and territorial coverage. Thereafter, the developer (or an intermediary) identifies and approaches the applicable rightsholders – music publishers, producers, and other intermediaries – to initiate negotiations. Upon successful conclusion[16] of these negotiations the developer is authorised, through a variety of legal instruments, to incorporate the musical track into the game.
2. **Fixed fees vs. royalties**: A key negotiation point concerns the model of compensation. Historically, flat-fee licences predominated: The developer pays a one-time fee, either upon signing or upon release of the video game, irrespective of its commercial performance. This approach aligns with industry practice in other creative sectors, such as film and television production. Royalties remain the exception and are generally reserved for cases in which a musical track is central to the gameplay experience or a core component of the game's identity. In such cases, the parties may negotiate revenue-sharing mechanisms, including advances on royalties, minimum guarantees, per-player fees, or percentages of game revenues.
3. **Most Favoured Nation (MFN) clauses**: The inclusion of MFN clauses is common in licensing agreements. These provisions – often requested by the licensor but occasionally initiated by the licensee for efficiency purposes – originate from international law. In a licensing context, an MFN clause requires the licensee to grant the licensor terms that are no less favourable than those granted to any other similarly situated licensor, including larger or more prominent rightsholders. The purpose is to ensure parity and prevent preferential treatment. In practice, this means that if a better financial arrangement is offered to another licensor for the same category of rights, the licensee (i.e. developer) must extend the same terms to all other licensors falling within that category. The sole existence of such clauses has raised questions about potential antitrust practises.[17]

E. Emerging issues and contemporary challenges

I. CMOs, direct licensing and territories

34 Anyone operating video games and dealing with music licensing in recent years – particularly within the European Union – is aware that **one of the most complex aspects** lies in the collective management of rights. While obtaining individual licences from music publishers and record labels may require time and resources, the process remains relatively straightforward: the licensee and the licensor negotiate terms, providing a degree of commercial predictability. In contrast, collective management is

[16] See → mn. 59 for more details regarding what should be considered as a successful conclusion.

[17] Winston & Strawn LLP, 'Antitrust 101: Most Favored Nation Clauses' (Winston & Strawn LLP, no date) https://www.winston.com/en/blogs-and-podcasts/competition-corner/antitrust-101-most-favored-nation-clauses (last accessed: 30.6.2025).

characterised by opacity and limited institutional adaptation to the video game sector, contributing to significant legal, financial and operational unpredictability. This section aims to offer an understanding of the stakes involved.

1. Purpose of CMOs and role in the gaming industry

CMOs were originally created to perform functions that individual authors or music publishers could not practically execute on their own – namely, the collection of royalties across multiple territories and platforms.[18] An individual author or music publisher is typically unable to monitor and enforce its rights worldwide, 24 hours a day. Conversely, a music user – such as a radio broadcaster – cannot feasibly negotiate licences with every rightsholder prior to using a musical work. The solution was the development of CMOs: By pooling their resources, **rightsholders mandate these organisations to issue licences**, collect royalties, and redistribute payments globally. While the general principle is that mandates are granted voluntarily by rightsholders to the CMOs, notable exceptions exist in the form of mandatory or extended collective management.[19] 35

This mutualised structure was a powerful innovation in traditional broadcasting contexts. For video game developers and publishers, it can be frustrating because **obtaining direct licences** from authors or their music publishers **is *generally* feasible**. This is precisely what occurs in the context of synchronisation licences, where terms for both incorporation into the game build and commercial exploitation *can be* agreed upon upfront (this direct model offering clarity and efficiency). 36

However, **in practice**, rights managed by CMOs are frequently excluded from licensing agreements between game developer and music rightsholders. The consequence is paradoxical: Although the parties involved would be capable of concluding direct licensing deals for *all* necessary rights (synchronisation but also reproduction and representation), payments must still be routed through CMOs. CMOs deduct their operational costs from the collected sums before redistribution, thereby reducing the income ultimately received by the rightsholders – who might otherwise have been paid directly, in full, and without delay. 37

The reason for this is that it is common, especially in Europe, for CMOs to be granted an **exclusive mandate**. While Directive 2014/26/EU of the European Parliament and of the Council of 26.2.2014 (on collective management of copyright and related rights and multi-territorial licensing of rights in musical works for online use in the internal market) and its local implementations has led CMOs to offer *à la carte* membership, allowing members to exclude certain fields (such as interactive services) or territories from their exclusive mandate,[20] this possibility remains rarely used *de facto*. Consequently, most of the time, authors and music publishers are redirecting video game developers and publishers towards CMOs in order to fully secure the necessary rights, rather than granting direct licences. 38

This would be manageable for the video game industry were it not for the following double-edged issue. First **CMOs operate mostly[21] on a country-by-country** basis through monoterritorial licences – which has generated intense discussions and case law with regards to competition law in Europe and in the US.[22] This is particularly true 39

---

[18] Ficsor, pp. 13–21 ; Uchtenhagen, pp. 14–15.

[19] Ficsor, pp. 104–107.

[20] SACEM, 'Informations générales sur vos apports à la SACEM' (SACEM, no date) https://createurs-editeurs.sacem.fr/brochures-documents/informations-generales-sur-vos-apports-la-sacem (last accessed: 30.6.2025).

[21] With the noticeable exception of pan-European initiatives, see Koskinen-Olsson/Lowe, p. 45.

[22] Chabaud et al., pp. 287–297; Ficsor, pp. 49–66; Uchtenhagen, pp. 19–22.

for offline uses that encompass physical distribution of games. Second, **they generally do not provide public-facing tariffs for video games.**[23] This means that, in theory, releasing a video game could require obtaining a licence from each CMO (bearing in mind that there may be several competing CMOs within a single territory) in every country where the game is distributed. Furthermore, in the absence of preset tariffs, obtaining a licence would entail entering into complex financial and legal negotiations, which could take months – or even years – to conclude. Given that music downloading and streaming platforms took several years to secure such licences, with fully dedicated legal and business teams, it is safe to assume that no video game company can currently undertake this process for each game release.

2. Enforceability of direct licences

40 The above **does not prevent direct licences** from being granted by authors and music publishers to users. There are four main reasons for this: **First**, as mentioned some CMOs allow their members to exclude certain fields from their collecting mandate; **second**, some memberships are non-exclusive, allowing members to grant direct licences[24]; **third**, some CMOs do not administer certain typologies of rights (e.g., the United States-based ASCAP and BMI do not administer the reproduction right, but only the representation right); and **fourth**, some rightsholders do not adhere to the principle that collective management should prevail over their ability to grant direct licences to users.

41 In this context, it is important to understand that CMOs operate under **reciprocal agreements.**[25] For example, SACEM (France) grants licences and collects revenues within the French territory for the use of works by members of GEMA (Germany), redistributes the corresponding sums - alongside usage data – to GEMA, which in turn redistributes these foreign-collected sums to its members, and *vice versa.*

42 This has several practical consequences: It is difficult for a **local CMO** to oppose the enforceability of a direct licence when it was granted in accordance with the statutes of the **foreign CMO** from which it obtained the mandate to administer a catalogue. For instance, when a European CMO attempts to collect reproduction fees in connection with an American repertoire, the developer has most likely obtained a direct reproduction licence from the music publisher (as a member of ASCAP or BMI, the publisher has not granted an exclusive licence to these entities). The European CMO will be obliged to recognise that the direct licence is enforceable and should not collect on this ground.

43 In a nutshell, **if a direct licence is valid under the statutes** of the CMO to which the licensor originally belongs, it should be recognised by any local CMO attempting to collect based on this licence. This covers excluded collecting fields, non-exclusive memberships, and types of rights not administered by the original CMO. The situation is more complicated for cases where music publishers and authors grant **direct licences despite an exclusive mandate**: CMOs generally do not recognise such licences, leading to the application of standard contractual law, particularly with regard to representations and warranties granted by music publishers and authors to the game developer. The approach taken by national courts in dealing with such conflicts varies.

---

[23] For more details on the way tariffs are established see Uchtenhagen, pp. 59–76.

[24] A good example of this is the Finnish Teosto, which declares itself as having 'the most flexible membership agreement in the copyright world'. 'Join Teosto – membership' (Teosto) https://www.teosto.fi/en/members/join-teosto/#the-membership-does-not-apply-to (last accessed: 9.1.2026).

[25] Koskinen-Olsson/Lowe, pp. 23–24.

3. Potential approaches

In order to facilitate the use of music administered by CMOs in video games – something that has historically posed substantial legal and logistical challenges – a combination of complementary strategies may be employed. The first strategy involves **establishing and maintaining commercial relationships with at least one European CMO**. This enables streamlined licensing discussions and may facilitate the acquisition of broader licences. In practice, this implies negotiating licensing terms on a per-game, per-rightholder or per-composition basis, addressing financial conditions (typically based on proportionality, as flat-rate fees are generally avoided by CMOs) and defining the scope of authorisation, including territorial extent, duration and types of allowed uses. Licensing structures may be bipartite (between the CMO and either the game developer or publisher) or tripartite, involving the CMO, the music publisher and the game developer (or game publisher) in a single agreement.[26] The latter offers the advantage of unified licensing and greater legal predictability, though it often requires a greater investment in time and resources. **44**

The **second strategic avenue concerns industry-wide lobbying**, particularly through collective representation at both national and European levels. Lobbying efforts should focus on ensuring that local CMOs are equipped to issue – at least – pan-European and – ideally – global licences. Video game developers, publishers and their professional associations must also remain united in advocating for public-facing, transparent and reasonable licensing tariffs.[27] **45**

Moreover, the industry must engage in a **substantive discussion about which stakeholder(s)** – game developers, publishers, distributors, manufacturers or platform operators – **should assume primary responsibility** in licensing negotiations. Although European legislation generally assigns the obligation to obtain CMO licences to the entity responsible for acts of reproduction or communication to the public, this often varies by case and continues to prompt significant contractual debates. A unified stance within the industry would greatly enhance legal clarity and operational efficiency. **46**

II. Impact of new technologies and business models

The distribution of video games and the business models underpinning it have always been subject to evolution. However, recent years have witnessed an unprecedented acceleration in the development of new modes of making video game content available to the public. **Two pivotal transformations** stand out. The first is the **digitalisation** of distribution, which has gradually replaced cartridge-based media with optical discs and, more recently, with downloadable and cloud-based streaming formats. The second transformation concerns the emergence of **new business models**, including the free-to-play component – often reliant on in-app purchases and in-game advertising – and subscription services that provide users with access to a broad catalogue of games in return for a recurring, typically monthly, fee. **47**

One significant consequence for music licensing arises from the **sustainable nature of video games in the digital era**. Whereas physical-only distribution models historically confined a game's availability to a limited window – spanning only months or a few years – digitally distributed games are now potentially available for decades. This **48**

[26] Chabaud et al., p. 75; Chabaud, pp. 226–230.

[27] Historically, a noteworthy model has been the Canadian SOCAN's Tariff 22.G, which allows for near-instantaneous licence acquisition.

longevity, however, clashes with the often time-limited scope of music licences. As a result, video game developers and publishers are increasingly faced with the risk that a licence may expire while the game remains commercially active. The consequences of such expiry are non-trivial: they may include the need to renegotiate licences under potentially unfavourable terms, issue corrective patches that remove or replace the affected content, or, where no viable solution is found, terminate the game's distribution entirely. To mitigate these risks, contractual mechanisms should be designed with greater foresight. Licences may include renewal options exercisable by the licensee for pre-agreed fees or be structured for longer initial durations. Moreover, adaptive licensing language that contemplates future distribution technologies and platforms may help preserve legal certainty and commercial continuity across the lifespan of a game.

49 Another significant consequence is the need to adapt the financial provisions of licensing agreements to accommodate **emerging and evolving business models**. During the era when video game distribution was predominantly – if not exclusively – sales-based, licences granted by music rightsholders were typically acquired in exchange for a fixed fee per composition or recording. In some instances, these licences included an additional fixed sum per unit of the game sold. This framework facilitated relatively straightforward financial negotiations and led to clear contractual arrangements. By contrast, the rise of new business models has introduced greater complexity into licensing discussions. Music licensors increasingly seek compensation that reflects the actual revenue generated in-game, whether from microtransactions (e.g., in-game purchases), advertising income, or subscriptions. In the subscription context, revenue-sharing models may be linked to metrics such as the number of subscribers, the total revenue generated, or the greater of the two. This necessitates a more granular contractual treatment of key financial definitions, including the delineation of applicable revenue, the identification and justification of permissible deductions (e.g., operational or distribution costs), and the scope of exclusions (e.g., free or promotional access). To ensure enforceability and transparency, the involvement of sales, financial and accounting teams during the drafting and negotiation phases is strongly advised. Furthermore, it is prudent to include contractual safeguards for future monetisation models not explicitly foreseen at the time of contracting. This can be achieved through the inclusion of renewal options, revenue-sharing triggers, or at the very least, a commitment to engage in good faith negotiations should new business practices emerge. Such provisions ensure that the licensing framework remains adaptable and resilient in a context of continuous industry innovation.

III. AI-generated music

50 One of the highest-stake current challenges around music revolves around the use of artificial intelligence (AI). There are **several aspects where there is no current music-specific challenge**: the question of authorship and surrounding good practices is the same for music and other contents, the legal uncertainty about who is the author *ab initio*, the difference between the different jurisdictions' approach and the contractual good practices that should be employed to ensure the game developers' and publishers' peaceful commercial exploitation of AI-generated content. This section will focus on certain music-specific aspects, with the understanding that this sector is so fast-paced that the questions raised may become outdated in a very short timeframe.

51 A particularly sensitive aspect of AI-generated music lies in the **use of training datasets**. While the development of text-to-text models necessitates vast amounts of textual data – which can, at least in theory, be sourced without infringing copyright – this is far less straightforward in the musical domain. Most music that falls outside the scope of copyright protection tends to be very old, thereby offering limited creative value for training models intended to produce contemporary-sounding music. Similarly, sound recordings that are unprotected under performers' rights are either antiquated or fall under narrow exceptions. As a result, the availability of legally usable, high-quality datasets for AI developers aiming to generate modern-style music is severely constrained. This scarcity means that developing commercially viable music-generation tools likely required the use of protected content, raising the need for licensing agreements with music publishers and record producers, who were initially reluctant to license their catalogues for this purpose.

Given these constraints, it can be suspected that the most effective **music-generating AI models currently in circulation** may have been trained on datasets of uncertain or infringing provenance although major licensing deals have been recently announced. This exposes not only the tool providers, but also game developers, publishers, and all downstream entities involved in the commercialisation of video games containing such music, to potential legal liability – or at least unpleasant discussions. 52

Accordingly, legal counsels should advise extreme caution when incorporating AI-generated music into video games unless **proper licensing agreements** are secured. As a best practice, developers should rely only on AI music providers that offer clear contractual representations and warranties regarding the lawfulness of their training datasets. '*As-is*' licence models that both disclaim liability and fail to disclose dataset provenance should be avoided. Furthermore, agreements should include indemnification clauses protecting the licensee from third-party claims, along with audit rights where feasible. These steps are essential to mitigate exposure to both legal and reputational risks, particularly as regulatory scrutiny and enforcement efforts in this area continue to intensify. 53

Beyond its use in generating original compositions, artificial intelligence plays an increasingly critical role in the **adaptation and contextualisation of music** within interactive game environments. AI-driven systems can dynamically modify tempo, instrumentation, or intensity of musical elements in response to in-game variables such as player behaviour, narrative progression, or gameplay tempo. Additionally, AI may assist in scaling or versioning music assets to accommodate various phases of a game's lifecycle, from initial launch to live service updates and promotional campaigns. While such adaptive capabilities enhance player immersion and operational efficiency, they also present distinct legal challenges. First: the need to verify that the rights granted to developers by composers cover not only fixed and linear uses, but also algorithmically modified and context-sensitive adaptations. Depending on the jurisdiction and the licensing structure, such modifications could be considered derivative works or transformations requiring specific authorisation. Legal counsels should thus ensure that commissioning or licensing agreements include explicit language permitting adaptive and interactive uses, as well as technology-neutral definitions of reproduction, representation and adaptation rights. Furthermore, when AI is used to generate contextualised variations or remixes, game developers and publishers should consider implementing internal version control and metadata tagging protocols to distinguish between the original music used as input and AI-modified outputs. A robust audit trail – combined with contractual warranties from AI tool providers regarding lawful use and training datasets will be useful to mitigate downstream liability and ensure regulatory compliance. 54

F. Frequently asked questions

55 This final section aims to address frequently asked questions and widespread misconceptions in a practical manner. While the objective is to offer accessible guidance, it is important to recognise that certain legal subtleties may apply. These should be considered on a **case-by-case basis** by legal counsels responding to such queries, in order to ensure that advice remains contextually accurate and legally sound.

I. Short excerpts and modifications

56 A **persistent misconception** in music law is the **belief that there is a minimum threshold** – such as a specific number of seconds or musical notes – below which the unlicensed use of a musical work would not constitute infringement. This is incorrect. The decisive factor is not the duration or length of the excerpt, but rather whether an original and legally protected element has been used without proper authorisation. In the context of authors' rights, even a very brief excerpt – such as a two-second segment of a distinctive melody, particularly when accompanied by its underlying harmony and rhythm – may suffice to trigger copyright protection and, if reused without a licence, give rise to an infringement claim.

57 This standard is even more stringent in the domain of related rights. The **unauthorised sampling** of even a single piano note from a sound recording can constitute a violation of performers rights, which are typically owned or administered by a record label. The reproduction of any part of a phonogram – if recognisable – can infringe the phonogram producer's exclusive rights, regardless of the length or originality of the sample.

58 The same principle applies to **modifications and adaptations**. In legal terms, the issue is not how much the new work differs from the original, but rather whether elements of the original remain recognisable and distinctive. Legal counsels frequently encounter questions about how many notes or chords must be altered in a melody to 'avoid infringement'. Such inquiries are misguided. If the adapted work retains a recognisable, original segment of the source composition or recording, it may still constitute an infringing use. This principle is particularly true in the context of remixes or edits of existing recordings. While such processes may obscure the source material to some extent, the decisive criteria remains whether the rightsholder can demonstrate that elements of the original recording have been used. If so, the existence of technical alterations or creative additions will not shield the unauthorised user from liability.

II. Split ownership and licensing complexities

59 One very common issue in the music licensing process is: *what happens if I cannot identify a minor rightsholder?* Even if there are subtleties across jurisdictions, it is safe to say that as per intellectual property laws, joint ownership of a composition or musical recordings generally means that all co-authors or co-owners of the recording, or their rightsholders, must consent to the use of the work and recording (an exception to this rule has been endorsed in a limited context by the United States Department of Justice, however, this interpretation remains controversial and is jurisdiction-specific).[28] This means that obtaining a licence to use a composition in-game can involve more than

[28] Ficsor, pp. 63–64.

a dozen licensors' authorisations[29] (especially in modern era music) and that if one of the stakeholders is not identified, or declines granting the licence, the musical work – or recording – should not be considered as cleared. Even **a tiny unlicensed share can block the entire use** of the composition or recording. This is *practically* true even if *legally* inaccurate in some jurisdictions. In this regard, one good practice consists in making sure that all involved licensors represent and warrant that they own a given percentage of the musical piece, and that the total of the licence shares leads to a total of one hundred percent, or more. If, for any reason, a developer decides to incorporate music in a video game or marketing asset while there is an unlicensed minority share, another minimum good practice would be to document exhaustive efforts made to locate the minority rightsholder, secure warranties and indemnities from intermediaries (e.g., external music supervisors or platforms), and consider escrow arrangements (holding fees in escrow for the missing rightsholder) – while recognising that none of these fully eliminate the risk of litigation. Under no circumstances should a composition be included in a video game **if a rightsholder has expressly denied a licence**.

Changes in ownership of music rights can occur after a licence has been granted or even after a musical work has been incorporated into a video game. Such changes may result from catalogue acquisitions, legal settlements, rights reversion, or other industry transactions. Generally, these developments do not raise legal issues for game developers or publishers, as they are standard practice within the music industry. In most cases, the new rightsholder – whether of a composition, a recording, or a share thereof – will either notify the licensee (e.g., to redirect royalty payments) or take no action if the change has no practical impact (such as when a one-time licence fee has already been paid). To ensure legal certainty in these scenarios, it is strongly recommended that licensing agreements include a clause stating that the licence shall remain valid and enforceable against any successor-in-interest. This provision ensures that the licensee's rights are preserved regardless of any subsequent transfer of ownership, thereby protecting the game's ongoing distribution. 60

Disputes among music owners may arise, particularly when parties disagree over ownership or the allocation of rights shares in a musical work. Two primary scenarios should be distinguished. The first occurs in relation to recently composed or unreleased works, where ownership **splits are often still under negotiation** between authors, performers, music publishers and record labels. In such cases, if the complete list of stakeholders is mutually recognised and there is no objection to the use from any party, it may be considered reasonably safe to proceed with the licensing process, even if this results in over-clearing (i.e., exceeding one hundred percent) of the rights. To manage financial uncertainty and reduce exposure, a prudent measure is to establish an escrow mechanism, whereby payments are held until the licensors formally resolve their internal allocations. 61

The second, more problematic, scenario involves a **persistent and active dispute** between two or more entities claiming overlapping or conflicting ownership rights. In such circumstances, proceeding with the licensing or incorporation of the disputed musical piece is not advisable. The risk of becoming embroiled in third-party litigation or receiving conflicting claims – particularly regarding royalty entitlements or injunctions – far outweighs the potential benefits. As a matter of risk management, the music should be withheld from the game or marketing asset until the conflict is resolved or an unambiguous rights chain can be established. 62

[29] See → mn. 19.

III. Music and video streaming

63 One of the most current and complex challenges faced by legal professionals in the field of music licensing for video games relates to the use of music in connection with video streaming platforms. Commercial, marketing, and executive teams within game companies frequently raise questions, often under **the assumption that platforms** such as YouTube, Twitch, or TikTok **hold comprehensive licences** that fully cover music use. While this assumption holds *some* truth, it is also a significant oversimplification.

64 Indeed, many of these platforms have entered into agreements with CMOs, music publishers, and record labels. However, **these licences are typically limited in scope.** They often only cover certain rights – most commonly, performance and communication to the public rights, and sometimes only in certain territories. More importantly, they sometimes do not extend to synchronisation rights. Additionally, these licences generally exclude the right to associate music with third-party brands or trademarks, a common feature in marketing assets.

65 Therefore, from a legal standpoint, the mere fact that a video streaming platform holds licensing agreements **does not imply that game developers or publishers are free to use any music in their promotional content** on these platforms. At best, platform-level licences may cover a subset of rights thereby relieving the game publisher from obtaining separate clearance for those particular rights. However, legal counsels should carefully assess the specific type of music usage involved, verify the exact coverage of the platform's licensing arrangements, and, where needed, obtain separate synchronisation or promotional licences to ensure full compliance, from both music publishers and record labels.

IV. Music and UGC

66 User-generated content (UGC) has become **a defining feature of modern video games**, offering players greater creative freedom and extending the lifespan of games through community-driven content. As UGC evolves, music has emerged as a central – and increasingly sensitive – category. Legal teams are now frequently confronted with the question: *should players be permitted to incorporate their own music into the game environment?*

67 At a conceptual level, there is no legal distinction between music and other forms of UGC items, such as character skins or level designs. However, *in practice*, **music presents distinct** and **elevated legal risks**. Players often use UGC functionalities to recreate or upload well-known copyrighted tracks, believing such use will enhance the game experience or simply be fun. While their intentions may be benign, the use of unauthorised, third-party music – particularly popular commercial tracks – exposes the game publisher to serious risks, including takedown notices, content blocking, and legal claims from rightsholders.

68 To address these challenges effectively, legal counsels should consider the following **best practices**. First define and limit UGC scope for music in the end-user licence agreements and terms of services, declare if musical UGC items are permitted, and if so, under what conditions. Then explicitly prohibit the inclusion of copyrighted third-party music, implement content moderation and reporting tools and establish technical and procedural safeguards to identify and remove infringing content. This may include automated content recognition systems (such as audio fingerprinting), community flagging mechanisms and clear notice-and-takedown protocols. In cases where musical UGC

items poses high risk (e.g., in games targeted at young people or AAA games), consider restricting upload features altogether, or limiting them to pre-cleared music libraries or in-game creation tools that avoid copyright conflicts. Lastly, it is recommended to monitor high-risk behaviour and proactively track patterns where users consistently replicate famous songs, which may require targeted intervention or preemptive removal. By embedding these principles into the design of music UGCs, legal teams can better manage the compliance burden and help development and community teams support player creativity while limiting litigation exposure.

§ 17
EU Trademark Protection in and for Games

Bibliography: European Union Property Office (EUIPO), 'Guidelines for examination of European Union Trademarks', (2025). Rauda, Marken- und Werktitelrecht im Zusammenhang mit Computerspielen, in Hentsch/Falk (eds), Games und Recht, Baden-Baden 2023.

A. Introduction 1
B. Protection of video games' trademarks 3
I. The role and importance of trademark registration in the video game industry 3
II. Territory 8
III. Goods and services 10
IV. Subject of protection and statutory requirements 13
1. Eligibility for protection 13
2. Absolute grounds for refusal 14
3. Relative grounds for refusal 18
V. Types of trademarks commonly registered in the game development industry 23
1. Video game title 24
2. Game's logotypes and other symbols 26
3. Characters' names 27
4. In-game assets 28
5. Slogans 30
6. Non-conventional trademarks 31
VI. Registration Strategy 32
C. Use of third-party trademarks within video games 39
I. Scope of protection – the texts 40
II. Case law in the EU 46

A. Introduction

1 Trademarks play a **pivotal role** within the video game industry. They are important at each stage of a game lifecycle irrespective of the size of the video game company, type of game or business model chosen for its distribution. Among the key legal and strategic considerations in game development is the need to ensure that the game's trademarks are sufficiently protected and – conversely – that the game does not infringe third-party trademarks.

2 Although trademark law intersects with the video game industry in numerous ways, this chapter focuses on the **two aspects** that are likely of greatest practical importance to developers and publishers: the protection of one's own trademarks and the use of third-party trademarks within games.

B. Protection of video games' trademarks

I. The role and importance of trademark registration in the video game industry

3 Trademarks constitute **invaluable assets** for any company operating within the industry and their strategic registration serves multiple essential purposes.

4 Foremost, trademark registration confers the proprietor with the **exclusive right** to use the sign and prevent others from using the same or confusingly similar signs –

e.g., in titles or as a logo. As such, they may establish clear market distinction and build brand recognition and reputation among players. Of note, timely clearing and registering a title and logo mitigates the risk of having to change those key game's identifiers after their public announcement if another has registered or used an identical or similar sign before.[1]

Second, trademark registration provides broad legal **protection against a wide range** 5
of unfair activities by third parties – such as the use of confusingly similar video game titles, distribution of look-a-like video games or the production and sale of counterfeit merchandise.

Third, well-structured trademark protection **enhances the commercial potential and** 6
economic value of both the game and the studio behind its development – not only by facilitating licensing opportunities, but also by strengthening the studio's credibility in the eyes of potential investors or acquirers.

Finally, compared to other types of IP rights, trademarks stand out in their **high** 7
enforceability,[2] **transparency and accessibility of the registries** and **potential broad application.**[3] Furthermore, even though a trademark right is initially granted for 10 years, it can be renewed an unlimited number of times, offering the opportunity for perpetual protection – something that is just not available for other types of IP rights.

II. Territory

Trademark rights are inherently **territorial**, i.e., their protection is limited to the 8
geographic areas covered by a specific registration regime. While each country has its own trademark laws and registration system, there are also several regional systems – such as the EU one governed by EUTMR and administered by the European Union Intellectual Protection Office (EUIPO). Additionally, trademark owners can use the Madrid System to seek protection in multiple jurisdictions through a single international application.[4]

This chapter will be primarily **focused on EU regional registration** under EUTMR. 9
Having said that, given the substantial harmonisation of trademark laws at both EU[5]

[1] The industry has seen many cases of the games needing to change their titles, logos or other key assets due to collision with some earlier trademark registrations. One of the recent widely commented on examples was 'The Day Before' game being removed from Steam due to a trademark dispute with calendar app developer. See e.g.: https://www.pcgamer.com/following-a-trademark-dispute-with-a-calendar-beleaguered-zombie-survival-game-the-day-before-looks-like-its-getting-a-new-name-but-this-one-might-already-be-in-use-too/.

[2] Practical experience shows that having a strong trademark portfolio significantly facilitates enforcement against counterfeit and lookalike products – particularly because trademark ownership is generally easier to prove than copyright ownership, which is not registrable in most jurisdictions.

[3] For example, Nintendo-based lawsuits against ROM platforms i.a. on claims regarding the use of Nintendo marks: https://www.gamesindustry.biz/nintendo-gets-permanent-injunction-against-romuniverse-owner.

[4] The Madrid System is governed by the Protocol Relating to the Madrid Agreement Concerning the International Registration of Marks. Notably, as much as the international registration system streamlines the process of obtaining registrations on numerous territories, international registration does not directly result in trademark protection in countries covered by it. Each applicable national or regional trademark office will independently conduct examination and, if application is accepted, grant independent national or regional trademark registration rights.

[5] See: Directive (EU) 2015/2436 of the European Parliament and of the Council of 16.12.2015 to approximate the laws of the Member States relating to trademarks.

and international[6] levels, the key principles and practical insights discussed here may serve as a broader reference for video game companies.

III. Goods and services

10 The **scope of protection** granted by trademark registration is determined by the specific goods and services for which registration is granted.

11 The **list of goods and services** for each trademark registration is organised with the use of the Nice Classification[7] system which serves administrative and practical purposes.

12 A review of EU and national trademark registries in the EU shows that **video game companies most commonly register their trademarks in Class 9** (e.g., computer games, video games, software) **and Class 41** (e.g., online gaming services, entertainment services, esports event organisation). Other frequently used classes include Class 16 (e.g., posters, books), Class 25 (e.g., clothing, headwear, footwear), and Class 28 (e.g., toys, collectible figures, board games, playing cards).

IV. Subject of protection and statutory requirements

1. Eligibility for protection

13 Unlike some other trademark systems, the EUTMR does not restrict registration to pre-defined types of signs. Art. 4 EUTMR provides that a **trademark may consist of 'any sign'**, listing examples such as words, designs, numerals, colours, shape of goods etc. According to the same article, to be eligible for protection a sign must meet two basic prerequisites: it must be capable of distinguishing the goods or services of one undertaking from those of others (i.e., possess distinguishing character) and it must be representable on the Register[8] in a manner that enables the competent authorities and the public to determine the clear and precise subject matter of the protection afforded to its proprietor. The absence of either of these basic requirements constitutes an absolute grounds for refusal (→ Section 2 below) under Art. 7(1)(a) EURMR.

2. Absolute grounds for refusal

14 Absolute grounds for refusal are obstacles to trademark registration that are **systematically examined by the EUIPO**. All absolute grounds for refusal are listed in Art. 7 EUTMR. Given the scope of this publication, we will focus on those absolute grounds most relevant in practice for video game companies.

15 First, under Art. 7(1)(b) EUTMR, no registration is available for the signs which are **devoid of any distinctive character** (so-called non-distinctive trademarks). Unlike the distinguishing character from Art. 4 EUTMR, distinctiveness shall be assessed in relation to particular goods and services for which registration is sought and from the perspective of the relevant public's perception of a given sign. While even a minimal degree of distinctiveness suffices to overcome this absolute ground for refusal, trademarks of

---

[6] As a result of set of international regulations and agreements adopted over time, starting from the Paris Convention for the Protection of Industrial Property from 1883.

[7] Established by the Nice Agreement Concerning the International Classification of Goods and Services for the Purposes of the Registration of Marks of 15.6.1957, administered by WIPO.

[8] Register of European Union trademarks.

low distinctiveness will typically be considered weak[9] and be vulnerable to invalidation. A complete non-distinctiveness would occur i.a. in case of signs that are purely descriptive (see following paragraph), simple figurative elements (e.g., single lines, basic circle) or typographical symbols (e.g., single coma). In most cases, however, the threshold will not be clear-cut and that is even if the sign is very simple. An example that may be of interest for video game companies are slogans. According to established EU case law and EUIPO's practice, slogans shouldn't be assessed through any stricter criteria than other signs[10] but they can be registered as trademarks only if the relevant public would perceive them not only as a promotional statement but also as indication of origin, e.g., if they bear particular originality or constitute a play on words.[11] Registered examples include: Nike's 'Just do it' (EUTM 000514984), Adidas' 'Impossible is nothing' (EUTM 003049756) or McDonalds' 'I'm lovin' it' (EUTM 003196581). Among well-known slogans which were refused registration in the EU is, e.g., Mastercard's 'More than just a card'.[12]

Second, Art. 7 (1)(c) EUTMR prohibits the registration of trademarks consisting of signs or indications which may serve, in trade, to designate the kind, quality, quantity, intended purpose, value (…) or other characteristics of the goods and services. This ground targets so-called ***descriptive* signs** – those which the relevant public would immediately perceive as conveying information about the nature or qualities of the goods or services in question. To trigger this absolute ground for refusal, a sign must be entirely descriptive; therefore, trademarks that are merely suggestive or allusive or that contain only some descriptive elements, would still be eligible for protection. Marks that are merely suggestive, allusive, or that include only partially descriptive elements may still be registrable. Basic examples of descriptive trademarks in the context of video games include word signs like 'video game', 'game', or 'computer game'. Such terms clearly describe the product type and do not function as indicators of commercial origin. However, the situation is rarely such evident. For instance, registration of the 'EURO TRACK SIMULATOR' (EUTM 017656141) for 'computer games, online games, simulation games, imitation driving games' was originally refused by EUIPO due to the lack of distinctiveness.[13] A negative decision was also issued for the trademark 'Ultimate Fighting' (EUTM 002766590) in relation to i.a. computer games. On the other hand, the word trademark 'Saga' (EUTM 010452911) is currently registered in EUIPO i.a. for 'computer games' and in *Kalypso v EUIPO*[14] the General Court confirmed that both the word 'Dungeon' and 'Dragon' possess a minimum degree of distinctiveness in relation to computer games. **16**

Other absolute grounds for refusal refer i.a. to trademarks which consist exclusively of signs or indications which have become **customary in the current language** or **bona fide and established practices of the trade** (Art. 7(1)(d) EUTMR) or signs of **misleading character** (Art. 7(1)(g) EUTMR). **17**

---

[9] From a practical perspective, original and untypical trademarks generally offer broader protection, e.g., the trademark owner is generally able to successfully use such trademark to prevent other companies from using a broader range of similar trademarks while, in the case of trademarks that barely meet the distinctiveness requirements, competitors would most probably be able to use even very similar trademarks without facing the risk of being held liable for trademark infringement.

[10] CJEU 12.07.2012 – case C-311/11 P, *Smart Technologies ULC v OHIM*, ECLI:EU:C:2012:460.

[11] GC 13.04.2011 – case T-523/09, *Smart Technologies ULC v OHIM*, ECLI:EU:T:2011:175; CJEU 21.01.2010 – case C-398/08 P, *Audi AG v OHIM*, ECLI:EU:T:2011:175.

[12] EUIPO 03/07/2008 – case R 1608/2007-4, More than just a card.

[13] The trademark was later successfully registered once the Applicant proved it acquired a secondary distinctiveness. See: *EUIPO BoA, 29.1.2019, No. R 1596/2018-5, SCS SOFTWARE S.R.O. v EUIPO.*

[14] GC 10.10.2019 – case T-700/18, *Kalypso Media Group GmbH v EUIPO*.

3. Relative grounds for refusal

18 Relative grounds for refusal are **not examined *ex officio* by the EUIPO.**[15] Instead, the Office would only consider them if an opposition is filed by a proprietor of an earlier right that may be in potential conflict with the application. It is then entirely up to the prior rightsholder to decide whether to challenge a colliding application or tolerate it. The opposition proceedings are held *inter partes*, requiring each party to provide its arguments and furnish factual evidence to support them.

19 The list of relative grounds for refusal is set out in Art. 8 EUTMR. The **most common basis for opposition is a previously registered trademark**, whether a European one or national registration from one of the Member States. While Art. 8 EUTMR also provides for opposition based on other types of earlier rights such as certain non-registered trademarks or other signs used in the course of trade of more than mere local significance, such cases are far less common in practice.

20 The primary grounds for opposing trademark registration are: 1) **double identity** (of trademarks and relevant goods and services) and 2) **likelihood of confusion** (that may arise from a combination of identity or similarity of the signs with identity or similarity of goods or services). Furthermore, an owner of the trademark with a reputation may use an additional ground: 3) even in the absence of any similarity between the goods or services, registration may be refused if the applied-for mark is similar and its use without due cause would take unfair advantage of, or be detrimental to, the distinctive character or **reputation of the earlier mark.**

21 In practice, the **most common ground for opposition is the likelihood of confusion** under Art. 8(1)(b) EUTMR. It refers to the potential risk that the relevant public might believe that the goods or services in question come from the same undertaking or from economically linked undertakings. The assessment of likelihood of confusion involves a global evaluation of several interdependent factors, notably: level of similarity of goods or services,[16] level of similarity of signs[17] and the distinctiveness of the earlier trademark.[18] These factors are examined from the perspective of the relevant public's perception,[19] taking into account their level of attention.[20] Each factor is assessed based on well-established principles developed through years of the Office's and judicial case law (in particular that of the CJEU).[21]

---

[15] Importantly, not all trademark registration systems require an objection from an interested party to assess relative grounds for refusal. In some jurisdictions, trademark offices examine relative grounds *ex officio*.

[16] The factors that must be considered when assessing similarity of goods or services have been described in the famous *Canon* case. CJEU 29.09.1998 – case C-39/97, *Canon Kabushiki Kaisha v Metro-Goldwyn Mayer Inc.*, ECLI:EU:C:1998:442.

[17] The signs are compared visually, aurally and conceptually. The comparison must be based on the overall impression of the mark on each of the aforementioned layers, bearing in mind their distinctive and dominant elements. See: CJEU 11.11.1997 – case C-251/95, *SABEL BV v Puma AG, Rudolf Dassler Sport*, ECLI:EU:C:1997:528.

[18] According to settled CJEU case law: the more distinctive is the earlier mark, the greater will be the likelihood of confusion (CJEU 11.11.1997 – case C-251/95, *SABEL BV v Puma AG, Rudolf Dassler Sport*, ECLI:EU:C:1997:528) and trademarks that are highly distinctive generally enjoy broader protection (See: CJEU 29.09.1998 – case C-39/97, *Canon Kabushiki Kaisha v Metro-Goldwyn Mayer Inc.*, ECLI:EU:C:1998:442).

[19] The *relevant public* (or the *average consumer*) is a legal concept encompassing both actual and potential purchasers of the goods or services in question.

[20] The degree of attention of the average consumer is assumed to vary depending on the nature of the relevant goods or services. For example, consumers are generally more attentive when purchasing expensive or technically complex products. Generally, the lower the level of attention, the higher the potential likelihood of confusion.

[21] In fact, those principles are quite universal across all jurisdictions and forums.

The video game industry has seen numerous **cases** in which the likelihood of confusion was examined by both the EUIPO and the EU courts. One notable example is case T-700/18, where the Court considered the registrability of the word mark 'DUNGEON' (Kalypso Media Group GmbH) in light of an opposition filed by the owner of the earlier word mark 'DUNGEON & DRAGONS' (Wizards of the Coast). The Court upheld the EUIPO's finding that a likelihood of confusion existed. Although the applicant argued that the previous 'DUNGEON & DRAGONS' trademark possessed a very low level of distinctiveness, the Court rejected that argument and assessed the distinctiveness of the earlier trademark as 'at very least normal'. The Court also undertook a detailed analysis of the relevant public for video games and its level of attention, finding i.a. that 'games and computer games are easily accessible to all, including those without special knowledge, and may therefore be assimilated to everyday consumer items, on the grounds that (...) they are no longer sold merely on "focused markets" but have gone "mainstream"'. Even though the Court did not exclude that some computer game buyers are particularly careful when choosing a given product, it emphasised that the assessment must be conducted from the perspective of the part of the relevant public with the lowest level of attention. Accordingly, the relevant level of attention was deemed to be 'average at best'. Similar interpretation has been taken in other EUIPO decisions involving video games.[22] 22

V. Types of trademarks commonly registered in the game development industry

As noted in Section III(1), the EUTMR imposes no restrictions on the types of signs that may be registered as trademarks. In theory, this allows video game companies to seek protection for a wide range of game-related elements. In practice, however, certain types of trademarks hold greater strategic importance or broader applicability, which is reflected in **common registration patterns across the industry**. 23

1. Video game title

A **game's title** is by far the **most important trademark** for a developer to register. It can be protected as a word mark, a figurative mark incorporating its graphic design (e.g., logotype), or both. However, word marks generally offer broader legal protection. Securing trademark rights for a title is crucial to ensure uninterrupted distribution and to defend against third parties. 24

Typical **challenges** faced by developers in registering their titles include not only avoiding collisions with previously registered titles but also, on some occasions, overcoming refusals based on descriptiveness – particularly since video game titles often contain elements referring to the game's type or genre (see Section III.3 above). Examples of titles refused registration by the EUIPO as word trademarks include: 'Bloody Good time' (EUTM 008187114), 'Racing Master' (EUTM 705031) and 'Rules of Survival' (EUTM 017496522). 25

---

[22] See, e.g., *EUIPO*, 30.5.2025, case No. W01748921; EUIPO, 17.7. 2014, case No. B 2 215 658, *Xompu GmbH v Ubisoft Entertainment, Société Anonyme*; EUIPO 29.9.2022, case No. R 588/2022–1, *CJ ENM Co., Ltd. v Ubisoft Entertainment.*

2. Game's logotypes and other symbols

26 In addition to registering the figurative version of a game's title, **developers often seek protection for other official game logotypes**. These may include graphic representations of title elements (e.g., , recently registered by Take-Two) or other distinctive symbols and emblems used to identify the game (e.g., , the symbol of Ubisoft's Assassin's Creed series).

3. Characters' names

27 **Some video game character names** are so distinctive and widely recognised that they function effectively as indicators of a game's commercial origin and can therefore be registered as trademarks. This strategy is especially useful for franchises featuring recurring protagonists. A notable example is *'Lara Croft'*, which has been widely registered, including in the EUIPO (EUTM 000549006). Square Enix has successfully enforced this trademark in the past – for instance, by opposing the registration of *"LoraCraft"* for goods in Class 22, including packaging materials, padding, and ropes.[23]

4. In-game assets

28 While the registration of **in-game assets** is **less common** than that of game titles or logos, it has become an increasingly visible trend among video game companies – particularly for elements that are highly distinctive or closely associated with a specific game or franchise. Such elements may include in-game logos, designs of in-game cosmetics, character appearances, symbols, emblems, etc.

29 To name several **examples** of EUIPO's registrations:

Witcher wolf medallion:

(EUTM 014374094)

pokeball design:

(EUTM 015964885)

and the design of the *Crash Bandicoot* character:

(EUTM 018539422)

5. Slogans

30 As discussed in Section III.2 above, only **particularly uncommon slogans** are generally capable of fulfilling the distinguishing function required for trademark protection. Among slogans that were successfully registered by video game companies are: *'GOTTA CATCH 'EM ALL'* (EUTM 001275221), *'IT'S IN THE GAME'* (EUTM 013855812), and *'PLAY HAS NO LIMITS'* (EUTM 018258312).

[23] *EUIPO, 30.11.2023, No. B 3 180 999, Square Enix Newco Limited v Wuhan Shuncheng Electronic Commerce Co., Ltd.*

6. Non-conventional trademarks

Registrations of **non-conventional trademarks** – such as sound, motion, multimedia, single colour, or hologram marks – remain **rare** in the video game industry. However, some companies have successfully obtained protection for such marks. For example, Ubisoft registered a sound trademark described as the 'yelling of a fictitious person characterised by a shrill cry', represented graphically by its acoustic spectrum (EUTM 005424171). 31

VI. Registration Strategy

Even among companies operating within the same industry – or those creating similar types of games – there is no universal trademark registration strategy that can be applied without custom analysis. A successful strategy must be **well-balanced and tailored to the individual needs of the company**. The number of factors involved in deciding whether and how to register trademarks can be considerable, so below we outline those that would typically serve as a starting point for most companies. 32

The registration strategy for a given game **begins with the choice of its title**. A common dilemma – often the source of heated debates between legal and marketing teams – is whether to opt for a more generic title that may be easier to market, or a distinctive, non-descriptive title that could evolve into a strong and widely protectable trademark but may not resonate as immediately with players. While there is no straightforward solution, if a company intends to use and benefit from trademark protection, it is advisable to choose a title that, in its word form, is not entirely descriptive – or to complement it with a highly distinctive graphic element to enhance its potential registrability as a figurative trademark. Equally important is conducting a trademark clearance search to ensure the proposed title does not conflict with existing rights. This process often involves several iterations between creative and legal teams before landing on a viable candidate. 33

The company must then determine **what** to register as trademark(s). To make this decision, the studio should assess which elements of the game are of key prominence and distinctiveness and which it would like to use as indications of the game's origin. In most cases, this will include the title and logo, but companies may also find value in registering additional trademarks, such as those discussed in Section IV above. 34

Next, the company should determine **where** to register its trademarks. Priority should generally be given to markets where the game is expected to generate the most revenue, have the largest player base, or where past or anticipated issues with unfair competition exist. 35

Finally, it is essential to consider the specific **goods and services** for which the company's trademarks should be registered. While registration for video games in Class 9 – often accompanied by Class 41 for online game services – is typically foundational for video game companies, additional classes may be relevant depending on the business plans for a given game, particularly when merchandise or ancillary works are planned. 36

Decisions regarding all the aforementioned aspects should, of course, be made **with due consideration to the budget** that the company can allocate to trademark registration. However, even for companies with substantial or unlimited resources, excessive filings are not advisable, as registered trademarks are subject to the genuine use requirement. In accordance with Art. 18(1) EUTMR, if within 5 years following the registration, the trademark owner has not put it into **genuine use** in the EU in connection with the goods or services for which it is registered, or if such use has been suspended during an 37 uninterrupted period of five years, the EU trademark is generally subject to cancellation for non-use. Similar regulations exist in other jurisdictions.

38 Last but not least, **timing** is a crucial element in any trademark registration strategy. No developer wants the title of an upcoming game to be prematurely revealed through a trademark filing. At the same time, delaying too long increases the risk of third parties filing bad-faith applications, which can lead to significant additional costs and prolonged legal proceedings. The best practice is typically to file the trademark application as close as possible to the public announcement of the game title or the release of other elements for which protection is sought.

C. Use of third-party trademarks within video games

39 Use of third-party trademarks within a video game is appealing to make the video game a more **realistic** and **immersive** experience. Also, technology now allows for the creation of more **lifelike** environments. Practices from studios vary: Some studios decide to obtain a license from the trademark holder, some decide to reproduce trademarks without asking and others just give up on the idea. Yet, the most common scenario is that studios avoid using third-party trademarks to avoid having to face a lawsuit but also mainly because that would amount to granting a brand a great promotion without the brand owner even having to pay for it. We nevertheless provide below an overview of the applicable texts and case law the authors have identified.

I. Scope of protection – the texts

40 The first thing to note is that the trademark protection is not absolute. There are rules **limiting the effects of a trademark**. As listed notably in B.III.3 above and under Art. 9 (2) of Regulation 2017/1001, the proprietor, should it want to oppose use of its trademark in a video game, if any, would have to prove that all statutory conditions are met.

41 Also, the recitals of Regulation 2017/1001, although not legally binding, give an idea of the **spirit of the legislation**. They provide that '*Use of a trade mark by third parties for the purpose of artistic expression should be considered as being fair as long as it is at the same time in accordance with honest practices in industrial and commercial matters*'.[24]

42 Further limits have been set by case law. In particular, in accordance with ECJ case law, a trademark owner can only exercise its right in cases in which a third party's use of the sign affects or is able to **affect the functions of the trademark**. In particular, its essential function of guaranteeing to consumers the **origin of the goods**.[25] That is the situation where the sign is used by the third party in relation to his goods or services in such a way that consumers are liable to interpret it as designating the origin of the goods or services in question.[26] In other words, the sign has to be 'used as a trademark' to be infringing.

43 Those functions include not only the essential function of the trademark, but also its other functions, in particular that of guaranteeing the **quality** of the goods or services in question and those of **communication**, **investment** or **advertising**.[27] Indeed, the proprietor of a trademark could have to demonstrate that use adversely affects the pro-

---

[24] Regulation 2017/1001, § 21.

[25] ECJ, case C-245/02, 16.11.2004, Anheuser-Busch, § 59.

[26] ECJ, case C-17/06, 11.9.2007, Céline, § 27.

[27] ECJ, case C-324/09, 12.7.2011, *L'Oréal and Others*, § 8; ECJ, joined cases C-236/08 to C-238/08, 23.3.2010, Google, § 77.

prietor's use of its mark as a factor in sales promotion or as an instrument of commercial strategy.[28]

In addition to its function of indicating origin and, as the case may be, its advertising function, a trademark may also be used by its proprietor to acquire or preserve a **reputation** capable of attracting consumers and retaining their loyalty. As such, the proprietor could have to demonstrate that the third party's use adversely affects the trademark's investment function.[29] **44**

In all the criteria reviewed, absence of risk of confusion and absence of 'use as a trademark' are likely the most common defences when it comes to assessing whether the use of a third-party trademark in a video game, often for reference purposes, is infringing. **45**

II. Case law in the EU

To the authors' knowledge, few judgments were rendered in relation to the depiction of trademarks in video games in the EU. Those concern the depiction of real-life **locations**, **cars** and **soccer clubs**. Although the cases do not provide harmonised clear guidelines, most of them have dismissed the claims against studios. **46**

In France, the owner of the trademark 'STADE DE FRANCE' which is the name of the largest stadium in France, filed an action against Electronic Arts (EA) for trademark infringement based on the use of its trademark in EA's sports video game titled "**RUGBY 08**".[30] According to the background outlined in the ruling, there had been discussions, which ultimately led to a deal, between the parties surrounding the reproduction of French stadiums in EA's game on the Rugby World Cup 2007 which was held in France. During these discussions, the trademark owner had set certain limits on use. Under the impression that these were not respected in the released version of the game, the trademark owner requested a complete ban of the game arguing that '*the "RUGBY 08" game included the reproduction of the STADE DE FRANCE trademark, in the game and in the accompanying booklet, without its authorization*'. EA defended that '*the information appearing on the game's cover and booklet* ***did not constitute trademark use****, but rather the* ***necessary reference*** *to the architects' moral rights*' and that said use complied with their deal. Ultimately, the court did not decide on this issue, ruling that there was an agreement between the parties allowing EA to '*include the name, trademarks, logos, images and designs of the Stade de France, including the architectural rights, in Rugby 08, on the cover and in the marketing for the game*'. **47**

Another French case[31] concerned two games of the ***Grand Theft Auto*** series, *GTA IV* and *GTA: San Andreas*, respectively set in New York City[32] and the fictional city of San Andreas.[33] The car manufacturer Ferrari filed multiple claims against its publisher, Take 2 Interactive, for the unauthorised imitation of its car models and notably its 360 Modena and F40 models. While the case is mostly a copyright and registered design case, it is interesting for the purpose of this chapter as Ferrari challenged the use of two logos on the in-game cars on the grounds of unfair competition. Despite this ground being distinct from trademark infringement, both tests require demonstration of **48**

---

[28] ECJ, joined cases C-236/08 to C-238/08, 23.3.2010, Google, § 92.

[29] ECJ, C-323/09 (*Interflora*), 22.9.2011, § 62.

[30] Paris First Instance Court, 28.4.2011, No. 09/10455, *Stade de France consortium v Electronic Arts.*

[31] Paris Court of Appeals, 26.1.2016, No. 14/10931.

[32] Grand Theft Auto IV – Rockstar Games (https://www.rockstargames.com/games/IV).

[33] Grand Theft Auto: San Andreas – Rockstar Games (https://www.rockstargames.com/games/sanandreas).

a likelihood of confusion which therefore sheds light on how a court could have ruled in a trademark case.

49 The Paris Court of Appeals, upon referral by the French *Cour de Cassation*, dismissed Ferrari's claims ruling that the **differences** between the real-world Ferrari logo and the ones reproduced in the video game were sufficient to exclude any likelihood of confusion. The Court ruled that the facts that there was a 'prancing rabbit' or a 'seated horse' and not a 'prancing horse' on the in-game logos, especially in different colours, and that the name displayed was 'Grotti' and not 'Ferrari' excluded likelihood of confusion even though both sound Italian. According to the court citing Porsche and Lamborghini as examples, this is especially the case since '*several car manufacturers use animals as emblems*' which makes them commonplace. Furthermore, many powerful car brands are Italian. The Court states that the player will consequently '*only perceive a **humorous intent** equally targeting all manufacturers of powerful vehicles*'.

50 The necessity to represent reality was also alluded to by the court which ruled to dismiss the free-riding claim that:

> *if the car is an important element of GTA (...), the main attraction of the game resides, not in driving cars (...), but in the ability for the player to be the main character of an interactive game embodying a character freely evolving in cities **represented in a realistic manner** in order to carry out successive missions (...).*

51 In Spain, a case concerned the reproduction of the name of a soccer club.[34] The soccer club BURJASSOT CLUB DE FÚTBOL filed a trademark action to prevent the defendant, EDITORIAL PLANETA DE AGOSTINI S.A., from using the name and shield of its soccer club in the video game titled **PC FÚTBOL**. The trademark appeared as one of the teams that the player could choose to play with. To dismiss the trademark owner's claim, the court held that the mark was **not used to identify the video game**, or any good or service, and that it was in any event purely **incidental** as the players could choose the club identified by the trademark from many more.

52 In Germany, a case also concerned the names and emblems of soccer clubs from the German Football League reproduced in a football management video game locally titled **'BDFL Manager'**.[35] Here, the outcome was in favour of the plaintiff. The court considered that the use was infringing to the extent that the player could assume that a license had been concluded. This is because the consumers assume that '*the names, brands, jerseys and the like may not be commercially exploited without the consent of the clubs or players, especially since this ancillary business with fan merchandise and other products represents a welcome and quite significant source of income*'. Buyers would therefore '*assume that the use of the names, jersey colors and designs has been expressly authorized by the respective rights holder*'.[36]

---

[34] Barcelona Provincial Court, 27.6.2008, No. 204/2008, *Burjassot CF v Planeta Deagostini*.
[35] OLG Frankfurt am Main, judgment of 22.11.2005 – 11 U 6/05, BeckRS 2011, 19270.
[36] EU Video Games Law, A Handbook, Hentsch, Rodenhausen, MacGreevy, trademark chapter.

There are other cases rendered in different fields regarding trademarks reproduced 53 in **various works or art** or **products** (e.g., audiovisuals works, paintings,[37] toys[38]) which could provide useful guidelines.

On the **EU level**, one case sheds light on the question at issue. It is the *Adam Opel* 54 *AG v Autec AG* case.[39] The dispute in the main proceedings concerned the affixing of the real-life logo of the car manufacturer Opel, illustrated below, on toys consisting in scale models cars marketed by Autec to reproduce it faithfully. One of the questions was whether that constituted trademark infringement. We can imagine that if applied to the video game field, the question would be equivalent to asking whether in-game cars can reproduce existing car brands.

The Court specified that the fact that the consumer of the toys is **used to and** 55 **expects car toys to reproduce real-life car models** and even '*accords great importance to absolute fidelity to the original*' can be a clue to find against infringement. Indeed, this could mean that the relevant public does not perceive the sign as an indication that the toys come from Opel or an undertaking economically linked to it.[40] Arguably, players may expect some fidelity to original products within games as well.

[37] District Court of Dusseldorf, 28.2.2007, No. 2a O 150/06.
[38] ECJ, case C-48/05, 25.1.2007, *Adam Opel AG v Autec AG.*
[39] ECJ, case C-48/05, 25.1.2007, *Adam Opel AG v Autec AG.*
[40] ECJ, case C-48/05, 25.1.2007, *Adam Opel AG v Autec AG, § 24.*

CHAPTER 4
LICENSING A VIDEO GAME

§ 18
Unpacking the European Video Game Publishing Landscape

A. Unpacking the European video game publishing landscape 1

B. The European video game market landscape 5
I. Market size and growth: a continental powerhouse 6
II. Diverse European markets: a multitude of choices 8
III. Platform distribution: from PC master race to mobile domination 10
IV. Digital vs. physical sales: the rise of the download 13

C. Localisation and the European gamer 16
I. Language localisation 17
II. Cultural nuances: sensitivity and adaptation 20
III. Case studies: successes and failures in localisation 23
IV. Impact of globalisation 25

D. Business models and revenue streams in the European games market 28
I. Traditional publishing 29
II. Indie publishing 32
III. Free-to-play and Games as a Service (GaaS) 36
IV. Esports and competitive gaming 40

E. Government support and regulation in Europe 43
I. Funding and incentives 44
II. PEGI and content regulation 46
III. Data protection and privacy: respecting user rights 50

F. Trends and challenges 53
I. Emerging Technologies: New Dimensions of Play 54
1. Cloud Gaming 55
2. Virtual Reality (VR) 57
3. Augmented Reality (AR/XR) 58
II. Brexit and its implications: navigating uncertainty 60
III. Sustainability and social responsibility 62
IV. Embracing the future of play 65

A. Unpacking the European video game publishing landscape

1 In 2022, over 454 million Europeans – that's more than the entire population of the United States – immersed themselves in the world of video games. From the bustling streets of London to the serene landscapes of the Nordic countries, gaming has become an undeniable force in European culture and a lucrative market for publishers worldwide. This thriving industry, however, is far from a homogenous entity. It is a **complex ecosystem** shaped by diverse cultural landscapes, fragmented markets, and evolving regulatory frameworks, presenting unique challenges and opportunities for those who seek to navigate the intricacies of video game publishing in Europe.

2 The roots of European game publishing can be traced back to the **early 1980s**, a period marked by the rise of home computers and iconic titles like *Pac-Man* and *Tetris* captivating audiences across the continent. Companies like Ocean Software in the UK and Infogrames in France emerged as early pioneers, laying the foundation for a growing industry. The subsequent decades witnessed the rise of console giants like Nintendo and Sony, further solidifying gaming's place in European homes. The dawn of the 21st century set the stage for a new era of online gaming, with titles like *World of Warcraft* and *League of Legends*, connecting millions of players across borders and laying the foundation for thriving online communities.

3 This chapter examines the **multifaceted nature of video game publishing** in this dynamic region. It takes a look into the unique challenges and opportunities faced by

publishers, focusing on market fragmentation, cultural diversity, localisation strategies, and the role of government support in supporting and growing a thriving industry. Video game publishers will be able to better understand and engage with European gamers by understanding the key elements of the complex gaming landscape.

4 The chapter is organised in the following way to achieve this goal:

- **Market Landscape**
  This section provides an overview of the European video game market, exploring its size, growth trends, and regional variations in player preferences and platform popularity. It highlights the challenges posed by market fragmentation and the need for publishers to adapt their strategies to different regional contexts.
- **Cultural Diversity and Localisation**
  Here, we take a look into the critical role of culturalisation and localisation in the European context. It examines how language, cultural nuances, and sensitivities impact game development and marketing, emphasising the importance of adapting content to resonate with diverse audiences.
- **Business Models and Revenue Streams**
  This section explores the wide landscape of business models and revenue streams employed by publishers in Europe. It examines traditional premium publishing models alongside free-to-play, Games as a Service (GaaS), and the growing influence of esports and competitive gaming.
- **Government Support and Regulation**
  This part focuses on the role of government policies and regulations in shaping the European gaming landscape. It examines government support initiatives, content regulation through the PEGI rating system, and the implications of data protection laws like GDPR for game publishers.
- **Future Trends and Challenges**
  The final section looks ahead to the future of video game publishing in Europe. It explores emerging technologies like cloud gaming, VR, and AR, and discusses the challenges posed by Brexit, sustainability concerns, and the evolving expectations of European gamers.

B. The European video game market landscape

5 The European video game market is a **dynamic and lucrative sector**, a testament to the continent's passion for interactive entertainment. However, beneath its impressive headline figures lies a complex tapestry of regional variations and evolving trends that publishers must carefully navigate. This part dives deeper into the key characteristics of this landscape, exploring its size, growth trajectory, regional nuances, and the ongoing shift towards digital distribution.

I. Market size and growth: a continental powerhouse

6 The European video game market is a force to be reckoned with, boasting an estimated value of **25.7 billion EUR in 2023**.[1] This represents a significant portion of the global gaming industry, driven by factors such as increasing smartphone penetration, the rise of esports, and the expanding popularity of online gaming. The market shows potential

[1] https://www.videogameseurope.eu/publication/2023-video-games-european-key-facts/.

for further growth, driven by technological advancements, innovative business models, and continued engagement across demographics. However, unforeseen challenges could arise.

Revenue streams within the European market are varied, encompassing traditional game sales, downloadable content (DLC), in-app purchases (IAP), subscription services, and advertising revenue from free-to-play games. The rise of Games as a Service (GaaS) has further diversified revenue generation, with ongoing content updates and micro-transactions contributing to a steady income stream for publishers. Esports and competitive gaming also represent a growing revenue source, with sponsorships, merchandise, and media rights adding to the industry's economic impact.[23] 7

II. Diverse European markets: a multitude of choices

While the European market has exhibited impressive overall growth, it's crucial to recognise the **significant regional variations** that exist within its borders. Player preferences, platform popularity, and spending habits can differ considerably from country to country, requiring publishers to adopt nuanced strategies for each target market. 8

- **The UK**[4]
  A long-standing console stronghold, the UK market is characterised by a high penetration of PlayStation and Xbox consoles. Mobile gaming is also prevalent, with a strong focus on casual and free-to-play titles. UK gamers are known for their early adoption of new technologies and a willingness to spend on premium games and DLC.
- **Germany**[5]
  PC gaming reigns supreme in Germany, with a strong tradition of PC development and a passionate community of PC enthusiasts. Mobile gaming is also popular, but German gamers tend to be more discerning in their spending habits, favouring high-quality titles and demonstrating a strong aversion to aggressive monetisation strategies.
- **France**[6]
  Similar to the UK, France has a strong console gaming culture, with a particular affinity for Nintendo consoles and family-friendly titles. French gamers are also known for their appreciation of narrative-driven games and a willingness to engage with local content and dubbing. France has also shown to be a stronghold for a lot of Asian influences, particularly Mangas enjoy a continued and high popularity.
- **Nordic Countries**
  The Nordic region, encompassing countries like Sweden, Finland, and Denmark, is a hotbed of innovation in the gaming industry. Mobile gaming is particularly popular, with a strong focus on social and competitive titles. The region also boasts a thriving esports scene and a strong tradition of PC gaming.

These are just a few examples of the regional variations that exist within the European market. Publishers are encouraged to conduct thorough market research to understand 9

---

[2] https://www.statista.com/search/?q=Video+Games+Revenue+Europe&p=1.

[3] https://www.videogameseurope.eu/publication/2023-video-games-european-key-facts/.

[4] https://ukie.org.uk/uk-games-map.

[5] https://www.game.de/en/facts-and-numbers/.

[6] https://newzoo.com/resources/trend-reports/key-insights-into-french-gamers-newzoo-gamer-insights-report.

the specific nuances of each region, **tailoring their marketing and localisation efforts** accordingly as the key to success in Europe clearly lies in understanding regional commonalities as well as differences.

III. Platform distribution: from PC master race to mobile domination[7]

10 The **distribution of gaming platforms** across Europe is another key aspect of the market landscape. While mobile gaming has witnessed explosive growth across all regions, the popularity of PC and console gaming varies considerably.[8]

11 **PC gaming** maintains a strong foothold in countries like Germany, Poland, and the Nordic region, where a culture of technology and a preference for high-performance gaming experiences have fuelled the platform's enduring appeal. Console gaming, on the other hand, is more prevalent in the UK, France, and Spain, driven by a console legacy and a preference for immersive living room experiences.

12 **Mobile gaming** has emerged as the dominant platform across Europe, fuelled by the accessibility and affordability of smartphones and tablets. Casual games, puzzle games, and social casino games are particularly popular on mobile devices, attracting a broad audience of casual and hardcore gamers alike.[9]

IV. Digital vs. physical sales: the rise of the download[10, 11]

13 The European market has witnessed a **significant shift towards digital distribution** in recent years. The convenience of downloading games directly to consoles and PCs, coupled with the rise of digital storefronts like Steam, PlayStation Store, and Nintendo eShop, just to name a few, has transformed the way games are purchased and consumed.

14 This shift has had a profound **impact on publishers**, reducing their reliance on physical retailers and empowering them to reach a wider audience through online platforms. Digital distribution also offers greater flexibility in pricing and promotional strategies, allowing publishers to experiment with different business models and monetisation techniques.

15 However, the rise of digital distribution also presents **challenges**. Publishers must now compete with a vast library of games on digital storefronts, making discoverability and visibility a key concern. They must also navigate the complexities of digital rights management (DRM) and address concerns about ownership and preservation in a digital-only world.

C. Localisation and the European gamer

16 The European video game market is a melting pot of languages, cultures, and traditions. While this diversity contributes to a vibrant and exciting landscape, it also presents

---

[7] https://newzoo.com/resources/trend-reports/newzoos-global-games-market-report-2024-free-version.

[8] https://gam3s.gg/news/european-gaming-industry-report/.

[9] https://www.thebusinessresearchcompany.com/report/mobile-gaming-global-market-report.

[10] https://www.statista.com/statistics/234664/digital-vs-non-digital-revenue-of-global-major-video-game-publishers/.

[11] https://www.game.de/en/6-in-10-pc-and-console-games-sold-in-2021-in-germany-were-purchased-as-downloads.

a unique set of challenges for publishers seeking to connect with players across the continent. This sub-chapter explores the critical role of **cultural diversity and localisation** in European video game publishing, examining the intricacies of language translation, cultural nuances, and the impact of globalisation on player preferences.

I. Language localisation

Language[12] is the cornerstone of cultural expression, and in the realm of video games, **effective localisation** is of utmost importance. It's not simply about translating text; it's about conveying the nuances of humour, emotion, and storytelling in a way that resonates with players from different linguistic backgrounds. 17

Europe is home to a multitude of languages, each with its own unique characteristics and regional dialects. A direct translation that works in one country might fall flat or even cause offense in another. For example, **humour** can be particularly challenging to translate, as jokes often rely on cultural references and wordplay that may not have equivalents in other languages. 18

Successful language localisation requires a deep understanding of the target audience's **linguistic and cultural context**. Publishers often collaborate with native-speaking translators, voice actors, and cultural consultants to ensure that the localised version of a game accurately reflects the source material while also feeling authentic to players in the target market. But we'll get into more details on localisation at a later point of this chapter in the book. 19

II. Cultural nuances: sensitivity and adaptation

Beyond language, **cultural sensitivities and preferences** play a crucial role in shaping the success of a video game in Europe. Values, beliefs, historical events, and social norms can all influence how players perceive and interact with game content. 20

For example, depictions of violence, sexuality, or religious themes may be subject to **different levels of acceptance** in different European countries. Publishers need to be mindful of these sensitivities, adapting their content or marketing materials to avoid causing offense or encountering regulatory hurdles. 21

Cultural nuances can also influence game design and mechanics. For instance, games that emphasise individual achievement and competition might resonate more strongly in some cultures, while games that promote cooperation and social interaction might be preferred in others. 22

III. Case studies: successes and failures in localisation

The history of video game publishing in Europe is full of examples of both successful and unsuccessful localisation efforts. 23

- **Success**
  A great example of successful localisation is CD Projekt Red and their approach with 'The Witcher' series. They didn't just translate the game, but they deeply understood the source material (the Polish novels) and ensured that the cultural nuances and

[12] https://ec.europa.eu/eurostat/databrowser/view/edat_aes_l22/default/table?lang=en.

tone were maintained in different languages. This helped 'The Witcher' resonate with global audiences while staying true to its origins.

- **Failure**
  In contrast, some publishers have faced criticism for inadequate localisation efforts. One notable example is the early European release of the role-playing game 'Final Fantasy VII', which suffered from poor translation and a lack of cultural adaptation, leading to confusion and frustration among players.

24 Looking at these examples we can easily understand the importance of investing in thorough localisation and culturalisation processes. When done well, **localisation can enhance the player experience**, broaden a game's appeal, and contribute to its commercial success.[13]

IV. Impact of globalisation

25 Globalisation and the internet have undeniably influenced cultural identities and consumption habits in Europe. The increased flow of information and cultural products across borders has led to a **convergence of tastes and preferences** in some areas, particularly among younger generations.

26 However, while globalisation has brought about a degree of cultural homogenisation, it has also ignited a renewed interest in **preserving and celebrating local identities** presenting both challenges and opportunities for publishers. On the one hand, they can leverage the global appeal of certain genres and franchises. On the other hand, they must also be mindful of the unique cultural values and preferences that persist within different European markets.

27 Overall, cultural diversity and localisation are integral to the success of video game publishing in Europe. By understanding the nuances of language, culture, and the impact of globalisation, publishers are able to create games that resonate with diverse audiences, reinforce meaningful connections, and contribute to a thriving and inclusive gaming ecosystem.[14]

D. Business models and revenue streams in the European games market

28 The European video game industry is a dynamic marketplace where creativity and commerce intersect. Publishers are constantly exploring new ways to connect with players and generate revenue, adapting their strategies to the evolving demands of the digital age. This sub-chapter digs into **business models and revenue streams** that shape the European gaming landscape, from traditional publishing partnerships to the rise of free-to-play and the growing influence of esports.

I. Traditional publishing

29 **Traditional publishing** remains a cornerstone of the European video game industry. In this model, publishers provide funding, marketing, and distribution support to developers in exchange for a share of the game's revenue. While this model has been the

[13] https://www.chargebee.com/blog/saas-business-growth-findings/.
[14] https://www.united-europe.eu/2018/01/globalization-and-the-eu-threat-or-opportunity/.

industry standard for decades, the relationship between publishers and developers is evolving.

In the past, publishers often exerted significant creative control over game development, dictating design choices and release schedules. However, the rise of **independent developers and digital distribution** has empowered developers to take more ownership of their projects. Publishers are increasingly adopting a more collaborative approach, recognising the value of supporting creative freedom and building strong relationships with talented developers. 30

This dynamic is reflected in the rise of **'indie-friendly' publishers** who offer more favourable terms to developers, allowing them to retain greater creative control and a larger share of the profits. These publishers often specialise in specific genres or niche markets, providing tailored support and expertise to developers. 31

II. Indie publishing

The European indie game development scene is thriving, fuelled by **digital distribution platforms** like Steam and GOG that allow developers to bypass traditional publishing gatekeepers and reach a global audience directly. This has democratised the game development process, empowering small teams and individual creators to bring their unique visions to life. 32

Indie developers often operate with **limited resources**, relying on creativity, innovation, and community engagement to achieve success. They are known for pushing creative boundaries, experimenting with new genres and gameplay mechanics, and fostering close relationships with their players. 33

However, indie publishing also presents **unique challenges**. Discoverability can be a major hurdle, as indie games often compete with a vast library of titles on digital storefronts. Marketing and promotion can also be challenging, requiring developers to wear multiple hats and find creative ways to generate buzz for their games. 34

Despite these challenges, the indie scene in Europe is a hotbed of innovation and creativity, contributing significantly to the diversity and vibrancy of the gaming landscape. 35

III. Free-to-play and Games as a Service (GaaS)

Free-to-play (F2P) and **Games as a Service (GaaS)** models have become increasingly prevalent in the European market. These models offer games for free or at a low cost, generating revenue through in-app purchases, subscriptions, or advertising.[15] 36

F2P games often employ **microtransactions**, allowing players to purchase virtual goods, cosmetic items, or gameplay advantages. GaaS games, on the other hand, provide **ongoing content updates and new features**, often funded by subscription fees or in-game purchases. 37

These models have proven to be highly successful, particularly in the mobile gaming sector. Popular titles like Fortnite, League of Legends, and Clash of Clans have demonstrated the immense revenue potential of F2P and GaaS, attracting millions of players and fostering dedicated communities. 38

However, these models also face criticism for their potential to exploit players through aggressive monetization strategies or create 'pay-to-win' scenarios where players who spend more money have an unfair advantage. Publishers must strike a **balance** 39

[15] https://clevertap.com/blog/games-as-a-service.

between generating revenue and maintaining a fair and enjoyable experience for all players.

IV. Esports and competitive gaming[16]

40 **Esports** has exploded in popularity across Europe, with millions of fans tuning in to watch professional gamers compete in tournaments for lucrative prizes. This phenomenon has created new opportunities for publishers and developers to generate revenue and engage with passionate communities.

41 **Publishers and developers are increasingly investing** in esports initiatives, sponsoring tournaments, supporting professional teams, and creating in-game features that promote competitive play. Esports also generate revenue through media rights, merchandise sales, and advertising.

42 The rise of esports has not only created **new revenue streams** but has also transformed the way games are designed and marketed. Publishers are now incorporating features that cater to competitive players, such as ranked matchmaking systems, spectator modes, and in-game tournaments.

E. Government support and regulation in Europe

43 The European video game industry thrives not only on creativity and innovation but also on a supportive **regulatory environment**. Governments across Europe recognise the economic and cultural significance of the gaming sector, implementing policies to support its growth while also ensuring responsible practices. This sub-chapter examines the key aspects of government support and regulation in the European video game market, focusing on funding initiatives, content regulation, and data protection.

I. Funding and incentives

44 Many European countries actively support their video game industries through a variety of **funding programs and incentives**. These initiatives aim to stimulate game development, attract investment, and promote the creation of local jobs.

- **Grants and Subsidies**[17]
  Governments offer grants and subsidies to game developers, particularly small and medium-sized enterprises (SMEs), to support the production of new games. These grants can cover various expenses, including development costs, marketing, and participation in international events.
- **Tax Breaks**
  Tax incentives, such as reduced corporate tax rates or tax credits for research and development, are common tools used to encourage investment in game development. These incentives can significantly reduce the financial burden on studios, allowing them to reinvest profits into creating new games and expanding their operations.

[16] https://www.gminsights.com/industry-analysis/esports-market.
[17] https://www.game.de/en/positions/german-games-fund/.

- **Regional Funds**[18]
  Some regions within Europe have established dedicated funds to support the growth of their local gaming industries. These funds may provide financing for game development projects, support the creation of incubators and co-working spaces, or offer training programs for aspiring game developers.

Examples of such initiatives include the UK Games Fund, which provides grants to SMEs in the gaming sector, the Centre National du Cinéma et de l'Image Animée (CNC) in France, which offers funding and support for video game production, and the German Games Fund, which provides financial support to German game developers. These programs demonstrate the commitment of European governments to fostering a thriving and competitive gaming industry. **45**

II. PEGI and content regulation[19, 20]

Content regulation is a crucial aspect of the European gaming landscape. The **Pan European Game Information (PEGI)** rating system plays a central role in ensuring that video games are appropriately classified and labelled based on their content. **46**

PEGI provides **age ratings and content descriptors** for video games, helping parents and consumers make informed decisions about the suitability of games for different age groups. The system uses age categories (e.g., 3+, 7+, 12+, 16+, 18+) and content descriptors (e.g., violence, bad language, fear, gambling) to provide clear and concise information about the content of a game. **47**

PEGI ratings are widely **adopted across Europe**, providing a consistent approach to content regulation and ensuring that games are marketed responsibly. This system helps protect children and young people from potentially harmful or inappropriate content while also providing valuable information to consumers. This book also touches deeper on PEGI in a separate section, → Ch. 22. **48**

In addition some countries maintain their own regional age rating systems. Germany, for example, uses the **Unterhaltungssoftware Selbstkontrolle (USK)** system, → Ch. 23. These systems work in conjunction with digital initiatives like the **International Age Rating Coalition (IARC)** to provide age ratings and content descriptors for video games. This helps parents and consumers make informed decisions about the suitability of games for different age groups. The systems typically use age categories and content descriptors to provide clear and concise information about the content of a game. **49**

III. Data protection and privacy: respecting user rights

Data protection and privacy are paramount concerns in the digital age, and the video game industry is no exception. The General Data Protection Regulation (GDPR), enacted in 2018, sets strict rules for the collection, processing, and storage of personal data. **50**

Game publishers operating in Europe must comply with **GDPR regulations**, ensuring that player data is collected and used transparently and responsibly. This includes obtaining consent for data collection, providing clear information about how data is used, and implementing measures to protect data from unauthorised access or misuse. **51**

---

[18] https://www.filmstiftung.de/en/news/official-launch-games-germany-gamescom-2017/.
[19] https://www.makeuseof.com/tag/video-game-ratings-guide-esrb-pegi/.
[20] https://pegi.info/.

52 GDPR compliance is not only a legal requirement but also an **ethical imperative**. By respecting user privacy and data protection rights, publishers can build trust with their players and contribute to a safer and more responsible gaming environment.

F. Trends and challenges

53 The European video game industry stands on the brink of a new era, shaped by technological advancements, shifting geopolitical landscapes, and evolving social consciousness. This sub-chapter explores the **future trends** and challenges that will define the next chapter of gaming in Europe, from the rise of immersive technologies to the implications of Brexit and the growing demand for sustainability and social responsibility.

I. Emerging Technologies: New Dimensions of Play

54 The future of gaming is tightly connected to emerging technologies that promise to revolutionise how we play and interact with virtual worlds.

1. Cloud Gaming

55 While services like Google Stadia have exited the market, other **cloud gaming** platforms like Xbox Cloud Gaming and GeForce Now continue to gain traction in Europe. These platforms offer several advantages to European gamers, including:

- **Accessibility**
  Cloud gaming removes the need for high-end hardware, making gaming accessible to a wider range of players, including those with limited budgets or technical expertise.
- **Reduced Hardware Costs**
  By streaming games from remote servers, players can save money on expensive consoles and PCs.
- **Cross-Platform Play**
  Cloud gaming services can enable cross-platform play between different devices, allowing friends and family to play together regardless of their preferred hardware.

56 European companies like Frontier Developments and Ubisoft are actively involved in cloud gaming, developing and publishing games specifically designed for this platform.

2. Virtual Reality (VR)

57 VR technology, which immerses players in fully realised **3D environments,** is poised to become more accessible and sophisticated. Advancements in VR headsets, motion tracking, and haptic feedback technology promise to create truly immersive and interactive experiences. European gamers are increasingly embracing VR, driven by the availability of high-quality content and the growing number of VR arcades and experiences.

3. Augmented Reality (AR/XR)

58 AR overlays digital content onto the real world, blurring the lines between the physical and virtual. Alongside AR, XR (extended reality), which encompasses AR, VR, and **MR (mixed reality)**, offers even greater potential for immersive experiences. European cities and cultural institutions are increasingly exploring the potential of AR and XR

to enhance visitor experiences and promote local heritage, which is a chance for the European gaming industry to expand its scope.

These emerging technologies will not only transform the gaming experience but also create **new opportunities** for publishers to innovate and engage with players in novel ways. 59

II. Brexit and its implications: navigating uncertainty

The UK's departure from the European Union has introduced a degree of uncertainty for the European gaming industry. Brexit is potentially impacting **UK-based publishers** in several ways: 60

- **Access to Talent**
  The free movement of labour between the UK and EU has ended, potentially making it more difficult for UK studios to recruit talent from across Europe.
- **Market Access**
  Trade barriers and regulatory differences could complicate the process of selling games and services between the UK and the EU.
- **Funding and Support**
  UK studios may no longer be eligible for certain EU funding programs and initiatives.

The long-term implications of Brexit are still unfolding, and publishers will need to adapt to the new realities of the post-Brexit landscape. 61

III. Sustainability and social responsibility

As the gaming industry matures, there is a growing awareness of the importance of **sustainability and social responsibility**. Players are increasingly demanding games that are environmentally conscious, ethically produced, and promote positive social values. 62

Publishers are responding to these demands by adopting **sustainable practices**, such as reducing their carbon footprint, using recycled materials in packaging, and promoting diversity and inclusion in their games and workplaces. They are also exploring ways to use games to address social issues, promote education, and raise awareness of important causes. The European video games industry is playing a leading role in driving sustainability and social responsibility in the gaming sector by supporting several initiatives that are underway to promote sustainable practices and positive social impact. 63

- **The Playing for the Planet Alliance** is a collaboration between the United Nations Environment Programme (UNEP) and leading game companies, including Ubisoft, Sony Interactive Entertainment, and Microsoft. The alliance aims to use games to raise awareness of environmental issues and promote sustainable behaviours.
- **The Green Game Jam** is an annual event that challenges game developers to create games that promote sustainability. The jam has been held since 2011 and has produced some innovative and thought-provoking games.

These initiatives are helping to raise awareness of sustainability and social responsibility in the gaming industry and are encouraging game companies to adopt more sustainable practices and create games that have a positive impact on society. 64

IV. Embracing the future of play

65 The European video game market is a dynamic and exciting landscape, with a pole position for continued growth and innovation. By embracing emerging technologies, adapting to new geopolitical realities, and prioritising sustainability and social responsibility, publishers can and will ensure a bright future for gaming in Europe.

66 However, **understanding the intricate differences and challenges** within Europe as well as when compared to other regions and cultures is key to unlocking Europe successfully for any company.

§ 19
Publishing Contracts

A. Introduction ... 1
I. Benefits of the publishing contract ... 1
II. Considerations when approaching a publishing contract ... 3
III. Negotiating the publishing contract ... 4
IV. Term sheets ... 6

B. The anatomy of a publishing deal ... 9
Mapping the contract ... 9

C. Operative provisions ... 11
I. Pre-release obligations, milestones and approvals ... 11
II. Post-release obligations ... 16
III. Limitations on licensing and exploitation ... 19
IV. IP ownership ... 23
V. Step-in and escrow ... 26
VI. Territory ... 28
VII. Term and termination ... 32
VIII. Derivative works ... 37

D. Financial provisions ... 40
I. Overview ... 40
II. Development budget ... 41
III. Publisher costs ... 44
IV. Recoupment ... 45
V. Reporting and payment ... 48

E. Legal terms and boilerplate ... 53
I. Warranties, indemnities and limitations on liability ... 53
II. Boilerplate ... 61

F. Conclusions ... 64

A. Introduction

I. Benefits of the publishing contract

The entering into of a publishing contract offers both challenges and opportunities for developers and publishers. Challenges, in that publishing contracts are complex documents, addressing a range of constantly evolving technical, creative and business concerns. Opportunities, in that a properly approached and thoughtfully executed publishing contract can play an important part in setting the stage for a happy and fruitful relationship between the parties. For the developer, the publishing contract is critical in ensuring the necessary flows of ongoing funding and support, enabling them to proceed with confidence to the creation of their work. For the publisher, the agreement is the best guarantor of a clear path to a return on investment, and that the various assumptions on which they are entering into the relationship will be validated. 1

The publishing contract, if approached correctly and with the necessary thought, has the potential to be the cornerstone of a healthy, high-functioning developer/publisher relationship. Likewise, if entered into hastily and without proper consideration it can set the stage for all manner of future misunderstanding, miscommunication and relationship dysfunction. In this chapter, we will explore some of the key opportunities and challenges of the publishing contract, taking in an overview of the document's anatomy, key clauses, and common pitfalls. 2

II. Considerations when approaching a publishing contract

3 The publishing contract is not, by its nature, a one-size-fits-all, generic product. Rather, these are **highly individuated, bespoke agreements** which need to be tailored to their circumstances. While, in this chapter, we will be focusing our analysis on the classic third-party publishing agreement (i.e., one where a publisher provides funding and/or various publishing services in exchange for the exclusive rights to distribute a game), a number of alternative forms of the contract exist. For example, 'ghost publishing' involves a publisher operating largely behind the scenes, and often not being the party to actually distribute the game. 'Co-publishing' is, as the name suggests, where a developer and publisher, or potentially multiple publishers, will share publishing responsibilities amongst themselves. And 'publishing as a service', a relatively new model, involves a publisher providing a more tailored, hands-off suite of services, often in exchange for payment on a time-spent or fixed-cost basis, rather than based on shared revenue. Given this evolution of what 'publishing' means as a concept, it is more important than ever to ensure from the outset that you are working from a template that is suited to the commercial arrangement you are aiming to document, and that both parties have established a clear common understanding of what is meant by 'publishing'. As ever, clear communication is the bedrock of any successful contractual relationship.

III. Negotiating the publishing contract

4 For the attentive lawyer, the negotiation of a publishing contract represents an opportunity to lay the groundwork for a long-term and **win-win collaboration**. This might take the form of helping to achieve the proper balance of incentives and disincentives, whereby each party is appropriately prompted to act in the overall interests of the shared venture. Or, alternatively, identifying points of disconnect and misunderstanding that risk flaring into greater significance as the relationship progresses. With these considerations in mind, the publishing contract is accurately viewed as an opportunity for pre-nuptial guidance counselling. To this end, an approach which emphasises the strength of the relationship is often optimal. Ask probing questions, explore under-inspected deal aspects, and, where possible, position contractual issues as common hurdles which will need to be resolved collaboratively. Build good relationship habits and clear patterns of communication between the parties which will help them iron out future issues and enable them to keep sight of the fact that either the success or failure of the project will, in most cases, ultimately be a shared experience.

5 As with any contract intended to underpin a long-term collaboration, it should also be borne in mind that most of the component clauses of the average publishing agreement will never be formally assessed in court, but will instead be stress-tested within the **equally testing theatre of the commercial relationship**. A party with strong relationship leverage might not need completely watertight drafting to use a clause to extract its intended concessions, and a clause that is potentially not strictly enforceable at law may still suffice for its proponent to demand action at a relationship level based purely on its intended spirit. Drafting should therefore be carefully viewed through the prism both of formal legal effect, but also relationship leverage; the ability of a party to point to what has been written and agreed and claim that the counterparty is not keeping up its end of the bargain, regardless of the precise formulation of words via which the bargain is expressed.

IV. Term sheets

Term sheets are an often misunderstood and under-used component of the negotiation toolbox. Comprised of a shorter form document, either in binding or non-binding form, they offer an opportunity to begin the negotiation by ensuring absolute clarity around key deal terms. Where used effectively, they can be an excellent means to root out misunderstandings and ensure alignment between the parties. However, they are also not without their risks. 6

The potential benefit of the term sheet is in ensuring clarity and setting the tone for what follows; once key deal terms such as IP ownership, financials, milestone schedule and headline obligations of the parties are clearly agreed, the long-form contract can be tackled with greater confidence and clarity. The risk of the term sheet is that, without good deal discipline, it can cost the parties time, adding an extra step to the negotiation. Without proper focus, the term sheet may also risk gradually transforming into a **proxy long-form document**, as the parties expand the term sheet's original scope to incorporate clauses best left for later negotiation. For this reason, where a term sheet is to be used, the parties should be clear upfront about what it will contain, primarily focusing on the commercial terms rather than legal, and ensure that this agreed scope is respected as discussions progress. 7

The discipline required to extract the proper benefits of the term sheet can become particularly challenging when the document is to be binding. Legal terms often play the role of offering key protections against their commercial counterparts, and a party might feel exposed without, for example, a key warranty to underwrite the commercial concessions they are offering. Likewise, a binding term sheet can occasionally risk a scenario where one party concludes upon signature that they are in no rush to proceed to long-form negotiation, having already secured a contractual position that gives them much of what they feel they might need. Careful consideration should therefore be given to ensuring at all times that the balance of the negotiation is not overturned or prejudiced in favour of one party or the other, and that the parties remain aligned that there will be a long form, and that it will be agreed to a mutually determined timescale and in good faith. 8

B. The anatomy of a publishing deal

Mapping the contract

As discussed above, the exact role of a publisher can vary significantly from deal to deal. However, this will typically include the provision of development and/or user acquisition funding as well as some combination of services spanning quality assurance, localisation, distribution, partner management, deal sourcing, sales management, revenue collection, age ratings, legal compliance, marketing and promotion, customer support, community management, event coordination and IP enforcement. This can also occasionally include actual development work, either on the core game itself, or developing ports for platforms where the main developer may have less experience. This means that publishing deals are often hugely complex agreements, covering a wide range of topics and regulating a relationship which will hopefully last for more than a decade. It is impossible to analyse all of this within a single chapter. However, in this section we will explore some of the cornerstone provisions of a traditional publishing deal, such as 9

IP ownership and termination rights and consequences, as well as some of the common pitfalls that can occur.

10 As with the majority of commercial agreements, the publishing deal's basic anatomy is best considered in four sections: the operative provisions, or 'front end' of the contract, in which the deal's various commercial specifics are set out; the classic legal terms (warranties, indemnities, limitations of liability) which establish protections against the various commitments contained in the commercial provisions; the 'boilerplate' sections at the back of the contract, which essentially describe rules for the operation of the agreement itself; and then finally the schedules or exhibits, which typically supplement the operative provisions and key legal terms with further detail.

C. Operative provisions

I. Pre-release obligations, milestones and approvals

11 The publishing agreement has at its heart a relatively simple exchange, from which all other details and complexities flow; the publisher will furnish money, publish the game, and provide certain associated services, in exchange for which the developer will either produce or otherwise provide the relevant game. There will also often be a mechanic to enable both parties to share in the upside of a high performing title. While this exchange may sound simple, the devil is, as ever, in the detail, and the publishing agreement is invariably full of nuances and pitfalls to which the effective video games lawyer should remain vigilant.

12 We must begin with a consideration of the deal's absolute centrepiece: the game itself. The agreement's definition of the game should be clear enough to describe the specific product, and include all its associated source code, object code, audiovisual content, music, sound effects and other elements. This may also include future additional downloadable content, updates and expansions. Care should be taken, however, that said definition is not so wide as to encompass sequels, ports, spin-offs, new versions (e.g., 'remasters' or 'director's editions') and derivative works, unless the developer is satisfied that it is receiving proper consideration for such potentially valuable assets. A proper understanding of this issue is often a prudent starting point for negotiation; before the parties can begin to arrive at a deal, they should ensure they have a clear, mutual understanding of what is actually in scope at the document's heart. For this reason, caution should be exercised where including in the definition of the game anything beyond the **base title**, unless otherwise explicitly agreed between the parties.

13 Once there is clarity around the game itself, and what it will encompass, attention may be turned to its actual production. If the agreement concerns a game that has yet to be developed, it will invariably contain a **milestone schedule**, setting out the pace at which development will be required to occur, and the various checkpoints agreed by the parties to ensure that the project remains on course for success and that key deliverables are provided on time. The precise shape of the milestone schedule will be determined by the commercial and technical considerations of the project at hand, but it is important that it is realistic and moored to the basic realities at play, with clear contractual consequences for repeated missing of milestones. An ill-conceived milestone schedule has the potential to set the parties up for conflict and confusion, particularly if not updated to reflect emerging needs and practicalities. To this end, the milestone schedule should be treated as a living, breathing mechanic that can be used to balance and rebalance expectations and responsibilities across the life of the development cycle.

Just as important as the milestone schedule is the **approval framework** built around it. A fundamental question for the parties to address will be the balance of creative control. Video games are inherently creative endeavours, and accordingly they can easily suffer where there is dispute as to with whom the final authority as to matters of quality lies. Where a publisher is investing heavily in a title, and particularly where the title involves the publisher's IP, the publisher is accordingly likely to push for a high level of creative approval. Where the relationship is more finely balanced, a developer may wish to seek clear contractual assurances that it will be granted final say on creative matters, albeit following close consultation, just as the publisher will retain final say over matters related to marketing and/or monetisation. 14

Once the appropriate milestones have been agreed, the parties will want to ensure that the approval process for each is fair and robust, with clear deadlines that avoid undue delay, clear grounds on which a publisher can validly reject a submission, and a requirement for the publisher to communicate its approval or rejection within a fixed time period. It is seldom helpful for a project to find itself bogged down with a sluggish approval process, and delays of this type can also have profound knock-on consequences for the developer's ability to meet its own obligations around timings, not least where it is engaging third parties to assist with development. The parties will also need to consider whether dates for subsequent milestones are automatically extended where a milestone is rejected and remediation work required. 15

II. Post-release obligations

Once the game has moved through its development cycle, the agreement's pendulum of responsibility will usually swing to the publisher. Invariably, a publisher will provide, in addition to finance, a range of services to support the game's launch and commercial success. Consideration should be given to the quality to which these services will be provided; is the publisher entitled to sublicense services to other, potentially less expert, third parties, and – if so – under what conditions; will there be a minimum monthly amount to be spent on marketing and user acquisition, or will the developer otherwise be consulted on marketing budgets; and are there metrics that might be agreed between the parties to gauge performance? These considerations are particularly pressing where the publisher has a deep stable of existing games, or a busy launch slate ahead; the developer will want to be reassured that their title will be given the appropriate level of priority. 16

Thought should also be given to the timing of the publisher's various activities. Is it obliged to release the game within a certain period of final approval – indeed, is it obliged to release the game at all? While the publisher enjoys the protections of the milestone schedule in respect of the developer's efforts, the contractual consequences for a delay on behalf of the publisher are often less clearly defined. Such delays have the potential to impact both the performance of the developer's own obligations under the agreement, and also its cashflow. Unexpected challenges are an inevitable fact of life in game development and publishing, and consequently care should be taken that unanticipated delay does not leave one or other party exposed. 17

The publishing agreement will also need to consider the developer's obligations and responsibilities post-launch. These might include a specified period of technical support for the game, in which additional development will occur as required to render any necessary bug fixes and patches, although the parties should be clear with one another as to whether this support will also be expected to include new or additional content, 18 and if so, whether further remuneration will be required. The publisher may also want to ensure clarity over the developer's role, or lack thereof, in the marketing of the game. The marketing campaign for a successful title is generally a tightly controlled process, focused around delivering key campaign 'beats' at the appropriate moments. While the developer may have in mind marketing it would like to conduct, perhaps to leverage an existing fan community with which it has an ongoing relationship, any such activities will need to be carefully coordinated with the publisher, and the publishing agreement should reflect as much.

III. Limitations on licensing and exploitation

19 In recent years the video games ecosystem has become increasingly complex, with what was once a fairly simple process of physical product release to bricks-and-mortar retailers splintering into a multiplicity of distribution options as digital delivery mechanics offer increased scope for experimentation and innovation. In such a context, it can be challenging to 'future-proof' the rights being granted, but developers should at minimum be mindful of the distribution paths already available and in-market. To this end, care should be taken that the rights being granted to the publisher – typically, to market, distribute and sell the game – are sufficiently clear as to what will and will not be in scope.

20 Developers should be conscious that publishers may have broader relationships with platforms and other industry stakeholders, and that **unexpected opportunities** may present themselves to leverage the game under development to the publisher's broader strategic benefit in ways which might not immediately be obvious. In such circumstances, the mutually aligned commercial goals which are the bedrock of a productive relationship may threaten to diverge, absent appropriate contractual guardrails. For example, the publisher may be offered opportunities to include the game in free giveaways, as part of exclusive deals or bundles, or via subscription or streaming services. In each instance, these forms of distribution might be lucrative or beneficial for the publisher, but may not be what the developer had in mind at the time the publishing agreement was negotiated. Indeed, dependent on the publishing agreement's financial terms, they may also deprive the developer of the opportunity to participate in the full value unlocked by such deals.

21 Careful watch should be kept on the detail of the agreement's licensed distribution rights with an eye to potential future developments in distribution. These matters are often particularly pressing where distribution rights are being offered on specific platforms or via specific commercial models only; for example, where the developer is granting console-only distribution rights, having already licensed PC rights elsewhere. What will be the position where a console port is streamed to PC via browser? Does this distribution remain an exploitation of console-specific rights, or does the use of the PC as the end destination device take such activities out of the scope of rights granted? It is essential for the developer that the license of rights is as clear as possible, particularly where any lack of clarity has the potential to reduce the value of other, neighbouring rights that are not being granted. As the industry and its distribution matrix becomes increasingly heterodox, such issues seem likely only to increase in urgency.

22 In addition to a clear delineation on permitted exploitation of the game, developers should also be watchful for any attempt within the agreement to limit their own wider commercial activities. While it is not unusual for a publisher to require that the developer should refrain from producing another, similar game that might compete with the

title being produced pursuant to the agreement, such clauses, where ill-defined, can threaten to materially undermine the developer's ability to go about its future business. Any such limitation should therefore always be completely clear as to what the developer will not be permitted to do (what type of game, for which platforms) and the period for which they will not be permitted to do it.

IV. IP ownership

IP ownership is, unsurprisingly, one of the core sections of any publishing deal. After all, games can cost millions, sometimes hundreds of millions, and take upwards of five years, to develop, so being clear who owns the output of such an investment of time and money is crucial. So, who typically owns the IP in a game? For larger game projects, this will generally be whichever party is funding development, often the publisher. The financial bets are simply too large for a publisher to justify investing in a project which it ultimately does not own. However, for smaller 'indie' titles this is usually the opposite, and in most cases 'indie' developers will remain the owner of their games. **23**

There are, of course, exceptions. Given that a game is a complex tapestry of code, tech, art, music and writing, it is not unusual for ownership of different aspects to be carved up and divided between the parties. For example, it may be agreed that the publisher is to own the audio-visual aspects of a game, such as its art and music, whilst the developer owns the underlying game code, technology and tools. Where a game's IP is split like this, it obviously becomes critical to consider the scope and duration of what licences are needed between the parties and, crucially, what happens to those on expiry or termination of the deal. The concept of **'jointly owning'** the IP in a game is often fleetingly mentioned by commercial counterparts but should generally be avoided without careful consideration of the attendant complex legal implications. Classically, a key risk posed by joint ownership is to potentially landlock the rights in the event of dispute; depending on the jurisdiction, jointly owned IP can require the ongoing consensus of the parties in order to ensure proper exploitation, and it is an optimistic lawyer indeed who allows themselves to assume that inter-party harmony will reign eternal. **24**

Parties should also be alive to the false sense of security that retaining IP ownership can give, due to the numerous contractual mechanics which can largely neuter the core benefits of 'owning' the IP. For example, if a developer retains ownership of the game but contractually agrees to grant a publisher sole and exclusive rights to exploit the game and its underlying IP on all platforms and in all mediums, including new games and TV/film adaptations, it is fair to question what benefits the 'owner' actually retains. **25**

V. Step-in and escrow

The issue of **'step in rights'** merits careful consideration. These are rights which essentially allow one party, usually the publisher, to assume control of game development when things have gone significantly off-track. One of the key points which the parties will need to agree upon with regard to such rights are appropriate trigger scenarios. Too loose and a developer could find itself easily removed from a project, a project where it 'owns' the underlying IP, partway through development. Too tight and a publisher could find its rights of limited use in practice. How long these step in rights last for, as well as any resultant changes to the financial parameters, are also key. **26**

27 Imagine a scenario where a developer suddenly shuts downs mid-project. Without access to the game's source code and other assets, a publisher could be left with a multi-million dollar nearly-finished game with no ability to complete it or support it. **Escrow** acts as a form of insurance for a publisher, as it requires a developer to backup essential game assets on a regular basis with a neutral third party, with such materials only ever being released if one of the pre-agreed 'release conditions' occurs. These release conditions might include where the developer becomes insolvent, but often also if there is significant delay on the development side, or if the underlying publishing deal is terminated early. Engaging an escrow agent will incur material costs and introduce additional admin and processes on the developer's side, given the requirement to frequently update the deposited materials. However, it can also be a valuable tool for a publisher to de-risk its investment in the event something goes seriously wrong on a project.

VI. Territory

28 Historically, and in many instances still today, a publisher will acquire rights to distribute the game on a worldwide basis. Some particularly ambitious publishers even expand this to include the entire universe. However, given the increasingly complex global video games ecosystem, such **territorial maximalism** is no longer ubiquitous.

29 China is one of the largest video games markets by both revenue and player numbers globally. However, in order to release a game officially within the country, certain regulatory approvals are required, and those regulatory approvals will only be granted to companies incorporated in China. As a result, it has become a legal necessity to have a China-based partner to release most types of game officially within the territory. Some other critical video games markets are beginning to consider similar restrictions.

30 This poses a question for developers: If a publisher will have to appoint a local sub-publisher to release a game in particular territory, what value is the original publisher actually providing in that particular territory, and should that publisher get a cut of revenues in a territory where a sub-publisher is undertaking most of the publishing responsibilities? In some circumstances, the answer will be obvious; savvy publishers will have built established relationships with partners and understand the local complexities, and can help build bridges with local partners that would otherwise be complex or even impossible for individual developers to negotiate on their own. They will also help shoulder the admin that comes with working with local sub-publishers.

31 Not all publishers are made equal though, and some have more experience in different markets than others. Developers should always stress-test their prospective publisher's experience in what are expected to be the game's core territories before signing the publishing deal, and if experience is lacking, the parties may agree to exclude limited territories from the scope of exclusive rights being granted to the publisher, or include a **reversion of rights** clause whereby rights revert to the developer if not exploited by the publisher within a set period of time.

VII. Term and termination

32 The term of the publishing agreement will typically run either for a specific number of years from the effective date, or from the effective date until a specific number of years after the game's commercial launch, with the latter option sometimes used to ensure a protracted development cycle does not risk eating into the publisher's period

of rights exploitation. This initial period represents the parties' mutual commitment to a minimum duration in which they will attempt to make a success of the game. Thereafter, the agreement may stipulate an auto-renewal of the term for successive periods, absent the objection of either party, or simply grant the publisher an option to renew its rights for an additional period of years. The precise duration of the term and the manner of its extension will generally be determined by the commercial balance of the deal and other practical considerations: what type of game is being developed; what is the length of the game's likely tail; how strong is the existing publisher-developer relationship and what is the likelihood that one or other might want to extricate themselves from said relationship in the medium, rather than long, term.

Standard termination rights in publishing agreements typically include provisions covering material breach and insolvency. Termination rights for material breach should usually permit a cure period to at least provide the breaching party an opportunity to correct their error, and parties may wish to specify certain breaches which would always be considered material. For example, a developer may seek to specify that material breach will have occurred where the publisher fails to meet its marketing spend obligations for any period of three successive months, or for three months in any six-month period. **33**

In certain circumstances, a publisher might push for an ability to **terminate for convenience**, although where any such right is granted, the developer will want to carefully consider the implications of such a termination at each of the various stages of the game's development and exploitation. Will the publisher be able to simply pay any outstanding amounts due and walk away? Where would that leave the developer if it has committed itself to ongoing development costs in the form of salaries and/or subcontractor agreements, and what is the developer's ability to manage those costs upon termination? In certain circumstances, and specifically where the developer is likely to find itself financially exposed, it might be appropriate to seek to negotiate an additional fee payable by the publisher in the event of termination without cause. **34**

So as to ensure an orderly exit from the relationship upon termination, publishing agreements will often set out a series of steps to be taken in such event during a prescribed 'wind-down period'. These might include the transfer of the game from the publisher back to the developer on relevant distribution platforms, return or destruction of each party's proprietary materials, and potentially a period of extended rights to enable the publisher to close down its operations with third parties in an orderly manner. In certain circumstances, the wind-down period might see the parties come together to negotiate in good faith a formal **wind-down plan** setting out in detail how the commercial relationship will be unpicked. Any such plan may want to consider as a priority issues such as: whether the game will continue to operate going forward; ongoing ownership of any consumer data acquired during the publishing activities to date; and whether the publisher should continue to receive a revenue stream from users it has previously paid to acquire for the game. **35**

In setting out a clear process for termination, the agreement can do a great service for both parties. As with any lengthy and important relationship, the publisher/developer association is best exited in an orderly fashion, and with a set of rules that creates the possibility of balanced negotiation between the parties. **36**

VIII. Derivative works

37 The video games industry is one of the richest sources of new IPs being made today. With engaging worlds, complex characters and emergent storytelling, games are prime for adaptation to other media formats such as film and TV. As a result, **derivative work rights** – the right to produce other content based on IP in the developed game – have re-emerged as one of the key points of discussion in recent years.

38 If the publisher owns the underlying game IP then the developer will often have little to no say in any derivative works being made. It may, however, be able to negotiate a 'right of first offer' to be the development partner for any future games in the series, and perhaps even some low residual revenue share for helping to build the original game. If the developer owns the game IP, then the developer will retain derivative work rights by default, and the publisher will only have whatever rights are explicitly set out in the publishing deal, if any.

39 Before giving up any such rights, a developer would be wise to query what experience their publisher actually has in bringing **transmedia** projects to life. Far too often, particularly in smaller 'indie' deals, transmedia rights are inelegantly wrapped up alongside merchandise and other ancillary products, given away on a sole and exclusive basis, but never actually exploited. Developers ought to seek to retain these rights, or at least include a rights reversion provision which would see those rights returned to the developer if not exploited within a pre-agreed time period.

D. Financial provisions

I. Overview

40 The financial provisions in a publishing deal will generally try to address two main topics – which party is paying for the game to get made, marketed and distributed, and how is any money coming in divided up. Whilst this sounds simple, the financial provisions are often one of the most hotly negotiated sections in any publishing agreement. This is partly because there is surprisingly little consistency throughout the industry regarding 'standard' deal terms. What is commonplace in 'AAA' deals will often not be in the 'indie' space, and even amongst deals in the same funding range financial terms can vary dramatically. As a result, financial provisions always need to be approached with alertness and a critical eye to ensure they are appropriate for the deal at hand and accurately reflect the commercial terms that have been agreed.

II. Development budget

41 In most publishing deals the publisher will be providing some amount of development funding to the developer to create the game. The amount of funding will naturally depend on the type of game being made, but also the stage at which a deal is being signed. It is common for developers to seek a publisher early in development, often right from game concept phase, or after having developed a limited playable prototype. However, some publishers provide what is known as 'finishing funding', which is intended to help developers bring an already in-development game to completion. The stage at which a publisher becomes involved will often impact a deal's financial terms, with

earlier-stage partnerships typically demanding more publisher-favoured terms to reflect the heightened investment risk.

Development funding will often be staggered out across a series of pre-agreed **milestones**, typically based around significant game development phases such as pre-production, alpha, beta, and release, with payment only being made after the publisher has approved the milestone in question. Each milestone will contain a description of the relevant deliverables expected, the due date for first submission to the publisher, and the amount of development funding attached. One exception to this is the frequently included 'on signing' milestone, which has no deliverables attached and is intended to kick-start the developer's initial work on the game. 42

The frequency of milestone submissions, and the corresponding payments attached, are two of the core factors determining a publisher's financial exposure during the development phase in any given deal. More frequent milestones with smaller payments attached can provide a publisher with greater visibility into progress on game development, which in turn can allow it to exercise its termination rights earlier and while minimising further financial investment into a project which is going significantly off-track. However, in the event that milestones occur too frequently, this can generate significant strain on the development team and impact its ability to make long-term investments. As with many aspects of the publishing deal, finding a fair balance is key. 43

III. Publisher costs

In addition to development funding, a publisher will typically incur a variety of other internal and external costs depending on the publishing services it is providing. Most publishers will be the one to incur these costs upfront but expect to recoup them once the game releases. Since these costs will eat into a game's profit, and in turn a developer's revenue share, developers often try to fight for some degree of control, or at the very least visibility, over these. Publishers often resist this on the basis that they require flexibility to leverage their expertise in determining how best to market and promote a product which, if done well, should result in greater sales and upside for all parties involved. As is often the case, with realistic expectations and open minds, reasonable compromises can be reached. This could include the parties mutually agreeing a high-level marketing strategy under which a publisher deploys a pre-agreed marketing budget. Or perhaps the publisher retains more day-to-day flexibility, but with a cap on the total amount of costs it can recoup. Or maybe a developer is granted a prior notification or consultation right, but not approval, over individual expenses above an agreed threshold. 44

IV. Recoupment

Once a game has released it will hopefully start generating revenue. This will typically be first collected by the distribution platforms through which a game is sold, though there are some exceptions where developers and publishers sell directly to their consumers. Those distribution platforms will collect the revenues, deduct applicable sales taxes, refunds, chargebacks and their platform distribution fee, and pay the remainder through to the publisher. Amounts received by the publisher are typically described as **'gross revenues'**. Most publishing deals are structured on a 'net revenue' sharing basis, with 'net' generally being the amount left after the publisher has recouped any agreed **'deductions'**. The list of permitted 'deductions' is therefore, unsurprisingly, a hotly 45 contested issue. This list typically includes a number of deductions that are made 'at source' (i.e., before money lands in a publisher's account), such as sales taxes, platform distribution fees and refunds and chargebacks. Items in contention could include costs surrounding engine fees, whether a publisher can recover its internal overhead costs, and costs paid out to third parties, such as development and distribution partners.

46 Some deals will be structured so that a publisher will recoup all of its costs, including the development funding and publishing costs, at a rate of 100% from gross revenues. This is the most pro-publisher model, as it is the fastest way for a publisher to recoup its investment. This model can be challenging for developers though, as it may result in serious cashflow issues, since they could be waiting months or even years before seeing any money from the project, even when it is a commercial success. As a result, another increasingly common approach in certain parts of the industry is a **day-zero** revenue share model. With this, the publisher would still receive the lion's share of revenues from day-zero in order to start recouping its investment, but the developer would start receiving a small revenue share as soon as the game releases. Once the publisher has recouped its costs, or potentially a multiple of its costs, the revenue share would flip to a more balanced **'post-recoup'** rate. This model can be of significant benefit to single-project developers with no alternative income sources.

47 Agreements should also state whether the publisher can recoup its costs incurred on one version of a game from profits derived from another version. This is generally known as **cross-collateralisation**, and mainly relevant where a developer and publisher are working on several games together, or a single game which is being ported to multiple platforms. Cross-collateralisation is frequently permitted. However, if a publisher holds the rights to make ports of a game without needing to involve the original developer, developers ought to consider this carefully to ensure profits from a successful base game are not being used to recoup costs from a less-successful port.

V. Reporting and payment

48 A publishing deal will typically require a publisher to provide some sort of **sales report** to the developer on a monthly or quarterly basis. These will be due within a set period of time after the end of each reporting period, as the publisher itself will need to obtain sales information from its own distribution partners.

49 There is generally little consistency between different publishers' sales reports, making it wise for a developer to ask for a publisher's template report prior to signing. At a minimum this should provide a developer with sufficient information to enable it to understand how its revenue share has been calculated, especially regarding any deductions or recoupment made by the publisher.

50 The agreement should also specify how long a publisher has to make payment following receipt of an invoice from the developer. Developers should seek to minimise this period where possible. When accounting for the time it takes for distribution platforms to report and pay out to publishers, publishers to report to developers, developers to invoice publishers, and publishers to pay out on those invoices, it is not uncommon for it to take close to six months between revenue being generated and that money actually landing in a developer's bank account.

51 Agreements should also often include standard provisions around matters such as payment currencies, currency conversions, de minimis payment thresholds, late interest and audit rights. **Audit provisions**, in particular, should be of keen interest to the savvy developer, given that it will often be paid a variable amount dependent on the

game's performance. Accordingly, developers will usually want to avail themselves of the necessary contractual tools to ensure that the sums they are being paid are accurate and contract-compliant.

Withholding taxes is an area which can often catch parties by surprise. These are taxes which are imposed by law when making cross-border payments. These can range from low single-digit percentages to 20% and upwards, and may be applicable on both development funding and royalties. It is therefore essential to establish from the outset if withholding taxes are going to apply, as this may require adjustment to the development budget itself. **52**

E. Legal terms and boilerplate

I. Warranties, indemnities and limitations on liability

Warranties are typically an opportunity for each party to consider and manage its particular areas of legal risk heading into a relationship. These provisions are therefore often highly bespoke, and tailored to the precise circumstances of the deal at hand. Nonetheless, there are certain warranties one might typically expect to encounter in a publishing agreement, since they speak to issues which tend to recur across such arrangements. **53**

Invariably, each party to a publishing agreement will warrant and represent that it has all necessary rights to offer their respective grant of rights thereunder, and to perform its respective obligations. From there, the developer will typically provide a series of warranties covering the game's contents, including that said contents will comply with applicable law, that they will be free from third-party rights infringement, defamation, invasion of privacy and moral rights, and that no royalties will be due to third parties in respect of such contents. These are important contractual guarantees to enable the publisher to proceed with exploitation of the rights granted in the game with full confidence that such exploitation will not create unprotected liabilities to third parties. **54**

Additional warranties are likely to be offered as to the technical quality of the game, assuring an absence of viruses or similar, and potentially that the software will be materially bug-free, and will not contain any unidentified 'Easter eggs', or other hidden content. Depending on the publisher's concerns, warranties may also be sought to the effect that the developer has the necessary technical resources and abilities to meet the various deadlines set out in the agreement, that it is not the subject of pending litigation, and that it does not have in place any policies or practices that might potentially adversely impact the publisher's reputation. **55**

The publisher, in turn, will generally be asked to similarly warrant that it will comply with all applicable laws in performance of its obligations and exercise of its rights pursuant to the agreement, that it will only exploit said rights per the terms of the agreement, and that it will promptly notify the developer of any third-party claims that have the potential to place the developer in breach. While the developer may request some degree of warranty protection as to the quality of the services publisher will be providing, typically, the publisher would not be expected to offer guarantees as to the extent of likely sales or revenues derived from the game, unless this has already been negotiated as a specific commercial deal point. **56**

The parties will want to give careful thought to the allocation of responsibility for any music rights which will be contained within the game. Often, this duty will sit with the developer, which is usually best placed to conduct selection and tracking of in-game **57** music, and which will accordingly be requested to provide warranties that all third-party fees which may be owed in connection with the sale or exploitation of the game have been paid, including synchronisation and mechanical royalties. In turn, the developer may wish to require that the publisher provides information necessary to facilitate such payment on an ongoing basis.

58 Ultimately, the agreement's warranties remain amongst the parties' best opportunities to set out their key concerns for the relationship ahead, to allocate responsibilities which are at particular risk of misunderstanding, and to ensure that there are no unexpected surprises. As with any long-term contractual relationship, the attentive lawyer should pay close attention to the wording of specific warranties, both in terms of its implications for the rights and liabilities of their client, and in terms of what said wording may reveal about the concerns and intentions of the counterparty. The contract negotiation process can deliver opportunities to address issues and misalignments before they can be allowed to fester, and often such opportunities manifest themselves most clearly during warranty discussions.

59 Given that there is likely to be a flow of services, and potentially intellectual property, in both directions, the publishing agreement will often see both parties provide **indemnities**, although as the originator of the agreement's key IP, the developer can typically expect to find itself granting the more fulsome indemnities of the pair. Mutual indemnities might cover breach of all representations and warranties under the agreement, and may also extend in some circumstances to any breach of obligation. The developer may also be requested to provide additional specific indemnity cover for third-party claims regarding IP in the game. As ever, careful thought should be given as to the precise circumstances of the deal, and the parties should be mindful to avoid 'double indemnities', whereby a liability that is already indemnified via warranty is also specified as an additional indemnified head using slightly different language, effectively giving two opportunities to claim against the same head of loss.

60 Depending on the respective bargaining strengths of the parties, the publishing agreement may also include a **limitation of liability** clause. Here, the parties may seek to identify heads of loss that are to be excluded for any claim (for example: indirect losses and/or punitive damages, such as lost profits and/or business interruption), and specify an overall liability cap for the quantum of each party's cumulative liabilities under the agreement. Commonly for agreements concerning themselves with a mix of services and intellectual property, one might anticipate a fiscal liability cap measured against some percentage of the overall fees paid and payable pursuant to the agreement, with carve outs to ensure that liabilities pursuant to indemnities and breach of confidentiality sit outside such cap. These carve outs are important, given that the potential losses to a party as a result of, for example, a third-party IP claim, or a fine for breach of applicable law, might be valued well in excess of the fees paid pursuant to the agreement.

II. Boilerplate

61 In common with any commercial contract, the publishing agreement contains a number of **boilerplate** provisions at its end which set out the rules by which the agreement itself will be governed. While it is tempting to consider these clauses as less material than those which precede them, close attention should still be paid to their fine detail, since these are provisions in which small variances in wording can have outsized consequences.

As with any agreement in which valuable IP is being licensed and/or assigned, the inclusion of an **insurance** provision should be regarded as non-negotiable. The transfer of IP invariably carries with it material contingent liabilities, and accordingly it is important for each party to know that the other is in a position to meet any financial commitments which may arise via the contract. A publisher will have cause for regret if it attempts to rely on its beautifully drafted, legally watertight indemnities and warranties, only to discover that all that care and precision has gone to waste because, even in the event of a successful claim, the developer cannot meet its financial obligations thereunder. Every rainbow must have the requisite pot of gold at its end, after all. The insurance provision, in which one or both parties commit to securing and maintaining insurance coverage sufficient to meet all their liabilities pursuant to the agreement, ideally with types of policy and limits of cover clearly specified, is therefore key to ensuring peace of mind. 62

The **assignment** clause is a provision that can seem, on the face of it, relatively benign, but which has the potential for material consequences down the line if not carefully thought through. The basic position of the clause is usually that no assignment of the agreement should occur without the consent of the other party, a relatively reasonable sounding concept which can easily create an unintended hostage to fortune in a number of common corporate scenarios. A publisher that is part of a larger corporate group may, for example, find itself subject to internal reorganisation from time to time, and accordingly may require an ability to freely assign the agreement, and its rights, to its affiliate companies to ensure that said rights can continue to be properly exploited. Likewise, a developer may have in mind future potential changes to its structure or ownership that would similarly necessitate that the agreement be transferred unencumbered, although it should be recognised that few publishers will relish the prospect of discovering mid-project that a new and unexpected third party is now responsible for the development of the game towards which they have been paying. The parties should be relatively open about their respective requirements in this area, and seek drafting solutions to balance any specific concerns around retaining the necessary flexibility for the road ahead with each party's need for reassurance that their carefully selected partner will not suddenly and without approval disappear. 63

F. Conclusions

The cornerstone of any good deal is finding a win-win arrangement that properly incentivises and rewards all parties involved. A recoupment structure that de-risks a project for a publisher but at the cost of the development partner's survivability is short-sighted, and a structure that is too favourable to a developer might de-incentivise a publisher from seriously investing on the marketing front if its potential upside is judged to be limited. A creative control clause or milestone approvals process which completely usurps a developer's creativity over its creative visions can build resentment, but a deal with no publisher control can pose an unacceptable financial risk or result in publishers exercising their kill-rights too eagerly to minimise further financial exposure. 64

The task of the lawyer when approaching a publishing agreement is to approach each of the contract's challenges looking to find the proper balance, and to be mindful that what might seem a win in the short term may often prove to be a loss over a longer horizon, as the publisher/developer relationship plays out across the life of the project. 65

By focusing on win-win, rather than either party seeking to maximise its own upside or minimise its exposure at all cost, the parties are more likely to strike a fair deal that 66 sets a solid foundation for what will hopefully be a long and fruitful relationship for all concerned. True mastery of the publishing agreement requires both the appetite to deliver such solid foundations, and the aptitude to consistently identify structures and solutions which will help to give the project its best chance of success.

§ 20
Game Localisation and Culturalisation: Navigating Creative Challenges on a Global Scale

Bibliography: Articy, 'Interview: Kate Edwards', (Articy, 17.9.2019), Detailed discussion on non-linguistic cultural elements. articy.com; Chandler/Deming, 'The Game Localization Handbook', 3rd edn, Sudbury, Massachusetts 2021; Edwards, 'Culturalization: The Geopolitical and Cultural Dimension of Content Localization', 2020 Geogrify White Paper; Hansen/Houlmont, 'A Snapshot into the Possibility of Video Game Machine Translation. arXiv.' (September 2022), Analyzes MT within game localization pipelines, arxiv.org; Henley, TheGamer, 'Interview: Kate Edwards On Culturalization In Gaming' (TheGamer, 6. August 2021), Edwards explains how she separates localisation from culturalization, https://www.thegamer.com/interview-kate-edwards-culturalization-gaming/; Mangiron, 'Culturalization in the Video Game Industry: Current Trends and Future Prospects', Perspectives: Studies in Translation Theory and Practice 2023, 147–163; National Geographic, '2022 Global Literacy and Cultural Awareness Survey' (2022), https://www.nationalgeographic.com/culture-survey; Nordic Game, 'When Worlds Collide: Creating Games in a Polarizing World – Kate Edwards' (21. May 2025). Retrieved from conference program. nordicgame.com; O'Hagan, 'Game Localization and Cultural Sensitivity: Case Studies from the Asia-Pacific'. Translation Spaces 2022, 23–47; OIGC, (2016), 'Cultural Challenges to Video Game Localization with Kate Edwards', Conference keynote overview; Rivas Ginel/Theroine, 'Gender in Video Games: Creativity for Inclusivity. arXiv.' (May 2024), Examines localisation's role in inclusive gender representation, https://arxiv.org/abs/2407.16536; The Doodle People, 'The Importance of Culturalization in Video Games: Insights from Kate Edwards' (The Doodle People, 31.5.2024), Highlights Edwards on history handling and early integration. thedoodlepeople.com; Unity Technologies, 'Game Localization Best Practices', (2023), retrieved from https://unity.com/resources/game-localization-best-practices; Wikipedia (2025-06), 'Video Game Localization', en.wikipedia.org, contains updated insights, including Edwards' 2006 'Fun vs. Offensive' GDC strategy; Zhang/Uyemura, 'Level Up Your Game Culturalization! With Insights from Kate Edwards', (GlobalSaké Growth Blog, 11. September 2025), an interview and practitioner-based overview featuring Edwards' role in advancing culturalization strategies. https://www.globalsakegrowth.com/post/level-up-your-game-culturalization-with-insights-from-kate-edwards.

A. The landscape of cultural perception 2
B. What is game localisation and how it works 9
C. When localisation should occur in development 13
D. The importance of game culturalisation 15
E. Degrees of culturalisation 18
F. Types of culturalisation challenges 23
 I. History: past and present 24
 II. Religion and faith: sacred vs. secular 25
 III. Ethnicity: inclusion vs. exclusion 26
 IV. Geopolitics: imaginations of sovereignty 27
G. The role of subject-matter expertise 29
H. Organisational considerations 32
I. Conclusion: key actions and a word about intent 39

Imagine that you've recently completed a long-term game project for a major publisher, and by all measures it's been a successful endeavour. Congratulations are exchanged all around, and the game is launched into the target markets while those involved move on to the next project. Months later, long after the glow of accomplishment has waned, you receive an unexpected e-mail from a government ministry in one of the target markets. The message outlines the government's great dissatisfaction with one of your game's content assets – the use of an icon that is considered **culturally offensive** to them – to a point where the release is being threatened with a local ban unless fixed immediately. As you quickly contact your legal, PR, development and other stakeholders to prepare for action, some thoughts may run through your mind: 'How did we miss 1 this?' 'What should we have done that we're not already doing?' 'How much does this specific market contribute to our global revenue?'

A. The landscape of cultural perception

2 Back in the earlier days of software creation and distribution, and around the time of the author's early career in the 1990s, the majority of software was distributed on CD-ROMs and DVDs as packaged products that were physically shipped to specific markets around the world. The source company had the ability to target their offerings to whichever markets they felt were strategically important, and in the event one of their product versions ended up in a non-targeted locale, they could rely upon a certain degree of **plausible deniability**. In other words, if the software's content was not culturally or geopolitically compatible with a local market, and the company had no intention of shipping the product there, then the company could blame it on the **black or grey markets** and sidestep (most) of their accountability.

3 However, through the years since then, software and game creation has evolved and at this point, the great majority of content is distributed via internet channels and less as physical media. When content is released today, it instantly becomes ubiquitous and exposed to a **broad multicultural audience**, often without the slow trickle effect of the past when companies had to wait to determine the cultural compatibility. And while many companies today still operate under the illusion that their content is geo-targeted and only available to whichever markets they prioritise, the reality is that all content that is released now is instantly global – regardless of what the company intends it to be. In short, the system that fuels content creation and global distribution has dramatically changed.

4 Another major shift over the past couple of decades that has changed the dynamic of content creation is the emergence of social media – i.e., **the enabling of instant, targeted feedback** from anyone, anywhere towards any content producer. In this often-harsh environment of the knee-jerk backlash and reactions without context, the creators' intentions have become mostly irrelevant. In the early days of the internet, we experienced many general discussions and mostly civil disagreements around issues discussed in nascent online forums. But these have now mutated into **full blown culture wars**, primarily fuelled by tech companies like Meta (Facebook), Alphabet (Google), and X (formerly Twitter) which generate a healthy profit off the phenomenon. There do remain some online forums where people can have constructive dialogues, but most people have been siloed into online echo chambers which reinforce the inclusion of like-minded people while excluding those who may think differently – to the point of 'cancelling' them (effectively erasing their digital existence). As a result, we have a plethora of toxic online environments where anything and everything is seemingly offered up for a vitriolic debate – from religion to politics, from reactions to a simple meme to the latest game release.

5 This has resulted in a wide range of effects depending on the type of media under scrutiny by the online masses. In the case of video games, they are still working to confirm the reality that they are truly a form of art which can address the same serious and challenging topics as would a film or a book. But games still must cope with the uninformed people (including many politicians) who conclude that **if a game isn't 'fun', then it must be regulated or banned.** This kind of thinking persists today, even though we've seen signs of positive change – such as the US Supreme Court's ruling in 2011 that games are protected free speech on the same artistic level as film, literature, art, etc.

So, creating content today is not only an issue of how we distribute it but also how we must manage the immediate reactions from a massive online audience and the toxicity that often comes with it. But there's yet another dimension that transcends and, in some ways, overshadows both the distribution and reaction issues, and that's the fundamental aspect of default audience, i.e., **for whom are we creating the content?** 6

For decades now, most companies often made their content with the Western mindset as the default version – namely, thinking of North America and Western Europe as their primary markets. The logic was that given the relatively **high levels of freedom of speech** and allowability of content in these regions, a company could create the default version of the content they are releasing (a film, a video game, etc.) and still maintain a very high degree of creative freedom and integrity. If the content of the default version was not going to align with certain local values or requirements, minor revisions could be made from market to market but for the most part, the great majority of the creative vision would remain intact. And then, this content produced with a default Western worldview could then be adapted as needed to locales beyond the region – to make localised and culturalised versions for the Middle East, South Asia, East Asia, and so on – to appease the general sensitivities in other worldviews. 7

Nowhere are cultural and geopolitical sensitivities more prominent than in video games. As global exports, games are among the most culturally expressive and potentially controversial forms of digital content. Localisation in games goes beyond translation – it includes adapting gameplay mechanics, character design, religious references, and political allusions to suit regional expectations. **Culturalisation, a deeper process, anticipates potential friction points** – such as religious symbolism, national identity, or gender portrayal – before they trigger rejection or censorship. 8

B. What is game localisation and how it works

Game localisation is the process of adapting the text content of video games for a specific target market, ensuring that it feels natural and relevant to the local audience. While it primarily involves translating the game's text and dialogue, localisation also extends to: 9

- **Voice acting** and lip-sync adjustments for dubbed versions
- **Cultural adaptation** of character names, jokes, idioms, and user interfaces
- **Technical adjustments** to time formats, currency, and legal disclaimers

This process is often facilitated by **localisation engineers, translators, and quality assurance testers** working collaboratively with development teams. It ensures that the user experience remains engaging and culturally appropriate across regions. 10

Localisation is not merely a technical step; it's a **strategic business decision**. The global video game market is highly segmented – regions such as Japan, South Korea, Germany, Brazil, and the MENA region each present distinct linguistic, regulatory, and cultural expectations. Effective localisation which is performed proactively in development can: 11

- **Boost market reach**: Games released in local languages are more likely to succeed in non-English-speaking regions.
- **Drive revenue growth**: According to industry reports, well-localised games can see up to 50 % greater revenue in international markets compared to unlocalised or poorly localised ones.

- **Protect brand reputation**: Avoiding translation and cultural missteps helps prevent PR crises, bans, or social media backlash.
- **Enhance player immersion**: Localisation increases emotional connection, especially in story-driven or culturally nuanced games.

12 Conversely, poorly localised games risk alienating players, appearing tone-deaf, or even worse, **being blocked from release by local authorities.**

C. When localisation should occur in development

13 **Ideally, localisation should be integrated early in the game development cycle, not added as a post-production step.** This proactive approach is called simultaneous or continuous localisation, and it offers several benefits:

- **Reduces cost and rework**: Content created with localisation in mind requires fewer retrofits.
- **Enables early cultural review**: Potential red flags can be flagged and resolved before art, narrative, or gameplay elements are locked.
- **Facilitates global launch strategies**: Sim-ship (simultaneous worldwide release) is only possible when localisation is part of the development pipeline.
- **Encourages collaboration**: Early involvement of localisation experts fosters more culturally inclusive design.

14 Many game studios now follow 'localisation-ready' practices from the earliest stages – starting with adaptable code, editable text strings, and modular game assets. **Planning for localisation upfront is both a production efficiency and a safeguard against unintended cultural fallout.**

D. The importance of game culturalisation

15 Culturalisation goes a step further beyond localisation as it takes a deeper look into a game's fundamental assumptions and content choices, and then gauges their viability in both the broad, multicultural marketplace as well as in specific geographic locales. **While localisation helps players comprehend the game's text content, culturalisation empowers players to potentially engage with the game's content at a deeper, more meaningful level.** Or conversely, culturalisation ensures that gamers will not be *disengaged* from the game by a piece of content that is considered incongruent or even offensive to their cultural worldview.

16 For most game developers and publishers, localisation is an assumed aspect of game distribution; most publishers already regularly localise their games into a wide variety of languages. However, with a significant portion of game industry revenue being generated through localisation and the trend of a growing global focus of the industry, **localisation alone isn't enough to sustain revenues and interest.** This is especially true as more local game development increases, putting home grown indie game content in competition with global IPs.

17 While the trend is slowly changing, most localisation efforts on a game title currently happen later in the development cycle which leaves little room for ensuring a completely thorough and effective localisation. Usually, the better examples of game localisation are cases where localisation considerations were addressed early on and throughout the project. This is particularly true of the process of content culturalisation. In order to

account for locale-specific content sensitivities, culturalisation requires a very *proactive* approach to content design and development, wherein the international viability of the content is considered throughout the cycle. Put simply, culturalisation isn't just a required step for selling overseas; it becomes a holistic *modus operandi* for the game's design, development and distribution which acknowledges the reality of global exposure on the first day of release. **At its core, culturalisation is about maximising the global inclusivity of a game's creative vision.**

E. Degrees of culturalisation

What we understand currently as 'localisation' is actually just one element in a broader scale of content culturalisation. **In its most rudimentary form, content culturalisation can be viewed as the following three phases:** 18

1. Avoid disruptive issues to allow a game to remain in the target market.
2. Perform 'typical' localisation to allow the game to be understood.
3. Adapt and provide locale-specific options to allow the game to be locally relevant.

Stated simply, a more straightforward way to view these three phases is as follows: 19

1. Reactive culturalisation: Make the content viable.
2. Localisation: Make the content legible.
3. Proactive culturalisation: Make the content meaningful.

Let's examine these three phases and elaborate further. Making content 'viable' essentially means allowing the content (and by implication, the product/service that contains it) to remain in the target locale. This means that there exists no issue in the content that could cause a local government and/or players to react negatively and thus initiate a potentially costly and embarrassing backlash episode, thus this step is labelled as 'reactive culturalisation. **Culturalisation at its most fundamental level tends to focus on the reactive aspect, i.e., identifying and removing potentially problematic issues from the release equation.** 20

Making game content more meaningful through proactive culturalisation is a step that many developers are starting to grasp and implement. It's arguably a more time-intensive and research-dependent aspect of content creation yet the return on the investment can potentially be very significant. We're talking about tailoring at a more fundamental level, so that gamers perceive the game as something as 'local' in nature or at least very locally relevant. From a game community aspect, **adding more local meaning to a game enhances the reputation of the game developer as they become known as a studio that truly cares about local-specific expectations**. Often times, this entails choosing a specific market or culture, and choosing to make extensive modifications to tailor the game to that narrowly-defined audience. 21

Strategic game culturalisation requires cross-functional collaboration between a variety of studio stakeholders – not only the designers, artists, producers, legal and marketing but also linguists, cultural consultants, and geopolitical experts. Many studios such as Ubisoft, Sony, and Microsoft have developed internal protocols for performing cultural risk review, while independent developers are increasingly outsourcing this expertise. In an era where digital content crosses borders instantly, culturalisation has become not only a best practice but a necessity for global market success. 22

F. Types of culturalisation challenges

23 In the global games industry, content reflects the culture of its origin—and inevitably encounters the values and sensitivities of the markets where it is distributed. **Game developers must navigate how design choices can be received abroad, especially in key areas where cultural conflicts frequently arise: history, religion, ethnicity, and geopolitics.**

I. History: past and present

24 **Games that draw on real history or reimagine past events can trigger strong reactions when cultural memory clashes with creative license. Even with factual grounding, interpretations can be contested.**

- *Assassin's Creed Mirage* (2023), which explores 9th-century Baghdad, received early praise for its attention to historical detail. However, prior *Assassin's Creed* titles have drawn criticism in countries like Italy and Turkey for perceived distortions of national or religious history.
- In *Call of Duty: Modern Warfare II* (2022), one mission set in a fictionalised Iranian context sparked backlash in Persian-language communities for reinforcing Western military narratives, despite being framed as fictional. Similarly, *Six Days in Fallujah* was revived in 2023 after years of dormancy – still surrounded by criticism for portraying a traumatic and recent real-world conflict.

II. Religion and faith: sacred vs. secular

25 **Religion remains one of the most sensitive aspects of culturalisation.** Content perceived as disrespectful toward sacred beliefs can lead to swift and widespread condemnation. Developers must consider that in sacred societies, context may not matter: simply including religious elements – regardless of intent – can be seen as transgressive.

- *Smite* (Hi-Rez Studios) continues to draw controversy for turning active deities – like Hindu gods and Japanese kami – into playable combatants. Hindu groups in particular have protested the depiction of gods like Kali and Ganesha in violent, player-controlled scenarios.
- In 2018, *Detroit: Become Human* faced criticism in some Islamic communities for including Quranic text in an in-game setting. Although meant as environmental detail, its use in a fictional, secular future was viewed as irreverent.

III. Ethnicity: inclusion vs. exclusion

26 **Representation of ethnicity continues to be a flashpoint**, particularly when stereotypes or colonial imagery are invoked – intentionally or otherwise. The growing demand for authentic, nuanced ethnic representation – especially from underrepresented groups – makes consultation and inclusion key to avoiding backlash.

- *Far Cry 5* (2018) reversed earlier franchise tropes by focusing on a white American doomsday cult. However, some critics noted that it avoided deeper commentary on U.S. racial and political tensions – suggesting that cultural sensitivity might have gone too far into caution.

- *Ghost of Tsushima* (2020), developed by a Western studio, was largely embraced by Japanese audiences, but it also reignited debates about authenticity and cultural ownership. Conversely, *Resident Evil Village* (2021) faced critique for its portrayal of Eastern European villagers as primitive and monstrous, echoing colonial-era depictions.

IV. Geopolitics: imaginations of sovereignty

Maps, flags, and territorial claims are highly politicised in many markets. Games that touch on real-world borders – even indirectly – can face government censorship or market exclusion. 27

- In 2020, *Animal Crossing: New Horizons* was pulled from Chinese platforms after Hong Kong protesters used the in-game customisation tools to display pro-democracy messages. This highlighted how even apolitical games can become geopolitical flashpoints.
- *PUBG Mobile* underwent regional modification in India and the Middle East due to both political tensions and content deemed inappropriate. It was rebranded as *Battlegrounds Mobile India* in 2021, with content changes reflecting local regulatory pressures.
- Even fictional maps are not immune. In *Arma 3*, modded content that included sensitive border representations led to takedown demands in regions like China and Turkey.

Culturalisation issues in games rarely fall into one category. History, religion, ethnicity, and geopolitics often overlap – making culturalisation a multidimensional challenge of intersecting sensitivities. While ignoring these concerns may seem easier, a proactive approach can help developers avoid backlash, maintain market access, and demonstrate respect for diverse audiences worldwide. 28

G. The role of subject-matter expertise

How one navigates the complexities will, of course, depend greatly on what knowledge and experience is at your disposal. **One of the most asked questions regarding the culturalisation process is: How can I know what I don't know?** 29

Without question, the fields of localisation and culturalisation contain a wide variety of subject-matter experts from very diverse backgrounds – from linguistics and translation technologies to sociology and anthropology (and even geography). But in any individual aspect of the culturalisation process, some skills are more tuned to the content need, and the situation with deep-level geopolitical and cultural content is no different. The skills found in the disciplines of geography, political science, international relations and other related fields are often not overtly and purposefully associated with this work, let alone game development. In order to achieve deeper levels of understanding of the local, non-traditional skills and experience are required. **It's critical to seek out additional voices, perspectives and approaches to culture that can inform a more comprehensive approach to content creation.** 30

In recent years, many developers have come to realise that **seeking out representatives (consultants, sensitivity readers, etc.) from local geographies, cultural groups, ethnicities, genders, and other demographic groups is the only path to success** when including real-world cultural themes and/or allegories in their game worlds. 31

H. Organisational considerations

32 **Just as important as the content types and their related risks are the organisational factors that contribute to overall risk**, namely, content management methodology and processes. In terms of consequences of a culturalisation-related misstep, the outcome will depend on several factors, some of which are as follows:

- Government relations: The state of the relationship of your company, your general industry, and/or your country/region of origin to the local government and/or consumers.
- Local media control: The degree to which the local government controls information and/or regulates international business within its boundaries.
- Issue severity: The severity of the cultural issue that was present in your content (that is, how deep was the offense?).
- Discoverability: The cultural issue in your product or service (how easy it was to find).

33 Most typically, all these factors combine into an overall assessment of the potential risk (if viewed proactively) or potential negative response (if viewed reactively). **General organisational acknowledgement of the potential risks is not typically sufficient to effectively find and resolve such culturalisation issues; and, sadly, many studios address such issues in a reactive mode.**

34 **Content must be developed and managed (and resolved, as necessary) with an overt organisational commitment to the cultural impact of game content.** The goal is to ensure that processes, whether existing or new, must contain the essential elements to ensure oversight and review of localisation and culturalisation issues, which implies consideration of necessary resources to conduct such reviews – both internal and external to the organisation. The form of the effective process to manage such content risks is highly dependent on a company's specific needs. At a fundamental level, there are three key organisational aspects that should be addressed:

35 **Process. Specific processes in place or inclusion in existing processes to identify and mitigate out such issues.**

36 **Ownership. Clear ownership of localisation and culturalisation issues in a game's development process.**

37 **Escalation. Create and reinforce escalation protocols that ensure timely communication between management and key stakeholders in the event of a crisis.**

38 Even partially addressing these three areas has been helpful to many creators, but fully addressing all the areas in the context of the organisation **will help foster a more proactive methodology.**

I. Conclusion: key actions and a word about intent

39 To return to the hypothetical scenario at the start of this article, hopefully the answers to 'How did we miss this?' and other questions are clearer. Given the nature of linguistic and cultural content challenges, some readers may feel daunted, but it's important to stress that **concrete actions can be taken to improve one's chances in dealing proactively and adeptly with such issues.**

40 **Be aware. Comprehension of the reality of cultural risks in content is often 50 % of the challenge in starting to address them.** Oftentimes in a US-based company, heavy reliance may be placed on subsidiary employees, localisation teams and/or non-US em-

ployees to provide the required local insight. All such resources are important to leverage, but ultimately the awareness of each employee – regardless of their origin – is critical to long-term success. Corporate inclusion efforts across many game studios have shown progress in broadening perspectives.

Be proactive. As the conventional saying goes, 'the early bird catches the worm'. 41
Without trying to be too trite, the saying is especially applicable in regards to culturalisation. Time and again, experience has shown that **finding and resolving such issues *as early as possible* during development will directly affect the time and costs expended to fix them later in the process**, not to mention the much greater costs if an issue is never found and then publicly exposed after release. This sentiment is shared among many in the localisation and culturalisation industry who must respond too late to any content changes – and it's likewise never too early to start considering the impact of the cultural dimension on content.

Be committed. The key to long-term success is to make the commitment to invest in resources, training and processes that are necessary to stay aware and proactive. 42
Business-specific and market-specific experience with such issues will demonstrate the need for specific resources, tools and more efficient processes to effectively manage these content considerations. The forms and combinations of resources and subject-matter expertise will greatly depend on the specific company, the specific game, target markets and other such variables.

In closing, one critical factor that requires mention is that of intent. Even if you take 43
all the proactive steps to become aware, to create an efficient organisational process and to verify content types as needed by leveraging subject-matter expertise, there remains the powerful force of local market perception – a fact that's common across all transnational businesses from the petroleum industry to IT to games. **In the author's experience, 99 % of culturalisation errors are the result of completely unintentional circumstances (note: unintentional, but not excusable). And yet in 99 % of those cases the local market perceived the errors to be completely intentional on the part of the game developer.** Players often raise questions such as 'Why did your company do this to us?' 'How could a huge publisher possibly get this wrong?' and so forth. Taking these comments in the context of the age-old differences between viewpoints, it's a natural reaction. However, while functioning in today's connected world, the affected company can't fall back on the age-old excuse of a lack of information. It might have worked in the Age of Exploration, but it's not very credible in the Age of Information. Intent is always a key issue to remember with offending content issues, and ultimately responding to the perception of intent is the key to resolution.

By proactively considering today's dynamic geopolitical and cultural landscape and how it affects your game project, it is entirely possible to more safely navigate the content issues and prepare for the uncertainties. With diligent planning and appropriate resources to develop the rationale, game creators can achieve a strategy of informed defensibility for their content choices and begin to view cultural content risks as positive opportunities to better serve the local player. 44

§ 21
Greener Play: EU Environmental Law and Games

A. Introduction 1
B. Environmental footprint of the video games sector 5
C. EU environmental legislation and video games 9
I. Corporate Sustainability Reporting Directive (CSRD) 10
II. Corporate Sustainability Due Diligence Directive (CSDDD) 16
III. Waste Electronic and Electric Equipment Directive (WEEED) 25
IV. Ecodesign Regulation and GCVA 29
V. Right to Repair Regulation 31
VI. Data centres reporting delegated regulation 33
D. Emerging trends and green technologies in gaming 35
I. Development 36
II. Publishing 38
III. Playing 41
E. Conclusion 42

A. Introduction

1 The EU's ambition to become the first climate-neutral continent by 2050 was heralded as 'Europe's man on the moon moment' by the European Commission at the start of the 2019–2024 legislature. The implementation of this 'European Green Deal' has led to the adoption of what has been described as a 'tsunami' of new **environment-related legislative texts** (often also comprising a social element), imposing far-reaching obligations on all sectors and industries.

2 While it is not the most affected sector, the video games industry is no exception. Under these new legislative developments, video game developers and publishers will be subject to **rules covering aspects ranging from general environmental reporting and specific data centre efficiency indicators reporting to due diligence obligations and the pursuit of carbon emission reduction objectives, in line with the Paris agreement**. Our aim in this chapter is to provide an overview of some of the more relevant EU legislative instruments in the context of development, publishing and distributing video games and consoles.

3 While the start of the 2024-2029 legislature has been characterised by an increasing focus on competitiveness, and a far-reaching simplification/recalibration agenda, the Commission has been adamant that it will **'stay firmly on course toward our decarbonisation goals'**, including by assisting EU businesses' decarbonation journey through the adoption of a new 'Clean Industrial Deal'. The direction of travel, and the main obligations imposed by EU environmental legislation, remain, especially for larger companies.

4 In this contribution, we will begin by looking at **what the main sources of emissions in the video games sector are**, before examining **how the most relevant new EU environmental legislation will apply to the sector**. Subsequently, we will look at some of the **initiatives already taken by the sector** which can be considered exemplary in the context of what is expected under existing law, and **what avenues of further 'greening' are possible.**

B. Environmental footprint of the video games sector

According to International Telecommunication Union (ITU), two thirds of the world's population are now online.[1] As a result, the overall internet and communication technology (ICT) sector's share of global carbon emissions ranges from 1.5 % to 4 %.[2] The video games sector is responsible for a fraction of this.[3] **Precise carbon emissions estimations for the video games sector are difficult to obtain**, but some estimates of its carbon footprint do exist: These carbon emissions stem from the development of games themselves,[4] the transport and distribution of hardware, and the actual playing of the games.[5] Carbon calculators, specifically designed towards addressing the particularities of the video games industry, are now beginning to enter the scene, which will contribute significantly towards **carbon emissions measurement**.[6] Additionally, a 2023 report by the Playing for the Planet Alliance explores the challenges of applying GHG Protocol accounting and reporting standards to organizations in the video gaming sector, could serve as a practical guide for video game businesses in measuring and reducing their emissions.[7] 5

The **majority of emissions from the video games sector as a whole stem from hardware manufacturing**, namely video game consoles and their peripherals. Also relevant (albeit shrinking) elements are the storage supports for physical copies of games (CDs, cartridges, and their packaging). Digital distribution has been increasing over recent years, and to do so, we have seen an increase in energy consumption of data centres and networks. Another relevant aspect pertains to the gaming hardware lifecycles, namely e-waste and associated recycling challenges. 6

One aspect that makes it difficult to calculate the aggregate impact of the games industry is that a very large proportion, estimated at 80–95 %,[8] of emissions related to 7

---

[1] ITU Press Release, 27.11.2024 https://www.itu.int/en/mediacentre/Pages/PR-2024-11-27-facts-and-figures.aspx.

[2] International Telecommunications Union/World Bank, 'Measuring the Emissions & Energy Footprint of the ICT Sector: Implications for Climate Action.' p. 1. <https://documents1.worldbank.org/curated/en/099121223165540890/pdf/P17859712a98880541a4b71d57876048abb.pdf>.

[3] In Sweden, it is estimated that the games sector corresponds to 0.015 % of the emissions from Swedish industry. This should take into consideration that games account for almost 0.3 % of jobs in the private sector and 1 % of Swedish exports. Source: The Swedish Games Industry, 'Climate Code Creativity' p. 17, https://dataspelsbranschen.se/nyheter/2024/10/24/new-report-code-climate-creativity-swedens-games-industry-aim-to-take-lead-in-green-transition.

[4] Estimated to represent around 0.04 % of global carbon emissions; Abraham, Digital Games After Climate Change, Palgrave & MacMillan, Switzerland 2022.

[5] The French Agency for Ecological Transition estimated that, in France, at least an hour of gaming amounts to an average of about 200g CO2e (carbon dioxide-equivalent emissions). This includes all of the upstream, use, and end-of-life emissions from the gaming console, TV, network transmission, and data centres. 78 % of this 200g CO2e comes from the console itself, 18 % from the TV, and the remaining 4 % from network transmission. Data centre emissions were considered negligible. As reported in Playing for the Planet/Carbon Trust 'Untangling the carbon complexities of the games industry report', pp. 19–20, https://www.playing4theplanet.org/project/carbon-complexities-report.

[6] For example, the Playing for the Planet calculator (https://www.playing4theplanet.org/carboncalculator), the French JYROS calculator (https://jyros-jeuvideo.com/en/home-english/), the Finnish calculator prepared by Neogames (https://neogames.fi/finnish-game-industry-model-for-co2-emissions-calculations-an-update/), or the Swedish Play Create Calculate (https://dataspelsbranschen.se/playcreatecalculate) project.

[7] Playing for the Planet/Carbon Trust 'Untangling the carbon complexities of the games industry report' https://www.playing4theplanet.org/project/carbon-complexities-report.

[8] Abraham, SGA Standard: Scope 3 issues briefing paper, 1.8.2024 <https://docs.google.com/document/d/10i_hpL6-FDt7GtN1cGhL_FMwmap09SxgF9cIYa_YErY/edit?ref=gtg.benabraham.net&tab=t.0#heading=h.6vchx3anglnz>.

video games are in the so-called **'Scope 3' category, namely emissions in a company's upstream and downstream value chain.**[9] The sourcing of raw materials necessary for the hardware is an obvious example.

8 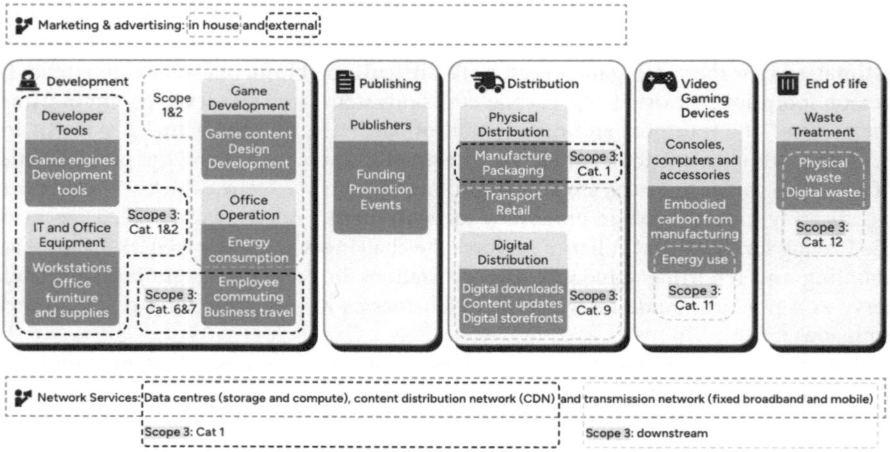

Fig.1: Scope of emissions in the video games sector value chain and their breakdown[10]

C. EU environmental legislation and video games

9 The European Green Deal is an ambitious roadmap for making the EU's economy sustainable. This entailed the passing of dozens of new regulations and directives during the 2019–2024 legislature, of which we have selected a few which we believe are most relevant for a law practitioner approaching this subject in relation to the video games sector. **We start our review with the two 'flagship' EU instruments, the CSRD and CSDDD**, as modified by the 'Omnibus I Simplification Package' adopted at the start of the 2024-2029 Commission mandate, before discussing a number of few sectoral instruments applicable to the video games industry.

I. Corporate Sustainability Reporting Directive (CSRD)

10 The CSRD,[11] which started to enter into application in 2025 for financial year 2024 for the largest in-scope companies,[12] **broadens the scope of application of the 2014**

[9] The Greenhouse Gas Protocol Corporate Standard classifies a company's greenhouse gas emissions into three 'scopes'. Scope 1 emissions are direct emissions from owned or controlled sources. Scope 2 emissions are indirect emissions from the generation of purchased energy. Scope 3 emissions are all indirect emissions (not included in scope 2) that occur in the value chain of the reporting company, including both upstream and downstream emissions.

[10] Source: Ibid, p.18.

[11] Officially titled 'Directive (EU) 2022/2464 of the European Parliament and of the Council of 14 December 2022 amending Regulation (EU) No 537/2014, Directive 2004/109/EC, Directive 2006/43/EC and Directive 2013/34/EU, as regards corporate sustainability reporting'.

[12] Following the adoption of the Omnibus I Simplification Package', the entry into application has been postponed to 2028 and 2029 (for the financial year starting on or after 1 January 2027/2028, respectively), depending on the size of the undertaking. Undertakings which are already reporting under the CSRD regime ("wave one" undertakings) which would fall out of scope on the basis of these revised tests will

Non-Financial Reporting Directive (NFRD)[13] and its obligations by requiring large companies (+1000 employees and/or meeting balance sheet and/or turnover thresholds), as well as parent companies of large groups, to include in a dedicated section of their annual management report not only the material information necessary to **understand how sustainability matters affect the company's development, performance and position**, but also the **material information necessary to understand the company's impacts on sustainability matters**. This so-called 'double-materiality' is groundbreaking, as no other non-financial information reporting regimes (such as IFRS standards) impose the second aspect.

Under the CSRD, specifically Art. 19a, companies in scope are expected to **report a** 11
number of aspects regarding their businesses, notably: a brief description of the undertaking's business model and strategy; a description of the time-bound targets related to sustainability matters set by the undertaking; a description of the role of the administrative, management and supervisory bodies with regard to sustainability matters, and relevant expertise and skills or access to them; a description of the undertaking's policies in relation to sustainability matters; a description of the due diligence process implemented by the undertaking with regard to sustainability matters; **the principal actual or potential adverse impacts connected with the undertaking's own operations and with its value chain**; any actions taken by the undertaking in relation to actual or potential adverse impacts, and the result of such actions; a description of the principal risks to the undertaking related to sustainability matters; required indicators relevant to the applicable disclosures requirements.

This information must be reported in accordance with the **European Sustainability** 12
Reporting Standards (ESRS), developed by the European Financial Reporting Advisory Group (EFRAG) and adopted by the Commission by means of delegated act in July 2023.[14] They specify the content and, where relevant, the structure to be used to present that information. In the context of the Commission's simplification agenda, EFRAG submitted its technical advice on revised ESRS on 3 December 2025.[15] EFRAG state they have implemented a 61% reduction of mandatory data points as compared to the existing set of ESRS.

The process for determining material sustainability matters, and information that 13
is reported, are subject to 'limited assurance' by the company's auditors (that may potentially evolve to the stricter standard of 'reasonable assurance' in the future).

The CSRD – and other EU disclosure regimes such as the Taxonomy Regulation[16] 14
and the Sustainable Finance Disclosure Regulation (SFDR)[17] – are designed to provide

---

need to continue reporting until the financial year starting on or after 1 January 2027 unless the relevant Member State opts to exempt them.

[13] Officially titled 'Directive 2014/95/EU of the European Parliament and of the Council of 22 October 2014 amending Directive 2013/34/EU as regards disclosure of non-financial and diversity information by certain large undertakings and groups'.

[14] Commission Delegated Regulation 2023/2772 of 31.7.2023.

[15] EFRAG Press release of 03.12.2025 <https://www.efrag.org/en/news-and-calendar/news/efrag-provides-its-technical-advice-on-draft-simplified-esrs-to-the-european-commission>.

[16] Officially tilted: 'Regulation (EU) 2020/852 of the European Parliament and of the Council of 18 June 2020 on the establishment of a framework to facilitate sustainable investment, and amending Regulation (EU) 2019/2088'. It requires companies and financial institutions covered by the CSRD to report on how (and to what extent) their activities are aligned with the so-called 'EU taxonomy', a classification system which establishes per economic activity technical sustainability criteria which must be met by the relevant economic activity in order for it to qualify as 'sustainable' under one of the six environmental objectives.

[17] Officially tilted: 'Regulation (EU) 2019/2088 of the European Parliament and of the Council of 27 November 2019 on sustainability-related disclosures in the financial services sector'. It lays down harmonised rules for financial market participants and financial advisers on transparency with regard

investors and other key stakeholders with **better, more comparable data**, so that they can make better informed decisions. They are also designed to help businesses **identify their sustainability risks and opportunities** so that this can be reflected in their wider business strategies. This will be of key relevance in effectively complying with the CSDDD, described in the next section: The more an enterprise is aware of its carbon footprint, and its potential and actual adverse impacts on the environment and human rights, the better positioned it will be to address and reduce them.

15 However, at the present, the sheer logistics of preparing for the first wave of CSRD reports, and unpicking how disclosure standards in other jurisdictions interact, is proving somewhat overwhelming. The impact of the Omnibus I Simplification Package remains to be determined. Paradoxically, publicly disclosing more sustainability data may also involve potentially increased (greenwashing) litigation risks. While the Commission has urged companies to be pragmatic and **apply common sense when reporting under the CSRD for the first time**, there is no doubt that complying with CSRD requirements (even as simplified) is a massive endeavour – from the sheer number of datapoints it covers, to the complexities of carrying out a double materiality assessment to obtaining data from global value chains.

II. Corporate Sustainability Due Diligence Directive (CSDDD)

16 The CSRD is limited to reporting obligations. In-scope companies must report on their transition plan for climate change mitigation or human rights and environmental due diligence policies but, in theory, they could report that they have nothing in place. This would obviously be challenging to defend vis-à-vis their stakeholders (investors, consumers, business partners, employees, etc.), meaning that disclosure obligations already lead to effective actions.

17 In addition, the next pillar of the EU sustainability agenda, the CSDDD,[18] **marks a shift from a 'duty to report' to a 'duty to act'**, by imposing on in-scope companies (large EU-incorporated companies and groups,[19] but also non-EU ones having substantial business activities in the EU)[20] the adoption and implementation of human rights and environmental due diligence measures. The CSDDD will be applicable as from 26 July 2029 (postponed from a start of application in 2027 for the largest companies by the Omnibus I Simplification Packages).

18 The pre-Omnibus version of the CSDDD also required in-scope companies to adopt and put into effect a transition plan aiming:

to ensure, through best efforts, that the business model and strategy of an entity are compatible with the transition to a sustainable economy and with the limiting of global warming to 1.5°C in line with the Paris Agreement and the objective of achieving climate neutrality as established in the EU Climate Law, including its intermediate and 2050 climate neutrality targets, and where relevant, the exposure of the entity to coal-, oil- and gas-related activities (Art. 22).

---

to the integration of sustainability risks and the consideration of adverse sustainability impacts in their processes and the provision of sustainability-related information with respect to financial products.

[18] Officially titled 'Directive (EU) 2024/1760 of the European Parliament and of the Council of 13 June 2024 on corporate sustainability due diligence'.

[19] With a worldwide turnover of above EUR 1.5 billion and more than 5,000 employees, on an individual or consolidated basis. Specific thresholds apply for franchise agreements.

[20] With a EU turnover of above EUR 1.5 billion, on an individual or consolidated basis. Specific thresholds apply for franchise agreements.

Many uncertainties on what this obligation would have effectively entailed existed.[21] What is clear, however, is that – despite the deletion of this obligation – **transition planning is becoming a core part of corporate strategy-setting and implementation and should not be mistaken for a tick-box disclosure exercise**. Notably, financial institutions, funds and other investors are already considering transition strategy as part of their due diligence and within credit and pricing conversations. 19

With **respect to human rights and environmental due diligence**, the CSDDD imposes on in-scope companies far-reaching obligations with respect to their own activities, but also those of **their subsidiaries and of their upstream and downstream business partners in the companies' 'chain of activities'** (as specifically defined in the Directive, and excluding the sale of goods and provision of most services as part of the downstream activities). 20

The due diligence obligations encompass the following six steps (in line, though not fully aligned, with existing international soft law standards, in particular the United Nations Guiding Principles on Business and Human Rights (UNGPs) and the OECD Guidelines for Multinational Enterprises): (i) **integrate** due diligence into companies' policies, (ii) **identify** actual and potential adverse human rights and environmental impacts (as defined in the CSDDD's annex), (iii) **prevent**, **cease** or **minimise** actual and potential adverse impacts (including by seeking contractual assurances from direct business partners that they will ensure compliance with the company's code of conduct and prevention action plan), (iv) **assess** the effectiveness of these measures, (v) **communicate** on these measures[22] and (vi) **remediate** the potential adverse impacts, i.e., drawing up a corrective action plan and neutralise the adverse impacts or, if impossible, minimise their extent (including by the payment of damages to the affected persons and by financial compensation to the affected communities). These due diligence expectations are likely to be cascaded throughout global value chains, and altering approaches to procurement, contracting and engagement strategies. 21

The respect of the Directive's obligations is ensured through strict public and private enforcement mechanisms. 22

For public enforcement, EU Member States are required to designate one or more **authorities to supervise compliance** with the Directive's obligations. They will have the **power to request information** and **carry out investigations**, on their own motion or as a result of substantiated concerns submitted to them by any natural or legal person who has reasons to believe a company is not complying. They will also have the power to order the cessation of infringements, **impose substantive administrative fines** (with a maximum of 3 % of the net worldwide turnover of the company in the financial year preceding the fining decision), and **adopt interim measures** in case of imminent risk of severe and irreparable harm. 23

The requirement for a harmonised EU-wide civil liability regime (including the harmonised position allowing trade unions or NGOs to bring claims on behalf of injured parties) has been deleted by the Omnibus I Simplification Package. However, **civil** 24

---

[21] The CSDDD provided in its Recitals that the transition planning requirement should be 'understood as an obligation of means and not of result'. This likely had to be interpreted as mostly coming into play at the stage of the implementation of the plan (as opposed to the obligation to have a plan and targets). The CSDDD did not define 'best efforts', although it did provide in its Recitals that the transition planning requirement should be 'understood as an obligation of means and not of result'. It therefore was unclear which actions a business would be expected to take to discharge its obligation to use best efforts to implement its transition plan, particularly as regards any Scope 3 emissions reduction targets.

[22] In order to avoid duplicating reporting obligations, the CSDDD does not introduce any new reporting obligations in addition to those under the CSRD. In-scope companies that do not fall under the proposed CSRD should publish on their website an annual statement in respect of their activities.

liability may still arise under the general tort law regimes of many Member States in case damage was directly caused by the breach of the due diligence obligation. National procedural laws may also allow activist organisations to bring claims and / or to support the alleged victim.

III. Waste Electronic and Electric Equipment Directive (WEEED)

25 The WEEED[23] requires the separate collection and proper treatment of WEEE and sets **targets for their collection, recovery and recycling**. Moreover, it is intended to help European countries fight illegal waste exports more effectively by making it harder for exporters to disguise illegal shipments of WEEE, and lastly, to reduce the administrative burden by calling for the harmonisation of national EEE[24] registers and of the reporting format.

26 Both physical copies of video games and video games consoles are covered within the scope of the WEEE Directive (as mentioned in its Annex II – Section 7), which complements the Waste Framework Directive for the processing of waste of electrical and electronic equipment.

27 One important element introduced by this legislation is the 'producer responsibility principle' (Art. 7) and, on that basis, **ensure that a minimum collection rate is achieved annually**. From 2016, the minimum collection rate shall be 45 % calculated on the basis of the total weight of WEEE collected in accordance with Art. 5 and 6 in a given year in the Member State concerned, expressed as a percentage of the average weight of EEE placed on the market in the three preceding years in that Member State.

28 The obligations under this Directive include, but are not limited to, product design (Art. 4) which facilitates the re-use, dismantling and recovery of WEEE, its components and materials. Additionally, producers (or third parties acting on their behalf) are obliged to set up systems to provide for the recovery of WEEE using best available techniques (Art. 8). These systems may be set up by producers individually or collectively. Moreover, **producers should provide information free of charge about preparation for re-use and treatment in respect of each type of new EEE placed for the first time on the Union market within one year after the equipment is placed on the market** (Art. 15).

IV. Ecodesign Regulation and GCVA

29 The Ecodesign Regulation[25] is the legal basis[26] for the GCVA (Games Consoles Voluntary Agreement), being itself the vehicle through which energy efficiency improvements are brought to consoles, and by extension to games. The Regulation only applies to physical goods (Art. 2(1)), and consequently will not cover video games themselves. It is important however to note that rec. 13 opens the door to interpretation as regards potential inclusion of digital content, as it stresses that:

[23] Official titled 'Directive 2012/19/EU of the European Parliament and of the Council of 4.7.2012 on waste electrical and electronic equipment'.

[24] Electrical and Electronic Equipment.

[25] Officially titled 'Regulation (EU) 2024/1781 of the European Parliament and of the Council of 13 June 2024 establishing a framework for the setting of ecodesign requirements for sustainable products'.

[26] Specifically, Art. 21 and Annex VI.

it is necessary to allow for the setting of ecodesign requirements on all physical goods placed on the market or put into service, including components such as tyres and intermediate products. Digital content that is an integral part of a physical product should also be included in the scope.

As stated above, the GCVA[27] is a self-regulatory initiative (SRI) under Art. 21, and **aims to achieve energy savings and material efficiency through improved design**, thus benefiting the environment without compromising console performance and gaming experience. It includes provisions to align with the European Commission's proposed action plan on the circular economy. It is the result of many years of work carried out by the signatories of the voluntary agreement (the three main console manufacturers: Microsoft, Nintendo and Sony) in consultation with the European Commission, civil society organisations and EU Member States. The agreement sets **energy and resource efficiency requirements** for various types of mains-powered games consoles placed on the market within EU countries and the UK. Signatories are also required to provide information regarding energy and resource efficiency. 30

V. Right to Repair Regulation

The Right to Repair Regulation (RRR)[28] looks to facilitate cross-border provision of services and competition among repairers of goods purchased by consumers in the internal market, and lays down **rules promoting the repair of goods**. In the context of the video games sector, this Regulation **will be relevant to manufacturers of video game consoles and game peripherals**. This will have little to no bearing on video games themselves. 31

Repairability of video game consoles is currently under some scrutiny, as it was preliminarily ranked as a top product category with repairability relevance, although the introduction of a repairability scoring system in the EU has not yet been proposed.[29] 32

VI. Data centres reporting delegated regulation

Under the Energy Efficiency Directive, the European Commission adopted the data centre sustainability rating scheme Delegated Regulation.[30] This Regulation **requires operators of data centres with an installed information technology power demand of at least 500 kW to report certain KPIs to the European Database on Data Centres**. These KPIs are listed in Annex II of the Delegated Regulation, and include, but are not limited to, total floor area, total energy consumption, water input, waste heat reusage, type of cooling, and total renewable energy consumption. 33

Moreover, as most of these indicators will be publicly available, economic operators contracting data centre services should, as part of their CSDDD obligations, consider these indicators before selecting a business partner. 34

---

[27] The GCVA, which is currently on its 5.1 version, can be accessed at <https://efficientgaming.info/eu-voluntary-agreement/eu-voluntary-agreement>.

[28] Officially titled 'Directive (EU) 2024/1799 of the European Parliament and of the Council of 13 June 2024 on common rules promoting the repair of goods'.

[29] European Commission, Joint Research Centre, 'Reparability Scoring System – Product relevance scoping study', Publications Office of the European Union (2025) https://data.europa.eu/doi/10.2760/4556439, JRC139725.

[30] Officially titled 'Commission Delegated Regulation (EU) 2024/1364 of 14 March 2024 on the first phase of the establishment of a common Union rating scheme for data centres'.

D. Emerging trends and green technologies in gaming

35 As is already clear from some examples flagged above (including the Games Consoles Voluntary Agreement), the video games industry has already put in place a number of noteworthy initiatives at multiple levels aimed at reducing the carbon intensity of the development, publishing and playing of games. Note that **not all measures are adequate for every games company**: they will vary from company to company, and the specific circumstances of each undertaking will be the most relevant in assessing how to reduce said undertaking's environmental footprint.

I. Development

36 In this regard, there is no great divergence from the video games sector in relation to general software development. Sourcing green energy to power the company premises, using reconditioned hardware, reducing redundant air travel, encouraging employees to use public transportation, choose suppliers with sustainability initiatives, to name a few – all of these are possible actions that can be taken. The usage of carbon calculators[31] is likely one of the better 'paths' of greening one's activities, as it allows for a **better understanding of the impact**, and consequently allow for better understanding of where improvements can be made.

37 Certain aspects of game design can also, in certain contexts, be tweaked and adjusted for increased efficiency. While it will vary from game to game, **optimisation of GPU power usage can often be performed with minimal impact on game visuals**. For example, the Xbox Developer Sustainability Toolkit includes analytical and visual systems, measurement tools, and resources to help creators make informed decisions about energy consumption and carbon emissions, associated with their game designs. A good example of environmentally conscious game design is one of the measures taken in *Halo Infinite*: The lowering of the resolution in the pause menu significantly reduced the load on the GPU, which decreased power consumption by 15 %.[32] Another practical example is that from Epic Games, in the context of *Fortnite*: The company managed, through **software optimisation**, to secure an estimate of 200 MWh per day of savings across their total player base, via a small amount of game side C++ code modification.[33] In April 2024, Ubisoft has introduced Eco Mode in their 2016 title *For Honor*, which allows players to significantly reduce their power consumption while playing the game without compromising the experience.[34] These are only three examples of several dozens of types of sustainability initiatives in game design.[35]

---

[31] See footnote 3 for some examples.

[32] Gaming Sustainability Halo Infinite Case Studies – Microsoft Game Dev | Microsoft Learn (https://learn.microsoft.com/en-us/gaming/sustainability/case-studies/case-studies-halo#power-consumption-in-gameplay-pause-menu).

[33] Epic Games, Reducing Fortnite's Power consumption (https://www.unrealengine.com/en-US/blog/white-paper-reducing-fortnite-s-power-consumption).

[34] On current gen consoles (PS5, Xbox Series S & X), a new Graphic Settings is added to enable an ECO Mode to save energy by reducing framerate, resolution, and graphic upgrades. Four modes are offered: Off, Minimal that activates only in the menus, Smart that activates after 2 minutes of idle time and Full that activates at all times. In the menus only, an ECO Mode icon will appear when it's activated.

Source: Patch 2.51.0 notes (https://www.ubisoft.com/en-gb/game/for-honor/news-updates/1OPoKzj6XD6FuzNQAFPWOu/patch-notes-2510-for-honor).

[35] The Green Game Design is a database of best practices, aimed at equipping developers with the tools they need to craft effective climate messaging into games and reduce production impact. < https://www.greengamedesign.com/>.

II. Publishing

Regarding video game publishing (and consequently distribution), as we have stated earlier, **video games are increasingly distributed digitally**, meaning that most users will no longer have a physical medium (CD/cartridge) of the game they are playing. Some games are not even viable for physical distribution, particularly for games with frequent updates such as certain simulators or MMORPGs.[36] While this transition has entailed significant reductions in plastic usage, it also meant an increase of energy usage for data centres and other connectivity infrastructure used in digital distribution. 38

Specifically on packaging, it is up to each publisher/distributor to ascertain where improvements can be made. However, **favouring the use of recycled plastic and paper**[37] are two obvious paths to make improvements with positive sustainability impacts. Trade-in or buyback programmes are also potential solutions – these are more present in the field of consoles.[38] Concerning physical copies of games, there are a number of dedicated market operators for second-hand games in most countries which see significant business. 39

Due to the need of reducing plastic waste, video games companies would be well advised to further stimulate digital distribution, while remaining cognizant of the drawbacks these entail in other non-sustainability related aspects. 40

III. Playing

Games can be powerful devices for storytelling and to convey messages. The Playing for the Planet Alliance has as one of its main goals the promotion of 'green activations',[39] and certain initiatives such as the Green Game Jam are helping drive and introduce these kind of green nudges into games. **This will not mean, however, that introducing green nudges in a game equals a sustainable operation**: A company's operations may be sustainable and not do any 'green activations', and the reverse may also be true. 41

E. Conclusion

Climate change, environmental and, more broadly, sustainability adverse impacts are rarely associated with the video games industry. However, the recent EU instruments presented above (despite their 'simplification/recalibration'), and the increased focus from all stakeholders (including from consumers, investors, employees and business partners), will mean that **companies in all sectors, including in the video games industry, will have to take additional precautions and considerations in this space**. Environmental – and broader sustainability – aspects will have to be actively taken into account (and documented) in decision-making processes and corporate strategies. 42

---

[36] Flight Simulator (2020), for example was almost exclusively distributed digitally, as widespread physical distribution of this title meant 10 discs per unit. Physical copies of the game were indeed sold, but were targeted at collectors and sold in small numbers.

[37] For example, SEGA has moved to recycled and recyclable cardboard packaging (https://www.gamesindustry.biz/sega-europe-rolls-out-fully-recyclable-packaging-for-all-pc-titles).

[38] The PlayStation Back Market or Microsoft trade-in programmes are examples of commercial encouragements of a circular economy, where consumers can either benefit from rebates in purchases of new equipment or simply sell back used hardware.

[39] The Playing for the Planet Alliance defines 'green activation' as 'an element that is added into a game or associated platform (e.g., social media) designed to engage a live game's audience on an environmental theme'.

43 The **obligations emerging from these legislative instruments will not apply homogenously**: each company will have specific circumstances to take into account. Favouring renewable energy to premises, increased digital distribution instead of physical, rationalising corporate travel, promoting lower-carbon forms of transportation, considering offsetting measures for unavoidable carbon emissions, all of these are options that should be considered with respect to each companies' own activities. Particular attention will have to be given by companies to their value chain, in view of the role played by scope 3 carbon emissions in the video game industry, as well as the higher risks of potential adverse impacts related to the sourcing of raw materials for hardware. Finally, companies can also generate a positive impact through game design, particularly by enhancing the educational dimension of games and their role in raising awareness.

§ 22
Protection of Minors – PEGI

A. Introduction 1

B. History of PEGI 5

C. Key background to the PEGI system 7
I. Organisation 7
II. Legal status of PEGI 11
III. Geographical scope of PEGI 15

D. How the PEGI system works 18
I. The PEGI age ratings and descriptors 18
II. Age rating criteria 24
III. Process to submit a game for age rating 29
1. Traditional age rating procedure (pre-release examination) 31
Process for obtaining an age rating 32
Sub-licensing 40
Downloadable content 41
Appeals 42
2. IARC age rating procedure 43

E. PEGI Code of Conduct 45
Legal requirements applicable to video games 46
Child rights and safety by design 47
Age ratings 48
In-game monetisation (Art. 8) 49
Safe online gameplay (Art. 9) 51
Privacy 53
Clear language 54
Labelling and advertising 55

F. PEGI labelling rules 56
UK 60

G. PEGI advertising rules 61

H. Enforcement 65

A. Introduction

1 For as long as video games have been commercially available, there have been concerns about the impact of playing games on young people. When video games innovated drastically in terms of graphic quality in the 1990s, coupled with their expanded reach, the debates intensified. The release of the popular yet controversial games *Mortal Kombat* and *Night Trap* in 1992 generated a political and academic discussion about the effects of video game content, violence in particular, on children. One immediate effect of this discussion was the founding in 1994 of three **self-regulatory** content rating systems for video games by: the UK trade association, the Entertainment and Leisure Software Publishers Association (ELSPA),[1] the US Entertainment Software Rating Board (ESRB) and the German '*Unterhaltungssoftware Selbstkontrolle*' (USK) which became mandatory in Germany in 2003 after an update of the German Youth Protection Act.[2]

2 Studies claiming that violence in video games had a **harmful effect** on players, particularly children, appeared frequently in the next two decades, until literature reviews, meta-analyses and new research[3] started pointing out contradictions and flaws in the

[1] https://playstation.fandom.com/wiki/Entertainment_and_Leisure_Software_Publishers_Association.
[2] https://usk.de/alle-lexikonbegriffe/jugendschutzgesetz/.
[3] https://pubmed.ncbi.nlm.nih.gov/37975654/.

existing research, and found that the impact was much smaller than initially claimed, or even non-existent, which led to some of these earlier studies being corrected or retracted[4] or recalibrated the debate to question the extent of any adverse impact.[5]

3 These evolving academic insights caused a shift in perception that diminished the attention to potentially harmful effects of video game content. Further, the generation of young players from the 1990s and early 21st century are now grown up with children of their own, seemingly without any broad societal impact by their pastime as children. The introduction of **efficient age classification** systems further helped to alleviate concerns.

4 The focus of concern today is less on content-related matters. The games market has undergone some drastic transformations. The rise of mobile video games and the general shift from physical to digital distribution and from offline to online experiences, have certainly broadened the appeal of games and brought along an expanded, more diverse audience (which in turn stimulated the development of a more diverse offering of and in video games). However, such new developments come with **new concerns**: parents still want to know what content is present in a game, but are also now concerned about user-generated content, toxic behaviour, in-game purchases and the length of time their children spend playing games.

B. History of PEGI

5 In February 2001, the Swedish presidency of the Council of the EU organised a workshop to discuss **self-regulation**, harmonised across the European Union, as a solution to protect minors against unsuitable content in video games.[6] A working group of classification experts was brought together by the Interactive Software Federation of Europe (now 'Video Games Europe' ('VGE')),[7] the European trade body representing the publishers of video games, to discuss the feasibility of a pan-European age rating standard for video games. A resolution by the EU Council from March 2002 further specified that consumers, in particular young people, should be protected via an age labelling system for video games acknowledging that self-regulation is an adequate means by which to do so.[8]

6 PEGI (Pan-European Game Information)[9] was founded by VGE in April 2003 and officially inaugurated by EU Commissioner Viviane Reding. Today, the PEGI rating system is used across all of Europe, with the exception of Germany. It has issued more than 40,000 age classification licences for video games. In 2008, the European Commission acknowledged it as a model of European **harmonisation** in the field of the protection of children.[10] A similar view was adopted on 26 November 2025 in the European Parliament Resolution on the Protection of Minors Online which "*highlights the video games industry's commitment to self-regulation as demonstrated by the implementation of age recommendations systems, which play a role in safeguarding younger audiences and promoting responsible gaming practices.*"[11]

---

[4] https://retractionwatch.com/2017/01/20/boom-headshot-disputed-video-game-paper-retracted/.
[5] https://www.sciencedirect.com/science/article/abs/pii/S0022103115300093.
[6] https://data.riksdagen.se/fil/81D9F8C0-1EFC-4A83-ADBE-3901BEF65DAE, pp. 111–119.
[7] https://www.videogameseurope.eu.
[8] https://eur-lex.europa.eu/LexUriServ/LexUriServ.do?uri=OJ:C:2002:065:0002:0002:EN:PDF.
[9] https://www.pegi.info.
[10] https://eur-lex.europa.eu/legal-content/EN/TXT/PDF/?uri=CELEX:52008DC0207.
[11] https://www.europarl.europa.eu/doceo/document/TA-10-2025-0299_EN.html.

C. Key background to the PEGI system

I. Organisation

The day-to-day management, supervision and development of the PEGI system is handled by PEGI s.a., an independent, not-for-profit company with a social purpose established under Belgian law. Drawing on wide experience, PEGI is steered by way of a number of boards and committees. Broad **stakeholder consultations** and participation form a key component of PEGI's success. This approach establishes a framework for continuous dialogue, which is crucial in a rapidly evolving market. 7

The **PEGI Management Board** provides guidance to the PEGI secretariat. The Board is made up of representatives of users of the PEGI system (games publishers and developers), the gatekeepers of PEGI (the game console manufacturers) and the promoters of PEGI (national trade associations) supplemented by the chairs of the PEGI Council and the PEGI Experts Group (see below). This board structure ensures there is proper oversight while maintaining PEGI's self-regulatory strength. 8

With PEGI in use in almost 40 countries it is vital that the system keeps in tune with social, political and legal developments in the entire region. The **PEGI Council** is responsible for making recommendations so that national as well as European developments are communicated and reflected in the PEGI system. Members of the Council are primarily recruited from the authorities in the PEGI countries, working as civil servants versed in the protection of minors in Europe. The Council gives the countries that use PEGI a voice but, equally important, it enables the policy makers in the PEGI countries to stay abreast of and involved in PEGI. The Council ensures this two-way flow of information. 9

With the Council's focus on country representation, PEGI also convenes with technical experts that have been an important source of advice for PEGI over the years. The **PEGI Experts Group** involves academics and specialists in the fields of media, psychology, age classification, legal matters, etc. They advise PEGI after considering technological and content-related developments raised by the PEGI Council, the PEGI Management Board or through circumstances brought to light by the classification procedure. 10

II. Legal status of PEGI

PEGI is a voluntary system. However, PEGI effectively becomes obligatory for publishers where a video game platform adopts a policy that it will not permit a game, developed for its devices, to be published without a PEGI age rating. To obtain that rating, the publisher of the game **must sign** the PEGI Agreement which includes the PEGI Code of Conduct (see → Section E: PEGI Code of Conduct). By doing so, the publisher agrees, as a matter of contract, to comply with all of PEGI's age rating and other requirements for each of its games published in countries where PEGI is recognised (see below). A breach of the PEGI Agreement, including the Code of Conduct, entitles PEGI to enforce the PEGI Agreement against the publisher, in accordance with the process set out in the Agreement, which includes the power to impose fines and ultimately to exclude products from the PEGI system (see → Section H: Enforcement). 11

Video game console manufacturers (Microsoft, Nintendo, and Sony) **require** that every game that is released for their devices has a PEGI rating. Google requires publishers of games and other apps to get a PEGI rating that is displayed to consumers in Europe. 12

Apple has developed its own age rating system that publishers must use. Steam does not require the display of age rating information in countries where PEGI is used.

13 Further, the PEGI system is recognised by national legal or regulatory frameworks giving PEGI what amounts to be a **co-regulatory basis** in certain countries. Some countries have laws providing for mandatory age rating of video games which directly or indirectly recognise PEGI, or which are satisfied by the use of the PEGI age rating system (France, Italy, Iceland, Israel, Lithuania, Netherlands, Switzerland, the UK and the Vienna region of Austria). Some countries' age rating boards officially accept PEGI ratings for video games (Finland, Ireland and Portugal) based on requirements in law while, in others, media authorities officially endorse PEGI (Denmark, Sweden and Norway). For most European countries, national support for PEGI is also secured by an official designation of representatives to sit on the PEGI Council by the responsible ministries or regulators (Austria, Belgium, Bulgaria, Denmark, Finland, France, Ireland, Italy, Luxembourg, Netherlands, Norway, Poland, Portugal, Spain, Sweden, Switzerland and the UK). Of course, there is *de facto* use of the PEGI system in those countries with no specific legislative or other formal basis.

14 As discussed, PEGI is a system of self-regulation by which PEGI Agreement signatories agree to obtain ratings, to comply with other rules set out in the PEGI Code of Conduct (see Section E: PEGI Code of Conduct), and to be subject to **enforcement** in the event of a breach. It is not the function of PEGI to enforce laws such as those which regulate the dissemination of certain types of content or ban it completely, such as national censorship laws, for which publishers remain responsible.

III. Geographical scope of PEGI

15 PEGI labels are used on game products published in Albania, Austria, Belgium, Bosnia and Herzegovina, Bulgaria, Croatia, Cyprus, the Czech Republic, Denmark, Estonia, Finland, France, Greece, Hungary, Iceland, Ireland, Italy, Kosovo, Latvia, Lithuania, Luxembourg, Malta, Moldova, Montenegro, the Netherlands, North Macedonia, Norway, Poland, Portugal, Romania, Serbia, Slovakia, Slovenia, Spain, Sweden, Switzerland, Ukraine and the United Kingdom.

16 The only EU country that does not recognise PEGI is **Germany**. Germany requires game publishers to display USK ratings which are explained in Chapter 23.

17 The PEGI age rating licence specifies the **countries** where a publisher can use the PEGI labels and descriptors based on the publisher's rating application. In most cases, publishers aim to distribute their game in all of these countries, but PEGI also provides the option to take a 'local licence' which limits distribution to a maximum of two countries, reducing the cost of the PEGI age rating licence fee.

D. How the PEGI system works

I. The PEGI age ratings and descriptors

18 The PEGI system provides players and parents with **two levels** of information: five age labels, advising the recommended minimum age of a player, and eight content descriptors that explain why a specific age rating has been given to a game. Aspects like violence, frightening scenes, depictions of or references to sex, drugs, gambling, and

inappropriate language are highlighted to assist parents and caretakers in making an informed decision.[12]

PEGI age ratings and descriptors are shown in Figure 22.1. 19

20

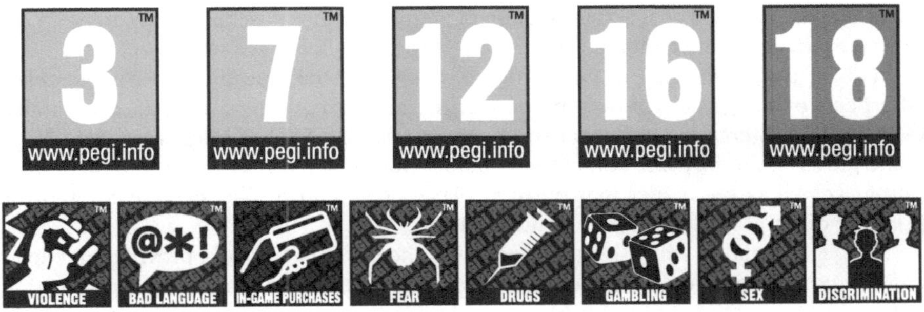

Figure 22.1

PEGI ratings consider the **age suitability** of a video game, not the level of difficulty. 21
Games with a PEGI 3 do not contain content that is inappropriate for children, but do not necessarily target young children; some of these games may be too difficult to master for younger players. Conversely, PEGI 18 games may be very easy to play, but they contain elements that make them only appropriate for an adult player.

Since 2020, there is a requirement to include an additional notice, in text form, in 22
games containing **paid random items** (e.g., loot boxes, card packs, surprise wheels, etc).

23

Figure 22.2

II. Age rating criteria

PEGI age ratings are determined by a set of assessment **criteria** which are translated 24
into simple yes/no questions that publishers must answer in a process of self-declaration. For example, in relation to violence in a game, the questionnaire asks several questions relating to the type and manner of depiction of the violence and whether it is perpetrated against humans, animals, fantasy or innocent characters. Depending on the answers to the questions, the system will open a further relevant set of questions and so on.

How often a certain type of content occurs is not necessarily relevant for the PEGI 25
rating of a game. For example, a single use of 'offensive language' within a game will result in a PEGI 12. This is where PEGI age ratings differ from movie classification systems that allow examiners to take the frequency of certain content into account as a mitigating factor. Video games are **non-linear**, which means there is no guarantee that certain content will only be seen or played once. However, the PEGI questionnaire also has an optional 'Theme' question where the Coder can disclose if the game contains

[12] https://pegi.info/what-do-the-labels-mean.

elements that have not been considered by the questionnaire but may have a bearing on the age rating.

26 The criteria set out in the questionnaire relate to the nature of the **game content.** Since 2018, the PEGI labels include an in-game purchases content descriptor. However, a 'yes' to the question of whether a game contains in-game purchases only triggers the in-game purchases descriptor, it does not affect the level of the age rating.

In 2026, around the time of publication of this Handbook, specific non-content-related aspects of the game will become part of the age rating criteria as well, comparable to the online interaction risks that the German system USK has integrated since 2023. Some purchases of in-game content (e.g. paid random items) may result in a higher age rating, as well as mechanics that pressure players to spend or play excessively, and the presence of unrestricted communication features.

27 The questionnaire, which is set out in full in the PEGI Handbook, provides an explanation and commentary on the criteria with some example footage. The classification criteria are monitored continuously by the PEGI Administrators and **updated regularly** by the PEGI Experts Group.

28 The eight PEGI **descriptors** which, like the age rating, are generated on the basis of the answers given to the PEGI questionnaire, serve to inform the purchaser or player why a game has received a certain age rating. For example, a parent may choose not to buy a game with any type of violence even though their child is above the age stated in the rating, or an adult may prefer not to play violent video games. Some descriptors will appear for certain age ratings only (e.g., bad language can only appear for games rated PEGI 12 and above). Games published with anything above a PEGI 3 will have at least one descriptor.

III. Process to submit a game for age rating

29 Like other classification systems around the world, the PEGI system was built to handle games that are released on a **physical carrier** (disc, cartridge or plug-n-play device), although PEGI also rates games that are **online-only**.

30 Since 2003, PEGI has issued between 1,600 and 2,400 licences per year to video game publishers. These licences are issued via the **'traditional'** rating system, where the PEGI administrators examine a game *prior* to its release to confirm the age rating for which the publisher is applying. This pre-release process is mandatory for physical releases, but publishers may also choose the traditional route for online-only game releases.

1. Traditional age rating procedure (pre-release examination)

31 This section provides an overview of the PEGI age rating process as set out in the PEGI Agreement and PEGI Handbook, which should be consulted for further details and instructions.

Process for obtaining an age rating

32 In order to get an age rating for a game, the publisher must first join PEGI (free of charge) by accepting an online version of the **PEGI Agreement**. PEGI will then require details of publisher individuals who will fulfil the role of Publisher Admin, Publisher Financial and Coder, the individual that can submit games for age rating. These individuals will then be provided with accounts and log-in details to get access to the PEGI rating site, an extranet that contains the online rating tool and all relevant

documentation (including the PEGI Handbook, Labelling Guidelines, graphic assets, etc.). Companies that have accepted the PEGI Agreement are called PEGI signatories.

The first step of the age rating process for a game is for the Coder to create a submission in PEGI's online rating tool. This involves submitting information on the type of product (e.g., online only or online and physical), the platform(s) on, and the countries in, which it will be released, the release date (and if available, a pre-order date) and consumer information relating to the game that will be included on the public websites of PEGI and the two **independent administrators** of the PEGI system, the NICAM institute in the Netherlands and the Games Rating Authority ('GRA') in the United Kingdom. The Coder can then complete the age rating questionnaire online for the game. This will generate a provisional age rating which can be used for pre-orders and pre-release marketing. 33

The publisher must then submit **examination** materials (e.g., actual gameplay, video footage, lyrics and scripts) either physically or digitally, as stipulated in the PEGI Handbook, which will be reviewed by NICAM if the provisional rating is a 3 or 7, or by GRA if the provisional rating is 12 or above. The examination cannot be completed unless the publisher has submitted all examination materials. The rating will then be confirmed within ten working days (unless the Coder has selected a faster Rate Track on submission). 34

The relevant administrator then plays through the game and examines the submitted materials to confirm or alter the **provisional** rating that was generated by the publisher's responses to the PEGI questionnaire. 35

An invoice is provided to the publisher, consisting of an examination **fee** which depends on the chosen Rate Track (normal (maximum ten working days), fast (four working days) or same day service) and a licence fee per platform (additional platforms are charged at a reduced fee). Lower licence fees apply for products with development costs of under 200,000 EUR. 36

Once the payment has been processed, a **licence** with the relevant PEGI age rating and content descriptors is issued to the Coder via email. The licence grants the right, solely to the publisher, to use the age rating and descriptors in connection with the game and on the platform(s) as specifically set out in the licence. The age rating and descriptors, as per the licence, must then be displayed on the game packaging, digital storefront listings and in promotional campaigns in accordance with the PEGI Labelling Guidelines (see Section F: PEGI Labelling Rules below). Failure to abide by the terms of the PEGI licence (e.g., display of an incorrect age rating or descriptor or a missing descriptor) will lead to a PEGI enforcement action (see Section H: Enforcement below). 37

It is possible to edit game information or modify or cancel game submissions in the rating tool on the PEGI extranet. 38

The publisher must finally provide a **copy** of every game published on physical media rated under the PEGI system within twenty working days of the game's release date. Amongst other things, this is to enable the PEGI Administrators to ensure compliance with the PEGI licence and the Labelling Guidelines. 39

Sub-licensing

Licences can be **sublicensed** via the PEGI extranet at no charge by the original licence holder only and only for an identical game. This is relevant, for example, where rights to publish a game are transferred to a different publisher. 40

Downloadable content

41 Where a game is expanded with new content via online delivery (**'DLC'**), this DLC must be separately rated if it is to be marketed as a new product, or has the potential to change the rating of the base game. If it does not fall within those criteria, the DLC must carry the rating of the base game. It is not permitted to allow players to access DLC that is rated higher than the game through which the DLC is accessed. IARC cannot be used to classify DLC of traditionally rated products (see 'IARC age rating procedure below).

Appeals

42 If a publisher wishes to contest the rating set out in a PEGI licence, it may do so on notice to the PEGI Administrator and, if an agreement cannot be reached, the matter will be heard by the PEGI **Complaints Board.** The decision of the PEGI Complaints Board is final and binding. Complaints by consumers about age rating decisions may also be brought to the PEGI Complaints Board.

2. IARC age rating procedure

43 The swift rise of online gaming and the quick expansion of mobile platforms for gaming changed the landscape in such a way that a quicker process to apply the same PEGI age rating criteria to **very high volumes** of products had to be explored. To deal with storefronts like Google Play where millions of mobile apps can be found, the International Age Rating Coalition (IARC)[13] was founded in 2013. In cooperation with rating boards from Australia, Brazil, Germany, South Korea and the United States, a technical solution was developed to allow a large number of online-only apps and games to get an age rating following a similar codified process to PEGI's.

44 When publishers submit a mobile game or app for age rating, they complete a questionnaire that aggregates the classification criteria of every participating rating board. Consequently, the app is published with an age classification for every region where it is published. By completing a single questionnaire, an app developer can therefore get a PEGI rating for Europe, a USK rating for Germany, the GRAC rating for South Korea, ESRB in the US, ClassInd in Brazil, etc. The administrators of the IARC rating boards perform continuous **rating checks,** both methodically (with a particular focus on the most popular titles) as well as at the request of game companies and players. The digital format of mobile storefronts allows the rating boards to alter any age rating inaccuracies immediately on-screen once these have been identified. As the underlying rating criteria for the traditional and IARC age rating methods are identical, both procedures will produce the same PEGI age rating.

E. PEGI Code of Conduct

45 The PEGI Code of Conduct ('Code') forms an Annex to the PEGI Agreement. Its stated aim is to reflect the industry's commitment to provide information on the content of video game products in a responsible manner and to ensure **safe online and offline gameplay** for all. The PEGI Agreement provides that all PEGI age rating licences are subject to full compliance with the Code. The Code itself stipulates that its terms apply to all games released by the signatory of the PEGI Agreement, intended for play in

[13] https://www.globalratings.com.

countries in which PEGI applies, whether distributed online or on physical media. An overview of the Code's provisions are set out below.

Legal requirements applicable to video games

The Code complements but does not replace or set out existing laws to which signatories may be bound with respect to the distribution or advertising of their game products. The Code highlights the need for signatories to take responsibility for such **legal compliance** as well as their requirements under the Code. 46

Child rights and safety by design

The Code was drafted with special consideration for the **rights of the child** as set out in the UN Convention for the Rights of the Child, including the responsibilities of parents to provide, in a manner consistent with the evolving capacities of the child, appropriate direction and guidance in the exercise by the child of these rights. The Code requires signatories to take account of children's perspectives, needs, interests and rights when designing and evaluating new products and services intended for children. 47

Age ratings

The Code sets out a description of the PEGI system and states the key requirement for signatories to apply for an age rating, prior to release, for each video game product and format. 48

In-game monetisation (Art. 8)[14]

The Code requires that any in-game purchase option must be fair and transparent, and signatories must display the PEGI in-game purchases descriptor and, where applicable, the additional 'includes random items' notice, at the point of download or purchase. Where paid random items (e.g., **loot boxes**) are available, signatories must provide clear and accessible probability information, which must be transparent and clear for all players, and must ensure and emphasise that paying for random items is never essential to gameplay. Signatories must maintain a policy to prohibit in-game items from being exchanged for monetary value for use in unlawful gambling or betting. 49

The cost of in-game currency must be clear and purchasers of in-game items with real money, including in-game currency, must always receive an **invoice or receipt**. Clear information must be provided when purchased in-game currency is used to acquire content. 50

Safe online gameplay (Art. 9)[15]

Signatories must provide easily understandable **'community standards'** for games that allow users to play against or otherwise communicate with other players online, 51

---

14 https://pegi.info/pegi-code-of-conduct#monetisation.
15 https://pegi.info/pegi-code-of-conduct#onlinegameplay.

or games that allow players to create, view, upload, stream or download user-generated content ('online gameplay environment'). These must prohibit players from introducing content or indulging in online behaviour that is **illegal** or **harmful**. Signatories must take reasonably practicable precautions to ensure that online gameplay environments that allow text, voice or video chat or image sharing protect children from age-inappropriate content introduced by other players.

52 Signatories must ensure that online gameplay environments are kept free of content or behaviour that breaches their community standards or other terms and conditions, including by acting expeditiously to remove user-generated content which exposes children to age-inappropriate content, provide user-friendly and easy-to-access grievance **reporting mechanisms**, have systems in place to review reports and process and take their decisions in respect of such reports in a timely, diligent and effective manner.

Privacy

53 Signatories engaging in the collection of personal information from players must maintain a legally compliant, effective and coherent **privacy policy**.

Clear language

54 Signatories providing online gameplay environments explicitly targeting children of a literate age must provide information relating to privacy or grievance reporting in clear and plain **language** or in a medium that children can understand.

Labelling and advertising

55 The Code of Conduct dedicates two articles to the importance of providing information to parents and consumers through consistent labelling and responsible advertising (see Section F: PEGI Labelling Rules below).

F. PEGI labelling rules

56 The PEGI Labelling and Advertising Guidelines stipulate how the PEGI icons should be displayed on **packaging** and **online** storefronts and in various types of advertising. The latest version of this document is available to companies that, as PEGI signatories, have access to the PEGI extranet.

57 PEGI age rating information must be clearly visible to consumers at the **point of purchase**. This includes games sold on physical media (including compilations, special editions, and bundles with consoles or peripherals), 'plug-and-play' devices, and boxes containing download codes, as well as cards sold in physical or online retail outlets containing a code to download game content. The PEGI icons must also be displayed in connection with DLC, games that can be accessed and played or streamed online, and early access versions of games. On its extranet, PEGI provides artwork for all the PEGI icons. In practice, these are automatically incorporated into the templates created by games platforms for use on physical media packaging and on online stores.

58 The display of other rating board icons alongside the PEGI labels is **prohibited**. Certain limited exceptions are provided for physical products such as for games for the German-speaking market with short print runs and bundles.

As discussed, a game must display a PEGI rating at the point of purchase or download. However, for **pre-order sales** and pre-release marketing, when the PEGI licence is pending, promotional materials must display the expected age rating, taking into account the highest rating in the case of doubt, with the word 'PROVISIONAL' underneath it. This will avoid confusion if the final age rating is different from the one used in pre-release marketing. 59

UK

Some of the rules discussed above reflect labelling provisions required under **UK law**, which came into force in 2012, for products age-rated PEGI 12, 16 and 18. These include the requirement to show certain age ratings on the physical media itself (e.g., disc label). As it is more efficient to create one packaging design for all PEGI markets, PEGI determined that such rules should apply to a product in all PEGI countries in which it is published. 60

G. PEGI advertising rules

The PEGI Code of Conduct sets out a number of principles to ensure that game advertising and promotion is conducted **responsibly**. These form the basis for the advertising rules in the PEGI Labelling and Advertising Guidelines. The principles include a prohibition on targeting advertisements for games rated 16 or 18 to consumers for whom the product is not rated as appropriate, a requirement for an advertisement to accurately reflect the nature and content of the game, and a restriction on advertisements causing serious or widespread offence to the average consumer. 61

The rules also restate the general commitment of the PEGI Agreement, namely, that advertising for a game shall, wherever practicable, show the **final or provisional** PEGI rating; there is no obligation to display descriptors in advertising. Specifically, the rules stipulate that the rating must be displayed in advertising via print and online media, online video produced by publishers (e.g., trailers, promotional game footage, and gameplay streams), TV, radio and cinema advertising and specific social media posts by publishers (if they contain trailers or display links to order or buy the game). 62

The rules set out in detail the size, **position** and duration for which the rating must appear and whether a voiceover is required. The display of other rating board age ratings alongside the PEGI rating is prohibited in video advertising that is regionalised or geo-segmented for a European audience. 63

The rules also set out guidance concerning **cross-promotions**, that is, the promotion of a game in or via another game or non-game product, or the promotion of a non-game product in or via a game. The main requirement is to ensure that the promoted product is appropriate for the audience that is targeted. In general, publishers are allowed to reference higher-rated games in lower-rated games, on the condition that the content introduced in the game remains in line with the age rating of the game and there are no direct links to buy the higher-rated product. 64

H. Enforcement

Breaches of the PEGI Agreement, including the Code, come to light via consumer complaints or following PEGI examination of the labelling or advertising of games on 65 or post release. It is the responsibility of the game publisher, as the PEGI Agreement signatory, to comply with PEGI rules, not the developer of the game (if different to the publisher) or the platform on which the game is released. The PEGI secretariat will write to the relevant publisher identifying the breach and requiring the publisher to respond with the steps it will take to rectify the breach and to avoid future similar breaches. The matter is then referred to the PEGI Enforcement Committee ('PEC'), which consists of a pool of six executives from PEGI signatories and six members from the PEGI Council and PEGI Experts Group. The PEC is responsible for enforcing the PEGI Agreement and Code in response to the notification of a breach by the PEGI Complaints Board or the PEGI secretariat. The PEC meets ad hoc, with a minimum of six serving members of the PEC (three PEGI signatories and three from the PEGI Council or Experts Group), to determine sanctions for breaches that have been notified to it. The sanction is then notified in writing to the publisher.

66 The level of **fines** stipulated under the PEGI Code depends on the seriousness of the breach. The highest fine of 100,000–250,000 EUR is for a deliberate failure, or gross negligence leading to failure, to disclose content in a game that would have led to a higher rating than that assigned to the product, or game advertising that targets consumers for whom the product is not rated as appropriate. The next level of fines, 5,000–20,000 EUR, can be imposed for a number of breaches such as for negligence leading to a failure to disclose content in a game that would have led to a higher rating than that assigned to the product, display of an incorrect rating or descriptor, or a missing descriptor. The final level of fines, up to 5,000 EUR, can be imposed for operational breaches such as the submission of inaccurate or incomplete submission materials. The Code provides for higher fines in the case of repeat offenders.

67 The Code also stipulates that **other sanctions** may be imposed in certain circumstances such as a period of disqualification from the PEGI system, recall and re-labelling of products, retraining of Coders and systematic screening of the publisher's future products at the publisher's expense.

68 The Code states that the PEC shall use reasonable and non-arbitrary discretion in examining the facts to enable determination of appropriate sanctions and shall be able to consider any or all extenuating circumstances justifying moderation of any sanction to be applied. All decisions regarding enforcement of the PEGI Agreement and Code are **published** on the PEGI public website.

§ 23
Protection of Minors – USK

Bibliography: BeckOK JugendschutzR/Liesching, 4th edn, Munich 2024; Binder/Vesting, Beck'scher Kommentar zum RundfunkR, 4th edn, Munich 2018; BZKJ, Gefährdungsatlas, 2nd edn, Bonn 2022; Erdemir, Das neue Jugendschutzgesetz, 1st edn, Baden-Baden 2021; Hentsch/von Petersdorff, Gesetzlicher Jugendschutz in der Games-Branche, MMR Supplement 2020, 3 seqq.; Hilgert/Sümmermann, Von Inhalt zu Interaktion: Neuerungen im Jugendschutzrecht, K&R 2021, 297; Hoeren/Sieber/Holznagel, Handbuch Multimedia-Recht, Munich 2024 (loose-leaf); Hopf/Braml, Die Entwicklung des Jugendmedienschutzes 2020, ZUM 2021, 427 seqq.; Liesching, Das Herkunftslandprinzip nach E-Commerce- und AVMD-Richtlinie, MMR Supplement 6/2020, 3 seqq.; Mast et al., Digital Services Act / Digital Markets Act (DAS / DMA), 1st edn, Munich 2024; Secker, Jugendschutz in der Games-Branche, MMR Supplement 2020, 1 seqq.

A. Introduction 1
I. Youth protection in the media in transition 3
II. Protection of minors in the gaming industry 5

B. Marketing of games in accordance with youth protection laws 7
I. Overview of the legal framework 8
1. The Youth Protection Act (JuSchG) 9
a) Defining developmental impairment 10
b) Impairment of personal integrity 13
c) Labeling requirements in accordance with JuSchG 18
d) Additional information/descriptors pursuant to § 14 2(a) 22
e) Precautionary measures 23
2. Interstate Treaty on the Protection of Minors in the Media (JMStV) 28
II. The Entertainment Software Self-Regulation Body (Unterhaltungssoftware Selbstkontrolle – USK) 33
1. Release of games in retail stores 36
a) Procedure 37
b) Review hierarchy and evaluation levels 40
c) Impact of usage risks on the ruling practice of the USK 43
2. Publishing games online 45
a) Structure and objectives of USK.online 45
b) International Age Rating Coalition 49
III. Monitoring compliance with regulations 52

C. Conclusion 53

A. Introduction

1 Legal youth media protection in Germany is considered one of the most restrictive in the world, which entails special requirements for game providers in the German market. Even though the German approach may seem the 'only show in town' to some publishers when it comes to age ratings – especially since the PEGI system is used throughout most of Europe – recent developments reveal that rating trends increasingly carry the label 'Made in Germany'. Amid ongoing debates at the European level on consumer protection and monetisation models, the reform of the Youth Protection Act has introduced a nuanced and pragmatic regulatory framework. It balances commercial realities with a high level of protection for minors. Rather than relying on blanket bans or rigid age thresholds, German youth protection follows a case-by-case approach that fosters both protection and empowerment. The **Entertainment Software Self-Regulation Body (USK)** implements this statutory framework in close cooperation with public authorities, serving as a 'one-stop shop' for game providers in Germany.

2 This chapter provides an overview of the basic legal framework for the statutory protection of minors in the media, which is particularly relevant for the games industry

and the publishing sector. It discusses the role of the USK as a **'one-stop shop'** and the legal framework for game providers and gaming platforms.

I. Youth protection in the media in transition

3 While the main goal of youth media protection has been to keep minors away from harmful media content for many years, modern youth media protection has had to face new challenges. Back in 2018, a resolution by the Conference of Ministers for Youth and Family Affairs addressed the need to further develop legal youth media protection in light of new risks associated with media content. Against the background of the UN Convention on the Rights of the Child, the goal of giving equal priority to **'promotion, protection, and participation'** was anchored in order to enable children to grow up safely with media in the long term.[1] This resolution led to an **amendment to the federal Youth Protection Act (JuSchG)**, which came into force on 1.5.2021. A shift in perspective had become necessary due to the rapid pace of digitalisation, the interlinked nature of online offerings, and the actual media usage patterns of minors. The previous system proved insufficient in light of constant online availability, social media, and user-generated content platforms. Additional risks – identified in the Risk Atlas of the Federal Center for Media Protection (BzKJ, formerly BPjM) – include unwanted contact, insults, disinformation, data misuse, excessive use, gambling-like mechanics (e.g., loot boxes), and issues originally classified as consumer protection issues, such as non-transparent payment obligations.[2]

4 Given the growing complexity of the digital world, proven risk mitigation tools like age ratings had to be further developed and adapted to new challenges. The German approach is to take into account risks associated with the **usage as part of a specific risk assessment** and weigh these against the protective measures already in place by providers. This allows a well-founded risk assessment for the specified age group to be made in combination with **additional information**. Terms such as empowerment, the right to control the collection and use of personal information, and resilience reflect the Zeitgeist, which is necessary to enable children and young people to act confidently and safely in the digital future.[3] The focus is on transparency, choice, and appropriate safeguards to create fundamental resilience against undesirable influences. European legislators have also taken action in the area of such intermediary services, where the Digital Services Act has been in force since February 2024 and now applies as a directly applicable EU regulation. However, aside from regulation, consistent monitoring of minors' media consumption by parents and educational professionals remains one of the most effective means of protecting children and young people in the long term.

II. Protection of minors in the gaming industry

5 Digital games have become an integral part of the lives of children and young people. According to the **JIM Study 2024**, 73 percent of 12- to 19-year-olds regularly – i.e., at least several times a week – play digital games across all platforms, including computers,

---

[1] See also JFMK, 'Beschluss der JFMK' (4.5.2018) <https://jfmk.de/wp-content/uploads/2018/12/a-JFMK-03._04.-Mai-2018_Protokoll-mit-Anlagen.pdf>.

[2] See also BZKJ, 'Gefährdungsatlas der BZKJ' (18.5.2022) <https://www.bzkj.de/bzkj/service/publikationen/gefaehrdungsatlas-digitales-aufwachsen-vom-kind-aus-denken-zukunftssicher-handeln-aktualisierte-und-erweiterte-2-auflage--197812>.

[3] See also Erdemir, p. 23 et seq.

consoles, tablets, and smartphones.[4] In the 6–13 age group, 60 percent regularly engage in digital games.[5] Games are now primarily played on smartphones, consoles, or PCs.

As a **voluntary self-regulation body for the games industry**, the USK has been ensuring compliance with the legal provisions for the protection of minors in the media in Germany for over 30 years. It is also committed to creating industry-wide standards that go beyond legal requirements. The USK is also highly valued by parents. According to a **representative survey** conducted by the USK in fall 2024, 92 % of parents say they are familiar with the age ratings, and around 4 out of 5 parents consider the USK to be an important institution when choosing digital games.[6] 6

B. Marketing of games in accordance with youth protection laws

When marketing games, providers are regularly confronted with the question of which legal regulations they must comply with in the area of German youth media protection. The regulatory framework is primarily derived from the **JuSchG (Youth Protection Act)** as federal law and the **JMStV (Interstate Treaty on the Protection of Minors in the Media)** of the federal states. Which of the aforementioned legal bases ultimately applies depends primarily on the distribution method. In many cases, this also applies after the amended JuSchG came into force in 2021, although a media-convergent approach was pursued. The JuSchG contains hardly any substantive legal consolidations that lead to uniform provisions and legal consequences for the various types of media. Rather, the core provisions – § 14a JuSchG for film and gaming platforms and § 24a JuSchG on precautionary measures, although the latter has now been largely superseded by **Art. 28 of the Digital Services Act (DSA)** – only regulate certain digital services, whereas a distinction continues to be made between digital services and carrier media with regard to legal consequences. If games are distributed on physical media or via a gaming platform as defined in the JuSchG, or presented publicly (e.g., at trade fairs or esports events), the JuSchG applies. Apart from these exceptions, the JMStV governs the online distribution of games and related media formats (trailers, streams, etc.). 7

I. Overview of the legal framework

The protection of minors has its origins in the personal rights of children and young people who need protection (Art. 1(1) in conjunction with Art. 2(1) GG) and in the restrictions on freedom of expression and freedom of the media under Art. 5 (2) GG, and thus has **constitutional status** in Germany. Accordingly, 'children and young people [...] have a right to develop their personality in accordance with these fundamental rights. They need protection and assistance in order to develop into responsible individuals within the social community'.[7] In addition, parents have the constitutionally guaranteed right to raise their children in accordance with Art. 6(2) GG (**parental privilege**). The state shall support the right of parents to raise their children by ensuring the protection of minors. 8

---

[4] LFK, 'JIM Studie 2024' (2024) <https://mpfs.de/app/uploads/2024/11/JIM_2024_PDF_barrierearm.pdf>.

[5] LFK, 'KIM Studie 2022' (2022) <https://mpfs.de/app/uploads/2024/11/KIM-Studie2022_website_final.pdf>.

[6] USK, press release (1.10.2024) <https://usk.de/pressemitteilung-4-von-5-eltern-setzen-beim-jugendschutz-in-games-auf-alterskennzeichen-der-usk/>.

[7] BVerfG 27.11.1990 – 1 BvR 402/87, NJW 1991, 1471 (1472) (translation by the author).

1. The Youth Protection Act (JuSchG)

9 The federal Youth Protection Act (JuSchG) regulates the protection of minors in the media. Accordingly, game providers in Germany may only offer games to children or adolescents in public if they have been rated by the USK. The aim of youth media protection is to protect children and young people from media that is likely to impair their development or their education as responsible and socially competent individuals or to endanger them. In 2021, the protection goals were also expanded to include promoting orientation for minors, persons with parental responsibility, and educational professionals in media use and education, as well as protecting the personal integrity of children and young people when using media. The expansion of the protection goals has had a significant impact compared to the previous age rating procedures. However, other provisions that are of central importance for the overall context must also be taken into account. These include, in particular, § 24a JuSchG, which links to the obligation for providers of online platforms under Art. 28 DSA, according to which online platforms accessible to minors must take appropriate and proportionate measures to ensure a high level of privacy, safety, and security for minors on their service (**precautionary measures**).

a) Defining developmental impairment

10 The term 'developmental impairment' forms the basis for age ratings, unlike the 'endangerment of minors', which excludes age ratings (§ 14(3) JuSchG) and may even fulfill criminal law standards. Until 2021, the term only covered **risks that could arise from the specific media content (so-called confrontation risks),** but it was extended to include risks that could arise from circumstances outside the media content (§ 10b (2) JuSchG), the so-called **usage risks** or **risks to the personal integrity** of minors.

11 As a general rule, children and young people must be protected from media that is unsuitable or harmful to their development. According to § 10a No. 1 JuSchG, media is considered likely to impair development if it hinders the education of minors into responsible and socially competent individuals. According to § 10b(1) JuSchG, this includes, in particular, media that is excessively frightening, promotes violence, or impairs social and ethical values. These risk areas, referred to as **content risks**, are defined in more detail in the Guidance Criteria of the USK (→ mn. 12).

12 The **Guidance Criteria of the USK**[8] support the USK rating committees (→ mn. 37 et seqq.) in their age classification and represent a rating standard that requires further expert interpretation in individual cases. An overall assessment of the medium is always necessary, whereby the aspects of its impact must be evaluated. The following areas of impact are particularly relevant: Pressure to act, violence, war themes, fear and threat, sexual content, discrimination, inappropriate language, drugs, gambling issues or socially and ethically disorienting role models. These can in turn be amplified or weakened by impact factors relating to the specific design of the test object and their influence on the areas of impact. The impact factors include: Visual and acoustic implementation of the game idea, gameplay, atmosphere, realism, credibility, human likeness, youth affinity and identification potential. Furthermore, particular importance is attached to the consideration of symbols of unconstitutional or terrorist organisations. The category of framing competence, which is attributed to minors in the cognitive and emotional-moral classification of media content and representations depending on their

[8] USK, 'Guidance Criteria of the USK' (1.1.2025) <https://usk.de/en//?smd_process_download=1&download_id=2272895>.

age, plays an important role in the decision-making process.[9] The assessment must take into account not only the average minor but also minors who are particularly vulnerable, excluding extreme cases.[10]

b) Impairment of personal integrity

While there is a long-established practice in the area of confrontation risks, the term 'personal integrity' needs to be defined more precisely and given substance in youth protection practice. According to the explanatory memorandum to the law, this pair of terms covers 'the protection of their [children and young people's] personal rights in the broadest sense in indirect third-party effect under Art. 2(1) in conjunction with Art. 1(1) GG and, associated with this, the right to informational self-determination and, overall, protection against identity violations'.[11] 13

This addresses the unimpaired development of the 'mental and emotional' integrity of children and adolescents. It includes the right to self-determination (formation of one's own identity), self-preservation (privacy and confidentiality) and self-presentation (right to personal honor, right to one's own word, right to one's own image, right to informational self-determination, right to guarantee the confidentiality and integrity of information technology systems).[12] The general right of personality is thus intended to ensure, overall, the conditions for the free and autonomous exercise of individuality within a community. Externally induced disturbances should be prevented during childhood and adolescence, and the path to a mentally healthy and strong personality – in cases of imminent violations of personality rights, also in the sense of a resilient personality – should be facilitated.[13] This means, for example, that impairments to **psychological integrity** (identity formation, inner autonomy, individual opinion formation), **social integrity** (claim to recognition in a community, identity and relationship management), **decision-making integrity** (freedom of choice, commercial autonomy) or **sexual integrity** (sexual self-determination) may be considered.[14] The central protective goal is therefore **psychological well-being** in the sense of a state in which the individual is at peace with themselves and with the world.[15] In disputes with third parties, this well-being may be impaired accordingly.[16] In addition, however, mechanisms contained in games or their design that start outside of the actual game activity can also pose a risk to the personal integrity of children and young people. This can include manipulative designs or processes that attempt to deliberately impair players' ability to control themselves ('dark patterns'), such as social, playtime-related or store designs.[17] A temporary (short-term) impairment of the child's well-being, such as mere irritation or 14

[9] USK, 'Guidance Criteria of the USK' (1.1.2025), p. 15 <https://usk.de/en//?smd_process_download=1&download_id=2272895>.

[10] USK, 'Guidance Criteria of the USK' (1.1.2025), p. 7 <https://usk.de/en//?smd_process_download=1&download_id=2272895>.

[11] BT-Drs. 19/24909, 43 (translation by the author).

[12] See also, in particular, on derivation: Dreyer in Erdemir, § 2 mn. 25.

[13] See also BzKJ, 'Gefährdungsatlas: Digitales Aufwachsen vom Kind aus denken – Zukunftssicher handeln', p. 73 et seqq.

[14] Dreyer in Erdemir, § 2 mn. 26.

[15] BVerfG 29.7.2009 – 1 BvR 1606/08, NVwZ 2009, 1494.

[16] Dreyer in Erdemir, § 2 mn. 26.

[17] USK, 'Guidance Criteria of the USK' (1.1.2025), p. 10. <https://usk.de/en//?smd_process_download=1&download_id=2272895>.

discomfort, is not sufficient; rather, a lasting disturbance is required for the existence of an impairment of development.[18]

15 For the age rating of games, this means that, in accordance with **§ 10b(2) JuSchG**, 'circumstances relating to the use of the medium that lie outside the scope of the media content may also be taken into account if they are an integral part of the medium and justify a different overall assessment beyond the labeling pursuant to § 14(2a)' (**risks of use**) (→ mn. 16).[19] This means that associated functionalities and their development-related risk potential must also be taken into account in the context of media use by minors.

16 This discretionary provision is supplemented by **§ 10b (3) JuSchG**. According to this provision:

> **risks to the personal integrity of children and young people that arise in connection with the use of the medium and are classified as significant following a specific risk assessment must be taken into account appropriately, taking into account any precautionary measures within the meaning of § 24a(1) and (2). These include, in particular, risks arising from communication and contact functions, purchasing functions, gambling-like mechanisms, mechanisms promoting excessive media use, the transfer of account data and usage data to third parties without consent, and age-inappropriate appeals to purchase, in particular through advertising references to other media.**[20]

17 Due to the respective wording of the two paragraphs ('may/shall provision'), there is initially an apparent contradiction, which can only be resolved in advance by means of interpretation and a strict **hierarchy of review** as well as a 'cursory' examination (→ mn. 40 et seqq.) of the functionalities.

c) Labeling requirements in accordance with JuSchG

18 According to § 12(1) of the JuSchG, data carriers are subject to a prohibition with reservation of permission, meaning that they may only be made accessible to minors if they have been approved and labeled for their age group by the highest state youth protection authorities (Oberste Landesjugendbehörden, OLJB) or a voluntary self-regulation organisation in accordance with the procedure laid down in § 14(6) of the JuSchG. A **labeling requirement** also applies to digital films and games offered via digital platforms (§ 14a (1) sent. 2 JuSchG).

19 **Film and gaming platforms** are defined in § 14a(1) sent. 1 of the JuSchG as service providers that compile games or films summarised in a overall offer and make them available for individual access at a time chosen by the user with the intention of making a profit. A **summary to an overall offer** should also be assumed if the service provider only makes a minor assessment of the content of the films and games before making them available and sorts them using automated procedures and publishes them on the offer.[21] According to the explanatory memorandum to the law, the question of whether content is 'own content' is to be determined in accordance with § 7(1) of the TMG (old version).[22] **Content is considered to be own content** if providers 'have direct influence on the selection and presentation of films and game programmes and curate them before making them available'. However, the legislative materials do not expressly state whether the term 'own content' also includes content that the service provider has

[18] See also Altenhain in Hoeren/Sieber/Holznagel, part 20, mn. 84 et seq.; Dreyer in Erdemir, § 2 mn. 27.

[19] Translation by the author.

[20] Translation by the author.

[21] BT-Drs. 19/24909, 47.

[22] The TMG has been repealed with effect from 14.5.2024 by Art. 37 of 'Gesetzes zur Durchführung des DSA' (6.5.2024), BGBl. 2024 I no. 149.

'adopted as its own' in accordance with the case law on the former § 7(1) TMG. According to established case law, an objective overall assessment of all relevant circumstances is decisive in this regard and restraint is required as a matter of principle. Under EU law, the principle of non-liability for third-party content applies (see Art. 14 E-Commerce Directive). The more the platform appears to be a mere host provider in relation to a piece of content offered, enabling another provider to distribute its content without its own review or decision, the less it can be assumed that the platform has made the content its own.[23] Neither the mere promotion or highlighting of third-party content nor purely economic participation, for example through advertising revenue or revenue sharing, constitutes 'appropriation' in itself. However, audiovisual offerings that, from the user's perspective, form part of an economically oriented overall offering curated by the platform provider are generally to be regarded as 'own content'.[24]

Service providers are **exempt from the labeling requirement** under § 14a(2) if they can prove there are fewer than one million users in Germany or restrict access to adults. Where access requires registration, the number of registered user accounts is generally decisive.[25] If no registration is required, user numbers can typically only be estimated – e.g., based on unique monthly visits, in line with § 91(2) No. 1 MStV. The burden of proof remains partially with the BzKJ pursuant to § 24 VwVfG and § 47 OWiG. 20

§ 14a (1) sent. 2 nos. 1–3 JuSchG also regulates **how age ratings are to be issued** within the framework of the labeling requirement. For digital games, they must either be obtained as result of a 'classic' JuSchG review procedure by a self-regulation body such as the USK with the involvement of the OLJB, or by a self-regulation body recognised under the JMStV such as USK.online. Labeling by a youth protection officer certified by a self-regulation body in accordance with § 7 JMStV or labeling by an automated rating system of a self-regulation body that has been submitted to the highest state youth protection authorities for approval is also possible. The **IARC system has been officially recognised** as such a system by the highest state youth protection authorities since 2025 (→ mn. 49). 21

d) Additional information/descriptors pursuant to § 14 2(a)

According to § 14 (2a) JuSchG, digital games must be labeled not only with the age rating but also with information on the main reasons for the age rating and indications of the potential impairment of personal integrity. The regulation adopts the system of additional information that had already been established on various online platforms through voluntary initiatives such as the IARC system and extends it to procedures under § 14(6) JuSchG. In order to meet the legislator's objectives of transparency, orientation and uniformity, the parties involved in the implementation have strived for the highest possible harmonisation within the framework of the implementation for the medium of games. Accordingly, following the involvement of relevant target groups consisting of parents, educational professionals and minors, precise information in text form (descriptor) has also been introduced for Germany, based on the IARC system.[26] 22

---

[23] Liesching in BeckOK JugendschutzR/Liesching, JuSchG § 14a mn. 13.
[24] Liesching in BeckOK JugendschutzR/Liesching, JuSchG § 14a mn. 16.
[25] Hilgert/Sümmermann K&R 2021, 297 (300).
[26] See also the current additional information (descriptors) of the USK <https://usk.de/en/the-usk-age-ratings/>.

e) Precautionary measures

23 According to **§ 24a of the JuSchG**, providers of online platforms that store or make available third-party information for users are obliged to take appropriate and effective structural precautions ('safety by design'). However, since the Digital Services Act came into force, Art. 28(1) DSA has largely replaced the previous regulation. **Art. 28(1) DSA** stipulates that 'Providers of online platforms accessible to minors shall put in place appropriate and proportionate measures to ensure a high level of privacy, safety, and security of minors on their service.' It is crucial that the measures are **appropriate and proportionate**. This means that they must have a positive effect on the three dimensions of protection mentioned above and the effort required to implement them must not be disproportionate to the risk reduction that can be achieved. The greater the potential harm that an online service poses to minors, the more extensive the measures that the provider must take. Proportionality must be assessed on the basis of a cost-benefit analysis, with the result that the assessment under Art. 28(1) DSA must always be carried out on a **case-by-case** basis. Both the technical characteristics of the service in question and their impact on the risk to the interests protected by law must be taken into account, as well as the human, technical and economic resources required by the provider. A clear limit is reached where the requirements for due diligence become so high that the permanent operation of the service is no longer possible or can only be implemented with considerable difficulty.[27]

24 In order to specify Art. 28(1) of the DSA, the EU Commission is authorised under Art. 28(4) of the DSA to issue guidelines to assist online platform providers in applying Art. 28(1). Accordingly, § 24a(2) JuSchG lists various possible precautionary measures to prevent or minimise the three relevant risk areas of content risks, interactive risks (**contact and conduct risks**) and other usage risks (**consumer and cross-cutting risks**). However, this list is likely to be largely superseded by the publication of the guidelines at the latest, as it is difficult to reconcile with full harmonisation under the DSA.[28]

25 An initial classification of the respective measures according to the risk dimensions has already been carried out by the BzKJ or the independent body responsible for Art. 28 DSA – the **Federal Office for the Enforcement of Children's Rights in Digital Services (KidD)** – using its assessment criteria, along with the requirements for the individual precautionary measures.[29] Within the scope of application, deviations are possible in individual cases due to the proportionality requirement. However, the assessment criteria will be continuously updated and further developed, in particular in light of the EU Commission's guidelines planned for 2025, which are to be given prior consideration.[30] The guiding principle of the **guidelines pursuant to Art. 28 (4) DSA** is to protect the rights and best interests of children and young people, pursuing a risk-based approach. Accordingly, online platforms must carry out a risk assessment and then implement proportionate, risk-minimising measures (→ Ch. 32 mn. 54). In addition, however, the German government's draft also provides for the possibility for the BZKJ to 'develop further

---

[27] Dreyer in Mast et al., DSA Art. 28 mn. 56.

[28] See also the draft of the 'Commission guidelines on measures to ensure a high level of privacy, safety and security for minors online' made available for public consultation (14.5.2025) <https://digital-strategy.ec.europa.eu/en/library/commission-seeks-feedback-guidelines-protection-minors-online-under-digital-services-act>.

[29] BZKJ, 'Prüfkriterien der BZKJ' (23.10.2023) <https://www.bzkj.de/bzkj/service/alle-meldungen/pruefkriterien-der-bzkj-fuer-anbieterseitige-vorsorgemassnahmen-231998> .

[30] See also EU Commission, press release (31.7.2024) <https://germany.representation.ec.europa.eu/news/schutz-minderjahriger-im-internet-eu-kommission-startet-sondierung-zu-dsa-leitlinien-2024-07-31_de?prefLang=en>.

precautionary measures, in particular to consider reporting and redress procedures for further offers, insofar as this does not contradict the provisions of the DSA.'[31]

In this complex situation, recommendations and positions from **self-regulatory bodies** such as the USK are also gaining legal and practical relevance.[32] They support their members in implementing protective measures and obligations relating to minors in a legally compliant and effective manner (→ mn. 45). With their expertise and established practices, they also contribute to the development of recognised minimum standards. In doing so, they offer guidance to providers, create realistic expectations and promote consistency and transparency in implementation. This role is in line with the European and international understanding of cooperative, multi-stakeholder-based youth media protection, as called for by the United Nations, among others.[33] Against this background, cooperation with recognised self-regulatory bodies such as the USK appears not only reasonable, but also an appropriate and responsible way of meeting regulatory requirements under the DSA. 26

The existing system of distribution restrictions applicable to telemedia under the JMStV remains unaffected and is supplemented by the overarching systematic requirements.[34] In this context, § 24a (2) No. 5 JuSchG, i.e., the provision of technical measures to control and monitor the use of online services by persons with legal guardianship (**parental controls**), should be highlighted. Accordingly, youth protection programmes **recognised by a self-regulation body** that enable access to telemedia within a 'closed system' in accordance with § 11(2) JMStV are likely to constitutute or at least complement as an appropriate precautionary measure.[35] Furthermore, the catalogue of measures in § 24a(2) JuSchG is not exhaustive and does not establish any order of priority. The obligation to take precautionary measures also applies to online games themselves, insofar as users have the opportunity to communicate with each other by providing their own content.[36] 27

2. Interstate Treaty on the Protection of Minors in the Media (JMStV)

The JMStV covers, in particular, the protection of minors from online content (telemedia), although some provisions have been replaced by the provisions of the Digital Services Act applicable to intermediary services, which also implements youth protection requirements in Art. 28 DSA. Due to the large number of services available on the internet, the concept of **'regulated self-regulation'** is particularly relevant in the context of the JMStV. This means that voluntary self-regulation bodies such as the USK are granted a 'decision-making framework' by law, which is only subject to 'limited' supervision by the media supervisory authorities, although state responsibility remains intact.[37] 28

[31] Cf. BT-Drs. 20/10031, 93.

[32] See also Holznagel in Müller-Terpitz/Köhler/Holznagel in DSA Art. 28 mn. 21–23; also Dreyer in Mast et al., DSA Art. 28 mn. 71 seq. which, within the scope of the 'protection' objective, highlights processes and procedures, including cooperation with external experts in child and youth media protection, the appointment of a child and youth protection officer (going beyond § 7 JMStV), or collaboration with external advisory and/or complaints bodies.

[33] Also see UN Committee on the Rights of the Child, General Comment No. 25 (2021), section V, 'C. Coordination', No. 27.

[34] BT-Drs. 19/24909, 62.

[35] Also see Dreyer in Erdemir, § 5 mn. 81. A system is considered 'closed' if the processes concerned, which are to be secured by the system's youth protection function, are essentially bound to the standards defined by the provider and cannot, in principle, leave the framework of the system.

[36] Recommendation for a decision, BT-Drs. 19/27289, p. 13 seq.; Hilgert/Sümmermann K&R 2021, 297 (300).

[37] Schulz/Held in Binder/Vesting, § 1 JMStV mn. 21.

For example, assessing the youth protection relevance of content falls to self-regulatory bodies, which are themselves overseen by supervisory authorities. The JMStV thus distinguishes between individual case decisions, handled by self-regulatory bodies, and the oversight of self-regulation as a system, which lies with media supervisory authorities.[38]

29 In the area covered by the JMStV, the principle of the provider's own responsibility applies. According to § 5 (1) JMStV, providers are obliged to assess media content that is potentially harmful to the development of minors themselves and to take protective measures to ensure that children and young people of the relevant age group 'do not normally perceive' such content (→ Ch. 34 mn. 58). However, the principle of individual responsibility is superseded in the area of telemedia by § 14a JuSchG, which creates a **labeling requirement for film and gaming platforms** through federal regulations that take precedence (→ mn. 18 et seqq.). In addition, § 6 JMStV contains several provisions on advertising that have become particularly relevant in relation to free-to-play models.

30 However, the JMStV also needs to be adapted to the circumstances of the digital media world. With the sixth Media Amendment Treaty (6. MÄStV), the heads of government of the federal states therefore decided on an amendment to the JMStV in December 2024.[39] The most important changes include, in particular, adjustments to the provisions of the DSA and the JuSchG that have come into force, stricter labeling requirements and further requirements in the area of technical youth media protection. For the first time, the law contains detailed requirements for **youth protection mechanisms for operating systems** 'commonly used by children and young people' and, in this context, relevant requirements for apps, browsers, distribution platforms and online search engines. The aim is to offer parents and guardians a (filter) mechanism that is as easy to use and secure as possible to protect their children (a so-called 'one-click solution') that combines and supplements existing youth protection measures and makes them more visible.

31 In line with § 10b (2) JuSchG, the **risks to the personal integrity** of children and young people will now also be taken into account as part of the scope of application of the **JMStV** when assessing developmental impairments (cf. § 5 (1) JMStV-E). In addition, telemedia providers must indicate the age rating of films, series and game programmes that they offer as their own content by **displaying a clearly visible rating** before or at the start of the content. They should also indicate the main reasons for the age rating and any risks to personal integrity (cf. § 5c (3) JMStV-E).

32 Many aspects of the JMStV-E will only be assessable after the amendment has been implemented. However, it should be noted that youth protection measures (e.g., through self-regulatory bodies such as **USK-certified parental controls**) within games and apps will become significantly more important under these regulations, as youth protection mechanisms at the operating system level will in future give preference to apps that have integrated parental controls, especially those certified by self-regulatory bodies such as the USK. It is also to be expected that ratings assigned by automated rating systems such as IARC (→ mn. 49) will become more important in this context, as they are intended to serve as a basis for youth protection measures at the operating system level. However, the adopted JMStV-E also raises concerns regarding its compliance with EU law. The EU Commission has already expressed criticism in its notification, particularly with regard to compliance with the country of origin principle under Art. 3 of the E-Commerce Directive and with regard to the full harmonisation effect of the DSA.

---

[38] Schulz/Held in Binder/Vesting, § 1 JMStV mn. 26.

[39] 6th MÄStV (26.3.2025) <https://www.ministerpraesident.sachsen.de/ministerpraesident/TOP-10-Sechster-Medienaenderungsstaatsvertrag.pdf>.

II. The Entertainment Software Self-Regulation Body (Unterhaltungssoftware Selbstkontrolle – USK)

The USK is legally **recognised under both the JuSchG and the JMStV of the federal states.** Its work focuses on implementing statutory youth media protection, particularly in the area of digital games. In the classic USK assessment procedure in accordance with the JuSchG, state representatives assign age ratings on the recommendation of independent youth protection experts. In addition, the USK also assigns age ratings within the global IARC system for online games and apps. Numerous companies have joined the USK as members in order to cooperate closely and on a permanent basis on the issue of youth protection. Through its press and public relations activities, the USK contributes to public information and opinion-forming on digital games and German youth media protection. This is particularly important in the context of **promoting media literacy** by educating parents, educational professionals and multipliers. It is also committed to the active promotion and further development of youth media protection.[40] 33

The shareholder of USK as a non-profit GmbH is the German Games Industry Association (game – Verband der deutschen Games-Branche e.V.). The shareholder bears the economic risk of the GmbH, but not the responsibility for the age ratings of the games. The USK is advised by a pluralistic **advisory board**,[41] which, among other things, determines the USK statutes and the guiding criteria for the assessment procedures. 34

As part of its assessment procedures, the USK ensures that games can be tested for technical and content-related issues on a wide variety of gaming platforms. It is also responsible for ensuring that the assessment procedures run smoothly. In addition, the USK provides further training for all experts involved in the assessment process and is a permanent partner of gamescom and other game fairs and public events where games are presented. Furthermore, the USK supports providers in implementing the diverse and complex requirements of the federal government, the states and Europe, in accompanying regulatory work, in picking up on new developments and in developing, implementing or **certifying innovative solutions in technical youth media protection** (→ mn. 32).[42] 35

1. Release of games in retail stores

If digital games are to be sold to children and young people in retail outlets or as data carriers, this is only permitted, regardless of their actual content, if they have been approved and rated for their age group in accordance with the procedure set out in § 14(6) of the JuSchG (**labeling requirement**). In Germany, only the USK offers such a procedure for digital games. 36

a) Procedure

Responsibility for age ratings delegated under the JuSchG is exercised by the competent ministry of North Rhine-Westphalia on behalf of all federal states, based on an interstate agreement. Under this agreement, staff of the responsible authority are appointed as permanent representatives of the OLJB to participate directly in the USK's standard classification process pursuant to the JuSchG and to issue **sovereign administra-** 37

[40] Also see 'Statut der Unterhaltungssoftware Selbstkontrolle' (1.1.2025) https://usk.de/wp-content/uploads/2024/12/Statut-der-USK.pdf.

[41] Advisory Board <https://usk.de/die-usk/grundlagen-und-struktur/beirat/>.

[42] Hentsch/von Petersdorff, MMR Supplement 2020, (3).

tive act at the end of the process. The procedure itself is based on an agreement between the shareholder of the USK (game – Verband der deutschen Games-Branche e.V.) and the competent authority in accordance with § 12 (1) and 14 (6) JuSchG. The procedure is based on the USK assessment principles[43] and the USK guiding criteria (→ mn. 12).

38 In accordance with the USK assessment principles, the material to be assessed is reviewed by a tester and presented to a pluralistic committee consisting of four youth protection experts and a permanent representative of the OLJB (chair). After discussion and consideration by the committee, the permanent representative of the OLJB adopts the review committee's recommendation for approval in its decision. The decision is justified in writing. In cases of doubt, the assessment procedure may be interrupted and an expert opinion from the BzKJ may be obtained. An **appeal** against the decision in the standard procedure may be made by the applicant or the OLJB. In order to consolidate and maintain the decision-making practice, a subsequent appeal may be submitted by the OLJB or the sponsoring association in borderline cases. The assessment results are based on the age groups specified in § 14 (2) JuSchG. USK ratings do not constitute educational recommendations.

39 If the result is 'no rating pursuant to § 14 JuSchG', a product may continue to be sold to adults, but pursuant to § 18(1) sent. 1 JuSchG, there is a risk that it will be listed as media harmful to minors (indexing) by the BzKJ due to its potential harmfulness, which would prevent it from being sold with legal certainty. In the event of **indexing by the BzKJ**, far-reaching trade restrictions apply.

b) Review hierarchy and evaluation levels

40 Age classification is based exclusively on youth media protection law and does not offer comprehensive legal protection with regard to compliance with other laws and regulations, such as general **consumer protection law**.[44] However, a high relevance to the protection of minors in terms of usage risks, as determined in the context of an age rating procedure at the USK or through **consultation services for members of the USK** (→ mn. 45 et seqq.), may indicate problematic constellations under consumer protection law and serve as a preventive risk assessment for providers.

41 The assessment hierarchy was developed based on the JuSchG and is defined in the USK's guiding criteria:[45] First, the content of the digital game must be evaluated. If functionalities (→ mn. 16) are identified that could lead to potential risks of use, these must be included in the assessment in a next step if the requirements set out in § 10b (2) and (3) JuSchG are met: At the time of the assessment, the functionalities must be **permanent** – i.e., they must not be temporary or short-term – and must be **contained in the individual game itself.**[46] It is not sufficient if the evaluation element only appears each time the surrounding platform is used, regardless of the use of the game in question, unless the game 'adopts' the platform's functionalities. The **same applies to precautionary measures** that have been adopted.[47]

---

[43] 'Prüfgrundsätze der USK' (1.1.2025), <https://usk.de/?smd_process_download=1&download_id=85141539>.

[44] Also see USK, 'Guidance Criteria of the USK' (1.1.2025), p. 11. <https://usk.de/en//?smd_process_download=1&download_id=2272895>.

[45] USK, 'Guidance Criteria of the USK' (1.1.2025), p. 11. <https://usk.de/en//?smd_process_download=1&download_id=2272895>.

[46] BT-Drs. 19/24909, p. 43: 'limited to cases where the circumstances are an integral part of the medium'. (translation by the author).

[47] Dreyer in Erdemir, § 2 mn. 43.

As part of a **specific risk prognosis**, it must be determined whether the functionalities contained therein pose a risk to the personal integrity of minors that can be classified as significant and thus justify a deviation from the age rating determined up to this point. The specific risk prognosis looks at the probability of a certain risk occurring and the potential damage that could result.[48] Corresponding risks must be identified and evaluated (**risk assessment**). For games, the question of the inevitability of the potential risk due to the gameplay or the focus, and thus the relevance of the function in the overall context of the game, can provide important clues.[49] In addition, factors that are structurally and effectively capable of minimising the probability of risks occurring or mitigating the potential damage (**risk mitigation**) must be taken into account. Besides giving priority to descriptors (**sensitising effect**) that especially take into account the participation rights of minors, as required by law, existing appropriate structural precautions must also be included (cf. § 24a (1) and (2) JuSchG). The stronger the interests are affected, the higher the requirements for such measures.[50] The reference to § 24a JuSchG in § 10b(3) JuSchG is to be understood merely as clarification of possible measures ('within the meaning of'). The extent to which the provider is actually obliged to implement corresponding measures in accordance with Art. 28(1) DSA is irrelevant for the consideration of their risk-reducing characteristics.[51] **42**

c) Impact of usage risks on the ruling practice of the USK

The protection of personal integrity has led to a structural expansion of the assessment scope for digital games, necessitating an adjustment of the USK's guiding criteria.[52] Proven practices developed by independent youth protection experts from child and youth welfare, media education, and media psychology have since been integrated into these criteria. A corresponding resolution was adopted by the USK Advisory Board (→ mn. 34). The 'risk dimensions in the use of digital games' referenced therein are based on the dimensions listed in § 10b(3) sentence 2 JuSchG (→ mn. 16), which do not constitute an exhaustive legal catalogue. In addition to outlining the relevant functions and their potential impact on minors' personal integrity, the assessment identifies possible aggravating and mitigating factors, as well as precautionary measures that may help address the identified risks of use. While technical protection and precautionary tools (→ mn. 16; 23; 27) have long been common in digital games and platforms, they are only now gaining relevance in the context of age ratings – and beyond (cf. § 24a JuSchG). **43**

The inclusion of usage risks has had a considerable **practical impact**: Nearly one third of games containing such risks have since received a higher age rating than they would have under the previous criteria. Since the introduction of the new assessment rules, the independent assessment bodies at the USK have placed particular focus on insufficiently secure chats, intrusive purchase requests and the non-transparent design of in-game shops. This includes complex monetisation systems and reward mechanisms tied to prolonged playtime necessary for in-game progress. According to current practice, such features can create pressure to play and increased incentives to purchase. Some remain despite existing precautionary measures (e.g., options to restrict or deactivate **44**

[48] Dreyer in Erdemir, § 2 mn. 49.
[49] Also see Wager/Waldeck in Erdemir, § 3 mn. 25.
[50] BT-Drs. 19/24909, 62.
[51] Also see Hilgert/Sümmermann K&R 2021, 297 (298); Dreyer in Erdemir, § 2 mn. 50.
[52] USK, press release (16.12.2024) <https://usk.de/update-der-leitkriterien-fuer-alterskennzeichen-usk-beirat-verankert-nutzungsrisiken-in-der-bewertung-digitaler-spiele/>; The revised guiding criteria are publicly available in English: <https://usk.de/en//?smd_process_download=1&download_id=2272895>.

functions) and can thus have a lasting negative impact on the **commercial autonomy** or **self-regulatory capacity of younger children** with regard to their gaming behaviour. **Additional information** has also become established in practice. '*Pressure to play a lot*', '*increased incentives to buy*', or '*increased communication risks*'[53] is information that parents in particular appreciate when buying games. A total of 86 percent of parents consider it helpful to have additional guidance in place alongside the traditional age ratings.[54]

2. Publishing games online

a) *Structure and objectives of USK.online*

45 USK.online supports providers of online content relevant to the protection of minors in implementing statutory youth media protection and in distinguishing between necessary legal safeguards and sensible or even superfluous youth protection measures, and **advises providers on compliance** with, further development and promotion of youth media protection. USK.online is an independent, established division of the USK that is recognised by the KJM pursuant to § 19 (3) JMStV for an indefinite period. The activities of USK.online are governed by the USK.online statutes,[55] which regulate the procedures and structure of USK.online.

46 In addition, USK.online offers its members guidance and a structured framework for the further development of practical standards in a dynamically evolving regulatory environment, in accordance with Art. 28 DSA (online protection of minors) and Art. 14(3) DSA (terms and conditions). The USK also supports its members within the framework of the so-called **'dialogic procedures' pursuant to § 24b JuSchG** in conjunction with Art. 28 DSA through professional exchange, statements or coordination and acts as a mediator in this role by advocating practical solutions. More than 50 companies have now joined USK.online as **members.**[56]

47 If a provider conforms to the statutes of a self-regulatory body recognised under the JMStV pursuant to § 20(5) JMStV or joins such a body as a **member**, any alleged violations of youth protection by the Commission for the Protection of Minors in the Media (KJM) must first be brought before that body within the framework of a supervisory procedure. Only if the decision exceeds the legal limits of the scope of discretion or if the self-regulation body fails to take a decision may supervisory measures be taken against the provider. This construct, known as **preliminary protection**, creates a 'safe harbour' for members of a self-regulation body under the JMStV. This protection is important and reasonable for providers, as the interpretation of legal terms in the field of youth media protection is sometimes subject to considerable variation due to their vagueness. The assessment and recognition of technical systems (→ mn. 32; 35) is also of particular importance here, as these are also covered by the scope of discretion of a self-regulatory body.

48 Unlike the procedures under the JuSchG, committee decisions are made by USK.online without government involvement, but still receive legal protection due to the limited

---

[53] Translation by the author: 'Druck zum Vielspielen', 'Erhöhte Kaufanreize', 'Erhöhte Kommunikationsrisiken'.

[54] Representative YouGov study commissioned by the USK (1.6.2024; n=1.001) among parents and guardians with children aged between 6 and 17 living in their household in Germany, according to which a total of 86 percent of parents find it helpful if there is additional guidance alongside the traditional age ratings.

[55] 'Statut der Unterhaltungssoftware Selbstkontrolle' (1.1.2025) <https://usk.de/die-usk/grundlagen-und-struktur/grundlagen/>.

[56] Overview of USK.online member companies <https://usk.de/fuer-unternehmen/service-angebot-der-usk/mitglieder/>.

possibility for the supervisory authorities to review the discretion exercised by a self-regulatory body. However, age ratings by committees under the JuSchG are considerably more relevant in practice, as USK.online primarily assigns its age ratings via the International Age Rating Coalition (→ mn. 49; Ch. 22 mn. 43 et seqq.). An age rating in accordance with the JuSchG also applies to the same content both on data carriers and online (cf. presumption rule pursuant to § 5 (2) sent. 1 JMStV and the duty to provide information pursuant to § 12 JMStV and § 14a No. 1 JuSchG). In addition to its assessment activities, USK.online also advises member companies on the relevance of media content for the protection of minors during the development phase (e.g., for games, trailers or journalistic reports).

b) International Age Rating Coalition

The International Age Rating Coalition (IARC) is an international association of institutions founded in 2013 that makes it possible to assign age ratings to online games and apps within a consistent, **global system**. Platforms and mobile app stores integrate the IARC system to automatically generate age ratings (→ Ch. 22 mn. 43 et seqq.) that are displayed across platforms and in accordance with the applicable regional regulations (e.g., USK for Germany, PEGI in Europe, ESRB for the USA, etc.). The IARC age ratings generated only provide information about the potential impairment to minors. Due to their high recognition value, the IARC ratings have been deliberately designed to look similar to the 'classic' USK JuSchG ratings, as the meaning of the USK age ratings is widely known and understood. IARC ratings may not be transferred to media carriers for stationary retail or for use at public events. 49

In addition to age ratings, the IARC system **displays descriptors** that provide information about the main reasons for the age rating (content and usage risks) and the features or interactive elements contained in the game. For Germany, the IARC system displays additional information that largely corresponds to the JuSchG procedure. These are automatically displayed for platforms participating in the IARC system. The Google Play Store, Nintendo eShop, Microsoft Windows Store, Xbox Store, Fortnite and Epic Store, PlayStation Store, Meta Quest, Pico and luna have already joined IARC.[57] 50

The IARC system has also convinced the highest state youth authorities in Germany, with the result that in 2025 it has been **officially recognised by the highest state youth authorities** as a system for labeling online gaming platforms in accordance with § 14a (1) No. 3 JuSchG. The IARC system thus offers conformity and sustainable legal and planning security in terms of ensuring compliance with the labeling obligation as an online gaming platform in accordance with § 14a JuSchG. In addition, this has also underlined the importance of the USK labels in the online sector: They ensure strong protection for children and young people and offer parents reliable guidance.[58] 51

III. Monitoring compliance with regulations

In the retail sector and at events, local public order offices and youth welfare offices are generally responsible for monitoring compliance. Violations can be penalised with fines of up to **50,000 EUR** in accordance with § 28(5) sent. 1 JuSchG, alongside additional criminal provisions. Pursuant to § 16(1) JMStV, the Commission for the Protec- 52

[57] Overview of participants in the IARC system <https://www.globalratings.com/about.aspx>.

[58] USK, press release (25.4.2025) <https://usk.de/starker-digitaler-kinder-und-jugendschutz-automatisiertes-system-der-usk-fuer-alterskennzeichen-auf-online-spieleplattformen-ueberzeugt-jugendschutzbehoerden-der-bundeslaender/>.

tion of Minors in the Media (KJM) is responsible for monitoring compliance with the provisions of the JMStV. With support of jugendschutz.net,[59] the KJM supervises online media as part of the state media authorities. It may impose fines of up to **500,000 EUR**, issue complaints, bans, or blocking orders. These are enforced by the competent state media authority. In the area of precautionary measures, enforcement lies with the BzKJ. If a prior 'dialogue procedure' fails, the BzKJ may impose binding measures and, as a last resort, fines of up **to 5 million EUR** pursuant to § 28(5) sent. 1 and 2 JuSchG. These measures can also be directed at providers based abroad. However, in the case of offers from other EU countries, the country of origin principle must be taken into account.[60]

C. Conclusion

53 Youth media protection in Germany has made significant structural progress in recent years. With the 2021 amendment to the JuSchG, the legislature has adopted well-functioning approaches of self-regulatory bodies, such as the legal anchoring of the promotion of orientation through additional information and the possibility of recognising automated rating systems of a self-regulatory body such as the IARC system. At the same time, the DSA and the associated due diligence obligations are creating increasing pressure for harmonisation at European level. National regulations such as the JuSchG and the JMStV are now more than ever caught between the conflicting demands of EU harmonisation and nationally established supervisory structures. It is positive to note that Germany has created structures at an early stage that can actively shape this change. For example, the consideration of usage risks alongside pure content risks in the context of differentiated case-by-case assessments and balanced consideration of rights represents a remarkable paradigm shift in German youth media protection that serves as a role model in an international context. Self-regulatory bodies such as the USK can be classified as reliable national partners with a European perspective in this area of tension, also with regard to their role and possibilities within the framework of Art. 28 DSA. However, in many areas, the focus is also on the development of secondary legislation, for example through specific guidelines on the application of Art. 28 DSA. It is also important to further strengthen pragmatic cooperation models between the state and industry. The cooperation in German youth media protection to date shows that such solutions are not only practicable but could also serve as a blueprint for other areas of regulation. Particularly noteworthy in this context is the **'one-stop shop' principle of self-regulatory bodies such as the USK** in the field of youth media protection and games. It is a forward-looking model for coherent, efficient and coordinated youth media protection at both national and European level.

---

[59] Jugendschutz.net is a joint youth protection agency of all federal states established by the highest state youth authorities in accordance with § 18 (1) JMStV and organisationally linked to the KJM.

[60] See also Liesching in MMR Supplement 8/2020, p. 18 seqq.; Liesching MMR Supplement 6/2020, p. 3 seqq.; Hopf/Braml in ZUM 2021, 421, 427 seq., 433.

CHAPTER 5
RETAILING A VIDEO GAME

§ 24
Business Models of the Games Industry

A. Introduction ... 1
B. Evolution of business models ... 3
C. Current business models and legal implications ... 13
I. Premium/buy-to-play ... 14
II. Free-to-play (F2P) and freemium ... 16
III. Subscription and cloud gaming ... 19
IV. Microtransactions and in-app purchases ... 22
V. Games as a Service (GaaS) ... 28
VI. Blockchain gaming and NFTs ... 31
D. Cross-cutting regulatory challenges ... 36
I. Consumer protection ... 40
II. Data protection ... 43
III. Protection of minors ... 45
IV. Competition law ... 48
E. Concluding remarks ... 50

A. Introduction

From coin-operated arcade machines to globally connected digital ecosystems, the video game industry has undergone a **profound transformation** over the last few decades. As the ways players engage with games have evolved, so too have the strategies used to sustain development, foster creativity, and community involvement. Each new **monetisation model** brings its own set of legal and ethical challenges – particularly within the EU's robust regulatory framework. 1

Gameplay innovation, shifting player demographics, and evolving monetisation strategies have developed hand-in-hand, reshaping the video game industry and often **democratising** not only how games generate revenue, but also how they are designed, marketed, and experienced. This chapter explores the evolution of business models in the industry, their legal implications, and the regulatory responses emerging within the EU. 2

B. Evolution of business models

Game monetisation[1] **has developed** significantly since the early days of the 'insert-coin-to-play' arcade model. Today, the industry employs a wide range of monetisation strategies, including, premium games,[2] downloadable content (DLC),[3] free-to-play mod- 3

[1] Monetisation refers to the process of generating revenue from a game. This is often achieved through advertising (e.g., banner advertisements, icon drops and incentivised downloads), limitation removal (e.g., removing advertisements for a price or paying for more energy, turns or lives), a virtual economy (e.g., paying for characters, resources, advantage-giving items, upgrades or customisations) and/or merchandising (e.g., branded shirts).

[2] Premium games are games that have a high up-front cost but do not feature in-app purchases.

[3] Downloadable content is additional content that can be downloaded for a game, such as extra maps or levels.

els,[4] subscription model,[5] season passes,[6] rewarded videos,[7] battle passes,[8] games as a service,[9] and in-game advertising.[10] Each model carries distinct public perceptions and raises different regulatory considerations.[11]

4 The earliest form of monetisation emerged with coin-operated arcade machines, where players paid per session and gameplay was limited by both skill and time. This model shaped early game design, encouraging short sessions and increasingly challenging levels. This dynamic shifted with the **arrival of home consoles**. Freed from the limitations of session-based revenue, developers could create story-driven titles based on longer, more immersive gameplay experiences and designed to be enjoyed over multiple sittings. The dominant monetisation model also evolved: Instead of paying per play, consumers purchased game cartridges or CDs at premium prices through physical retail, making the one-time purchase model – granting a license to play – a new industry standard.

5 This mainstream monetisation strategy began to change with the success of 989 Studio's *EverQuest*, followed by Activision Blizzard's *World of Warcraft*, which introduced a **subscription-based model** at the turn of the millennium, requiring monthly payments to access the game. This new approach proved that players were willing to pay continuously for access to a game, marking a fundamental shift from one-time purchases to ongoing revenue streams and opening new possibilities for long-term monetisation.

6 The true revolution, however, came with **digital distribution**. Services like Steam on PC paved the way for an era where developers could bypass traditional publishers and reach players directly. Mobile gaming followed suit, with app stores making games more accessible than ever. Console platforms, such as PlayStation Network and Xbox Live, later integrated digital storefronts, further reducing the reliance on physical media.

7 With so many games entering the digital market, developers have hoped that allowing players to try their game with no upfront costs might attract players who eventually would pay for game-related downloadable content and microtransactions.[12] While the **free-to-play model** has taken on different iterations, it has revolutionised the industry by making most games available to the public at no cost and yet by 2024 accounted for

---

[4] Free-to-play models are games that are free but often make heavy use of in-app purchases.

[5] A subscription model is a model in which players pay at regular intervals, e.g., monthly, to access the game, and there are often continual releases of new content. There is also another type of subscription model that is closer to the Netflix model, in which a payment is made on a monthly basis to access a library of content. Apple Arcade is an example of this type of model.

[6] Season passes are discounted packages for current and future DLC packs for a video game, in addition to its base price.

[7] Rewarded videos are video advertisements placed in games that reward users, for example, with free in-game items, virtual goods or content.

[8] Battle passes are season passes that encourage further gameplay to unlock tiered cosmetic items and/or in-game currency to progress in the game. Most battle passes include a free option to unlock some items. There is also an option to pay a premium to obtain greater rewards from the battle pass. This is the monetisation model used in popular games such as *Fortnite* and *Apex Legends*.

[9] Games as a service is a business model where games are treated as ongoing services, receiving continuous updates, new content, and support over an extended period, often years, rather than being a one-time purchase with limited post-launch support.

[10] In-game advertising corresponds to advertisements within games, including, but not limited to, rewarded video advertisements, playable advertisements, interstitial advertisements and banner advertisements.

[11] Generally see Greenspan/Dimita, Mastering the Game, 2nd edition, WIPO, 2022. Sections 1.7, 1.8, 9.3.2 and Chapter 10. Available online at https://tind.wipo.int/record/45851?ln=en&v=pdf.

[12] Microtransactions typically involve in-game purchases, for a small amount of money, of various virtual items. These may include costumes, weapons, skins, and power-ups, which allow gamers to move through a game more quickly.

117 billion USD in revenue for over 80 % of the total digital games revenue.[13] Games like *League of Legends* and *Fortnite* demonstrated that players were willing to spend money on cosmetic items, battle passes, and other in-game purchases, leading to a dramatic shift in game design. Developers began designing games with monetisation strategies that generated revenue without requiring an upfront purchase.

Subscription-based services, such as Xbox Game Pass and PlayStation Plus, have also introduced a Netflix-style model to gaming. Players now pay a **monthly fee** for access to a rotating library of games, changing how they discover and engage with new titles. Meanwhile, cloud gaming services, like Nvidia GeForce Now and Xbox Cloud Gaming, promise a future where games can be streamed instantly without requiring powerful hardware. **8**

These evolving monetisation strategies have not only influenced how players buy games but also how developers create them. Many modern titles are designed with **live-service elements**, ensuring continuous updates and content releases to maintain engagement. Meanwhile, independent developers have gained more opportunities to self-publish and experiment with niche monetisation methods that would not have been viable in a retail-dominated industry. **9**

This technological transition introduced new legal and regulatory considerations, prompting debates over distribution rights, the applicability of the exhaustion doctrine, and the enforcement of age-rating systems.[14] **10**

As technology continues to advance, new monetisation strategies will likely emerge, whether through **AI-driven game personalisation**, blockchain-based ownership models, or deeper integrations between gaming and social platforms. What remains clear is that the industry will continue evolving, shaped by both technological advancements and changing player expectations. **11**

Gaming is no longer just about selling a product – it is about sustaining a **long-term experience** that keeps players engaged, invested, and willing to support ongoing development. The industry's transformation over the past two decades shows how innovation drives not only profits but also the evolution of gaming itself. **12**

C. Current business models and legal implications

Each video game monetisation model presents distinct legal and regulatory challenges. As developers continue to innovate – often offering games for free while relying on in-game purchases to generate revenue – these models attract increasing legal scrutiny. The **use of in-game currency**, for instance, may trigger obligations under banking, consumer protection, or tax laws. Similarly, certain monetisation features such as **loot boxes** have raised concerns under gambling regulations, with some jurisdictions classifying them as games of chance. In many cases, evolving legal frameworks have directly influenced the development of new business models. This section examines the most prevalent monetisation strategies in the industry today, as shown in the chart below, with premium games, free-to-download titles, and in-game purchases all playing a significant role in shaping the regulatory landscape. **13**

[13] Statista, Gaming Monetisation, 2025. Available at https://www.statista.com/study/41424/gaming-monetisation-statista-dossier/.

[14] As discussed in → Ch. 22 and Ch. 23 of this book.

I. Premium/buy-to-play

14 The premium model – based on a **one-time payment for full access to a game** – emerged as the first transformative business model of the video game industry and remains highly relevant today. A majority of developers report working on premium titles, making it the most widely used business model globally.[15] This model continues to dominate in the console and PC markets, particularly within AAA development, where titles like *Elden Ring* and *Hogwarts Legacy* exemplify full-price releases often followed by downloadable content or expansion packs. It is also favoured for narrative-driven and single-player experiences, which benefit from upfront pricing structures that support self-contained, offline gameplay. Independent developers on platforms such as Steam, GOG, and Nintendo Switch also commonly use this model due to its simplicity and clearer revenue path, without the infrastructure demands of live-service frameworks.

15 Even where the premium model persists, it has evolved: Developers often supplement base game sales with downloadable content (DLC), deluxe editions, and season passes to extend monetisation. Legal and commercial considerations such as digital rights management (DRM), content licensing, and regional pricing also shape how the model functions in today's market.

II. Free-to-play (F2P) and freemium

16 Free-to-play (F2P) models allow players to access **games at no cost**, with optional purchases for cosmetic items, in-game advantages, or faster progression. This model has proven especially **successful in mobile and multiplayer environments**, where large player bases and frequent engagement create opportunities for recurring revenue. Mobile platforms have notably transitioned from premium-priced games to F2P ecosystems dominated by microtransactions, advertisements, and hybrid monetisation approaches that blend ads, in-app purchases, and subscription tiers. Today, a significant portion of app store revenue – up to 95 % – comes from in-app purchases, including loot boxes, experience boosts, and time-saving features.[16]

17 This shift in monetisation was driven in part by the open marketplace models of platforms like Apple's App Store and Google Play, which initially offered little editorial filtering and encouraged mass distribution of free or low-cost apps. In this competitive landscape, developers experimented with various business models, often adapting monetisation strategies from browser and online games. Developers must also remain **responsive to user behaviour and platform constraints**: For example, switching from a free model to a paid one may not be feasible due to consumer expectations or app store policies. Furthermore, successful monetisation can depend heavily on brand strength, user engagement, and technical flexibility, making the selection and execution of a business model a strategic concern.

18 Legal and regulatory issues accompany the rise of these models, particularly around **transparency, consumer protection, and child-directed monetisation**. The EU's Unfair Commercial Practices Directive (UCPD), for example, has been cited in cases involving non-transparent pricing or manipulative game mechanics. Despite concerns,

---

[15] According to recent data, 57 % of game developers report working on premium games, making it the most commonly used business model among developers worldwide. Statista.

[16] A trove of information and data can be found in the court documents of the *Epic v Apple* cases in the US. *Epic Games, Inc. v Apple Inc.*, 20-cv-05640-YGR; *Epic Games, Inc. v Apple Inc.*, No. 21–16506 (9th Cir. 2023).

F2P models have proven financially lucrative – even if only a small percentage of players make purchases, their contributions are significant.

III. Subscription and cloud gaming

Subscription-based models, such as Xbox Game Pass or PlayStation Plus, offer players access to a broad library of games in exchange for a **monthly fee**. Cloud gaming services, like GeForce Now or Xbox Cloud Gaming, further expand accessibility by enabling users to stream games without high-end hardware. While these models can enhance player retention and broaden access, they also raise important legal issues around licensing agreements, access rights, exclusivity clauses, competition law and data protection.[17] **19**

Although not yet the dominant monetisation method, subscription models are growing in popularity. They often include features like **season passes** or **battle passes**, which provide users with access to periodic content or in-game rewards. These mechanisms encourage ongoing engagement but require a compelling value proposition to persuade players to commit financially. Importantly, platform holders who control these services determine not only what content is included, but also how revenue is shared, which may limit how developers monetise their games independently. **This centralisation of control by distribution platforms** represents a notable shift in commercial dynamics. **20**

The **viability of subscription models** depends on various factors, including the volume and quality of available games, pricing, and the economic terms for developers. For smaller studios, subscriptions can offer valuable exposure and financial support, especially if the distributor provides guarantees or marketing backing. Conversely, established developers may be reluctant to cede control over monetisation or distribution. In such cases, subscription services might still be appealing for back-catalogue titles or lower-risk projects. While the model can limit direct monetisation options, it provides access to a curated audience and greater discoverability – advantages that may offset reduced per-game earnings in a saturated digital marketplace. **21**

IV. Microtransactions and in-app purchases

Microtransactions and in-app purchases have become core components of modern video game monetisation, particularly within F2P models. These transactions typically involve the purchase of non-essential items such as cosmetic upgrades, character skins, time-saving features, or additional gameplay advantages. While technically optional, these purchases can significantly alter a player's experience, offering aesthetic customisation or faster progression. As a result, many games are now designed with this form of monetisation in mind, integrating mechanisms that allow spending while playing the game without requiring an upfront payment. This strategy has proven especially lucrative in mobile and online multiplayer games, where player engagement is high and frequent content updates support continuous monetisation. **22**

One specific form of in-app purchase that has generated considerable attention is the **loot box** – a randomised reward mechanism where players pay to receive a mystery item of variable rarity and desirability which has caused growing regulatory scrutiny and consumer frustration.[18] **23**

---

[17] Generally see Mitchell et al., Mich. Tech. L. Rev. 1 2022, 29.

[18] → Ch. 27.

24 The legal implications of microtransactions and loot boxes are increasingly complex and vary significantly across jurisdictions. Key concerns include the **applicability of gambling laws**, the **lack of transparency in pricing and probabilities**, the **potential for psychological manipulation**, and **insufficient safeguards for underage users**. Several countries, including Belgium and the Netherlands, have taken regulatory action, while others continue to evaluate whether such systems should be classified as gambling. In response, some developers have introduced voluntary disclosures of drop rates or removed loot boxes altogether.

25 The scrutiny by various regulatory bodies has shown that the concept of consumer vulnerability needs to be redefined in light of **immersive and psychologically targeted digital environments**, where all users – regardless of age or mental capacity – can be susceptible to manipulation. Traditional legal tools like transparency requirements and narrow definitions of misleading practices are insufficient to address the complex, integrated nature of freemium ecosystems that use data-driven design to maximise engagement and spending. Instead, legal frameworks should focus more on concepts like aggressive commercial practices and undue influence, recognising the structural and behavioural strategies that shape user decisions across an entire digital ecosystem.[19] More detailed discussions of loot box regulation, advertising practices, and marketing can be found in the relevant sections of this book.

26 In more recent regulatory developments, in March 2025, the EU's Consumer Protection Cooperation Network (the 'CPC Network') published a set of principles to promote transparency and fairness in the online gaming industry's use of virtual currencies (the 'Principles').[20] These Principles apply primarily to **'Hard Virtual Currency'** – (Hard VC) currency purchased with real money. Depending on interpretation, under the concept of 'payment with data' within the EU existing consumer protection laws, users providing personal data beyond what is necessary to access a digital service, or if that data is used for other purposes (such as marketing), this may constitute a paid transaction. This means that even items obtained via data exchange or significant gameplay effort ('Soft Virtual Currency' – Soft VC) could trigger consumer protection rights, including conformity standards, withdrawal rights, and remedies – contrary to the assumptions of many publishers who treat such items as non-contractual or exempt from liability.[21]

27 The regulatory implications become even more significant when Hard VC transactions are viewed as separate business-to-consumer (B2C) contracts. This interpretation, supported by the BEUC (European consumer organisation), could require publishers to treat each **in-game purchase as a distinct transaction subject to EU consumer rights**. That would necessitate changes in game store design, such as implementing withdrawal waivers and user consent tick boxes to limit refund obligations. Depending on whether such purchases are classified as digital content or digital services contracts, different refund rules may apply. For digital content, if the withdrawal right is properly waived, no refund is due. For digital services, refunds must be offered on a pro-rata basis if the consumer cancels within the withdrawal period. These developments signal

[19] Honer, IELR 4(2), available at: https://www.elgaronline.com/view/journals/ielr/4/1/article-p63.xml.

[20] Key principles on in-game virtual currencies, 21.3.2025, https://commission.europa.eu/document/8af13e88-6540-436c-b137-9853e7fe866a_en.

[21] Deller, 'European consumer organisation challenges in-game monetisation landscape as unfair' (Bird & Bird, 10.1.2024) available at: https://www.twobirds.com/en/insights/2024/global/european-consumer-organisation-challenges-in-game-monetisation-landscape-as-unfair'; and Deller, 'Regulatory spotlight: virtual currency vs. consumer law (part 2)', (Bird & Bird 2.4.2025) available at: https://www.twobirds.com/en/insights/2025/global/regulatory-spotlight-virtual-currency-vs-consumer-law-part-2.

a growing regulatory focus on in-game monetisation practices, particularly regarding transparent pricing, player rights, and contract enforcement – potentially requiring significant adjustments to how game economies, storefronts, and refund mechanisms are structured across the industry.[22]

V. Games as a Service (GaaS)

Building on the success of the FTP model, many publishers have adopted the **'games-as-a-service' (GaaS)** approach, offering ongoing content and features for a fee.[23] Rather than relying on traditional sequels or one-time purchases, GaaS titles offer players a dynamic, evolving experience in exchange for recurring payments, such as season passes, battle passes, or in-game purchases. This model not only reduces the cost and risk associated with releasing entirely new titles but also allows publishers to maintain long-term engagement with their player base. For example, Electronic Arts reported that live services accounted for 73 % of its net revenue in 2024, rising from 51 % by 2020, illustrating the growing importance of recurring monetisation in the gaming economy.[24] 28

One outcome of the growing popularity of live services is that major publishers might invest less in new AAA properties, especially with the combination of increased development costs and the uncertainty that accompanies the release of a new title. 29

The GaaS model introduces several legal and regulatory challenges. Questions arise around **content ownership** – particularly whether players have any rights to digital items or expansions they have paid for. The classification of virtual goods remains ambiguous under many legal systems, affecting taxation, refunds, and resale rights. Additionally, when live-service games are shut down, players may lose access to content they have purchased or invested time in, raising issues of consumer rights and contractual fairness. These concerns are magnified when games rely on server-side architecture that makes offline play impossible once support is discontinued.[25] 30

VI. Blockchain gaming and NFTs

Blockchain-based games have introduced a new layer of monetisation and digital ownership through non-fungible tokens (NFTs), which are cryptographically unique assets recorded on a blockchain. These NFTs often serve as in-game items – such as characters, skins, or digital real estate – and are marketed as a way for players to truly 'own' their virtual goods. This is achieved through the tokenisation of digital or physical assets into blockchain-based metadata files, which users can buy, sell, or trade using crypto wallets. However, most NFTs are 'off-chain,' meaning the underlying asset is stored elsewhere and accessed via a link – posing durability and value risks if that link becomes broken. While NFTs promise decentralisation, traceable provenance, and 31

[22] Gardner, 'In-game currencies – are they for real?' IELR 8(2), available at: https://www.elgaronline.com/view/journals/ielr/aop/article-10.4337-ielr.2025.0009/article-10.4337-ielr.2025.0009.xml.

[23] This type of monetisation is often referred to as a 'live service' because the game is continually evolving with new updates. The key to a live service is the ability of the developer to retain users.

[24] EA Annual Report 2024.

[25] Geradin/Huijts, 'Dark clouds gather – The development of cloud gaming, and competition agencies' efforts to enable it on mobile app stores', IELR 6(1), available at: https://www.elgaronline.com/view/journals/ielr/6/1/article-p3.xml.

potential revenue for creators, they also raise concerns over environmental sustainability, speculative bubbles, and exposure to fraud.[26]

32 Blockchain gaming and NFTs have seen a mixed reception within the industry and from players. While they offer the potential for true digital asset ownership and new monetisation opportunities, they also face challenges like complex onboarding, scalability issues, and fluctuating **tokenomics**. Ubisoft has experimented with NFTs in games like *Ghost Recon: Breakpoint*, allowing players to acquire limited-edition in-game items (Quartz Digits) through their Tezos partnership and *Off The Grid*, a battle royale game, uses blockchain as an optional feature, allowing players to opt-in to NFT integration for cosmetic items and potential marketplace trading. Both games are rare examples of successes, demonstrating a viable path for integration.

33 To conclude, today's most widely used monetisation models, whether premium, free-to-play, or hybrid, almost universally involve some form of **payment**, either upfront or during gameplay. At the 'Start Game' stage, players may pay to access the game, as in Premium or Paymium models, or begin playing for free under freemium, ad-supported, or demo-based models. As the game progresses, users often have the option to make purchases that enhance or accelerate their experience – such as unlocking new characters, acquiring cosmetic upgrades, or gaining gameplay advantages. While these purchases are technically optional, they can significantly reduce the time or effort needed to complete a game, especially in titles designed around progression gates.

34 It is increasingly common for games – particularly casual and mobile titles – to blend **multiple monetisation strategies**. For instance, a game may offer in-app purchases alongside rewarded advertisements or combine subscription features with cosmetic microtransactions. This convergence of business models allows developers to diversify revenue streams and tailor monetisation to player behaviour, but it also blurs the line between gameplay and commercial transaction, raising new challenges for transparency and fairness.

35 As these models evolve and overlap, so do the legal and ethical questions surrounding them. From consumer protection and data privacy to gambling regulation and competition law, the legal implications of modern game monetisation extend far beyond any single model. The next section explores these cross-cutting regulatory issues, highlighting how the EU and other jurisdictions are responding to the complex legal landscape emerging from today's digital gaming economy.

D. Cross-cutting regulatory challenges

36 As the video game industry continues to expand and innovate, it faces an increasingly complex and evolving **regulatory landscape**. This section offers a high-level overview of the cross-cutting legal and policy challenges that underpin video game business models across jurisdictions. While many of the topics addressed here are explored in greater detail in individual chapters, the aim is to provide context for the broader legal

[26] From a legal standpoint, the introduction of NFTs into gaming triggers complex questions around ownership, intellectual property, and consumer rights. Purchasing an NFT does not usually confer ownership of the underlying asset, nor of any associated IP rights, unless explicitly granted through a licence agreement. Courts in jurisdictions such as the UK, US, and China have begun to define NFTs as a form of property, separate from the asset they represent, but legal consensus is still emerging. See Dimita, et al., 'IP and Metaverse(s) – an externally commissioned research report' (UKIPO February 2023) available at: https://www.gov.uk/government/publications/ip-and-metaverses-an-externally-commissioned-research-report/ip-and-metaverses-an-externally-commissioned-research-report#metaverse-specific-ip-issues.

frameworks shaping the sector, from consumer protection and competition law to child safety, data governance, and platform regulation.

Although traditionally seen as a relatively unregulated space, the game industry is now encountering a range of legal constraints that go well beyond content and IP rights. Physical products, such as boxed games and merchandise, remain subject to product liability and labelling laws. But more pressing today **are digital-age challenges involving antitrust enforcement, monetisation design, data privacy, and child protection**. Prominent cases such as *Epic Games v Apple and Google* have drawn global attention to platform dominance and the fee structures imposed on developers. Even where courts stopped short of calling Apple a monopoly, they acknowledged the anti-competitive nature of certain practices, setting a precedent that continues to evolve through litigation and legislation worldwide.[27] The judicial scrutiny highlighted growing global concern over platform dominance and developer restrictions. It has also intensified discussions around developer monetisation, with courts and commentators questioning the legitimacy of Apple's commission model and considering whether future legal challenges might push for broader changes to platform practices. Developers may benefit from greater freedom in how they monetise their apps, but smaller studios could struggle with the technical and financial barriers of bypassing integrated payment systems.[28] **37**

The regulatory reach is also extending into new domains. The growing overlap between games, esports, social media, and online broadcasting platforms is triggering scrutiny under **sports law, broadcasting regulation, and content moderation standards**. As games move further into cloud-based infrastructure and integrate blockchain, NFTs, and AI, they increasingly intersect with emerging digital economy frameworks. This convergence across creative industries brings with it both regulatory uncertainty and rising political interest, particularly within the EU. **38**

At the heart of this shift are several EU legislative initiatives poised to reshape how games are monetised, distributed, and experienced. The Digital Services Act (DSA)[29] imposes new obligations on games with social features, including impact assessments on minors and stronger marketing safeguards. The UK has also introduced a comprehensive regulation designed to **protect users from illegal and harmful content online** – Online Safety Act (OSA).[30] Both legal frameworks focus on high-risk digital services, imposing stricter obligations on platforms in these categories. The OSA primarily targets providers of user-generated content (UGC), mandating actions against criminal and harmful material, while the DSA applies more broadly to all intermediaries and addresses a wider array of illegal content and systemic risks. The Digital Markets Act (DMA)[31] seeks to break the grip of dominant app store platforms by regulating in-app payment structures and subscription restrictions. Meanwhile, the anticipated Digital **39**

27 → Ch. 33.

28 Ward/Farsimadan, 'The impact of the Epic Games v. Apple case on developer monetization and payment systems', IELR 5(2), available at: https://www.elgaronline.com/view/journals/ielr/5/2/article-p101.xml.

29 Regulation (EU) 2022/2065 on a single market for digital services and amending Directive 2000/31/EC (Digital Services Act), available at: https://eur-lex.europa.eu/legal-content/EN/TXT/?uri=legissum:4625430.

30 Online Safety Act 2023.

31 Regulation (EU) 2022/1925 of the European Parliament and of the Council of 14.9.2022 on contestable and fair markets in the digital sector and amending Directives (EU) 2019/1937 and (EU) 2020/1828 (Digital Markets Act), available at: https://eur-lex.europa.eu/eli/reg/2022/1925/oj/eng.

Fairness Act,[32] expected in late 2026, targets manipulative design practices – such as dark patterns, loot boxes, and addictive mechanics – especially those affecting children.

I. Consumer protection

40 EU consumer protection law plays a critical role in regulating the video game industry, ensuring players – particularly minors – are safeguarded as consumers of digital content and services. Key legal instruments such as the Unfair Commercial Practices Directive (UCPD) and the Digital Content Directive[33] establish rights around refund eligibility, product quality, and protection from misleading or aggressive commercial tactics. These laws apply to a wide range of gaming practices, from deceptive advertising and in-game promotions to problematic monetisation schemes like loot boxes. As video games often involve digital service or content contracts, developers and platforms must ensure their commercial practices meet **EU standards for transparency, fairness, and informed consent**.[34]

41 The rise of aggressive monetisation practices and premature game shutdowns has led to increased scrutiny from regulators and growing consumer backlash. In response, platforms such as Steam have implemented **user-friendly refund policies to help address dissatisfaction with defective or misleading releases**. Additionally, EU product safety legislation extends to both the software and hardware aspects of gaming, with recent updates introducing cybersecurity requirements to ensure the safe functioning of connected devices.[35] Taken together, these frameworks provide a robust legal foundation aimed at holding game developers and distributors accountable while empowering consumers to push back when their rights are not respected.

42 Game developers must strike a careful balance between effective monetisation and delivering a fair, enjoyable player experience. While aggressive strategies can boost short-term revenue, they often come at the cost of player trust and long-term engagement. By prioritising **ethical design** – such as transparent pricing, optional purchases, and avoiding manipulative mechanics – developers can protect consumers from exploitation while still achieving sustainable profitability and fostering loyal communities.

II. Data protection

43 As online gaming continues to dominate the entertainment industry, data privacy has become a central concern. Game developers must comply with strict regulations such as the EU's General Data Protection Regulation (GDPR) and the U.S. Children's Online Privacy Protection Act (COPPA), which set clear rules around the collection, storage, and use of personal data – particularly for minors. These laws require companies to implement **robust age verification systems**, obtain valid consent before collecting data,

---

[32] Digital Fairness Act and Digital Fairness Fitness Check, available at: https://www.digital-fairness-act.com/#:~:text=The%20Digital%20Fairness%20Act%20deals,and%20other%20challenges%20for%20consumers.

[33] Directive 2011/83/EU of the European Parliament and of the Council of 25.10.2011 on consumer rights; Directive 2005/29/EC of the European Parliament and of the Council of 11.5.2005 concerning unfair business-to-consumer commercial practices in the internal market.

[34] → Ch. 25.

[35] Directive 2001/95/EC of the European Parliament and of the Council of 3.12.2001 on general product safety (General Product Safety Directive), updated with Regulation 2023/988 of the European Parliament and of the Council on General Product Safety (Regulation on General Product Safety).

and maintain transparency about how user data is processed. Failing to meet these obligations can result in severe financial penalties and damage to a company's reputation.

Modern video games often rely on data-driven models that collect user behaviour and gameplay metrics to personalise experiences, refine game design, and improve accessibility. While these practices can enhance the user experience, they also raise significant **privacy concerns**. Under EU data protection and e-privacy laws,[36] developers must clearly inform players about what data is being collected, why it is needed, and how it will be used. This includes providing a comprehensive privacy notice and ensuring appropriate data security measures are in place. According to the video game industry, the majority of data collected by publishers relates to gameplay patterns and is considered non-personal information. **44**

III. Protection of minors

Given that players under 18 make up a significant demographic within the video game community, **regulating minors' access** to and engagement with video games has been a long-standing priority for policymakers. In Europe, this has involved a combination of industry-led initiatives, most notably the Pan-European Game Information (PEGI) system, and technical tools provided by game companies. In addition to PEGI and strict privacy tools, parental controls for blocking by age-rating, limiting time spent, controlling purchases and restricting communication are made available by video game companies on all major video games platforms. **45**

Several online risks are particularly relevant to the protection of minors, many of which extend beyond video games to digital environments more broadly, such as social media and messaging platforms. These include concerns about **gaming addiction**, especially among children still developing self-regulation skills, as well as exposure to toxic behaviours like harassment and offensive content in online multiplayer games. Commercial influences also raise concerns, as minors are more vulnerable to manipulative marketing tactics, particularly in freemium games where the distinction between paid and free content can be unclear. Additionally, there is growing awareness around the misuse of gaming platforms for **grooming, exploitation, or radicalisation**, prompting policymakers and the video game industry to take a more proactive role in safeguarding young users.[37] **46**

Across the board, calls for **stricter child protection** are intensifying, with proposals ranging from robust age verification tools (like the EU's Digital Identity Wallet) to harmonised standards for digital consent and spending limits. As these reforms take shape, developers and publishers will need to reassess design choices, monetisation strategies, and compliance frameworks to meet new regulatory expectations. **47**

IV. Competition law

Competition law has become a central regulatory concern in the video game industry, particularly in the areas of antitrust enforcement and merger control. While the industry was once dominated by a few major players like Nintendo and Sony, the rise of new distribution platforms such as Google Play, Apple's App Store, and Steam, along with innovations like cloud gaming, has reshaped the **competitive landscape**. As a **48**

[36] → Ch. 29.

[37] → Ch. 22 et seq.

result, practices related to licensing fees, market access, data use, and platform control are facing growing scrutiny from competition authorities and within the video game the industry (as evidenced by the *Epic v Apple & Google* cases). In January 2021, for instance, the European Commission fined Valve and five game publishers 7.8 million EUR for geo-blocking, a practice that restricted cross-border game purchases within the EU and violated the principles of the Digital Single Market.[38]

49 In recent years, the industry's rapid consolidation through high-profile acquisitions has further intensified regulatory attention. In 2022 alone, major deals included Sony acquiring Bungie, Take-Two buying Zynga, and Embracer Group expanding its portfolio, while Saudi Arabia's Savvy Games Group made significant investments. However, the most prominent transaction was Microsoft's acquisition of Activision Blizzard, a move that drew antitrust investigations from regulators in the EU, UK, and US. Authorities focused on whether the deal could harm competition in game development, publishing, and digital distribution – particularly given Microsoft's increasing presence across gaming platforms and services. These developments underscore the growing importance of competition law in shaping the future of the global gaming industry.[39] In response to such concerns, the DMA aims to **prevent anti-competitive practices** by imposing stricter rules on dominant digital platforms, including app stores and cloud gaming services, to ensure fairer access and market conditions for developers and consumers alike.

E. Concluding remarks

50 The future of video game monetisation will be shaped by **ongoing technological innovation and evolving regulatory priorities**. Advancements such as AI-driven content personalisation and dynamic pricing offer new ways to enhance player experiences and optimise revenue. However, they also raise complex questions around fairness, transparency, and algorithmic accountability, challenging existing legal frameworks and requiring careful oversight to ensure that player trust is not compromised by manipulative or opaque systems.

51 At the same time, regulators around the world are moving toward greater alignment on issues such as in-game monetisation, gambling mechanics, and digital market fairness. Growing consolidation among major distribution platforms has drawn increased scrutiny, as these gatekeepers wield significant influence over how games are monetised and accessed. Initiatives like the EU's Digital Markets Act reflect a broader push to curb anti-competitive practices and ensure a more level playing field for developers, while safeguarding consumer interests.

---

[38] 'Antitrust: Commission fines Valve and five publishers of PC video games 7.8 million EUR for 'geo-blocking' Practices', 20.1.2021. Commission Decision of 20.1.2021 in cases AT.40413; 40414; 40420; 40422; 40424.

[39] MacDonald, 'Definitions: what constitutes a video game?', Legal challenges and market dynamics in the video games sector, European Audiovisual Observatory, Strasbourg, 2024.

§ 25
Consumer Contracts*

Bibliography: Anderie, Games Industry Management: Gründung, Strategie und Leadership – Theoretische Grundlagen, Berlin/Heidelberg 2016; Billing/Vetter, 'Der Widerrufsbutton – offene Umsetzungsfragen und praktische Probleme', K&R 2024, 387; Boyd/Pyne/Kane, Video Game Law – Everything You Need to know About Legal and Business Issues in the Game Industry, Boca Raton 2019; Busch, 'Implementation of the Consumer Rights Directive – Germany', euvr 2014, 119; Damjan/Lutman, 'Administrative Enforcement of EU Consumer Law: A Disoriented Tiger in the Regulatory Jungle of E-Commerce', EuCML 2022, 130; Dannenberg, Legal Guide to Video Game Development, 2nd edn, Chicago 2016; DiMatteo et al. (eds), International Sales Law – A Handbook, 2nd edn, Munich/Baden-Baden 2021; Föhlisch/Stariradeff, 'Zahlungsmittel und Vertragsschluss im Internet', NJW 2016, 353; Gsell, 'Informationspflichten im europäischen Verbraucherrecht', ZfPW 2022, 130; Hau/Poseck (eds), Beck'scher Online-Kommentar zum BGB, 73rd edn, Munich 2025; Hentsch/Falk (eds), Games und Recht – Games Entwicklung, Publishing Vertrieb, Plattformen, Marketing, Praxishandbuch, Baden-Baden 2023; Hunzinger, 'Änderungsbefugnisse des Unternehmers nach § 327r BGB Auslegung und Vertragsgestaltung im Lichte der AGB-Rechtsprechung (§ 327r BGB)', CR 2022, 349; Legner, 'Informationspflichten des europäischen Verbrauchervertragsrechts im digitalen Zeitalter – Quo Vadis?', ZEuP 2024, 649; Lang/Rösch, 'Besonderheiten des Widerrufs von Verbraucherverträgen über digitale Produkte', NJW 2024, 118; Liesching, 'National games regulation for the EU area – Observance of the country-of-origin principle of the E-Commerce Directive within the framework of German regulation of online games', MMR Suppl.. 2020, 48; Limpach, The Publishing Challenge for Independent Video Game Developers – A Practical Guide, Boca Raton 2020; Loos, 'Standard terms for the use of the Apple App Store and the Google Play Store', EuCML 2016, 10; Mankowski (eds), Commercial Law – Article-by-Article Commentary, Munich/Baden-Baden 2019; Mann, 'Commercial Contracts in Germany', 2nd edn, Munich 2024; Maume, 'Bestehen und Grenzen des virtuellen Hausrechts', MMR 2007, 620; Möllnitz, 'Änderungsbefugnis des Unternehmers bei digitalen Produkten – Auslegung und Folgen des § 327r BGB-RefE', MMR 2021, 116; Narciso, 'The Unfair Commercial Practices Directive – Fit for Digital Challenges?, An Analysis of the European Commission's Guidance (C/2021/9320)', EuCML 2022, 147; Op Heij, 'The Digital Content Contract in a B2C Legal Relationship from a European Consumer Protection Perspective – Recommendations for the Pre-Contractual and (Post-)Contractual Phase', EuCML 2022, 53; Rauda, 'Verbraucherrechtliche Dauerbrenner in der Games Branche – Informationspflichten, Widerrufsrecht, Auto-Renewals und AGB-Kontrolle bei den Pionieren des Digitalvertriebs, MMR 2022, 705; Rauda, Recht der Computerspiele, München 2013; Säcker et al. (eds), Münchener Kommentar zum Bürgerlichen Gesetzbuch, Vol. 3, §§ 311–432 BGB, 9th edn, München 2022; Schmidt, 'Einbeziehung von AGB im Verbraucherverkehr', NJW 2011, 1633; Schulze/Staudenmayer (eds), EU Digital Law – Article-by-Article Commentary, Munich/Baden-Baden 2020; Spindler, 'Ausgewählte Rechtsfragen der Umsetzung der digitalen Inhalte-Richtlinie in das BGB – Schwerpunkt 2: Rechtsbehelfe, Beweislastregelungen und Regress zwischen Unternehmern', MMR 2021, 528; Stiegler, 'Der Kündigungsbutton', VuR 2021, 443; von Walter, 'Leitlinien der EU-Kommission zur UGP-Richtlinie und das UWG – Digitale Geschäftspraktiken im Fokus des EU-Verbraucherschutzes', MMR 2022, 719; Wiebe/Sengül, 'Der Widerrufsbutton: Gesetzliche Vorgaben und offene Fragen', WRP 2025, 574.

A. Introduction 1
B. Effective conclusion of the contract 14
I. Offer and acceptance 15
II. Inclusion of terms and conditions 18
III. Written form 19
IV. Information requirements 20
C. The right of withdrawal 27
I. The right of withdrawal – background 28
II. Exclusion of the right of withdrawal for digital content 31
III. Exclusion of the right of withdrawal for digital services 32
IV. Withdrawal button 34
D. Modifications of the contract 35
I. Modification of the digital content or digital service 36
II. Price adjustment (clause) 40

* The authors thank Sophie Kraus, Trainee at Osborne Clarke, for her valuable support in the preparation of this contribution.

III. T&Cs adjustment clause ... 43
E. Term and termination rules ... 46
I. Term and automatic renewal ... 47
II. Termination ... 49
III. Termination button ... 51
F. Sanctioning of players ... 52

A. Introduction

1 Under EU law there is no express definition of a '**consumer contract**'. The Consumer Rights Directive (EU) 2011/83 (**Consumer Rights Directive**) only defines the terms 'consumer' and 'trader' which suggests that a consumer contract is a contract concluded between a consumer and a trader.[1] According to Art. 2(1) Consumer Rights Directive, a consumer is 'any natural person who, in contracts covered by this Directive, is acting for purposes which are outside his trade, business, craft or profession.' Art. 2(2) Consumer Rights Directive states that a trader is 'any natural person or any legal person, irrespective of whether privately or publicly owned, who is acting, including through any other person acting in his name or on his behalf, for purposes relating to his trade, business, craft or profession in relation to contracts covered by this Directive.' Consumers are therefore those who do not act for commercial purposes, i.e., primarily for private purposes. Traders, on the other hand, conclude transactions for commercial or professional purposes, and game providers will regularly fulfil this characteristic. It should be noted that the consumer may be defined differently in each EU legal act, depending on its purpose and content, and each act may therefore provide for its own definition. In addition, EU Member States may also have their own definition of a consumer as a result of the implementation of the Consumer Rights Directive.[2] However, **consistency** in EU law must be taken into account in the interpretation of the concept of consumer,[3] so the definition of consumer in the Consumer Rights Directive can generally be used as a basis. This means that contracts concluded between a consumer and another consumer are not covered, so the following rules do not apply to these contracts. The consumer contracts are regularly designed as **terms and conditions (T&Cs)** that the trader, i.e., game provider, unilaterally submits to the consumer. Consumer contracts and T&Cs are regulated by specific legal norms.

2 On the one hand, **EU legislation** must be considered when concluding contracts with consumers in the EU. EU legal acts refer to both directives (i.e., those that the national legislator in the EU Member States must first transpose into national law and which also may have a certain degree of implementation flexibility) and regulations (which apply directly in the EU Member States).

3 In particular, the following **EU legal acts** must be considered:

4 The **Unfair Contract Terms Directive (EC) 93/13** protects consumers from unfair standard contract terms in contracts they conclude with traders. Contract terms are unfair and therefore not binding on consumers if, contrary to the requirements of good faith, they cause a significant imbalance in the parties' rights and obligations to the detriment of the consumer (Art. 3 no. 1 Unfair Contract Terms Directive (EC) 93/13). A list of examples of terms which may be regarded as unfair is given in the Annex of this Directive. EU Member States must ensure that national law enforces these rights and

[1] For the individual types of contracts, see Sester/Kastner in Games und Recht § 18 para. 1 et seqq.
[2] Busch euvr 2014, 119 (122) on the broader definition of the consumer in Germany.
[3] ECJ 8.6.2023 – case C-570/21, ECLI:EU:C:2023:456 para. 40 – I.S., K.S v YYY.S.A.

prevents the continued use of unfair contract terms. The aim is to ensure fairness and transparency in consumer contracts.

The **e-Commerce Directive (EC) (2001/31) (EC Directive)** ensures the free movement of information society services between the EU Member States by establishing a legal framework for online services in the EU and removing obstacles to cross-border online services. It sets out rules on transparency and information requirements, commercial communications, electronic contracts, and limitations of liability of intermediary service providers. The Directive aims to increase consumer confidence and legal certainty in the digital single market. 5

The **Unfair Commercial Practice Directive (EC) 2005/29 (UCPD)** is intended to protect consumers from unfair business-to-consumer commercial practices. It prohibits misleading and aggressive commercial practices, ensuring that consumers are not misled or coerced in their decisions. Recently, the EU and consumer organisations have increasingly focussed on online games with regard to potentially unfair business practices.[4] The Directive promotes overall fair competition and consumer confidence in the internal market. 6

The **Consumer Rights Directive** mentioned above strengthens consumer protection by harmonising regulations on contracts concluded between consumers and traders. It covers areas such as information requirements, the right of withdrawal and delivery conditions. The aim is to achieve a high level of consumer protection across the EU and thus ensure the proper functioning of the internal market. 7

The **Digital Content Directive (EU) 2019/770 (DCD)** covers contracts between traders and consumers for the supply of digital content and digital services. It sets out rules on warranty rights, liability and the modification of contracts for digital content or services.[5] An important new aspect is that traders must provide updates such as functional and security updates.[6] The aim is to ensure a high level of consumer protection in the digital environment while contributing to the proper functioning of the internal market. 8

The **Sale of Goods Directive (EU) 2019/771** follows a similar line, introducing specific rules for goods with digital elements that are not digital products. This should not only improve consumer rights but also benefit the digital internal market. 9

The **Omnibus Directive (EU) 2019/2161** strengthens consumer rights by amending several existing EU consumer protection directives (such as the Unfair Commercial Practices Directive, the UCPD and the Consumer Rights Directive). It introduces new harmonised rules on transparency and information requirements (in particular on price indication), sanctions for infringements and effective remedies. The directive aims at better enforcement and modernisation of consumer protection law. 10

By regulating online intermediaries and platforms, the **Digital Services Act (DSA)** ensures user safety, fundamental rights and a fair and open online platform environment. It introduces a graduated catalogue of obligations for digital service providers, depending on the type of intermediary service in question. One of the main obligations is for providers to remove illegal content. In addition, there are instructive **delegated** 11

[4] Narciso EuCML 2022, 147 (152); BEUC Report, 'Game over: Consumers fight for fairer in-game purchases' (12.09.2024), https://www.beuc.eu/reports/game-over-consumers-fight-fairer-game-purchases, p. 29; CPC-Network, 'The Consumer Protection Cooperation Network's Key Principles on In-game Virtual Currencies' (March 2025), https://ec.europa.eu/commission/presscorner/detail/en/ip_25_831, p. 7; also mentioned by Narciso EuCML 2022, 147 (153).

[5] Op Heij EuCML 2022, 53 (59) on the criticism of the Directive's inadequate provisions in the pre-contractual phase.

[6] Op Heij EuCML 2022, 53 (60).

acts on the DSA,[7] and the Commission publishes so-called **Guidance Notes** for many directives which can be helpful in understanding and complying with the requirements (for example, in the case of the withdrawal → mn. 31, 33).[8]

12 On the other hand, there are **national regulations**, some of which have implemented directives that go beyond what is necessary and whose special features must be taken into account by the game provider. In addition, there is an **extensive body of European and national case law** that must be followed. The European regulations and case law have a common purpose: they serve a **harmonised consumer protection law**. To create the highest possible level of consumer protection, the fragmented regulations in the EU Member States must be standardised. This should also benefit the European internal market. Otherwise, strictly speaking, game providers would have to offer a contract in every country in every language with different content. The goal of harmonisation has not yet been achieved, in particular because of many divergent or excessive national rules.[9] Therefore, it is a challenge for game providers to draw up largely compliant contracts in view of this density of regulation. Game providers must adapt their T&Cs to the laws of the country of residence of the consumers targeted by the games. The rules of the country in which consumers are to be addressed with the games apply. If game providers do not adapt their T&Cs, they run the risk of non-compliance with applicable consumer laws leading to possible legal consequences. Admittedly, game providers could incorporate a choice of law clause in their contracts, thereby choosing the law of a country that does not have such stringent consumer protection rules. Nevertheless, consumer law always prevails in international private law, as consumers must not be deprived of their protection (see Art. 6(2) sent. 2 Rome I Regulation (EC) 593/2008). The *ECJ* has ruled against a corresponding choice of law clause, as it would be unfair not to inform the consumer that the consumer protection provisions under Art. 6(2) Rome I Regulation are mandatory.[10]

13 In view of this complex legal framework, this chapter focuses on a **few typical and current problems**.

B. Effective conclusion of the contract

14 Consumer contracts in the context of video games are usually concluded **online**. Certain aspects must be taken into consideration when offering an online contract, not only at the time of contract conclusion, but also pre- and post-conclusion.

---

[7] The delegated acts on the DSA: Commission, 'Delegated Regulation (EU) 2024/436 supplementing Regulation (EU) 2022/2065 of the European Parliament and of the Council, by laying down rules on the performance of audits for very large online platforms and very large online search engines' (2.2.2024), L 436; Commission, 'Delegated Regulation (EU) 2023/1127 supplementing Regulation (EU) 2022/2065 of the European Parliament and of the Council with the detailed methodologies and procedures regarding the supervisory fees charged by the Commission on providers of very large online platforms and very large online search engines' (9.6.2023), L 149/16.

[8] A list of the most important Guidance Notes: Commission, 'Guidance on the interpretation and application of Directive 2005/29/EC of the European Parliament and of the Council concerning unfair business-to-consumer commercial practices in the internal market' (29.12.2021), 2021/C 526/01; Commission, 'Guidance on the interpretation and application of Directive 2011/83/EU of the European Parliament and of the Council on consumer rights' (29.12.2021), 2021/C 525/01; Commission, 'Guidance on the interpretation and application of Council Directive 93/13/EEC on unfair terms in consumer contracts' (27.9.2019), 2019/C 323/04; For an overview of the Guidance Notes on the UCPD see von Walter, MMR 2022, 719.

[9] Therefore, the use of 'paste & copy' contracts is risky for game providers, similar to Anderie, p. 50.

[10] ECJ 28.7.2016 – case C-191/15, ECLI:EU:C:2016:612 para. 71 – *Verein für Konsumenteninformation v Amazon EU Sàrl.*

I. Offer and acceptance

15 As a general rule, in order to conclude a contract, there must be an **offer** and an **acceptance.**[11] It is up to the trader to decide whether he wishes to enter into a contract and how this process is to be structured.[12] By presenting its games online, the game provider generally does not want to legally bind itself, but only to present its games to the consumer. So, the presentation of the games online is only an invitation to make an offer. It is a so-called invitatio ad offerendum (invitation to treat) which is not a legally binding offer.[13] Usually the contract conclusion process is designed in a way that the consumer makes an offer that the trader accepts. In the event of the provision of an order button by the game provider, the submission of an offer by the consumer is constituted by clicking on such button, which the game provider must accept. The fact that the order button with the words 'order with obligation to pay' or a corresponding unambiguous formulation constitutes a legally binding offer is established by Art. 8(2) and (3) Consumer Rights Directive, which indicates that the placing of the order entails an obligation to pay the trader. Acceptance may be expressed or implied and only occurs when one party to the contract expresses an intention to be bound by the offer. The pure confirmation of receipt of the order, which is a requirement under Art. 11 EC Directive, is not deemed an acceptance. This is usually (implicitly) the case when game providers grant the user access to the online game or when they send the consumer the game in physical form or a hyperlink to download the file or software or when the game provider allows the user to play online in the browser. Because the use of the order button is a **mandatory obligation** of the trader, it is not possible to conclude implied contracts online.[14]

16 Conversely, game providers could make a binding offer which the consumer then accepts by clicking on the order button which then leads to the conclusion of the contract.

17 When concluding the contract, game providers must in any case observe the following: The contract conclusion process should be described in detail in the T&Cs. This description, together with the specific design and organisation of the order process, is also decisive for the question which declaration constitutes the offer, and which declaration constitutes the acceptance of the offer in legal terms. Moreover, information on the use of an order button must also be provided (for information requirements → mn. 20 et seqq.). In addition, when designing the order button, the **correct labelling** should be 'order with obligation to pay' (Art. 8(2) Consumer Rights Directive) and any different labelling bears the risk that the consumer is not bound by the contract. As a consequence, the consumer could later ask for a refund of the money paid until the statute of limitations expires.[15] Although Art. 8(2) Consumer Rights Directive states that a corresponding unambiguous formulation is also permitted, it must be very close to the wording of the law so that the consumer's obligation to pay is clear.[16] *German courts* have already decided cases in which providers have tried to deviate from this formulation in creative ways: 'register' ("Anmelden"), 'order' ("Bestellen"), 'send order' ("Bestellung abschicken"), 'continue' ("Weiter") are misleading as they do not clearly indicate the

[11] Dannenberg, p. 49; Eckert in BeckOK BGB § 145 para. 2; Schulze in DiMatteo/et al. International Sales Law Chapter 8 para. 26.

[12] There is no obligation to contract according to Sester/Kastner in Games und Recht § 18 para. 21.

[13] Schulze in DiMatteo/et al. International Sales Law Chapter 8 para. 46.

[14] Maume in BeckOK BGB § 312j para. 20.

[15] An incorrectly labelled order button can be life-threatening therefore says Sester/Kastner in Games und Recht § 18 para. 20.

[16] Maume in BeckOK BGB § 312j para. 26 et seqq.

obligation to pay.[17] Similarly, 'Subscribe' ("Abonnieren")[18] or 'Try now for free – then pay' ("Jetzt gratis testen – danach kostenpflichtig")[19] are not sufficient. Therefore, game providers must ensure that their order button is correctly labelled so that a contract is concluded.

II. Inclusion of terms and conditions

18 The T&Cs must be effectively incorporated into the contract. The consumer must be informed in advance of the conditions and consequences of the contract conclusion.[20] This means that the consumer must be aware of the provider's T&Cs when the consumer enters into the contract. The *Commission* requires that the consumer must have a real **opportunity of becoming acquainted** with a contract term before the conclusion of the contract.[21] Similarly, German Law (§ 305(2) BGB) states that the trader must refer to T&Cs expressly and the consumer must be given a reasonable opportunity to take note of the content. If the contract is concluded online, the trader should explicitly refer to the T&Cs at the time the contract is concluded. The customer's acknowledgement can also be confirmed by activating a checkbox.[22] However, this is not legally required, as it is sufficient if the T&Cs can be accessed and printed out via a clearly visible link on the order page.[23] But a checkbox would be the safer way and serve as evidence.[24] Lastly, it is necessary that the reference to the T&Cs is clearly emphasised for the consumers so that they do not have to spend a lot of time searching for them on the website.[25] If a game is sold physically, a contract is usually concluded between the consumer and the retail store. The consumer is then subject to the T&Cs of the retail store and not those of the game provider. However, it is usually necessary for the consumer to conclude an additional contract between the consumer and the game provider, for example, because an online account has to be set up. In this case, the consumer must have the opportunity to obtain knowledge of the game provider's T&Cs before purchasing the game. This can be achieved by providing clear information on the packaging of the game,[26] and a link or QR code to the T&Cs of the game provider. In the case of digital distribution of games including via third parties such as platforms, a **hyperlink** to the fully accessible T&Cs can be placed before the contract is concluded.[27] Including links in the app stores to allow users to read the T&Cs when signing a contract can be a challenge for game providers, but this is usually solved by including a link to the T&Cs on the product detail pages. Finally, it must be observed that the T&Cs must be drawn up in plain, intelligible

[17] LG Hildesheim 7.3.2023 – 6 O 156/22, MMR 2023, 790 para. 27.

[18] OLG Düsseldorf 8.2.2024 – I-20 UKl 4/23, MMR 2024, 969 para. 22 et seqq.

[19] OLG Köln 3.2.2016 – 6 U 39/15, MMR 2016, 602 (604).

[20] ECJ 30.4.2014 – case C-26/13, ECLI:EU:C:2014:282 para. 70 – Kásler and Káslerné Rábai v OTP Jelzálogbank Zrt.

[21] Commission, 'Guidance on the interpretation and application of Council Directive 93/13/EEC on unfair terms in consumer contracts' (27.9.2019), 2019/C 323/04, point 3.3.1.

[22] Loos EuCML 2016, 10 (11); Mann in Commercial Contracts in Germany Chapter 2 para. 32.

[23] BGH 14.6.2006 – I ZR 75/03, NJW 2006, 2976 para. 16; according to LG Essen 13.2.2003 – 16 O 416/02, NJW-RR 2003, 1207, it is sufficient that the reference to the T&Cs is made on the order form above the order bar and separated from the other data and that the T&Cs can be accessed online.

[24] Also recommended by Schmidt NJW 2011, 1633 (1638).

[25] Loos EuCML 2016, 10 (12).

[26] Rauda, para. 689.

[27] ECJ 24.11.2022 – case C-358/21, ECLI:EU:C:2022:923 para. 59 – *Tilman SA v Unilever Supply Chain Company AG* has ruled on the jurisdiction clause that it is validly concluded if it is contained in T&Cs to which a written contract refers by the inclusion of a hypertext link to a website where these T&Cs can be viewed, downloaded and printed prior to that contract being signed.

language, as required by Art. 5 Unfair Contract Terms Directive (EC) 93/13. This means that the T&Cs must be written in clear, understandable language so that consumers can comprehend them. This is even more important when contracting with minors. Any provisions in the T&Cs that are not transparent therefore do not fulfil this requirement and run the risk of being invalid.

III. Written form

The **written form** is generally not required for contracts between game providers and consumers in the EU. In practice, this means that game providers can present their games and T&Cs electronically and obtain the consumer's consent by clicking an order button (→ mn. 15). This electronic consent or consent through other similar mechanisms is legally binding. 19

IV. Information requirements

As online contracts are so-called distance contracts (see Art. 2(7) Consumer Rights Directive), game providers must comply with several extensive **information requirements** in order to provide consumers with comprehensive information.[28] 20

The consumer must be informed clearly and comprehensibly about the essential terms of the contract before the contract is concluded. This includes information on the main characteristics of the goods or services, the total price and the arrangements for payment, delivery and performance (see Art. 6(1) Consumer Rights Directive). In practice, this means that game providers must ensure that all relevant information is presented in an **easily accessible and comprehensible manner**, which can also be done in their T&Cs. However, the information must then be made available in a clear and comprehensible manner in a prominent position immediately before the consumers place their orders. 21

In addition, consumers must be informed of their **right of withdrawal**, including the conditions, time limit and procedures for exercising this right in accordance with Art. 11(1) Consumer Rights Directive and the model withdrawal form in accordance with Annex I(B) Consumer Rights Directive (Art. 6(1)(h) Consumer Rights Directive). This can be included in the game provider's T&Cs but must be specifically highlighted for the consumers so that they are aware of it. If game providers have properly informed the consumer, the consumer has a withdrawal period of 14 days during which he can withdraw from the contract without giving reasons. If game providers do not comply with this information obligation, the consumer can still withdraw from the contract 12 months after the withdrawal period has expired (Art. 10(1) Consumer Rights Directive). In addition, where a right of withdrawal is not provided for in accordance with Art. 16 Consumer Rights Directive, game providers must inform the consumer that he will not benefit from a right of withdrawal or, where applicable, the circumstances under which the consumer loses his right of withdrawal. If the goods, by their nature, cannot normally be returned by post, the cost of returning the goods must be mentioned by the trader in a case of distance contracts (Art. 6(1)(i) Consumer Rights Directive). 22

Game providers must ensure that they also comply with the information obligations under Art. 6 and Art. 7 UCPD, which partly overlap with those under Art. 6 Consumer 23

---

[28] Op Heij EuCML 2022, 53 (54); For the weaknesses of the 'information model', see: Legner ZEuP 2024, 649 (670 et seqq.); Gsell ZfPW 2022, 130 (137 et seqq.).

Rights Directive; in particular, **price information** must be transparent:[29] According to Art. 6(1)(d) UCPD, no misleading or false information may be given about the price, the manner in which the price is calculated, or the existence of a specific price advantage. At the same time, traders must not omit material information before the conclusion of the distance or off-premises contract, including the total price of the goods or services inclusive of taxes or, where the nature of the goods or services is such that the price cannot reasonably be calculated in advance, the manner in which the price is to be calculated, as well as, where applicable, all additional freight, delivery or postal charges any other costs or, where those charges cannot reasonably be calculated in advance, the fact that such additional charges may be payable (Art. 6(1)(e) Consumer Rights Directive, Art. 7(4)(c) UCPD).

24 According to Art. 8(1) Consumer Rights Directive, the trader shall give the required information of Art. 6(1) Consumer Rights Directive to the consumer in a way appropriate to the means of distance communication used in plain and intelligible language. Therefore, the trader must provide the consumer with the **following information**: the main characteristics of the goods or services, to the extent appropriate to the medium and to the goods or services (a), the identity of the trader, such as his trading name (b), the geographical address at which the trader is established as well as the trader's telephone number and email address; in addition, where the trader provides other means of online communication which guarantee that the consumer can keep any written correspondence, including the date and time of such correspondence, with the trader on a durable medium, the information shall also include details of those other means (c), if different from the address provided, the geographical address of the place of business of the trader, and, where applicable, that of the trader on whose behalf he is acting, where the consumer can address any complaints (d), the price information ((e) → mn. 23), the cost of using the means of distance communication for the conclusion of the contract where that cost is calculated other than at the basic rate (f), the arrangements for payment, delivery, performance, the time by which the trader undertakes to deliver the goods or to perform the services and, where applicable, the trader's complaint handling policy (g), where a right of withdrawal exists, everything relating to the right of withdrawal, in particular the model withdrawal form set out in Annex I(B) ((h)-(k) → mn. 22), a reminder of the existence of a legal guarantee of conformity for goods, digital content and digital services (l), the duration of the contract, where applicable, or, if the contract is of indeterminate duration or is to be extended automatically, the conditions for terminating the contract (o), and where applicable, the minimum duration of the consumer's obligations under the contract (p).

25 The trader must provide this information on a **durable medium** according to Art. 8(1) Consumer Rights Directive. Durable medium is defined in Art. 2 no. 10 Consumer Rights Directive as 'any instrument which enables the consumer or the trader to store information addressed personally to him in a way accessible for future reference for a period of time adequate for the purposes of the information and which allows the unchanged reproduction of the information stored'. According to the *Commission*, this means that the trader must send the consumer a confirmation of the contract with all the necessary information, for example in a text message or email, before the conclusion

[29] For these requirements and the problem with advertising, see Commission, 'Guidance the interpretation and application of Directive 2005/29/EC of the European Parliament and of the Council concerning unfair business-to-consumer commercial practices in the internal market' (29.12.2021), 2021/C 526/01, point 4.2.9.

of the contract.[30] A website only fulfils these requirements for a durable medium under very specific conditions.[31] Providing information on a normal website is usually not sufficient to fulfil the obligation to provide the necessary information on a durable medium. Therefore, game providers generally send an e-mail with the relevant information to the consumer to fulfil such requirement. In addition, the trader must provide the consumer with a confirmation of the concluded contract after the conclusion of the distance contract on a durable medium in accordance with Art. 8(7) Consumer Rights Directive. The trader must also communicate the acknowledgement of receipt of the withdrawal on a durable medium in the event of withdrawal if consumers can electronically fill in and submit either the model withdrawal form set out in Annex I(B) or any other unequivocal statement on the trader's website.

In addition, Art. 5(1) EC Directive requires game providers to provide the company name, the geographical address and contact details; if the game provider is registered in a trade or similar public register, the trade register and registration number or equivalent means of identification in that register; and, if the activity is subject to an authorisation scheme, the relevant supervisory authority. National peculiarities apply here, as the EU Member States have implemented this rule differently: In Germany and France, stricter regulations apply regarding this so-called **imprint obligation**, according to which more detailed information must be provided in the imprint of a website: In Germany, this is regulated in § 5 DDG and in § 18 MStV, according to which the service provider is obliged to designate a person responsible for journalistic-editorial content, stating their name and address. In France, the Loi n° 2004-575 requires the name of the person responsible for the content of the website ('Directeur de la publication') in addition to the mandatory provision of a telephone number for communication. As the **country-of-origin principle** applies (see Art. 3(1) and (2) EC Directive), the provider should observe the law of the country in which it has its registered office.[32] According to the *ECJ*, this is not a specific conflict-of-laws rule but merely requires that the provider of an e-commerce service in the host Member State is not subject to stricter requirements than those laid down by the substantive law of the Member State in which the service provider is established.[33] Therefore, the individual EU Member States may also apply their own substantive law to foreign providers of e-commerce services as long as these regulations are not stricter than in the country of origin.[34] The determination is left to the Member States themselves. In Germany, for example, the law (§ 3 DDG) stipulates that digital service providers are subject to German regulations if they explicitly target their digital services at consumers in Germany or (also) address consumers in Germany. The *ECJ* has developed criteria for assessing when there is such targeting:[35] An overall assessment must be made on the basis of various criteria, which are not considered to be exhaustive, and in particular the international nature of the activity or the use of a language or currency other than the language or currency normally used in the EU Member State in 26

[30] Commission, 'Guidance on the interpretation and application of Directive 2011/83/EU of the European Parliament and of the Council on consumer rights' (29.12.2021), 2021/C 525/01, point 4.4.

[31] For these requirements: Commission, 'Guidance on the interpretation and application of Directive 2011/83/EU of the European Parliament and of the Council on consumer rights' (29.12.2021), 2021/C 525/01, point 4.4.

[32] According to Liesching MMR Suppl. 2020, 48 (51) the country-of-origin principle is applicable in the games sector.

[33] ECJ 25.10.2011 – joined cases C-509/09 and C-161/10, ECLI:EU:C:2011:685 para. 68 – *eDateAdvertisingGmbH v X* and *Martinez v MGN Limited.*

[34] Damjan/Lutman EuCML 2022, 130 (132).

[35] ECJ 7.12.2010 – joined cases C-585/08 and C-144/09, ECLI:EU:C:2010:740 para. 80 et seq. – *Pammer v Karl Schlüter GmbH & Co. KG* and *Hotel Alpenhof GesmbH v Heller.*

which the trader is established, with the possibility of booking and confirming bookings in that other language or currency, should be taken into account. In general, the service providers whose web shop or online presence is also targeted at a country other than their own country of origin should therefore also comply with the information requirements under this legal regime (for the limited possibility of a choice of law clause → mn. 12).

C. The right of withdrawal

27 The **right of withdrawal** allows consumers to withdraw from a contract within a period of 14 days from the day the contract is concluded without giving reasons.

I. The right of withdrawal – background

28 Following the adoption of the Consumer Rights Directive on 25.10.2011, the EU legislator created **uniform rules** for the right of withdrawal. However, this was not a new development as the right of withdrawal had already been regulated at EU law level, in two separate legal acts: Council Directive 85/577/EEC of 20.12.1985 on the protection of consumers in respect of contracts negotiated away from business premises and Directive 97/7/EC of the European Parliament and of the Council of 20.5.1997 on the protection of consumers in respect of distance contracts. This right exists to protect consumers who have no opportunity to see the product or take note of the service's characteristics before concluding a distance or off-premises contract. They should therefore be granted a right of withdrawal retrospectively (see rec. 14 sent. 1 Directive 97/7/EC, rec. 37 Consumer Rights Directive). This would be different in the case of a contract concluded on the business premises, where the consumer can inspect the product or service, assess whether to purchase or utilise it based on its nature, characteristics and functioning. In addition, in the case of off-premises contracts (e.g., doorstep selling) may involve surprise elements or psychological pressure. A corresponding right of withdrawal for the consumers should take this circumstance into account (see rec. 37 sent. 3 Consumer Rights Directive). The EU legislator has combined these two directives with the Consumer Rights Directive, harmonising the regulations on the right of withdrawal in contracts concluded at a distance or away from business premises. This is intended to contribute to a high level of consumer protection and improve the functioning of the business-to-consumer internal market (see rec. 5 sent. 7 Consumer Rights Directive).

29 If the consumer contract is a distance or off-premises contract, the consumer has the right to withdraw in accordance with Art. 9(1) Consumer Rights Directive. Therefore, the consumer may withdraw from the contract without giving any reason and without incurring any costs other than those provided for in Art. 13(2) and Art. 14 Consumer Rights Directive. A **distance contract** is a contract concluded between the trader and the consumer under an organised distance sales or service-provision scheme without the simultaneous physical presence of the trader and the consumer, with the exclusive use of one or more means of distance communication up to and including the time at which the contract is concluded (Art. 2 no. 7 Consumer Rights Directive). Online contracts for games between game providers and consumers constitute a distance contract, so the rules regarding the right of withdrawal apply. However, there are also **exceptions** to the right of withdrawal, which are defined in Art. 16 Consumer Rights Directive. Particularly relevant exceptions for games are those for digital services in Art. 16(1)(a) Consumer Rights Directive and for digital content according to Art. 16(1)(m) Consumer

Rights Directive (→ mn. 31 et seqq.). This is because, in certain cases, a right of withdrawal would be inappropriate given the nature of particular goods or services (see rec. 49 sent. 2 Consumer Rights Directive). If no exception applies, consumers can withdraw within a 14-day withdrawal period. If the trader does not provide the consumer with adequate information, the withdrawal period is extended to 12 months (see rec. 43 Consumer Rights Directive).

According to Art. 12 Consumer Rights Directive, the obligations of the contracting parties are terminated if the consumer withdraws from the contract. In the event of withdrawal, the trader and the consumer then have **different obligations**. The trader shall reimburse all payments received from the consumer without delay (Art. 13(1) Consumer Rights Directive). In return, the consumer shall send back or hand over the goods to the trader or an authorised person without delay (Art. 14(1) Consumer Rights Directive). 30

II. Exclusion of the right of withdrawal for digital content

Digital content is data produced and supplied in digital form and not on a tangible medium (Art. 2 no. 2 DCD). In this case, a special rule applies to the exclusion for digital content (Art. (1)(m) Consumer Rights Directive after its amendment by Art. 4 no. 12 Omnibus Directive (EU) 2019/2161). According to this, the trader must have started to perform the contract, in contrast to digital services, where the service must be fully performed. The following conditions must then be met for consumers to waive their right of withdrawal if the contract obliges the consumer to pay (which is usually the case): Firstly, the consumer must have given prior express consent to the beginning of the performance during the withdrawal period. Secondly, consumers must confirm that they are aware that they will lose their right of withdrawal upon performance of the contract. In addition, the trader must have provided the consumer with confirmation of the concluded contract on a durable medium. If these three mentioned conditions are met, the right of withdrawal is **excluded or waived**.[36] The Consumer Rights Directive Guidance[37] provides a model language for such a declaration: 'I hereby consent to immediate performance of the contract and acknowledge that I will lose my right of withdrawal from the contract once the download or streaming of the digital content has begun.' In practice, game providers must ensure that consumers are informed of the legal consequences of the expiry of the right of withdrawal before the download or streaming or the playing of games in a browser begins and that they expressly agree to waive their right of withdrawal beforehand. 31

III. Exclusion of the right of withdrawal for digital services

The right of withdrawal could be excluded if the provision of the game constitutes a **digital service:** Digital services are services that allow the consumer to create, process, store, access and to share such data in digital form, as well as any other interaction with data in digital form (Art. 2 no. 2 DCD). If the performance has begun with the consumer's prior express consent and with acknowledgement that he will lose his right of withdrawal once the contract has been fully performed by the trader, the right of with- 32

---

[36] Terryn/Vandenbulcke in Schulze/Staudenmayer EU Digital Law Art. 14 CRD para. 8.

[37] Commission, 'Guidance on the interpretation and application of Directive 2011/83/EU of the European Parliament and of the Council on consumer rights' (29.12.2021), 2021/C 525/01, point 5.7.

drawal is excluded in accordance with Art. 16(1)(a) Consumer Rights Directive. The difference to digital content is therefore that digital services must be fully performed for the consumer's right of withdrawal to be excluded or waived. The purpose of this regulation is to give consumers the opportunity to test the quality of the service during the withdrawal period, which they would not be able to do if they lost their right of withdrawal at the start of the contract performance.[38]

33 The Consumer Rights Directive Guidance provides the following model declaration for a waiver: 'I hereby request immediate performance of the service contract and acknowledge that I will lose my right of withdrawal from the contract once the service contract is fully performed.'[39] As a result, in the case of a withdrawal, the consumer owes a **pro-rata refund** (as opposed to digital content, Art. 14(3) Consumer Rights Directive). If the consumer waives the right of withdrawal, the payment of the refund will depend on the length of time the service has been provided: If the service is provided for more than 14 days, the digital service is not fully performed within the withdrawal period and the consumer owes a pro-rata refund. If the service has been provided for a shorter period, the withdrawal is not possible as the digital service has been fully performed.

IV. Withdrawal button

34 To make withdrawal easier for consumers, the EU has planned to introduce a **withdrawal button** for all distance contracts from the end of 2025.[40] With the adoption of Directive (EU) 2023/2673, the EU legislator inserted Art. 11a into the Consumer Rights Directive, which regulates the procedure for this withdrawal button or 'withdrawal function':[41] This takes place in two stages. The withdrawal function is labelled with the words 'withdraw from contract here' or an unambiguous corresponding formulation in an easy legible way. As soon as the consumer activates it, he must be able to send his online withdrawal statement informing the game provider of his decision to withdraw from the contract. Once the consumer has completed the online withdrawal statement, the trader shall enable the consumer to submit it to them by means of a confirmation function. Accordingly, the trader must inform the consumer pre-contractually about the existence and placement of the withdrawal function (Art. 6(1)(h) Consumer Rights Directive by Art. 1 no. 2 Directive (EU) 2023/2673). However, the existing mechanisms, such as the exercise of the right of withdrawal by means of an unequivocal statement setting out his decision to withdraw from the contract or the use of the model withdrawal form, will remain in place.

D. Modifications of the contract

35 Various circumstances can lead to game providers wanting to **modify the contract**. This may, for example, involve changing the content of the game, the price or even the T&Cs. The reason for this is that T&Cs need to be adapted to current legal developments or the game might be further developed or have been technically modified. In

[38] Terryn/Vandenbulcke in Schulze/Staudenmayer EU Digital Law Art. 16 CRD para. 6.

[39] Commission, 'Guidance on the interpretation and application of Directive 2011/83/EU of the European Parliament and of the Council on consumer rights' (29.12.2021), 2021/C 525/01, point 5.6.1.

[40] The EU Member States must transpose the directive by 19.12.2025 and the corresponding transposition provisions must be applied from 19.6.2026, Art. 2(1) Directive (EU) 2023/2673.

[41] For the legal requirements and open issues of the withdrawal button, see Billing/Vetter K&R 2024, 387; Wiebe/Sengül WRP 2025, 574.

all these cases, changes are necessary. Finally, prices can be adjusted due to economic factors. The changes also benefit the consumer as they improve the digital products overall (rec. 75 sent. 3 DCD).

I. Modification of the digital content or digital service

A modification to the game is subject to specific requirements as digital content or digital service, which are regulated in Art. 19 DCD. According to this, modifications that are not only intended to maintain the contractual condition,[42] but go beyond this, are possible. But this rule is only applicable if the digital content or digital service is to be supplied or made accessible to the consumer over a period of time. This means that only in the case of continuing obligations are game providers authorised to modify the digital content or digital service, not in the case of one-off provision. Then a modification is allowed under **three conditions** which Art. 19(1) DCD stated: 36

The contract must first allow and provide a '**valid reason**' for such a modification (first condition). Game providers should therefore have already contractually granted themselves the right to make modifications. If this is not the case, the nature of the contract can allow the modification.[43] The question then arises as to whether the modification provides a 'valid reason'. Such valid reasons could encompass cases where the modification is necessary to adapt the digital content or digital services to a new technical environment or to an increased number of users or for other important operational reasons (see rec. 75 sent. 2 DCD). This regulation applies even to graphical changes that do not affect the game's functionality.[44] It is irrelevant whether the change affects a subordinate function or the core of the digital product.[45] Significant modifications are, for example, those that remove or add to the main content of the game or those that change the game mechanics, while insignificant modifications are more likely to be minor updates and bug fixes or cosmetic adjustments that do not affect the game mechanics. Modifications which generally have a valid reason could therefore be, in addition to technical adjustments, the correction of errors, the change of content or the introduction of new content and functions.[46] To avoid legal uncertainty, the objective reasons legitimising a modification should be defined in more detail in the contract.[47] 37

The second condition is that the modification is made **without additional costs** to the consumer. This includes all costs caused by changing the digital product. These may not be passed on to the consumer. In addition, the consumer must be **informed of the modification** in a clear and comprehensible manner (third condition). The information enables the consumer to decide if he is willing to accept the modification or not. 38

If the modification negatively impacts the consumer's access to the content or its use by the consumer to a more than minor extent, there is a further condition: The consumer must be **informed reasonably in advance** on a durable medium of the features and time of the modification and of the right to terminate the contract. To qualify such impacts, several circumstances must be taken into account. Rec. 75 sent. 6 DCD indicates that the extent to which modifications negatively impact the use of or access to the digital content or digital service by the consumer should consider 'the nature 39

42 Möllnitz MMR 2021, 116 (117); Spindler MMR 2021, 528 (531).

43 Wendland in Schulze/Staudenmayer EU Digital Law Art. 19 CRD para. 12.

44 Hunzinger CR 2022, 349 (350).

45 Hunzinger CR 2022, 349 (350); According to Möllnitz MMR 2021, 116 (118); Spindler MMR 2021, 528 (531) the core of the digital product must be preserved.

46 A list of possible modifications in Hunzinger CR 2022, 349 (351).

47 Hunzinger CR 2022, 349 (355); Möllnitz MMR 2021, 116 (118).

and purpose of the digital content or digital service and to the quality, functionality, compatibility and other main features which are normal for digital content or digital services of the same type.' An example of a negative impact that is more than minor is where the consumer must meet additional hardware requirements due to functional improvements.[48] The consumer may therefore terminate the contract in such a case. However, the consumer cannot terminate the contract if the trader has enabled him to maintain without additional costs the content without the modification and if the digital content remains in conformity (Art. 19(4) DCD).

II. Price adjustment (clause)

40 If game providers incur additional costs due to certain circumstances, such as a change in technological conditions, game providers may consider **changing the price later**.

41 In principle, price modifications are legally possible and can be agreed in the game provider's T&Cs. Game providers can only change the price following contract conclusion by including a corresponding clause in the T&Cs. However, in some jurisdictions such as Germany the design of the price modification clauses is almost always ineffective in practice, as the requirements for them are particularly high: According to Art. 3(1)(i) in conjunction with Annex no. 1(l) Unfair Contract Terms Directive (EC) 93/13, price modification in T&Cs are **unfair** and therefore **invalid** if the seller of goods or supplier of services can set or increase the price at the time of delivery without giving the consumer the corresponding right to cancel the contract and if the final price is too high in relation to the price agreed when the contract was concluded. The relevant clause must therefore always grant the consumer the right to terminate the contract in the event of a price modification. In addition, the price must not be too high compared to the price agreed when the contract was concluded. When exactly the price is too high is not explained in detail and depends on the individual case.

42 In Germany, for example, the *BGH* has ruled as follows: In any case, the trader may not increase the agreed price beyond the passing on of specific cost increases without any limitation, whereby he would not only avoid a reduction in profit but would also make an additional profit.[49] This could otherwise be unfair within the meaning of Art. 6(1) Unfair Contract Terms Directive (EC) 93/13. Accordingly, price adjustments are only permissible if they pass on a real cost increase to the contractual partner. However, there must be **valid reasons** for this, as otherwise the contractual balance is shifted and the consumer is unreasonably disadvantaged. Price adjustment clauses should therefore specify the costs on which their prices (and price increases) depend and how the individual cost elements are weighted, as well as disclose the weighting in the calculation of the total price, so that the consumer can estimate what price increases he may face in future.[50] In addition, the consumer must be informed of the price change in advance. As a result, a price increase is usually only possible with the **user's consent** due to the high requirements.

---

[48] Wendland in Schulze/Staudenmayer EU Digital Law Art. 19 CRD para. 17.
[49] BGH 11.10.2007 – III ZR 63/07, NJW-RR 2008, 134 para. 19.
[50] BGH 15.11.2007 – III ZR 247/06, NJW 2008, 360 para. 10 et seqq.

III. T&Cs adjustment clause

Game providers may include in their T&Cs the right to subsequently amend the T&Cs. However, a **blanket T&Cs adjustment clause** in which the consumer's non-response is deemed to be consent will generally be ineffective. Although this has not yet been decided by the *ECJ*, in some jurisdictions national courts have ruled that such a clause is invalid regarding the implementation standards of the Unfair Contract Terms Directive (EC) 93/13, as it unilaterally provides for a contract modification to the detriment of the consumer and thus unreasonably disadvantages the consumer contrary to the requirement of good faith.[51] The consumer then has to take action against the contract amendment rather than in favour of it, which disadvantages the 'unsophisticated consumer' who does not react, for example, due to lethargy, lack of interest, intellectual overload or clumsiness. In addition, such a clause violates the principles of contract law, as this always provides for an offer and an acceptance to conclude a contract. Instead, the silence of the contractual partner would be inadmissibly qualified as consent to the conclusion of the contract. **43**

For the subsequent modification of the T&Cs to be effective, an adjustment clause must fulfil specific requirements: Firstly, just as with the price modification clause, it must set out when a modification to the T&Cs is possible. There must be a **valid reason** for a modification. A valid reason may, for example, exist if a change in legislation or case law makes it necessary to modify the T&Cs to remedy a significant disruption to the equivalence of the contract that was not foreseen when the contract was concluded.[52] Such a reason is valid and would not unreasonably disadvantage the consumer, as the elimination of a disruption of the equivalence relationship is also in the consumer's interest. **44**

In addition, the clause should stipulate that game providers must inform consumers transparently and in good time in advance about the changes to the T&Cs. Moreover, they should have a reasonable period (at least 30 days) to object. Game providers must inform them that no objection is equivalent to consent. If the consumer remains silent, the modified terms and conditions will apply. However, the right to modify certain clauses may not extend to the **main performance obligations**, as this would be unreasonably disadvantageous, as the user of the T&Cs would otherwise be able to shift the equivalence of performance and consideration significantly in their favour and thus devalue the position of the contractual partner.[53] A corresponding clause must therefore explicitly exclude the main performance obligations to be effective. **45**

E. Term and termination rules

Contracts for video games can be for a limited or unlimited period and have different terms. The termination rules can also vary accordingly. The decision as to when and under what circumstances a consumer contract can be terminated is a decision of **significant economic importance**, as well as the decision on the duration of the consumer contract.[54] Nevertheless, game providers need to consider that there are certain limits to the contractual design of termination and term clauses. **46**

---

[51] BGH 27.4. 2021 – XI ZR 26/20, NJW 2021, 2273 para. 19 et seqq.

[52] Fornasier in MüKoBGB § 305 para. 94.

[53] BGH 27.4.2021 – XI ZR 26/20, NJW 2021, 2273 para. 26, 38.

[54] According to Boyd/Pyne/Kane, p. 59 everyone in the games industry has to think about term and termination, among other things.

I. Term and automatic renewal

47 In the case of fixed-term contracts, it is important that the consumer is informed about the term and the conditions of automatic renewal. **Automatic renewals** are only allowed to a limited extent under EU consumer law. They are ineffective if the consumer does not object against the auto renewal and if the time limit set for the consumer to express his wish not to renew the contract is unreasonably early (Art. 3(1) in conjunction with Annex no. 1(h) Unfair Contract Terms Directive (EC) 93/13).

48 In some Member States like Germany, special rules for automatic contract renewal in the case of so-called **continuing obligations** exist. A continuing obligation is considered to exist if new performance and protection obligations arise during the term of the contract, which is characterised by time.[55] This applies in particular to so-called pay-to-play contracts, in which a fee is paid for temporary participation in the game, as well as in the case of subscriptions. In these situations, the initial contract term may not exceed two years. As of 1.3.2022, the contract may also not be tacitly renewed for a specific period. The automatic renewal is only possible if the contract is considered to continue indefinitely, and the consumer can terminate the contract at any time with one month's notice. In addition, the cancellation period before the end of the initially intended contract term may not be longer than one month before the end of this contract term. In practice, it is therefore necessary to consider in advance how the term and the right of termination are to be structured when pricing the games.[56] At least in Germany, it must be taken into account that only a maximum term of two years and no tacit extension of the contract for a specific term are permitted. However, the right to ask for an explicit extension of the contract remains unaffected. Overall, game providers should provide clear and comprehensible information on the term of the contract and the conditions for automatic renewal. They should also ensure that consumers are informed of the impending renewal in good time before the end of the contract term and are given the opportunity to object to the renewal.

II. Termination

49 The consumer has the right to terminate the contract as a remedy for lack of conformity by means of a statement to the trader expressing their decision to terminate the contract (Art. 15 DCD). The right of withdrawal is different from the right of termination as it does not depend on the lack of conformity with the product or service.[57] Continuing obligations can be terminated with effect for the future by ordinary or extraordinary notice. An **ordinary right of termination** should be agreed, whereby both parties can terminate the contract with a reasonable notice period. This should be possible for open-ended contracts and should be defined accordingly in the contract. A period of two weeks for ordinary termination by game providers is recommended so that the player of an online game has, for example, the opportunity to use the virtual items in the game.[58]

50 In addition, both parties can be given the option to terminate the contract without a notice period if there is a **good cause** for the termination that makes it unreasonable to continue the contractual relationship until the end of the notice period (**extraordinary**

[55] Gaier in MükoBGB § 314 BGB para 10.
[56] Rauda MMR 2022, 705 (706).
[57] Twigg-Flesner in Schulze/Staudenmayer EU Digital Law Art. 15 DCD para. 4.
[58] Rauda, para. 737; Sester/Kastner in Games und Recht § 18 para. 70.

notice). It should be noted that under certain national legal systems, such as German law (§ 314(1) BGB), a continuing obligation can be lawfully terminated without a notice period if there is a valid reason. Such good causes may be that the consumer is in arrears with the payment of fees, culpably violates laws despite warnings, grossly disregards the terms of use or uses technical aids such as bots to manipulate the course of the game.[59] Such important reasons should be redefined accordingly in the contract. Game providers should therefore present the grounds for termination in a transparent manner and provide clear provisions on notice periods and the (written or electronic) form of termination.

III. Termination button

To simplify termination for the consumer, a game provider can offer a **termination button** on its website. The obligation to provide a termination button exists in Germany (§ 312k BGB)[60] and in France (le décret d'application de l'article 17 de la loi n°2022–1158). In Germany, the trader must include a clearly legible termination button on its website with the wording 'Terminate contracts here' or a similarly clear wording, which must be permanently, directly and easily accessible. The consumer must then be directed to a confirmation page on which only the data required for termination may be requested and on which there is a confirmation button with the same clarity as the termination button. If these criteria are not met, the consumer can terminate the contract at any time without observing a termination period. In France, the three-click termination ('la résiliation en trois clics') applies, with which consumers should be able to terminate from the contract in three clicks: First, as under German law, the consumer clicks on the function 'Terminate your contract' or another clear wording that must be legible and easily accessible. Then, with the second click, the consumer lands on a website where information on the termination is summarised and can be changed if necessary. With the third click, the consumer should then also notify the trader of the termination of the contract by clicking on the legible function 'Notification of termination' or another clear formulation. However, these two constellations are not based on a European legal act. It therefore remains to be seen whether the EU, after the introduction of the withdrawal button, will also make the termination button mandatory throughout the EU. **51**

F. Sanctioning of players

To successfully communicate and market a game, it is necessary to build and maintain a trouble-free community for the game.[61] If individual players increasingly violate the T&Cs and disrupt this community due to certain behaviours, the question arises as to whether such players may be **sanctioned**. This includes behaviour that affects communication between players (e.g., insults) or that abuses the game mechanics, for example by deliberately losing in a group game.[62] It also means other misconduct, such **52**

---

[59] Rauda, para. 740.

[60] For an overview of the termination button in Germany see Stiegler VuR 2021, 443.

[61] Hilgert in Games und Recht § 26 para. 2; Limpach in The Publishing Challenge for Independent Video Game Developers Chapter 3 p. 76.

[62] Emmerich/Krekhov/Krüger, '"Pls Uninstall": On the Interplay of the COVID-19 Pandemic and Toxic Player Behavior in Competitive Gaming', pp. 224–228, available at https://doi.org/10.1145/3383668.341989.

as punishable content and behaviour, as these are already undesirable by law,[63] bots and cheats as abusive behaviour,[64] and the passing on of virtual teams or user accounts may be prohibited.[65] It is also conceivable to restrict behaviour in communication where players express their political or ideological positions in order to ensure trouble-free gameplay, protect individual players from discrimination and avoid disputes over interpretation under criminal law.[66] Corresponding clauses in the terms of use that sanction such behaviour constitute T&Cs. They must therefore be transparent. The clause must be detailed enough to allow the user to assess in advance and without separate legal advice which behaviour is specifically covered, so that the trader has no unjustified room for interpretation.[67] If game providers are then accused of a lack of transparency, they can defend themselves by arguing that excessively detailed regulations would lead to the consumer being overwhelmed by their abundance and complexity, which contradicts the idea of transparency.[68] The sanctions must be **proportionate**, so warnings, bans or similar must be considered first, and only in the case of serious offences can they be refrained from.[69]

53 In some cases, it is also assumed that game providers have virtual domiciliary rights and are therefore authorised to take measures such as the exclusion of players.[70] Regardless of whether such rights exist, the possibility of sanctions can be defined in the T&Cs. In addition, it must be noted that the game operator may also have **legal obligations** to intervene, for example, hosting services as intermediary services are obliged to remove illegal content under the conditions of Art. 16 DSA,[71] or it may arise from a contractual duty of protection.[72]

---

[63] A list of the error behaviour in Hilgert in Games und Recht § 26 para. 5 and 28.

[64] BGH 12.1.2017 – I ZR 253/14, MMR 2017, 394.

[65] BGH 11.2.2010 – I ZR 178/08, MMR 2010, 771.

[66] Hilgert in Games und Recht § 26 para. 29.

[67] BGH 17.10.2023 – VI ZR 27/23, NJW 2024, 144 para. 9; BGH 1.10.2019 – VI ZR 156/18, NJW-RR 2020, 112 para. 23.

[68] BGH 5.10.2023 – III ZR 216/22, NJW 2023, 3794 para. 23; BGH 9.6.2011 – III ZR 157/10, NJW-RR 2011, 1628 para. 27.

[69] Hilgert in Games und Recht § 26 para. 19, 32.

[70] On the legal nature of the virtual domiciliary right, see Rauda, para. 711; Maume MMR 2007, 620 (622).

[71] Similar obligations may also arise from national regulations, for example in Germany from the JuSchG or NetzDG.

[72] Hilgert in Games und Recht § 26 para. 8 et seqq.

§ 26
Digital Items – Consumer Protection

Bibliography: Baumgartner/Ewald, Apps und Recht, 2nd edn, Munich 2016; Borges/Hilber, BeckOK IT-Recht, 19th edn, Munich 2025; Hau/Posek, BeckOK BGB, 74th edn, Munich 2025; Kaufmann, Erwerb von Lootboxen und die vertragstypologische Erfassung der Leistungspflichten MMR 2023, 739; Rauda, Recht der Computerspiele, Munich 2013; Söbbing/Schwarz, Wie kann man einen virtuellen Gegenstand in einem Metaverse erwerben? CR 2024, 346.

A. Introduction 1
B. Legislative framework for consumer law 8
C. Acquisition of the digital items by the player 9
I. Acquisition through payment 10
II. Acquisition through gameplay 14
III. Acquisition via exchange of personal data 15
IV. Acquisition through random elements 17
V. Acquisition via exchange of in-game currency 18
1. Legal position as digital content 18
2. Digital representation of value 21
D. Loot Boxes 24
I. Legislation 24
1. European Union guidance on the UCPD 27
2. Digital Fairness Act 28
3. Upcoming national legislation 31
II. Industry self- and co-regulation 35
1. The Pan European Game Information System – PEGI 35
2. Unterhaltungssoftware Selbstkontrolle – USK 37
E. Current enforcement activities surrounding Loot Boxes 41
I. Consumer protection enforcement 41
1. Italy: AGCM decision on the application of the Unfair Commercial Practices Directive 41
2. PEGI enforcement 44
3. UK: Advertising Standards Authority rulings 46
4. European Commission: letter to the European trade associations 49
II. Enforcement based on gambling laws 50
1. Belgium 51
2. The Netherlands 56
3. Austria 66

A. Introduction

Digital items have become an increasingly important part of video game ecosystems, particularly since the rapid growth of 'free-to-play' gaming in the late 2000s and early 2010s, where the base game is downloadable for free but further digital items can be purchased (or otherwise acquired). 1

There is typically a representation of the digital item in the context of the game – visual or otherwise – (the "**Representation**"). This Representation might for instance be an image, a sound or 3D model, stored as a digital file or group of files. It may be subject to intellectual property rights that have to be cleared – this is further discussed in the → following chapter. 2

At its very core, however, a digital item really is an entitlement to do something in the context of a game (the "**Entitlement**"). This Entitlement may mean, inter alia, that a character in the game world has different physical characteristics, a prettier cloak, new abilities, a virtual companion or the ability to travel to new places. It some cases it may 3 also have a more direct impact on gameplay, for example speeding up the building of a new base.

4 Many digital items are purchased directly with real-world money. However, in many situations they may also be exchangeable for other digital items, often referred to as in-game currency (**IGC**). IGC can take several forms; (a) it can be earned as part of gameplay – for example, as a prize for achieving a certain objective or as a log-in reward ("**Soft Currency**"); (b) purchased with real-world money ("**Hard Currency**"), which is purchasable from and spendable with the same games company (i.e. in a 'closed loop') and; (c) in some cases it can be a combination of the two – currency which is both earned and that can be purchased with real-world money ("**Mixed Currency**").

5 Digital items can attract particular scrutiny when they are granted based on a randomised mechanism. While the particulars of such mechanisms vary widely, they are collectively referred to as "**Loot Boxes**".

6 **Loot Boxes** have been given many names over the years, including 'gacha', 'random reward mechanism', 'paid random items' and 'prize crate'. In short, Loot Boxes are considered a subcategory of digital items, which when 'opened', provide the player with a random reward – therefore one Entitlement is replaced with another Entitlement or group of Entitlements released in the process.

7 We further discuss IGC and Loot Boxes as part of this chapter.

B. Legislative framework for consumer law

8 Outside of intellectual property law (discussed in the next chapter), the acquisition and use of digital items, the compliance framework is primarily based in consumer protection law. The key consumer protection legislation applying to digital content is:

- **The Unfair Commercial Practices Directive**[1] **(UCPD).** The UCPD covers prohibited unfair commercial acts and omissions – those that are considered either misleading or aggressive. Annex 1 of the Directive contains a list of acts which will always be considered unfair. The European Commission has published a related guidance document (the **UCPD Guidance**) that, among other matters, lays out its interpretation of certain rules of the UCPD insofar as they concern the distribution of video games and digital items, including Loot Boxes.[2] For a more general overview of the UCPD in the context of marketing, → Ch. 36, I.1.
- **The Consumer Rights Directive**[3] **(CRD).** The CRD covers a couple of key areas relevant to digital content, including the right of withdrawal and certain information requirements for 'distance' contracts (including those concluded over the internet).

---

[1] Directive 2005/29/EC of the European Parliament and of the Council of 11.5.2005 concerning unfair business-to-consumer commercial practices in the internal market and amending Council Directive 84/450/EEC, Directives 97/7/EC, 98/27/EC and 2002/65/EC of the European Parliament and of the Council and Regulation (EC) No. 2006/2004 of the European Parliament and of the Council ('Unfair Commercial Practices Directive').

[2] Guidance on the interpretation and application of Directive 2005/29/EC of the European Parliament and of the Council concerning unfair business-to-consumer commercial practices in the internal market of 29.12.2021, (2021/C 526/01).

[3] Directive 2011/83/EU of the European Parliament and of the Council of 25.10.2011 on consumer rights, amending Council Directive 93/13/EEC and Directive 1999/44/EC of the European Parliament and of the Council and repealing Council Directive 85/577/EEC and Directive 97/7/EC of the European Parliament and of the Council.

- **The Digital Content Directive[4] (DCD).** The DCD includes rules around providing features and updates to digital content, what happens if a trader does not conform with their contract with a user and obligations of the trader to the user in the event of termination
- **Unfair Contract Terms Directive[5] (UCTD).** The UCTD sets out rules for contracts between businesses and consumers, including terms which are always considered unfair on consumers.
- **The Enforcement and Modernisation Directive[6] (EMD).** The EMD made several updates to existing consumer laws, and introduced percentage-based fines for breaches of consumer protection rules (maximum fines of 4 % of the trader's annual turnover, or €2 million where it cannot be calculated). The EMD also included the expansion of the UCPD to expressly cover digital content.

C. Acquisition of the digital items by the player

Players can acquire the Entitlement to digital items through various means within the game environment. The **method of acquisition is significant** for the legal classification of the underlying transaction.[7] 9

I. Acquisition through payment

A common method of acquiring digital items is through **a real-world money payment**, typically via in-game purchases. In-game purchases encompass any paid acquisition of content or services during the use of a game or the associated user account. Whether the game itself is free or paid for is irrelevant for the legal classification of the in-game purchase.[8] 10

The UCPD Guidance sets out that in-game purchases that **'enhance the playing experience of the respective user, such as digital items'** would normally qualify as a contract for 'digital content'.[9] According to this interpretation, EU consumer protection rules in relation to paid-for digital content (e.g. the CRD, UCTD and DCD) would apply when purchasing a digital item with real-world money. Such digital items have also been confirmed to be **'digital content'** in German case law.[10] 11

However, it bears repeating that the **UCPD Guidance** is neither binding law, nor must its existence replace individual legal analysis. To give an example, the Entitlement provided by a digital item might not add access to any new 'content' in a game but merely shorten the waiting time in a multiplayer game's matchmaking lobby or otherwise 12

---

[4] Directive (EU) 2019/770 of the European Parliament and of the Council of 20.5.2019 on certain aspects concerning contracts for the supply of digital content and digital services.

[5] Council Directive 93/13/EEC of 5.4.1993 on unfair terms in consumer contracts.

[6] Directive (EU) 2019/2161 of the European Parliament and of the Council of 27.11.2019 amending Council Directive 93/13/EEC and Directives 98/6/EC, 2005/29/EC and 2011/83/EU of the European Parliament and of the Council as regards the better enforcement and modernisation of Union consumer protection rules.

[7] Kaufmann MMR 2023 739 (740).

[8] Baumgartner/Ewald, Chapter 2 no. 36; Hilber in BeckOK IT-Recht, BGB § 453 mn. 5.

[9] Guidance on the interpretation and application of Directive 2011/83/EU of the European Parliament and of the Council on consumer rights.

[10] 6 U 108/16 – 11.07.2018 – Higher Regional Court of Karlsruhe; and 18 O 7/16, BeckRS 2016, 12084 – 25.05.2016 – Regional Court of Karlsruhe.

improve the quality of services in connection with the game (so may perhaps in some cases be considered a digital service).

13 In the German legal discourse, the acquisition of digital items via a purchase with real-world money has been classified as a purchase of rights (**Rechtskauf**) under § 453(1) var. 1 BGB, or a purchase of other objects under § 453(1) var. 2 BGB, as the digital items themselves are not considered "things" (§ 90 BGB).[11] Instead, the transaction often involves the transfer of rights, such as licences for the use of additional app functions or the digital items themselves.[12]

II. Acquisition through gameplay

14 Players can also **acquire digital items simply by engaging with the game**, such as earning them as rewards for completing specific tasks or challenges. This method contrasts with explicit monetary purchase. Generally, events and interactions occurring solely within the game are not considered legal transactions.[13] The acquisition of items earned through gameplay (e.g. via a **Soft Currency**) is typically seen as part of the user's interaction with the software rather than a contractual acquisition event.

III. Acquisition via exchange of personal data

15 In some circumstances, digital items will obtain **some of the EU consumer rights protections afforded to paid digital content** (as set out in C(I) above) if the digital content has been exchanged for the consumer's personal data – but only where the personal data is not just processed for the purpose of performing the contract and complying with legal requirements[14] – this includes where a consumer is '*exposed to advertisements exclusively in order to gain access to digital content*'.[15] Many consumer rights obtained via the provision of non-mandatory personal data are set out in the DCD, although the CRD (as amended by the EMD) should also be referred to.

16 The processing of personal data will of course be subject to data protection law, further discussed in → Ch. 29.

IV. Acquisition through random elements

17 A specific and often debated method of acquisition is through random elements, which are often referred to as **Loot Boxes**. Given the specific scrutiny that Loot Boxes have been subjected to in recent years, these are discussed in a separate section of this chapter (→ section D below).

---

[11] Rauda, p. 266; Fritzsche in BeckOK BGB § 90 mn. 29; disputed by Söbbing/Schwarz CR 2024, pp. 346–352.

[12] Hilber in BeckOK IT-Recht, BGB § 453 mn. 6.

[13] Kaufmann MMR 2023, 739 (743).

[14] Guidance on the interpretation and application of Directive 2011/83/EU of the European Parliament and of the Council on consumer rights.

[15] Recital 25 of the DCD.

V. Acquisition via exchange of in-game currency

1. Legal position as digital content

As described in the introduction of this chapter, 'digital content' is defined as "*data produced and supplied in a digital form*".[16] Therefore, use of IGC to acquire other digital items would be considered the exchange of two types of 'digital content' (**"Game Exchange"**). 18

Even where 'digital content' is not acquired for a 'price'[17] (like during a Game Exchange), much of consumer law still applies; for example, the **acquisition of digital content via personal data** (as described in subsection III above). The UCTD will also apply to the relationship between the player and games company more broadly regardless of whether there is "*monetary consideration*" or not.[18] 19

As highlighted in section CI, European case law has also confirmed that in-game content such as IGC is 'digital content'. 20

2. Digital representation of value

Recent debate has questioned whether a Game Exchange should be classified as a separate contract.[19] This viewpoint sets out that IGC should be considered a **'digital representation of value'** rather than 'digital content' under consumer protection law. This position is, however, **flawed for a number of reasons**: 21

(a) The concept of 'digital representation of value' (**DRV**) is borrowed from the DCD. However, the recitals of the DCD makes it clear that virtual currencies should only be considered DRV to the extent that they are "*recognised by national law*",[20] which no IGC currently is.

(b) The examples of DRV provided in the DCD capture methods of payment such as "*electronic vouchers or e-coupons*" commonly associated with the concept of 'e-money' under financial services legislation.[21] As further explained in the DCD, these methods of payment are used to pay for "*different*" goods or services in the digital single market, not within one closed-loop ecosystem such as a video game. **IGC is also not transferable or exchangeable for cash** or other legal tender, unlike many types of e-coupon or voucher.

(c) If IGC was considered DRV, IGC itself **would lose the protection it has as 'digital content'**. As highlighted in the DCD: "*since digital representations of value have no other purpose than to serve as a method of payment, they themselves should not be considered digital content or a digital service within the meaning of this Directive*".[22] This would mean that users would have – for example – no right of withdrawal when purchasing Hard Currency with real-world money.

---

[16] Article 2(1) of the DCD.

[17] Article 2(7) of the DCD.

[18] See 1.2.1.2. of the Commission's Notice on guidance on the interpretation and application of the UTD: https://eur-lex.europa.eu/legal-content/EN/TXT/HTML/?uri=CELEX:52019XC0927(01).

[19] The Consumer Protection Cooperation Network's Key Principles on In-game virtual currencies: https://commission.europa.eu/document/download/8af13e88-6540-436c-b137-9853e7fe866a_en?filename=Key+principles+on+in-game+virtual+currencies.pdf.

[20] Recital 23 of the DCD.

[21] See the definition of 'electronic money' in Article 2(2) of Directive 2009/110/EC: https://eur-lex.europa.eu/legal-content/EN/TXT/HTML/?uri=CELEX:32009L0110.

[22] Recital 23 of the DCD.

(d) A Game Exchange is **not subject to any separate contractual process**: a player agrees to terms of the game at the initial download or first access of the game. As flagged above, the terms of that contract will still be subject to the UCTD regardless of how a digital item is later obtained during the game.

22 The classification of IGC as DRV would result in a worse position for consumers; instead of the vast majority of consumer law obligations triggering at the point of purchase of IGC, they would instead trigger at every instance of a Game Exchange (which would include the use of IGC in very small denominations, potentially several times during one gameplay session). This would include receiving a contract on a durable medium on each instance of a Game Exchange and agreeing to a right of withdrawal waiver at the point of each Game Exchange.[23] This **multiplication of contracts** would also have negative implications for companies, increasing complexity and costs of managing customer relations.

23 **Other knock-on effects** would likely occur too under the UCPD – including that digital items would need to be shown both in their IGC price and 'real-world price'.[24] Again, due to the way video game ecosystems work, this is more likely to cause confusion for consumers, implying that digital items have monetary value (when they do not, since in the vast majority of cases digital items are not resaleable or otherwise transferable) – and may not actually represent an accurate 'real-world price' depending on how IGC itself can be obtained (e.g. if it is Mixed Currency, or if Hard Currency can be bought in different denominations or bundles). This would also have implications for companies, as they would need to add legal caveats that the displayed price does not actually represent an accurate 'real-world price'. At its core, use of IGC is part of the gameplay experience and not a separate legal relationship with the player. As flagged in earlier UK guidance[25] which was later referred to as part of the common position by the EU's CPC Network,[26] the commercial transaction occurs at the point the user spends their real-world money, and that this should not be combined with gameplay.

D. Loot Boxes

I. Legislation

24 As discussed above in relation to digital items broadly, **most Loot Boxes are considered 'digital content'** under European Union consumer legislation.

25 As digital content, Loot Boxes must comply with these pieces of legislation. If the Loot Box is **paid for**, then generally the consumer legislation applicable to it will be increased (for example, there are certain statutory rights under the CRD that apply only where digital content has been paid for).

26 The UCTD is further discussed in → Ch. 25 in relation to consumer contracts.

---

[23] See Article 8(7)(a) and Article 16(m) of the CRD.

[24] See 4.2.9 of the Commission Notice – Guidance on the interpretation and application of Directive 2005/29/EC of the European Parliament and of the Council concerning unfair business-to-consumer commercial practices in the internal market (2021): https://eur-lex.europa.eu/legal-content/EN/TXT/?uri=CELEX%3A52021XC1229%2805%29&qid=1640961745514.

[25] See the OFT's principles for online and app-based games: https://www.gov.uk/government/publications/principles-for-online-and-app-based-games.

[26] See both the common positions of national authorities within the CPC from December 2013.

1. European Union guidance on the UCPD

The European Commission's Notice on the interpretation and application of the UCPD ('**UCPD Guidance**') raises a few points specifically targeted at Loot Boxes:[27] 27

- Using algorithms to personalise the timing of in-game offerings for Loot Boxes to target those more likely to take 'risks' and increase in-game spending may constitute an '**aggressive practice**'.
- Merchants should clearly disclose to players the probabilities of receiving each digital item/prize from a Loot Box.
- The sale of Loot Boxes must also comply with the information obligations under the CRD and the UCPD concerning the price and main characteristics of the Loot Box.

2. Digital Fairness Act

Following the publication of the European Commission Staff Working Document on the digital fairness fitness check[28] ("**DFFC**"), it is possible that Loot Boxes will feature in the upcoming Digital Fairness Act. 28

Loot Boxes are **mentioned a handful of times in the DFFC**, primarily in relation to the section on 'Addictive design and gaming', which in a video games context focuses on digital items and in-game currencies more broadly. The DFFC considers that Loot Boxes could be considered an '*addictive design*' and that concern is '*amplified*' due to the accessibility of apps to children. 29

The European Commission has published a public consultation and call for evidence on the topic.[29] Depending on the result of the public consultation, and the impact assessment, the European Commission could decide to move forward with a **legislative proposal for Digital Fairness Act in 2026, or in 2027**. Depending on the provisions included in a future Act, the self and co-regulatory instruments PEGI and USK would likely need to be updated. 30

3. Upcoming national legislation

The **Draft Bill on the Protection of Minors in Digital Environments, published by the Spanish government** on 4.6.2024, aims to ensure the safety and well-being of minors in digital spaces, addressing the benefits and risks associated with technology.[30] The draft bill was approved by the Council of Ministers on 25.3.2025, and is currently undergoing parliamentary process. 31

The proposal establishes rights for minors, including protection from harmful content and access to educational resources. Article 5 proposes **regulate random reward mechanisms** in video games, i.e. Loot Boxes, by prohibiting their access to minors: 32

- Article 5 'Regulation of Access to and Activation of Random Reward Mechanisms' defines random reward mechanisms as virtual feature present in video games or other electronic games which is
  - (i) activated using legal tender or a digital item, such as a code, key, in-game currency, cryptocurrency or other element,

---

[27] See section 4.2.9 of footnote 24.

[28] Fitness check – SWD(2024)230.

[29] https://ec.europa.eu/info/law/better-regulation/have-your-say/initiatives/14622-Digital-Fairness-Act_en.

[30] https://www.congreso.es/en/proyectos-de-ley?p_p_id=iniciativas&p_p_lifecycle=0&p_p_state=normal&p_p_mode=view&_iniciativas_mode=mostrarDetalle&_iniciativas_legislatura=XV&_iniciativas_id=121/000052.

(ii) acquired directly or indirectly with money, and,
(iii) where the result of such activation is random and,
(iv) leads to obtaining a digital item that can be exchanged for money or other digital items.

- The Article further states that regulations may define exceptional cases in which the prohibition for minors to access paid random items may be exempted, provided that the principle of child protection underpinning the proposal is fully respected.
- The final provision (provision eleven) designates the departments (consumer protection and gambling departments, and the ministry responsible for digital transformation), that may adopt relevant technical provisions to allow verification of the age of the users. It states that the adoption of such measures must comply with EU regulations and, in particular, those of the DSA addressing unethical commercial techniques and practices in relation to "dark patterns", influencer marketing, addictive design of digital products and online profiling, especially when they exploit consumer vulnerabilities for commercial purposes.

33 Should the proposal be adopted at the end of the legislative proceedings, game developers, publishers and distributors would need to adapt their services accordingly in Spain, or alternatively put in place geographical limitations to restrict access to the game, or to certain features of the game. As for the rest of the EU, as discussed earlier in this chapter, **existing laws on consumer protection apply**, including the PEGI Code of Conduct should the game carry a PEGI age rating, and in Germany the provisions established by the USK.

34 The Spanish proposal establishes a **market fragmentation** within the internal market of the EU as regards paid random reward mechanisms, at a time where the European Commission is preparing a future Digital Fairness Act, which could regulate the use of paid random items in games. Spain notified the proposal to the European Commission, and during the TRIS procedure the European Commission did not oppose Spain proceeding with the proposal, subject to certain amendments.

II. Industry self- and co-regulation

1. The Pan European Game Information System – PEGI

35 As discussed in the PEGI chapter (→ Ch. 22) the game age rating bodies also have certain requirements around Loot Boxes. For PEGI, its **Code of Conduct** includes specific rules around the disclosure and information requirements in relation to Loot Boxes[31] – although the presence of Loot Boxes in and of themselves do not affect the PEGI age rating granted. PEGI Code of Conduct signatories must:

- display the PEGI 'Paid Random Item' notice at the point of purchase of the game to support consumers in making an informed decision about whether or not to purchase or download the game;
- ensure and emphasise that paying for such random in-game content is never essential to gameplay, but is always optional;
- ensure that probabilities are transparent and equivalent for all players, that random items are distributed without any disadvantageous manipulation based on unfair processing of personal data, and in compliance with applicable data protection and privacy laws; and

[31] Sections 8.2 and 8.3 of the PEGI Code of Conduct: https://pegi.info/pegi-code-of-conduct.

- signatories of the Code of Conduct must have a policy that explicitly prohibits players from using in-game content to engage in unlawful gambling or betting activities (so-called skin gambling or skin betting). These policies should include clear wording on the enforcement of potential penalties such as suspending or banning players in the case of illegal trading.

Signatories that do not comply with these requirements are in breach of the Code of Conduct and would be subject to corrective measures, including financial sanctions. 36

2. Unterhaltungssoftware Selbstkontrolle – USK

Conversely for **USK ratings** (further discussed in → Ch. 23) that are applicable in Germany, Loot Boxes can be considered a 'risk factor' when determining the age rating of a game, which could lead to an increased age rating.[32] 37

In May 2021, the amended **Youth Protection Act (JuSchG)** came into force in Germany. This extension brought significant changes to the review of computer and video games. The aim of the legislator was to improve the protection of children in the "digital space" and to better counter possible risks from online functions (so-called "usage risks"). In order to put the new provisions for the protection of minors into practice, the USK has been working on their implementation in cooperation with the responsible authorities of the supreme state youth authorities. In order to implement the amended JuSchG in a practical and, above all, targeted manner for families, the development of the proposals involved stakeholders in German youth media protection, the USK Advisory Board, but also children and young people themselves as well as educational professionals and parents. 38

By law, risks of use must therefore be appropriately taken into account in an assessment under youth protection law if they are to be classified as significant risks to the personal integrity of children and young people according to a **concrete risk prognosis**. When considering whether these circumstances justify a higher age level, priority is given to both sensitising information (e.g. in-game purchases and random items) and existing protective measures (e.g. parental control systems) of the game providers. The USK age ratings have also been expanded to include additional information on content and use or the main reasons for the age rating (e.g. pressure to play a lot or increased incentives to buy). The updated guiding criteria have been in use since January 2023. 39

Since January 2025, the latest findings from two years of adjudication practice on risks posed by Loot Boxes or purchase functions have also been incorporated into the **USK guiding criteria**. The new USK test rules have led to higher age ratings for around a third of the games assessed with online functions. 40

E. Current enforcement activities surrounding Loot Boxes

I. Consumer protection enforcement

1. Italy: AGCM decision on the application of the Unfair Commercial Practices Directive[33]

In 2020, the **Italian Competition and Market Authority (AGCM)** closed an investigation that originated from complaints by consumers associations that the information 41

[32] https://usk.de/en/the-usk-age-ratings/.
[33] Bulletin no. 41–20: https://www.agcm.it/dotcmsdoc/bollettini/2020/41-20.pdf.

about the presence of in-game purchases (including Loot Boxes) was not clearly and easily highlighted. In addition, free-to-play games were presented as free, while providing in-game purchases within the game, without the contextual indications clarifying the presence of such purchases.

42 AGCM, without ascertaining the infringement of the consumer code for incorrect commercial practice, made binding the commitments proposed by the video game company as it considered the company *"capable of remedying the profiles of possible impropriety of the disputed commercial practices".*

- **Transparency commitments:** the video game company was required to update their digital platform and the Italian website to include the PEGI descriptor for in-game purchases and to provide clear information about these purchases in product descriptions by 31.12.2020. Additionally, the company had to implement the descriptors on physical game boxes and ensure users are informed about their right to withdrawal and refund options.
- **User protection measures:** the company committed to set a default spending limit to zero for adolescent accounts and provided a tutorial link during account registration to help users manage spending limits. They were required to inform platform owners about these commitments by the end of 2020.

43 In its assessment of the undertakings submitted by the companies, the AGCM highlights, inter alia, the following:

> **The commitments proposed by the [...] should be assessed in the context of a commercial trend that has introduced into video games, also intended for children and adolescents, in-game purchases and purchases via loot-box. The video game business model is gradually shifting from selling copies of a certain game at a remunerative price to building an engaging environment that induces the user to purchase content and functionality within the game itself. In-game purchases are becoming more and more a significant source of remuneration (if not the only one as in the case of free to play games) for operators in the sector.**
> **In this context, as video games are also intended for vulnerable users such as children and adolescents who may not have a clear awareness of the economic and psychological mechanisms underlying in-game purchases, maximum clarity and transparency is needed for consumers and parents as to whether such purchases can be made. This is all the more true in relation to video games that contain in-game purchases in the form of a loot-box, where randomness is a feature.**

2. PEGI enforcement

44 **PEGI has enforced against video games companies** in relation to inaccurate or incomplete display of information related to paid Loot Boxes. These are cases where publishers did not display the **'Paid Random Items'** notice while the games did in fact include paid random items: (i) *Diablo Immortal* (Activision Blizzard) and (ii) *Hunt: Showdown Bounty Hunter* – Limited Edition (Plaion).

45 In both cases the presence of paid random items (like Loot Boxes), was not disclosed to PEGI when the games were submitted for a rating license. Since this amounted to **a violation of the rules in the PEGI Code of Conduct**, the PEGI Enforcement Committee sanctioned both companies with a fine of 5,000 EUR. The companies took immediate action to update relevant store listings and marketing materials.

3. UK: Advertising Standards Authority rulings

46 The UK's advertising guidelines are largely based on the Consumer Protection from Unfair Trading Regulations 2008 (which has since been repealed but now forms part of the Digital Markets, Competition and Consumers Act 2025), which was the transposed version of the UCPD prior to the United Kingdom exiting the European Union. There-

fore, as of the date of this book, the **UK approach to these topics is still largely in alignment with the European Union.**

The Committee of Advertising Practice in 2021 published its Guidance for advertising in-game purchases (**CAP Guidance**), which includes specific guidance in relation to Loot Boxes.[34] The CAP Guidance highlights that: (a) the presence of Loot Boxes should be clear in all advertising for the game; and (b) that marketing messaging should not be misleading (for example, the marketer must not suggest that the next Loot Box purchase will result in a rare or specific item if that is not the case, or suggest that the outcome is based on skill when it is not). **47**

On the basis of this guidance, the **Advertising Standards Authority (the ASA)** has ruled against several games companies for failing to disclose the presence of Loot Boxes in the advertising for their games.[35] In one instance, the video games company did make the disclosure, but it was deemed to be insufficient by the ASA, as the text of the disclosure was too small and too difficult to read.[36] Games companies should therefore ensure that any Loot Box disclosures are clear in all advertising. **48**

4. European Commission: letter to the European trade associations

In September 2022, the **European Commission (EC) sent a letter**[37] to the International Software Federation of Europe (ISFE – now Video Games Europe) and the European Games Developer Federation (EGDF) reminding the video games industry of their obligations under consumer protection law in relation to the sale of Loot Boxes. No further action was taken by the EC. **49**

II. Enforcement based on gambling laws

On the other end of the Loot Box legislation spectrum sits gambling legislation; unlike consumer protection legislation, **gambling laws are not harmonised across the European Union**, nor does the European Union have competence to legislate on gambling issues. This means each Member State has its own unique laws and guidance that have to be complied with in relation to Loot Boxes. This chapter is not exhaustive of each Member State's laws, but we have focussed on some countries that have specifically looked at Loot Boxes under gambling legislation. As highlighted above, the direction of travel for the regulation of Loot Boxes in the EU is a combination of consumer protection legislation and self-regulatory rules (such as PEGI). **50**

---

[34] https://www.asa.org.uk/static/69722495-6217-45c3-aee0181c2b72a437/220524-Guidance-CAP.pdf.

[35] There have been two ASA rulings against Hutch Games (https://www.asa.org.uk/rulings/hutch-games-ltd-a23-1196857-hutch-games-ltd.html, https://www.asa.org.uk/rulings/hutch-games-ltd-a23-1196862-hutch-games-ltd.html), one against Miniclip (https://www.asa.org.uk/rulings/miniclip--uk--ltd-a23-1216455-miniclip--uk--ltd.html) and one against Electronic Arts (https://www.asa.org.uk/rulings/electronic-arts-ltd-a23-1222185-electronic-arts-ltd.html) for the failure to disclose Loot Boxes in advertising.

[36] Electronic Arts (https://www.asa.org.uk/rulings/electronic-arts-ltd-a24-1239057-electronic-arts-ltd.html).

[37] https://commission.europa.eu/document/download/2cd696bd-6a6c-4012-8257-e72b423346be_en?filename=Commission%20letter%20to%20ISFE%20EGDF%20on%20loot%20boxes%20from%20September%202022.pdf.

1. Belgium

51 The main framework for gambling in Belgium is the Gaming and Betting Act of 7.5.1999 (**GBA**) which regulates 'games of chance'. The Belgian Gaming Commission (**BGC**) is responsible for the enforcement of the GBA.

52 Under the GBA, a 'game of chance' is defined as:

any game whereby a bet of any kind that is placed leads to the loss of this bet by at least one of the players, or a win of any kind for at least one of the players or organisers of the game, and whereby chance may be a secondary element in the course of the game, indication of the winner or determination of the size of winnings.

53 Therefore, any Loot Box needs to be a 'game', include a 'bet' and lead to a 'chance' of a 'win' and/or 'loss'. The **BGC's report in 2018** on Loot Boxes applied this test to Loot Boxes found in four games, *Overwatch, Star Wars Battlefront II, FIFA 2018* and *Counter-Strike: Global Offensive.* Looking at each limb in turn:

(a) **Game.** Although there is no definitive definition of a 'game', leading legal literature refers to a 'contract of chance' whereby two parties enter into a transaction with an uncertain outcome (according to the rules of that game). In any event, the opinion of the BGC was that a Loot Box did constitute a 'game'.
(b) **Bet.** A 'game of chance' also requires a bet, wager or stake to be made. In other words, a purely 'free' Loot Box would fail under this limb. The bet does not need to be money, but it must be possible to attribute a value to this wager. BGC expanded on this further, setting out that purchases with either real-world money or Hard Currency would constitute a 'wager', but that Soft Currency would not.
(c) **Chance.** 'Chance' will often be present as the player is usually not aware of the contents of the Loot Box. In order to fail this limb, a player would need to know what they would 'win' by opening a Loot Box (which has been seen in some games, such as FIFA's Preview Packs).
(d) **Win and/or loss.** The GBA sets out that any loss by at least one player or any wins by at least one player (or the organiser of the game) is sufficient for this condition to be met. The 'win' does not have to be monetary and can be '*of any kind*'. Therefore a Loot Box 'win' of a cosmetic or an advantage over another player would meet this definition.

54 Therefore, following the 2018 report, it is not possible to offer paid Loot Boxes in compliance with the GBA. Although technically not banned, there is **no specific 'game of chance' license** offered to cover Loot Boxes, hence their de facto illegality.

55 In 2024, following a workshop with stakeholders (academia, gambling regulators across Europe and the industry),[38] the BGC set out that a combination of EU consumer law and **self-regulation would likely be the most suitable avenue** of regulation for Loot Boxes:

The law of the European Union, in particular consumer protection law, seems to be the most appropriate instrument to implement the substance of these rules. Lastly, tools of self-regulation can tailor this framework to the needs of specific products and industries.[39]

---

[38] https://gamingcommission.be/en/workshop-paid-random-items.
[39] Workshop – paid random items report – FPS Justice Gaming Commission: https://gamingcommission.paddlecms.net/sites/default/files/2024-12/Workshop%2020240130%20-%20Report%20(EN).pdf.

2. The Netherlands

The **Betting and Gambling Act 2021 (BGA)** prohibits the offering and promotion of "games of chance" in the Netherlands without holding the correct license. 56

A 'game of chance' requires **two conditions to be met under the BGA.**[40] The first is that there must be an opportunity for participants to '*compete for prizes or premiums*' and that the winners of these prizes or premiums are '*designated by means of any calculation of probably over which over which the players are generally unable to exercise a dominant influence*'. Notably, there is no requirement for a stake, wager or bet in order to meet the definition of 'game of chance'. 57

The **concept of** "*prizes or premiums*" has been subject to little case law and there is little further explanation of this in the legislation. However, the Dutch Betting and Gaming Tax Act (**DBGTA**), as well as the courts, have however approached the topic of 'virtual goods'. The DBGTA sets out that '*all goods to which an economic value can be attached, which accrue to the participants in the games of chance by virtue of their participation*'.[41] The explanatory notes of the DBGTA also explains that the definition of 'prizes' is '*very broad*'. 58

The Netherlands gaming authority (Kansspelautoriteit or 'KSA') in 2018 released its **'Guide on Assessing Games of Chance'** (*Leidraad beoordeling kanspelen)*[42] which helps the KSA assess whether a game falls in scope of the BGA. The guide indicates that tradability of items awarded from a Loot Box is necessary for said item to be considered a 'prize' under the BGA. 59

Whether or not a Loot Box could constitute a 'game of chance' was put to the test in 2019 when **The Hague District Court** ruled that Electronic Arts was offering 'games of chance' in *FIFA 19*[43] via its FUT Packs. In this ruling, the District Court set out that the internal virtual game economy could be regarded as a real economy, and therefore the value of digital items had real economic value and therefore would constitute '*prizes or premiums*'. This was due to the fact that the football players awarded in FUT Packs could be traded for FUT Coins within the game – i.e. that there was tradability and "supply and demand" within the game economy. An additional indication of real economic value was the existence of an unauthorised 'black market' outside of the game where FUT Coins could be traded for FUT Points, which in turn could be converted into euros. In the District Court's view, the first condition of the 'game of chance' test was met. 60

The District Court also set out that the players could not exercise any "*dominant influence*" on winning a prize from FUT Packs – i.e. it was based on chance. Therefore, the second condition of the test was also met according to the District Court. As noted earlier, the way a Loot Box is acquired (whether paid or free) has no impact under the Dutch test for a 'game of chance'. 61

However, the **ruling of the District Court was later overturned.**[44] The Court of Appeal's decision hinged on the fact that the FUT Packs were part of a wider 'game of skill' and not a standalone 'game of chance'. The Court of Appeal took a practical approach and said it was important to look at how the game is played *in practice* by the majority of players. The Court also highlighted that – in the case of *FIFA 19* – that the 'chance' and wider 'game of skill' aspect could not be separated. 62

---

[40] Article 1(1)(a) BGA.

[41] Article 3(2) of the DBGTA.

[42] https://kansspelautoriteit.nl/over-ons/publicaties/regels-leidraden/overige-regels/leidraad-beoordeling/.

[43] https://kansspelautoriteit.nl/aanpak-misstanden/sanctiebesluiten/electronic-arts/.

[44] https://www.raadvanstate.nl/uitspraken/@130150/202005769-1-a3/.

63 Although this decision was favourable to Electronic Arts, it no doubt does leave **questions unanswered** – because the KSA fell at the first question as to whether or not FUT Packs are a 'game of chance'; the limb regarding whether or not the prizes from the FUT Packs would be considered '*prizes or premiums*' was left unexplored. Loot Boxes could also – at least in theory – be considered 'games of chance' in some video games; this would need to be assessed on a case-by-case basis.

64 Games companies should therefore ensure their wider game contains a **sufficient level of 'skill'** to counterbalance any 'chance' present in Loot Boxes, as well as ensuring that the majority of players only engage with Loot Boxes as part of the wider game.

65 Despite this, it appears that the **Dutch consumer authority** ('Autoriteit Consument & Market' or 'ACM') has turned towards consumer law in order to further regulate Loot Boxes. In its non-paper for the EU Fitness Check on Digital Fairness,[45] the ACM requested that an EU-wide prohibition be considered for Loot Boxes, specifically in relation to children.

3. Austria

66 The legal status of Loot Boxes under gambling legislation in Austria has been under considerable debate, which has predominantly played out in several court cases.

67 However the highest court to rule in Austria on the matter so far has been the **Vienna Higher Regional Court,**[46] which heard an appeal from the Vienna Regional Court for Civil Matters.[47] The Higher Court in this instance dismissed a player's lawsuit against Electronic Arts, determining that FIFA's FUT Packs did not qualify as a game of chance under Austrian law, primarily because of the player's intention to use any FUT Pack prizes (i.e. player cards) for in-game use and not for any 'cash-out' purpose.

68 There is currently no Supreme Court ruling on this matter (although the Vienna Higher Regional Court has permitted the above case to be appealed), and with **several court cases related to Loot Boxes pending**, it is likely that uncertainty in relation to Loot Boxes under Austrian gambling law will continue.

---

[45] See Section 3.2: https://www.acm.nl/en/publications/acms-response-eu-fitness-check-digital-fairness.

[46] 13 R 30/24p – 30.09.2024 – Denis Delic v EA Swiss Sarl and Sony Interactive Entertainment Network Europe Limited.

[47] 66 cg 11/22f-51 – 19.12.2023 – Denis Delic v EA Swiss Sarl and Sony Interactive Entertainment Network Europe Limited.

§ 27
Digital Items – Intellectual Property

Bibliography: Borges/Hilber, BeckOK IT-Recht, 19th edn, Munich 2025; Daum, Outfits, Coins und Tools im Metaverse: Wie übertrage ich digitale Assets von einer Welt in die andere?, DSRITB 2022, p. 345; Daum, Multiplayer Games und Virtuelle Gegenstände, InTeR 2022, p. 142; Daum, Die Plattform-Ökonomie von Online-Games und der Anspruch auf "angemessene Vergütung", ZfPC 2023, p. 250; Hugenholtz/Quintais, Copyright and Artificial Creation: Does EU Copyright Law Protect AI-Assisted Output?, IIC 2021, 1190; Lober/Trunk, Lootboxen im Regulierungsdschungel – Überblick über den bestehenden Rechtsrahmen MMR 2024 p. 651; Söbbing/Schwarz, Wie kann man einen virtuellen Gegenstand in einem Metaverse erwerben? CR 2024, 346; Stieper/Klumpp/Singer/Herrler (eds), Staudinger BGB – Buch 1: Allgemeiner Teil, Cologne 2021.

A. Introduction ... 1
B. Legislative Framework under Intellectual Property Law ... 5
C. Properties of Digital items ... 6
I. Origin of a Digital item ... 10
1. Sources ... 11
a) *In-House Creation* ... 11
b) *User-Generated Content* ... 13
c) *Third-Party IP* ... 17
2. Impact on IP ... 20
a) *Copyright* ... 21
b) *Design Rights* ... 26
II. Transferability ... 29
III. Centralised or De-Centralised Administration ... 42
IV. Uniqueness ... 53

A. Introduction

As with many legally relevant topics surrounding the digital economy, the video game industry has been ahead of the curve in relation to digital items and their interplay with intellectual property. This chapter has been structured with key intellectual property concepts in mind, such as the origin of digital items and how that may impact the IP rights attached to it. 1

Outside the industry, the surge of interest in non-fungible tokens (**NFTs**) in 2021 catalysed a broader discourse, bringing longstanding questions around the ownership, transferability, and legal nature of digital items into sharper focus. While NFTs represent only one subset of virtual property and the hype surrounding them seems to have waned, their emergence into mainstream discourse has prompted renewed scrutiny of more established forms of in-game content as well — ranging from character skins and cosmetic assets to player-tradable goods and competitive advantages purchasable through real-world currency. 2

For European legal counsel, the analysis must account not only for national private law regimes, but also for the framework of relevant EU directives, including those on intellectual property – the focus of this chapter. 3

As a starting point for such an overview, the term "digital item", depending on context, may mean substantially different things. 4

B. Legislative Framework under Intellectual Property Law

For the **Representation** of a digital item (see previous chapter for the definition), the most practically relevant legal norms are those dealing with **intellectual property**, in 5 particular copyright. These have been discussed in chapters 13 to 15 of this Handbook but are further explored in section C below, particularly in relation to the origin of digital items. Provided that the game's or game platform's terms of service are sufficiently clear concerning the permitted use and potential compensation and furthermore do not pre-emptively transfer rights in future works, but only provide a framework for a future transfer of such works upon upload, it is possible to collect the necessary rights in UGC for use in digital items.[1]

C. Properties of Digital items

6 A central difficulty in any legal or even informal discussion surrounding digital items – be it among colleagues, clients, or regulators – is the persistent misconception that there exists a singular legal construct of *the* digital item. In reality, this notion is fundamentally flawed. Digital items are not monolithic, and their legal character cannot be universally prescribed. Their nature, function, and associated legal challenges vary significantly depending on the technical architecture of the game and the intended player interactions. Consequently, each digital item must be considered within the specific context of the individual title in which it appears, rather than in abstraction.

7 To bring analytical structure to this intellectual property complexity, we propose a classification framework grounded in three interdependent dimensions that commonly influence the legal treatment of digital items. These are:

- **Origin** – What is the origin of the Representation of an item, including whether it is developer-created, procedurally generated, licensed in as part of an established third-party franchise or user-generated content ("**UGC**"). This characteristic is instrumental to determining the challenges associated with initial rights clearance by the developer and what permanence the item may have (e.g. if rights are being licensed in).
- **Transferability** – The extent to which the item can be traded or gifted between users after the initial acquisition, and the mechanics and limitations of such transfers – the vast majority of digital items in video games are non-transferable and there will be no functionality that permits transfers. For example, in-game currencies (see previous chapter) – which can be optionally purchased with real world money in some games and then exchanged for other digital content in that game – cannot be exchanged back into real world money nor are they transferable, at least not in the vast majority of games. Transferability rather is a characteristic commonly associated with items such as NFTs.
- **Uniqueness** – Whether the item has a persistent, unique identity (e.g. a token ID), which may affect rights of attribution, enforcement, or recovery; uniqueness is commonly associated with NFTs.

8 It is essential to understand that these dimensions do not function in isolation, but instead influence each other in meaningful ways. The path to acquisition of the digital item is also relevant, albeit more closely interplays with consumer protection law so is discussed in the previous chapter.

9 This framework does not aim to impose a rigid taxonomy, but rather to serve as a heuristic for European legal practitioners navigating the patchwork of relevant doctrines across intellectual property law and contract law. By segmenting the analysis along

[1] See Cour d'Appel de Paris, decision of 21 October 2022, RG 20/15768, confirmed by French Cour de Cassation, decision of 23 October, 2024, G 23–13.738.

these axes, we seek to move beyond generalised statements and instead offer a nuanced, context-sensitive perspective – one that recognises the legal heterogeneity of digital items and the importance of their embeddedness in specific technical and commercial environments.

I. Origin of a Digital item

As any asset in a game, the Representation of a digital item has to be cleared from an IP perspective. 10

1. Sources

a) In-House Creation

The most straightforward case arises when the Representation is wholly created by a member of the game studio's internal development team. In other words, an artist or a group of artists creates an image, a 3D model, a custom sound effect, an animation, a virtual map to explore etc. 11

In such instances, the Representation is typically protected under copyright law, assuming the required threshold of originality is met[2], and the relevant rights are either held directly by the employer under national employment law[3], or validly assigned via contract. This scenario introduces essentially the same challenges as any other inbound licensing for a game project does under applicable IP law.[4] 12

b) User-Generated Content

Matters become considerably more complex, however, in relation to UGC. Historically, UGC has been primarily associated with PC gaming, where open architecture and modding culture have long enabled players to develop and share their own content. Increasingly, though, developers and publishers are seeking to bring UGC into more controlled environments – including console platforms – by facilitating uploads through curated platforms such as *mod.io* or integrating external creations from services like *moddb* or the *Steam Workshop* via licensing agreements. 13

In some cases, developers proactively curate community-generated content for formal integration into the game, either by direct commission or via competitions and reward programmes. A notable example is Valve's approach in *Counter-Strike 2*, where community-designed weapon skins are reviewed, selected, and implemented by the developer, with creators receiving substantial financial compensation – often exceeding what full-time industry professionals might earn. 14

The legal implications differ significantly depending on whether the UGC is curated or freely distributed. In curated models, where the developer selects and integrates community content into the official version of the game, it is generally possible to structure rights acquisition similarly to contracts with freelance creators. Such models allow for a higher degree of editorial oversight and legal predictability. By contrast, *open UGC ecosystems* – such as those envisioned by proponents of the "metaverse"—allow players to create, distribute, and sometimes even monetise content with little or no oversight 15

---

[2] It is clear from the overall context of the Berne Convention, in particular from its Art. 2 para. 5 and 8, that the protection of works art presupposes that they are individual intellectual creations.

[3] In some European countries, there are statutory licenses, e.g. in Germany for software code (§ 69b Copyright Act). However, most countries rely on the transfer of rights in the employment contract.

[4] See → Ch. 13–16 of this handbook.

from the game provider. This raises intricate questions around authorship, licensing and liability, especially when content creators reside in multiple jurisdictions and do not operate as professionals.

16 Sourcing the Representation of a future digital item from the player community adds an additional layer of legal complexity due to consumer protection laws being applicable.[5]

c) *Third-Party IP*

17 Licensing an established franchise for your game offers a significant advantage in terms of immediate brand recognition and a pre-existing audience. The main pro is the **instantaneous attention and built-in fanbase** that comes with a well-known intellectual property (**IP**). This obviously does not just apply when basing an entire game on a well-known IP, but also when only a set of items is introduced through digital items as a cross-licensing deal.

18 However, the benefits of licensing are often counterbalanced by the significant drawback of **limited license durations and restrictive terms** as well as **substantial license fees**. The main con is that these licenses are typically not perpetual and come with a defined expiry date, creating a ticking clock for development and market saturation. This can lead to rushed development cycles to maximise the window of opportunity, potentially compromising game quality. Moreover, license agreements often include stringent creative controls from the IP holder, limiting developer freedom and potentially stifling innovation. There can also be substantial upfront costs and ongoing royalties, impacting profitability.

19 The eventual expiration of the license means the game, even if successful, can no longer be sold or updated containing the branded item, essentially leaving the developer with a previously well-received game that might lose appeal for new users and cause open conflict with existing users. This can necessitate a complete re-branding or the abandonment of the project, posing a significant long-term risk.

2. Impact on IP

20 Intellectual Property Rights are discussed in-depth in → Ch. 13–17 of this handbook. The below should therefore only be seen as supplemental aspects that are of particular relevance for digital items.

a) *Copyright*

21 One critical issue is **copyright eligibility**. While it is broadly accepted that Representations of digital items can be protected under copyright law if they meet the relevant standard of originality, some such items – particularly those with a functional or utilitarian design – may fall short of this threshold.

22 This is particularly relevant where the item's appearance originates with generative AI[6], it is procedurally generated or based on templates.

23 Moreover, EU law and certain national regimes do not extend related rights (e.g., those for photographs or simple graphical representations) to content generated solely

---

[5] For an overview of European consumer protection law that may be applicable to digital items, see the previous chapter and → Ch. 25 of this handbook.

[6] Output wholly generated by an AI system without any human intellectual effort is excluded from copyright protection, see Hugenholtz/Quintais IIC 2021, 1190, (1196).

by software processes. Thus, the legal protectability of digital items often depends not only on their aesthetics, but also on the creative process behind them.

The **acquisition of rights by the game developer** is another area requiring careful structuring. When dealing with in-house teams or professional freelancers, comprehensive contractual arrangements can be negotiated. These allow for specific and enforceable rights transfers and are generally insulated from consumer rights scrutiny. By contrast, when content is generated by end users under standard terms of service, rights assignments must be crafted in ways that comply with consumer protection law, including rules on transparency, fairness, and jurisdiction. This presents additional challenges, as platforms must often contend with diverging national copyright regimes and the cross-border enforceability of choice-of-law clauses. 24

The situation is further complicated in practice by the **international composition of development teams and user bases**. Co-authorship across jurisdictions can give rise to significant conflicts of law, particularly between systems based on continental European *droit d'auteur* and the more economic-rights-oriented copyright regimes of common law jurisdictions. Concepts such as "work for hire" (common in US law[7]) or Germany's simplified collection of licenses from co-creators for certain types of collaborative works[8] do not always translate across borders. The enforceability of contractual provisions governing IP ownership, royalty waivers, or exploitative rights – especially when entered into by non-legal professionals – remains an area of legal uncertainty. 25

b) Design Rights

Finally, some developers have explored **design rights** as an additional or alternative means of protecting digital items, particularly where copyright eligibility is uncertain. Despite the relatively low cost of registration and the potential breadth of protection, the use of design law remains limited. 26

In all cases, the **novelty requirement** under EU design law must be carefully observed. This necessitates integrating the design registration process into the game's development timeline, especially where early previews or community teasers risk compromising future applications. Failure to do so may leave valuable assets unprotected and open to exploitation by third parties, including unauthorised manufacturers who, in some instances, have even secured design registrations themselves to exclude others from the merchandising market. 27

Ultimately, the legal character of a digital item begins with its creation. Whether developer-designed, algorithmically generated, or user-submitted, the origin of the item determines not only who owns it, but what kind of protection – and legal certainty – it can realistically enjoy. 28

[7] Section 101 of the US Copyright Act defines a "work made for hire" as a) a work prepared by an employee within the scope of his or her employment or b) a work specially ordered or commissioned for use as a contribution to a collective work, or as a part of a motion picture or other audiovisual work, or as a translation, or as a supplementary work, or as a compilation, or as an instructional text, or as a test, or as answer material for a test, or as an atlas, if the parties expressly agree in a written instrument signed by them that the work shall be considered a work made for hire.

[8] See sections 69b and 89 of the German copyright act (Urheberrechtsgesetz).

II. Transferability

29 The question of if or how a digital item can be transferred is a central aspect for its legal evaluation. This is intrinsically linked to how the item is bound to a player and the legal and technical regulations governing this tie.

30 The vast majority of games that include optional purchases of digital items to use in the game do not allow transferability, since the underlying license for the digital content will often be limited and subject to restrictions. There will also often be technical bars on transferring digital items to other users or accounts. Fundamentally, in most games digital items are designed to be used only by the user who acquired them.

31 In some situations, users may attempt to evade technical restrictions – for example by attempting to sell or transfer whole accounts that contain digital items to other users. Again, this in the vast majority of cases would be considered a breach of the game's license terms.

32 Beyond any applicable license terms, the legal treatment of digital items is complex, partly because digital items are generally not considered physical objects due to their lack of physical form[9] (and rules can vary under Member State law); they are often viewed as electronic data[10]. Consequently, traditional rules regarding the transfer of ownership of physical goods are not directly applicable[11].

33 This is why transactions involving digital items are frequently classified legally as the purchase of rights or other objects[12]. As mentioned above, this means that acquiring a digital item often involves receiving a license or a right to use the digital content, rather than obtaining ownership of a physical copy[13].

34 A key legal issue related to transferability concerns European Union copyright law, specifically the distribution right and the doctrine of exhaustion. Video games are considered complex works, comprising not just a computer program, but also significant creative elements like graphics, sound, and story[14].

35 These elements mean video games are protected by the general copyright Directive 2001/29/CE (InfoSoc Directive), although Directive 2009/24/CE (Software Directive) is a *lex specialis* for the computer program component.[15] Under the Infosoc Directive, the exhaustion of the distribution right applies only to tangible articles[16]. The online provision or downloading of a digital game is classified as a "communication to the public", a right that is not subject to exhaustion under this directive[17].

36 While the UsedSoft decision related to Directive 2009/24/CE found that exhaustion could apply to downloaded software licenses upon a "first sale or transfer of owner-

[9] Under German law, they are not "Sachen" (physical objects) pursuant to § 90 BGB). Staudinger Stieper 2021 S.BGB 90 Rn 12–19; Söbbing/Schwarz CR 2024 pp. 346–352.

[10] Stieper in Klumpp/Singer/Herrler BGB § 90 mn. 12–19; Söbbing/Schwarz CR 2024 pp. 346–352.

[11] Stieper in Klumpp/Singer/Herrler BGB § 90 mn. 12–19.

[12] For Germany, see § 453 BGB. Söbbing/Schwarz CR 2024 pp. 346–352; Hilber in BeckOK IT-Recht, BGB § 453 mn. 5–8.

[13] Söbbing/Schwarz CR 2024, 346–352.

[14] Opinion of Advocate General Bot delivered on 24 April 2012 in re UsedSoft GmbH v Oracle International Corp.

[15] Opinion of Advocate General Bot delivered on 24 April 2012 in re UsedSoft GmbH v Oracle International Corp.

[16] Opinion of Advocate General Bot delivered on 24 April 2012 in re UsedSoft GmbH v Oracle International Corp.

[17] Opinion of Advocate General Bot delivered on 24 April 2012 in re UsedSoft GmbH v Oracle International Corp.

ship"[18, 19], this is specific to computer programs and does not override the application of Directive 2001/29/CE to the other protected elements of a complex work like a video game. The Tom Kabinet ruling on e-books, where the creative content was deemed the essential element, suggests a similar approach for video games where the intellectual and artistic creation is central[20].

This view was confirmed by the highest French court in a decision of October 23, 2024, in which it confirmed that the terms of the Steam Subscriber Agreement prohibiting the transfer of digital content on Steam were validly enforceable under French law.[21] These terms do not just govern full games but notably also in-game digital items. 37

Furthermore, even rights related to data, such as the right to data portability under GDPR Article 20 or potential rights under the Data Act, primarily relate to the user's personal data or data generated through product usage[22, 23]. These rights do not necessarily entitle a user to transfer the digital item itself between different platforms or game world. The Data Act, for example, is generally limited to physical products, and data resulting from a software process might not be covered[24]. 38

Technical and contractual restrictions on transferability may in certain cases be a strategic choice by platform operators to maintain closed ecosystems. Closed ecosystems allow operators to track all payment streams and earn revenue from the sale of assets on their platform[25]. Permitting transferability to other platforms could make it harder for operators to control content usage and participate in transactions occurring elsewhere. The ability to transfer assets between different game worlds or hardware platforms faces significant technical hurdles due to a lack of common standards and, importantly, legal restrictions imposed by providers who want to keep their worlds "sealed off"[26]. 39

However, while it may be tempting for self-described consumer advocates to criticise such transfer restrictions as unfair, it is worth noting that the default legal situation as intended by law is that intellectual property rights grant the owner a legal monopoly over their subject. Likewise, civil law typically makes any transfer of an agreement for the provision of services dependent on the consent of the service provider. Accordingly, terms that prohibit the transfer of user accounts or Entitlements related to such accounts really do not impose a deviation from the legal norm but merely confirm the statutory status quo. 40

Even if not explicitly presented to the user as unique, many digital items managed on centralised databases are internally identifiable, allowing operators to track their history for purposes like fraud prevention. NFTs specifically highlight this aspect of non-replaceability. Beyond purchases, players may also acquire digital items through other means, such as receiving them as gifts. 41

---

[18] CJEU C-128–11 – Oracle vs Usedsoft.

[19] Opinion of Advocate General Bot delivered on 24 April 2012 in re UsedSoft GmbH v Oracle International Corp.

[20] Opinion of Advocate General Bot delivered on 24 April 2012 in re UsedSoft GmbH v Oracle International Corp.

[21] Arret de la Cour de Cassation, première chambre civile, du 23 Octobre 2024, Pourvoi no G 23–13.738, Arret no 555 FS-D.

[22] Daum DSRITB 2022, 345.

[23] Daum InTeR 2022, 142–147.

[24] Daum InTeR 2022, 142–147.

[25] Daum ZfPC 2023, 263.

[26] Daum InTeR 2022, 142–147; Lober/Trunk MMR 2024, 651.

III. Centralised or De-Centralised Administration

42 An official solution for the transferability of digital items can be developed specifically for the game, based on a central platform that supports a variety of games, or decentralised and buzzword-friendly on a blockchain basis.

43 The arguments for and against a **game-specific solution** are ultimately the same as for any other important middleware. A solution that is completely controlled by the game developer has the highest development costs, but has the advantage that it can be adapted and expanded according to individual requirements.

44 An **external platform** such as administration via Steamworks[27] or mod.io[28] has less flexibility, but has already internalised the not inconsiderable development effort. The use of such pre-existing platform tools sometimes makes the inclusion of certain features in a game possible in the first place.[29]

45 The management of the ownership of in-game items via the **blockchain** has been the subject of much discussion, especially under the heading of NFTs.

46 Given the target audience of this book, there is probably no need to explain in detail what a blockchain[30] actually is. It is currently being proposed by some market participants as the future of virtual asset management.[31]

47 However, it is precisely the core promise of decentralised administration that the blockchain-based products actually in widespread use today fail to deliver. It also seems at least doubtful whether a truly decentralised technology is at the end of the current development.

48 The blockchain servers that regulate the ownership of virtual objects run in the background on distributed systems. However, interaction with these servers today almost always takes place de facto via centralised interfaces of a few companies, such as by selling API access[32] to a node of the Ethereum blockchain[33], which they operate as a service. The majority of the decentralised applications or DApps working on this basis use the services of just a handful of companies to interact with the blockchain. The client APIs through which end users access the system do nothing to verify the blockchain status or the authenticity of the responses from these interface companies.[34]

49 Trading in NFTs also currently takes place via centralised marketplaces. The delisting of a virtual asset on a major marketplace such as results in its economic insignificance, regardless of whether it still exists in principle on the blockchain. Due to its market power, objects removed from OpenSEA even disappear from users' wallets.[35] Whether OpenSEA in particular will retain the same central position for trading NFTs in the medium term is questionable; however, based on past experience, it seems at least likely that there will be market concentrations among interface operators and marketplaces in the future, which will de facto counteract the distributed management of NFTs running in the background.

50 In addition to interfaces and marketplaces, there is a third aspect of NFTs that leads to a concentration that does not do justice to the ideal of the distributed database. Due

---

[27] https://partner.steamgames.com/doc/features/microtransactions#5.
[28] https://mod.io/.
[29] E.g. with Arma III, https://www.bohemia.net/blog/arma3-steam-dev-blog.
[30] https://de.wikipedia.org/wiki/Blockchain.
[31] E.g. Ubisoft, https://news.ubisoft.com/en-us/article/kujZ0Njdh6cojf6rzlEN0/ubisofts-vision-for-blockchain?isSso=true&refreshStatus=noLoginData.
[32] API=Application Programming Interface.
[33] https://de.wikipedia.org/wiki/Ethereum.
[34] https://moxie.org/2022/01/07/web3-first-impressions.html.
[35] https://moxie.org/2022/01/07/web3-first-impressions.html.

to the cost of decentralised storage, only the absolute minimum of data is ever stored on the blockchain. In today's art NFTs, this may include a URL that refers to an Internet address on which an image is stored, for example. However, the actual image file is then stored on a classic web server, e.g. from AWS, not on the blockchain.[36]

On a positive note, a rights holder who feels infringed by an NFT does not have to expend energy on deleting it from the blockchain – they have other centralised points of attack through which they can sink the NFT into irrelevance, even if it still formally exists on the blockchain. **51**

The extent to which the actual implementations of NFTs will come closer to their ideals in the future remains to be seen; whether it can ever actually be economical or desirable for every user to mirror the entire database of ownership and not access the blockchain via the API of a central service is at least doubtful. This is all the more true as even the major proponents of blockchain within the games industry consider it necessary for large, established market players to regulate access.[37] **52**

IV. Uniqueness

From a civil contract law perspective, it is also relevant whether a virtual object is uniquely defined in the game logic or freely interchangeable. NFTs, for example, already bear the "non-fungibility" in their name. The uniqueness of a NFT isn't necessarily their Representation (e.g. the IP in the visual representation of the NFT), but the string of metadata attached to it. **53**

However, this uniqueness is not a special feature of NFTs. Virtual objects that are managed on classic centralised databases can of course also be unique in that one defined instance of such an item can only be associated with one user account at a time. **54**

Even if the uniqueness is not emphasised in the user interface, many database systems for digital items not only store internally for fraud prevention purposes that, for example, player X has a virtual weapon of a certain type, but it is also possible to trace back that this instance of the item was in player Y's inventory up to a certain point in time and, with a little effort, even that player Z fired the decisive shot in a major esports tournament with precisely this one instance of the weapon. **55**

It is to be expected that such "unique" virtual objects will continue to gain in importance in the coming years, regardless of the technology on which they are based. **56**

Even when a digital item is not "unique" it can still hold subjective value to the player. For completeness, these concepts of value must not be confused with 'monetary value': the vast majority of digital items in video games does not possess monetary value – further explored in the previous chapter. **57**

Even digital items that are purely cosmetic in nature, i.e. have no properties that make them practically advantageous in the game, can have a subjective "utility value" consisting of the ability to express one's personality in the game towards one's peers via a particular Representation. **58**

Anyone who finds this disconcerting may ask themselves whether they have ever spent money on a product in the physical world that had a higher value to them than **59**

---

[36] https://blog.mollywhite.net/blockchains-are-not-what-they-say/.

[37] "First and foremost, established industry actors need to act as gatekeepers and create the conditions for trust by implementing this technology in safe, familiar environments, and in ways that make sense both for the medium and ultimately for the players." https://news.ubisoft.com/en-us/article/kujZ0Njdh6cojf6rzlEN0/ubisofts-vision-for-blockchain?isSso=true&refreshStatus=noLoginData.

a functionally identical competitor's product due to its appealing design, the prestigious brand printed on it or the image otherwise associated with it.

60 The "exchange value" of a virtual object is less difficult to convey to an uninvolved party than its "utility value" – although as explained in section C III above is less common in the video games industry. This is probably one of the reasons why reporting outside of specialised media tends to focus on their reported sales prices.

§ 28
Enforcement

Bibliography: Communication from the Commission to the European Parliament, the Council and the European Economic and Social Committee, 'Guidance on certain aspects of Directive 2004/48/EC of the European Parliament and of the Council on the enforcement of Intellectual Property Rights', COM (2017) 708 final, 21; EUIPO, 'Study on dynamic blocking injunctions in the European Union', March 2021; European Commission Directorate-General for Communications Networks, 'Overview of the legal framework of notice-and-action procedures in Member States' SMART 2016/0039 – Final report, 2018

A. IP enforcement by video game companies 7
I. Direct action against infringers 9
1. Identifying the infringer 9
2. First step: cease and desist 16
3. Civil proceedings 19
a) Ex-parte or inter-parte proceedings 21
b) Proceedings on the merits or preliminary injunctions 24
4. Criminal proceedings 29
II. Intermediaries and blocking injunctions 35
1. Definitions 37
2. Blocking injunctions in theory 46
3. Blocking injunctions in practice 51
a) Applicants 51
b) Targets 53
c) Intellectual property rights 56
d) Evidence required 58
e) Implementing the blocking 60
III. Focus on hosting provider's liability 63
1. General considerations 64
2. Streaming and let's play 69

B. Enforcement against video game companies 73
I. Consumer law enforcement 76
1. National authorities and the CPC 77
2. Consumer protection organisations 85
3. Players 90
a) Friction areas 90
b) In court and out of court 94
II. Dealing with law enforcement 99

'Enforcement' is a very broad legal term. It is defined by the Cambridge Dictionary as 'the process of making people obey a law or rule, or making a particular situation happen or be accepted'. We have chosen to define 'enforcement', for the purpose of this chapter, as all **actions taken by a rightsholder** to uphold their rights (for example, intellectual property rights) and obligations (for example, consumer law obligations). 1

A classic **example** of enforcement would be an IP infringement claim brought by a video game company against a competitor releasing a highly similar game (a 'copycat' or 'clone' game) with the intent of stopping the infringement, preventing further violations and remedying the prejudice caused. 2

In a world where IP rights are considered as some of the most valuable assets of a video game company, it is simply not enough to merely secure these rights (for example, filing a trademark or a registered design). This is just the initial step in safeguarding one's business. If these rights are filed, but not actually enforced, they hold little value. Their enforcement is **crucial** to the success of their holder, especially in a creative industry. 3

Reflecting on our experience as outside counsel for video game companies, we look in this chapter at the **two sides** of enforcement: when a video game company enforces its 4 rights against a third party and when it finds itself in the opposite situation, i.e., when it becomes the target of such enforcement by a third party (e.g., a regulator or a player).

5 This chapter focuses primarily on **intellectual property**. Yet it also addresses other areas of law generating rights and obligations, such as consumer, contractual, and even criminal law.

6 It is divided into **two sections**: The first section explores the distinctive characteristics of offensive enforcement strategies employed by video game companies to assert their rights against third parties. The second section seeks to highlight the diversity of sources from which enforcement actions may arise against video game companies.

A. IP enforcement by video game companies

7 This section goes over the **different actors**, along the value chain of video game distribution, which rightsholders may turn against to enforce their rights, from direct infringers to intermediaries.

8 Some key features of the sector, including the weight of digital distribution, the global nature of games' distribution and the **complex nature** of video games, combining multiple intellectual property rights, may affect a company's enforcement and need to be kept in mind throughout.

I. Direct action against infringers

1. Identifying the infringer

9 With the ever-growing share of digital distribution over tangible copies and the development of mobile gaming, **clone games** are a common concern for the industry.

10 The most straightforward approach consists in taking action directly against the **infringer**, who is responsible for developing and/or marketing the game. However, identifying the infringer for enforcement purposes is often a first major hurdle faced by rightsholders.

11 While all websites should include legal notices identifying the publisher, obviously few infringers include their contact information. Likewise, most common app stores require the disclosure of the publisher details and/or the developer's basic identity. However, the publicly available information is often **lacklustre**, merely mentioning a company name, and sometimes address in an exotic jurisdiction.

12 If the rightsholder manages to identify the infringer's website, **Whois** can be a helpful tool to attempt to obtain more information about the infringer. Whois information refers to the publicly accessible data about the registered owners of a domain name. When someone registers a domain name, they are required to provide certain contact and administrative details. This information is stored in a central database and can be queried using the 'Whois' protocol or through various online Whois lookup tools. However, due to privacy concerns, many registrars now offer privacy protection services that mask the registrant's personal information in the public Whois database.

13 In addition, website publishers may use various intermediaries to conceal their identity. Reverse proxy services, such as those offered by Cloudflare, centralise all incoming and outgoing connections to and from a website in order to protect the website against potential attacks. However, this has the effect of masking the IP address and identity of the actual host of a website, thereby anonymising it. These reverse **proxy services** are often slow to answer disclosure requests, if they ever answer.

The most effective method remains carrying out detailed research online, **recouping information** from sources such as websites' terms of services, games' copyright notices, privacy policies, trade registries and Whois information. 14

Once the target has been identified, **pre-litigation** may start. 15

2. First step: cease and desist

Most actions will start with a **cease and desist letter**. A cease and desist is a formal written notice sent by one party to another, explaining the rights owned, the alleged infringing actions and demanding that they stop now and in the future an identified action which the sending party believes to be unlawful. In simple terms, it is an official warning telling someone to stop doing something that could get them into legal trouble. 16

A cease and desist is often a **mandatory step** before initiating a litigation. Indeed, many jurisdictions require the claimant to demonstrate that they have attempted to contact the defendant but were unable to resolve the issue out of court. 17

A cease and desist can also be an effective and cost-efficient tool to put an end to some infringing behaviour, leveraging the **threat** of further action to encourage compliance. 18

3. Civil proceedings

For most video game infringements in the EU, **civil litigation** is the primary and most flexible route, offering direct remedies for the rightsholder. 19

Broadly speaking, the claimant may consider **ex-parte or inter-parte** proceedings, as well as proceedings on the **merits or summary** proceedings. 20

a) Ex-parte or inter-parte proceedings

Ex parte proceedings refer to legal actions taken by a rightsholder without the presence of the alleged infringer. Such proceedings are often used when there is a risk that evidence of infringement, such as unauthorised copies of a game, evidence of source code copying, or accounting documents might be concealed, altered, or destroyed if the alleged infringer is alerted in advance. Courts in the EU may grant ex parte orders to protect the rightsholder's interests and ensure effective enforcement of intellectual property rights. 21

However, these proceedings are subject to strict legal safeguards to **balance the interests** of both parties. For instance, in France, Voodoo, a prominent hyper casual video game publisher, used ex parte proceedings against alleged clone games on several occasions. They justified these actions to the judges by arguing that hyper casual games have a very short lifespan after their launch, so that an injunction should be awarded swiftly. They also argued that it was impossible to quickly obtain an *inter parte* injunction against the alleged infringers, located in Ukraine and Israel. The Paris Court of Appeals,[1] as well as the French Supreme Court,[2] found that the reasons given to justify ex parte proceedings were insufficient. The Court argued that claimants may only be granted ex parte injunctions if the defendants are 'unidentified, unknown or unreachable'. This was not the case here, where Voodoo had exchanged emails with the defendants. 22

On the contrary, **inter-parte** proceedings refer to the most common legal action, with the alleged infringer being summoned before court and having the opportunity to present their arguments in defence. Whether the defendant chooses to appear or 23

---

[1] Paris Court of Appeals, 26.3.2021, No. 20/08441.

[2] French Supreme Court, 8.2.2023, No. 21–17.582.

not, inter-parte proceedings are often lengthier, as they require service of documents, through official channels. When service needs to be done abroad, especially outside the EU, this may significantly lengthen the proceedings. Inter-parte proceedings are also often costlier, as they require rounds of pleadings to rebut the adverse side's arguments.

b) Proceedings on the merits or preliminary injunctions

24 Proceedings on the merits are the most common type of proceedings. The duration varies greatly, from one jurisdiction to another. In Italy, on average, intellectual property infringement proceedings may last two to three years in the first instance. In Germany, intellectual property proceedings are usually quicker, typically taking 10–18 months in the first instance. When the defendant is in the business of game cloning, by the time a decision is issued, it would have already recouped the funds invested in the clone and **moved on** to another video game. Therefore, other proceedings may be available, with quicker outcomes.

25 National courts may issue, at video game companies' request, preliminary injunctions. These allow the rightsholders to **quickly** obtain an injunction restraining an alleged infringer from continuing the alleged infringing act, while the case is pending or progressing to a trial. The time frame to obtain a preliminary injunction is significantly shortened. For instance, while patent lawyers may be familiar with the Italian torpedo,[3] a video game company seeking to act against a clone game may want to look into the **'German torpedo'**. German courts can issue ex-parte preliminary injunctions in obvious intellectual property infringement in a matter of days. This may allow rightsholders to quickly obtain an injunction and then use it to request a takedown of the clone game from platforms.

26 National jurisdictions set the requirements for granting preliminary injunctions, which are often tied to demonstrating **urgency**.

27 However, preliminary injunctions may be a **double-edged sword**, if the decision is overturned on the merits. Some jurisdictions, such as Germany, France or the Netherlands provide for strict liability, meaning that if the preliminary injunction is ultimately overturned, the initial defendant can directly claim damages caused while the injunction was in force. If the injunction banned the game in a specific jurisdiction, the affected party may request damages based on lost sales during the time of the ban. Other jurisdictions, such as Italy, do not provide for strict liability. The affected party must demonstrate that the initial claimant was negligent or demonstrate fault in bringing a request for a preliminary injunction.

28 In January 2024, the CJEU ruled that **strict liability regimes** for losses caused by preliminary injunctions were admissible under EU law, as they were consistent with the Enforcement Directive.[4]

4. Criminal proceedings

29 Intellectual property infringement may also lead to **criminal penalties**. Criminal law is a matter of national law, with little harmonisation at the EU level.

30 Criminal proceedings usually serve as a stronger deterrent because sentences may include imprisonment (in practice more commonly suspended sentences). In addition,

[3] A litigation strategy consisting in bringing a patent infringement case before a national jurisdiction which is known for lengthy judicial proceedings, such as Italy. Other EU jurisdictions may then be forced to stay the proceedings until the first court seized rules. This allows the claimant to delay the judicial resolution of the dispute.

[4] ECJ, 11.1.2024 – case C-473/22, ECLI:EU:C:2024:8 – *Mylan v Gilead.*

the involvement of law enforcement and public prosecutors can bring additional and free-of-charge **investigative resources**, which are not usually available in civil proceedings. This may be helpful in uncovering large-scale organised or cross-border **piracy** operations targeting video games.

Other legal differences which may be of interest to rightsholders is the weight of the **burden of proof**. In France, for criminally prosecuted copyright infringement cases, the concerned works are presumed original, until the defendant proves otherwise.[5] This is the exact opposite of civil cases, where the claimant must demonstrate originality of each work, an often burdensome task. 31

However, as the case is handled by the state, the rightsholders have **less control** over the proceedings. Criminal proceedings may also be significantly **lengthier** than that of civil proceedings. 32

There are a **few precedents** of video game actors which have taken criminal action against infringers. 33

In **Italy**, in 2017, the Supreme Court upheld criminal sentences against the sellers of circumvention devices which enabled Nintendo consoles to run pirated games. The sellers were sentenced to jail time, as well as large fines.[6] In **France**, in 2011, the Paris Court of Appeals convicted sellers of circumvention devices for the Nintendo DS, known as 'linkers'. It handed down heavy criminal penalties, including fines, damages totalling more than 4.8 million EUR, and suspended prison sentences.[7] 34

II. Intermediaries and blocking injunctions

Enforcement against **online intermediaries** may be of interest to rightsholders for various reasons. In particular, when the infringers cannot be identified (→ Rn. 12) or when they are unresponsive to actions taken against them, not answering cease and desist letters. 35

If the infringers are located **outside the EU**, in particular in unfamiliar jurisdictions, rightsholders may prefer turning to well-established intermediaries, often located in their own jurisdictions or other EU jurisdictions. Actions against intermediaries can also be helpful in conjunction with a direct action, for added efficiency. One interesting action against intermediaries is blocking injunctions. 36

1. Definitions

Online intermediaries is a term that refers to the entities that enable users to connect to the internet and transmit content. Online intermediaries play a significant role in the **distribution and accessibility** of video games. Unfortunately, they can also be misused to facilitate video game infringement. 37

Infringement in the video game sector may occur on the platforms of various intermediaries: on a file-sharing platform, where a user uploads a cracked version of a game; on online marketplaces where sellers may list infringing products such as technical protection measure circumvention devices, unauthorised physical copies or digital download codes for pirated games; on a game distribution platform, where an infringer may upload a clone game; on streaming platforms, where users can broadcast entire games. These are only a few examples of the plethora of online intermediaries 38

[5] CSPLA, 'Rapport de Mission: la preuve de l'originalité' (15.12.2020), 19.
[6] Italian Supreme Court, case Nos. 57858/2017 and 38204/2017.
[7] Paris Court of Appeals, 26.9.2011, No. 10/01053.

which may be involved in some capacity in video game infringement. In each of these scenarios, the online intermediary provides the **technological means** or platform that enables or facilitates the infringement, even if they are not directly involved in the act of copying or distributing the game themselves.

39 The **liability exemption** for online intermediaries is a cornerstone of internet regulation, ensuring that it is possible to tackle illegal content swiftly, but also that platforms are not incentivised to remove legitimate content and are not obliged to monitor their users. The EU has passed a series of directives governing online intermediary liability.

40 The EC Directive first established a general framework for the liability and obligations of online intermediaries providing information society services in the EU. It introduced a **safe harbour principle**, under which three types of online intermediaries who host or transmit content provided by a third party are exempt from liability under certain conditions. The DSA updated these provisions as follows:

- Art. 4 provides for a 'mere conduit' exception, exempting online intermediaries from liability when the service provider is only passively involved in the transmission of data. This exception covers, for example, internet service providers (ISPs) and network infrastructure.
- Art. 5 provides for a 'caching' exception, which exempts online intermediaries from liability when they temporarily and automatically store data in order to make transmission more efficient, provided the technical conditions for storing the information are met. This exception covers, for example, the use of proxy servers or content delivery networks.
- Art. 6 provides for a 'hosting' exception, which exempts online intermediaries from liability for the storage of data for their users, as long as they do not have actual knowledge of the illegal activity or information, or, act expeditiously to remove or disable access to the illegal information. This exception covers, for example, the provision of web hosting, cloud storage, or online platforms for user-generated content.

41 The **InfoSoc Directive** does not explicitly address the liability of online intermediaries, but it does require the Member States to ensure that rightsholders have the possibility of applying for injunctions against intermediaries whose services are used by a third party to infringe their rights.[8]

42 The **Enforcement Directive** sets out the measures, procedures, and remedies that the Member States must provide for the enforcement of intellectual property rights, including copyright and related rights, in the EU. It requires the Member States to ensure that rightsholders have the possibility of applying for injunctions against intermediaries whose services are used by a third party to infringe their rights.[9] It also provides that national courts may order the disclosure of information on the origin and distribution networks of the infringing goods or services from the infringer or any person involved in the infringement, including intermediaries.[10]

43 Lastly, the **DSM Directive** created a new kind of online intermediary: online content-sharing platforms (OCSSPs), whose goal is to give the public access to a large amount of copyright-protected works uploaded by its users, which it organises and promotes for profit-making purposes.

44 OCSSPs shall obtain a licence from the rightsholder to give the public access to copyright-protected works. If no authorisation is granted, their liability may be sought

---

[8] Art. 8(3) InfoSoc.
[9] Art. 11 Enforcement Directive.
[10] Art. 8 Enforcement Directive.

unless they demonstrate that they have, cumulatively, made best efforts to obtain an authorisation, made **best efforts** to ensure the unavailability of said copyright-protected works; and in any event acted expeditiously in response to notices received from the rightsholder to remove the works and made best efforts to prevent their future uploads.[11]

Some national authorities have already hinted at which platforms would qualify as OCSSPs in their opinion. The most relevant for the video game industry would be traditional social media platforms, but also **streaming platforms**, where a significant portion of the content is gaming related.[12] Therefore, streaming platforms that permit users to upload gameplay videos will require authorisation from video game publishers, unless an exception or limitation applies. In the absence of a licence, they will have to employ best practices to ensure the unavailability of gameplays uploaded by their users, in the terms that prospective national laws will determine. **45**

2. Blocking injunctions in theory

A '**blocking injunction**' refers to 'an order requiring an internet intermediary to implement technical measures directed at preventing or disabling access to a specific internet location'.[13] **46**

Once a blocking injunction has been ordered, a further step may be a **dynamic blocking injunction**. 'Dynamic blocking injunction' refers to 'injunctions which can be issued, for example, in cases in which materially the same website becomes available immediately after issuing the injunction with a different IP address or URL, and which are drafted in a way that makes it possible to also cover the new IP address or URL, without the need for a new judicial procedure to obtain a new injunction'.[14] **47**

In the EU, blocking injunctions find their legal basis in Art. 18(1) of the EC Directive, Art. 8(3) of the InfoSoc Directive and Art. 11 of the Enforcement Directive. Rec. 59 of the InfoSoc Directive acknowledges that intermediaries' services may be used by third parties for infringement, so that they are **best placed** to stop such infringement. **48**

The CJEU has confirmed blocking injunctions' compatibility with EU law, in particular in the *UPC Telekabel decision*.[15] The European Court of Human Rights found that blocking injunctions are not per se contrary to the provision in Art. 10 ECHR, as long as they are available within a balanced and carefully drafted legislative framework which contains a robust and articulated set of **safeguards** against abuse.[16] **49**

The conditions and modalities for blocking injunctions are a matter of **national** law. **50**

3. Blocking injunctions in practice

a) Applicants

The majority of blocking injunctions applicants are collective management organisations or professional organisations, representing the interests of **several companies** in **51**

---

[11] Art. 17 DSM copyright directive.

[12] See for instance for France, CSPLA 'Rapport de Mission – Les outils de reconnaissance des contenus sur les plateformes numériques de partage: Propositions pour la mise en oeuvre de l'article 17 de la Directive européenne sur le droit d'auteur (15.12.2020), 62 et seq.

[13] EUIPO, 'Study on dynamic blocking injunctions in the European Union', March 2021.

[14] Communication from the Commission to the European Parliament, the Council and the European Economic and Social Committee, 'Guidance on certain aspects of Directive 2004/48/EC of the European Parliament and of the Council on the enforcement of Intellectual Property Rights', COM (2017) 708 final, 21.

[15] ECJ 27.3.2014 – case C-314/12, ECLI:EU:C:2014:192 – *UPC Telekabel Wien GmbH.*

[16] ECtHR, 23.6.2020 – App. No. 10795/14 – *Kharitonov v Russia.*

the same creative sector. Indeed, most infringing websites make available very large quantities of works, owned by various rightsholders.

52 Yet **individual rightsholders** have also successfully requested blocking injunctions, including in the video game industry. Nintendo for instance has obtained blocking injunctions against websites allowing access to unlawful video game copies in several jurisdictions, including the UK,[17] Germany[18] and France.[19]

b) Targets

53 While originally rightsholders mainly targeted ISPs, the possibility to bypass these blocks recently led to actions against **other intermediaries**, including search engines, domain name resolution (DNS) providers and virtual private network (VPN) providers.

54 There is **no hierarchy** to these targets, meaning that the claimant does not need to provide evidence that they have attempted to act against the publisher, the hosting provider or the ISP before acting against other intermediaries.[20]

55 When deciding against which intermediary they wish to act, rightsholders should keep in mind that which intermediary is targeted may significantly change a case's **strategy**: while ISPs, which have been the subject of online blocking injunctions for years, generally do not object to a blocking request, VPN and DNS providers still fight tooth and nail, which results in lengthier, and therefore costlier, actions. Likewise, the place of establishment of the intermediary may significantly lengthen the duration of the action, as summoning companies established abroad often requires service through national authorities, which may cause delays.

c) Intellectual property rights

56 Blocking injunctions were initially focused on **copyright infringement** but have also been used in the context of trademark infringements.[21] Some EU Member States, such as France, still have specific provisions for copyright infringement, whereas other intellectual property rights may fall under the general provisions, applicable to various unlawful content.[22] Other Member States, such as Germany or Belgium have more general provisions, relating to all IP infringement.[23]

57 In at least some EU jurisdictions, the scope extends to blocking access to websites offering devices and software that allow for the circumvention of **TPMs**. In Italy, Spain[24] and the UK,[25] rightsholders have successfully requested blocking injunctions against ISPs to block access to websites advertising, distributing, offering for sale and/or selling devices that allowed console TPMs to be circumvented.

d) Evidence required

58 Generally, to request a blocking injunction a rightsholder must provide **evidence** (i) of the validity of the rights infringed, whether it be copyright, related right trademark,

---

[17] *Nintendo Co. Ltd. v British Telecommunications Plc* [2021] EWHC 3488.

[18] CUII, 6.4.2021, No. 4/2021.

[19] Paris first instance Court, 17.2.2022, No. 21/15799.

[20] See for instance in France Paris first instance Court, 28.3.2025, No. 25/01443, *Canal + v Cloudlfare.*

[21] See for instance in the UK, Cartier, Montblanc, *Richemont International SA v BskyB, EE, TalkTalk and Virgin* [2016] EWCA Civ 6358.

[22] EUIPO, 'Study on dynamic blocking injunctions in the European Union', March 2021, 31.

[23] See Art. 7(4) German Telemedia Act.

[24] Rosati, 'TPM circumvention and website blocking orders: An EU perspective' (The IPKat, 26.11.2020) <https://ipkitten.blogspot.com/2020/11/tpm-circumvention-and-website-blocking.html>.

[25] *Nintendo Co. Ltd. v Sky UK Ltd & Ors* [2019] EWHC 2376.

or another IPR; (ii) that there are infringing acts; (iii) that the requested blocking injunction is proportionate, appropriate, reasonable and/or necessary. However, the evidence required largely varies depending on whether voluntary arrangements are in place between ISP and rightsholders or relevant authorities.

In Germany, a **voluntary agreement** between German ISPs and rightsholders let to the creation of the *Clearingstelle Urheberrecht im Internet* (Clearing Body for Copyright on the Internet – CUII), which targets 'structurally copyright-infringing websites' without the intervention of a court. The CUII's decision is reviewed by an administrative authority, BNetzA, which ensures compliance with EU Net Neutrality Regulation, before being implemented by ISPs. 59

e) Implementing the blocking

Some jurisdictions clearly provide for **time-limited** blocking, which must be regularly renewed. In Finland for instance, injunctions are available for a maximum of one year while in France the usual duration is 18 months. Other jurisdictions do not provide any explicit time limitation. This is the case for Belgium, Denmark (in principle), Germany, Italy and Spain.[26] 60

There are **two** main types of blocking: DNS blocking and IP address blocking: 61

- When an intermediary implements a domain name blocking measure, it generally configures its DNS service to provide users with an invalid hosting address for the site to be blocked. This is known as DNS blocking.
- IP blocking involves the intermediary prohibiting or diverting exchanges between users on its network and the IP address of a web server. However, this raises the problem of overblocking, as a single IP address can host several websites. If other legitimate services are also hosted on the server (and therefore use the same IP address), they may also be blocked as a side effect.

While some jurisdictions specify the **technical solution** to be applied, others leave the intermediary free to determine their preferred solution. 62

III. Focus on hosting provider's liability

Among the various categories of online intermediaries, **hosting providers** are particularly interesting. Video game companies may make use of the 'notice-and-takedown' mechanisms to attempt to enforce their rights. 63

1. General considerations

As mentioned above, Art. 6 of the DSA, like its predecessor, Art. 14 of the InfoSoc Directive, provides for a **liability exemption** for hosting providers, as long as they do not have actual knowledge of the illegal activity or information, or, act expeditiously to remove or disable access to the illegal information. Such a regime was first introduced in the US, and a few years later in EU law, followed by national transpositions. 64

Before the DSA entered into force, there were no harmonised requirements regarding information to be included in a notification to a hosting provider. As a result, the content and form of a valid notification, and thus what would trigger 'actual knowledge', 65

[26] EUIPO, 'Study on dynamic blocking injunctions in the European Union', March 2021, p. 34.

varied from one jurisdiction to another.[27] Rightsholders sometimes faced difficulties ensuring their notices were effective in multiple jurisdictions and cross-border enforcement suffered as a result.

66 The DSA sought to **harmonise** notice-and-takedown. Art. 16 of the DSA goes over the information to be included in notices to hosting providers.

67 Video game stakeholders seeking to enforce their right against an anonymous or unresponsive infringer operating online may therefore **notify hosting providers**, in accordance with the DSA.

68 While this may be a time- and cost-efficient strategy, it largely depends on the hosting providers' **willingness to cooperate**. Despite some unresponsive hosting providers being sentenced to pay large sums in damages for failing to take down properly notified unlawful video game copies,[28] not all hosting providers defer to notice-and-takedowns promptly, if at all.

2. Streaming and let's play

69 Notice-and-takedown can be particularly useful for video game companies wishing to control **live-streaming or let's play** of their games. While streaming and let's play are an important marketing tool for publishers and developers, they may also be perceived as a threat: They give audiences access to the video game without requiring them to purchase it, they may undermine the player experience, in particular for story-focused game; and they may be monetised by a third party, without any monetary compensation to the rightsholder.

70 From an IP perspective, unauthorised streaming involves the reproduction, public performance, making available to the public and/or communication to the public rights of the video game, and its different elements. Therefore, it is generally accepted that unauthorised streaming may constitute **copyright infringement**. In addition, it may also constitute a contractual breach, depending on the game's EULA.

71 Some video game publishers have a **permissive approach** to streaming, allowing it under certain easily fulfilled conditions. For instance, Square Enix's live streaming guidelines for Final Fantasy VII Rebirth allow players to stream on Twitch or YouTube but not on paid-per-view platforms and require the streamer to display a 'spoiler alert' 'to prevent ruining the experience for people who have not played that scene yet'.[29] Likewise, Ubisoft allows players to monetise videos of its games, provided that the videos include the streamer's 'creative spin on [their] owned content' and is generally appropriate.[30]

72 Video game companies that wish to further **restrict streaming** of their content rarely act against the streamers directly, to avoid any public relations backlash. They will more likely make use of streaming platforms' notice-and-takedown systems.[31]

[27] European Commission Directorate-General for Communications Networks, 'Overview of the legal framework of notice-and-action procedures in Member States' SMART 2016/0039 – Final report, 2018, p. 140-161.

[28] See for instance, French Supreme Court, 26.2.2025, No. 23–15.966.

[29] Square Enix, 'Live Streaming and Video/Image Posting Guidelines for FINAL FANTASY VII REBIRTH' <https://www.square-enix-games.com/en_GB/documents/live-streaming-and-video-image-posting-guidelines-for-final-fantasy-vii-rebirth>.

[30] Ubisoft, 'Ubisoft Video Policy' <https://www.ubisoft.com/legal/documents/VideoPolicy/en-INTL>.

[31] See, e.g., for Twitch <https://legal.twitch.com/en/legal/dmca-guidelines>.

B. Enforcement against video game companies

This section identifies legal **risk areas** which may give rise to enforcement against video game companies. It focuses on dealing with national authorities, consumer watchdogs, players and local law enforcement but other actors may be involved, in particular, competitors. 73

It highlights **specific practices** within a video game's lifecycle that present unique challenges. 74

This section purposefully does not go over the scenario where a video game company acts as the defendant to an IP infringement action, as it would be redundant with the first section. 75

I. Consumer law enforcement

Consumer law is increasingly discussed in the EU due to ongoing efforts to adapt it to the digital age and address emerging issues such as 'dark patterns'.[32] According to the European Commission, video games feature a variety of commercial practices that may raise fairness concerns under applicable consumer protection law, in particular for vulnerable consumers such as children.[33] 76

1. National authorities and the CPC

Consumer law enforcement actions may come from **national authorities** in charge of consumer protection, such as the AGCM in Italy,[34] the Konsumentverket is Sweden, the DGCCRF in France,[35] or the ACM in the Netherlands.[36] These authorities are responsible for enforcing consumer protection laws, handling complaints, and ensuring compliance with both national and EU consumer law. 77

They usually take an interest in a **specific sector**, such as the video game industry, if there is a concerted action at EU level; and/or they receive multiple consumer complaints on the same topic; and/or they receive complaints from consumer protection organisations. 78

National authorities usually carry out their **own investigations** before reaching out to the trader. They may ask for a meeting to discuss the results of their investigations or send a letter requesting explanations on compliance. 79

They may then send a formal cease-and-desist to the trader. If they are not satisfied with the trader's answers, which is often the case, they may issue a **sanction**, which generally consists in: 80

- Administrative fines for failure to comply with consumer law provisions. As per Directive 2019/2161, the maximum amount of such fines is at least 4 % of the trader's annual turnover in the Member State or Member States concerned.
- Injunctions to stop certain practices. Some authorities may also request that a sanctioned trader publishes a disclaimer on their website, for a few weeks, to inform

---

[32] A 'dark pattern' refers to a type of malicious nudging, generally incorporated into digital design interfaces, which may be scrutinised under consumer law.

[33] European Commission, 'Commission Notice on the interpretation and application of the Unfair Commercial Practices Directive' (2021/C 526/01).

[34] *Autorità Garante della Concorrenza e del Mercato* – Italian Competition Authority.

[35] *Direction générale de la concurrence, de la consommation et de la répression des fraudes* – Directorate General for Competition Policy Consumer Affairs and Fraud Control.

[36] *Autoriteit Consument & Markt* – The Netherlands Authority for Consumers and Markets.

consumers of the sanctions. In 2018, several video game distribution platforms, including Ubisoft, were sanctioned by the French DGCCRF, which resulted in a disclaimer being published on their website's homepage.

- Some authorities may also publish a summary of the sanction on their own website, in a 'name and shame' fashion.
- Lastly, for the most serious breaches, the case may be referred to the public prosecutor, which may initiate criminal proceedings.

81 Since 2020, Reg. 2017/2394 provides for a network of competent public enforcers tackling consumer protection in a coordinated manner, the **Consumer Protection Cooperation Network** (CPC), with the Commission playing a larger role. The CPC has been involved in various initiatives targeting the video game industry.

82 In 2013/2014, the CPC alongside the European Commission engaged in a joint enforcement action to improve the protection of children regarding **in-app purchases** in online games. The joint action was directed at Apple, Google and the Interactive Software Federation of Europe (ISFE) and encouraged them to adopt consumer protection measures, such as not using the word 'free' for games that include in-app purchases.

83 In 2018, the CPC collected and analysed complaints about **loot boxes** and related mechanisms filed with national consumer organisations. The analysis showed that gambling authorities in Belgium and the Netherlands have found that loot boxes fell under national gambling regulation, whereas most Member States did not, relying on consumer protection. In particular, Electronic Arts faced legal challenges with the Dutch Gambling Authority concerning FIFA's loot boxes.[37]

84 In March 2025, the CPC published key principles on **in-game virtual currencies**, which were heavily criticised by the video game industry.[38] At the same time, the CPC announced an enforcement action against publisher Star Stable Entertainment AB for unfair commercial practices in the context of virtual currency and minors.

2. Consumer protection organisations

85 Authorities are not the only actors in enforcing consumer regulation. Local or regional **consumer protection organisations** also play a key role. They are often the first point of contact for displeased players. Once they receive multiple complaints, such organisations usually reach out to the trader, either informally or through a cease and desist. If they are not satisfied with the trader's answers, which is often the case, they may initiate civil proceedings, file criminal complaints or ask the national authority to step in.

86 As an example, in 2012, **German** consumer watchdog group *Verbraucherzentrale Bundesverband* (The Federation of German Consumer Organisations – vzbv) brought a case against Valve, publisher of the digital distribution platform Steam, claiming that they were in breach of several consumer law and intellectual property provisions.

87 Similarly, in **France**, in 2014 French consumer protection association *UFC Que Choisir* initiated proceedings against several big tech companies, including Valve, based both on consumer law, intellectual property rights and data privacy. The Paris first instance Court found that several provisions of these companies' terms and conditions

---

[37] Kansppelautoriteit, 'Electronic Arts Swiss Sàrl en Electronic Arts Inc' (29.11.2020) <https://kansspelautoriteit.nl/aanpak-misstanden/sanctiebesluiten/electronic-arts/>.

[38] EGDF and VGE, 'Joint statement from European Game Developers Federation and Video Games Europe on the Consumer Protection Cooperation Network's principles on in-game virtual currencies' (22.3.2025) <https://www.videogameseurope.eu/news/video-games-europe-and-egdf-statement-on-cpcs-principles-on-in-game-virtual-currencies/>.

were abusive and ordered them to be removed,[39] although the main intellectual property question was ultimately decided in Valve's favour.[40]

At the regional level, the **European Consumer Organisation** (BEUC) brings together national consumer organisations from 32 European countries, undertaking coordinated consumer protection enforcement actions. 88

In 2024, the BEUC filed a complaint with the EU Commission and the CPC citing alleged **unfair commercial practices** of some of the largest video game companies, Activision Blizzard, Electronic Arts, Epic Games, Mojang Studios, Roblox Corporation, Supercell and Ubisoft.[41] The complaint mentions issues such as alleged lack of transparency over the use of virtual currencies and 'manipulative tactics' affecting children. 89

3. Players

a) *Friction areas*

Players themselves may be the initiators of legal actions against video game companies, often invoking consumer law protection. As they are considered to be the weaker party in the asymmetric relationship with traders, consumers are particularly protected under EU law. 90

Consumer complaints often crystallise around sanctions for cheating, including **bans and refund rights**. In 2024, the French consumer protection organisation *UFC Que Choisir* published a press release announcing it had been contacted by multiple players banned from Call of Duty without clear justification, which intended to initiate proceedings against Activision.[42] 91

Increasingly, players have transformed from mere consumers of video games into active contributors in the creation and development of gaming experiences. This shift is particularly evident in light of the success of sandbox games, such as Minecraft or Roblox. By providing tools to encourage **user-generated content**, some games blur the lines between developer and player. In addition, some players have made a living out of their video game skills, through esports. 92

From a legal standpoint, this may alter the relationship between video game companies and these **'professional' players**. Banning a casual player is one thing, banning a creator who makes their living by developing user-generated content is another. What about sunsetting a game on which monetised tournaments are organised? Video game companies should be wary of the legal risks associated with this environment. 93

b) *In court and out of court*

Several pieces of EU legislation aim at ensuring consumers have access to effective **redress mechanisms**, both in court and out of court, for resolving disputes with traders, particularly in online transactions. 94

Out of court, Reg. No. 524/2013 required online traders to provide, on their website, an easily accessible link to the European **Online Dispute Resolution** (ODR) platform. ODR offered a single point of entry to consumers and traders seeking the out-of-court resolution of disputes arising from online sales or service contracts. Yet given the very 95

---

[39] Paris First instance Court, 17.9.2019, No. 16/01008.

[40] French Supreme Court, 23.10.2024, No. 23–13.738.

[41] BEUC, 'Game over: Consumers fight for fairer in-game purchases' (12.9.2024) <https://www.beuc.eu/reports/game-over-consumers-fight-fairer-game-purchases>.

[42] UFC Que Choisir, 'Deux plaintes pour bannissement abusif de joueurs' (26.9.2024) <https://www.quechoisir.org/action-ufc-que-choisir-activision-deux-plaintes-pour-bannissement-abusif-de-joueurs-n131658/>.

low adoption of the platform, it has recently been discontinued.[43] Despite this recent change, alternative dispute resolution remains an easy avenue for EU consumers to settle their disputes, in particular under the consumer Mediation Directive.[44]

96 In court, although video game companies may attempt to limit their exposure, for instance by including choice of jurisdiction clauses or mandatory arbitration provisions in the player-agreed contractual terms, such provisions are generally **unenforceable** in the EU, as a consumer may not be deprived of their right to sue in their home country.

97 Players may also consider **mass actions**. Also called class action or group action, these are actions brought by multiple claimants against the same defendant in relation to similar claims. The EU Directive on Representative Actions for the Protection of the Collective Interests of Consumers sets minimum standards for consumers to seek collective redress regarding European consumer laws. It requires EU Member States to establish at least one procedural mechanism, which meets these requirements by June 2023.

98 Although mass actions have not yet made a big impact on the EU video game landscape, this may well change in the **future**. Starting in 2024, the Dutch non-profit foundation, *Stichting Massaschade & Consument* – Foundation for Mass Damage & Consumer Protection – started carrying out investigations into Sony, related to alleged abuse of dominant position. They claim that by locking the market of digital PlayStation 4 and 5 games and in-game content, Sony would be artificially maintaining high prices. Consequently, an action was brought by a group of Dutch residents who have purchased at least one Playstation 4 or 5 game in the Sony Playstation Store.[45]

II. Dealing with law enforcement

99 **'Law enforcement'** refers to the agencies responsible for enforcing laws, maintaining public order, and managing public safety.

100 Video game companies operating in the EU can play a crucial role as communication intermediaries for large online communities. Like any intermediary, these companies may be approached by local law enforcement authorities asking for help to obtain **information on players** for their investigations. As an example, law enforcement may have information on the fact that players have used a specific game's chat to coordinate a crime. They may approach the game's publisher to request said players' contact information or activity logs.

101 As mentioned before (→ Rn. 29), criminal law is largely **unharmonised** at the EU level. How to address these requests is often a balancing exercise between, on the one hand, the cooperation with law enforcement for efficient enforcement and ultimately, a safer video game platform and, on the other hand, applicable EU laws and regulations, including data privacy. Companies should establish clear internal procedures for responding to lawful requests, ensuring that any disclosure of user information is made to legitimate law enforcement officers, based on valid legal grounds and is limited to what is strictly necessary for the investigation.

---

[43] Regulation (EU) 2024/3228 of the European Parliament and of the Council of 19.12.2024 repealing Regulation (EU) No. 524/2013, and amending Regulations (EU) 2017/2394 and (EU) 2018/1724 with regard to the discontinuation of the European Online Dispute Resolution Platform.

[44] Directive 2013/11/EU of the European Parliament and of the Council of 21.5.2013 on alternative dispute resolution for consumer disputes and amending Regulation (EC) No. 2006/2004 and Directive 2009/22/EC.

[45] Stichting Massaschade & Consument, 'Jij betaalt te veel voor PlayStation games' (24.6.2025) <https://www.massaschadeconsument.nl/collectieve-acties/playstation/#steun>.

Maintaining transparency, safeguarding user rights, and documenting all interactions with authorities are essential to uphold **users' trust** while staying compliant with applicable legal obligations. **102**

§ 29
Data Protection and Privacy in the Video Games Industry

Bibliography: Bauckhage et al., How Players Lose Interest in Playing a Game: An Empirical Study Based on Distributions of Total Playing Times, Institute of Electrical and Electronics Engineers (IEEE) Conference on Computational Intelligence and Games, Granda, Spain, 2012; González Fuster, Study on the essence of the fundamental rights to privacy and to protection of personal data, Brussels, 2022; Hentsch/Bänsch, 'Datenverarbeitungen in der Games-Branche', MMR Zeitschrift für IT-Recht und Recht der Digitalisierung, 08/2021, 3; Kröger et al., 'Surveilling the gamers: Privacy impacts of the video game industry', Entertainment Computing, Vol. 44, January 2023; Lober/Klein, 'Datenschutz bei Multiplayer-Games und Spielen auf sozialen Netzwerken', MMR Zeitschrift für IT-Recht und Recht der Digitalisierung, 08/2021, 17; Przybysz/Kubit, Data protection in the video games sector in Cappello (ed), Legal challenges and market dynamics in the video games sector, IRIS European Audiovisual Observatory, Strasbourg, 2024, 93.

A. Introduction: The importance of data for the video games industry 1
B. Data categories enabling video game play 5
  I. Device and network data 6
  II. Account data 9
  III. Gameplay data 11
  IV. Communication and interaction data 14
  V. Third-party data 16
C. Grounds for lawful data processing in video games 18
  I. Processing necessary for the performance of a contract 19
  II. Legitimate interests 21
  III. Consent 25
  IV. Processing for legal compliance or to protect vital data subject interests 30
D. GDPR obligations of particular importance to video game companies 32
  I. Transparency 33
  II. Processing of personal data of minors 37
  III. Fraud prevention 45
  IV. Data transfers outside the European Union 49
E. Conclusion 52

A. Introduction: The importance of data for the video games industry

1 In the European Union, the **General Data Protection Regulation** (GDPR)[1] and the **ePrivacy Directive** (ePD)[2] are the **two key instruments** for the protection of personal data and privacy of EU citizens. Both are distinctly different. The right to privacy or private life is a universal human right and enshrined in Art. 12 of the Universal Declaration of Human Rights, Art. 8 of the European Convention of Human Rights and Art. 7 of the European Charter of Fundamental Rights. The notion of data protection originates from the right to privacy and is explicitly stated in Art. 8 of the European Charter of Fundamental Rights.[3]

2 The ePD focuses on **privacy in electronic communications**, including rules for cookies, online tracking, and marketing communications. A review proposal for an ePrivacy regulation did not manage to get adopted and was officially withdrawn. The GDPR, on the other hand, sets rules for the **fair processing (collection, use and**

[1] European Parliament and Council, 'Regulation (EU) 2016/679 of 27.4.2016 on the protection of natural persons with regard to the processing of personal data and on the free movement of such data, and repealing Directive 95/46/EC', OJ 2016 L 119, 1.

[2] European Parliament and Council, 'Directive 2002/58/EC of 12.7.2002 concerning the processing of personal data and the protection of privacy in the electronic communications sector', OJ 2002 L 201, 37.

[3] González Fuster, p. 8 et seq.

storage) of personal data, e.g., any information relating to an identified or identifiable natural person, by automated means or as part of a filing system (Art. 2.1 GDPR). It sets out the principles, including different legal grounds, for lawful processing, and the requirements that companies, individuals and public authorities who determine the purpose and the means of the processing (data controllers) and those who process the data on their behalf (data processors) must fulfil. It also outlines the conditions for transferring personal data to third countries and the rights of citizens to access, correct, and delete their own personal data.

Both legal instruments have been firmly implemented in the daily working practice of video games companies which depend on data of its users to **enable an interactive gameplay experience** and, above all, to constantly improve and optimise this experience according to the gaming habits of its users. Data is collected and processed in a video game for many different reasons: to enable game play and communication in multiplayer mode, to purchase and provide content, or to improve the game experience and develop new games. 3

In this chapter, we will first provide an overview of the different types of data processing operations that are essential for the functioning of a game. Then, we will explain how these can be based on the different legal grounds for lawful data processing that exist under the GDPR. Finally, we will outline in detail the legal requirements in relation to transparency, the processing of data of minors, fraud prevention and data transfers outside of the European Union. Each of these is of particular importance for video game companies. 4

B. Data categories enabling video game play

The essence of a video game is to provide a digital and interactive service enabling a gameplay experience. To deliver this service to the player, **several categories of data are required**. This includes functional and technical data, account information, gameplay metrics, communication and interaction data, as well as third-party data.[4] 5

I. Device and network data

For every video game – whether played on a PC, console or mobile device – a connection between the servers of the provider and the device of the player needs to be established. This requires the collection and processing of **technical information** related to the configurations of the network, the device and the connected peripherals such as controllers and headsets. Examples of such device and network data include MAC and IP addresses, device serial numbers, internet service provider or mobile carrier data, etc. This type of data may also encompass information about the software or applications that are installed on the device and how the player interacts with them. 6

Although of a technical nature, this type of data should be considered personal data as it may allow the identity of the player to be revealed directly or indirectly. In the latter case, the ability of a third party to lawfully **combine the data with complementary identifiable information** should always be presumed but only if such an activity would 7

[4] Hentsch/Bänsch, MMR 2021, 3(3 et seqq.).

constitute a 'means likely reasonably to be used'[5] and the risk of identification is significant.[6]

8 The collection and processing of this type of data often require direct access to information and processing and storage capabilities of the device of the player by using **cookies or similar technologies** and is then subject to different legal requirements under ePrivacy law. Art. 5(3) of the ePD requires the user's consent when cookies or similar technologies are used, except where such storage or access is necessary for carrying out the transmission of a communication or for the provision of an information society service explicitly requested by a user.

II. Account data

9 Joining an online gameplay service usually requires registration of an account whereby, at minimum, **basic contact information and profile information** is provided by the player in addition to choosing a username and password of choice. While names and e-mail addresses are always processed upon registration, age may also be collected to comply with relevant data protection and consumer protection regulations. In some cases, the free use of an online game only requires an e-mail address, username and password. However, to enable the purchasing of content, essential billing information such as the physical address and credit card number is needed as well. Finally, telephone numbers may also be processed in addition to the name, address and e-mail for handling enquiries and providing customer support.

10 Account data can contain sensitive information and is **often linked to other personalised information** about popular game titles, scores and achievements, communication and marketing preferences, purchasing history, etc. Usernames or gamer tags are a commonly used form of pseudonymisation and allow players to interact with each other while protecting their identity. Passwords are usually stored in a hashed form which does not allow the actual password to be reconstructed.

III. Gameplay data

11 As players engage with video game content or with other players, data about their activity is generated encompassing actions such as player movements, duration, and engagement with game characters and interfaces. This data, also called **telemetry data**, plays an essential role in the way companies are detecting software errors or bugs. It is instrumental in enhancing the gameplay quality by identifying areas that need improvement, for example to find bottlenecks within the game, where many players fail the tasks at hand. By collectively analysing players' data, a video game company can identify if there is a large problem being experienced by the majority of the players and learn how it needs to be fixed. Developers and publishers therefore regularly provide updates and patches to games that add to and improve existing content and user experiences.

12 Telemetry data also allows cheating behaviours to be detected and can uncover unfair practices, thereby **ensuring a fair level playing field** for all players. It helps match players based on non-precise location, skill and performance without having to further identify them. Players have a more enjoyable experience if they are matched with other

---

[5] ECJ 19.10.2016 – case C-582/14, ECLI:EU:C:2016:779, mn. 42 – *Patrick Breyer v Bundesrepublik Deutschland.*

[6] AG Spielmann 6.2.2025 – case C-413/23 P 06.02.25, mn. 57 – *European Data Protection Supervisor v Single Resolution Board.*

players of similar skill levels and the location is required to ensure that players are placed together on the most appropriately located servers to prevent their connections from being interrupted.[7]

Similar to device and network data, gameplay data may, often only indirectly, allow the identity of the player to be revealed and should then be considered as personal data. More controversially, some argue that it may also disclose **details about a player's biometric identity**, gender, emotions, and personality traits which could be classified as sensitive data under Art. 9 GDPR.[8] Processing such data would require obtaining the explicit consent of the players. This view is however not widely supported. 13

IV. Communication and interaction data

Gameplay services typically incorporate communication features within the game software that enable communication **between players or between the player and the provider** of the service. These supplementary communication tools support the gameplay activities by allowing players to plan a gameplay session ahead and to communicate during gameplay. They also allow the player to report malfunctions, inappropriate content or abusive behaviour. Communication with the provider may occur outside the game software where it is necessary to respond to requests, provide product support, or enable membership features, such as the ability to receive exclusive content, redeem prizes for competitions, or receive newsletters. The content of a communication as well as the related metadata processed for the purpose of its conveyance may reveal very sensitive and personal information and is therefore in principle subject to strict confidentiality requirements under ePrivacy law. 14

Communication services in video games, such as a chat function in an online game, are however **not regularly considered as an interpersonal telecommunications service** according to Art. 2(5) of the European Electronic Communications Code. The Code provides for the corresponding legal basis in the ePD and excludes communication services that are a minor and purely ancillary feature to another service. Furthermore, interpersonal telecommunications services are defined as services that allow connectivity between a finite number of users who can decide themselves with whom to connect, thereby excluding 'open' chat rooms in which the communications are visible for all participants.[9] A retracted review proposal by the European Commission suggested to expand the scope of this definition which would have required video game companies to obtain consent to continue to actively or reactively monitor chat functions to ensure a high level of safety and security for the players.[10] 15

V. Third-party data

Online gameplay services not only process data received or collected from the player directly. Information is also shared from, or shared with, external third-party service providers. The majority of them are providers involved in the **technical supply of the** 16

[7] Bauckhagen, p. 1 et seqq.

[8] Kröger et al., EC, 1 (12).

[9] Rec. 17 of the European Electronic Communications Code explicitly mentions communication channels in online games as examples that do not fall under the concept of an 'interpersonal communication service'.

[10] European Commission, Proposal for a 'Regulation on Privacy and Electronic Communications', 2017/0003 (COD), 24.

service, e.g., gaming platforms, data analytics companies and financial institutions that verify payment transactions. In addition, data may also be shared with administrative or judicial authorities to comply with a legal obligation, e.g., in connection with an investigation of fraud or intellectual property infringement, or to protect the rights and safety of the players.

17 This category of data may also encompass information processed to deliver **personalised advertisements or tailored content** to players. Sometimes data is directly shared with marketing companies. Targeted advertising does not, however, always require an analysis of a player's personal data to identify characteristics or behavioural patterns with a view to make predictions. If players opt to link their account to social networking sites or other video game publishers, that information may be shared from those platforms. Where the processing of this data is based solely on automated processing, including profiling, and has an impact on a player's legal rights or a similarly significant effect, Art. 22 of the GDPR imposes strict rules and safeguards, including a right to object.[11] Targeted advertising has allowed video game companies, in particular SMEs who do not have large marketing budgets at their disposal, to acquire a dedicated user base. However, it is not the prevalent business model in the games industry. Unlike in other media industries, **revenue primarily comes from the sales** of games, in-game purchases as well as subscription models and fees for services.

C. Grounds for lawful data processing in video games

18 The above-mentioned processing activities in video games must of course be carried out in compliance with the law. If the processing is subject to the GDPR, it should be grounded on one of the six legal bases outlined in Art. 6(1). In this regard, it should be underlined that GDPR does not establish any hierarchy between them. If, however, the ePD applies, consent of the player must be required except where the processing is necessary for the provision of the service. The purposes for processing the personal data and their legal grounds need to be carefully documented and communicated in a mandatory privacy notice.[12]

I. Processing necessary for the performance of a contract

19 The provider of the digital and interactive service enabling a gameplay experience and the player will be bound by a contractual relationship, usually called an **End User License Agreement (EULA)** or Account User Agreement. This contract requires the provider to make the game available and ensure that it runs smoothly from a technical point of view which is a conformity requirement under EU contract law.[13] In order to fulfil these contractual obligations, device and network data must be collected so that the game can be played on the user's device. The collection of data to detect bugs, cheats, bots or trolls, as well as to support multiplayer functions, maintain the gameplay balance or enable purchasing options contribute to the smooth functioning of the game and is therefore covered by the contract.

---

[11] Art. 29 Data Protection Working Party, 'Guidelines on Automated individual decision-making and Profiling for the purposes of Regulation 2016/679', 3.10.2017, 17/EN WP 251, 10.

[12] Przybysz/Kubit in Cappello, p. 93 (95).

[13] European Parliament and Council, 'Directive of 20 May 2019 on certain aspects concerning contracts for the supply of digital content and digital services', OJ 2019 L 136, 20.

The collection of communication data **can be covered by the contract** when such a feature is part of the gameplay or when reporting mechanisms are provided. The transfer of personal data to third parties may also be considered as part of the contract as far as it supports the provision of the gameplay or the billing process. However, processing based on the performance of a contract should always align closely with the purpose of the contract. Where marketing activities have no relation to the gameplay, the processing will need to be based on other lawful grounds. 20

II. Legitimate interests

Legitimate interests also play an important role in the lawful processing of personal data in video games. They should not, however, be considered as a legal basis 'by default'. Before relying on such a legal basis, data controllers should carefully assess whether the interest that is pursued is legitimate and lawful. Secondly, it should be examined whether the processing of the data is necessary to pursue this interest and cannot be achieved otherwise. Finally, a so-called "**balancing test**" must establish if the pursued interest is not overridden by the interests or fundamental rights and freedoms of the player, in particular if the player is a child. The latter includes an assessment of whether he or she can reasonably expect that processing for that purpose may take place.[14] 21

A **commercial interest of the controller** can constitute a legitimate interest which should not be interpreted narrowly.[15] Rec. 47 of the GDPR explicitly acknowledges that the legitimate interest basis can be invoked for the purposes of preventing fraud and for direct marketing purposes. These are two processing purposes of particular importance for the video games industry. Many publishers offer players individually tailored additional content. This may include special skins or equipment, new levels or expansion packs as well as comparable game titles from the same publisher. These services are not part of the contract and are acquired through in-game purchases as a separate legal transaction. 22

Furthermore, video game companies need to deploy **safety and security mechanisms** that process data not just to protect video game software and licensed content from unauthorised access (hacking), but also to prevent fraudulent behaviour, protect the safety of players and the confidentiality of their personal data. Requiring consent in such fraud detection scenarios would be both impractical and ineffective, as malicious actors would simply decline to provide it. 23

Finally, the legitimate interest basis can also be invoked for product improvement processing activities that are not covered by the contract, provided that they are limited to what is necessary in relation to the purpose for which they are processed and do not have a significant impact on the user.[16] 24

III. Consent

Art. 4(11) of the GDPR defines consent as: 'any freely given, specific, informed and unambiguous indication of the data subject's wishes by which he or she, **by a statement** 25

[14] EDPB, 'Guidelines 1/2024 on processing of personal data based on Art. 6(1)(f) GDPR', 8.10.2024, 26 et seq.

[15] ECJ 4.10.2024 – case C-621/22, ECLI:EU:C:2024:858 mn. 57 – *Koninklijke Nederlandse Lawn Tennisbond v Autoriteit Persoonsgegevens.*

[16] ECJ 4.7.2023 – case C-252/21, ECLI:EU:C:2023:537 mn.123 – *Meta Platforms Inc. and Others v Bundeskartellamt.*

or by a clear affirmative action, signifies agreement to the processing of personal data relating to him or her'. It can only be an appropriate lawful basis if a data subject is sufficiently informed about all aspects of the processing operations and about his or her rights as a data subject and is **offered a genuine choice** with regard to accepting the terms offered or declining them without detriment. Consent must be clearly given with an affirmative action; it cannot be given with a pre-ticked checkbox that users have to uncheck to opt out, or assumed or bundled with other consents, and it must be able to be withdrawn at any time.[17]

26 In video games, relying on consent may become **problematic when processing personal data is crucial for the game's proper functioning**, as consent under these circumstances may not be considered freely given. It is therefore typically obtained in the context of processing operations that cannot be covered by the contract and cannot be reasonably expected by the data subject. Examples include the provision of personalised advertising or personalised content, in particular in games that operate via social networks or where the player's account is linked to such services.[18]

27 The processing of special categories of personal data according to Art. 9 GDPR, the use of automated individual decision-making, including profiling, according to Art. 22 GDPR, and the transfer of data to a third country or international organisation according to Art. 49 GDPR are all subject to the even **higher standard of 'explicit consent'**. Explicit consent generally means that the data subject must give an express statement of consent. It will be required when a video game collects biometric data, for instance through the use of the VR headset or specific types of gameplay data. It may also be necessary in case of automated processing of personal data to evaluate certain personal aspects relating to a natural person, for instance for the purpose of advertising, although other legal grounds can sometimes be invoked in this context as well.

28 Consent is the **only valid legal basis under the ePD**. It is always required when cookies or similar technologies access information, which may be personal and non-personal data, or make use of the processing and storage capabilities on the device of the player. An exception applies when cookies are strictly necessary for a service requested by the user or for the sole purpose of carrying out the transmission of a communication. These **first-party or functional cookies** are indispensable for the operation of the game and often provided for device recognition, for enabling the desired or acquired settings, for displaying the correct language version and for preventing mass registrations.[19]

29 **Third-party cookies**, on the other hand, are cookies from authorised third-party providers. They are often used to track a provider's webpage visits and views. They can be necessary for the detection of download problems or other software issues, for fraud prevention or for the protection against spam. Third-party cookies are also used for marketing purposes. They can allow networks to display advertisements, attribute marketing campaigns to a specific partner and optimise marketing efforts on the basis of conversion figures.

---

[17] ECJ 1.10.2019 – case C-673/17, ECLI:EU:C:2019:801 mn. 65 – *Bundesverband der Verbraucherzentralen und Verbraucherverbände – Verbraucherzentrale Bundesverband e.V. v Planet49 GmbH.*

[18] Lober/Klein, MMR 2021, 17 (19 et seqq.).

[19] EDPB, 'Guidelines 05/2020 on consent under Regulation 2016/679', 4.5.2020, 7 et seqq.

IV. Processing for legal compliance or to protect vital data subject interests

Lawful processing under the GDPR can also be carried out in accordance with a legal obligation to which the controller is subject or where processing is necessary for the performance of a task carried out in the public interest or in the exercise of official authority. In these cases, the processing should **have a basis in Union or Member State law**. In the video games industry, these legal grounds may for instance be invoked when a player's account data is being processed to report suspicious financial transactions to financial institutions, or when grooming must be reported to the authorities. 30

Processing personal data to protect the vital interests of an individual should in principle only take place where the processing cannot be manifestly based on another legal basis. It involves mostly medical or healthcare situations and is therefore less relevant to video game companies. 31

D. GDPR obligations of particular importance to video game companies

Under the GDPR, data controllers are responsible for ensuring that their processing activities comply with the law. They must implement appropriate and effective measures to ensure security of the processing, allow individuals to exercise their rights, conduct impact assessment, notify data breaches, comply with the data processing principles and conditions for international data transfers, and much more. In this section, we will highlight the obligations that are of particular importance for those types of data that are typically collected in the games industry. 32

I. Transparency

Transparency is one of the key data protection principles for lawful processing under the GDPR and is closely linked to the principles of fairness and accountability. It is an **overarching obligation** that applies to specific types of information which must be communicated by data controllers in different scenarios. It must be provided in a concise, transparent, intelligible and easily accessible form, using clear and plain language, in particular for any information addressed specifically to a child. 33

This information must be easy to find and accessible in a clear and prominent place. It typically takes the form of a **privacy notice** and includes the identity and contact details of the organisation, the different categories of collected data, its recipients and retention period, the purposes and legal grounds of the processing activities, the details about the transfer of the data to a third country, the statutory rights of the data subject and how he or she can exercise them, and whether any automated decision making or profiling is being used. 34

The privacy notice plays a key role, as it empowers the user of a service to exercise control over its personal data and hold data controllers accountable. It also helps children, as well as their parents, to make properly informed decisions about whether to provide the information required to access or sign up to a service. In such case, the information must be presented in a way that is **likely to appeal to the age of the child** who is accessing the service and in clear and plain language that the child can easily 35 understand. A one-size-fits-all approach does not recognise that children have different needs at different stages of their development.[20]

36 Video game companies have transposed these requirements by using less legal jargon and more clear language in privacy notices which are often presented in a layered form or accompanied by concise and easy-to-read summaries. Icons and symbols are also regularly used to support children's understanding and to present the information in a child-friendly way.[21] However, there may be a tension between the amount of information the controller needs to provide and the requirement that it must be concise. Data processing activities in the video game industry are often complex and involve large amounts of data, so companies may need to prioritise information provided to individuals and adjust its depth and the level of detail based on the degree of underlying risk of the processing.

II. Processing of personal data of minors

37 Rec. 38 of the GDPR states that **children merit specific protection** when it comes to the processing of their personal data because they may be less aware of the risks, consequences and safeguards involved and their rights in relation to the processing of personal data. It suggests that age, maturity and developmental capacity will impact children's ability to mitigate these risks and that additional protection measures would be required. Data protection authorities have interpreted the legal obligations and necessary protection measures relating to the processing of children's data from the perspective of **the 1989 United Nations Convention on the Rights of the Child**. State parties that have ratified this Convention or have acceded to it are bound by international law and must respect it. In addition, Art. 24 of the Charter of Fundamental Rights specifically recognises the rights of children and the need for public authorities or private institutions to make the child's best interests a primary consideration.

38 Art. 3 of the Convention gives every child the right to have his or her **best interests taken into account** as a primary consideration in all actions or decisions that concern him or her, which includes the processing of his or her personal data. The UN Committee on the Rights of the Child identified in its General Comment No. 25 the best interest of the child as one of the four general principles through which the implementation of all other rights under the Convention should be viewed. The Committee also acknowledges that the best interest of the child is a dynamic concept that requires an assessment appropriate to the specific context. It stressed that **due regard should be given to all children's rights**, that children should have equal and effective access to the digital environment in ways that are meaningful for them such as culture, leisure and play, and that their views should be given due weight.[22]

39 The Information Commissioner's Office in the UK was the first to translate this perspective into detailed guidance on how online services should appropriately safeguard children's personal data. The 2018 Data Protection Act requested the Commissioner to prepare a code of practice which contains guidance on the appropriate **standards of age-appropriate design** of relevant information society services which are likely to be accessed by children. The code was adopted on 27.1.2020 and consists of a set of 15

[20] Art. 29 Data Protection Working Party, 'Guidelines on transparency under Regulation 2016/679', 11.04.2018, 17/EN WP260 rev.01, 10 et seq.

[21] An example of such a practice is the 'King Privacy Saga' < https://tcs.king.com/privacy-saga/>.

[22] United Nations, 'General comment No. 25 (2021) on children's rights in relation to the digital environment', 2.3.2021, CRC/C/GC/25, 2 et seqq.

technology-neutral principles which are enforceable under UK law and intended to be built into the design of online services to safeguard children's personal data.[23] Since then, other national authorities have developed similar guidelines for their respective jurisdictions.[24]

Of particular importance is that the UK code requires these standards to be applied in relation to the risks that arise from the processing of data of individual users. This requires establishing the age of individual users with an appropriate level of certainty. Alternatively, the standards could also be applied to all users of the service. The code is not prescriptive about the methods of age assurance that should be used, nor about the level of certainty required. They should depend on the type of service and the specific circumstances, notably in relation to the risks they may poses to child users. **40**

The potential negative impact, harm or damage, caused by the processing of children's data in the games industry is however very limited, as safeguards are widely implemented. Video games companies use various **solutions appropriate to the identified risks** to distinguish children from adults and comply with minor protection rules, but also to ensure wider safety and security of their services. In addition, the industry has innovated in flexible and granular **parental tool systems** which allow parents to set up accounts for their children and confirm user age for account- or subscription-based services. They can ensure access to age-appropriate video game content according to the PEGI age classifications and allow parents to accompany their children in their online activities and use the tools to set fair rules adapted to the child's maturity. The European Data Protection Board (EDPB) accepted that parental control mechanisms can be relied on as an alternative to age verification.[25] **41**

It is important to note that **age assurance solutions** are not explicitly mentioned in the GDPR. The EDPB considers however that such solutions may be implicitly required as a means to undertake reasonable efforts to verify age in complying with the provisions of Art. 8 of the GDPR if consent is the legal basis of the processing.[26] Art. 8 of the GDPR provides that the processing of the personal data of a child in relation to an information society service offered directly to that child shall only be lawful if the child is at least 16 years old, or if the consent is given or authorised by the holder of parental responsibility over the child. Member States of the EU can, nonetheless, reduce the age threshold for consent to a minimum of 13 years. Parental consent is in the context of a video game often obtained through the parental control tool settings. **42**

Rec. 38 of the GDPR also states that children merit specific protection when their personal data is 'used for the purpose of marketing or creating personality or user profiles'. When marketing activities are carried out through the sending of emails, (parental) consent will always be the legal basis as such activities are governed by the ePD. However, if general marketing activities are executed on a legitimate interest basis, particular attention is required to ensure that the interests or fundamental rights and freedoms of the child are not affected. The same holds true for **automated processing, including profiling, of children's data** which is not prohibited in theory, but may produce 'legal or similarly significant effects' on the child. **43**

---

[23] Information Commissioner's Office, 'Age-appropriate design: a code of practice for online services' 27.1.2020, 7 et seqq.

[24] Irish DPC, 'Fundamentals for a Child-Oriented Approach to Data Processing', 12.2021; Dutch Ministry of Interior, 'Code for Children's Rights', 7.12.2021; French CNIL, '8 recommendations to enhance the protection of children online' <https://www.cnil.fr/en/cnil- publishes-8-recommendations-enhance-protection-children-online> (9.8.2021).

[25] EDPB/EDPS, 'Joint Opinion 04/2022 on the Proposal for a Regulation of the European Parliament and of the Council laying down rules to prevent and combat child sexual abuse', 28.7.2022, mn. 93.

[26] EDPB, 'Guidelines 05/2020 on consent under Regulation 2016/679', 4.5.2020, 28.

44 It should be noted in this context that rec. 71 GDPR states that measures relating to 'solely automated decision-making, including profiling, with legal or similarly significant effects (...) should not concern a child'. Data protection authorities have argued that children can be particularly susceptible in the online environment and more easily influenced by behavioural advertising. They maintain that using data for advertising purposes is not in their best interests and produces such a legal or similarly significant effect on them that companies are advised to refrain in general from profiling altogether.[27] The **UN Committee on the Rights of the Child** has even called for the complete prohibition of profiling or targeting of children for commercial purposes on the basis of a digital record of their actual or inferred characteristics.[28] Finally, it should be noted that profiling of children is already prohibited for online platforms under the Digital Services Act and upcoming legislation is expected to broaden that scope even further.

III. Fraud prevention

45 As mentioned above, the GDPR has recognised that data controllers can have a legitimate interest to process personal data if it is strictly necessary for the purposes of preventing fraud. Video game companies need to deploy **safety and security mechanisms** to address cybersecurity threats and protect video game software and licensed content from unauthorised access. They also need to protect the safety of players, the integrity of their gameplay experience and that of their terminal equipment, as well as the confidentiality of their personal data.

46 Video game companies therefore implement protection measures that typically aim to detect hacking attempts and prevent **fraudulent behaviour**, such as cheating, bullying/harassing, spoofing (e.g., impersonating other players) and malicious reporting. Such behaviour deprives genuine players of an authentic and fair gameplay experience, for example, by allowing cheaters to 'level up' faster than other players, disrupting the gameplay experience and hindering progression in the game. It creates negative player sentiment, which causes genuine players to disengage from games, leading to impacts on revenue.

47 **Hacking** is often done by professional organisations that make use of unauthorised access to the game code to illegally download video game content in order to sell it to players and make large profits. Such companies often operate in an organised crime environment and do not hesitate to engage in other criminal activities. Hacking may also compromise the security of the personal data of players which puts companies as data controllers under a legal obligation to implement appropriate measures to contain this risk.

48 Information about the functioning of propriety detection methods would allow a user of the service to circumvent the software and go undetected in the future. Such information is, therefore, considered a **trade secret**. The EDPB has recognised that trade secrets may preclude the disclosure of the player's personal data where the player has requested access to his personal data according to Art. 14 GDPR.[29] This right of access is subject to the limitations that result from Art. 15(4) GDPR which says that the right to obtain a copy shall not adversely affect the rights and freedoms of others. Conflicting rights and

---

[27] Irish DPC, 'Fundamentals for a Child-Oriented Approach to Data Processing', 12.2021, 54 et seqq.

[28] United Nations, 'General comment No. 25 (2021) on children's rights in relation to the digital environment', 2.3.2021, CRC/C/GC/25, 7.

[29] EDPB, 'Guidelines 01/2022 on data subject rights – Right of access', 28.3.2023, 54 et seq.

freedoms that are explicitly mentioned in the corresponding rec. 63 GDPR include trade secrets or intellectual property and copyright protecting of the software.

IV. Data transfers outside the European Union

The video games industry is an **international business**, and many video game companies are offering their services globally. Companies are only able to deliver services to their customers if they are in a position to process user data from around the world. Video game companies, like any other companies, also often commission a range of selected service providers externally. Global SaaS providers, for instance, are typically used for supportive functions, such as company email, payment processing, document storage, customer relationship management, customer support, analytics, user testing, and background checking services. Group subsidiaries often also rely on central services infrastructure, such as centralised human resources, information security systems, and privacy management systems, procured by the parent company in one head office and managed and supported by specialised teams locally. 49

Video games companies therefore depend on a reliable legal framework which allows the transfer of data securely across borders. If processing operations need personal data from EU citizens to be transferred to a 'third country' outside the EU, the GDPR requires that the level of protection in this country is essentially equivalent to the level in the EU. Therefore, an **adequacy decision** pursuant to Art. 45 GDPR must be in place. Data flows between EU and US economies, which are of particular importance for video game companies, have been disrupted due to the subsequent invalidations by the Court of Justice of the two previous EU-US adequacy decisions, the Privacy Shield[30] and its predecessor the Safe Harbour Agreement.[31] The new 'EU-US Data Privacy Framework' which was adopted in July 2023 may provide a more durable basis for transatlantic data transfers in compliance with EU standards.[32] 50

If no adequacy decision with the third country has been issued, personal data may only be transferred by using tools containing appropriate safeguards pursuant to Art. 46 GDPR, such as **standard contractual clauses** adopted by the European Commission or a supervisory authority. The companies that are using such clauses remain however responsible for verifying on a case-by-case basis if the law or practice of the third country impinges on the effectiveness of the appropriate safeguards. They may need to implement supplementary measures that fill any gaps in the protection to bring it up to the level required by EU law.[33] Alternatively, companies can also use binding corporate rules that, once approved by the EDPB, allow for transfers of personal data within a group of companies. 51

30 ECJ 16.7.2020 – case C-311/18, ECLI:EU:C:2020:559 mn.. 201 – *Data Protection Commissioner v Facebook Ireland Limited and Maximillian Schrems.*

31 ECJ 6.10.2015 – case C-362/14, ECLI:EU:C:2015:650 mn. 106 – *Maximillian Schrems v Data Protection Commissioner.*

32 European Commission, 'Implementing Decision EU 2023/1795 of 10.7.2023 pursuant to Regulation (EU) 2016/679', OJ 2023, L 231, 118.

33 EDPB, 'Recommendations 01/2020 on measures that supplement transfer tools to ensure compliance with the EU level of protection of personal data', 18.6.2021, 10 et seqq.

E. Conclusion

52 Video games do not exist without the processing of (personal) data. **Several types of data** need to be collected, processed and stored to allow for the functioning of a video game. Gameplay metrics constitute a particularly important category of data as they are essential in ensuring that players are provided with a smooth, enjoyable and challenging gameplay experience. As data controllers, video game companies are responsible for ensuring that these processing activities comply with the legal framework. Its fundamental principles of transparency and accountability allow individuals to understand how their personal data is being used and to hold organisations accountable.

53 Among the **many regulatory requirements**, video game companies need to ensure, in particular, that their, often complex, processing operations are covered by clear, justified lawful grounds and that the processing is well documented in mandatory, easy to find and understandable privacy notices. Furthermore, as children may be less aware of risks, consequences and rights in relation to the processing of personal data, companies must implement specific safeguards appropriate to the identified risk and the age of the child. They also need to deploy safety and security mechanisms to address cybersecurity threats and ensure that they can transfer data securely across borders to continue to offer their services globally.

54 As a digital industry known for its **data-driven innovations** and technological progress, the video game sector heavily depends on a predictable and reliable legal framework that provides for consistent, uniform rules across territories. While the Europe-wide harmonised standards of the GDPR are a great added value for the sector, the 2024 review report of the European Commission demonstrated a lack of progress towards a consistent application of its rules.[34] Concerns exist in relation diverging national interpretations, fragmented implementation where Member States have a possibility to specify the rules and a lack of harmonised enforcement. Furthermore, a potential review of the ePD in the future will bring another regulatory challenge as this may affect how companies keep in-game communication services such as chatrooms safe and secure. Video game companies will need to adapt to forthcoming legal reforms and ensure that their operational practices are taken into account.

[34] European Commission, 'Second Report on the application of the General Data Protection Regulation' (25.7.2024), COM(2024) 357 final, 2 et seqq.

§ 30
Value Added Tax

A. Introduction and scope 1

B. EU VAT 3
I. Nature of supply – electronically provided services 4
II. Key elements of EU VAT 5
1. Supply for consideration 5
2. Place of supply 7
3. VAT rates 11
4. When does VAT become due? 13
5. Invoicing 16
6. Filing of VAT returns 18
III. Platform business 23
1. Fiction of a supply chain 24
2. Denial of a supply chain 31

C. General consumption taxes outside the EU 35
I. Background 35
II. Steps to check tax liability in the third country 40
III. Tax registration, calculation and declaration of VAT 42

Annex 1 – EU VAT rates (May 2025) 47

Annex 2 – VAT on electronic services outside the EU (not a complete list) .. 48

A. Introduction and scope

In terms of revenue, **value added tax** (VAT) is the most important tax not only in Germany (with approx. 300 billion EUR or 30 % of total tax revenue in 2024) but also in many other countries. The tax is linked to sales and therefore relevant for every company – apart from small businesses (the current threshold in Germany is 25,000 EUR of annual turnover) which are exempt from VAT. 1

Compared to other taxes, in particular (corporate) income tax, VAT (or more generally: any consumption-based indirect tax) has two special features: Firstly, errors are much more difficult to correct. This is because VAT is a component of the price under civil law (i.e., it is supposed to be passed on to the purchaser of goods or services) and the tax liability must be checked for every individual sales transaction or sales invoice. On the purchase side, VAT is generally paid for every good or service and its deduction as input VAT requires a **correct and complete VAT invoice**. Errors which are detected in tax determination or tax calculation can therefore cost a lot of money if the relevant invoice cannot be corrected anymore. Secondly, a tax liability of a particular company in another state can quickly arise from the fact that goods are sold or services are provided to customers abroad – unlike in the area of income-based taxes, this does not require a physical presence in the other country. In particular with regard to electronic services provided via the internet by a gaming company, it is not reasonable to exclude customers from other countries (i.e., by geo-blocking), if the range of services can be scaled with marginal costs of almost zero across borders. As a consequence, a gaming company generally has a worldwide customer base and quickly gets in touch with VAT and other general consumption taxes in other states. It is therefore not reasonable to ignore those indirect consumption taxes. 2

B. EU VAT

3 The Common Market of the European Union started about 30 years ago, on 1.1.1993. From that date, also the application of value added tax was harmonised across all Member States, based on the **European VAT Directive**. This means that the main components of the tax (determination of the place of supply, tax base, tax point, right to recover input, invoicing, etc.) are comparable in all Member States. There are of course lots of differences to be taken into account, due to different interpretation and implementation but also with regard to tax administration, interest and penalty schemes.

I. Nature of supply – electronically provided services

4 The core feature of the services provided by games companies is their automated transmission via electronic networks.[1] Such '**electronically supplied services**' (cp. Art. 7 IR 282/2011) are services 'which are delivered over the Internet or an electronic network and the nature of which renders their supply essentially automated and involving minimal human intervention, and impossible to ensure in the absence of information technology'. In other words, computer and mobile games, irrespective of whether they are played online or provided as a download, can be delivered automatically without a person being involved at the side of the supplier at the moment of supply. Access to the game as well as the purchase of in-game content is largely automated. The fact that a game has been programmed by humans is as irrelevant as the fact that there may be a customer helpline and staff which make sure that servers work properly and the game gets upgrades, etc.

II. Key elements of EU VAT

1. Supply for consideration

5 Generally, VAT is linked to a payment in currency (legal tender or crypto which has to be converted for declaration and tax payment purposes). '**Consideration**' in the meaning of the EU VAT Directive[2] is the amount spent by the customer to receive a service in return. In case payment services providers (such as Paypal or credit card companies) deduct a fee from the payout to the gaming company, this fee is a cost and does not reduce the taxable consideration for the sale made to the customer.

6 As regards the concept of consideration, the following is worth mentioning:

(1) **F2P and provision of data**
It is an iron principle of capitalism that nothing in life is for free. With regard to F2P games (free-to-play) it is therefore not surprising that tax authorities are suspicious. Is it really reasonable that computer and mobile games can be downloaded/played for free? And indeed, about 10 years ago a discussion started, if internet users actually pay for free content with their personal data as part of a barter-like transac-

---

[1] If computer games are sold on a carrier, i.e., CD or memory card this is to be seen as a sale of goods which follows different rules (not discussed herein).

[2] Council Directive 2006/112/EC of 28.112006 on the common system of value added tax.

tion[3] which would give rise to VAT liabilities.[4] Fortunately, the VAT Committee[5] rejected such views about 7 years ago and it has been quiet on this topic for a while. However, this can change quickly as a recent case in Italy shows[6] – the Italian tax administration has addressed the question to the EU VAT committee and claimed VAT in particular from Facebook, Meta and LinkedIn. If user data is seen as a consideration for free content this will of course also affect gaming companies. The matter needs to be monitored closely and it is not unlikely that the ECJ will have to decide.

(2) **Donations**

The concept of VAT says that there must be a close link or relationship between the service provided and the payment made. Interestingly, about 30 years ago[7] the European Court of Justice denied the applicability of VAT on money received by a street musician, arguing that there is no such link between the music and the money paid by people passing by. However, 30 years later and with regard to a YouTube streamer, the Lower Tax court of Dusseldorf/Germany[8] has confirmed that voluntary payments of followers are subject to VAT. Without deep diving into the circumstances it is not evident where the difference between such cases is to justify a different handling for VAT. Further case law can be expected[9] and also in this matter it may be helpful if the ECJ would bring further clarification.

(3) **Crowdfunding**

A gaming company might collect money by crowdfunding to develop and market its products. It depends on the nature of the return given to the investor to determine whether or not VAT becomes due:

- Equity-based: Paying into the project establishes co-ownership rights. Subsequent profit shares are not subject to VAT but have the nature of a dividend.
- Lending-based: The deposit is made in the form of a loan. Potential interest flowing back later is exempt from VAT.
- Donation-based: If the payment does not give rise to any returns or rights for the investor, such a donation is (potentially, see point above) out of scope of VAT.
- Reward-based crowdfunding: If the investor is given a specific benefit (such as exclusive content, pre-release access) his payment is a consideration in terms of

---

3 For discussion in Germany cp. Grambeck, 'Keine Umsatzsteuerpflicht bei kostenlosen Internetdiensten und Smartphone-Apps', DStR 2016, 2026; in English: Pfeiffer, VAT on 'Free' Electronic Services? International VAT Monitor May/June 2016, 158.

4 Additionally, it shall be noted that a situation where a user provides personal data in return for the use of digital content falls under the German Civil Code (§ 327). However, as VAT is a tax which is harmonised across the EU, this cannot lead to the conclusion that in such a situation a barter transaction is in place which triggers VAT.

5 VAT Committee working paper 982, taxud.c.1(2018)6248826 – EN, 30.10.2018, https://circabc.europa.eu/sd/a/ee8603b3-9d86-444f-921c-003e3bee08ce/WP%20958%20-%20Art%202%20-%20Internet%20services.pdf.

6 See https://www.vatcalc.com/italy/italy-assess-facebook-for-vat-on-users-data-in-return-for-free-portal-access/.

7 ECJ decision, 3.3.1994, R. J. Tolsma, C-16/93 (If a musician who performs on the public highway receives donations from passers-by, those receipts cannot be regarded as the consideration for a service supplied to them').

8 Lower Fiscal Court Duesseldorf, 4.3.2022, 1 K 2812/19 U https://nrwe.justiz.nrw.de/fgs/duesseldorf/j2022/1_K_2812_19_U_Urteil_20220304.html.

9 The Lower Fiscal Court Berlin Brandenburg, 25. April 2025, 2 K 2085/21 came to a different conclusion than the Lower Fiscal Court Duesseldorf, the matter is now pending at the German Supreme Court, V R 10/25 https://dejure.org/dienste/vernetzung/rechtsprechung?Gericht=FG%20Berlin-Brandenburg&Datum=25.04.2025&Aktenzeichen=2%20K%202085/21.

VAT. If the project fails (and nothing can be provided to the investor) VAT may have to be adjusted.

2. Place of supply

7 The concept of EU VAT as a general consumption tax is based on the **destination principle** – services shall be taxed where they are received and consumed. In B2C business this is generally the place where the consumer is resident (Art. 58 EC VAT Directive).

8 With regard to providers of electronic services from outside the EU this scheme was introduced on 1.7.2003. Suppliers seated in the EU have applied the VAT in their member state of residence until 2014 (for simplification); from 1.1.2015 they have to apply the destination principle. Exceptions apply for companies whose annual revenues from customers resident in other EU Member States do not exceed 10,000 EUR. They still have the right to remit all EU VAT in their EU Member State of residence (Art. 59c EC VAT Directive).

9 In principle, the place of residence of the B2C customer must be **proven on the basis of two non-contradictory criteria**, such as IP address, bank details, mobile country code of mobile phone, location of landline/internet connection or other 'relevant' information (such as country-specific payment systems or the customer's purchase history).[10] A gaming company can also rely on information provided by other parties, such as payment service providers. For reasons of simplification, for companies with a total revenue from customers in other EU Member States of not more than 100,000 EUR/year, one element is sufficient to prove the place of supply.

10 Even after more than 10 years in operation, there is only little practical experience on how the tax authorities handle **potential errors** in documentation of the place of supply (i.e., there is only one item of evidence or there is a mismatch between two items). This may be due to the fact that a tax inspector in Member State A (where the provider is resident), may have only little interest in auditing and shifting the tax base and tax revenue from Member State B to a potential other Member State C. Stricter standards may be applicable if a gaming company applies different prices in different Member States (i.e., because the purchasing power is different) and does not take sufficient measures to prevent price shopping by consumers. If customers try to technically 'migrate' to low-price countries (i.e., with proxy IP and VPN exploitation) a gaming company should be prepared to present sufficient evidence of the place of supply of customers across the EU.

3. VAT rates

11 All EU Member States apply a **regular or standard VAT rate** as shown in Annex 1.[11] Reduced rates or exemptions are not relevant for the games sector.

12 Incidentally, tax rates are proving to be relatively stable. However, since VAT has a stable tax base it is also a good way to close funding gaps in the state budget. In particular in the context of the Euro crisis in 2010 VAT was increased in a number of EU Member States (i.e., in Ireland from 21 % to 23 %, in Spain from 18 % to 21 %, in Portugal from 21 % to 23 %, in Greece from 23 % to 24 %, in Italy from 20 % to 22 %). Germany

[10] Explanatory notes on the EU VAT changes to the place of supply of telecommunications, broadcasting and electronic services that enter into force in 2015 (Council Implementing Regulation (EU) No. 1042/2013), published on 3.4.2014, https://vat-one-stop-shop.ec.europa.eu/system/files/2021-07/explanatory_notes_2015_en_0.pdf.

[11] Source: https://ec.europa.eu/taxation_customs/taxation-1/value-added-tax-vat_en.

now ranks at the lower end of the scale with a rate of 19 %. In the long run it is foreseeable that VAT rates will further increase across the EU.

4. When does VAT become due?

VAT becomes **due at the time a service is provided to the customer** (even if the money is received later) or if a payment is received before the service is provided. This gives rise to the question of when a service is supposed to be provided if a customer has to buy in-game currency first which is then used to acquire in-game items. One could argue that there is no service until the in-game currency is spent in the game. However, it could also be argued that legal tender is finally spent (and the service is provided) at the time the in-game currency is purchased. The latter approach seems to be correct in particular if it is taken into account that according to T&Cs of a gaming company in-game currency cannot be changed back into legal tender. Whether at all or when the customer uses his in-game currency in the game is therefore irrelevant for VAT purposes. If the credit expires (because the player closes his gaming account or no longer uses it for other reasons), this does not entitle the provider to adjust the VAT that has already been incurred or paid. The VAT would only have to be adjusted if the gaming company refunds the remuneration (e.g., as a gesture of goodwill). 13

In VAT there is a particular issue with **vouchers**. Because there was no harmonisation across the EU and doubt about the correct VAT handling, rules were harmonised in 2019 (cp. Art. 30a, 30b EC VAT Directive). Basically, there are two different scenarios: 14

(1) The VAT can be calculated at the time the voucher is issued (single purpose voucher). This is the case if it is defined that a voucher can only be used for a particular type of service (so that it is clear that – as an example – the standard VAT rate applies) and only in a particular Member State.[12] If those criteria are met, VAT has to be declared at the time the voucher is issued. If the voucher is redeemed nothing happens in terms of VAT; and if the voucher is not redeemed at all, VAT cannot be corrected.

(2) The VAT cannot be calculated at the time the voucher is issued (multi-purpose voucher). This is the case if the voucher can be redeemed for several types of goods/services and/or in several jurisdictions. The VAT can only be calculated correctly at the time of redemption. Thus, VAT becomes due when the voucher is redeemed. If no redemption takes place, VAT does not occur.

Hence, if a gaming company decides to make use of vouchers it needs to be determined if they are single or multi purpose vouchers to correctly apply EU VAT. 15

5. Invoicing

As a general principle, there is an obligation to raise a VAT **invoice for commercial sales**. However, there are several simplifications in place, i.e., if it is a B2C transaction (there may not be an obligation to raise a VAT invoice at all, such as in Germany) or if it is a small invoice (in Germany = up to 250 EUR, limited content of invoices). For cross-border sales within the EU the VAT Directive stipulates that a supplier has to apply the rules on invoicing of the Member State where the VAT place of supply is (which is the Member State where the customer lives). If, however, the supplier of electronic services makes use of the simplified One Stop Shop (see next section), he can apply the rules on 16

[12] See ECJ Case C-68/23, 18.4.2024.

invoicing of the member state of his residence. Example: A German gaming company provides electronic services to

- German customers: There is no obligation to raise a VAT invoice for B2C sales, cp Art. 14 German VAT Act. From a VAT perspective, it would be sufficient to issue a receipt which only shows the gross amount.[13]
- Customers in other EU Member States: Since the place of supply is where the customer is, local rules apply. There may be a need to raise a complete VAT invoice. However, if the gaming company makes use of the One Stop Shop, it can apply German rules and insofar has no obligation to raise a VAT invoice.
- Consumers outside the EU: There is no need to raise a VAT invoice from a German perspective. Of course, local rules in the state where the customer lives, should be checked (see section C.).

17 Where allowed, a gaming company should not issue an invoice which shows the VAT amount. This is because in case of mistakes and changes (i.e., the VAT rate changes or it turns out the VAT place of supply is in another jurisdiction), the correction of the VAT declared may be linked to the correction of the invoice. If the receipt does not show the VAT amount, the correction of VAT does not require the correction of the receipt.[14]

6. Filing of VAT returns

18 Generally, VAT needs to be **declared to the tax authority of the Member State** where the VAT place of supply is. A gaming company from outside the EU as well as an EU resident gaming company with B2C sales across the EU would therefore have to register for VAT in multiple jurisdictions. Due to the language barriers and the non-harmonised administrative rules, this is difficult to manage and involves considerable administrative costs.

19 The legislator recognised this problem in the course of the implementation of the regulations on the place of supply for electronic services (on 1.1.2015) and those changes where accompanied by the introduction of the so-called Mini One Stop Shop (**MOSS**). This means that an EU resident provider of electronic services can submit a VAT report with all cross-border EU B2C revenues sales in his EU Member State of residence. The calculated VAT is passed on by the tax office to the authorities in all other EU Member States. The scheme can also be used by companies not resident in the EU; they can decide in which EU Member State they want to submit the simplified VAT return.

20 On 1.7.2021, the MOSS was renamed **OSS** (One Stop Shop). The scheme is not anymore limited to electronic services but now also covers other types of services as well as B2C distance sales of goods. At the same time two improvements were adopted:

- The submission deadline was extended from the 20th of the month following the reporting quarter to the end of this month (e.g., 31 April instead of 20 April for the Q1 VAT report).
- Corrections of a previously calculated VAT (e.g., due to cancellations, refunds or chargebacks of the payment service providers) can be done in the next OSS return due, instead of correcting historic OSS returns in which the original transaction was reported.

---

[13] The issuance of an invoice may of course be necessary for non-tax reasons (cf., e.g., § 368 BGB on the issuance of a receipt).

[14] Fortunately, the ECJ has confirmed that a correction of VAT is possible without a correction of a VAT invoice if it is evident that the customer is not allowed to deduct input VAT, i.e., because he is not in business or because the service received is for private use only (8.12.2022, P GmbH, C-378/21).

A gaming company making use of OSS should be aware of the following aspects of the special scheme: 21

- It is not possible to claim and deduct input VAT under OSS. If local input tax is incurred in other EU Member States, the gaming company has to make use of the special refund procedure for non-established businesses (Art. 170 EC VAT Directive, based on Council Directive 2008/9/EC of 12.2.2008). The application is to be made until 30 September of the following year. If the gaming company is established outside the EU, input VAT can be reclaimed accordingly, and the application is due until 30 June of the following year (Thirteenth Council Directive 86/560/EEC of 17.11.1986).
- OSS is 'all-in or all-out'. If a gaming company decides to apply OSS, this implies the special scheme has to be applied for all EU Member States (with the exception of sales in Member States where the gaming company is established or maintains a permanent establishment; in those Member States the gaming company has to file regular VAT returns).
- OSS cannot be accessed with retrospective effect. If a gaming company failed to register for OSS upfront, it has to regularise the past first (by submitting voluntary disclosures to the tax authorities in the respective EU member state), register for OSS and report future sales via OSS.
- The tax authority of the EU member state where the OSS returns are filed only acts as a mailbox with regard to the VAT amounts belonging to the other EU Member States. Any particular issues (i.e., clarification of tax rate, scope of the concept of electronically supplied services, penalties and interest in case of late filing and payment of VAT) are subject to the regulations of the Member State where the VAT place of supply is. Also, tax audits are likely to be carried out by the Member States to which the VAT belongs. Thus, even if OSS is a simplification, there may still be a need for local consultants.

Notwithstanding these problems and special features of the OSS procedure, it is a welcome simplification for the suppliers of electronic services. 22

III. Platform business

Where electronic content is not delivered and sold directly to the final consumer (i.e., via the website of the gaming company), **platforms** such as Steam, Google or Apple play an important role. In such a case it needs to be decided for VAT purposes if the gaming company has to report a direct sale to the customer (of the platform) or if there is a sale to the platform (which in a subsequent step sells to the customer). Whilst in the beginning of such internet business it was not entirely clear if VAT on the sale to the consumer was to be paid by the platform or by the gaming company[15] the legislator addressed this issue and implemented a rule which defines under what circumstances the platform is directly responsible for the collection of VAT (this is called a fiction of a supply chain). 23

[15] On 10.4.2025 the General Advocate has given his opinion in Xyrality (C-101/24) and confirmed that under the circumstances given the platform is also liable to account for VAT for sales made prior 1.1.2015. Even though the decision is welcome and in line with today's practice, it comes a little late since for most businesses any tax assessments prior to 2015 are already time barred.

1. Fiction of a supply chain

24 'Where electronically supplied services are supplied through a telecommunications network, an interface or a portal such as a marketplace for applications, a taxable person taking part in that supply shall be presumed to be acting in his own name but on behalf of the provider of those services', if the conditions of Art. 9a IR[16] are met. This is the case if the intermediary (such as Steam, Google or Apple)

- authorises the charge to the customer or the delivery of the services, or
- sets the general terms and conditions of the supply.

25 If those conditions are met, the gaming company is deemed to provide the electronic service to the intermediary whereas the intermediary provides the service to the gamer (final consumer).

26

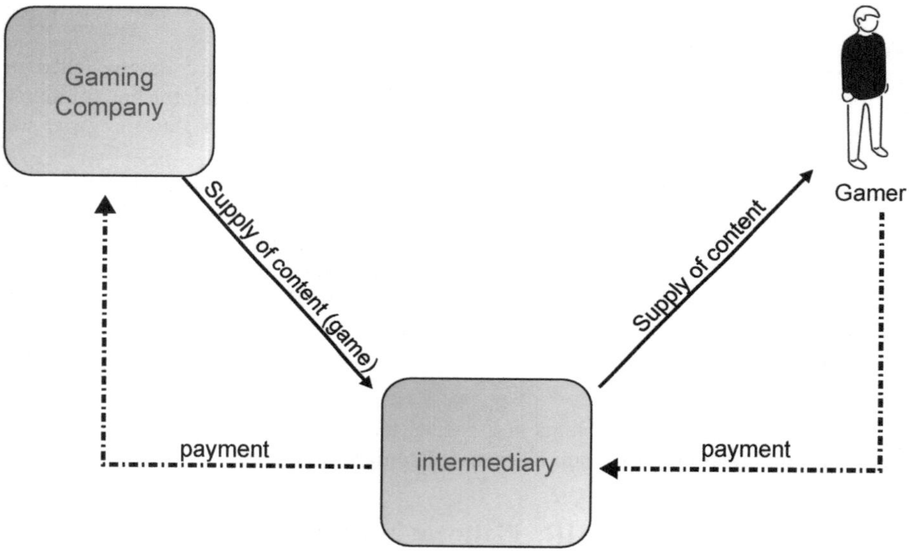

Fig. 30.1: Fiction of the supply chain (gaming company → intermediary → gamer)

27 The fiscal idea of the concept is that it is much easier for the tax authorities to tax (and audit) the big platforms (such as Google and Apple operating the PlayStore or AppStore) on their B2C business than to collect the VAT from numbers of gaming companies.

28 If under the conditions of Art. 9a IR the gaming company makes a (deemed) sale to the intermediary this transaction is subject to B2B rules. The VAT **place of supply** for the service provided by the gaming company to the intermediary is the place from which the platform operates its business (Art. 44 EC VAT Directive), usually the place of residence. If the intermediary is

- based in Germany, the payout received by a German gaming company is subject to German VAT. The gaming company is liable to remit the VAT and the platform has a right to deduct it as input VAT;

[16] Council Implementing Regulation (EU) No. 282/2011 of 15.3.2011, current consolidated text can be down- loaded https://eur-lex.europa.eu/legal-content/EN/TXT/?uri=CELEX%3A02011R0282-20250414.

- resident in another EU Member State, the payout is taxable in that EU Member State. The intermediary has to self-account for VAT under the reverse charge mechanism and has a right to deduct that VAT as input VAT (Art. 196 EC VAT Directive). The gaming company needs to document the EU VAT ID number of the intermediary, and this VAT ID number must be checked for validity and included in the EC Sales Lists to be filed by the gaming company.
- resident outside the EU, the payout is out of scope of DE VAT.

The issuance of an **invoice** by the gaming company to the intermediary/platform is mandatory (as it is a deemed B2B sale), whereby the parties can agree on self-billing. The tax base is calculated on the basis of the payout made by the intermediary/platform to the gaming company. 29

The intermediary/platform provides an electronic service to the final consumer, in accordance with the principles set out in section B.2. It can apply OSS to report its EU VAT liabilities. 30

2. Denial of a supply chain

If the requirements of Art. 9a IR are not met or if the intermediary merely processes payments[17] in relation to the services provided by the gaming company the intermediary is not part of a (fictitious) supply chain: 31

32

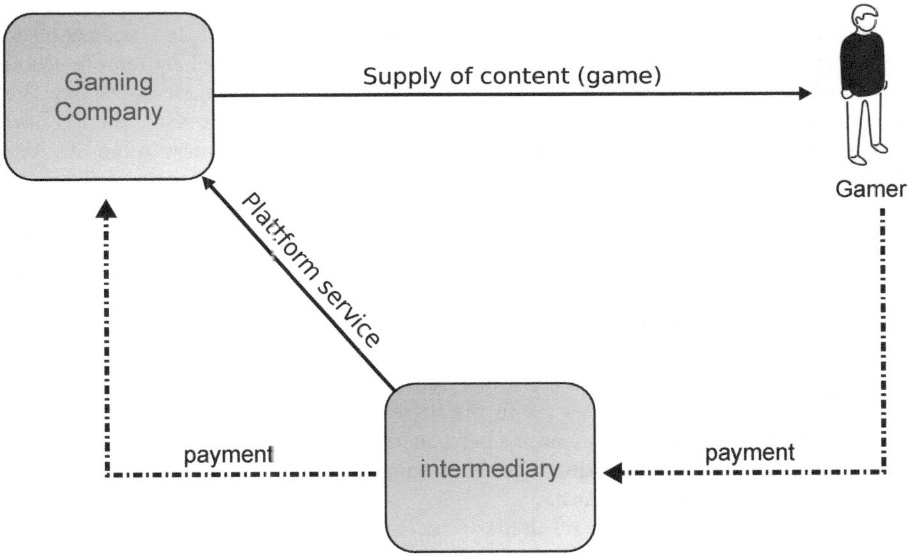

Fig. 30.2: Negation of the supply chain

In this scenario, the gaming company provides the service to the final consumer (B2C) which follows the rules set out in section B II. Tax is calculated on the basis of what the customer spends to receive the service. That means the gaming company cannot calculate its VAT on the basis of the payout received from the intermediary! 33

[17] It should be mentioned here that EU law requires payment processors to record and report details of cross-border payments according to Art. 243a – 243d EC VAT Directive. This measure was taken to give tax authorities an additional instrument to expose tax fraud.

34 The intermediary provides a **platform service** to the gaming company. VAT is calculated on the basis of its revenue share. Its VAT handling is subject to B2B rules as set out in section B.III.1. As an example, if a German-based gaming company receives platform services from an intermediary being resident

- in Germany, this remuneration is settled with VAT, which has to be declared by the intermediary and which can be claimed by the gaming company as input VAT for the services received.
- outside Germany, this remuneration is settled without VAT, whereas the gaming company has to self-account for German VAT (reverse charge) which is deductible as input VAT.

C. General consumption taxes outside the EU

I. Background

35 There are 193 countries on earth (member countries of the United Nations). Basically in every country outside the EU an indirect general consumption tax on private consumption is applied which is more or less comparable to the design of the EU VAT. There are only a few **exceptions** (e.g., Kuwait, Qatar, as well as some states of the US, such as Montana or Delaware) where no general consumption tax is in place.

36 In the meantime many of those countries have regulations in place according to which the consumption tax applies on **electronic content** provided by remote sellers (see Annex 2 which does not claim to be complete and correct). It looks like this development was triggered by the EU itself, where companies from outside the EU have had to register since 1.7.2003 if they sell electronic content to consumers in the EU. Also the OECD in their International VAT/GST Guidelines[18] as well as in their 'VAT Digital Toolkits'[19] for Latin America,[20] Asia and Africa[21] suggests to follow that path. This is not only a measure to broaden the tax base but also a matter of neutrality to tax local and remote traders equally. As a matter of fact, no country can afford not to tax the digital economy which is gaining in importance.

37 For gaming companies which act globally by nature (and which have fewer restrictions than companies trading with goods) the handling of consumption taxes is a big challenge. In principle, any end consumer sale, no matter how small, can trigger an obligation to pay a consumption tax in the respective countries. Unlike in the area of direct taxes, this does not even require a permanent establishment in the sense of human or technical resources on site since the tax is triggered merely by the fact that the end consumer is resident in this country.

38 Experience has shown (so far) that the tax administrations are still rather passive when thinking about taxation of **remote sellers**. They set up (more or less comfortable) portals and basically rely on the wish of decision makers in companies to be compliant and to register voluntarily. Some pressure on companies may be built up by exchange of information between the tax administrations (such as between Norway and the EU) or by the publication of names of companies which already registered (such as in

[18] OECD (2017), International VAT/GST Guidelines, OECD Publishing, Paris https://doi.org/10.1787/9789264271401-en.

[19] https://www.oecd.org/en/topics/sub-issues/vat-policy-and-administration/vat-digital-toolkits.html.

[20] See also Bal, beck.digitax 2024, 389.

[21] See also Bal, beck.digitax 2025, 14.

Russia, Mexico, Chile or South Korea). There are also a few states which send letters to the companies which they think should register as remote sellers of digital content (recently such as Kenia, Peru or Moldova). Other countries rely on the agreements of international legal assistance so that the gaming company receives a respective request from its own local tax office which has been contacted by the tax authorities of the country where the content is sold (such as Indonesia).

To summarise, it is a matter of fact that the need to pay **tax outside the EU** cannot be ignored by gaming companies. Otherwise there is a risk of facing an unexpected tax liability not only for future years but also for the past. It is much better to take the matter seriously, to register and – where possible – to include the local VAT in the price calculation. **39**

II. Steps to check tax liability in the third country

In order to clarify potential **tax obligations and risks outside the EU** a gaming company must first obtain an overview (e.g., by means of geolocation software) of its worldwide revenues. In a next step it is necessary to examine whether there is a tax liability in the countries. By nature, this is not an easy task since there is no general source where respective information can be obtained. If a gaming company does not want to rely on newsletters of tax professionals it is necessary to reach out to the local tax administration or a local advisor. **40**

Once a potential tax liability has been identified, in a next step it is necessary to check if there is a general exemption. This may be for different reasons, in particular: **41**

- Digital/intangible products are explicitly excluded from local consumption taxes (this applies to selected states of the US, e.g., Georgia and Virginia), or
- The local revenue from B2C sales is below a given threshold. High thresholds are applied for instance in Japan (10 million JPY or approx. 75,000 EUR), Singapore (100,000 SGD or approx. 65,000 EUR) and Australia (75,000 AUD or approx. 50,000 EUR) whilst many countries do not apply a threshold at all (such as the EU does), i.e., Turkey or Switzerland. Other states, such as Norway (50,000 NOK, or approx. 5,000 EUR) apply a rather low threshold which is quickly exceeded. Many US states also apply a second type of threshold which is the number of transactions/year.
- The tax is owed by a different party involved, in particular platforms such as Google or Apple (which are actually registered in most of the countries on earth, comparable to the model applied in the EU) or payment processors (such as in many countries in South America).

III. Tax registration, calculation and declaration of VAT

If a VAT liability for the gaming company is confirmed, it may be necessary to clarify the handling of **historical tax liabilities**. Most countries have general limitation periods. Depending on when the rules for the taxation of remote sellers were introduced in the respective country, a retroactive assessment of up to 5 years may be required. Any interest and penalties due to late registration and payment of the tax need to be taken into account (those may be negligible, such as in Norway or considerable, such as in Russia, Chile or the Kingdom of Saudi Arabia). **42**

43 **Tax registration** and filing can usually be carried out by the gaming company itself or by a tax specialist. In many cases (such as Norway, Australia, UK, Turkey or Chile) the portals are very comfortable and the process of registration, filing and payment is straightforward. Only in a few cases (in particular in Switzerland, Japan and Mexico) is it necessary to appoint a local fiscal representative – this makes it easier for the gaming company but (where the representative can be held jointly liable) also more expensive (such as in Mexico where the costs for fiscal representation can reach 10,000 USD/year). It may also be considered to outsource tax compliance to technical service providers such as Avalara or Taxamo.

44 In most countries, the **calculation of the tax** is based on the gross revenues received. In countries with sales tax (especially the US, Canada), it is common to add the tax upon check-out. Such differences need to be taken into account when setting up the web shop and defining the prices to be charged to consumers. With regard to the VAT rate to be applied, almost all countries have nationwide rates for electronic services. The situation is different in Canada (where at provincial and state levels different rates are applied) and the US (where the tax rate depends on the post code of the living address of the consumer).

45 The **filing frequency** is quarterly in most cases, it may also be monthly, bi-monthly or (if there is only little revenue) annually (such as in Saskatchewan and British Columbia, both Canada). The last obstacle of being compliant is the transfer of the tax to the local tax authorities. This is of course easy where SEPA is in place (Single European Payment Area) and also manageable where the payment can be made via credit card (i.e. Turkey) or by simple money transfer (i.e. Australia, New Zealand or Canada). It is a however a real challenge in the US where some states require the payment to be made from a US bank account.

46 In most cases invoicing is not an issue since there is no obligation to raise a specific invoice on B2C sales. Also here, exceptions apply, such as in Taiwan, where it is necessary to upload invoices to a portal of the tax authorities.

Annex 1 – EU VAT rates (May 2025)

47

EU member state	Country code	Standard VAT rate in % on 1.1.2026
Belgium	BE	21
Bulgaria	BG	20
Czech Republic	CZ	21
Denmark	DK	25
Germany	DE	19
Estonia	EE	24
Ireland	IE	23
Greece	GR	24
Spain	ES	21
France	FR	20
Croatia	HR	25
Italy	IT	22

EU member state	Country code	Standard VAT rate in % on 1.1.2026
Cyprus	CY	19
Latvia	LV	21
Lithuania	LT	21
Luxembourg	LU	17
Hungary	HU	27
Malta	MT	18
Netherlands	NL	21
Austria	AT	20
Poland	PL	23
Portugal	PT	23
Romania	RO	21
Slovenia	SI	22
Slovakia	SK	23
Finland	FI	25.5
Sweden	SE	25

Annex 2 – VAT on electronic services outside the EU (not a complete list)

48

	Country	Implementation date	Threshold in local currency	Threshold in Euro	Tax rate	Fiscal representative required?
1	Switzerland (incl. Liechtenstein)	01.01.2010	0 (worldwide income 100,000 CHF)		8.1 %	yes
2	Canaries	01.01.2010	0		7 %	
3	Norway	01.07.2011	50,000 NOK	5,000 EUR	25 %	
4	Iceland	01.11.2011	2,000,000 ISK	16,000 EUR	24 %	
5	Kenya	01.09.2013	0		16 %	
6	South Africa	01.06.2014	1,000,000 ZAR	58,300 EUR	15 %	
7	Albania	01.01.2015	0		20 %	
9	South Korea	01.07.2015	0		10 %	
10	Japan	01.10.2015	10,000,000 JPY	75,000 EUR	10 %	yes
11	Egypt	01.09.2016	0		14 %	
12	New Zealand	01.10.2016	60,000 NZD	35,000 EUR	15 %	
13	United States	from 2017/ depending on the state	usually 100,000 USD and/or 200 transactions per year	85,000 EUR	approx. 8 %	
14	India	01.01.2017	0		18 %	

	Country	Implementation date	Threshold in local currency	Threshold in Euro	Tax rate	Fiscal representative required?
15	Russia	01.01.2017	0		20 %	
16	Serbia	01.04.2017	0		20 %	yes
17	Taiwan	01.05.2017	480,000 NTD	14,000 EUR	5 %	
19	Australia	01.07.2017	75,000 AUD	50,000 EUR	10 %	
20	Belarus	01.01.2018	0		20 %	
21	Turkey	01.01.2018	0		20 %	
22	Saudi Arabia	01.01.2018	0		15 %	
23	United Arab Emirates	01.01.2018	0		5 %	
24	Uruguay	01.01.2018	0		22 %	
25	Colombia	01.01.2018	0		19 %	
26	Argentina	01.04.2018	0		21 %	
27	Canada (Quebec)	01.01.2019	30,000 CAD	20,000 EUR	9.975 %	
28	Canada (Saskatchewan-wan)	01.01.2019	0		6 %	
29	Bahrain	01.01.2019	0		10 %	
30	Singapore	01.01.2020	100,000 SGD	65,000 EUR	9 %	
31	Tunisia	01.01.2020	0	0	19 %	
34	Cameroon	01.01.2020	50,000,000 XAF	75,000 EUR	19.5 %	
35	Uzbekistan	01.01.2020	0		12 %	
37	Malaysia	01.01.2020	500,000 RM	100,000 EUR	10 %	
38	Uganda	01.01.2020	0		18 %	
40	Zimbabwe	01.01.2020	0		15 %	
41	Vietnam	01.01.2020	0		8 %	
42	Moldova	01.04.2020	0		20 %	
43	Mexico	01.06.2020	0		16 %	yes
44	Chile	01.07.2020	0		19 %	
45	Indonesia	01.07.2020	600,000,000 IDR	30,000 EUR	12 %	
47	Great Britain (BREXIT)	01.01.2021	0		20 %	
48	Paraguay	01.01.2021	0		10 %	
50	Tajikistan	01.01.2021	0		14 %	
51	Kenya	01.02.2021	0		16 %	
52	Canada (British Columbia)	01.04.2021	10,000 CAD	6,500 EUR	7 %	
53	Oman	01.04.2021	0		5 %	

	Country	Implementation date	Threshold in local currency	Threshold in Euro	Tax rate	Fiscal representative required?
54	Pakistan	01.06.2021	0		18 %	
49	Philippines	01.01.2021	3,000,000 PHP	50,000 EUR	12 %	
55	Canada (state)	01.07.2021	30,000 CAD		5–15 %	
56	Thailand	01.09.2021	1,800,000 Baht	47,500 EUR	7 % (10 % from 1.10.2024)	
57	Georgia	01.10.2021	0		18 %	
58	Canada (Manitoba)	01.12.2021	10,000 CAD	6,500 EUR	7 %	
59	Cambodia	01.01.2022	250,000,000 KHR	55,000 EUR	10 %	
60	Ukraine	01.01.2022	1,000,000 UAH	30,000 EUR	20 %	
61	Armenia	01.01.2022	0		20 %	
62	Panama	01.01.2022	0		7 %	
63	Kazakhstan	01.01.2022	0		12 %	
64	Bhutan	01.07.2022	5,000,000 BTN	60,000 EUR	7 %	

CHAPTER 6
DISTRIBUTING A VIDEO GAME

§ 31
Consoles and Platforms

Bibliography: Baumgartner/Ewald, 'Apps und Recht', 2nd edn, München 2016; Forster, 'Spielkonsolen und Heimcomputer 1972 bis 2015', 5th edn, Utting 2015; Iwata, in Hobonichi (ed), Ask Iwata, San Francisco 2019; Schwiering/Zurel, 'Gaming & Recht – Zwei Bereiche wachsen zusammen!', MMR 2016, 440.

A. The relevance of content ... 1
B. Types of consoles and platforms ... 4
I. Consoles ... 7
II. Digital platforms ... 11
III. Mobile games platforms ... 14
C. The relevance of consoles and platforms ... 15
I. Development ... 16
II. Release ... 17
III. Distribution ... 20
IV. Marketing ... 22
V. Responsibility as a platform and commission ... 24
D. Account systems ... 29
E. First-party games, third-party games and information barriers ... 34
F. Summary ... 41

A. The relevance of content

'Content is King'[1] – this phrase, originally referring to the internet, is commonly used in the video game industry today. It expresses that a video game console or (digital) platform can only have lasting success if the available content, the games, are appealing to consumers. A console or platform that cannot offer attractive games to its users, meaning no games that animate users to frequently and regularly use the console or platform, will not have sustainable success, irrespective of any other unique functionalities it may offer. 1

On the other hand, this does not mean that it is enough to offer appealing content in order to be successful Or in the words of Nintendo's former president Satoru Iwata: '[…], there are loads of enjoyable games out there that people would love playing, if they only knew that they existed.'[2] Without a **channel to consumers** and without the consumer's attention to the product, even a unique or exceptional game will hardly achieve commercial success. Content is key but it needs a way to find an audience. 2

How does content reach the consumer and how can individual games gain the attention of consumers – in particular in a more and more **digital environment**, amongst a cacophony of other offers that vie for the users' attention? This is where consoles and platforms play a relevant role in today's video game business. 3

B. Types of consoles and platforms

Consoles and platforms for games can roughly be categorised as follows, keeping in mind that one may consider consoles as the original form of platform: 4

[1] Gates, 'Content is King' (3.1.1996). <https://web.archive.org/web/20010126005200/http://www.microsoft.com/billgates/columns/1996essay/essay960103.asp>.
[2] Iwata, p. 97.

- **Dedicated video game consoles** as proprietary systems consisting of a specific hardware, software and digital sales channel ('shop'),
- **Digital platforms** mostly available on PC, and
- So-called **mobile games platforms**.

5 All three types of consoles and platforms have in common that a developer or publisher that wants to offer a game for a console or on a platform needs to conclude an **agreement with the respective console manufacturer or platform provider**. Commonly, the maximum autonomy possible for release date, price, and method of marketing still rests with the developer respectively publisher so that the decisions about release date, end-consumer price of the game, and marketing (positioning of the game in terms of genre (although genre is becoming less and less relevant and the lines between genres are becoming more and more blurry), target group(s), preferred marketing channels, pre-order rebates, etc.) remain with the developer respectively publisher.

6 Many console manufacturers and platform providers are also publishing games and, thus, acting as a publisher themselves. These games, released by the console maker or platform provider, are commonly referred to as **first-party games** whereas the games released by other publishers are referred to as **third-party games**. The developers and publishers of third-party games are, therefore, regularly referred to as third-party developers respectively third-party publishers.

I. Consoles

7 In the course of the 1970s video game consoles as **dedicated gaming hardware** became commercially available to consumers[3] and had the aim of offering different dedicated gaming experiences. Well-known video game console manufacturers today are Nintendo, headquartered in Kyoto (Japan) and present on the European market since 1986[4] with their newest console being the Nintendo Switch 2, Sony PlayStation, present on the European market for video game consoles since 1995,[5] and Microsoft Xbox, which started on the European market in 2002.[6] Many users use multiple of these consoles simultaneously, often also in parallel to a gaming PC.[7] Irrespectively, and despite the fact that the majority of games is released for several or all consoles and platforms (so-called multiplatform titles), particularly the individual consoles but nowadays also certain game franchises or developer studios have their own active fanbase that sometimes highly emotionally supports their favourite manufacturer or franchise/developer – be it organised as part of a fan community or be it in public discussions (often in internet forums or on social media). These communities are of high value to the companies, and are highly appreciated and supported through community activities.[8]

8 Typically, consoles consist of a carefully synchronised package of specifically designed **hardware** (console including input devices, referred to as controllers), an **operating**

---

[3] Forster, p. 10 et seq.

[4] See <https://www.nintendo.com/en-gb/Hardware/Nintendo-History/Nintendo-History-625945.html>.

[5] See <https://web.archive.org/web/20040422074254/http:/www.scei.co.jp/corporate/data/bizdataeu_e.html.

[6] See <https://www.nytimes.com/2001/11/08/technology/game-theory-console-shootout-the-sequel.html>.

[7] Key facts about the European video games sector, 2023, Video Games Europe, p. 9. <https://www.videogameseurope.eu/wp-content/uploads/2024/09/Video-Games-Europe-2023-Key-Facts-Report_FINAL.pdf>.

[8] See, e.g., <https://www.xbox.com/en-gb/community/for-everyone>.

system specifically developed for or adjusted to this hardware, and – nowadays – a **shop** offering games for download as well as online services for the console. A console is dedicated to the purpose of playing video games so that it can provide relatively more gaming power with an existing hardware than, e.g., a PC with an operating system that has to support many different purposes. At the same time, this aspect of dedicated video game hardware also allows developers to focus on one hardware configuration when optimising their games instead of having to consider zillions of different possible combinations of hardware components such as in the PC gaming world.

9 The design philosophy and creative approach of the relevant manufacturer are regularly reflected in this package, leading to **unique features** of each console which can gain the relevant console a competitive advantage in the video games business, provided compelling contents are available that make appropriate use of such unique features ('Content is King' → mn. 1). For example, Nintendo's Wii with its novel motion controls used innovatively by games of Nintendo and other publishers was a major success with 101 million units sold worldwide.[9] The unique combination of integrated hardware and games can offer users an **all-embracing experience** and is regularly only possible in this way on consoles. Some, such as *Alan Kay* already 40 years ago, go as far as saying: 'People who are really serious about software should make their own hardware.'[10]

10 In 2023, consoles (astride mobile games platforms) were the type of platform via which the video game industry in Europe was able to create the **highest revenues** – 41 % of the video game turnover in the biggest European markets was conducted through consoles respectively games for consoles.[11] More than 69 million people enjoyed games on consoles in Europe in 2023.[12]

II. Digital platforms

11 Well-known examples for digital platforms are Valve's Steam,[13] Electronic Art's Origin,[14] Ubisoft's Ubisoft Connect,[15] and the Epic Games Store.[16] The first digital platform that was able to broadly establish itself was probably Steam, not least due to the game 'Half-Life 2' that was only playable when linked to Steam.[17]

12 Typical elements of such kind of platform are that they allow the user to **obtain digital games** (respectively licenses) for download to their device, typically an internet-connected PC, and associated **services** such as automatic download of updates, online multiplayer, game subscriptions, etc. Some digital platforms, in particular those that are operated by a publisher, offer only games published by such publisher. Other platforms offer games published by third-party publishers as well, similar to consoles.

---

[9] <https://www.nintendo.co.jp/ir/en/finance/hard_soft/index.html>.

[10] Kay, 'Creative Think' (20 7.1982) <https://www.folklore.org/StoryView.py?story=Creative_Think.txt>.

[11] Key Facts about the European video games sector, ©2023, Video Games Europe, p. 14 <https://www.videogameseurope.eu/wp-content/uploads/2024/09/Video-Games-Europe-2023-Key-Facts-Report_FINAL.pdf>.

[12] Key Facts about the European video games sector, ©2023, Video Games Europe, p. 8 et seq <https://www.videogameseurope.eu/wp-content/uploads/2024/09/Video-Games-Europe-2023-Key-Facts-Report_FINAL.pdf>.

[13] See <https://store.steampowered.com/>.

[14] See <https://www.origin.com/>.

[15] See <https://ubisoftconnect.com/>.

[16] See <https://www.epicgames.com/>.

[17] Kogel, '10 Jahre Steam – Die Geschichte des Dampfs' (GameStar, 28.9.2013) <https://www.gamestar.de/artikel/,3028364.html>.

13 The landscape of digital platforms is evolving quite rapidly and represents an innovative business that offers many more models for obtaining games than one-time payment and download. **Game subscriptions** offered by digital platforms, such as Ubisoft+[18] or EA Play[19], enable users a different way to enjoy a varying library of games for a monthly or annual fee. **Game creator platforms** such as Roblox[20] enable users to express their creativity and potentially receive some revenues for their works but also present a large variety of new challenges, for example in the fields of intellectual property rights and youth protection,[21] as well as in relation to a platform's responsibility to remove inappropriate or illegal content (→ Ch. 33 mn. 19). Some digital platforms may also offer users to receive games via **streaming** rather than as download, although the probably most prominent offering of game streaming in the last couple years, Google's Stadia, was discontinued on 18 January 2023.[22] In the case of streaming, the games are not downloaded and executed on the user's device. Rather, a server's computing power is used for the operation of the game so that users can enjoy even games that their device might not be sufficiently powerful for, provided the user's internet connection is sufficient for the data streamed and aspects such as input lag are addressed.

III. Mobile games platforms

14 The most widely known platforms for smart devices such as mobile phones or tablets, which also offer games in the form of so-called **mobile games**, may be Apple's iOS and Google's Android. Both platforms offer a shop for applications, including games specifically designed for or adjusted to smart devices, the aforementioned mobile games. In the case of iOS, the App Store operated by Apple[23] is the official option to obtain digital games for the platform, with other stores being possible alternatives in the EU since March 2024.[24] Android, on the other hand, has been designed globally as a more open platform that enables in addition to Google's official store, the Google Play Store or simply Google Play,[25] also third-party sources for downloading and installing games – at the user's own risk and responsibility because third-party sources are outside of the platform provider's review and check mechanisms as well as developer guidelines[26] (more on this → mn. 19).

C. The relevance of consoles and platforms

15 As already indicated (→ mn. 3), consoles and platforms offer developers and publishers of games a **digital distribution channel** to consumers that is open for business seven days per week, 24 hours per day and enables consumers to obtain games at any time as they please. Through continuous investment into development and marketing of their console or platform, console manufacturers and platform providers acquire

---

[18] See <https://store.ubisoft.com/en/ubisoftplus>.

[19] See <https://www.ea.com/en-gb/ea-play>.

[20] See <https://www.roblox.com>.

[21] See <https://usk.de/game-creator-plattformen-auf-dem-pruefstand-aenderung-der-alterskennzeichen-bei-unzureichendem-jugendschutz/>.

[22] See <https://stadia.google.com/gg/>.

[23] See <https://www.apple.com/app-store/>.

[24] See <https://www.apple.com/newsroom/2024/01/apple-announces-changes-to-ios-safari-and-the-app-store-in-the-european-union/>.

[25] See <https://play.google.com/>.

[26] See <https://support.google.com/android/answer/9457058?hl=en&ref_topic=7311596>.

and maintain a **large user-base and customer-base** that developers and publishers can address if they decide to distribute their game on the respective console or platform. However, this establishing, sustaining and making accessible of a valuable user and customer base over years and sometimes even decades is not the only role of consoles and platforms in the **ecosystem of the video game industry** and in the lifecycle of games.

I. Development

The role of consoles and platforms already begins in the phase of game development 16
(→ Ch. 12 mn. 30). Regularly, game developers are given access to so-called **development kits** of the console manufacturer or platform provider that the developers can use in the course of the creation of their game.[27] In the case of consoles, these development kits do not only consist of **specific software libraries** (so-called software development kits or SDK)[28] but also special **hardware with additional interfaces** (so-called developer consoles). Often, developers can even contact free of charge a dedicated technical support team for third-party developers of the respective console manufacturer in case they face technical issues.

II. Release

In the context of the **release of games**, consoles and platforms support the developers 17
and publishers further, for example by enabling them to obtain age rating classification for their digital game free of charge through the groundbreaking **IARC system** (→ Ch. 22 mn. 43, Ch. 23 mn. 49). The IARC (International Age Rating Coalition) is a cooperation of organisations in multiple countries responsible for the classification of games, which includes the European age rating organisation PEGI and the German age rating body USK.[29] Thanks to the shop's (i.e., the console's or platform's) participation in IARC, it is free of charge for developers and publishers to obtain age ratings through IARC for games distributed digitally only, but of course the age rating can also only be used in a shop participating in (and contributing to) IARC.[30] This means that for a game distributed only digitally, the shop essentially bears the **cost of the age rating classification**, whereas for games distributed on physical media the publishers have to bear the cost of the age rating classification themselves.

In addition, the consoles and platforms provide **technical protection measures** 18
(TPM) to developers and publishers to protect their games against unauthorised copying, i.e., against **software piracy** that continues to cause high economic damage each year to the copyright owners and further rights holders in games. In this area, the European Court of Justice (ECJ) and other relevant courts have already issued decisions multiple times.[31]

---

[27] See, e.g., <https://developer.nintendo.com/ (last accessed: 2.5.2025), https://partners.playstation.net/> (last accessed: 2.5.2025), <https://www.xbox.com/en-gb/developers/id> (last accessed: 2.5.2025), <https://partner.steamgames.com/>.

[28] For more details about SDK in the case of mobile apps see Baumgartner/Ewald, lit. 13 et seqq.

[29] See <https://globalratings.com/about.aspx>.

[30] See <https://globalratings.com/for-developers.aspx>.

[31] See, e.g., *Bundesgerichtshof* (Federal Court of Justice – BGH), 27.11.2014 – I ZR 124/11, GRUR 2015, 672; ECJ, 23.1.2014 – case C-355/12, ECLI:EU:C:2014:25 – *Nintendo Co. Ltd and Others v PC Box Srl and 9Net Srl*, GRUR 2014, 255.

19 For the users and with respect to the distribution of games, consoles and platforms offer security through technical reviews ensuring that games are free from errors to the degree reasonably possible and free from malware. This is often referred to as 'Lotcheck'. In addition, developer guidelines of consoles and platforms require compliance of the games with applicable legal requirements, in particular data protection. Contrary to popular belief, the review of a game's content (so-called 'content approval') is not part of Lotcheck or developer guidelines – consoles and platforms regularly only conduct **technical reviews**. Regarding the content the providers of consoles and platforms have to rely on the review by the age rating organisations, in particular by PEGI or USK, and on contractual warranties from developers respectively publishers that any legal requirements relevant to the content are complied with. Consoles and platforms have less control over the type of games that are published for their console or platform than is often assumed.

III. Distribution

20 Naturally, the provider of the console or platform also develops and operates the shop, or in other words the **digital sales channel** to the consumer. In this respect, they manage the compliance of the shop with all applicable legal requirements such as regulation on the transparency of prices as well as general consumer protection regulations and youth protection requirements. The consoles and platforms face the same issues that many operators of online shops face, however, multiplied by the nature of video games as a digital product or service protected by intellectual property rights (→ Ch.13 mn. 5). A video game can be completed within a timeframe of days or weeks, which means fully enjoyed or consumed, in particular if it is a linear, story-driven game with little appeal to play it another time, or if **unauthorised copies** are created before returning it (respectively, in the digital world, deleting the license from the associated account). This can create issues for example in the scenario of refund requests by parents or guardians due to supposedly unauthorised purchases by children. Naturally, the reaction of consoles and platforms as operators of the shop is **lenient and consumer-friendly** in such situations – after all, they invested heavily and over a long period of time into the acquisition of a large user-base. However, courts and regulators should not condone fraudulent or irresponsible behaviour by consumers, in particular where claims are raised after many months of supposedly not checking credit card statements or of complete neglect to use parental control tools or other purchase restriction options offered by the console or platform. Otherwise, consumer protection inadvertently tips from endorsing behaviour in good faith to one-sidedly disadvantaging creative industries and, ultimately, **game designers and authors**.

21 The acquisition and maintaining of a large user-base and customer-base that developers and publishers can easily address was already mentioned (→ mn. 15). This is certainly one of the most valuable and appealing benefits that releasing a game for a console or platform offers to developers and especially smaller publishers. Instead of having to make their own investments into the development and operation of a well-functioning shop, instead of having to incur expenses for the promotion of such shop to consumers in order to convince the users of creating an account for the shop, and instead of having to advertise the game to the consumers and convince them to obtain the game in this shop, the developer or publisher can use an **existing infrastructure** and directly address a **relevant user and customer base**. And consumers can easily obtain the game in a

shop they know and trust, without having to create a new account and without having to entrust their data and payment information to yet another new shop.

IV. Marketing

Providers of consoles and platforms additionally play a role in the promotion of games. For instance, they regularly communicate newly released games for the console or platform via **email newsletters** or **news systems** on the console respectively platform, they organise sales, i.e., **discount activities** in which developers and publishers can participate with their titles, and communicate these to some degree on owned channels and to some degree on paid channels operated by media companies or influencers. 22

Specifically for small developers, which often publish their games on their own (so-called self-publishing) and are often referred to as '**Indies**', the providers of consoles in particular offer specific support programmes with presentations only for **Indie games**, special Indie sales or similar marketing activities in order to provide increased publicity to Indie titles. Among gamers the Indie games enjoy increased popularity, which is why a certain level of solicitation for and with Indie developers respectively their games has been established. 23

V. Responsibility as a platform and commission

Lastly, the consoles and platforms also face a responsibility as **operators of systems and online services**. To address this responsibility, activities in fields such as technical youth protection or parental control systems (→ Ch. 34 mn. 16), combatting inappropriate or illegal content online (→ Ch. 33 mn. 19), and community management have been implemented. 24

In the field of technical youth protection, the providers of consoles and platforms accepted already many years ago the challenge to provide parents and guardians with the information and the tools they need to protect their children on the console or platform and to effectively prevent unauthorised purchases. Especially the providers of consoles have done ground-breaking work on technical youth protection measures.[32] The current consoles of Nintendo, Sony PlayStation and Microsoft Xbox all provide free of charge elaborated, pre-installed **parental control systems** and provide notices about these, e.g., on packaging, in the initial boot sequence of the console, and in further communication on websites, YouTube channels or manuals.[33] Parents or guardians can not only restrict children from starting up a game that has not been rated as suitable for their age by PEGI or USK, they can also restrict or limit spending in the shop, block the download of games above a certain age rating and decide whether (and with whom) their child can communicate as well as share information possibly provided in their user account, such as birth date or email address. 25

Combatting inappropriate or illegal content online is a task not only for consoles or platforms. All parties in the value chain of a video game, in particular the publishers which will often be the actual operator of the online service, have a role to play in this. Thankfully, online video games and associated platforms are not particularly vulnerable to being misused for dissemination of inappropriate or even illegal content, especially 26

---

[32] See, e.g., <https://www.seizethecontrols.eu/> (last accessed: 2.5.2025).

[33] See <https://pegi.info/parental-controls> (last accessed: 2.5.2025).

when compared to other types of online services or social media platforms.[34] However, video game companies operating online services have a keen sense for maintaining an **ethical online environment** in their platform or game, as is often demonstrated by committing to the **PEGI Code of Conduct** (→ Ch. 22 mn. 45),[35] and consoles have a particularly strong interest in ensuring the safety of their ecosystem, as is demonstrated by aforementioned efforts on providing sophisticated parental control systems, in order to ensure their offering is particularly appealing to parents and guardians.

27 In the area of **community management** consoles and platforms are working together with their users to provide a positive and encouraging atmosphere among gamers and to avoid negative, so-called 'toxic' behaviour or cyber-bullying. The three console-makers Nintendo, Sony PlayStation and Microsoft Xbox, for example, published joint principles for safe gaming already in 2020.[36]

28 For their services as described in section C, the providers of consoles and platforms receive a remuneration from the publishers of the titles distributed digitally on the console or platform, most commonly in the form of a **commission** depending on net sales turnover. The amount of this commission is not publicly available for most providers and is handled confidentially. However, based on some publicly available sources, the amount of the commission is usually between 30 % and 12 % of the end-consumer net price of the game in the shop as determined by the publisher.[37]

D. Account systems

29 The relation between console respectively platform and user is handled through account systems. Accordingly, the **user account** plays a major role in the interaction between provider and user which today goes far beyond the mere obtaining of licenses and the processing of payments.

30 While consoles still allow at least an offline-only functionality without creation of a user account, the use of **online functionalities** such as the shop or community systems with the ability to create friend lists or exchange user-generated content ('UGC') as well as the use of a platform in general require the creation of a user account. It is this user account that any **licenses** for games obtained are linked to and, in addition, this user account effectively serves as an **online persona**, which is relevant for the online interaction with other users, especially in multiplayer games, but also for the enforcement of community rules through measures such as temporary or permanent ban of accounts for certain online services by the provider in case of repeated violation of community rules, e.g,. through insulting or harassing other users.

31 Further, users can enjoy a **multitude of services** through the user account, such as the automatic download of game updates and patches or the download of games to several systems used by the user with the same account as well as the re-download of games eventually deleted locally from the user's system.[38] In the past, it was controver-

[34] See, e.g., Ofcom, 'Internet users' experience of potential online harms: summary of survey research', page 78 (2020) <https://www.ofcom.org.uk/siteassets/resources/documents/research-and-data/online-research/online-harms/2020/concerns-and-experiences-online-harms-2020-chart-pack.pdf> (last accessed: 2.5.2025).

[35] See, e.g., <https://pegi.info/pegi-code-of-conduct> (last accessed: 2.5.2025).

[36] See <https://news.xbox.com/en-us/2020/12/14/shared-safety-principles/> (last accessed: 2.5.2025).

[37] Apple: Commission of 15–30 %, see <https://developer.apple.com/app-store/small-business-program/> (last accessed: 2.5.2025); Epic Games Store: commission of 12 %, see <https://store.epicgames.com/en-US/distribution> (last accessed: 2.5.2025).

[38] See, e.g., Schwiering/Zurel, MMR 2016, 440.

sially discussed – in particular with the example of the platform Steam – whether the providers may refuse the **transfer of a user account** to another person in the light of those services by referring to dedicated clauses in their terms and conditions, which was ultimately widely accepted.[39]

In connection with all these services there is, of course, processing of **personal data**. However, the level of personal data collected by providers of dedicated video game consoles and platforms is often on a rather low and non-intrusive level as the providers regularly use **pseudonymisation** and aggregation of data so that the amount of information available that could directly identify an individual is very limited. Often, no real name, no physical address and – especially for child accounts – not even an email address are required to create an account. A username (pseudonym), an email address for adult accounts, a date of birth as well as the country of residence are required, in addition to a password. In case of payments certain additional data needs to be collected, however such transactions are regularly conducted via specialised payment service providers (and in any case in alignment with the requirements of the credit card organisations – the Payment Card Industry Data Security Standard or PCI-DSS) so that the provider itself usually has no or only very limited access to such data. 32

Due to users increasingly obtaining games exclusively digitally through shops, the amount of games linked to the individual account has increased as well. This means that user accounts have become more valuable for the individual consumer. In order to address the resulting increased need for security and to avoid the takeover of accounts by unauthorised persons, providers have implemented additional security features. In particular, the option of so-called **two-factor authentication** ('2FA') can be considered as market standard by now. Moreover, users receive transaction statements via email and can access their login history, i.e., date, time and IP address used for the last successful login to their account so that any successful **unauthorised login attempts** can be swiftly identified and countermeasures such as changing the password taken. The offered level of security of course stands and falls with the question of how responsible the users are in making use of the security features. Especially multiple use of the same combination of username/email address and password with different online services leads to vulnerabilities and can, if the user did not activate 2FA, lead of access to the account by unauthorised persons or even complete account takeover. In this respect, it can be considered advantageous for the user that it is regularly not possible to remove individual licenses from an account and transfer them individually to other accounts. This way, the provider can often assist the user in regaining control over the account, including all associated licenses. 33

E. First-party games, third-party games and information barriers

Many console manufacturers and providers of platforms are also video game publishers. Commonly, the games published by console makers and platform providers are referred to as first-party games and games published by other publishers are usually referred to as third-party games. 34

This means that console manufacturers and platform providers are at the same time partner and competitor of developers and publishers for such console or platform. They are business partners as provider of the console or platform for which the developers 35

---

[39] BGH, judgment of 11.2.2010 – I ZR 178/08, MMR 2010, 771; Kammergericht (Higher Regional Court of Berlin, KG), decision of 10.8.2015 – 23 U 42/14, MMR 2016, 340; Cour de cassation (French Supreme Court), première chambre civile, ruling of 23.10.2024, No. 23–13.738.

and publishers release their games as well as operator of the – often exclusive – shop on such console or platform. They are competitors as publisher of games that may compete for the same or a similar target group of players. To manage this dual role in the spirit of fair competition, the providers of consoles and platforms generally have implemented sophisticated internal **information barriers**, also referred to as 'garden walls', in their organisations.

36 This means that, firstly, the teams responsible for decision making on first-party games (for example concerning pricing, release date, positioning of the title relating to genre or target group, etc.) are both **organisationally as well as in terms of staff** separated from the teams responsible for the so-called third-party business, i.e., the management of the cooperation with and support of third-party developers and publishers. It is ensured in this way that no information is shared within the organisation that could influence business decisions in any direction – and even if only subconsciously.

37 In addition, **internal guidelines** require that no sensitive information is shared between staff members in the first-party business and staff members in the third-party business. Usually, the in-house legal department is in charge of **supervising and monitoring** the compliance with such internal rules and obtains external support for regular training of all relevant staff as wells internal audits hereon.

38 This separation is commonly also reflected in the technical systems. To the degree systems are not completely different anyhow, it is regulated at minimum on the level of **user rights management** that the first-party business teams and the third-party business teams respectively each only have access to their own data.

39 In some other areas, for example the team operating the shop, it may be unavoidable that information from both the first-party business and the third-party business are required on an operational level. If this is the case, such areas will generally be separated organisationally and in terms of staff from both the first-party business and the third-party business. This for example relates to the preparation of the respective shop page for a game prior to its release for which release date and potentially end-consumer price may already be required before the announcement so that post-announcement pre-orders are possible immediately. In such cases, information is shared on a strict **need-to-know basis** exclusively and sometimes third-party publishers even handle the input of the information into the provider's system directly through remote access.

40 This way, providers of consoles and platforms want to ensure that even the slightest misconception is avoided in relation to any unethical behaviour in order to maintain the trust of third-party developers and publishers at all times. Every console and platform requires for its lasting success strong third-party games in addition to its own (potentially exclusive) first-party games in order to attract a large target audience with an **attractive range of content**.

F. Summary

41 In conclusion, consoles and platforms play (or can play, depending on the developer's or publisher's decisions) a vital role in all phases of the **development and marketing cycle** of a video game if the developer or publisher decides to publish their game for a console or platform. Certain legal aspects of what has been described in this chapter are addressed in more detail in the following chapters.

§ 32
Platform Obligations

Bibliography: Berberich/Seip, 'Der Entwurf des Digital Services Act', GRUR-Prax 2021, 4; Geppert/Schütz (eds), Beck'scher Kommentar zum TKG V, Munich 2023; Gersdorf/Paal (eds), Beck'scher Online-Kommentar Informations- und Medienrecht, Munich 2023; Grünwald/Nüßing, 'Vom NetzDG zum DSA: Wachablösung im Kampf gegen Hatespeech', MMR 2021, 282; Hauck, 'Die außergerichtliche Streitbeilegungsstelle nach Art. 21 DSA', GRUR 2024, 1185; Hentsch/Rodenhausen, 'Einsatzfelder von KI in Games – Games und die KI-VO – ein Überblick', MMR 2024, 714; Hilgert, 'Toxic Players' in Hentsch/Falk (eds), Games und Recht, Baden-Baden 2023, 447; Hofmann/Raue (eds), 'Digital Services Act – Gesetz über digitale Dienste', Baden-Baden 2023; Janal, 'Friendly Fire? Das Urheberrechts-Diensteanbieter-Gesetz und sein Verhältnis zum künftigen Digital Services Act', GRUR 2022, 211; Liesching (ed), BeckOK Jugendschutzrecht IV, Munich 2024; Maamar, 'Sorgfaltspflichten für Anbieter von Vermittlungsdiensten' in Kraul (ed), Das neue Recht der digitalen Dienste – Digital Services Act (DSA), Baden-Baden 2023, 92; Martini/Botta, 'Der Staat und das Metaversum', MMR 2023, 887; Müller-Terpitz/Köhler (eds), 'DSA – Digital Services Act', München 2024; Nathanail, 'Ziele, Anwendungsbereich und Verhältnis zu anderen Rechtsakten' in Kraul (ed), Das neue Recht der digitalen Dienste – Digital Services Act (DSA), Baden-Baden 2023, 44; Nothelfer/Trunk, 'Die Verletzung der Wettkampfintegrität im eSport durch Umgehen spielinterner Ranking-Systeme', SpoPrax 2022, 341; Spindler, 'Der Vorschlag für ein neues Haftungsregime für Internetprovider – der EU-Digital Services Act (Teil 1)', GRUR 2021, 545; Trunk, 'Das Gesetz über digitale Dienste (Digital Services Act) und der eSport', SpoPrax 2023, 329; Voigt/Bastians, 'Pflicht zur Benennung von EU-Vertretern im europäischen Digitalrecht', MMR 2022, 930.

A. Playing it safe in the EU 1

B. Digital Services Act 5
- I. Scope 6
- II. Applicability to online games 12
  1. Communication features 13
  2. User-generated content 16
  3. Gameplay 19
  4. Workarounds 22
- III. Provider obligations 24
  1. Points of contact 25
  2. Terms and conditions 27
     a) Formal requirements 28
     b) Content requirements 29
     c) Specific requirements for services that are directed towards minors 35
  3. Transparency reports 36
  4. Obligations for hosting services 38
  5. Obligations for online platforms 43
     a) Disclosure of monthly active users 44
     b) Internal complaint-handling system and out-of-court dispute resolution 45
     c) Trusted flaggers 48
     d) Measures and protection against misuse 49
     e) Transparency 50
     f) Prohibition of manipulative and deceptive practices 53
     g) Online protection of minors 54
     h) Special platforms 57
- IV. Conclusion 58

C. Platform obligations under other EU legal acts 59
- I. Digital Markets Act 60
- II. Platform-to-Business-Regulation 61
- III. Artificial Intelligence Act 63
- IV. E-evidence package 67
- V. CSAM-Regulation (Draft) 70

D. Summary 71

A. Playing it safe in the EU

1 As there is no single definition of the term **'platform'**, this chapter is intended to provide an overview of the main obligations under EU law that apply to games-related online services that serve as a platform for interaction between players.

2 The **Digital Services Act** [1] **(DSA)** represents a significant development in the European Union's regulatory framework for digital services designed to create a safe online environment (the UK's Online Safety Act has a similar goal).

3 Regulating online platforms such as social networks is at the DSA's core, but games-related services are not exempt, and even online games can, under certain circumstances, be considered platforms under the DSA. They have undergone significant developments in the last two decades and have changed user behaviour considerably. They have become a **pivotal component of the European cultural and creative ecosystem,**[2] providing a distinctive environment for creative virtual interaction among users. In addition to their primary function as a form of entertainment, online games also serve a crucial social role, for example for individuals who experience social disconnection or isolation in real-life environments.[3] Online games such as *Roblox,*[4] *Fortnite*[5] and *Minecraft*[6] give users nearly unlimited opportunities to create their own content (user-generated content, 'UGC'). They are also considered pioneers of the Metaverse.[7] In Minecraft, for example, players work together to recreate well-known buildings such as the Brandenburg Gate.[8] At the same time, online games also bear risks. These can include cyberbullying, harmful UGC (→ Ch. 33), and risks such as cyber grooming.[9] These risks are the subject of existing and proposed EU legislation.

4 It is therefore important for games companies to assess the DSA's applicability and the potential obligations that may arise if their services fall within the scope of the Regulation (B.). Further obligations may also stem from other EU legislation (C.).

B. Digital Services Act

5 The DSA aims to create a level playing field for so-called **intermediary services such as hosting services and online platforms**. This comprehensive set of rules seeks to create a safer and more transparent online environment, with a focus on protecting consumers and their fundamental rights online (rec. 9 sent. 1 DSA). It applies to all intermediary services offered to recipients in the European Union, irrespective of where the service provider is located (Art. 2 (1) DSA). Compliance obligations under the DSA vary depending on the type of intermediary services provided. In addition, the DSA preserves the conditional exemptions from liability for providers of intermediary services, which

---

[1] Regulation (EU) 2022/2065 of the European Parliament and of the Council of 19.10.2022 on a Single Market For Digital Services and amending Directive 2000/31/EC (Digital Services Act).

[2] Rec. D of the European Parliament resolution of 18.1.2023 on consumer protection in online video games: a European single market approach (2022/2014(INI)).

[3] No. 29 of the European Parliament resolution of 18.1.2023 on consumer protection in online video games: a European single market approach (2022/2014(INI)).

[4] Roblox is a gaming platform developed by Roblox Corporation.

[5] Fortnite is a third-person shooter published by Epic Games.

[6] Minecraft is a sandbox computer game developed by Mojang Studios.

[7] Martini/Botta MMR 2023, 887 (889).

[8] Günsch, Mammutprojekt: Die ganze Erde als 1:1-Kopie in Minecraft (ComputerBase, 30.3.2020) https://www.computerbase.de/2020-03/build-the-earth-erde-1-1-kopie-minecraft/.

[9] Nos. 46 and 47 of the European Parliament resolution of 18.1.2023 on consumer protection in online video games: a European single market approach (2022/2014(INI)).

were previously provided for in Art. 12 to 15 E-Commerce Directive[10] (rec. 16 DSA). Consequently, providers of intermediary services are generally under no obligation to actively monitor third-party content and, with some exceptions, are not responsible for such content.[11]

I. Scope

The DSA makes the providers of **intermediary services** responsible for mitigating certain risks arising from the use of their services.[12] In this regard, the due diligence obligations depend on the type, size and nature of the intermediary service (rec. 41 sent. 1 DSA). 6

7

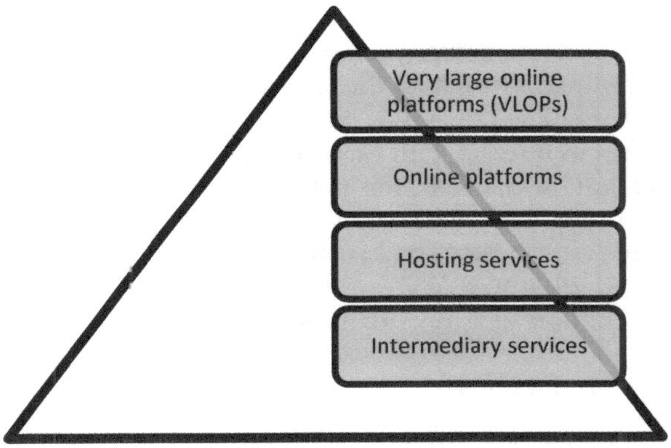

Figure 32.1

Art. 3 (g) DSA defines three different types of intermediary services: 'mere conduit' services, 'caching' services and 'hosting' services. The DSA further highlights 'online platforms' as a special form of hosting services (Art. 3 (i) DSA). The term **'hosting service'** is of particular relevance, as it is a broad term that can trigger several additional due diligence obligations. It is defined as 8

information society service consisting of the storage of information provided by, and at the request of, a recipient of the service (Art. 3 (g) (iii) DSA).

'Online platforms' are a subcategory of hosting services which must comply with an even greater number of obligations (→ mn. 43). An online platform is defined in Art. 3 (i) DSA as 9

hosting service that, at the request of a recipient of the service, stores and disseminates information to the public, unless that activity is a minor and purely ancillary feature of another service or a minor functionality of the principal service and, for objective and technical reasons, cannot be used without that other service, and the integration of the feature or functionality into the other service is not a means to circumvent the applicability of this Regulation.

[10] Directive 2000/31/EC of the European Parliament and of the Council of 8.6.2000 on certain legal aspects of information society services, in particular electronic commerce, in the Internal Market ('Directive on electronic commerce').
[11] Berberich/Seip GRUR-Prax 2021, 4; Hilgert in Hentsch/Falk, p. 447 (450).
[12] Nathanail in Kraul, p. 44 (45).

10 In simple terms, online platforms are hosting services which allow users to publicly **disseminate information provided by the users**, unless this possibility is only a minor and purely ancillary feature. The DSA explicitly mentions social networks and online marketplaces that allow consumers to conclude distance contracts with traders as examples for online platforms (rec. 13 sent. 2 DSA).

11 Additional obligations apply to **very large online platforms** (and very large online search engines). These are services which have an average number of at least 45 million active recipients of the service in the European Union and which have been designated by the European Commission as such (Art. 33 (1) DSA). No video game has yet been classified as a very large online platform.

II. Applicability to online games

12 A central feature of an intermediary service is its role as an intermediary of information provided by third parties, without the service provider exercising any control over this information.[13] For online games, this means that in particular games which provide a platform for **players to interact with each other**, create and share their own content, or provide communication channels, can potentially be classified as intermediary services. The following technical classification is intended to provide an initial overview. As intermediary services can be offered standalone or in connection with other intermediary services (rec. 29 sent. 5 DSA), a detailed examination may be necessary for technically complex services such as video games.

1. Communication features

13 When players **communicate** with each other via voice or text channels in the game, the publisher is passing on third-party user information. These functions can be either 'mere conduit' services or hosting services, depending on how the communication is technically carried out.

14 A **'mere conduit'** service is a 'service, consisting of the transmission in a communication network of information provided by a recipient of the service' (Art. 3 (g) (i) 1. DSA). The service provided is a purely technical process of information transmission.[14] Examples mentioned in the DSA include Voice-over-IP communication and interpersonal communication services (rec. 29 sent. 2 DSA). Such **interpersonal communication services** may also fall within the extended scope of the European Electronic Communications Code[15] (EECCD) which also covers online services that are functionally comparable to traditional telecommunication services.[16] The EECCD even mentions communication channels in online games as potential interpersonal communication services (rec. 17 sent. 6 EECCD) which shows that game chats can be 'mere conduit' services.[17]

15 If the communication is not only transmitted but also stored on online servers on behalf of the user, the service qualifies as a **'hosting' service** (Art. 3 (g) (iii) DSA). This applies even if the communication is only stored temporarily or deleted after the match.[18]

---

[13] F. Hofmann in Hofmann/Raue DSA Art. 3 mn. 45.

[14] Hennemann in Gersdorf/Paal TMG § 8 mn. 14.

[15] Directive (EU) 2018/1972 of the European Parliament and of the Council of 11.12. 2018 establishing the European Electronic Communications Code (Recast).

[16] Schütz in Geppert/Schütz TKG § 3 mn. 142.

[17] Trunk SpoPrax 2023, 329 (331).

[18] Holznagel in Müller-Terpitz/Köhler DSA Art. 3 mn. 89.

However, these types of chats do not usually qualify as an online platform (Art. 3 (i) DSA) as the chats are typically not publicly disseminated. Such dissemination would require making information available to a potentially unlimited number of third parties, which is not the case with interpersonal communication between limited user groups (rec. 14 sent. 3 DSA). This may be different in the case of dissemination in public groups or open channels (rec. 14 sent. 4 DSA).

2. User-generated content

16 Online games with UGC offer players extensive **creative freedom**. This ranges from designing an avatar or vehicle bodywork to creating entire game worlds. Users also often have the option of personalising their profile with an individually selected username and additional information such as texts. Some games also allow users to create their own logos or to organise in-game tournaments with further information that is visible for others online. This content may be illegal or contradict the rules of the game. By storing such information on the server, at the request of the recipient, the publisher provides a hosting service (Art. 3 (g) (iii) DSA). However, if players only have a very limited degree of freedom, i.e., they can only choose from certain presets, we hold that these choices should not be regarded as 'information provided by the by the recipient of the service'.

17 If UGC is also visible to other players, i.e., if it is 'publicly disseminated', the game (or, more precisely, the hosting service of the game) may even constitute an **online platform** (Art. 3 (i) DSA) (→ mn. 9). Art. 3 (k) DSA defines **'dissemination to the public'** as making information available, at the request of the recipient of the service who provided the information, to a potentially unlimited number of third parties. This can be understood as the provision of easy access to users in general and irrespective of whether the information is accessed by other users (rec. 14 sent. 1 DSA). Information may also be publicly disseminated despite the need to register if users are automatically accepted without any human decision to grant access (rec. 14 sent. 2 DSA).

18 However, hosting services are not qualified as an online platform when the function of disseminating information to the public is – simply speaking – a **'minor and purely ancillary feature'** and the integration of the function is not 'meant to circumvent the applicability of the DSA' (cf. Art. 3 (i) DSA). This exception is intended to avoid over-regulation (rec. 13 sent. 3 DSA) and requires a case-by-case assessment, whereas the DSA only very roughly outlines the legal framework. As an example, the comments section in an online newspaper can be minor and clearly ancillary if the main service is the publication of news by a publisher (rec. 13 sent. 4 DSA). However, the legislator does not consider the comment function in social media to be a minor feature (rec. 13 sent. 5 DSA). Arguably, for most online games, the main purpose is enjoying gameplay itself. In story-based role-playing games, for example, solving tasks and experiencing the story together are of central importance. In particular, esports focussed games are primarily about competing against each other, for example through in-game ranking systems.[19] The range of game functions is as extensive as it is varied. However, there are also online games that put much more emphasis on UGC. In these games, users may be able to create entire worlds and share them with other users. The greater the importance of these functions, the more difficult it is to argue against the classification of these services as an online platform. Consequently, UGC-driven online games such as Roblox or Fortnite have started to disclose their estimated monthly active users in the EU, which is one of the obligations for online platforms (Art. 24 (2) DSA) (→ mn 44).

[19] Nothelfer/Trunk SpoPrax 2022, 341 (342).

3. Gameplay

19 It is questionable whether **core gameplay features** lead to the online game being classified as an intermediary service. This depends primarily on the question whether the interaction in the game, i.e., the input of commands, is considered as 'information provided by and stored upon request of the recipient of the service'.

20 In online chess, for example, a player's move is transmitted to their opponent via the server. In an online shooter, on the other hand, the positions, statuses (e.g., health points and equipment) and actions (e.g., shots fired and movements made) of all players must be synchronised in real time via the server and transmitted to the respective clients of the other players.

21 The term '**information**' is not legally defined in the DSA, nor in the E-Commerce Directive. The German and French versions also lack any indication of its meaning under EU law. There is a definition of illegal content in Art. 3 (h) DSA that covers 'any information that, in itself or in relation to an activity' is 'not in compliance with Union law or the law of any Member State'. This implies that the player must have the possibility to create such information in-game. Comparing the DSA with other digital legislation, such as the Data Act[20] (DA), the term 'information' seems less comprehensive than the term 'data' which is defined as 'any digital representation of acts, facts or information and any compilation of such acts, facts or information, including in the form of sound, visual or audio-visual recording' (Art. 2 (1) DA). The purpose of the DSA is to create a safe, predictable and trustworthy online environment that counteracts the spread of illegal online content and social risks such as disinformation. These risks are generally not present when players are limited to pre-programmed actions, such as, for example, controlling the characters in a football match.[21] If the term was to be understood so broadly under the DSA, any storage of settings in an online service would also have to be classified as a hosting service. In our view, such a broad understanding was not intended and would lead to significant over-regulation, the benefits of which are questionable at best.

4. Workarounds

22 Publishers of online games face the challenge of designing their offerings in such a way that they either **meet the requirements of the DSA** or, if necessary, fall outside its scope. For example, they can consider whether certain features, such as chat systems or the ability to create UGC, are essential to their game. If these features are of minor importance, removing them could help to avoid extensive technical burdens, such as the implementation of a notice-and-takedown mechanism (→ mn. 38). Another strategy could be not to include certain features, such as chats or the sharing of UGC, and instead suggest using external platforms such as Discord, Xbox Live, PlayStation Network or TeamSpeak. This would allow the publisher to relinquish direct control over these aspects of the game, potentially removing them from the scope of the DSA.

23 With regard to the qualification as an online platform, it could be argued that certain sharing functionalities only represent a subordinate function. This would mean that these functions are not of central importance in the overall context of the game and may therefore not be subject to the strict requirements of the DSA for online platforms (→ mn. 43). In this respect, additional functionalities could shift the focus of the online game. However, it is important that such adaptations should not be seen as an attempt

[20] Regulation (EU) 2023/2854 of the European Parliament and of the Council of 13.12.2023 on harmonised rules on fair access to and use of data and amending Regulation (EU) 2017/2394 and Directive 2020/1828 (Data Act).

[21] Trunk SpoPrax 2023, 329 (331).

to circumvent the provisions of the DSA. In this case, the provider cannot rely on the subordinate importance of the function.

III. Provider obligations

The **DSA sets out basic obligations** for all intermediary service providers as well as additional obligations for hosting service providers (→ mn. 38), in particular online platform providers (→ mn. 43) and very large online platforms (rec. 41 sent. 2 DSA). 24

1. Points of contact

All providers of intermediary services must designate a point of contact for enquiries by the competent authorities, the European Commission and the European Board for Digital Services (Art. 11 (1) DSA). Additionally, they must designate a point of contact for the users of their service (Art. 12 (1) DSA). Both must enable a **direct communication by electronic means.** Information about the points of contact must be public and easily accessible. In the case of the point of contact for the users, the DSA requires additionally a fast communication in a user-friendly manner, including by allowing the users to choose the means of communication which shall not solely rely on automated tools. 25

If the service provider does not have an establishment in the EU, it must also designate a **legal representative** that is based in one of the EU Member States (Art. 13 (1) DSA). This appears to be necessary in order to ensure enforcement of the DSA (rec. 44 DSA) and has become increasingly common under EU law.[22] The legal representative can be held liable for compliance under the DSA in addition to or instead of the service provider (Art. 13 (3) DSA). 26

2. Terms and conditions

Under the DSA, the terms and conditions of the service, defined in Art. 3 (u) DSA as 'clauses which govern the contractual relationship between the provider and the recipient of the service', must clearly inform recipients of any restrictions that the provider may impose on them in relation to the information they provide (Art. 14 (1) sent. 1 DSA). Users must be able to anticipate when and how to expect content moderation and be put in a position to review its admissibility afterwards.[23] 27

a) Formal requirements

The information shall be set out in clear, plain, intelligible, user-friendly and unambiguous language, and shall be publicly available in an **easily accessible and machine-readable format** (Art. 14 (1) sent. 3 DSA). Moreover, significant changes to the terms and conditions must be communicated to the recipients of the service according to Art. 14 (2) DSA. Providers of very large online platforms must further publish their terms and conditions in the official languages of all EU Member States in which the service is offered and provide their users with a concise, easily-accessible and machine-readable summary (Art. 14 (5), (6) DSA). 28

---

[22] Voigt/Bastians MMR 2022, 930.

[23] Raue in Hofmann/Raue DSA Art. 14 mn. 3.

b) Content requirements

29 Many online games also contained rules of conduct in their **end user license agreements** or other guidelines before the DSA entered into force. As the DSA requires a clear and predictable legal framework for users when moderating content, providers must ensure that their terms and conditions also cover the topics mentioned in Art. 14 (1) sent. 2 DSA.

30 'Content moderation' in the sense of Art. 3 (t) DSA means the

> **activities, whether automated or not, [...] that are aimed, in particular, at detecting [...] and addressing illegal content or information incompatible with [the service providers'] terms and conditions, provided by [users], including measures taken that affect the availability, visibility, and accessibility of that illegal content or that information, such as demotion, demonetisation, disabling of access to, or removal thereof, or that affect the ability of [users] to provide that information, such as the termination or suspension of a [user] account.**

31 The information shall include **information** on any policies, procedures, measures and tools used for the purpose of content moderation, including algorithmic decision-making and human review, as well as the rules of procedure of the internal complaint-handling system (Art. 14 (1) sent. 2 DSA).

32 **Policies** include the permission or prohibition of particular content and the way it is expressed.[24] These shall serve as a clear indication of the reasons why providers may restrict the provision of their service. This can be done in two ways: First, service providers may consider restricting content by topic.[25] For example, they may restrict discussions in an online forum to game-related topics. Second, explicit prohibitions can be useful to ensure clarity. For example, the creation of user names and avatars may be prohibited if they contain swearwords, sexual innuendo or hate speech. This requires foresight and a careful consideration of possible cases for content moderation. Overly broad clauses and clauses that leave it entirely to the service provider's discretion as to what is and what is not permissible do not meet the requirements of Art. 14 DSA.

33 **Procedures** shall mean any process that aims to implement statutory provisions and other policies to restrict information on the service. This includes the rules for the internal complaint-handling system as set out in Art. 20 DSA (at least for online platforms) (→ mn. 45).

34 Moreover, information on the **measures and tools** to detect and identify illegal content needs to be provided. This includes human review by employees and third-party service providers.[26] Moreover, this includes tools that are used for the automated moderation of content. In online games, this relates in particular to the monitoring of communication channels, for example with self-learning AI tools to prevent abusive chats and offensive language.[27] These tools are now so advanced that they can issue real-time warnings to toxic players, even during voice chats. Simpler programmes such as word filters, which censor swearwords found on a publisher's list in chat, can also be considered tools. The reporting and redress procedure in Art. 16 DSA can also be seen as a tool for restricting content.

---

[24] Raue in Hofmann/Raue DSA Art. 14 mn. 38.
[25] Janal GRUR 2022, 211 (217).
[26] Raue in Hoffmann/Raue DSA Art. 14 mn. 42.
[27] Just, 'Neuartige Voicechat-KI soll toxischen Spielern automatisch den Mund verbieten' (GameStar 18.12.2020) <https://www.gamestar.de/artikel/neue-voicechat-ki-gegen-toxische-spieler,3365337.html>.

c) *Specific requirements for services that are directed towards minors*

35 Where a service is primarily directed at minors or is predominantly used by minors, the Provider shall explain the conditions for, and any restrictions on, **the use of the service in a way that minors can understand** (Art. 14 (3) DSA). This may be assumed if more than 50 % of the users are minors.[28] Providers can consider using graphical elements in their terms, such as icons or images, to illustrate the main elements of the information requirements (rec. 45 sent. 5 DSA).

3. Transparency reports

36 All service providers are required to publish **transparency reports** at least once a year unless they qualify as micro or small enterprises (Art. 15 (1) sent. 1 DSA). These transparency reports must contain information on orders received from authorities (a), meaningful and comprehensible information about the content moderation engaged in at the provider's own initiative (c), and the number of complaints received through the internal complaint-handling systems in accordance with the service provider's terms and conditions (d). Providers of hosting services must further add information on the number of notices in accordance with Art. 16 DSA (b). This information must be categorised by the type of alleged illegal content; the number of notices submitted by trusted flaggers; and it should give further insights on the action taken. Further information obligations apply to the providers of online platforms and very large online platforms.

37 **The report must be clear, and easily comprehensible.** It must be published in a machine-readable format and in an easily accessible manner. The European Commission has adopted an implementing act in accordance with Art. 15 (3) DSA to lay down an obligatory template, concerning the form and content of transparency reports and to harmonise the reporting periods.[29]

4. Obligations for hosting services

38 Section 2 of Chapter III of the DSA contains additional obligations for providers of hosting services, including online platforms. As they play a particularly important role in tackling illegal content online (see rec. 50 sent. 1 DSA), providers of hosting services, regardless of their size, must put in place an easily accessible and user-friendly **notice and action mechanism** that enables users to report illegal content ('notice'), on the basis of which the provider must decide whether it agrees with the assessment and possibly moderate the content ('action') (Art. 16 (1) DSA). Failure to do so may result in the loss of their liability privileges (Art. 16 (3) DSA).

39 The mechanism shall facilitate the submission of sufficiently precise and adequately substantiated notices (Art. 16 (2) DSA). It must be easily accessible to everyone, i.e., not only users but also third parties, such as authorities.[30] Consequently, it would not be enough to enable only logged-in users to report content. User-friendliness requires that the notice and action mechanism be located close to the information to be reported (rec. 50 sent. 3 DSA). It should also be possible to report multiple items of illegal content at once (rec. 50 sent. 4 DSA).

40 These harmonised requirements may make sense for static websites. However, they do not seem to take into account the particularities that games companies may face in

[28] Maamar in Kraul, p. 92 (107); Raue in Hofmann/Raue DSA Art. 14 mn. 70.

[29] Commission Implementing Regulation (EU) 2024/2835 of 4.112024 laying down templates concerning the transparency reporting obligations of providers of intermediary services and of providers of online platforms under Regulation (EU) 2022/2065 of the European Parliament and of the Council.

[30] Spindler GRUR 2021, 545 (552); Raue in Hoffmann/Raue DSA Art. 16 mn. 16.

this context. It remains more than questionable how unregistered third parties, such as authorities, should be able use an **in-game reporting tool** without login, if the game in question is only accessible after login.

41 Filed notices must be processed in a timely, diligent, non-arbitrary and objective manner (Art. 16 (6) DSA). Upon receipt of the notice, to provider must send the reporting user a notification of receipt (Art. 16 (4) DSA). Moreover, the provider must inform the individual or entity of its decision in respect of the information to which the notice relates, providing information on the possibilities of redress (Art. 16 (5) DSA). If the provider restricts information provided by a user on the grounds that it contains illegal content or is incompatible with the terms and conditions, a clear and specific **statement of reasons** must be given (Art. 17 DSA). In particular, the statement of reasons shall reasonably allow the affected user to effectively exercise the possibilities for redress (Art. 17 (4) DSA).[31]

42 Information giving rise to a suspicion that a **criminal offence involving a threat to the life or safety of a person or persons** has taken place, is taking place or is likely to take place, shall be promptly reported to law enforcement of the Member State concerned of the suspicion (Art. 18 (1) DSA). All relevant information available shall be provided.[32] In case the hosting service provider cannot identify with certainty the Member State concerned, it shall inform the authorities of the Member State in which it is established or Europol, or both (Art. 18 (2) DSA).

5. Obligations for online platforms

43 Additional obligations for online platforms can be found in Section 3 of Chapter III of the DSA. They do not apply to providers of online platforms that qualify as micro or small enterprises as defined in Recommendation 2003/361/EC,[33] unless they are designated as a **very large online platform** (Art. 19 DSA; rec. 57 DSA).

a) Disclosure of monthly active users

44 Online platforms are obliged to publish the **average number of their monthly active users** in the Union at least every six months (Art. 24 (2) DSA). This number is relevant to identify very large online platforms (→ mn. 11). The monthly average number of active users should reflect the total number of individuals who have used the service at least once by engaging with the information disseminated via the online platform, for instance by viewing, listening to or providing user information (rec. 77 sent. 2 DSA). If a game consists of several different components, not all of which can be classified as an online platform, we believe there are good arguments for using the number only of these users as the relevant benchmark and not the total number of all active players of the game. In this case, only those players who have used the respective game component are exposed to information from the online platform, so that the other players are not at risk of potentially illegal third-party information. It is generally difficult to reliably determine these figures due to restrictions on user tracking imposed by data protection laws.

b) Internal complaint-handling system and out-of-court dispute resolution

45 Users of online platforms must have access to an effective, free **complaint-handling system** to appeal against content removals or account suspensions (Art. 20 (1) DSA).

---

31 Maamar in Kraul, p. 92 (120).

32 Raue in Hofmann/Raue DSA Art. 18 mn. 41.

33 Commission Recommendation of 6.5.2003 concerning the definition of micro, small and medium-sized enterprises.

At the same time, the complaint-handling system enables users who have submitted a notice in accordance with Art. 16 DSA (→ mn. 38) to lodge a complaint against the decision taken by the provider based on the notice.[34] It must be possible to lodge a complaint for a period of at least six months after the decision in question. Complaints must be handled in a timely, non-discriminatory, diligent and non-arbitrary matter (Art. 20 (4) DSA). The complaint-handling system must be easy to access, user-friendly and enable and facilitate the submission of sufficiently precise and adequately substantiated complaints (Art. 20 (3) DSA). The service providers shall not set formal requirements, such as referral to specific, relevant legal provisions or elaborate legal explanations (rec. 58 sent. 3 DSA).

The internal complaints procedure may be followed by an **out-of-court dispute resolution** procedure. Online platform providers must work with certified independent dispute resolution bodies to resolve disputes relating to such decisions (Art 21 (1) sent. 1 DSA). Providers of online platforms must ensure that the information about the out-of-court dispute settlement is easily accessible, clear and user-friendly (Art. 21 (1) sent. 2 DSA). Unlike other out-of-court dispute resolution mechanisms, the participation of the online platform provider is mandatory, unless the dispute has been settled or is pending before a competent court or another out-of-court dispute resolution body (Art. 21 (2) DSA).[35] The out-of-court dispute resolution bodies must be certified by the Digital Services Coordinator of the EU Member State in which it has its establishment (Art. 21 (3) DSA). 46

As for the notice-and-takedown mechanism, the technical implementation of an internal complaint-handling system can be very complicated for online games that qualify as online platforms. 47

c) *Trusted flaggers*

Trusted flaggers are special entities under the DSA that detect specific potentially illegal content and notify the online platforms. Providers of online platforms must prioritise reports from trusted flaggers and process them without delay (Art. 22 (1) DSA).[36] Trusted flaggers are designated by the competent Digital Services Coordinator in the state where they have their establishment if they meet the respective criteria. They have special expertise in their field of competence which is taken into account by the service providers who receive the notice. 48

d) *Measures and protection against misuse*

If users frequently submit manifestly unfounded false notices or complaints, platforms shall suspend their privileges for a reasonable period of time and after having issued a prior warning (Art. 23 (1), (2) DSA). This may include the use of the services in general but also the processing of notices and complaints, if these tools were frequently misused. 49

e) *Transparency*

Providers of online platforms face additional transparency obligations. Among other things, their transparency reports must include information on the out-of-court dispute 50

[34] Grünwald/Nüßing MMR 2021, 283 (285); Raue in Hofmann/Raue DSA Art. 20 mn. 2.

[35] Hauck GRUR 2024, 1185 (1186); Maamar in Kraul, p. 92 (127).

[36] European Commission, 'Trusted flaggers under the Digital Services Act', (European Commission, 15 April 2025) <https://digital-strategy.ec.europa.eu/en/policies/trusted-flaggers-under-dsa>.

settlement procedures pursuant to Art. 21 DSA (→ mn. 46) and the number of suspensions pursuant to Art. 23 DSA (→ mn. 49). If they present **advertising** on their online interfaces, they must ensure that the recipients of the service who are shown advertisements are able to recognise that the information presented is advertising and, among other things, the natural or legal person on whose behalf the advertising is presented and who has paid for the advertising (Art. 26 (1) DSA).

51 More important, providers of online platforms shall set out in their terms and conditions, in plain and intelligible language, the main parameters used in their **recommender systems,** as well as any options for the users to modify those main parameters (Art. 27 (1) DSA). Recommender systems mean

> **a[ny] fully or partially automated system used by an online platform to suggest in its online interface specific information to recipients of the service or prioritise that information, including as a result of a search initiated by the recipient of the service or otherwise determining the relative order or prominence of information displayed (Art. 3 (s) DSA).**

52 These **recommender systems are filter tools** that help users prioritise the content that is presented to them.[37] For online games this might be a catalogue of UGC that is suggested for the player or offerings on a user-to-user marketplace, for example based on preferences during previous gameplay sessions. The transparency obligation to is intended to explain to the user why certain information is suggested. The way in which information is prioritised and presented to users has a significant impact on their ability to retrieve and interact with information online (rec. 70 sent. 3 DSA).

f) Prohibition of manipulative and deceptive practices

53 Art. 25 (1) DSA prohibits the use of manipulative or deceptive practices, such as **dark patterns,** described in rec. 67 sent. 1 DSA as 'practices that materially distort or impair the ability of recipients of the service to make autonomous or informed choices or decisions'. The scope of this prohibition is comparably small as it shall not apply to practices which are covered by the Unfair Commercial Practices Directive[38] (UCPD) or the General Data Protection Regulation[39] (GDPR → Ch. 29 mn. 25) (Art. 25 (2) DSA).[40] Among other things, the UCPD, for example, prohibits misleading or aggressive commercial practices towards consumers. The GDPR applies to dark patterns that aim to influence the data subject's consent to the processing of personal data.[41] So, the DSA does not add anything more to what has already been excluded for dark patterns.[42]

g) Online protection of minors

54 The protection of minors is an **important policy objective** for the legislators in the European Union (rec. 71 sent. 1 DSA). Consequently, online platforms which are accessible to minors shall put in place appropriate and proportionate measures to ensure a high level of privacy, safety, and security for minors on their service (Art. 28 (1) DSA).

---

[37] Grisse in Hofmann/Raue DSA Art. 27 mn. 13.

[38] Directive 2005/29/EC of the European Parliament and of the Council of 11.5.2005 concerning unfair business-to-consumer commercial practices in the internal market and amending Council Directive 84/450/EEC, Directives 97/7/EC, 98/27/EC and 2002/65/EC of the European Parliament and of the Council and Regulation (EC) No 2006/2004 of the European Parliament and of the Council.

[39] Regulation (EU) 2016/679 of the European Parliament and of the Council of 27.4.2016 on the protection of natural persons with regard to the processing of personal data and on the free movement of such data, and repealing Directive 95/46/EC (General Data Protection Regulation).

[40] Raue in Hofmann/Raue DSA Art. 25 mn. 7.

[41] Raue in Hofmann/Raue DSA Art. 25 mn. 101.

[42] Higher Regional Court Bamberg 8.1.2025 – 3 UKl 11/24 e, GRUR-RS 2025, 6221.

The obligation applies to all providers of online platforms who permit minors to use their service, those whose service is directed at or predominantly used by minors, or who are otherwise aware that some of their users are minors (rec. 71 sent. 2 DSA). Targeted advertising towards minors is prohibited (Art. 28 (2) DSA), i.e., not even allowed based on consent – contrary to the GDPR. As the DSA fully harmonises the rules applicable to intermediary services in the internal market (rec. 9 sent. 1 DSA), the EU Member States may not adopt or maintain additional national requirements falling within the scope of the DSA.[43] Further obligations to protect minors imposed on online platforms under national law could therefore infringe on Union law.[44]

A significant number of online games already rely on **youth protection tools** that **55** have been implemented by the console manufacturer.[45] The objective of these tools is to provide customised youth protection measures, with consideration for the vulnerabilities of children (→ Ch. 34 mn. 7). The implications of the DSA extend the reach of such obligations. In particular, such obligations not only apply to the console manufacturer but to the provider of the online platform, i.e., the online game. The competent German authority for youth protection measures under Art. 28 DSA, the so-called *Stelle zur Durchsetzung von Kinderrechten in digitalen Diensten (Centre for the enforcement of children's rights in digital services* – KidD), has identified the following measures (which are non-exhaustive):

- Notice- and action mechanisms through which children can easily report harassment, for example;
- Safe default settings that ensure, among other things, that children can no longer be easily found with their profiles or approached by third parties;
- Provider-independent help and reporting centres;
- Instruments for monitoring the online use by parents and other persons with custody rights.[46]

In July 2024, the European Commission launched a call for evidence for **guidelines** **56** **on compliance with Art. 28 DSA**.[47] The draft guidelines were published on 13.5.2025.[48] In these, the European Commission emphasises that any measures should adhere to the general principle of proportionality, take into account the rights of children set out in the Charter and the United Nations Convention on the Rights of the Child, incorporate the highest standards of privacy, safety and security, and design services that take into account the developmental, cognitive and emotional needs of minors (→ Ch. 34 mn. 26). The final guidelines are scheduled for adoption in Summer 2025, though they were not available at the time of writing this chapter.

---

[43] BzKJ, 'Der Digital Services Act und seine Auswirkungen auf die Anbietervorsorge' (BzKJ, January 2024) <https://www.bzkj.de/rsource/blob/236652/391378483407530522cf1b5388d0e249/20241-der-dsa-und-seine-auswirkungen-auf-die-anbietervorsorge-data.pdf>.

[44] Liesching in BeckOK JugendschutzR JuSchG § 24a mn. 15 et seq.

[45] For example: Nintendo Parental Controls; Playstation Safety; Epic Games Cabined Accounts.

[46] BzKJ, 'Strukturelle Vorsorgemaßnahmen' (BzKJ) <https://www.kidd.bund.de/kidd/risikobegegnung/strukturelle-vorsorgemassnahmen-239568>.

[47] European Commission, 'Commission launches call for evidence for guidelines on protection of minors online under the Digital Services Act' (European Commission, 31.7.2024) <https://digital-strategy.ec.europa.eu/en/news/commission-launches-call-evidence-guidelines-protection-minors-online-under-digital-services-act>.

[48] European Commission, 'Commission publishes draft guidelines on protection of minors online under the Digital Services Act' (European Commission, 13.5.2025) <https://digital-strategy.ec.europa.eu/en/news/commission-publishes-draft-guidelines-protection-minors-online-under-digital-services-act>.

h) Special platforms

57 Further obligations may apply to very large online platforms (→ mn. 11) or online platforms that allow consumers to conclude distance contracts with other traders (Chapter III Section 4 of the DSA).

IV. Conclusion

58 The classification of online games under the DSA as an **intermediary service** depends on its features and their technical implementation. Interactive and social features can be in the scope of the DSA. Due to the differences in content and technology, each online game must be examined individually. The due diligence obligations require game companies to act and make changes, in particular to their live services and their terms and conditions. This may have positive effects for both, players and publishers, as transparent and comprehensible communication between each other creates legal certainty and promotes a trustworthy online environment. However, the additional effort, especially for small game companies, seems unreasonable if they only offer very limited hosting functionalities, such as for user names. Future developments in case law and guidelines issued by the competent authorities on a national and EU level may reveal a need for more specific action.

C. Platform obligations under other EU legal acts

59 In addition to the Digital Services Act, several other legal instruments at the EU level impose specific obligations on platform providers, including those operating online games. These frameworks address issues ranging from **fair platform-business relations and competition regulation to AI usage, cross-border access to electronic evidence, and child protection**. While their scope and applicability vary, each can have a significant impact on how online games and gaming platforms are designed, operated, and moderated. The following section provides a brief overview of key legislative acts relevant to game companies active in the EU.

I. Digital Markets Act

60 Under the Digital Markets Act (DMA),[49] further platform obligations apply to so-called 'core platform services' provided by large operators with significant economic power ('gatekeepers'). For further details, (→ Ch. 34 mn. 62).

II. Platform-to-Business-Regulation

61 The Platform-to-Business Regulation[50] aims to establish a set of mandatory rules between to so-called 'online intermediation services', a term that is similar to 'intermediary services' under the DSA, and their business users. This may be particularly relevant for

[49] Regulation (EU) 2022/1925 of the European Parliament and of the Council of 14.9.2022 on contestable and fair markets in the digital sector and amending Directives (EU) 2019/1937 and (EU) 2020/1828.

[50] Regulation (EU) 2019/1150 of the European Parliament and of the Council of 20.6.2019 on promoting fairness and transparency for business users of online intermediation services.

certain online games, especially those with a UGC-driven content creator economy. In games that allow players to monetise their UGC and sell it to other players, players may act as both consumers and business users under the Regulation.

The Platform-to-Business Regulation is predicated on two fundamental principles: firstly, the establishment of minimum requirements for the general terms and conditions, and secondly, the implementation of transparent, fair and effective redress possibilities. Given that the DSA's is without prejudice to the Platform-to-Business Regulation (Art. 2 (4) (e) DSA) and its application to all users, including business users, there is some overlap between both regulations. **62**

III. Artificial Intelligence Act

The Artificial Intelligence Act[51] (AI Act) entered into force in August 2024. Its purpose is to promote the development and deployment of human-centric and trustworthy artificial intelligence while ensuring a high level of protection of health, safety and fundamental rights (rec. 1 sent. 1 AI Act). The regulation adopts a **risk-based approach** and tailors the type and content of rules, especially for the AI's providers and deployers, to the intensity and scope of the risks that the AI system can generate (rec. 26 AI sent. 1 AI Act): from minimal risk to high-risk and even prohibited AI practices. **63**

Most game features, particularly the game engine, generally fall outside the scope of the AI Act because they do not constitute an AI system. According to Art. 3 (1) AI Act, an AI system is defined as **64**

a machine-based system that is designed to operate with varying levels of autonomy and that may exhibit adaptiveness after deployment, and that, for explicit or implicit objectives, infers, from the input it receives, how to generate outputs such as predictions, content, recommendations, or decisions that can influence physical or virtual environments.

In this regard, games' engines lack autonomy and adaptability, i.e., they aren't self-learning, as they follow strict rules of the game, even though they may appear to the user to be artificial intelligence.[52] **65**

For online games (platforms), however, AI systems can be used to **improve the user experience**, for example by detecting cheats and moderating content.[53] In most cases, these are neither developed nor placed on the market by the publisher, so that the publisher does not qualify as provider pursuant to Art. 3 (3) AI Act. Rather, they are deployers who only have limited obligations under the AI Act (if any at all).[54] **66**

---

[51] Regulation (EU) 2024/1689 of the European Parliament and of the Council of 13.6.2024 laying down harmonised rules on artificial intelligence and amending Regulations (EC) No 300/2008, (EU) No 167/2013, (EU) No 168/2013, (EU) 2018/858, (EU) 2018/1139 and (EU) 2019/2144 and Directives 2014/90/EU, (EU) 2016/797 and (EU) 2020/1828 (Artificial Intelligence Act).

[52] Hentsch/Rodenhausen MMR 2024, 714.

[53] Hentsch/Rodenhausen MMR 2024, 714 (716).

[54] Hentsch/Rodenhausen MMR 2024, 714 (717).

IV. E-evidence package

67 Further platform obligations regarding cross-border access to electronic evidence apply from 2026. The **e-evidence package**, comprising a Regulation[55] and a Directive,[56] is intended to facilitate the process of obtaining electronic evidence for law enforcement and judicial authorities, thus enabling more efficient investigation and prosecution of criminals.[57]

68 The scope of the package is broad and covers services, including electronic communication services within the meaning of Art. 2 (4) EECCD (→ mn 14), as well as services that enable players to communicate with each other or that enable data to be stored or otherwise processed on their behalf (Art. 3 (3) e-Evidence Regulation).

69 Most importantly, the e-Evidence Regulation allows judicial authorities to request the **provision and preservation of electronic evidence** (such as communication and personal information) from a service provider who is established in another EU Member State. As for the DSA, service providers are required to either have an establishment or appoint a legal representative in the European Union.

V. CSAM-Regulation (Draft)

70 In May 2022, the European Commission proposed a regulation to prevent and combat child sexual abuse online (CSAM-Regulation Proposal),[58] requiring technical and human efforts by online service providers to proactively detect and remove child sexual abuse material (CSAM) and to combat cyber grooming online. The draft was amended by the LIBE committee in November 2023 and contains due diligence obligations for providers of online games with chat functionalities, irrespective of their size or their substantial exposure to online child sexual abuse.[59]

D. Summary

71 The provision of live services, such as online games, is subject to a wide range of additional platform obligations covering various aspects to enhance player safety and level the playing field across the European Union. The legal landscape is characterised by a **progressive increase in complexity**. For games companies wishing to offer their services in the European Union, it is crucial to keep abreast of these developments and, above all, to anticipate the upcoming changes so that they can adapt their technical and organisational processes in good time to prepare and ensure compliance.

---

[55] Regulation (EU) 2023/1543 of the European Parliament and of the Council of 12.7.2023 on European Production Orders and European Preservation Orders for electronic evidence in criminal proceedings and for the execution of custodial sentences following criminal proceedings.

[56] Directive (EU) 2023/1544 of the European Parliament and of the Council of 12.7.2023 laying down harmonised rules on the designation of designated establishments and the appointment of legal representatives for the purpose of gathering electronic evidence in criminal proceedings.

[57] European Commission, 'E-evidence – cross-border access to electronic evidence' (European Commission) <https://commission.europa.eu/law/cross-border-cases/judicial-cooperation/types-judicial-cooperation/e-evidence-cross-border-access-electronic-evidence_en>.

[58] Proposal for a Regulation of the European Parliament and of the Council laying down rules to prevent and combat child sexual abuse (COM(2022/209 final) – 2022/0155 (COD).

[59] Committee on Civil Liberties, Justice and Home Affairs, Draft report on the proposal for a regulation of the European Parliament and of the Council Laying down rules to prevent and combat child sexual abuse (COM(2022)0209 – C9–0174/2022 – 2022/0155(COD)).

§ 33
Illegal Content and Activity on Game Platforms

Bibliography: Hilgert, 'Toxic Players' in Hentsch/Falk (eds), Games und Recht. Games – Entwicklung – Publishing Vertrieb – Plattformen – Marketing. Praxishandbuch, Baden-Baden, 2023; De Streel et al., 'Online Platforms' Moderation of Illegal Content Online: Law, Practices and Options for Reform', European Parliament, Policy Department for Economic, Scientific and Quality of Life Policies, June 2020.

A. Terminology ... 2
I. Video game platforms ... 2
II. Third-party content and activity: the case of toxic players ... 5
III. Information, activity and content ... 9
IV. Illegal and inappropriate ... 13
B. Video game platform providers' obligations to act and liability exposure ... 18
I. Illegal content under EU law ... 20
II. Illegal content under Member State law ... 25
1. Public morality ... 26
2. Youth protection ... 28
3. Hate speech and discrimination ... 31
4. Consumer protection and economic law ... 33
5. Moral integrity, harassment, stalking and defamation ... 34
6. Conclusion ... 38
III. Obligations to act against illegal content ... 41
1. Sectoral obligations and charters ... 42
2. The DSA ... 55
3. TCO ... 63
4. Contractual obligation to act ... 66
C. Video game platform providers' freedom to act ... 69
I. General legal provisions ... 70
II. Terms of Use ... 73
III. Burden of proof ... 76
D. Conclusion ... 77

The present chapter considers the main types of **illegal content and activity** that video game platforms are concerned with. The topic of illegal content and activity on video game platforms is analysed from a double angle. First, we examine various types of content and behaviour which are illegal under Union or Member State law, and which may lead to an objective *obligation* to act on behalf of the video game platform provider further to either sector-specific obligations, Union law instruments, or contractual obligations (**B**). Second, we examine when and how that same provider can invoke a subjective *right* to act against certain forms of content or behaviour which the provider deems illegal or even simply inappropriate (**C**).[1] Prior to this double analysis, however, it is necessary to clarify several terminology items (**A**). We end with a brief conclusion (**D**). 1

A. Terminology

I. Video game platforms

For the purposes of this chapter, **'video game platform'** is to be understood broadly as either (i) a stand-alone online video game or (ii) an online repository or 'library' of 2

[1] For a similar approach, see Hilgert, 'Toxic Players' in Hentsch/Falk (eds), Games und Recht. Games-Entwicklung – Publishing Vertrieb – Plattformen – Marketing. Praxishandbuch, Baden-Baden, 2023, 447.

video games, in both cases allowing for player interactions. With 'player interactions' we mean interactive player features such as group chats, community posts, or the possibility for players to access and create game-specific additional content.

3 An example of a stand-alone online video game allowing for player interaction is Roblox. Examples of 'libraries' allowing for player interaction are for instance Steam, GOG, or the EA App.

4 Video game platforms within the meaning of this chapter qualify as **providers of an information society service**, since they provide services for remuneration, at a distance, by electronic means and at the individual request of a recipient of services.[2] Such video game platforms will typically qualify as a hosting services provider within the meaning of the DSA[3, 4] because they host third-party content, consisting either of entire video games[5] and/or of user-generated content such as community posts. In some cases, the video game platform may not only qualify as a hosting services provider, but in addition as a platform within the meaning of the DSA.[6]

II. Third-party content and activity: the case of toxic players

5 In line with chapter I, the present chapter does not address the responsibility of video game platforms for 'own' content or activity. Rather, this chapter focuses on **third-party, i.e., player-generated, content and activity**. Player-generated content or activity can come about in different fashions.

6 First, players can create content within a video game itself. A growing number of video games allow for varying degrees of alteration and personalisation through a process initially called **'modding'** (short for modifying) and now more generically known as **'UGC'** (user-generated content). Games like *Fortnite*, *Halo Forge*, *Minecraft* and *Roblox* have seen considerable success, in part due to their ability to support UGC. While player-generated content may sometimes be embedded within the video games, it may also be generated and made separately accessible via the game platform. For example, the Steam Workshop feature allows not only game developers but also game users to share and download modifications of the game.

7 Second, as a corollary to the main function of providing video game content, video game platform providers increasingly offer **additional functionality** to post messages or

[2] Art. 1 (1), point b) of Directive 2015/1535 of the European Parliament and of the Council of 9.9.2015 laying down a procedure for the provision of information in the field of technical regulations and of rules on Information Society services.

[3] 'Hosting services provider' within the meaning of Art. 3 (g), (iii) DSA.

[4] See for instance Ubisoft, that considers itself as a hosting services provider, as is apparent from its DSA transparency report available on https://www.ubisoft.com/legal/documents/transparencyreport/en-US.

[5] Imagine an online library of online video games uploaded by the third-party video game publishers. Whether a video game platform can, in its capacity of 'host', also benefit from the associated liability exemption, will inter alia depend on the extent to which it can be considered passive. A platform that quasi-automatically allows any publisher to make available its games can benefit from the hosting exemption (e.g., Steam). In contrast, a platform that engages in a deep editorial review, vetting and selection of video games may be denied the exemption (very much like an audiovisual streaming platform may assume liability for the movies it decides to make available). See judgment of the CJEU of 12.7.2011, *L'Oréal/EB eBay*, case C-324/09, EU:C:2011:474, point 116; Judgment of the CJEU of 23.3.2010, *Google France and Google*, cases C-236/08 to C-238/08, EU:C:2010:159, point 114.

[6] See for instance Roblox, which consider itself a platform within the meaning of the DSA, as is apparent from its online reporting: https://en.help.roblox.com/hc/en-us/articles/13061336948244-EU-Digital-Services-Act. Other video game platform providers that qualify as a platform within the meaning of the DSA are for instance Xbox Console Store, Xbox.com Website Store, Pc Games Store.

share files and content with a potentially indiscriminate audience, thereby going beyond person-to-person communications. Players may thus generate content that is stored on and possibly disseminated by means of the video game platform.

In both instances, players may (knowingly or unknowingly) disseminate content and/or display behaviour that is either illegal or inappropriate – the case of so-called **'toxic players'**. 8

III. Information, activity and content

It is important to consider that players can not only disseminate problematic[7] *information*, but can also display problematic *activity*.[8] The two concepts should be carefully distinguished.[9] The DSA does employ both concepts but does not define them.[10] Next to *information* and *activity*, the DSA also relies on the concept of *illegal content*, defined as 'any information that, in itself or in relation to an activity, including the sale of products or the provision of services, is not in compliance with Union law or the law of any Member State which is in compliance with Union law, irrespective of the precise subject matter or nature of that law'.[11] 9

Through the concept of **illegal content**, and especially through the phrase 'in relation to an activity', the DSA suggests that information, which is per se lawful, could become unlawful if the underlying activity also is unlawful. This begs the question whether information qualifies as unlawful, and therefore constitutes 'illegal content', *as soon as* that information frames within an activity that is unlawful, or whether in addition it is required that the information *itself* must explicitly be prohibited by a Union or Member 10

[7] Illegal or inappropriate, cfr. *infra*.

[8] Consider, for instance, a player on a platform inviting in a public chat another (minor of age) player to meet up in real life. Such invitation is, from an *informational* perspective, unproblematic. Indeed, one can reasonably assume that no EU Member State has speech laws curtailing the right to invite someone to meet. From a *behavioural* perspective, however, the invitation may very well be illegal if the inviting player turns out to be an adult, knew that the invited player was minor of age, and sent the invitation with sexual intent. Indeed: this is called 'grooming', an activity that is criminally prohibited and sanctioned in the EU Member States (see, for instance, Art. 251 of the Dutch Criminal Code ('Wetboek van Strafrecht') and Art. 417/24 of the Belgian Criminal Code ('Code penal').

[9] Knowledge of information does not necessarily lead to knowledge of the underlying activity. Conversely, without knowledge of the underlying activity, it is sometimes difficult or simply impossible to assess whether certain information is illegal or not.

[10] The DSA's Chapter II governing the liability of providers of intermediary services. In this chapter, the DSA exempts mere conduit (Art. 4), caching (Art. 5), and hosting (Art. 6) service providers from liability for third-party '*information*' that is transmitted or accessed and/or stored. In particular, one of the conditions to benefit from the liability exemption for information stored by hosting providers is that the latter does not have actual knowledge (for criminal claims) of illegal '*activity*' is and not aware of facts or circumstances (for damages claims) from which the illegal '*activity*' is apparent. Thus, the DSA seems to implicitly link a hosting provider's liability for unlawful '*information*', to a contextual awareness of underlying '*activity*'. This link was already present in the Directive on electronic commerce (Directive 2000/31/EC of the European Parliament and of the Council of 8.6.2000 on certain legal aspects of information society services, in particular electronic commerce, in the Internal Market ('Directive on electronic commerce'), OJ L 178, 17.7.2000, 1–16. See in particular Art. 14.1(a). The corresponding no-monitoring provision in the DSA (Art. 8, DSA) exempting intermediary service providers from a general monitoring obligation applies not only to '*information*' but also to seeking facts or circumstances indicating illegal '*activity*'. Again, also the Directive on electronic commerce previously imposed a ban on general monitoring obligations for both '*information*' and '*activity*' (Art. 15.1, Directive on electronic commerce).

[11] Art. 3(h), DSA.

State law. The question is not without importance.[12] The DSA's recitals provide some help to answer this question.

11 The recitals state that for the purpose of the DSA the concept of 'illegal content' should be

> **defined broadly to cover information relating to illegal content, products, services and activities. In particular, that concept should be understood to refer to information, irrespective of its form, that under the applicable law is either itself illegal, such as illegal hate speech or terrorist content and unlawful discriminatory content, *or that the applicable rules render illegal in view of the fact that it relates to illegal activities* [emphasis added]. Illustrative examples include the sharing of images depicting child sexual abuse, the unlawful non-consensual sharing of private images, online stalking, the sale of non-compliant or counterfeit products, the sale of products or the provision of services in infringement of consumer protection law, the non-authorised use of copyright protected material, the illegal offer of accommodation services or the illegal sale of live animals. In contrast, an eyewitness video of a potential crime should not be considered to constitute illegal content, merely because it depicts an illegal act, where recording or disseminating such a video to the public is not illegal under national or Union law.**[13]

12 The recitals thus are not entirely conclusive,[14] but through the used wording and examples cited do seem to indicate that 'illegal content' must be broadly understood to encompass information that is 'contextually' illegal, *i.e.*, that frames within an activity prohibited by Union or Member State legislation.

IV. Illegal and inappropriate

13 In the section above, we have focused on the distinction between information, activity and content. Below we focus on the *illegal* respectively *inappropriate* nature thereof.

14 First, let's turn to the topic of **illegality**. In its plain meaning, anything that runs against or is prohibited by the rule of law is illegal. What constitutes 'illegal content' also derives clearly from the DSA. It is any information that is not in compliance with either Union law or Member State law. Importantly, the Union legislator has been wise enough to include in the legal definition of 'illegal content' a proviso further to which account should only be taken of Member State law that is in turn 'in compliance with Union law'.[15, 16] This is important in light of the growing concern that some Member States resort to censorship laws under the cover of, for instance, minor protection. Reference can be made to the situation in Hungary, which has given rise to infringement proceedings by the Commission.[17, 18]

---

[12] Turning to our fictitious example above, does the 'information' (consisting of the invitation to meet up) constitute 'illegal content' merely because the underlying 'activity' (the act of grooming) is illegal? Or is it required that Union or Member State legislation explicitly prohibits the information itself?

[13] Recital 12, DSA.

[14] One can argue that the concept of 'illegal content' is to be understood to only encompass information that is illegal per se, since the recitals require that 'the applicable rules render [the information itself] illegal'.

[15] Art. 3(h), DSA.

[16] Interestingly, the proviso only applies to *Member State* law that is incompatible with Union law. It should be noted, however, that also secondary Union law (regulations and directives) may very well be found incompatible with primary (Treaty) Union law. See for example judgment of the CJEU of 8.4.2014, *Digital Rights Ireland and Seitlinger and Others*, cases C-293/12 and C-594/12, EU:C:2014:238.

[17] Case C-769/22, *Commission v Hungary*, OJ C 54, 13.2.2023 (Action brought in December 2022, currently pending).

[18] Another example of where the Union legislator's proviso may have significant importance is in games of chance. Some Member States impose particularly sweeping blanket prohibitions that are over-inclusive and, for instance, also ban elements of video games that contain a 'surprise' element, the so-called loot boxes.

On the topic of illegality, grey zones may appear. Whether a certain type of information (or the underlying activity) is illegal under a given Union or Member State law may in and of itself already be cause for debate. Even within one single Member State differences in opinion may exist between different authorities and/or courts of law. In addition, as set out in the previous paragraph, the conformity of Member State law with Union law can be contested, and the process to determine such incompatibility before a court of law may take years. The DSA leaves the question unanswered how third parties, including video game platform providers, should consider illegal content when confronted with such challenges.[19] It is beyond doubt that the Union legislator was more than aware of the issue. For instance, on several occasions the DSA refers to 'allegedly' illegal content.[20] 15

Second, let's turn to the topic of **inappropriateness**. Content or behaviour is inappropriate when it is not 'proper or suitable in the circumstances'[21] – a highly subjective and circumstantial assessment indeed. Whilst there may be a category or set of types of behaviour that any reasonable person would consider inappropriate, there is certainly also a grey zone. What is appropriate to a 16-year-old adolescent may not be appropriate to a 10-year-old child. Also, the boundary between 'inappropriate' and 'illegal' is not always clear. An isolated insult may be inappropriate yet legal – but if repeated it may become illegal harassment. 16

Although these elements are self-evident and require little further explanation, the subjective and circumstantial nature of inappropriateness will prove important to assess to what extent video game platform providers can or must intervene to rule out inappropriate player behaviour on their platforms, in particular when considering sectoral or contractual obligations.[22] 17

B. Video game platform providers' obligations to act and liability exposure

After exploring the conceptual landscape of illegal respectively inappropriate third-party information, activity and content, we now turn to a more substantive analysis of applicable EU and Member State legislation. 18

Video game platform providers can be exposed to content that is illegal under Union law (I) or Member State law (II) and may have obligations to act against toxic players (III) that can derive from sectoral obligations, from the DSA and the TCO, or from contractual obligations. 19

I. Illegal content under EU law

On Union level, four types of content have been subjected to harmonized legislation rendering such content illegal.[23] 20

---

19 With regard to 'orders to act', that will be discussed below, it is for the Member State to decide which authority is competent for issuing said orders. In addition, as will be discussed below, while 'orders to act' are aimed at tackling illegal content, operators receiving an order on the basis of a national legislation that is contrary to EU law may refrain from acting against the alleged illegal content.

20 See Artt. 15.1(b), 17.1(d), 21.2 para. 2, and 22.3(b), DSA.

21 Oxford language dictionary.

22 Cfr. *infra*, section C.

23 For a detailed overview, see the study (predating the adoption of the DSA) by De Streel et al. requested by the European Parliament's IMCO Committee, 'Online Platforms' Moderation of Illegal Content Online: Law, Practices and Options for Reform', European Parliament, Policy Department for

21 The **Counter-Terrorism Directive** ('CTD')[24] obliges Member States to make punishable as a criminal offence the intentional distribution or making available – including online – of any message to the public with the intent to incite and advocate the commission of terrorist acts as defined by the CTD.[25] The CTD also requires Member States to make punishable the recruitment[26] and the provision of instructions – including online – of weapons, hazardous substances, methods or techniques to commit the same terrorist acts.[27]

22 The **Child Sexual Abuse and Exploitation Directive** ('CSAED')[28] defines child pornography[29] and obliges Member States to make punishable the distribution, dissemination or transmission thereof – including online. The same goes for grooming and soliciting children to provide child pornography through 'information and communication technology'.[30] A review of the CSAED is currently pending with a view to replacing it by a 'Child Sexual Abuse Regulation' or 'CSAR'.[31] After failed attempts by the Belgian and Hungarian presidencies of the Council of the EU, the Polish Presidency currently aims to find a compromise on Council level.[32]

23 The **Counter-Racism Framework Decision** or 'CRFD'[33] obliges Member States to make punishable various racist and xenophobic acts, such as public incitation to (racist or xenophobic) violence,[34] the public dissemination of content ('tracts, pictures or other material') containing the same,[35] and publicly condoning, denying or grossly trivialising crimes of genocide, crimes against humanity and war crimes, and crimes against peace on racist or xenophobic grounds.[36]

24 Finally, reference can be made to the EU harmonised body of law on intellectual property law, particularly in the field of copyright, trademarks, and designs and models,[37] with horizontally applicable provisions across different fields. Under the InfoSoc

---

Economic, Scientific and Quality of Life Policies, June 2020, available at http://www.europarl.europa.eu/supporting-analyses.

[24] Directive (EU) 2017/541 of the European Parliament and of the Council of 15.3.2017 on combating terrorism and replacing Council Framework Decision 2002/475/JHA and amending Council Decision 2005/671/JHA, OJ L 88/6 of 31.3.2017 (hereinafter referred to as the 'Counter-Terrorism Directive' or 'CTD').

[25] See Art. 5, CTD, which in turn refers to the offences listed in points (a) to (i) of Art. 3.1.

[26] Art. 6, CTD.

[27] Art. 7, CTD.

[28] Directive 2011/93/EU of the European Parliament and of the Council of 13.12.2011 on combating the sexual abuse and sexual exploitation of children and child pornography, and replacing Council Framework Decision 2004/68/JHA, OJ L335 of 17.12.2011 (hereinafter referred to as the 'Child Sexual Abuse and Exploitation Directive' or 'CSAED').

[29] Art. 2(c), CSAED.

[30] Art. 6.1 and Art. 6.2, CSAED.

[31] See the European Commission's Proposal for a Regulation of the European Parliament and of the Council laying down rules to prevent and combat child sexual abuse, COM/2022/209 final, available on https://eur-lex.europa.eu/legal-content/EN/TXT/?uri=COM%3A2022%3A209%3AFIN&qid=1652451192472.

[32] See the European Parliament's 'Legislative Train Schedule – New legislation to fight child sexual abuse online': https://www.europarl.europa.eu/legislative-train/spotlight-JD22/file-combating-child-sexual-abuse-online#:~:text=At%20the%20Council%2C%20work%20is,Council%20on%2029%20April%202024.

[33] Council Framework Decision 2008/913/JHA of 28.11.2008 on combating certain forms and expressions of racism and xenophobia by means of criminal law, OJ L 328, 6.12.2008 (hereinafter referred to as the 'Counter-Racism Framework Decision' or 'CRFD').

[34] Art. 1(a) CRFD.

[35] Art. 1(b) CFRD.

[36] Art. 1(c) and (d) CFRD.

[37] De Streel et al. limit their overview of intellectual property-related content that is harmonised at Union level at the Directive (EU) 2019/790 of the European Parliament and of the Council of 17.4.2019

Directive,[38] infringements of copyrights, namely the reproduction right,[39] the right of communication to the public[40] and the distribution right,[41] are to be considered as illegal content. The same can be said for trademark or design rights infringements, where any unlawful use of a registered trademark[42] or registered design[43] will be regarded as illegal content.[44] Furthermore, the CDSM Directive contains a provision applicable specifically to online-content sharing service providers.[45] Those providers must remove copyright-infringing contents from their services and prevent future uploads thereof to avoid liability for unauthorised acts of communication to the public of copyright-protected works, *i.e.*, illegal content.[46]

II. Illegal content under Member State law

Unsurprisingly, Member State laws contain a patchwork of legal provisions that render certain content unlawful, either on a purely civil law level, or also on a criminal law level. A detailed and exhaustive overview of individual Member State legislation would take us too far, and we therefore limit ourselves to a high-level categorization of legislation prohibiting certain illegal content. 25

1. Public morality

Member States have the right to legislate on **public morality**. Both the Union Treaties and the CJEU share the view that the power to determine what is public morality, and to legislate the same, preeminently falls under Member State jurisdiction.[47] In principle it is for each Member State to determine in accordance with its own scale of values and in the form selected by it the requirements of public morality in its territory.[48] 26

on copyright and related rights in the Digital Single Market and amending Directives 96/9/EC and 2001/29/EC, OJ L 130, 17.5.2019 (hereinafter referred to as the 'CDSM Directive').

[38] Directive 2001/29/EC of the European Parliament and of the Council of 22.5.2001 on the harmonisation of certain aspects of copyright and related rights in the information society, OJ L 167, 22.6.2001 (hereinafter referred to as the 'InfoSoc Directive').

[39] Art. 2 of the InfoSoc Directive.

[40] Art. 3 of the InfoSoc Directive.

[41] Art. 4 of the InfoSoc Directive.

[42] Art. 9 of Regulation (EU) 2017/1001 of the European Parliament and of the Council of 14.6.2017 on the European Union trademark, OJ L 154/1, 16.6.2017; and Art. 10 of Directive (EU) 2015/2436 of the European Parliament and of the Council of 16.12.2015 to approximate the laws of the Member States relating to trademarks, OJ L 336, 23.12.2015.

[43] Art. 16 of Directive (EU) 2024/2823 of the European Parliament and of the Council of 23.10.2024 on the legal protection of designs, OJ L 2024/2823, 18.11.2024. Art. 19 of Council Regulation (EC) No 6/2002 of 12.12.2001 on Community designs, OJ L 3, 5.1.2002, as last amended by Regulation (EU) 2024/2822 of the European Parliament and of the Council of 23.10.2024 amending Council Regulation (EC) No 6/2002 on Community designs and repealing Commission Regulation (EC) No 2246/2002, OJ L 2024/2822, 18.11.2024.

[44] See judgment of the CJEU of 12.7.2011, *L'Oreal v eBay*, case C-324/09, EU:C:2011:474, point 120. The Court specifically referred to trademark infringement as 'illegal activity'.

[45] Art. 17 of the CDSM Directive. Art. 17 (4) (c) provides for a 'notice and take down' and 'notice and stay down' system where online content-sharing service providers must use their best efforts to prevent the uploading of unauthorised copyrighted material and obtain licenses from rightsholders in order to avoid liability for copyright infringements.

[46] *See* judgment of the CJEU of 22.6.2021, *Frank Peterson*, cases C-682/18 and 683/18, EU:C:2021:503, point 71 and opinion of AG Saugmandsgaard Øe of 15.7.2021, *Poland v Parliament and Council*, case C-401/19, EU:C:2021:613, both referring expressly to 'illegal content' in the context of Art. 17 of the CDSM Directive.

[47] See Art. 4.2 TEU.

[48] Judgment of the CJEU of 14.12.1979, case C-34/79, *Henn and Darby*, ECR 1979, 3795.

However, Member States' sovereignty in the matter is not absolute. The CJEU has held that no inherent general exception can be inferred from the TFEU that would exclude all measures taken for reasons of law and order or public security from the scope of European Union law.[49]

27 Member States are entitled to impose limitations to the free movement of goods and services on grounds of public morality.[50] However, in accordance with standing case law, such limitations will need to be necessary and proportionate.[51] Specifically relevant for video game platform providers is the *Omega Spielhallen* case,[52] where the CJEU examined, under the angle of the freedom to provide services,[53] an administrative prohibition issued by the Bonn (Germany) police authority on a 'laser drome' that allowed 'playing at killing people'.[54] Somewhat surprisingly, the CJEU held in this case that the prohibition was permitted under Union law, arguing that it corresponds to the level of protection of human dignity which the German Constitution sought to guarantee, and that by prohibiting only the variant of the game that focused on 'playing at killing' people, the contested order did not go beyond what was necessary.[55] It is important to add that the CJEU[56] has considered that the proportionality test of a certain restriction on the freedom to provide services is 'not static but dynamic'. This means that a finding of proportionality does not indefinitely stand over time, and that due note should be taken of the evolution of circumstances after adoption of a given restriction.[57] This leads to the consideration that 20 years later, *Omega Spielhallen* could arguably be decided differently in light of evolving customs, the evolving exposure to shooter games and convincing scientific evidence that there is no correlation between playing shooter games and propensity to real-world violence.

2. Youth protection

28 **Youth and child protection laws** traditionally constitute a second important pillar of Member State regulation of content. Reference can for instance be made to the German federal youth protection law or 'JuSchG'[58] which predates the DSA and already featured important obligations for platform providers in relation to youth protection.

29 As is the case with public morality, youth protection undoubtedly constitutes an overriding ground of public interest that can serve as a justification to limitations on the

---

[49] Judgment of the CJUE of 2.4.2020, *Commission v Poland, Hungary and Czech Republic*, case C-715/17, C-718/17 and C-719/17, EU:C:2020:257, point 143.
point 143.

[50] The latter constitutes a compelling ground that is subsumed by the CJEU under grounds of public policy. Public policy is mentioned in Art. 36 TFEU as a ground to limit the free movement of goods provided in Art. 34 TFEU. Similarly, public policy is mentioned as a justification ground in Art. 52.1 TFEU, which by virtue of Art. 62 applies to the free movement of services provided by Art. 56 TFEU.

[51] For instance, the CJEU took issue with the UK customs authorities prohibiting the import of inflatable dolls, qualified as 'indecent or obscene', whilst no restrictions existed in the UK to manufacture or market similar products. See judgment of the CJEU of 11.3.1986, case C-121/85, *Conegate v HM Customs & Excise*, ECR 1986, 1007, point 14.

[52] Judgment of the CJEU of 14.10.2004, case C-36/02, *Omega Spielhallen- und Automatenaufstellungs-GmbH v Oberbürgermeisterin der Bundesstadt Bonn*, EU:C:2004:614.

[53] CJEU, *Omega Spielhallen*, point 27.

[54] CJEU, *Omega Spielhallen*, points 2–6.

[55] CJEU, *Omega Spielhallen*, point 39.

[56] In a matter relating to games of chance.

[57] Judgment of the CJEU of 18.5.2021, *Fluctus Fluentum*, case C-920/19, EU:C:2021:395, point 46. See also judgment of the CJEU of 14.6.2017, *Online Games et al.*, case C-685/15, EU:C:2017:452, point 53.

[58] Jugendschutzgesetz of 23.7.2002 (BGBl. I p. 2730), last changed by Art. 12 of the Law of 6.5.2024 (BGBl. 2024 I No. 149), available on https://www.gesetze-im-internet.de/juschg/BJNR273000002.html.

free circulation of goods and the freedom to provide services. In addition, youth and child protection considerations can justify interferences with certain fundamental rights, such as the right to respect for private and family life.[59]

Youth protection considerations can however also be abused, as is apparent from Advocate-General Capeta's opinion[60] in the case *Commission v Hungary*, already mentioned above.[61] Whilst the CJEU is still to pass judgment, the Advocate-General's position was quite non-equivocal.[62] As a result, the Advocate-General found that Hungary not only infringed Directive 2000/31/EC,[63] Directive 2006/123/EC,[64] Directive 2010/13/EU,[65] Regulation 2016/679[66] and Art. 56 TFEU, but also Art. 2 TEU and Artt. 1, 7, 8(2), 11 and 21 of the Charter of Fundamental Rights ('CFR'). 30

3. Hate speech and discrimination

As set out above, the **criminalisation** of some forms of hate, racist and xenophobic speech has been harmonised at Union level through the CTD and CRFD. However, this by no means constitutes a maximum harmonisation and important Member State differences exist (and will arguably continue to exist for a long while). 31

For instance, a small number of Union and EEA Member States prohibit denial of the **Armenian genocide**, whilst the majority does not. Switzerland has been condemned by the European Court of Human Rights ('ECtHR')[67] on grounds that its criminal repression[68] of a Turkish politician, denying that the Ottoman Empire had committed an act of genocide in Armenia, constituted an unjustified restriction to the freedom of expression[69] that could not be outweighed by an interest to protect the right to respect for private life.[70, 71] 32

---

[59] Judgment of the ECHR of 19.12.2017, case 22338/15, *AR and LR v Switzerland,* http://hudoc.echr.coe.int/eng-press?i=003-5977739-7646199.

[60] Opinion of Advocate-General Capeta of 5.6.2025, *European Commission v Hungary,* case C-769/22, EU:C:2025:408.

[61] The Hungarian legislator has adopted a rehaul of Hungarian minor protection legislation, whose main aim was to protect minors from 'LGBTI content'. The Commission initiated proceedings against Hungary for violation of both secondary and primary Union law.

[62] Opinion of Advocate-General Capeta, point 41: 'Hungary's decision to protect minors from "LGBTI content" is not based on any scientific proof of its potential harmfulness for the physical, mental or moral development of children. It is, therefore, based on a value judgement, or, as the European Parliament referred to it, on a prejudice that homosexual and non-cisgender life is not of equal value or status as heterosexual and cisgender life. That is why Hungary believes that 'access of minors to such content might be susceptible to negatively affect their image of themselves or of the world.'.

[63] The E-Commerce Directive.

[64] The freedom of services or 'Bolkestein' Directive.

[65] The Audiovisual Media Services (AMSD) Directive.

[66] The General Data Protection Regulation.

[67] Judgment of the ECHR of 15.10.2015, case 27510/08, *Perinçek v Switzerland,* https://hudoc.echr.coe.int/eng?i=001-158235.

[68] Set forth in Art. 261*bis* § 4 of the Criminal Code.

[69] As laid down in Art. 10 ECHR.

[70] As laid down in Art. 8 ECHR.

[71] This was inter alia decided because of the remote connection of Switzerland to Armenia and Turkey, which could have led Switzerland to adopt less repressive measures than criminal sanctions. Also at play was the time factor since the tragic events in Armenia as well as the fact that the Turkish politician would have adopted a historic and legal discourse, would have addressed his own constituents and not the public forum, and would have refrained from hate speech.

4. Consumer protection and economic law

33 In the ambit of consumer protection and economic law, an increasing number of Member State legislations render **specific types of content and activity illegal**. In some instances, the illegality may apply across virtually all Member States.[72] In other cases, individual Member States may adopt legislation that is very specific, for instance legislation criminalising the resale of event tickets[73] or legislation prohibiting the reproduction of cultural heritage without due authorisation from the competent authority.[74]

5. Moral integrity, harassment, stalking and defamation

34 Finally, a very important category of illegal content relates to the moral integrity of individuals. This includes a person's right to be protected from repeated undue interferences that could lead to fear for that person's (or others') safety or emotional distress – in other words, to be protected from **stalking and harassment**. It also includes the person's right to be protected from untrue allegations – in other words, to be protected from libellous or defamatory statements.

35 Regarding stalking, the **Istanbul Convention of the Council of Europe** requires that adhering States criminalise the intentional and repeated engaging in threatening conduct directed at another person, causing her or him to fear for her or his safety.[75] Driven by this Council of Europe convention, and aside from some notable exceptions[76], most Member States have legislation in place further to which different acts or types of conduct – even if not individually punishable – can result to stalking when taken together. However, important differences persist, especially regarding whether online or cyberstalking is subsumed under the criminalisation.[77]

36 Whilst the Council of Europe is an active proponent of the criminalisation of stalking, an opposite trend can be observed regarding defamation,[78] with the ECtHR clearly leaning towards the prevalence of freedom of expression and being highly critical of the proportionality of defamation laws.[79]

---

72 For instance: identity fraud or bank fraud.

73 For example, Art. 5 of the Belgian Act of 30.7.2023 relating to the resale of tickets to events, Art. 313–6–2 of the French Criminal Code, the so-called 'Battelli law' amending the Italian Budget Law No. 145 of 30.12.2018.

74 See Art. 107.1 of the Italian Cultural Heritage and Landscape Code (*Codice dei beni culturali e del paesaggio*) providing that the Italian authorities may ***allow the reproduction and instrumental*** and temporary use of cultural heritage in their possession, without prejudice to the provisions on copyright. *See* also in Greece the Law 4858/2021 (A 220/19–11–2021): For the protection of antiquities and cultural heritage in general (*Νόμος 4858/2021 (Α 220/19–11–2021): Για την προστασία των αρχαιοτήτων και εν γένει της πολιτιστικής κληρονομιάς*).

75 Art. 34 of the Council of Europe Convention on preventing and combating violence against women and domestic violence (CETS 210).

76 *For example*, the case of Sweden, see van der Aa, 'New Trends in the Criminalization of Stalking in the EU Member States, *Eur J Crim Policy Res* 2018.

77 See for instance the study of the European Institute for Gender Equality, 'Analysis of National Definitions of Stalking', October 2016, Annex 1. Available on https://eige.europa.eu/sites/default/files/documents/database/gbv_natdefn_stalking.pdf.

78 See Resolution 1577 'Towards decriminalisation of defamation' of the Parliamentary Assembly of the Council of Europe and the corresponding Recommendation 1814, available on https://pace.coe.int/en/files/17588#trace-3.

79 See Council of Europe, Directorate General of Human Rights and Legal Affairs, 'Study on the alignment of laws and practices concerning defamation with the relevant case-law of the European Court of Human Rights on freedom of expression, particularly with regard to the principle of proportionality', CDMSI(2012)Miscl1Rev2, available on https://rm.coe.int/study-on-the-alignment-of-laws-and-practices-concerning-alignment-of-l/16804915c5.

Once more, it should be noted that whether stalking and defamation laws are violated, is highly context dependent. In addition, compliance of Member State defamation laws with Union law is not a given, considering the ECtHR's case law combined with the applicability of the CFR. As a result, it is not always self-evident for video game platform providers – even after receiving a detailed and motivated notice – to assess whether they are facing 'illegal' content. 37

6. Conclusion

In conclusion, it can be safely stated that Member State legislation banning certain content on grounds such as public morality, youth protection, hate speech, intellectual property or moral integrity poses several challenges to video game platform providers. 38

Member State provisions are at times phrased in vague wording (what is 'indecent or obscene'?) and may be at odds with various fundamental EU freedoms – not only free movement of goods and freedom to provide services, but also the basic freedoms of expression and of information. It is therefore not straightforward for video game platform providers to assess whether certain content violates a Member State law and, even more fundamentally, whether that Member State law is compatible with Union law. 39

Furthermore, video game platform operators may be caught between a rock and a hard stone. On the one hand, they have an interest (and as the case may be an obligation) to protect their players from harmful behaviour by toxic players. On the other hand, it is well-known that toxic players may at times be extremely vocal in claiming their right to keep playing. It is therefore tantamount to video game platform operators to dispose of a fair, balanced and predictable regulatory environment that allows them to assess whether they either have the obligation or the right to act against certain player content or actions. In the next two sections we delve deeper into this topic. 40

III. Obligations to act against illegal content

In this section, we investigate which norms can give rise to a positive obligation to act on behalf of a video game platform provider. We first look at sectoral obligations and charters (**1**), since these have paved the way for content management and moderation in the video game sector since the early 2000s, and this often in more detail than the DSA (**2**). We also briefly discuss the rules under the TCO (**3**) and assess when providers must act against a toxic player based on their contractual duty to protect other players (**4**). 41

1. Sectoral obligations and charters

For the purposes of this analysis, **sectoral obligations** shall be understood as duties, standards, or practices that, although not imposed by binding statutory or regulatory law, are widely recognised within the video game industry as normative benchmarks of responsible conduct. Such obligations may arise either from the formal ratification of industry codes or charters – such as the Pan-European Game Information (PEGI) system – or from voluntary, self-binding commitments freely adopted by industry participants. 42

Unlike statutory obligations, sectoral obligations do not derive their normative force from legislative enactments or regulatory mandates. Rather, they rest upon industry consensus, established customary practice, or the voluntary assumption of governance responsibilities by stakeholders. Their binding effect is thus contingent upon either explicit acceptance through ratification processes or through contractual or self-regulatory commitments voluntarily undertaken by industry actors. 43

44 As widely recognised, the prevailing regulatory framework establishes definitive legal mechanisms to prohibit and sanction illicit and illegal content on video game platforms. These statutory provisions constitute the primary instruments for preventing the dissemination and proliferation of unlawful material, including but not limited to hate speech, child sexual exploitation, incitement to violence, and other proscribed conduct as set out above in Sections I and II.

45 In a complementary manner, sectoral obligations form an integral component of the video game industry's multi-layered governance framework. Operating alongside formal legal duties, they enable the sector to effectively address challenges relating to illicit and illegal content and to foster safe, lawful, and responsible digital environments tailored to its operational context.

46 Within this self-regulatory regime, the **Pan-European Game Information (PEGI) system** occupies a central position by providing age classifications and standardised content descriptors grounded in the assessment of content compliant with applicable legal standards. PEGI's classifications are designed to furnish consumers – especially parents and guardians – with reliable guidance regarding the nature and suitability of video game content.

47 While the PEGI system is based on voluntary adherence by industry participants, it operates within a **robust self-regulatory framework** supported by enforceable rules. Signatories commit to compliance with the PEGI Code of Conduct, overseen by the PEGI Enforcement Committee (PEC), a mixed body of industry and independent representatives. The PEC has the authority to investigate violations, require corrective measures, and impose sanctions – including product disqualification, public disclosure of breaches, and fines up to 500,000 EUR per violation.[80]

48 This enforcement capacity is particularly relevant to the standards for safe online gameplay set forth in Art. 9 of the PEGI Code of Conduct. Although PEGI does not determine the legal status of content under national or EU law, these standards function as a normative tool for managing online gaming environments. They impose **proactive duties** on signatories to reduce risks linked to user-generated content, hate speech, and other illegal or harmful conduct – especially where minors are involved.

49 By requiring moderation systems, reporting mechanisms, and privacy protections, the Art. 9 standards serve as an internal compliance framework that complements wider legal frameworks addressing illicit content. The Art. 9 standards enable PEGI to contribute to the prevention, detection, and mitigation of online harms, thereby reinforcing its role as a co-regulatory system aligning industry practices with public interest safeguards.

50 Specifically, Art. 9.2 requires signatories to include clear and understandable Community Standards in their terms of service for online gameplay. These terms of service, generally set out in End User License Agreements (EULAs), represent the primary contractual vehicle through which video game publishers define acceptable user behaviour and implement the preventive and corrective measures mandated by Art. 9.

51 By explicitly prohibiting illicit and illegal content, EULAs establish binding contractual obligations that protect the integrity, security, and safety of digital gaming spaces. These Community Standards are more than guidelines; they are enforceable covenants clarifying user responsibilities and enabling content moderation, including content removal and sanctions against violators.

52 This contractual framework reflects the video game industry's duty of care – especially toward vulnerable groups like minors – and exemplifies a governance approach that

[80] As set out in Artt. 14 and 15.

goes beyond voluntary compliance. EULAs thus fulfil both preventive and remedial functions: setting behavioural expectations in advance and providing the legal basis for enforcement when breaches occur.

Therefore, embedding Community Standards in EULAs is a vital point where self-regulation meets enforceability, strengthening PEGI's effectiveness within the broader regulatory landscape. This alignment also supports compliance with relevant legislation such as the DSA, which requires swift action against illegal content and emphasizes responsible platform governance. 53

Through this combined contractual and regulatory approach, compliance with the PEGI standards can serve as mitigating evidence in regulatory or judicial proceedings regarding liability for unlawful third-party content, reducing the risk of sanctions and protecting reputational interests. 54

2. The DSA

Below, we look at the DSA's ruleset for both *illegal* and *inappropriate* content. 55

First, let's turn to **illegal content**. As commonly known, the DSA does not establish itself positive criteria for establishing when an online service provider can be held liable for illegal content. This is for the applicable Union or Member State legislation to determine,[81] and we have examined above some categories of content that are thus qualified as illegal. As stated at the start of this contribution, video game platform providers that store information provided by players can qualify as a 'host' under the DSA,[82] and possibly as an 'online platform' provided the information is not only stored but also disseminated.[83] 56

A video game platform provider qualifying as a 'hosting service provider' will be exempted from liability for third-party information on condition that it (a) does not have actual knowledge of illegal activity or illegal content, and (b) upon obtaining such knowledge or awareness, acts expeditiously to remove or disable access to the illegal content.[84] Conversely, this implies that in order to avoid liability, video game platform providers *do* have an obligation to act and remove illegal content as soon as they acquire circumstantial (for damages claims) or actual (for criminal claims) knowledge of such illegal content. 57

As set out above, the question what constitutes 'illegal content' is not straightforward and often requires a highly context-driven analysis, where the provider must not only have regard to the information *per se*, but also to the underlying activity. As a result, it will be hard to assess when a video game platform provider was deemed to have either circumstantial or actual 'knowledge' of such illegal content. 58

In this respect, the DSA clarifies that, when notices are given to a provider of hosting services pursuant to the notice and action mechanism (this includes notices by trusted flaggers to online platforms),[85] such notice is considered to give rise to actual knowledge or awareness of illegal content only if it allows 'a diligent provider of hosting services 59

[81] Recital 17, DSA.
[82] Art. 3(g) point (iii), DSA.
[83] Unless that activity is considered a minor and purely ancillary feature, or a minor functionality of the service of making video games available and, for objective and technical reasons cannot be used without the video game service, and the feature or functionality is not a means to circumvent the DSA. See Art. 3(i), DSA.
[84] Art. 6.1, DSA.
[85] See Art. 22.1, DSA.

to identify the illegality of the relevant activity or information without a detailed legal examination'.[86]

60 Even then, the provider may be confronted with Union or Member State legislation that is not in conformity with higher-ranking provisions of Union law. It can be argued that, in case the video game platform provider has findings (either on own initiative or provided by a third party) that indicate a lack of conformity, the provider is not deemed to have 'actual knowledge of illegal content', since in such cases the law on the very basis of which illegality is argued is questionable *per se*. A similar remark can be made relating to orders to act against illegal content issued by relevant national judicial or administrative authorities.[87] Also here, the DSA clearly gives leeway to providers in case the legal basis for the alleged illegality is questionable. As a matter of fact, the DSA does not require hosts and other intermediary service providers to give *effect* to the order; it merely states that these providers shall *inform* the authority of any effect given to the order without undue delay, specifying *if* (and if so, when) effect was given. In addition, the DSA requires that orders to act contain a statement of reasons explaining why the information is illegal content, by reference to one or more specific provisions of Union law or national law 'in compliance with Union law'.[88] The latter addition may indicate that providers have no obligation to act if they have reasonable grounds to believe that the legislation serving as the basis for the order to act is incompatible with Union law.

61 So, let's now turn to *inappropriate* content – a highly context- and person-dependent concept, and thus difficult to define. Although at first sight the DSA deals with 'illegal content', the topic of **'inappropriate content'** comes peeking through the backdoor in the case of online platforms. Indeed, the latter are obliged to put in place 'appropriate and proportionate measures to ensure a high level of privacy, safety, and security of minors'.[89] In a public consultation ending on 10.6.2025, the Commission has requested stakeholder comments on its proposed guidelines on measures to ensure a high level of privacy, safety and security for minors online in furtherance of the DSA.[90] In this context, it is clear that the Commission expects that online platforms do their part in defining inappropriate content, and tackling access thereto by minors.[91] Although obviously well-intentioned, it will be important to ensure that the Commission's guidelines (even if not binding) do not cause online platforms to engage in very difficult policy decisions on what is 'inappropriate' and/or to avoid a 'chilling effect' in case of platforms – like games - that are used by minors and adults alike.

62 In conclusion, whether one is concerned with *illegal* or *inappropriate* content, and whilst it provides for extensive 'procedural' rules (inter alia on liability and reporting), the DSA leaves quite some margin of discretion in the exact ways in which video game operators should work 'on the merits' (i.e. in carrying out their moderation activity).

---

[86] Art. 16.3, DSA.

[87] Art. 9.1, DSA.

[88] Art. 9.2, DSA.

[89] Art. 28.1, DSA.

[90] Communication from the Commission – Commission guidelines on measures to ensure a high level of privacy, safety and security for minors online pursuant to Art. 28(4) of Regulation (EU)2022/2065, available on https://ec.europa.eu/newsroom/dae/redirection/document/115476.

[91] For instance, the Commission considers age restrictions an effective means to 'protect minors from accessing age-inappropriate content online' (p. 8), and considers that online platforms accessible to minors should set up reporting, feedback and complaints mechanisms that allow users to report not just illegal content, but also 'content, activities, individuals, accounts, or groups that they deem inappropriate or undesirable for minors' or where they are uncomfortable that these categories are accessible to minors (p. 27). Finally, minors must be availed with clear, easily identifiable and accessible support tools to seek help when encountering inappropriate content, accounts or behaviour that 'make them feel uncomfortable' (p. 29).

This is where self-regulation and sectoral rules (see the above-mentioned PEGI system) can fully play their role.

3. TCO

The **Terrorist Content Online Regulation**[92] ('TCO') imposes obligations on hosting service providers to remove or block 'terrorist content', as defined in the Counter-Terrorism Directive, which are stricter than in the DSA: competent authorities have the power to issue binding removal orders. The terrorist content must be removed by the hosting service as soon as possible and in any event within one hour of receipt of the removal order. **63**

Moreover, hosting services providers must set out in their terms and conditions their policy for addressing the dissemination of terrorist content. Where a hosting service provider had to take measures to prevent the dissemination of the terrorist content, it must publish a report containing information on that subject. **64**

In practice, we observe that video game platform providers will often issue a single report, combining reporting obligations further to the DSA and to the TCO, and detailing for each type of illegal content (whether terrorism, hate speech, or any other category) the moderating interventions, interventions further to a notice, and interventions further to an order to act. **65**

4. Contractual obligation to act

Finally, beyond sectoral obligations and legislation, a video game platform provider may be subject to obligations to act that arise from a contractual obligation in the contractual relationship engaged in with the player community. A prerequisite is of course that any such obligation is not in conflict with higher-ranking mandatory legal provisions. Even absent an explicit obligation to intervene against toxic behaviour or toxic players, it is in some cases possible that applicable national rules of contract law may lead to an implied duty on the platform provider to protect compliant players.[93] **66**

The DSA provides for a specific regime for 'online platforms'. Video game platform providers meeting the definition of 'online platform' are required under the DSA to suspend, for a reasonable period of time and after issuing a prior warning, the account of a player that 'frequently' provided 'manifestly' illegal content.[94] Conversely, online platforms must also suspend, for a reasonable period of time and after having issued a prior warning, the processing of notices and complaints through notice and action mechanisms and internal complaints-handling systems[95] in case of individuals or entities that 'frequently' submit notices or complaints that are 'manifestly' unfounded.[96] Online platform providers must also explain in a clear and detailed manner in their terms and conditions what their policy is in respect of such 'frequent' and 'manifest' **67**

---

[92] Regulation (EU) 2021/784 of the European Parliament and of the Council of 29.4.2021 on addressing the dissemination of terrorist content online, OJ L 172 of 17.5.2021.

[93] In this regard, see Hilgert, 'Toxic players', 450 who argues that § 241 para. 2 of the German Civil Code (Bürgerliches Gesetzbuch or 'BGB') may imply a general duty to take duly into account the rights, legally protected goods and interests of the contractual counterpart. In other jurisdictions, in particular those with a Napoleontic Code civil-tradition, a similar conclusion may be reached on the basis of the principle of good faith ('*bonne foi*') that is required when performing contracts (see for France: Art. 1104 of the Civil Code and for Belgium: Art. 1134 of the old Civil Code and Art. 5.73 of the new Civil Code).

[94] Art. 23.1, DSA.

[95] As referred to in Artt. 16 and 20, DSA.

[96] Art. 23.2, DSA.

misuse by either players disseminating illegal content, or players, trusted flaggers or third parties issuing complaints.[97]

68 As already stated above, whatever their qualification under the DSA ('host' or 'platform') video game platform providers are often caught between a rock and a hard stone when taking up their duty to protect compliant players. Toxic players will not shy away from invoking their own (perceived) rights, such as the right to free speech and freedom of expression, and may try to argue that *their* rights are violated, rather than those of, for instance, a bullied or harassed player.[98] It may therefore be important for video game platform providers to explicitly foresee in contractual terms (general terms and conditions or EULAs) when and how they are entitled to intervene. This is the subject matter of the next section.

C. Video game platform providers' freedom to act

69 In Section **B** above, we have focused on the obligations that befall upon providers of video game platform to act against illegal content. In this Section **C**, we investigate the freedom of providers to act against content and/or behaviour which they deem problematic.

I. General legal provisions

70 As a general principle, any business or trader – including video game platform providers – is free to choose with whom it engages into a contractual relationship, provided of course non-discrimination[99] and competition law[100] is respected. This principle and the absence of *Kontrahierungszwang* follows from the fundamental freedom of enterprise.[101]

71 In line with the **freedom to engage into a contractual relationship**, video game platform providers also have the liberty of ending such relationship, provided that the contractual terms for termination are met. Most, if not all, legal systems in the Union provide two types of contract termination. One is a termination 'at will', in which case the platform provider will not need to give any justification for the termination, but will need to observe a notice period. The other is a termination 'for cause', in which case the platform provider can terminate immediately and without notice period, but will need to give a justification (for instance: a serious breach, or a series of small breaches that have continued despite an earlier warning or notice of default). Any B2C clause that allows for immediate termination without serious cause is highly likely to be regarded as unfair.[102] What constitutes a 'serious cause' is very much open to the parties' contractual freedom, and the EULA can contractually define what behaviour is considered as illegal or inappropriate. Similarly, platforms can provide that inappropriate behaviour or activi-

[97] Art. 23.4, DSA.

[98] See also the U.S. Supreme Court's decision that considers moderation part of the editorial freedom of an online platform: *Moody v NetChoice, LLC*, 602 U.S. (2024) (Nos. 22–277 & 22–555) (U.S. 1.7.2024).

[99] Council Directive 2000/43/EC of 29.6.2000 implementing the principle of equal treatment between persons irrespective of racial or ethnic origin, OJ L 180, 19.7.2000.

[100] Judgment of 26.11.1988, *Bronner*, case C-7/97, EU:C:1998:569.

[101] Art. 16 of the CFR.

[102] See Art. 3.3 of Council Directive 93/13/EEC of 5.4.1993 on unfair terms in consumer contracts, OJ L95 21.4.1993 refers to a set of clauses that 'may' be regarded as unfair. The annex to the Directive lists in its Art. 1(g) the clause 'enabling the seller or supplier to terminate a contract of indeterminate duration without reasonable notice except where there are serious grounds for doing so'.

ty may constitute a small breach by itself but may, if repeated, result in a serious breach and in the termination of the relation. It is also possible to contractually determine whether prior notices of default are required before acting against the user at issue, or whether partial termination is possible, *e.g.*, disabling access to one game or community channel made available on a video game platform instead of full termination of a user's account. Any B2C clause (and use thereof) must be compliant with general consumer protection rules and cannot, as such, be unfair towards consumers[103] and contrary to good faith.

In the following section, we highlight a few elements that should be considered when preparing Terms of Use or EULAs for video game platforms. 72

II. Terms of Use

Video game platforms must (and typically do) ensure their **Terms of Use** are transparent and clearly written, avoiding vague or overly complex language. Users should be able to easily understand their rights and responsibilities when engaging with the platform, including understanding which behaviours may constitute a cause breach for termination or content removal. 73

Regardless of any requirements under the DSA or TCO, video game platforms are recommended to clearly reserve the right to control and moderate content. This includes the ability to remove or restrict access to content that violates rules or legal obligations. It is also recommended to make a proviso that there is no obligation to proactively monitor or moderate user-generated content, unless when required by law. 74

In addition, the Terms of Use must outline clear procedures for reporting, reviewing, and addressing violations, including timelines and potential consequences. These procedures should be fair, accessible, and consistently applied to maintain user trust and legal compliance. Typical Terms of Use may list the various 'escalation levels' that the video game platform's moderation department can engage in (e.g., short- or long-term 'silencing' of the player; short- or long-term suspension of the player account;[104] or termination). 75

III. Burden of proof

Under the DSA, when a platform acts against a user or their content, it carries the burden of proof to justify that decision. This means platforms must be able to clearly demonstrate the basis for removals, suspensions, or bans, especially if challenged by the user. Documentation and internal review processes should support such actions and be made available during appeals or legal scrutiny, and the Terms of Use should facilitate the means to **prove violations** found on the platform. However, video game 76

103 Pursuant to Art. 3 of Council Directive 93/13/EEC of 5.4.1993 on unfair terms in consumer contracts, OJ L 95, 21.4.1993, pp. 29–34 (hereinafter referred to as the 'Unfair Terms in Consumer Contracts Directive'), a contractual term which has not been individually negotiated 'shall be regarded as unfair if, contrary to the requirement of good faith, it causes a significant imbalance in the parties' rights and obligations arising under the contract, to the detriment of the consumer'.

104 Such suspension can be operated on the level of an individual game, but also on the level of an entire player profile or account, possibly also affecting games where the toxic player did not misbehave. This can be decided for technical reasons (e.g., if the profile or account cannot technically be suspended for only one game) or legal reasons (e.g., if there is a reasonable concern that the toxic player will also misbehave in the future on other games, in which case it can be justified to take a pre-emptive and conservatory measure).

platforms cannot unduly restrict the evidence available to the consumer or impose on the consumer a burden of proof which should lie on the platform in the first place.[105]

D. Conclusion

77 Video game platform providers operate within a complex and expanding legal framework that governs their obligations and rights to act against illegal or inappropriate user content and behaviour. This framework arises from sector-specific standards, regulatory instruments, and contractual arrangements.

78 The volume of legislation prohibiting or criminalising certain types of content or conduct continues to grow, often without harmonisation at Union level. Providers must therefore navigate significant legal uncertainty, including inconsistent interpretations and the risk that Member State laws may conflict with higher-ranking Union law.

79 In addition, providers must balance competing interests. While protecting players – particularly minors – is essential, users who engage in disruptive behaviour may invoke rights such as freedom of expression or consumer protection when subject to moderation. Well-drafted Terms of Use or EULAs are therefore critical. These instruments should grant providers the discretion necessary to reconcile user protection with individual rights, within the limits of applicable law.

[105] Art. 1 (q) of the Annex to the Unfair Terms in Consumer Contracts Directive.

§ 34
Technical Youth Protection on Platforms

Bibliography: Grisse in Hofmann/Raue, Digital Services Act, Munich/Baden-Baden/Oxford/New York 2025; Hilgert, Technischer Jugendmedienschutz, in Hentsch/Falk (eds), Games und Recht, Baden-Baden 2023, 431; Hilgert/Sümmermann, Youth Protection Compliance by Technical Means, Supplement MMR 8/2020, 56; Liesching, National games regulation for the EU area, Supplement MMR 8/2020, 48.

A. Introduction 1

B. Basic concepts of technical youth protection 7
I. Age assurance 8
1. Age verification 10
2. Age estimation 12
3. Self-declaration 14
II. Parental control systems 16
III. Proactive content monitoring permitted but not required 19

C. Harmonised youth protection requirements 20
I. Digital Services Act 20
1. Statutory protection requirements 22
2. General regulatory strategy guidance 25
3. Specific DSA guidance 26
a) Age assurance 29
b) Default settings 34
c) Parental controls 39
II. General Data Protection Regulation 40
1. Express statutory requirements 41
2. Implied statutory requirements 44
3. Regulatory guidance 46
III. Audiovisual Media Services Directive 48
1. Scope 49
2. Statutory requirements 50

D. Non-harmonised youth protection requirements 52
I. Germany 56
II. France 60
III. Ireland 64
IV. Spain 65
V. Italy 66

A. Introduction

Among the guiding principles of European, and indeed global, youth protection law is the focus on the **best interests of the child.**[1] These interests include not only protection from harm, but also access and participation. Children's personal data is entitled to special protection, yet additional data processing may be required to protect the children themselves. Accordingly, the regulatory framework for platforms is complex, and it can be a challenge to balance structurally competing interests and requirements. 1

To a large and increasing extent, **digital platforms** are replacing physical retail distribution of games (→ Ch. 24 mn. 19 et seqq.; Ch. 31 mn. 11 et seqq.), and they play a key role in enabling and organising multiplayer experiences and the creation and distribution of content by players themselves. These functions put platform providers 2

[1] Cf. Art. 3 (1) of the United Nations Convention on the Rights of the Child; rec. 89 of the DSA; Further examples in Livingstone et al., 'The best interests of the child in the digital environment', 2024, p. 7 et seqq, <https://www.digital-futures-for-children.net/digitalfutures-assets/digitalfutures-documents/Best-Interests-of-the-Child-FINAL.pdf>.

in the place of both the retailer checking a young-looking buyer's ID, and the referee responsible for regulating the content and interactions that players are exposed to in the game.

3 While the main game content available through the platform will generally carry an **age rating** issued by a third party (→ Ch. 22 et seq.), platforms face the challenge of determining which of their players make up which age group. And while their responsibility for individual pieces of user content and individual user interactions is limited (→ Ch. 28 mn. 64), they are expected to provide **safe feature design** and to effectively react to youth protection concerns.

4 One thing, however, is clear: Technical youth protection cannot work without the involvement of parents and guardians. They are closest to their children and know them best, and it is their fundamental right to make certain educational decisions for their children. Therefore, any technical youth protection concept should include **parental controls** to enable such choices.

5 While some Member States have historically had very detailed and granular statutory technical youth protection requirements, the current, relatively recent EU level regulation is more openly worded, **principles-based and flexible**. While this raises the challenge of lower legal certainty at least until detailed guidance and case law is established, it can make the regulation more **future-proof** and give platforms and regulators the tools to cooperate for the sake of practical and pragmatic youth protection.

6 Finally, it should be noted that EU law is **not entirely harmonised** on all aspects of technical youth protection. To the extent a platform provider does not only distribute third-party content, but also populates the platform with its own content, it falls within the scope of application of Member States' national youth protection laws – subject to the Country of Origin principle for such providers domiciled in the EU (→ mn. 52 et seqq.).

B. Basic concepts of technical youth protection

7 Before exploring the legal requirements for the implementation of technical youth protection measures, it is worth examining the basic concepts underlying this field of law.

I. Age assurance

8 When it comes to establishing the age of a given player, as a prerequisite of providing them with age-appropriate content, features and interaction,[2] the available legislation, guidance and policy discussions all differentiate between various approaches that **balance competing interests** in different ways. These interests include reliability and protection against circumvention, protection of user privacy, and user experience. Generally, a more **reliable method** comes with **higher privacy concerns** and a less smooth user experience.

9 The terminology for these categories is not entirely settled yet, but most guidance documents in the European context use **'age assurance'** as an umbrella term for a **three-part taxonomy**: In descending order of reliability, individual methods can be

[2] Occasionally, age verification can also be used to achieve the opposite goal, i.e., to prevent adults from impersonating minors, which can be a cyber-grooming technique.

categorised as age **verification**, age **estimation**, and **self-declaration**,[3] also sometimes referred to as 'age gating'.[4]

1. Age verification

Age verification refers to a system that relies on **hard (physical) identifiers** and/or **verified sources** of identification that provide a **high degree of certainty** in determining the age of a user. It can establish the identity of a user, but can also be used in an anonymous setup to establish only whether the user attempting to access a given service at a given moment is over a certain minimum or under a certain maximum age, without sharing any further personal data with the provider.[5] 10

This type of verification is also referred to as 'highly effective age assurance'[6] and must generally satisfy requirements of **accuracy**, meaning the ability to determine an accurate age or age range; **reliability**, meaning the ability to function in real-world circumstances; **robustness**, meaning resistance to circumvention attempts; **non-intrusiveness**, meaning a fair balance of effectiveness and protection of user privacy; and **non-discrimination**, meaning availability regardless of factors like ethnicity or disability.[7] 11

2. Age estimation

Age estimation consists of methods which establish that a user is **likely** to be above or below a certain age or within a certain age range. This includes estimation based on facial features, automated analysis of behavioural and environmental data, comparing the way a user interacts with a device with other users of the same age, and metrics derived from motion analysis or by testing their capacity or knowledge.[8] 12

With regards to age estimation based on **facial features**, some regulators take the view that this may even satisfy the requirements of age verification, provided the estimation technology is sufficiently advanced and/or the system is configured with a **safety margin**.[9] 13

---

[3] European Data Protection Board, Statement 1/25 on Age Assurance (11.2.2025) (EDPB Age Assurance Guidance); EU Commission, 'Research report: Mapping age assurance typologies and requirements', February 2024 (EU Age Assurance Typology Report), <https://better-internet-for-kids.europa.eu/en/age-assurance-guide/research-report>; EU Commission, 'Commission guidelines on measures to ensure a high level of privacy, safety and security for minors online pursuant to Article 28 (4) of Regulation (EU) 2022/2065' (Art. 28 (4) Guidance), para. 24, <https://eur-lex.europa.eu/legal-content/EN/TXT/?uri=OJ:C_202505519>; OFCOM, 'Guidance on highly effective age assurance' (24.4.2025) (OFCOM Guidance), <https://www.ofcom.org.uk/online-safety/protecting-children/statement-age-assurance-and-childrens-access>; ICO, 'Commissioner's Opinion on age assurance for the Children's Code' (18.1.2024), Sec. 1.1, <https://ico.org.uk/about-the-ico/what-we-do/information-commissioners-opinions/age-assurance-for-the-children-s-code>; one notable exception being the Irish privacy regulator, whose guidance (still) opts for 'age verification' as the generic umbrella term: see Data Protection Commission, 'Fundamentals for a Child-Oriented Approach to Data Processing' (December 2021) (DPC Fundamentals), p. 44, <https://www.dataprotection.ie/sites/default/files/uploads/2021-12/Fundamentals%20for%20a%20Child-Oriented%20Approach%20to%20Data%20Processing_FINAL_EN.pdf>.

[4] Facia.ai, 'Global Age Assurance Standards; Age Restrictions & Child Privacy Laws', 12.4.2025 <https://facia.ai/blog/global-age-assurance-standards-age-restrictions-child-privacy-laws/>.

[5] EU Age Assurance Typology Report (fn. 3), adopted by EDPB Age Assurance Guidance (fn. 3).

[6] OFCOM Guidance (fn. 3).

[7] Art. 28 (4) Guidance (fn. 3), para. 49; OFCOM Guidance (fn. 3), Sec. 4 combines non-intrusiveness and non-discrimination into a broader category of 'fairness'.

[8] EU Age Assurance Typology Report (fn. 3), adopted by EDPB Age Assurance Guidance (fn. 3).

[9] OFCOM Guidance (fn. 3); The German regulator Kommission für Jugendmedienschutz (KJM) has considered a five year margin sufficient (so access to 18+ content requires an estimated age of 23+), see: KJM, 'KJM bewertet Altersverifikationssystem mit biometrischer Alterskontrolle positiv', 7.11.2022,

3. Self-declaration

14 Self-declaration consists of methods that rely on a user to declare their age or confirm their age range, **without providing any evidence**. Examples of self-declaration methods include declaring one's date of birth or declaring that one is above 18 years of age.[10]

15 Many European guidance and policy documents consider pure self-declaration of age **insufficient** to comply with rules requiring a technical solution to prevent underage users from accessing content or features.[11] Only in limited cases may self-declaration be a feasible tool, such as when the self-declaration puts the user under a threshold age and therefore causes the most protective settings and practices to apply.[12] Some guidance also contemplates **design choices** that make self-declaration slightly more reliable – such as asking open questions about age without communicating the applicable threshold, and/or preventing users from going back to change their answer if their initial answer puts them under the threshold for access to certain content or features.[13]

II. Parental control systems

16 Parental control systems are mentioned in Art. 35 (1) (j) DSA as an example of a youth protection measure, but are not further defined either in the text or in the recitals of the regulation. Generally, the term is understood to refer to systems that allow parents to **limit** or **monitor** the types of content or interactions available to underage users, including by limiting the **time** and/or the **monetary amounts** that children can spend in a game.[14] Parental control systems can be deployed at platform, device, or ecosystem level.

17 In previous guidance relating to unfair commercial practices, the European Commission had already pointed out a potential use case for such systems on a platform to limit or disable minors' **in-game purchases.**[15]

18 In **Germany**, so-called 'youth protection programmes' have long been the subject of **official evaluation and approval** by government regulators or industry self-regulation bodies. Such systems include filter software that parents can install on a child's device or directly on the home WiFi router and that blocks content that is inappropriate or harmful for the relevant age group, based on white- and blacklists, age rating content labels, and on ad-hoc screening of unknown and unlabelled sites.[16]

<https://www.kjm-online.de/presse/pressemitteilungen/kjm-bewertet-altersverifikationssystem-mit-biometrischer-alterskontrolle-positiv/>.

[10] EU Age Assurance Typology Report (fn. 3), adopted by EDPB Age Assurance Guidance (fn. 3).

[11] Art. 28 (4) Guidance (fn. 3), para. 52; Coimisiún na Meán, Online Safety Code, October 2024 ('OSC'), <https://www.cnam.ie/app/uploads/2024/11/Coimisiun-na-Mean-Online-Safety-Code.pdf>; OFCOM Guidance (fn. 3).

[12] ICO, Age appropriate design: a code of practice for online services ('AADC'), sec. 3, <https://ico.org.uk/for-organisations/uk-gdpr-guidance-and-resources/childrens-information/childrens-code-guidance-and-resources/age-appropriate-design-a-code-of-practice-for-online-services/>.

[13] AADC (fn. 12), sec. 3.

[14] Cf. Art. 28 (4) Guidance (fn. 8), para. 82.

[15] EU Commission, Notice C/2021/9320, Guidance on the interpretation and application of Directive 2005/29/EC of the European Parliament and of the Council concerning unfair business-to-consumer commercial practices in the internal market, 29.12.2021, Sec. 4.2.9.

[16] See further details at <https://www.jugendschutzprogramm.de/en/parents>.

III. Proactive content monitoring permitted but not required

European regulation makes a point of not requiring across-the-board proactive content monitoring, e.g., in Art. 15 of the E-Commerce Directive[17], or in Art. 8 DSA. This does not mean, however, that providers cannot or should not implement **filters** as one component of a youth protection concept in the context of age-appropriate design. Art. 7 DSA expressly permits 'investigations' and 'other measures', including those aimed at disabling access to certain content or otherwise complying with EU and national laws, without losing the protection of **safe harbour** provisions in the context of **liability for user-generated content**. 19

C. Harmonised youth protection requirements

I. Digital Services Act

The DSA applies to online intermediary services, including online platforms (Art. 2, 3 (g) (iii) DSA). The definition of 'online platform' is broad, covering hosting services that 'at the request of a recipient of the service, store and disseminate information to the public' (Art. 3 (i) DSA). This does not cover offline games, nor necessarily all multiplayer games, but it does include such online video games and game platforms that allow players to create and share their own content and otherwise interact with other players (→ Ch. 32 mn. 12 et seqq.). 20

Like many more recent pieces of EU legislation, the DSA follows a **tiered approach**, with stricter and more onerous rules for larger providers. The European Commission can designate such **Very Large Online Platforms** (VLOPs), but this generally requires reaching a number of average monthly active users corresponding to 10 % of the population of the EU (currently, the threshold is 45 million), and no video games platforms have been designated as VLOPs at the time of writing.[18] 21

1. Statutory protection requirements

The dedicated youth protection provisions of the DSA are set out in the quite short Art. 28, which does not provide much legal clarity.[19] Its first paragraph merely requires platforms to implement appropriate and proportionate measures to ensure a high level of privacy, safety, and security of minors. According to rec. 71 of the DSA, this broad and openly worded obligation is intended to refer providers of online platforms to existing best practices and guidance, such as the EU's 'Better Internet for Kids' or 'BIK+' strategy, published in 2022.[20] 22

For **VLOPs**, Art. 35 (1) DSA appears to create a separate standard – it is here that the DSA contains its only mention of parental controls (→ mn. 16, 39, 58 et seqq.), for example – which raises the question of whether the legislator actually meant to impose **more stringent technical youth protection obligations** on VLOPs (and conversely, a re- 23

---

[17] Directive 2000/31/EC of the European Parliament and of the Council of 8.6.2000 on certain legal aspects of information society services, in particular electronic commerce, in the Internal Market.

[18] The official list of VLOPs is available at <https://digital-strategy.ec.europa.eu/en/policies/list-designated-vlops-and-vloses>.

[19] As here: Grisse in Hofmann/Raue, DSA, Art. 28 mn. 15.

[20] EU Commission, A Digital Decade for children and youth: the new European strategy for a better internet for kids (BIK+), <https //eur-lex.europa.eu/legal-content/EN/TXT/?uri=COM:2022:212:FIN>.

laxed set of requirements for smaller platforms, including online games platforms).[21] The open wording of Art. 35 (1) (j) DSA is not helpful here and could be interpreted either way, so that providers will need to look to developing guidance and case law in this matter.

24 Art. 28 (3) DSA further clarifies one important aspect of the protection concept that the DSA embraces: Compliance with the DSA's youth protection rules does **not oblige** a provider to process **'additional' personal information**, i.e., such information that it does not otherwise collect.[22] Of course, there may be other reasons why the provider of a game may want or need to collect age information from players, and where this is the case, Art. 28 (3) does not absolve the provider from using this information in the context of technical youth protection as well. In other words, and as rec. 71 further clarifies, Art. 28 (3) DSA does not permit the provider to close their eyes to age information they actually possess.[23]

2. General regulatory strategy guidance

25 The **BIK+ strategy** that rec. 71 of the DSA alludes to is not helpful. It provides strategic objectives, but not detailed rules.[24] While it reiterates that mere self-reporting of age is not an effective age or parental control mechanism, it otherwise only mentions in broad strokes the need for age verification that **respects privacy rights**, alluding to EU-wide eID services allowing trusted and verified age disclosure without having to disclose other personal information.

3. Specific DSA guidance

26 In addition, Art. 28 (4) DSA enables the European Commission to issue dedicated guidance specific to the DSA's (technical) youth protection requirements, which it has done in a comprehensive guidance document setting forth its interpretation of what constitutes appropriate and proportionate measures.[25] Together with the initially published call for evidence,[26] this document provides a clear indication of the direction of travel.

27 In particular, both the call for evidence and the guidance itself refer to the **'5C model' of risk classification**, under which risks for minors can result from content, conduct, contact, the consumer role, and 'cross-cutting' risks,[27] and examine technical and non-technical measures to promote minor safety, including age-appropriate default settings, content moderation systems, '**age assurance and verification** processes' and parental controls.[28]

28 However, the guidance does not answer the question whether VLOPs will in fact be held to stricter standards than smaller platforms in the context of Art. 28 (4) DSA

---

[21] Grisse in Hofmann/Raue, DSA, Art. 28 mn. 15.

[22] Also see rec. 71 of the DSA, clarifying that a provider should not be incentivized to 'collect the age of the recipient of the service prior to use'.

[23] As here: Grisse in Hofmann/Raue, DSA, Art. 28 mn. 21.

[24] As here: Grisse in Hofmann/Raue, DSA, Art. 28 mn. 13.

[25] Art. 28 (4) Guidance (fn. 3).

[26] The call for evidence is available for download at <https://ec.europa.eu/info/law/better-regulation/have-your-say/initiatives/14352-Protection-of-minors-guidelines_en>.

[27] OECD Working Party on Data Governance and Privacy in the Digital Economy, Children in the Digital Environment: Revised Typology of Risks (12.1.2021), <https://one.oecd.org/document/DSTI/CDEP/DGP(2020)3/FINAL/en/pdf>.

[28] Call for evidence, available for download at <https://ec.europa.eu/info/law/better-regulation/have-your-say/initiatives/14352-Protection-of-minors-guidelines_en>.

(→ mn. 23); it only states – unsurprisingly – that compliance with the guidance does not automatically imply compliance with specific VLOP obligations under Art. 34, 35, 38 and 40 DSA.[29] Its **practical utility** specifically with regards to age assurance is also **diminished** somewhat because some technologies it refers to – the EU Digital Identity Wallet and an (interim) EU age verification solution – are not yet available.[30] Nevertheless, any alternative technologies must meet the criteria described in the guidance to be compliant.[31] In particular, the final version of the guidance repeatedly stresses a strong preference for trusted **third-party verification** methods that limit the potentially sensitive information that each provider might obtain about their users if they performed their own age verification from start to finish.[32]

a) Age assurance

Age assurance is **only one building block** of what the European Commission considers appropriate minor safety measures under the DSA, and the guidance reminds providers that any such mechanism also always shuts out younger users from certain offerings, which also impacts their rights and legitimate interests. The guidance therefore encourages providers to limit age gates to such parts of a service that actually require them.[33] 29

Age verification is discussed as a tool to exclude minors from the **most high-risk** content – examples stated in the guidance include gambling, pornography, and alcohol sales,[34] and therefore do not appear to focus on games. However, other parts of the guidance do mention virtual currencies and lootboxes[35] as content that may be unsuitable for all minors, and the guidance also leaves the door open to restrictions under national laws, which may in particular include violence (→ mn. 52, 57, 60, 64, 65). 30

Age estimation is discussed as a tool for **medium-risk** content (without offering detail on what specifically that might mean), and where content risks affect only younger minors (and not everyone under the age of 18).[36] 31

Self-declaration is considered structurally insufficient to satisfy robustness and accuracy requirements (→ mn. 15).[37] 32

To prevent users from being excluded merely because a method of age assurance fails for them, the guidance calls for **'more than one' methods** of age assurance, as well as a **redress mechanism** to challenge an allegedly inaccurate outcome.[38] 33

b) Default settings

Section 6.3.1 of the Art. 28 (4) Guidance contains extremely **detailed** and **prescriptive** language on what the European Commission considers mandatory default settings. 34

As written, the list reads like prescribing **mandatory product features** rather than just settings regarding otherwise existing features. This would make the guidance quite far-reaching beyond the wording of the DSA, and **raises questions** as to the extent of rule-making authority that Art. 28 (4) actually confers on the European Commission. 35

---

[29] Art. 28 (4) Guidance (fn. 3), para. 9.
[30] Art. 28 (4) Guidance (fn. 3), para. 42.
[31] Art. 28 (4) Guidance (fn. 3), paras. 45 et seq.
[32] Art. 28 (4) Guidance (fn. 3), paras. 39, 41, 46.
[33] Art. 28 (4) Guidance (fn. 3), para. 31.
[34] Art. 28 (4) Guidance (fn. 3), para. 37.
[35] Art. 28 (4) Guidance (fn. 3), para. 69 (k).
[36] Art. 28 (4) Guidance (fn. 3), para. 47 (a).
[37] Art. 28 (4) Guidance (fn. 3), para 52.
[38] Art. 28 (4) Guidance (fn. 3), para. 48.

36 For instance, the list of required default settings implies the existence of **screenshot blockers**[39] or granular messaging and **notification settings** that take into account unspecified 'core sleep hours' of minors (without however providing any indication as to what bedtimes the European Commission deems adequate at what age).[40]

37 Any features encouraging **'excessive use'** should be deactivated – and the European Commission has a **broad understanding** of what might fall in this category, including such features as 'number of likes' or 'communication streaks'.[41] While the examples seem targeted at social media sites, this could raise particular issues for games as well, as there is no consensus on what 'excessive' gameplay is and where to draw the line between engaging but entirely benign gameplay mechanics and artificial pressure tactics.

38 Furthermore, minors should not be 'encouraged' to change any of the default settings,[42] and some changes, like activating geolocation, microphones or cameras, should trigger an **'obvious' cue** throughout the duration they are activated,[43] and **revert to their default** off state after each use.[44]

c) *Parental controls*

39 The guidance calls parental controls 'tools for guardians' and clarifies that such tools can only **supplement**, but not replace, age assurance and protective default settings.[45] It emphasises the need for **transparency** to inform minors of when they are being monitored by guardians, and generally calls for an appropriate balance between protective restrictions and minors' privacy and information access rights.[46]

II. General Data Protection Regulation

40 The GDPR contains its own set of **technical requirements** related to the protection of minors. Art. 8 GDPR governs data protection consent for information society services that are offered directly to a minor.[47] This includes online games and games platforms. Minors can only effectively consent to the processing of their personal data in the context of such offerings from a certain threshold age, the default being 16 years, but with flexibility for Member States to lower this threshold down to 13 years. For minors under the applicable age limit, the so-called holder of **parental responsibility** must either approve the minor's previously articulated consent, or must themselves consent on behalf of the minor.

1. Express statutory requirements

41 The only express assurance requirement in Art. 8 (2) GDPR concerns not the age of the person consenting, but only the **status** of a purported holder of **parental responsibility**. The GDPR does not specify concrete technical review or verification procedures.

[39] Art. 28 (4) Guidance (fn. 3), para. 57 (b) (ii).
[40] Art. 28 (4) Guidance (fn. 3), para. 57 (b) (vii).
[41] Art. 28 (4) Guidance (fn. 3), para. 57 (b) (viii).
[42] Art. 28 (4) Guidance (fn. 3), para. 57 (e).
[43] Art. 28 (4) Guidance (fn. 3), para. 58 (f).
[44] Art. 28 (4) Guidance (fn. 3), para. 58 (e).
[45] Art. 28 (4) Guidance (fn. 3), para. 79.
[46] Art. 28 (4) Guidance (fn. 3), para. 81.
[47] The GDPR uses the term 'child', but this is generally understood as anyone under the age of 18 and therefore the same as a minor for the purposes of this analysis; see Art. 1 of the UN Convention on the Rights of the Child.

However, Art. 8 (2) GDPR makes the controller's obligations subject to appropriateness and available technology.

The GDPR therefore (only) requires **reasonable efforts** that do not disproportionately restrict any of the guarantees for the data subject. To assess the appropriateness, the financial and organisational efforts of the controller must be weighed against the nature, scope and importance of the data processing. 42

Furthermore, Art. 5 (1) (c) GDPR states that the **processing** of personal data must be **limited** to what is necessary for the purposes of the processing (principle of data minimisation). In particular, this means that not only is there no 'register of holders of parental responsibility', it would also be unreasonable and incompatible with the principle of data minimisation to attempt to set one up, or to attempt verification by obliging users to submit identification documents. This general approach is in line with Art. 28 (3) of the DSA (→ mn. 24), which also expressly limits the providers' obligation to collect additional data for age assurance purposes. However, **secure digital identity wallets** may provide a solution to this problem by allowing parents to link their children's wallets to their own, thus creating a trusted source of affiliation information.[48] 43

2. Implied statutory requirements

In contrast to the requirement to verify the parental authority of a person purporting to validate a minor's consent, the GDPR does not contain any express requirement to ascertain whether the person they are interacting with has in fact reached the **digital age of consent** or not. However, the existence of Art. 8 GDPR and particularly the verification obligations of Art. 8 (2), **imply** that some level of age assurance is required. 44

The details are however unclear, and the GDPR itself does not suggest a specific level of reliability, so that at the outset, **self-declaration** (→ mn. 14) should be sufficient. In line with the principle of data minimisation, even a purely binary query ('Are you at least 16 years old?') or a checkbox ('I am at least 16 years old') seems feasible and sufficient. 45

3. Regulatory guidance

The Irish Data Protection Commissioner[49] and the EDPB[50] consider that an age 'verification' obligation is indeed **implied** by Art. 8 (2) GDPR, even though under the more recent terminology used here, this should more accurately be termed an **age assurance obligation**. The guidance emphasises that any such age assurance should not lead to excessive data processing, but is otherwise scant on details as to what appropriate age assurance under the GDPR would look like. Crucially, however, it does not categorically exclude **self-declaration** in this context.[51] 46

The Art. 29 Working Party, the predecessor of the EDPB, describes a **possible procedure** using an example in which a platform for online games wants to make the use of services by minors dependent on parental consent.[52] This procedure involves three or four steps: 47

---

[48] This technology was recently adopted in Greece; see: Burt, 'Greece launches children's digital wallet for online age assurance', 6.5.2025, <https://www.biometricupdate.com/202505/greece-launches-childrens-digital-wallet-for-online-age-assurance>.

[49] DPC Fundamentals (fn. 3), p. 44.

[50] EDPB, Guidelines 05/2020 on consent under Regulation 2016/679 (4.5.2020) (EDPB Consent Guidance), mn. 133, <https://www.edpb.europa.eu/sites/default/files/files/file1/edpb_guidelines_202005_consent_en.pdf>.

[51] EDPB Consent Guidance (fn. 51), mn. 135.

[52] Art. 29 Working Party, 'Guidelines on consent under regulation 2016/679', 28.11.2017, last revised 10.4.2018, WP259 rev. 01.

- **Ask** the **user** whether they are under or over 16 years of age (or alternative age of digital consent). If the user indicates that they have not reached the age of digital consent, proceed to the next step.
- **Inform** the **child** that a parent or legal guardian must agree or authorise the processing before the service is made available. Ask the user to provide the email address of a parent or legal guardian.
- **Contact** the **parent** or guardian, obtain their consent to the processing by email and take reasonable steps to confirm that the consenting party does indeed have parental responsibility.
- Only in the event of complaints, take **additional steps** to verify the user's age.

III. Audiovisual Media Services Directive

48 For the sake of completeness, Art. 6a (1) and 28b (3) of the Audiovisual Media Services Directive (AVMSD) also contain requirements for audiovisual media services to implement youth protection mechanisms, which may specifically include **'age verification' tools** and other **technical measures**. Such measures must be **proportional** to the possible harm to or impairment of the physical, mental, or moral development of minors that results from a given piece of content, with the strictest measures required for gratuitous violence and pornography.

1. Scope

49 These requirements however only apply to **audiovisual media services**, which are essentially television broadcasts and on-demand audiovisual media services, including video-sharing platforms. The definition in Art. 1 (1) (g) of the AVMSD refers to a 'viewing of programmes', and 'programmes' are defined in Art. 1 (1) (b) AVMSD as 'a set of moving images', with examples referring to different types of traditional non-interactive TV and movie content. This definition **does not cover** the core **interactive** functionalities of a video games platform. However, under Art. 1 (1) (a) (ii) AVMSD, audiovisual commercial communication is expressly covered by the Directive, and this can cover advertisements that may be shown within games.

2. Statutory requirements

50 Even if most aspects of a game will therefore be out of scope of the Directive, Art. 28b AVMSD does set forth a **detailed catalogue** of **technical measures** that the EU legislator considers possible building blocks for an appropriate youth protection system as it concerns user-generated video content. A platform implementing such measures to content created by players in an interactive environment would in the very last be able to argue that it has made good faith efforts to meet the European standard for an 'appropriate' youth protection system under Art. 28 (1) DSA.

51 The measures specifically contemplated in Art. 28b (3) AVMSD include addressing youth protection questions in the user **terms and conditions**, and enforcing those terms (also required under Art. 14 (4) DSA), letting users flag their own content as unsuitable for minors (thereby facilitating and improving the operation of filters and other parental control tools), implementing **reporting** functionalities, implementing **'age verification'** systems, implementing parental control systems, and providing and raising awareness of **media literacy** tools.

D. Non-harmonised youth protection requirements

52 Not all aspects of a games platform are necessarily covered by harmonised EU (platform) legislation, and even where Member States' laws[53] primarily implement the AVMSD to regulate online games, these laws can go beyond the scope required by that Directive.

53 Where a platform provider gives access to their own content not covered by the AVMSD, such as by distributing its **own games** alongside third party games, or where the platform offers a **metaverse** style experience with third party content embedded within a game or interactive world (as might be the case on platforms like Roblox or Fortnite), that first-party content is governed by Member States' **non-harmonised** national laws.

54 However, for providers domiciled in an EU Member State, the **Country of Origin** principle of Art. 3 of the E-Commerce Directive, echoed in Art. 3 and 4 of the AVMSD, states that absent specific individual circumstances, only the law of their domicile applies to their services. This means, for example, that a provider domiciled in Ireland does not need to comply with a German regulation, nor can a German regulator take action against them, **except in very serious cases** of violation of certain core public policy laws including public health and safety and consumer protection, and even then only after consultation with the European Commission.[54] These laws can include youth protection laws, which are often framed as a matter at least related to public health and consumer protection.

55 The exceptions to the Country of Origin principle **only cover specific enforcement** actions in specific cases. They do not permit a Member State to impose abstract obligations on all providers of a certain category,[55] such as requiring a specific level of age assurance, or the designation of a point of contact, or of a youth protection officer.

I. Germany

56 German law requires age assurance for all online media, not limited to sites and platforms covered by the DSA and/or the AVMSD, when there is a real potential for danger or impairment. It takes a **graduated approach** that differentiates according to the content concerned and the degree of possible danger or impairment.

57 The highest degree of reliability is required for the most **harmful** content, including pornographic content, certain content declared harmful by a federal regulator, and content that is 'obviously severely harmful' to minors, for instance because of highly detailed depictions of **violence** and gore. For such content, the law requires state of the art **age verification** systems with a **two-level structure**, involving at least a one-time identification of the user by personal contact and comparison of official identification documents (identity card or passport), and then the authentication of the user for each

---

53 The author is grateful to Pauline Bonnet, Claire Bouchenard, Julia Darcel, Lluis Ferre, Rafael Garcia del Poyo, Mario Gras, Gianluigi Marino and Alessandra Potini for their invaluable input on the Member State laws and guidance documents discussed in this section.

54 For a detailed discussion of the implications of the Country of Origin principle on EU Member States' video games laws, see Liesching, supplement MMR 8/2020, 18 ff.

55 ECJ 19.12.2019 – case C-390/18, ECLI:EU:C:2019:1112 – *Airbnb Ireland*; ECJ 9.11.2023 – case C-376/22, ECLI:EU:C:2023:835 – *Google Ireland and others*; for a recent example from Member State national case law implementing this jurisprudence, see Administrative Court of Düsseldorf 19.11.2025 – case 27 L 1350/24, ECLI:DE:VGD:2025:1119.27L1350.24.00.

individual access to relevant content.[56] The regulator for online youth protection has issued strict guidelines to determine an appropriate level of protection, based on case law from the German Federal Court of Justice, and publishes a list of age verification systems it deems appropriate.[57]

58 For content that is not outright harmful but **inappropriate for minors**, e.g., because it has received a corresponding age rating from USK/IARC (→ Ch. 23), providers have a duty to ensure that it is **not usually seen** by minors of the age groups concerned. The measures do not have to make access impossible: It is sufficient if access is made significantly more difficult. The law provides several options to comply with this duty, including by applying access **time limits**, by specifying an age rating that can be read by (client-side) **parental control software**, or through other technical **age assurance** mechanisms that do not have to rise to the standard of actual age verification.[58] Self-declaration however is not a suitable age assurance mechanism under German youth protection law.[59]

59 In addition, an amendment to the State Treaty on Youth Protection in the Media, jointly enacted by the German federal states and in force since 1.12.2025,[60] requires **providers of operating systems** to implement **parental controls**, which must be active by default, although the constitutionality of this law as well as its compliance with the DSA and the Country of Origin principle (→ mn. 54) are contested,[61] and the matter is not fully settled.

II. France

60 Art. 227–24 of the French Penal Code makes it a criminal offence to produce, disseminate or trade a message that is **likely to be seen** by a child and is of a **violent nature**, incites terrorism, is pornographic, or is of a nature that seriously **undermines human dignity** or incites children to engage in games that physically endanger them. Providers of such content cannot rely on a user's self-declaration of their age to argue their content was not likely to be seen by a minor.[62]

61 A new law[63] further specifically requires **providers of pornographic content** to implement **age verification** technologies and thereby verify the age of each user before

---

[56] Hilgert in Hentsch/Falk, p. 433; Hilgert/Sümmermann, Supplement MMR 8/2020, 56, 57.

[57] KJM, Criteria for evaluating concepts for age verification systems as elements for ensuring closed user groups in telemedia (…) ('AVS Matrix') (valid since 12.05.2022), <https://www.kjm-online.de/fileadmin/user_upload/KJM/Themen/Technischer_Jugendmedienschutz/AVS-Raster_gueltig_seit_12.05.2022-ENG.pdf>; list of appropriate systems available at <https://www.kjm-online.de/themen/technischer-jugendmedienschutz/unzulaessige-inhalte/#c3798>.

[58] For further details see Hilgert in Hentsch/Falk, p. 435; Hilgert/Sümmermann, Supplement MMR 8/2020, 56, 57; Darcel et al., 'Age assurance is focus of European regulatory action for online protection of minors', <https://www.osborneclarke.com/insights/age-assurance-focus-european-regulatory-action-online-protection-minors>.

[59] Hilgert in Hentsch/Falk, p. 435 (with additional references).

[60] Full text of the final draft: BW LT-Drs. 17/8818 of 13.5.2025, <https://www.landtag-bw.de/resource/blob/573526/8b31631c6393adeae0dc1804e47ed3c5/17_8818.pdf>.

[61] EU Commission Messages C(2024) 4659 final (4.7.2024) and TRIS/(2024) 3018 (11.11.2024), relating to TRIS notification 2024/0188/DE, <https://technical-regulation-information-system.ec.europa.eu/en/notification/25746> .

[62] Cf. Darcel et al., 'Age assurance is focus of European regulatory action for online protection of minors', <https://www.osborneclarke.com/insights/age-assurance-focus-european-regulatory-action-online-protection-minors>.

[63] Law No. 2024–449 of 21.5.2024 aiming to secure and regulate the digital space (Loi SREN), <https://www.legifrance.gouv.fr/jorf/id/JORFTEXT000049563368>.

displaying any such content. This specific law does not cover the other types of harmful content listed in the penal code, but it has already been proposed to extend its scope, including to general social media websites.[64] The French audiovisual communications regulator, ARCOM, is charged with enforcing these rules and can fine non-compliant providers, as well as block such websites.[65]

ARCOM has issued guidance after consultation with the privacy regulator, CNIL, to establish a frame of reference for age verification technologies sufficient to satisfy these requirements.[66] This guidance considers **privacy implications** and the need to counteract **circumvention** and credential sharing in similar ways as the various guidance documents from European regulators (→ mn. 46 et seq.). It does consider that **age estimation** technologies can be sufficient as long as they are configured to 'exclude the risk' of overestimating a minor's age to let them access pornographic content, which likely requires a very significant safety margin. 62

Finally, and similar to Germany (→ mn. 59), the so-called Studer law[67] requires manufacturers of connected devices (computers, smartphones, tablets, video game consoles, and other connected devices such as TVs, watches, and speakers) to **install parental control software** and offer **free activation** when the device is first used. 63

III. Ireland

The Irish Online Safety Code (OSC) is **limited in scope** to video-sharing platforms, but its Section 12.10 does expressly require the implementation of age assurance measures for what it calls 'adult-only' videos. These are defined in Section 11 OSC as including not only **pornography**, but also realistic representations of gross or **gratuitous violence** or acts of cruelty. Sections 11 and 12.10 of the OSC further clarify that age assurance for this purpose may include age estimation, but not self-declaration. 64

IV. Spain

Likewise in **Spain**, Art. 89 of the General Audiovisual Law (Law 13/2022 of 7.7.2022) requires age assurance only from video-sharing platforms, and includes both **pornography** and gratuitous **violence** as categories of harmful content to which this requirement applies. The **privacy regulator** AEPD has issued comprehensive guidance on privacy-preserving age assurance measures, but there is no clear rule specifying the cases in which their use would be mandatory.[68] Furthermore, Art. 25, 26 of Royal Decree 958/2020 of 3.11.2020 (regulating advertising requirements in relation to gambling ac- 65

---

64 Le Monde, '*Réseaux sociaux : la France veut imposer la vérification d'âge au niveau européen*', 10.5.2025, <https://www.lemonde.fr/pixels/article/2025/05/10/reseaux-sociaux-la-france-veut-imposer-la-verification-d-age-au-niveau-europeen_6604843_4408996.html>.

65 Taverne et al., 'France enacts new rules on pornographic content in the digital environment', <https://www.osborneclarke.com/insights/france-enacts-new-rules-pornographic-content-digital-environment>.

66 ARCOM, 'Référentiel technique sur la vérification de l'âge pour la protection des mineurs contre la pornographie en ligne' (ARCOM Guidance), <https://www.arcom.fr/se-documenter/espace-juridique/textes-juridiques/referentiel-technique-sur-la-verification-de-lage-pour-la-protection-des-mineurs-contre-la-pornographie-en-ligne>.

67 Law No. 2022–300 of 2.3.2022 aiming to strengthen parental control over means of internet access (Loi Studer), <https://www.legifrance.gouv.fr/jorf/id/JORFTEXT000045287677>.

68 AEPD, 'Decalogue of principles – Age verification and protection of minors from inappropriate content', December 2023, <https://www.aepd.es/guides/decalogue-principles-age-verification-minors-protection.pdf>.

tivities) set out that **gambling-related ads** may not be served in video-sharing platforms or **social media** unless providers establish means to **effectively avoid** that advertisements are addressed to minors.

V. Italy

66 In **Italy**, the law commonly known as the Caivano Decree (Law Decree No. 123 of 15.9.2023, converted with Law No. 159 of 13.11.2023) introduced age verification measures (only) for website operators and video-sharing platforms that distribute **pornographic** content on Italian territory.[69] The Italian Communications Authority (AGCOM) subsequently established detailed technical modalities for age verification,[70] requiring the mandatory involvement of **certified independent third parties** and based on the principle of **double anonymity**, meaning that the provider does not know which site the user is visiting, while the site receives only the certification without knowing the user's identity.[71]

67 Significantly, systems based on self-declaration, direct collection of identity documents, browsing history analysis, and biometric data processing are expressly considered **not compliant** with GDPR data minimisation and privacy-by-design principles.[72]

[69] Law Decree No. 123 of 15.9.2023, converted with amendments by Law No. 159 of 13.11.2023 (art. 13-bis).

[70] AGCOM, Resolution No. 96/25/CONS of 8.4.2025; also see European Platform of Regulatory Authorities EPRA, Towards a new Framework for Child Protection: AGCOM Approves Age Verification Regulation for Online Platforms, <https://www.epra.org/news_items/italian-agcom-approves-age-verification-regulation-for-online-platforms>.

[71] AGCOM Resolution No. 96/25/CONS, Annex A, Art. 3.

[72] AGCOM Resolution No. 96/25/CONS, Annex A, Art. 3, point ii.

§ 35
Antitrust Law and Related Regulation

A. Introduction ... 1
B. Anticompetitive collusion ... 5
I. Art. 101 TFEU ... 5
1. EU examples of prohibited agreements ... 10
a) Pricing restrictions ... 10
b) Territorial restrictions ... 13
2. Block exemption regulations ... 17
a) Vertical Block Exemption Regulation (VBER) ... 18
b) Technology Transfer Block Exemption Regulation (TTBER) ... 23
II. Damages litigation ... 28
C. Merger control ... 29
I. Notifiability of acquisitions under the EUMR ... 29
Recent example: Microsoft/Activision ... 36
II. Jurisdictional issues and scope of notifiability of minority acquisitions; potential acqui-hire issues for developers/publishers ... 42
1. Jurisdiction ... 42
2. Minority acquisitions ... 44
3. Acqui-hires ... 48
D. Abuse of dominance ... 50
I. Art. 102 TFEU ... 50
II. Recent example: Epic Games and Apple ... 56
E. Digital regulations ... 58
I. EU Digital Markets Act ... 58
1. Overview ... 58
2. Relevance to video games ... 62
II. Geo-blocking regulation ... 67

A. Introduction

European antitrust law is intended to **ensure effective competition between market participants**, in order to protect consumers (e.g., as regards prices and innovation of video games and related services) as well as competing market participants (e.g., from being excluded from the market by an alleged dominant company). 1

Antitrust law has two main provisions: the prohibition of anti-competitive collusion and the prohibition of an abuse of a dominant position, which are both enshrined in the Treaty of the Functioning of the EU (TFEU). In addition, the EU's merger control regulation (EUMR) ensures that concentrations between companies do not impede competition. In recent years, this **legal framework has been complemented by additional EU regulations** pursuing similar objects: the Digital Markets Act (DMA) and the regulation addressing unjustified geo-blocking. 2

Antitrust law is **becoming increasingly relevant for the video games industry**, not only since the European Commission's (EC) geo-blocking proceedings and the *Microsoft/Activision* transaction.[1] In general, creative industries such as the video games industry as well as the tech industry have been a key focus of EU antitrust enforcement over the last decade and will likely persist for the decades to come. For video game developers and publishers, as tech-driven companies (e.g., driven by AI technologies), this increases the risk of landing in the crosshairs of European antitrust enforcers. At the 3

[1] Commission decision from 15.5.2023; see https://ec.europa.eu/commission/presscorner/api/files/document/print/en/ip_23_2705/IP_23_2705_EN.pdf.

same time, video game companies are also discovering antitrust as a powerful tool to defend their business interests,[2] potentially creating business opportunities.

4 The following sections address antitrust from the practical perspective of a video games company. The below lists examples of scenarios in which a video games company should think about antitrust law and related regulation, including when:

- Considering whether (or not) to enter into an agreement with another video games company or supplier of services necessary for developing video games (e.g., third-party software company) or distributor for video games – see section B. below;
- Considering whether to acquire another video games company, supplier or distributor – see section C. below;
- Dealing with a company that wields significant power over a resource necessary for the development or distribution of video games, for example an app store – see section D. below;
- Facing digital regulation in the EU – see section E. below.

B. Anticompetitive collusion

I. Art. 101 TFEU

5 It is unlawful for companies to engage in conduct with (actual or potential) competitors having the **object or effect of preventing, restricting or distorting competition**. Agreements, partnerships and other forms of collaboration, however informal, which restrict competition are prohibited in principle under Art. 101 TFEU.

6 Parties to prohibited agreements can be sanctioned with **fines of up to 10 %** of the group's global annual turnover under the Council of the EU's Regulation 1/2003. The EC has issued fines for players in the video games sector amounting to several millions of euros in recent years for alleged agreement (see below).

7 Any agreements found to be restrictive of competition can be **deemed null and void** *ab initio*, generally without any severability of permissible content of the contracts – irrespective of the language of any related clauses. It is not necessary to enter into a formal, binding or written agreement to be found to have engaged in prohibited conduct. It is sufficient if the parties concerned have entered into a verbal agreement or have a 'gentleman's understanding' as to how they will co-ordinate their behaviour. An agreement may be inferred from a course of conduct and, in actual practice, often is inferred.

8 In this assessment, a key factor is the **determination of whether agreements involve competitors**, or if they are instead in a vertical relationship with each other. Whilst horizontal agreements are those between parties at the same level of an industry, i.e., direct competitors, e.g., two video game publishers, vertical agreements are concluded between companies at different levels of the distribution chain, e.g., one video game publisher and one video game developer.

9 This **distinction between horizontal and vertical** in the video games industry is complicated because although developers and publishersstand in a vertical relationship – with development occurring prior to publishing – many developers engage in digital distribution and leave physical distribution to publishers. As such, developers can

[2] For example as part of the *Epic v Apple* case in the USA: Court of Appeals of the 9th Circuit decision from 17.7.2023; see https://law.justia.com/cases/federal/appellate-courts/ca9/21-16506/21-16506-2023-07-17.html.

compete with publishers insofar as digital and physical distribution is considered to take place at the same level. Meanwhile, console manufacturers are active at multiple levels: manufacturing and supplying consoles; offering digital distribution services; and publishing games, which are often developed by their own studios. In the exercise of each of these functions, console manufacturers might be considered vertical contractual partners and direct competitors of external video game developers and publishers.

1. EU examples of prohibited agreements

a) *Pricing restrictions*

Agreements to fix or set prices between competitors are prohibited. It is also prohibited for companies with vertical relationships to agree on a minimum resale price for products. 10

An example from outside the video games world illustrates what would also be prohibited in the video games sector: In 2019, the EC fined two manufacturers of canned vegetables over 30 million EUR – a third was afforded full immunity as the leniency applicant – after finding that they had participated in agreements to fix (by maintaining or increasing) selling prices of their products across the EEA over a 13-year period. A fourth company was fined 20 million EUR one year later.[3] Together, the companies set prices; agreed on market shares and volume quotas; allocated customers and markets; coordinated replies to tenders; and also exchanged commercially sensitive information. 11

Non-binding price recommendations, however, are generally permissible as long as they are de facto non-binding. There should be no express or implicit pressure to apply the recommended prices, e.g., threats to revoke publishing agreements if the recommended prices are not implemented. Equally, no 'rewards' can be offered for adherence with recommendations as this would detract from the non-binding nature of the recommendation. 12

b) *Territorial restrictions*

Agreements to assign or designate sales territories between competitors are also prohibited. 13

However, companies in a vertical relationship may designate exclusive territories under certain circumstances. 14

The EC has issued fines in the video games industry in recent years for alleged agreements to restrict cross-border sales. Undertakings must not actively prevent cross-border passive sales and deny consumers in the EEA the benefits to find the most suitable offers between EU Member States. The General Court has also upheld that Art. 101 TFEU must apply in the context of agreements between parties with a vertical relationship. 15

It is clear that platforms, publishers and distributors must not undertake any conduct that has the objective or could have the effect of **restricting parallel trade between EU Member States**. Individual exemptions under Art. 101 (3) TFEU are possible, but this can result in a burdensome exercise for companies – which is why block exemptions play such an important role in practice, as set out below. 16

[3] Case AT.40127 – *Canned Vegetables*.

2. Block exemption regulations

17 Agreements that restrict competition can be justified, or 'exempted' under block exemption regulations. The benefit for companies is that if they compete with one another only to a limited degree, the agreements made with suppliers or distributors will face a lower risk of antitrust enforcement. Such increased level of legal clarity ('**safe harbour**') also enables companies to plan and invest accordingly.

a) Vertical Block Exemption Regulation (VBER)

18 The VBER provides a general exemption from the application of Art. 101 TFEU for agreements between suppliers and buyers of services or goods, provided certain conditions are met.

19 The VBER focuses on agreements facilitating the distribution of goods or services (distribution agreements). In particular, the focus is on **agreements facilitating dual distribution** where a supplier sells its goods through independent distributors and directly to end customers itself. For instance, agreements between video game developers and publishers for the physical distribution of games whilst retaining responsibility for concurrent digital distribution would fall under the VBER.

20 The VBER presumes these vertical agreements are **legal if parties possess less than 30 % market share**, individually, in the supply of a relevant good or service, e.g., video games. The agreement would not be presumed illegal if this safe harbour threshold was exceeded, although the parties would be considered to have significant market power.

21 However, certain **hardcore restrictions** also prevent the exemption from applying to the agreement as a whole, including resale price maintenance;[4] territorial resale restrictions; and online sales restrictions. Moreover, cross-platform retail parity obligations and certain non-compete obligations will also cause the VBER to be disapplied but only to the extent that those obligations cannot be severed from the broader distribution agreement.

22 The EC may also choose to disapply the block exemption if it finds that multiple similar agreements (e.g., between game developers and publishers) govern more than 50 % of the distribution of a particular good or service in a given geographic market.

b) Technology Transfer Block Exemption Regulation (TTBER)

23 The provisions of the VBER do not apply to agreements concerning, as a primary focus, assignment or licensing of technology or intellectual property (IP) rights. The TTBER covers agreements involving rights such as know-how, rights over patents, utility models, design and software copyrights.

24 The TTBER applies only to technology transfer agreements in the form of either **licensing agreements**, where the licensee will produce contract products, or the assignment of rights where some risk associated with exploitation remains with the assignor. Unlike the VBER, the TTBER covers only agreements between two companies, but the TTBER also applies to the connected companies of either the licensor or the licensee.[5]

25 Like the VBER, the TTBER can be of significant use for video game companies by providing a 'safe harbour' and thereby also reducing compliance costs. This block exemption safe harbour from Art. 101 TFEU is applied for all technology transfer agreements insofar as either the parties to the agreement are competitors with a **combined**

---

[4] See, for example, the e-books case.

[5] TTBER, Art. 2, 'connected undertakings' being those over which either party to the agreement may exercise control, have control exercised over them, or share control rights with.

market share of 20 %, are not competitors with a market share of 30 % or none of the hardcore restrictions apply.

The TTBER's **hardcore restrictions** also lead to disapplication of the block exemption for licensing agreements. These include retail price maintenance (RPM, i.e., vertical price fixing) and territorial restrictions, which cannot be severed from the agreement. Restrictions on licensees from using their own IP, to grant back an exclusive licence to facilitate improvements, do not benefit from the application of the block exemption. 26

Conversely, obligations to grant exclusive licence or assignment for the IP, restrictions against IP legal challenges within the EU and restrictions on the usage of proprietary technology also do not fall under the TTBER, although these terms may be severed from the agreement so the broader agreement can still benefit from the block exemption. 27

II. Damages litigation

Any parties harmed by conduct stemming from an agreement found to be restrictive of competition may lodge **claims for damages through the EU national courts**. However, this has not occurred in relation to video games in the EU to date. 28

C. Merger control

I. Notifiability of acquisitions under the EUMR

Merger control has played a significant role in the video games industry, particularly when a platform or publisher seeks to purchase other publishers or development studios. This has been particularly relevant in the past few years, such as when Microsoft acquired Activision Blizzard in 2022. However, EU merger control can also be relevant for far smaller mergers or acquisitions. 29

The EU operates a **mandatory pre-closing merger control notification regime under the EUMR** for concentrations, including mergers and acquisitions of sole or joint control of the whole or parts of companies (Council Regulation (EC) No 139/2004).[6] If a transaction meets the EUMR's thresholds set out below, the transaction must be notified to the EC and a bar on closing the transaction is enforced until approval is received from the EC. 30

Transactions are **notifiable to the EC if**: 31

a) The parties' combined worldwide turnover exceeds 5 billion EUR and each of at least two of the parties' turnover in all EU Member States exceeds 250 million EUR, unless each party realises more than two-thirds of their EU-wide turnover in one single Member State; or
b) The parties' combined worldwide turnover exceeds 2.5 billion EUR and each of at least two of the parties has EU-wide turnover exceeding 100 million EUR, and in each of at least three EU Member States, the parties' combined turnover exceeds 100 million EUR with each party having at least 25 million EUR turnover in each of the same three Member States, unless each party realises more than two-thirds of its EU-wide turnover in a single Member State.

---

[6] For the purposes of the EUMR, control is defined as the possibility of exercising decisive influence over a company. This can involve powers such as approving annual budgets or appointing board members.

32 In addition to the EUMR, **EU Member States have their own national merger control laws**. When a transaction does not meet either of the EUMR thresholds depicted above but does meet the national merger control thresholds of any three EU Member States, the parties can request in writing that the EC examine the transaction before notifying any of the national competition authorities. This will only be refused if a Member State objects within 15 days of a communication from the EC, but is uncommon. National laws are pre-empted by the EUMR when the EC assumes jurisdiction.

33 Once a transaction has been notified to the EC, a **Phase I review** period takes 25 working days from the day after the notification is received.[7] The EC uses this time to gather thoughts on the transaction from the parties' competitors and customers in the relevant markets to identify the potential effects on competition of the transaction.

34 Should the EC identify potential concerns during Phase I, the parties may choose to offer remedies to assuage these. Consideration of these remedies will extend the Phase I by ten working days to allow for it to be tested amongst market participants, i.e., ask competitors and customers for feedback on how the remedy would be implemented in relation to the relevant product and geographic markets.

35 Absent remedies being offered, however, the EC could look to refer the transaction to an **in-depth investigation in Phase II** where the concerns will be further considered through intensive requests for additional data and documents as further evidence for the EC to make its decision on the transaction. Phase II lasts for a duration of 90 working days from the day immediately following the decision to open the investigation. This may be extended to 105 working days if remedies are offered after working day 54 of Phase II. The EC may also extend the review period by 20 working days if the notifying parties agree.[8]

Recent example: Microsoft/Activision

36 **Microsoft agreed to acquire Activision** for USD 68.7 billion in January 2022 and notified the EC in September 2022.[9] In the course of the EC's Phase I review, concerns were identified regarding the potential for reduced competition in relation to (i) the distribution of console and PC games, including through multi-game subscription platforms and/or cloud gaming and streaming; and (ii) the supply of PC operating systems.

37 Both Microsoft and Activision comprise development studios and publishers of video games for PCs, consoles and mobiles whilst distributing games – Microsoft for PC and console; and Activision for PC, consoles and mobiles. Microsoft also provides the Xbox console and a cloud game streaming platform, Game Pass, in addition to adjacent products, such as the PC operating system, Windows, and cloud computing system, Azure.

38 Through the Phase II in-depth review, the EC was able to rule out most of the concerns identified in its Phase I review, by finding that **Microsoft would have no incentive to refuse to distribute Activision's game to competing platforms**, especially

[7] Ordinarily, a pre-notification period of at least two months will precede the formal notification, wherein the parties will introduce the EC to the relevant markets and demonstrate with internal documents and data why no negative effects on competition on the relevant product and geographic markets are possible, so the transaction should be approved.

[8] In practice, the EC may also stop the review clock in the event it is waiting for responses to requests for information, particularly for documents or data. Although work and analysis may continue, the review period is effectively suspended.

[9] Microsoft/Activision was simultaneously notified to competition authorities in the EU, UK and a number of other jurisdictions. For the purpose of this handbook, this section will only discuss the review undertaken by the EC.

Sony. In particular, as there are reportedly four times as many PlayStation consoles than Xbox consoles in the EEA, the EC determined that even if Microsoft did withdraw Activision's console games from PlayStation, competition would not be harmed significantly. Furthermore, the EC found that Activision would not have shared its games with multi-game subscription services absent the transaction, and as such, third-party multi-game subscription service providers would not have been affected.

However, the EC did not find anything in the course of the review to alleviate the **concern that there might be harm to competition in the distribution of PC and console games via cloud gaming streaming platforms** and relatedly that Microsoft might be able to foreclose other distributors from cloud game streaming if it made Activision games exclusive to Game Pass. The EC also maintained that Microsoft would be able to strengthen the position of the Windows PC operating system if it chose to make Activision's games exclusive to Game Pass whilst degrading the quality of Activision's games streamed on PCs that use different operating systems. 39

Microsoft agreed on two commitments that would address the EC's concerns in full as two licences in relation to cloud game streaming. First, a free licence to consumers for ten years to facilitate streaming of all current and future Activision PC and console games via their own choice of cloud game streaming services. Second, Microsoft afforded a licence to cloud game streaming providers for the same time period, to ensure EEA-based gamers may stream any Activision PC or console game. This case is therefore a good example of how competition concerns in merger control can sometimes be remedied through significant behavioural commitments. 40

Video game companies should, however, be aware that sometimes competition authorities – including the EC and UK Competition and Markets Authority (CMA) – may consider behavioural commitments such as these to be inadequate to address the competition concerns at hand, alone. Instead, the **competition authorities might require structural remedies**, which may involve divestment of development studios or other assets to third parties who are active in the industry and would enable the studios or assets to continue operating (and competing) at the same level as they had been before the transaction. 41

II. Jurisdictional issues and scope of notifiability of minority acquisitions; potential acqui-hire issues for developers/publishers

1. Jurisdiction

In the event the EUMR thresholds are not met by a given transaction, the EC can only review it if one or more **Member States refer it to the EC** under the procedure in Art. 22 EUMR. 42

In order to be referred to the EC by a Member State's national competition authority, the transaction must meet the merger control thresholds of that Member State, or the national competition authority must have the power under national law to call in the transaction for review.[10] 43

[10] See ECJ decision in *Illumina/Grail*, determining that the EC cannot review a transaction that does not meet EUMR thresholds based on a referral from an EU Member State whose own thresholds were not met by the transaction and who does not have power under its national law to review transactions that do not meet its national merger control thresholds.

2. Minority acquisitions

44 Acquisitions of minority shareholdings are notifiable if the acquiring party could be considered to exercise **de facto control over the target entity** following the acquisition. Lately, European competition authorities, including the EC, CMA and German Federal Cartel Office (FCO, *Bundeskartellamt*), have considered a number of transactions involving partnerships and commercial arrangements relating to Artificial Intelligence (AI) development.

45 These transactions have not involved the acquisition of control rights. Such a situation could be foreseen if a publisher wished to invest in a studio to ensure the development of a particular video game or franchise over time.

46 The first transaction of this kind subject to regulatory scrutiny was Microsoft's USD 13 billion investment in OpenAI between 2019 and 2023. The EC, FCO and CMA all considered the investment and eventually concluded, for separate reasons, that it was not notifiable.[11] Although not notifiable, these investments were considered very closely and over long periods of time.[12]

47 The risk of separate competition authority investigations with significant duration can **risk the value of the investment** as it may prevent the investee's access to the invested funds. Parties should be ready to highlight the lack of influence and control the investment affords the investor to avoid sustained competition authority interest or concern.

3. Acqui-hires

48 A recent development in merger control is the **hiring of talent for the purposes of advancing projects** such as software development in-house. Known informally as 'acqui-hires', the EC has considered such transactions to be concentrations notifiable under the EUMR. This could be pertinent to the hiring of video game developers by other developers or publishers to bolster their development teams.

49 In 2024, Microsoft hired the two founders and a number of staff at the technology company and Pi (personal intelligence) AI chatbot developer, Inflection. The two companies also agreed on a non-exclusive licence for Inflection's IP and a waiver of legal rights by Inflection for hiring their staff. The EC considered that these engagements involved substantially all of the assets necessary to transfer Inflection's competitive position for generative AI foundation models and AI chatbots to Microsoft such that it should be considered a concentration notifiable under the EUMR. However, in this case, the EC could not investigate further as the transaction met neither the EUMR thresholds, nor any EU Member State thresholds.

---

[11] The EC determined the investment did not qualify as a 'concentration' under EUMR due to Microsoft's lack of control over OpenAI following the investment. The FCO determined the investment qualified as a 'concentration' under German law but that OpenAI did not have 'substantial activities' in Germany as required for notification by national transaction value merger control thresholds. The CMA determined the investment would not result in any change from 'material influence' to 'control' for Microsoft over OpenAI.

[12] The FCO concluded its review in November 2023; the EC in June 2024; and the CMA in March 2025.

D. Abuse of dominance

I. Art. 102 TFEU

Complementing the EUMR and the cartel prohibition of Art. 101 TFEU, Art. 102 TFEU includes the third pillar of EU antitrust law: the prohibition of certain unilateral conduct. Any **unilateral conduct** by one or more companies that hold a dominant position in a relevant product or geographic market within the internal market that has a restrictive effect on trade between EU Member States is prohibited under Art. 102 TFEU. 50

Sanctions for abusing a dominant position usually involve **significant fines**, although commitments may also be required to remedy the conduct at issue. In the most severe cases, structural or behavioural remedies proportionate to the infringement may be required. 51

A **dominant position** is understood to mean a position of 'economic strength' enabling a company to prevent effective competition, which is itself understood to mean considerable market share in relevant markets for at least two consecutive years.[13] Generally, market shares below 40 % will be considered an absence of market power, but other factors will also be considered. 52

Specific factors that may be considered in the context of an abuse of dominance include the competitive constraints imposed by existing competitors, the potential for expansion or new entry of prospective competitors and the prevalence of countervailing buyer power. Any barriers to entry will also be scrutinised. 53

Art. 102 TFEU also prohibits abuses of dominance by one or more companies. **Collective dominance** can exist when multiple companies act together such that they may be perceived as a collective entity. This is particularly the case if companies have concluded cooperation agreements to coordinate market conduct. It can also be found without formal links. 54

Important to note is that the existence of a dominant position on its own does not infringe EU competition law; only the combination with certain behaviour (abuses) may lead to an infringement of Art. 102 TFEU. Abuses are most commonly found in the form of price discrimination or predatory pricing, refusals to supply, tying and, most recently, self-preferencing. 55

II. Recent example: Epic Games and Apple

Epic Games filed a formal antitrust complaint to the EC about Apple in 2021, one year after Epic's most popular game Fortnite was banned from the Apple App Store. The complaint alleged that **Apple had leveraged its market power** to eliminate competition for app distribution and payment processes. Epic did not seek damages as it had done in proceedings in the US, Australia and the UK, but sought to encourage the EC to take action and impose sanctions on Apple. 56

The complaint was also filed one year after the EC launched an investigation into Apple's App Store for an alleged abuse of dominance following complaints relating to the App Store's rules for music streaming providers from Spotify and Rakuten. The latter resulted in a EUR 1.8 billion fine for Apple in March 2024, which Apple appealed. The EC has never acknowledged Epic's complaint formally. 57

---

[13] Judgment of the Court of 13 February 1979 – Hoffmann-La Roche & Co. AG v Commission of the European Communities – Dominant position – Case 85/76.

E. Digital regulations

I. EU Digital Markets Act

1. Overview

58 The DMA is a recent regulation, relevant for companies active in digital markets within the EU and, to some extent, relates to the concepts of unilateral conduct developed under traditional EU antitrust law. Unlike traditional antitrust law such as Art. 102 TFEU, which grants the EC enforcement powers when a company has committed an infringement ('ex post' regulation), the prohibitions of the DMA apply to certain designated companies up-front (**'ex ante' regulation**). The DMA entered into force in November 2022 with the purpose of imposing additional strict obligations for certain digital platforms with significant numbers of EU users ('gatekeepers') for the provision of certain services ('core platform services').

59 Core platform services include **online intermediation services** (including app stores), online advertising services, social networks and messaging services, web browsers and online search engines, as well as virtual assistants.

60 Art. 3 establishes qualitative and quantitative criteria for identifying and assigning **gatekeepers**. Qualitatively, gatekeepers are digital platforms having a significant impact on the internal market, providing a core platform service as an important gateway for business users to reach end users and enjoying entrenched and durable positions. Quantitatively, this translates, for each of the prior three financial years, to:

a) Annual turnover within the EU of at least 7.5 billion EUR in each of the three prior financial years or an average market capitalization (or fair market value) of at least 7.5 billion EUR with a same core platform service provided in at least three EU Member States; and
b) At least 45 million monthly active users of the core platform services who are located in the EU and at least 10 thousand yearly active business users.

61 Under the regulation, gatekeepers must comply with obligations and prohibitions, which target fairness and contestability of digital markets. These largely relate to the collection, processing and usage of end users' personal data, as well as the interactions between end users and business users that the gatekeepers must facilitate through the core platform service.

2. Relevance to video games

62 Of these core platform services and obligations and prohibitions specified in the DMA, some are particularly pertinent to the video games industry. **Online intermediation stores**, including app stores, are identified as core platform services and gatekeepers are obliged to not require the interoperation of end users with specific payment systems for in-app purchases.

63 In general, the DMA is an area of **high importance for all digital and creative sectors**, including for the video games industry, particularly for the distribution of mobile games. Mobile platforms are crucial partners for video game companies and have helped the industry to grow. At the same time, the EC's stated aim of the DMA is to provide for consistent enforcement of the DMA to benefit European consumers through cheaper prices, more choice, and enabling the industry to reinvest in new games.

One example of the DMA in action concerning video games relates to the disputes between Apple's App Store and Epic Games (see above). Following the enforcement of the DMA's obligations on designated gatekeepers' core platform services, Apple was required to permit Epic and others to establish alternative app stores on the iOS operating system to facilitate broader opportunities for app distribution. However, Apple was found to have terminated Epic's app developer account because it did not trust Epic to comply with the App Store terms. Apple reinstated Epic's developer status four months later, after the EC asked for clarifications on this decision. 64

After one year of investigations, the EC adopted a **non-compliance decision against Apple** on 23.4.2025, finding that Apple used technical and commercial restrictions to breach the 'anti-steering' provisions under Art. 5 (4) of the DMA, which require gatekeepers to permit developers to inform customers of alternative offers outside its own app store and facilitate navigation to those offers to make purchases. The EC fined the company EUR 500 million. Apple has submitted an appeal against the decision with the EU General Court. 65

A similar proceeding was opened against Alphabet's Google Play Store. The EC adopted a preliminary finding, on 19.3.2025, that the Google Play Store would not comply with Art. 5 (4) of the DMA because app developers are prevented – as a result of unjustifiable fees – from freely steering consumers to other channels for better offers. The DMA affords companies an opportunity to respond to preliminary findings and fines of up to 10 % of global annual turnover may be imposed for a confirmed breach. 66

II. Geo-blocking regulation

Another relatively new regulation, related to ideas developed under antitrust law and potentially relevant for companies in the digital and creative sectors, addresses so-called geo-blocking (see also above). 67

In 2015, the EC proposed to address so-called 'unjustified geo-blocking', which is defined as 'discrimination between EU customers to segment markets along national borders and increase profits to the detriment of foreign customers', with the objective of improving the conditions of cross-border e-commerce within the EU.[14] The geo-blocking regulation (2018/302) that entered into force in December 2018 prohibits **unilateral practices leading to market partitioning** that are not covered by competition law, i.e., unilateral conduct of non-dominant companies. 68

Both **direct and indirect discrimination** are targeted by the regulation, based on data indicating customers' physical location. Companies may not generally use measures to block or limit customers' access to traders' online interfaces, and traders may not apply different levels of access to their goods or services for cross-border transactions. 69

Particularly pertinent to the video games industry, Art. 4 (1) (b), which deals with access to goods and services, provides an **exemption for electronically supplied copyright protected content**. This means that services providing access to and use of electronically delivered copyright-protected works, such as video games, are excluded from the general rule that traders must not apply different conditions for accessing goods or services based on a customer's nationality, place of residence or place of establishment. 70

This exclusion is specific to Art. 4 and **video game companies services' remain subject to all other provisions** in the Regulation, including the prohibition to block or limit access to online interfaces on the basis of the nationality, residence or establishment of the customer (Art. 3) and the non-discrimination for reasons linked to payment means 71

[14] https://digital-strategy.ec.europa.eu/en/policies/geoblocking.

(Art. 5). This means that video game companies cannot block access to their online interface, i.e., websites or apps, where the consumer can access different types of information like the price.

CHAPTER 7
MARKETING A VIDEO GAME

§ 36
Gaming Marketing Law, Tools and Partnerships

A. Introduction ... 1
I. The people and players ... 2
II. Choice in gaming ... 4
III. Gaming as big business ... 6
IV. Author's disclaimer ... 9

B. Gaming marketing and the law ... 11
I. Art of persuasion ... 12
II. Supporting act ... 13
III. Power of words ... 15
IV. Marketing slogans vs. marketing claims ... 16

C. The legal framework governing gaming marketing ... 19
I. One team ... 21
II. Prepare for change ... 24
III. Overview of the key laws ... 31
1. General Data Protection Regulation (GDPR) ... 32
2. Digital Services Act (DSA) and Digital Markets Act (DMA) ... 33
3. Consumer protection directives ... 34
4. The EU AI Act ... 35
5. Sustainability laws ... 36
IV. Conclusion on legal frameworks ... 37

D. Marketing tools and partnerships ... 40
I. Defining marketing tools ... 41
II. Above the line (ATL) marketing ... 42
III. Below the line (BTL) marketing ... 45
IV. Digital marketing ... 48
V. Online tools ... 51
VI. Promotions and competitions ... 54
VII. Artificial intelligence ... 57
VIII. Defining marketing partnerships ... 60
IX. Traditional brand partnerships ... 61
X. Celebrity endorsements and influencer collaborations ... 64
XI. Partnering with 'the competition' ... 66
XII. Co-branding with other entertainment verticals ... 68
XIII. Agency relationships ... 70

E. Final thoughts ... 74
I. 'The department of "No"' ... 76
II. The bigger picture ... 79
III. Conclusion ... 80

A. Introduction

The fact you are reading this EU Video Game Law Handbook means the chances are high that you already know the immense size and reach of the **video gaming industry**. Nevertheless, it is worth repeating because across the board, whether it is the players, the games, or the revenue generated, the figures are staggering. Put simply, gaming touches more people, takes more forms, and generates more money, than any other entertainment vertical in the world. 1

I. The people and players

'Dads, moms, millennials, Gen Z, financial advisors, lawyers, and others from all walks of life are among the billions of consumers logging innumerable hours across a multitude of purpose-built and generalized consumer devices across one of the largest and rapidly growing media ecosystems in the world—video gaming.'[1] Jonathan Stringfield, Get In the Game

2 Where else can we start but with the **players**? Whatever image the word 'gamer' conjures up for you, it is estimated that well over a third of the world's population plays video games in one form or another, so unless we are willing to generalise across approximately 3 billion people, it is fair to assume that no one type of person fits the description. At the time of writing, Pope Leo XIV was recently inaugurated, with the gaming press taking great pleasure in labelling him the first 'casual gamer Pope'[2] following the revelation that he regularly plays Wordle with his brother.

3 Closer to home and less hallowed, there was a member of each generation of my own family that could be considered a **gamer**, all the way from my grandmother, born almost a century ago who enjoyed *Solitaire* on her iPad, to my twelve year old nephew who loves nothing more than playing EA Sports FC with his friends (sometimes letting me join in, too). There are dedicated gamers who spend hundreds, even thousands, on consoles, gaming PCs, accessories, and access to the latest titles, and log many hours playing; and there are occasional gamers who exclusively stick to free to play games only. There are those who enjoy gaming as an integral part of their social life, using their leisure time to go virtual bowling with friends and family, or those who are physically at home but part of an international cohort, meeting up online to take down bad guys any time of the day or night. Take a second to look up on the bus or train during your morning commute and you will see people immersed in mobile games on their phones as they go about their daily lives. Gamers are all around.

II. Choice in gaming

'Video Games are magic'[3]

4 Next, we move on to the **games** themselves. Just as there is no one type of player, there is also no one type of video game. Even the term 'video game' feels somehow deficient, outdated, and narrow now given the variety available. From the recently disclosed papal favourite, Wordle, to the arcade classic *Pacman*; from the imaginative and creative build-your-own worlds of *Minecraft* and Roblox, to the grittier yet equally immersive missions of *Call of Duty* and *Grand Theft Auto*; from the singular *Solitaire* to the worldwide *Fortnite* community; from the data-rich strategic Football Manager played on a PC, to the block simplicity of *Tetris* on the Gameboy, the list goes on, representing decades of technological development and cultural relevance. And all of this without even touching on the hybrid world of esports which sees gamers physically come together to compete with one another in digital worlds and is covered in more detail later in this handbook at → **Ch. 41 Esports**.

---

[1] Stringfield, Jonathan. *Get in the Game: How to Level Up Your Business with Gaming, Esports, and Emerging Technologies*. 1st ed. Hoboken, NJ: John Wiley & Sons, 2022.

[2] Gould, Elie. "First we do Wordle: Pope Leo XIV plays games like Wordle and Words With Friends with his brother, and did so before the Conclave." *PC Gamer*, May 9, 2025. https://www.pcgamer.com/.

[3] Gaetano Dimita, Yin Harn Lee, Michaela MacDonald & Marc Mimler, "Video Games Are Magic," *Interactive Entertainment Law Review* 5, no. 1 (June 2022).

Gaming has evolved and there is also **no one way to play**. Growing up, it was simple: if you were a gamer, you either spent your pocket money in an arcade or bought your own gaming machine which took cartridges or discs, and you played. Multiplayer meant your friend came over to your house, and sharing a gaming experience meant lending them your copy of *Golden Axe* for the weekend. Today, you can still game on a console or your PC, but you can also use your TV, mobile phone, tablet, handheld, headset, even your smart watch! It is possible to start playing on one screen at home and pick up from the exact same place on a different screen hours later on the train. You can still buy physical discs, but you can also stream and download, accessing games on- and offline. To borrow and paraphrase from PlayStation, nowadays, play really does have no limits. 5

III. Gaming as big business

> *'Over the past few decades, beneath the bright lights of Hollywood blockbusters and amid chart-topping music hits, a silent yet powerful revolution has been steadily unfolding: the meteoric rise of the gaming industry.'*[4]

Although my parents taught me that it was impolite to talk about money, we must acknowledge the fact that the **gaming industry is big business**. As you might expect when assessing such large numbers, there are wildly differing estimates on the global value of the gaming industry. According to Statista, revenues in gaming are set to exceed 500 billion USD in 2025;[5] Precedence projects a more conservative (but still eye-watering) 300 billion USD in 2025.[6] Even accounting for the disparity of these figures, it is clear we are dealing with an industry experiencing revolutionary growth, driven by increasing internet penetration and smartphone adoption globally. The global gaming market is expected to reach **circa 437 billion USD by 2030** – an enviable compound annual growth rate of over 10% during the forecast period.[7] 6

Since the **pandemic gaming has become far more accepted**, but even now it can be seen as part of the sub-culture rather than the firmly established fixture of mainstream entertainment that it is, especially when compared to watching TV, going to the movies, or listening to music. To put it into context, paid TV and streaming is estimated to be worth around 200 billion USD, with both the film and music industries estimated at approximately 100 billion USD each, paling into comparison against the gaming industry. 7

So how do those working in the gaming industry, the creators, storytellers, designers, programmers, artists, developers, publishers, platform engineers, and hardware manufacturers go about the enormous task of reaching all these people all over the planet to promote such a variety of products? How do they drive demand for even more people to express curiosity and cross over the Rubicon to becoming a gamer? How does an industry which experienced such an enormous boom during the pandemic years continue to grow revenue and raise awareness of its continued innovation now that we are no longer all confined to our homes? **The answer is incredibly complex and yet can be summarised in one simple word: Marketing.** 8

---

[4] Arora, Krishan. "The Gaming Industry: A Behemoth With Unprecedented Global Reach." *Forbes*, November 17, 2023.

[5] Statista Market Insights, "Games – Worldwide," Statista, updated October 2025, https://www.statista.com/outlook/amo/media/games/worldwide.

[6] Precedence Research, "Video Games Market Size to Hit USD 721.77 Billion By 2034," July 28, 2025, https://www.precedenceresearch.com/video-game-market.

[7] Mordor Intelligence, "Gaming Market Size, Share, Growth, Trends & Industry Analysis 2030," accessed July 2025, https://www.mordorintelligence.com/industry-reports/global-gaming-market.

IV. Author's disclaimer

9 Before we go any further, I am a firm believer in transparency, so full disclosure: I am not a marketer, I am a lawyer. But importantly, **this is not a gaming marketing handbook, it is a legal one**. For that reason, while as the chapter suggests, we will explore various types of marketing, tools and partnerships, we will do so by applying a legal lens and tackling issues from the perspective of the lawyer. I am not about to assess the efficacy of one marketing tool over the other, or highlight why one brand partnership might yield more than an influencer campaign; I am not qualified to do this. Instead, using my experience from over a decade as in-house legal counsel supporting a wide range of consumer products and gaming services, including Xbox, I plan to set out how I believe a good in-house or outside counsel lawyer can use their skills to help marketing teams with the exciting – and daunting – mission of promoting our industry, one still so rich in potential.

10 Final point of disclosure: I work for Microsoft. I say this because it is important that you, the reader, understand that I am not being partisan throughout this chapter if my focus or examples come more from the Xbox ecosystem, it is simply because this is where the majority of my experience on these topics has come from and I intend to follow the age old wisdom of 'write what you know'.

B. Gaming marketing and the law

11 It might not seem like an obvious or immediate connection, but there are several important overlaps between the role of a marketer and a lawyer.

I. Art of persuasion

12 Both marketing and legal professionals are in the business of building cases to support their objectives: a marketer needs to convince the customer that their product is superior over another product to convince consumers to buy it; a lawyer must convince a regulator, judge or those on the other side of a negotiation, that their application of the rules or position is the most compelling.

II. Supporting act

13 Marketing agencies and internal marketing teams, like law firms and in-house lawyers, are often in the supporting role. The ultimate aim of marketing is not usually an end in itself, but an integral part of the full go to market journey, culminating in a sale.

14 Similarly, a law firm does not exist solely to advise on the law, but to advise on how the law can be applied to help the business clients achieve their main goal: a merger, making or defending a claim, protecting their IP, promoting a video game, whatever it might be.

III. Power of words

15 What is marketing if not the utilisation of the power of words? Whether it is a product claim ('The Most Powerful Console in the World'), earworm phrases that are repeated for years ('It's in the game'), or a combination making for an aspirational

mission statement ('Play Has No Limits'), words are often the marketers' most valuable instrument. A lawyer might say the same, but the circumstances are different, and this is reflected in the language used. A marketer uses words to connect, inspire, promote and sell; a lawyer to protect, convince, prove, and clarify. So where should the lawyer be leaning in, and where should they be taking a backseat? An illustration can be found by looking in more detail at the differences between marketing slogans and marketing claims.

IV. Marketing slogans vs. marketing claims

A marketer must speak to the audience in a way that engages them, piques their curiosity, and draws them in. Think of your favourite brand, snack, or car… go on: *Just Do It. Taste the Rainbow. Vorsprung Durch Technik.* We can all quickly recall slogans and often we cannot explain why these short amalgam of words linger long in our memory. Whilst some lawyers may argue their jobs involve creativity – creativity in problem solving, creativity in argument building, creativity in the application of the law – the reality is that when it comes to reviewing a marketing slogan, the true creativity comes from the marketer, and the lawyer's role is to tread lightly. I make it a rule to leave the **creative work to the marketers** and only **offer my view if there is a specific legal issue** with a slogan, for example, a potential copyright infringement. **16**

There is an important distinction to draw between a marketing slogan and a marketing claim. Whilst sometimes they may overlap, the primary difference from a legal perspective is that while one is usually a catchy sequence of words with any claims contained amounting to puffery and requiring no substantiation (slogan), the other can be heavily reliant on the legal team to prove it and permit its use (claim). **17**

The Most Powerful Console in the World was the bold claim that Microsoft made about the Xbox Series X on release. While it is a simple message, the amount of testing and substantiation that was required in order to demonstrate it was true and permit the Xbox marketing team to use it was anything but simple. As the lawyer, assessing whether your client is creating a slogan or making a claim can be important in understanding how much involvement you should have in this stage of the marketing process. **18**

C. The legal framework governing gaming marketing

A significant challenge of rules and regulations is the perception that they exist solely to restrict companies by stifling creativity and innovation. By working with clients to change this perception and instead view governing laws as a safe framework for marketers to operate within, rather than something to push against, we can reduce that view of the law as an obstacle. **19**

In this world where consumers are increasingly aware of their rights, applied correctly, the law can even be a marketing advantage. Over the years, I have found it beneficial to act in partnership with the marketing teams I support, helping them understand the basics of the legislation that forms the framework governing gaming marketing now, and looking at how it might evolve. This approach ensures that what they create is not only compliant with the law from the outset, meaning it should require fewer modifications during end stage legal review, but also has the added bonus of building trust in the brand. **20**

I. One team

21 **Building a close relationship with marketing clients is crucial**, and you can build this trust by accompanying each other on your respective journeys.

22 For the marketing teams, this means bringing their legal team in from the start. Speaking from my own experience, being invited to the initial meetings and involved in the inception of an idea always helped me to **develop a better understanding** of what the team was trying to achieve. If it was necessary to take some risk, understanding the context of that risk and being able to suggest mitigation steps that the business could take meant not only that the business would be more likely to better execute their idea, but that there would be far less change required at the final review stage.

23 For the lawyer, this means becoming part of the team. You of course need to maintain some separation to maintain the impartial, and sometimes difficult messages that a lawyer needs to deliver. However, showing willingness to attend team meetings, sharing excitement about campaigns, being available to answer initial questions, responding quickly, and showing enthusiasm for the product or game being promoted, are all ways that you can integrate.

II. Prepare for change

24 Once you have built that relationship, an existential role of the lawyer is **helping your business clients avoid unforeseen issues** that may be triggered by regulatory change. An effective legal counsel can provide enormous value to their marketing teams through early visibility into the rule-making process. This proactive approach allows the business to advocate for amendments to unworkable proposals or, at the very least, be prepared for upcoming legislative changes, especially where engineering modifications are needed.

25 Taking my own learnings from occasions where it has felt like a new law has come out of nowhere and taken the business by surprise, here is a step-by-step guide to handling regulatory change:

26 **Set up a listening system:** Whether you are a large well-resourced company that has access to an internal team of government affairs professionals, an outsourced policy agency, or a regional trade association (e.g., Video Games Europe in the case of Gaming in the EU) – or you have to rely solely on your own alerts and research to monitor legislative proposals – it is vital to seek early notification of changes that impact your business. Top tip: Many law firms that specialise in gaming offer these types of services free of charge simply by signing up to receive regulatory updates. Trade association newsletters are another excellent way of staying up to date.

27 **(Optional) Early notice to business:** Whether you do this now or choose to wait depends on the size of the business you are supporting, the potential impact of the rule change, and your marketing team's preference. It is not a lawyer's job to create panic amongst their clients by being alarmist, so you may choose to hold off notifying them at the beginning stages of hearing about new rules or draft legislation process, but I have worked with individuals and teams who want to know of proposed changes as soon as I hear about them. From a practical perspective, sometimes providing a short note to inform key stakeholders that changes are being considered, you will continue to monitor, and if they would like to hear more, they can contact you, is sufficient.

28 **Proactive feedback:** In both the EU and UK, there are usually many opportunities throughout the legislative process to provide comments on draft versions of proposed

legislation and rule changes, from consultation documents to direct calls with those drafting the legislation seeking feedback. It is rare that an issue will impact only your business, so consider using trade associations to provide aggregated industry feedback.

Notify the business: Once proposals are close to being finalised is a good moment to prepare your business more fully. By this stage, you should understand the main changes, how they will impact your business, and what the timelines are. 29

Consider carefully what your business needs to know and keep the information relevant and targeted. If the team wants more information, they can ask. Often compliance with a new law is not straightforward and there will be areas where a certain amount of interpretation is required, so provide an FAQ where you can pre-empt the more routine questions the business might ask on topics like enforcement and deadlines. 30

III. Overview of the key laws

Much of this has already been covered in depth in previous chapters, including in chapter 4 EU Video Game Law, and indeed in the next chapter 37 on Advertisement Law in Gaming Marketing, so I will not go into too much detail here. However, it is beneficial to set out some of the key pieces of legislation and what they are trying to achieve so that you can work together with your marketing team to help them work with, rather than against, the law. 31

1. General Data Protection Regulation (GDPR)

The **GDPR**, which came into effect in 2018, is one of the most well-known and broad data privacy laws globally. Its impact on marketing is profound, particularly in areas such as targeted advertising and data collection. Under the GDPR, gaming companies must obtain explicit consent before collecting or processing personal data, ensuring that the consent is freely given, informed, and revocable. Additionally, the GDPR mandates data minimisation and secure deletion of data once it is no longer needed. 32

2. Digital Services Act (DSA) and Digital Markets Act (DMA)

The **DSA and DMA are EU regulations** designed to **create a safer and fairer digital environment**. The DSA focuses on protecting users' fundamental rights online, ensuring accountability for digital platforms, and preventing illegal and harmful activities such as disinformation. The DMA, on the other hand, aims to regulate large tech companies (known as 'gatekeepers') including some gaming platforms, to promote fair competition and prevent monopolistic practices. 33

3. Consumer protection directives

Consumer protection is a cornerstone of EU law, and the gaming industry is no exception. The Unfair Commercial Practices Directive (UCPD) prohibits misleading and aggressive marketing practices, including false claims about game features and hidden in-game costs. The Consumer Rights Directive enhances consumer protection by requiring clear information about terms of sale and transparent pricing practices for games and gaming products. 34

4. The EU AI Act

The **EU AI Act**, officially adopted in 2024 and gradually coming into force through 2030, is the world's first comprehensive legal framework for artificial intelligence – and 35 will not be the last. It aims to ensure that AI systems used in the EU are safe, transparent, and respect fundamental rights, while fostering innovation and trust in AI technologies.

5. Sustainability laws

36 EU sustainability laws aim to make eco-friendly products and services the norm by ensuring they are durable, repairable, recyclable, and energy efficient. The **Ecodesign for Sustainable Products Regulation (ESPR)** sets strict requirements to reduce environmental impact, promote circular economy practices, and eliminate harmful substances. Consumers benefit from lower costs, better product longevity, and more transparency, while businesses are encouraged to innovate and compete fairly in a greener market. These laws support the EU's climate goals and aim to create a sustainable, resource-efficient economy.

IV. Conclusion on legal frameworks

37 So, what are these laws and regulations really trying to achieve? At their core the focus is about protecting people. Under GDPR, Gaming companies should adequately guard customer data and not unreasonably share or profit from using an individual's personal data without their permission. Under the DSA and DMA companies must make sure the most vulnerable users of this evolving technology are adequately protected online from seeing and experiencing things that they should not and provide a level playing field for competition, especially where the larger tech companies are involved. The various consumer protection laws in place are aimed at making sure the players who spend money on your products are treated fairly before, during and after they choose your product. The AI Act is a pioneering piece of legislation seeking to ensure this incredibly powerful new technology is used in a way that harnesses its contribution to worldwide economic growth and outweighs the risks that come with seismic innovative change. The various sustainability laws are focused on creating less waste and pushing companies to be honest in how they communicate the environmental impact of their product.

38 Set out as above (acknowledging that the list is not exhaustive, the summary is a gross over-simplification of what amounts to thousands of pages of complex written legislation, and regulators do not always get it right) the legal environment does not in fact look too bad for marketers. It is worth remembering the same rules apply to your competitors, too, so even if something seems unfair, it is at least the same for everyone. Operating within the confines of the law does not mean you cannot make a bold claim about your product, the claim just needs to be true and capable of substantiation. Complying with GDPR does not mean you cannot market to a potential customer, but it means you need to do so with appropriate safeguards in place to ensure you are respecting their privacy.

39 As a lawyer you can bring value to your clients by helping them **focus on what they can do and say, rather than what they cannot**. The laws exist for a reason and that cohort of people who chose not to be marketed to were probably not your best customers. If you cannot make a claim because it is potentially misleading, that is not necessarily preventing sales, but it is almost certainly saving the company from reputational damage down the line, bad reviews from disappointed customers, and likely a good deal of costly returns and wasted resources.

D. Marketing tools and partnerships

In this next section, we delve into the **essential tools and partnerships** that marketers use to drive engagement and promote gaming products and services. We will focus on the legal considerations and the important role that supporting legal counsel plays in safeguarding the business while assisting marketers in achieving their objectives (see → Ch. 38). 40

I. Defining marketing tools

Of course, as a lawyer, the starting place is to provide a **definition of marketing tools**, acknowledging this is a tough exercise because the word tool can mean anything a marketer uses to promote products or services to consumers. For the purposes of this chapter, we'll narrow the scope to the most common tools used in marketing, set out below. 41

II. Above the line (ATL) marketing

ATL is a collective word for **traditional marketing tools** that include print and online adverts, television and radio commercials, and outdoor ads such as billboards or those you see plastered on the side of public transport (sometimes abbreviated as Out of Home or OOH marketing). This type of marketing is usually the most expensive, using mass media to reach a broad audience and create brand awareness. The marketing team will have booked media at great cost and often have strict deadlines for creative assets to be ready by, and when it goes up, it will be viewable to a wide audience. For this reason, marketers will often need the specific expertise of the legal team to make sure their ATL campaign is compliant because it can be heavily scrutinised by regulators and consumers alike. As a lawyer, supporting this form of marketing can be some of the most interesting and high stakes work you will do. I will admit to occasionally pausing live TV to check a disclaimer I have drafted on a commercial, or pointed out a little too excitedly to my unimpressed daughter that 'Daddy reviewed that' as a red bus trundles by with a picture of an Xbox on it. 42

Legal considerations: When reviewing ATL marketing, first assess the basic facts about the marketing asset itself and where it will be displayed. Consider the medium being used, the deadlines, and if there are claims being made are they honestly made and capable of being substantiated. Does the asset require additional superimposed text to provide the consumer further information? Ensure the product is portrayed accurately, reflecting its true capabilities and features. If it is showing in-game play footage, be clear, and ask if sequences have been shortened and what is being shown reflects the experience a user will have playing at home. Identify early any barriers to entry or clearances required to meet deadlines. For instance, in the UK, each TV advert must pass through the UK clearance body, Clearcast, which rigorously checks that all claims are substantiated. In France, certain performance claims must be objectively verified by an independent notary. Many countries across Europe have their own unique requirements. 43

It is crucial that the media buying team, creative team, and legal team are aligned on the strategy moving forward. Typically, ATL campaigns require bespoke legal input at several stages, so be prepared to be part of the process, making suggestions, changes, and reviewing multiple iterations of a campaign before it goes live. 44

III. Below the line (BTL) marketing

45 **BTL** is an example of marketing tools that include more targeted advertising practices, such as trade events, emails, telemarketing, or leaflet dropping in a particular geography. This type of marketing uses less traditional forms of advertising with the purpose of generating sales and tends to be more budget friendly. For this reason, it usually receives less publicity and scrutiny, and so while you will need to work with the marketing team to make sure that they are complying with applicable laws, the potential risks might be different.

46 **Legal considerations**: Because BTL is less about mass marketing and more about targeting individuals or groups, the potential reputational damage of getting something wrong may not be the main concern, but it might be that you need to ask more targeted questions about data protection measures your marketing team is taking. While compliance with the rules remains essential for BTL marketing, it might be easier to provide marketers with training, playbooks, templates and self-help guidance to help them stay compliant, rather than the continual and iterative involvement required for an ATL campaign.

47 Consider if you can set up a legal review process for your clients working on BTL: If they plan to send a marketing email out to customers, make sure the recipient is someone the business has the right consents to contact, the email template contains the correct company, contact, and opt-out information, and the business is aware of the need to communicate information in a truthful manner and honour any offers that are made. If they do all of this then you have helped them deal with the main legal risks up front and may only need to provide a final legal review prior to launch.

IV. Digital marketing

48 Less traditional, but increasingly vital marketing tools that drive awareness and engagement with products are **social media platforms**. In addition to platforms such as TikTok, Instagram, Facebook and X, are the platforms particularly popular with gamers like Twitch, Steam, Discord, and YouTube. These platforms allow companies to tailor messages to target groups and create stories that inspire and resonate with the huge audiences they attract.

49 **Legal considerations**: Familiarise yourself with these platforms and how they work. They will all have their own terms and if your clients are using them regularly, you should be familiar with the main areas of risks for your business when using them.

50 Digital marketing is an evolving space and with the DSA, DMA, and the newly proposed Digital Fairness Act (DFA), is being increasingly proactively regulated. In the last couple of years both Meta[8] and TikTok[9] have found themselves under the spotlight of the European Commission for their models or alleged lack of transparency when it comes to targeted ads. One of the reasons digital marketing is so popular with marketers is the same reason that it is carries so much potential legal risk: The content often does

---

[8] European Commission, "Commission Sends Preliminary Findings to Meta over Its 'Pay or Consent' Model for Breach of the Digital Markets Act," press release, July 1, 2024, https://digital-markets-act.ec.europa.eu/commission-sends-preliminary-findings-meta-over-its-pay-or-consent-model-breach-digital-markets-act-2024-07-01_en.

[9] European Commission, "Commission Preliminarily Finds TikTok's Ad Repository in Breach of the Digital Services Act", press release, May 15, 2025, https://digital-strategy.ec.europa.eu/en/news/commission-preliminarily-finds-tiktoks-ad-repository-breach-digital-services-act.

not look like marketing. Remembering these important points will help you and your clients avoid the most egregious of breaches:

- **The campaigns are ads:** Remember, while the content on social media is often deliberately built to appear organic, it is vital to disclose that it is marketing. The most commonly upheld complaints about social media marketing are about its lack of transparency.
- **The rules apply:** The influencer you are working with may be known for having a particular sense of humour, for targeting a certain audience demographic, or for hosting content in a particular style, but it's important that they still make sure what they say complies with the law when it comes to marketing your product. If they are promoting a particularly great feature of the game, that is fine, but they cannot mislead their followers by making unsubstantiated claims about performance metrics, or say things that are untrue about the product to drive engagement.

V. Online tools

Moving away from the tools marketers use to reach their audience and on to the tools they use to measure the efficacy of their campaigns, there are a wealth of data insight, performance analytic, and CRM tools available that marketers and agencies employ. Data-driven marketing has become an industry within the marketing industry, and ensuring your clients are working with the right tools can prevent a lot of problems down the road. 51

Legal considerations: As the lawyer, you will be working with clients who wish to use tools which maximise the information they can access to measure the success of their campaigns. Clients may want to sign up to third-party terms and conditions in return for access to specific data insights, they may want to allow a third-party tool to access your company data in order to provide analytical services. Apply a level of circumspection to the tool at the outset. Just because it lists established brands as users and has been available for a number of years does not mean it is compliant. 52

Conduct your own checks on the data provided, make sure you are not taking commercially sensitive or competitive data from other companies that exposes your clients or business to legal risk. Understand that often these tools require some level of interoperability with your own company's systems, and often they have 'click to accept' terms which are heavily weighted in their favour and provide the user with little or no protection should something go wrong. 53

VI. Promotions and competitions

Sweepstakes, contests, challenges, games of skill, these are tried-and-tested ways of **engaging potential customers** in proactive and fun ways. Often participants of promotions and competitions will be considered some of the most valuable potential customers and their interaction with your brand can generate a special relationship if handled correctly. However, there are a number of potential legal pitfalls because promotions and competitions involve working directly with consumers, (often requiring a consumer to take a certain action like reposting a message, completing a task, or answering a question), and they can be high risk and damage the brand if they go wrong. 54

Legal considerations: As a lawyer working for a gaming marketing company, you may find yourself spending a lot of time working on promotions and competitions. Be 55 clear what the clients are seeking to achieve. Are they running a game of skill or a game of chance? Is there a risk that what they are doing in certain jurisdictions might amount to gambling, and therefore be subject to even more regulation, or possibly even require a license? Some up front guidance and training is essential here, as is a set of template terms and conditions that you can repurpose for different types of promotions.

56 Consider, too, that even within the EU, each country will likely have different consumer protection requirements, for example, to make sure the terms are translated into the consumer's local language, so a one-size-fits-all approach may not work.

VII. Artificial intelligence

57 It is 2025, so no chapter would be complete without acknowledging the seismic **impact AI** is having across the world, including the gaming industry, and both the marketing and legal professions. Whole books, let alone chapters, have been and are being written on the opportunities, influence, transformation, skills, challenges, and potential pitfalls of AI. What is becoming very clear is that AI is viewed by businesses and governments across Europe and the rest of the world as key to economic growth, and leveraging AI will be essential to industries seeking to expand, including gaming.

58 **Legal considerations:** As a legal professional, whatever stage you are in your career, AI adoption will become (and arguably already is) an existential skill. As someone working in Microsoft's legal department at the cutting edge of the AI revolution, here are some suggestions for developing your own AI adoption strategy:

- **Experiment:** Like most new technology, taking the first step can be daunting. If you are new to using AI, start small. Despite the perception on social media and professional networking platforms, very few became AI experts overnight and everyone started somewhere. I was upfront with my team about using AI and the fact we were all part of experimenting with something new at the time added to the enjoyment of the activity.
- **Integrate:** As you gain comfort and confidence, begin to integrate it into areas of your work that make sense to you. Ask it to summarise an article or long email chain you have been added to. Then check the summary so you know nothing material to you was missed. The more you use it, you will see the value it can bring, and begin to rely and trust the output. You will also get better at working with it, improving the questions and prompts you use to drive results that suit you.
- **Internal guardrails:** A commonly heard phrases is 'responsible AI'. Whether you are a single practitioner advising a small studio or part of the legal team working for a AAA publisher or a multinational platform, a key role you can play is laying the groundwork for your clients to benefit from AI in a responsible, ethical and positive way. Many legal and compliance organisations have already set up teams which provide guidelines and policies dedicated to educating those in their business on the best ways to use AI, so look at upskilling in this area as a career development opportunity, too.
- **Continuous learning:** There are myriad ways of using AI; the above are some of the basics. If you take those initial steps, it will not be long before you should feel comfortable using AI to help plan your day, take notes in meetings, find that elusive document that you know is stored somewhere on your PC, or even provide tips to redraft a memo so that is more accessible for your audience.

These tools not only enhance the value of your output, but free up time so you can focus on the more strategic aspects of your role. 59

VIII. Defining marketing partnerships

As we did with Tools, we shall start with a definition. Marketing partnerships naturally involve some form of collaboration between brands, companies, individuals, other entertainment verticals, and even competitors, in order to co-create and execute campaigns, or form strategic alliances. Again, there are many types of partnerships, and the list below is not exhaustive, but focuses on the most common. 60

IX. Traditional brand partnerships

Traditional brand partnerships involve companies coming together to create a campaign with many benefits to the parties: 61

- **Broader audience and greater reach** – two companies operating in different spaces will likely have at least some variances in their customer base, allowing each to effectively target more customers.
- **Complementary products and services** – many partnerships involve two complementary brands of products coming together to provide a more complete consumer offering, a good example would be a television manufacturer and a console maker.
- **Positive and refreshing associations** – aligning your brand with another strong and trusted brand can bring about enormous associative and reputational benefits.
- **Cost savings** – consider the costs of a 30-second TV spot, a poster on a billboard, even an online banner during Black Friday. In most cases, the advertiser pays for the space, not the content, so an effective partnership can lead to a significant reduction to media spend and other shared campaign costs.

The above is not exhaustive and there are, of course, many other positives, with the hope being that the partnership leads to an increase in sales and revenue for your product. 62

Legal considerations: Alongside the benefits come potential pitfalls. As the legal advisor to a marketing client employing a brand partnership strategy, it is your role to both highlight, and where possible, protect your brand from these. The following are a list of things to look out for and possible actions to take to mitigate any problems down the line: 63

- **Ensure alignment and clarity on gives and gets** – although this might be seen as something the marketing team should take care of, apply extra caution when reviewing the respective obligations of each party. Consider issues like which party will book the media, is it well understood what will happen at the end of the partnership, and who will be responsible for handling any complaints if something goes wrong?
- **Regular check-ins** – the initial stages of a marketing partnership can (and should) be full of optimism and excitement, but it is necessary to think about what happens if things are going off track and need to be brought back on course. Insert regular mandatory check-ins into the agreement and have a dispute resolution process if something cannot be agreed. Try to avoid too many vague terms in the agreement like 'to be agreed at the time between the parties', especially over important issues.

As the legal support, your job is sometimes to be the calm voice in the room and the person willing to have the difficult conversations.

- **Reputational damage** – this can arise before, during or even after a campaign has launched. Make sure your clients have done their due diligence before choosing to work with a certain brand or individual and ask them to consider if it fits not just the product you are trying to promote, but the overall ethos of your company. If it is necessary and you have one, bring in your PR team to confirm the company values are aligned. Remember, by teaming up with another brand, or even an individual, you relinquish some control of your marketing. As a lawyer, you can help by drafting robust provisions in the contract to protect your business, but damage to brand reputation are hard to repair, let alone quantify financially. If brand partnerships are a regular occurrence in your business, it is worth designing a due diligence template to guide your clients safely through the partner selection process.

X. Celebrity endorsements and influencer collaborations

64 Partnering with a famous celebrity to boost the image of a brand is nothing new (think of Michael Jordan's incredibly successful relationship with Nike, that was nearly half a century ago, in 1984!). However, with the rapid growth of social media the individuals that brands are partnering with now are no longer traditional VIPs, but a whole variety of digital influencers. According to Influencer Market Hub: '*In 2024, influencer marketing propelled social media to become the world's largest advertising channel, surpassing paid search with a staggering $247.3B, reaching **$266.92B** by end of 2025 in global spend, cementing its role as the epicenter of consumer influence and engagement*'.[10]

65 **Legal considerations**: There is little doubt the positive outweighs the negative if the brand you are working with has the money, time and desire to build a trusted, long-term relationship with an individual. However, these types of brand endorsements can be even more risky than when companies pair up. With a company, there is a PR machine, codes of conduct, trainings, rules that govern how they behave, and often shareholders to answer to. Celebrities and influencers while often having a team of people behind them, are still human and prone to missteps (or worse), so expect the unexpected when contracting and working with individuals. Of course, in many cases you will be largely liaising with an agent or management company, but there can still be the odd ad-hoc request that can take you by surprise and challenge your standard compliance model. Consider carefully exclusivity provisions, you do not want the celebrity you are marketing with popping up all over the place as this can dilute the perceived authenticity of the campaign. Make sure you have an easy way to exit any relationship should the celebrity or influencer find themselves mired in controversy. While it is more one for the PR team, having a good crisis management process ready is advisable in the event that something goes seriously wrong.

XI. Partnering with 'the competition'

66 Some partnerships are obvious and complementary, for example, a car rental company partnering with a flight operator. There are other types of partnerships that are not so obvious, especially when two supposedly rival companies come together as happened

[10] Influencer Marketing Hub, *Influencer Marketing Benchmark Report 2025*, April 25, 2025, https://influencermarketinghub.com/influencer-marketing-benchmark-report/.

in 2019. As competitors in the so-called console wars for over two decades, Microsoft's partnership with Sony, for Sony to run their cloud services on Microsoft Azure, took the whole market by surprise. Since this announcement, the competition and collaboration between the two companies has continued showing that even rivals can benefit from working together.

Legal considerations: The above brand partnership considerations still apply, but here additional focus should also be on making sure up front that there are no legal issues with the formation of the partnership from a competition law perspective. Again, you may also want to bring in PR to guard against communications concerns, such as diluting your brand or perhaps even alienating your existing fanbase or customers. If you are granting access to buildings or systems to competitors, ensure you are able to do so in a way that prioritises security, both for your company and your customers. Brief the business team working on the partnership on the type of information they should be sharing and importantly, what is off limits and could place the company at risk of having its commercially sensitive data mistakenly shared. **67**

XII. Co-branding with other entertainment verticals

It is often noted that gaming occupies a unique place in the entertainment industry, a kind of Leonardo DaVinci straddling the creative and the scientific worlds, where imagination, art, coding, and program engineering all comes together in harmony. There has long been overlap between different entertainment verticals, from comic book adaptations which have been made into blockbuster films and hit video games, we're now seeing the trend going the other way with successful game franchises crossing over into TV, movies and music. In 2023, the year of Barbenheimer (Barbie and Oppenheimer) a small Italian plumber named Mario inserted himself between the two most hyped titles of the year, securing the number 2 spot in the highest grossing list of films from that year, generating 1.36 billion USD worldwide.[11] Also occupying the no. 2 position for 2025 at the time of writing is the Minecraft movie, grossing just under 1 billion USD so far.[12] On TV, from kids' cartoons like Pokémon and Angry Birds, to critical hits like the Last of Us and Fallout, **games have long been an inspiration for great TV**. **68**

Legal considerations: I work closely with colleagues that have provided legal support for the Minecraft movie and have colleagues supporting studios designing titles such as Fallout and Halo which have been made into successful TV series, so I know this is an area that could benefit from its own book, let alone a chapter of a book. Media, TV and film law is its own specialist subject covering music licensing, talent and image rights, international shipping and trade laws, studio and location agreements… the list of legal support goes on and on. If this type of entertainment vertical crossover is being considered by your clients, the best thing you can do is consult expert counsel as soon as possible, so your business is able to factor in the additional legal costs early. **69**

---

[11] Box Office Mojo, "2023 Worldwide Box Office", accessed July 2025, https://www.boxofficemojo.com/year/world/2023/.

[12] Box Office Mojo, "2025 Worldwide Box Office", accessed July 2025, https://www.boxofficemojo.com/year/world/2025/.

XIII. Agency relationships

70 An obvious but sometimes overlooked form of partnership is between the brand and its marketing agencies. Even companies that have their own marketing teams will use agencies to execute a campaign, and agencies come in all shapes and sizes.

71 **Legal considerations:** The role a lawyer can play here is generally more traditional, for example assisting negotiating the scope of work and services agreements needed to capture what is expected from each party and ensure the right protections are in place. At a minimum, an agency that is working with you should always be providing work that complies with applicable rules, codes, regulations, and laws. If that is in Europe, it could mean the GDPR applies to how they treat data, if it is in the UK, it could mean the CAP or BCAP code, in France, it could be the Toubon Law requiring advertising be translated into French. There is no point in clients paying for non-compliant work that the brand either cannot use, or worse, that could harm the brand's reputation, so a basic legal check should be a de-minimis threshold that you are all aligned upon before getting to the contractual stage.

72 Consider the type of agency you client wants to work with. A small boutique video production agency that has a specific USP is unlikely to be able to sign that unlimited indemnity clause, no matter how much they desire to work with your team. Getting ahead of issues like this and ensuring the business teams are aware of and have approval for the risks they may be taking can save difficult conversations in the future, which can delay a campaign or even a product launch.

73 When negotiating, consider other options: If the other side cannot provide the financial assurances you need, think about other ways to protect your clients. For example, having extra review steps clearly set out so that your marketers have the right to check the work at more stages and are comfortable that it represents the brand and what they want. **No deal is risk-free**, especially in gaming marketing. If you are a risk-averse company, make it clear to your marketers that this may impact the types of companies they can work with, and perhaps they can only use larger global agencies from a pre-approved list. Sometimes, these agencies will take on the risk for you, but your business should know that this will come at a financial cost. Ultimately, it is about finding what works for you and your team.

E. Final thoughts

74 I will end with a quote from the protagonist of one of 2023's most played games, *Spiderman*: 'With great power comes great responsibility'. At the outset of this chapter, I sought to establish the size and scale of the gaming industry, and what an opportunity that is for those marketing it. If it is the marketers who largely have the 'great power', it is fair to say their **legal teams share the 'great responsibility'**. I have offered suggestions to help build a strong and trusted relationship between the marketing team and their legal support. I have outlined the legal framework and key regulations impacting marketers in the gaming industry, and how lawyers can help clients view these regulations differently. Additionally, I have explored how marketers can compliantly leverage traditional marketing tools and partnerships, and some of the key considerations for the legal team supporting.

75 All that remains is to offer a final few words of advice that might help you to take that trusted advisor relationship to the next level and be considered a true business

partner to your marketing team, someone that really adds commercial value, as opposed to being seen as part of a box checking exercise, or worse...

I. 'The department of "No"'

As a legal professional, supporting an industry as creative and innovative as gaming presents exciting opportunities, and it is why many of us choose this area of law. **76**

Gaming is one of, if not the most inventive and creative of all the industries to be part of, and requires innovation in its marketing to tell that story. Bringing to life a unique campaign and being the lawyer who helped it happen can be as close as some of us get to feeling that creative buzz in our professional lives. But as the claims get bolder and the ideas more extreme, the legal risks get bigger. No legal or compliance team wants to be seen as *'the department of "No"'*, or, as I've unkindly heard (of course, not in reference to me), *'the place great ideas go to die'*,[13] which means that striking the right balance on acceptable risk tolerance is critical. **77**

As a lawyer supporting marketing teams, especially in gaming, it is inevitable that you will get some interesting (unworkable) and bold (crazy) ideas brought to you. How you handle these can be vital in how you build trust with your clients. A response that entirely shuts an idea down and offers no alternative solutions may be the quickest and most straightforward way to deal with another thing hitting your inbox. However, consider whether that means you are likely to be someone that the business will want to involve next time. **78**

II. The bigger picture

Legal professionals love to rely on the phrase 'the devil is in the detail', but sometimes it also helps to take a big step back. A good lawyer will know and be able to apply the law. **The best lawyers will be trusted advisors**, helping the company see around corners, and able to deliver the ultimate marketing goal. The ability to do this is a common trait shared amongst all the most successful business leaders I have worked with. They can assume the mindset and the roles of all the functions, from sales and marketing, legal, finance, supply chain and logistics to understand where the business is and how to get it to where it needs to be. I recall seeing an email from a junior marketer celebrating the number of impressions a campaign they had worked on had received. The campaign was promoting a product which was not hitting its targets and the first thing the senior leader of the team wrote back was to inquire into how many of those impressions had converted into sales? This might seem harsh, and there is nothing wrong with marketers using impressions, click-thrus, reach, tracking sentiment, or any other similar tools to measure the success of a marketing campaign, but the point the senior leader was making is that impressions are not what drive the bottom line and make or break the success of a product. As the lawyer, your role is also to help the clients see the bigger picture. Even when advising a marketing team, your focus should not just be on the marketing, but on the whole go-to-market strategy and how it ties in with the broader goals of the business you are supporting. **79**

---

[13] Anonymous marketer who shall remain unnamed.

III. Conclusion

80 It is not possible, nor is it the job of the in-house or outside legal counsel, to make sure a company never takes any risk, a world without risk would not be an exciting one for a marketer or the consumer, especially in an industry like gaming. It is the job of the lawyer to help the marketing and business teams understand the size of those risks, and how best to reduce them.

81 The stereotype would have you believe that the marketer and the lawyer are in diametrically opposite positions: The marketer wants to do something outlandish and daring that will gain the most attention; the lawyer wants to do something safe and reliable that will attract the least liability. The reality is neither of these positions is true. There are conservative marketers and there are risk-taking lawyers. The key to the relationship is understanding the expertise and the value that each party brings to the campaign. Navigating the complexities of gaming marketing law requires a collaborative approach between marketers and legal professionals. By understanding the legal framework, leveraging marketing tools and partnerships, and maintaining open communication, both teams can achieve their goals while mitigating risks. Ultimately, the key to success lies in finding a balance between creativity and compliance, ensuring that innovative campaigns can thrive within the boundaries of the law (see → Ch. 32–35 for more details).

§ 37
Advertisement Law in Games Marketing

Bibliography: Apostolopoulos 'Neuere Entwicklungen im europäischen Lauterkeitsrecht: Problematische Aspekte und Vorschläge', WRP 2004, 843; Boyd/Pyne/Kane, Video Game Law: Everything you Need to Know About Legal and Business Issues in the Game Industry, 2018; Ciancio, 'The Unfair Commercial Practices Directive and the UK Consumer Protection from Unfair Trading Regulations: A Possible Conceptual Convergence of General, Flexible European Standards and English Law Concepts Relevant to Fairness in the EU Context of Consumer Protection', SSRN 2008; Dauses/Sturm, 'Prawne podstawy ochrony konsumenta na wewnętrznym rynku Unii Europejskiej', Kwartalnik Prawa Prywatnego 1997, 34; Harte-Bavendamm/Henning-Bodewig (eds), Gesetz gegen den unlauteren Wettbewerb, Kommentar, München 2004; Howells/Micklitz/Wilhelmsson, European Fair Trading Law: The Unfair Commercial Practices Directive, Farnham 2006; Howells/Twigg-Flesner, 'What sort of Europe do consumers want?', Consumer Policy Review 2005, 168; Howells/Wilhelmsson, 'EC Consumer Law: has it come of age?', European Law Review 2003, 368; Lipson/Brain, Videogame Law: Cases, Statutes, Forms, Problems and Materials, 2nd edn, 2016; Maliszewska-Nienartowicz, 'Programy ochrony konsumenta w prawie Wspólnot Europejskich', Studia Europejskie 2003, 113; Mokrysz-Olszyńska, 'Swoboda promocji a ochrona przed nieuczciwymi praktykami handlowymi w projektach prawa Unii Europejskiej', Państwo i Prawo 2005, 54; Namysłowska, 'Projekt reformy prawa zwalczania nieuczciwej konkurencji państw członkowskich UE – zagadnienia materialnoprawne', Monitor Prawniczy 2004, 130; Nestoruk, 'Europejskie prawo o zwalczaniu nieuczciwej konkurencji? (Prezentacja projektu dyrektywy o nieuczciwych praktykach handlowych)', PIP-WI UJ 2005, 147; Scelsi/Dannenberg, Computer Games and Immersive Entertainment: Next Frontiers in Intellectual Property Law, 2nd edn, 2020; Sieradzka, Ustawa o przeciwdziałaniu nieuczciwym praktykom rynkowym. Komentarz, Warszawa 2008; Sikora, Marketing gier wideo, 2013; Stuyck/Terryn/Van Dyck, 'Confidence through fairness? The New Directive on unfair business-to-consumer commercial practices In the internal market?', CML Rev. 2006, 115; van Boom/Garde (eds), The European Unfair Commercial Practices Directive: Impact, Enforcement Strategies and National Legal Systems, Farnham 2014; Weatherill/Bernitz (eds), The Regulation of Unfair Commercial Practices under EC Directive 2005/29: New Rules and New Techniques, Oxford 2007; Wesley/Barczak, Innovation and Marketing in the Video Game Industry: Avoiding the Performance Trap, London 2010; Zackariasson/Dymek, Video Game Marketing: A Student Textbook, London 2016.

A. General remarks 1
B. Unfair commercial practices 5
C. DSA and dark patterns 17
D. Advertising ethics 21
E. Unfair competition 22
F. Practical examples 31
  I. Comarketing, partnership deals 32
  II. Trailers, TV, AV, radio, print commercials 36
  III. Dynamic web advertisements, mass mailing, push notifications, pop-ups 43
  IV. Competitions, lotteries, draws 44
  V. Price reductions, bundles, game or discount in exchange for data 48

A. General remarks

Just as any other medium or product, video games need advertising to present their appeal to an ever-widening audience. Depending on that audience and type of marketing communication, these may trigger many **legal regimes and issues**. 1

Regardless of the type of games developed, published or either way marketed, there are some general topics which need to be covered, i.e., **(i) unfair commercial practices (ii) dark patterns, (iii) advertising ethics and (iv) unfair competition**. 2

There are also considerations towards **marketing materials** which are commonly used and may require legal review from a specific angle, e.g., TV, audiovisual and radio 3 ad content restrictions in the AVMSD, which will be covered later in this chapter as a practical outline of popular marketing law queries.

4 **Advertising of video games** is merely an extension of games distribution and marketing, so all regimes discussed elsewhere will be impacted or be applicable, esp. privacy (→ Ch. 29), taxes (→ Ch. 11 and → Ch. 30), use of intellectual property (→ Ch. 12 till → Ch. 17), consumer law (esp. on warranty and conformity requirements for digital content, → Ch. 24 till → Ch. 28).

B. Unfair commercial practices

5 The regime of unfair commercial practices is harmonised throughout the EU with the Unfair Commercial Practices Directive or UCPD. There are two conditions to be met for any commercial practice to be established as unfair: it is contrary to the requirements of professional diligence and this distorts the consumer's economic behaviour.[1]

6 **Misleading commercial practices** take place if the practices contain false information and are therefore untruthful or in any way, including overall presentation, deceive or are likely to deceive the average consumer, even if the information is factually correct, in relation to one or more of the following elements, and in either case cause or is **likely to cause the consumer to take a transactional decision** that he would not have taken otherwise:

(a) the existence or nature of the product;
(b) the main characteristics of the product, such as its availability, benefits, risks, execution, composition, accessories, after-sale customer assistance and complaint handling, method and date of manufacture or provision, delivery, fitness for purpose, usage, quantity, specification, geographical or commercial origin or the results to be expected from its use, or the results and material features of tests or checks carried out on the product;
(c) the extent of the trader's commitments, the motives for the commercial practice and the nature of the sales process, any statement or symbol in relation to direct or indirect sponsorship or approval of the trader or the product;
(d) the price or the manner in which the price is calculated, or the existence of a specific price advantage;
(e) the need for a service, part, replacement or repair;
(f) the nature, attributes and rights of the trader or his agent, such as his identity and assets, his qualifications, status, approval, affiliation or connection and ownership of industrial, commercial or intellectual property rights or his awards and distinctions;
(g) the consumer's rights or the risks they may face.
Comment: This may encompass information on when the game will be available for purchase, what are the core elements of a game like mechanics, inclusion of specific assets (think roster of football teams, or celebrity actor's appearance), use of a game engine or compatibility on a specific device, where the game was made and whether it is still a work-in-progress (beta, alpha builds, Steam early access) or a fully-fledged QA-tested release (with an assumption that most game-crashing bugs would be fixed with a day-zero patch), but also any symbols or affiliation marks, the need for updates

[1] It materially distorts or is likely to materially distort the economic behaviour with regard to the product of the average consumer whom it reaches or to whom it is addressed, or of the average member of the group when a commercial practice is directed to a particular group of consumers.

and consumer rights (including the withdrawal right, or right to replacement or reimbursement).

If any of these are communicated explicitly to a consumer and found to be false, and that could influence whether said consumer would purchase a game or not – a risk of misleading practices may become real. 7

The UCPD regime comprises a **blacklist** of commercial practices which in all circumstances are regarded as unfair. The list is established by means of the annex to the UCPD and should apply in all Member States and may only be modified by revision of this Directive. 8

From a video games industry standpoint, nearly all misleading commercial practices may occur and may be categorised as: 9

(a) pertaining to code of conduct, trust marks or approvals,[2] e.g., PEGI;
(b) bait advertising,[3] bait and switch;[4]
(c) false limited time offers;[5]
(d) false assertions on legality;[6]
(e) presenting consumer laws as a feature;[7]
(f) advertorials[8] – without making that clear in the content or by images or sounds clearly identifiable by the consumer;
(g) vague threats on consumer's or his family's security;[9]
(h) copycatting and misleading origin;[10]
(i) pyramid schemes;[11]
(j) false going-out-of-business and moving sales;[12]
(k) claims on aiding odds with games of chance;
(l) snake oil claims;[13]

---

[2] Claiming to be a signatory to a code of conduct when the trader is not; displaying a trust mark, quality mark or equivalent without having obtained the necessary authorisation; Claiming that a code of conduct has an endorsement from a public or other body which it does not have; claiming that a trader (including their commercial practices) or a product has been approved, endorsed or authorised by a public or private body when they have not or making such a claim without complying with the terms of the approval, endorsement or authorisation.

[3] Making an invitation to purchase products at a specified price without disclosing the existence of any reasonable grounds the trader may have for believing that they will not be able to offer for supply, or to procure another trader to supply, those products or equivalent products at that price for a period that is, and in quantities that are reasonable, having regard to the product, the scale of advertising of the product and the price offered.

[4] Making an invitation to purchase products at a specified price and then: (a) refusing to show the advertised item to consumers; or (b) refusing to take orders for it or deliver it within a reasonable time; or (c) demonstrating a defective sample of it, with the intention of promoting a different product.

[5] Falsely stating that a product will only be available for a very limited time, or that it will only be available on particular terms for a very limited time, in order to elicit an immediate decision and deprive consumers of sufficient opportunity or time to make an informed choice.

[6] Stating or otherwise creating the impression that a product can legally be sold when it cannot.

[7] Presenting rights given to consumers in law as a distinctive feature of the trader's offer.

[8] Using editorial content in the media to promote a product where a trader has paid for the promotion.

[9] Making a materially inaccurate claim concerning the nature and extent of the risk to the personal security of the consumer or their family if the consumer does not purchase the product.

[10] Promoting a product similar to a product made by a particular manufacturer in such a manner as deliberately to mislead the consumer into believing that the product is made by that same manufacturer when it is not.

[11] Establishing, operating or promoting a pyramid promotional scheme where a consumer gives consideration for the opportunity to receive compensation that is derived primarily from the introduction of other consumers into the scheme rather than from the sale or consumption of products.

[12] Claiming that the trader is about to cease trading or move premises when they are not.

[13] Falsely claiming that a product is able to cure illnesses, dysfunction or malformations.

(m) inducing consumer to buy at conditions less favourable than normal market conditions when passing on materially inaccurate information on market conditions or on the possibility of finding the product;
(n) promising awards and not giving them out;[14]
(o) saying that something is free when it is not;[15]
(p) fake invoices and similar documents seeking payment;[16]
(q) falsely representing oneself as a consumer or not as a trader;[17]
(r) deceiving aftersales services[18] or false claims on the durability or reparability and any commercial communication of products with designed obsolescence;[19]
(s) fake consumer reviews, hiding advertising in search results and e-scalping (reselling tickets that the trader has acquired using automated means, i.e., bots);[20]
(t) greenwashing (generic environmental claims, sustainability labels not based on certification; claims of neutral, reduced or positive impact on the environment if based solely on offsetting greenhouse emissions).[21]

10 The **UCPD blacklist** also contains a list of aggressive commercial practices, which is a practice whereby harassment, coercion, including the use of physical force, or undue influence, it significantly impairs or is likely to significantly impair the average consumer's freedom of choice or conduct with regard to the product and thereby causes him or is likely to cause him to take a transactional decision that he would not have taken otherwise, esp.:

(a) creating the impression that the consumer cannot leave the premises until a contract is formed;
(b) commercial stalking of consumer's home[22] or unwanted distance solicitation;[23]
(c) direct exhortation to children to buy advertised products or persuade their parents or other adults to buy advertised products for them;
(d) explicitly threats on the trader's job or livelihood;[24]
(e) creating the false impression that the consumer has already won, will win, or will on doing a particular act win, a prize or other equivalent benefit, when in fact

[14] Claiming in a commercial practice to offer a competition or prize promotion without awarding the prizes described or a reasonable equivalent.

[15] Describing a product as 'gratis', 'free', 'without charge' or similar if the consumer has to pay anything other than the unavoidable cost of responding to the commercial practice and collecting or paying for delivery of the item.

[16] Including in marketing material an invoice or similar document seeking payment which gives the consumer the impression that they have already ordered the marketed product when they have not.

[17] Falsely claiming or creating the impression that the trader is not acting for purposes relating to his trade, business, craft or profession, or falsely representing oneself as a consumer.

[18] Undertaking to provide after-sales service to consumers with whom the trader has communicated prior to a transaction in a language which is not an official language of the Member State where the trader is located and then making such service available only in another language without clearly disclosing this to the consumer before the consumer is committed to the transaction; creating the false impression that after-sales service in relation to a product is available in a Member State other than the one in which the product is sold.

[19] On the basis Directive (EU) 2024/825 as is to be implemented by EU Member States by 27.3.2026.

[20] Amendments made by Directive (EU) 2019/2161.

[21] On the basis Directive (EU) 2024/825 as is to be implemented by EU Member States by 27.3.2026.

[22] Conducting personal visits to the consumer's home ignoring the consumer's request to leave or not to return except in circumstances and to the extent justified, under national law, to enforce a contractual obligation.

[23] Making persistent and unwanted solicitations by telephone, fax, e-mail or other remote media except in circumstances and to the extent justified under national law to enforce a contractual obligation.

[24] Explicitly informing a consumer that if he does not buy the product or service, the trader's job or livelihood will be in jeopardy.

either: there is no prize or other equivalent benefit, or taking any action in relation to claiming the prize or other equivalent benefit is subject to the consumer paying money or incurring a cost.

Misleading omissions are also subject to the UCPD regime – if, in its factual context, taking account of all its features and circumstances and the limitations of the communication medium, the practice omits **material** information that the average consumer needs, according to the context, to take an informed transactional decision and thereby causes or is likely to cause the average consumer to take a transactional decision that they would not have taken otherwise. 11

The following information may well be regarded as material: 12

(a) pertaining to the trader's consideration – the main characteristics of the product, to an extent appropriate to the medium and the product; (e.g., whether a game is playable or not on a given platform, whether accessories or internet connection are required); the geographical address and the identity of the trader; the arrangements for payment, delivery, performance and the complaint handling policy; for products and transactions involving a right of withdrawal or cancellation, the existence of such a right.
(b) and pertaining to the consumer's consideration: the price or the manner in which the price is calculated, any charges (e.g., whether the game is distributed as a subscription or one-time fee).

In late 2021 the European Commission issued a **Guidance on the interpretation and application of UCPD**[25] with a section addressing video games, mobile games and online games. Although the UCPD Guidance is a body of *soft-law* and does not create a direct ban or obligation, this may act as a standard measure by some local authorities. The UCPD Guidance points out: 13

a) in-game promotions and advertisements, which increase the risk of hidden marketing and could amount to a misleading practice under UCPD regardless if concerning in-game purchases or products available outside of the game;
b) exhorting to children – children are less likely to notice and understand the commercial intent of advertisements in games, as compared to more direct advertisements on television;[26]
c) prices of virtual items must be clearly and prominently displayed (also) in real currency;
d) **early access games**, meaning games that are still in development, traders should be clear about what the consumer can expect, for example in terms of the content of the early access game and its development prospects;
e) traders should make use of **platform-level parental controls;**
f) consumers must be clearly informed about the **arrangements for payment** before each purchase;

[25] Commission notice – Guidance on the interpretation and application of Directive 2005/29/EC of the European Parliament and of the Council concerning unfair business-to-consumer commercial practices in the internal market (text with EEA relevance) (2021/C 526/01).

[26] European Commission, London School of Economics and Political Science; Fundació per a la Universitàt Oberta de Catalunya; Block de ideas SL, Tech4i2, March 2016, 'Study on the impact of marketing through social media, online games and mobile applications on children's behaviour' (EACH/FWC/2013/85/08), https://commission.europa.eu/system/files/2018-03/online_marketing_children_final_report_en.pdf (last accessed: 12.1.2026), p. 94.

g) **embedded advertisements** could amount to an aggressive practice, like the timing of offers within the gameplay, pervasive nagging or the use of visual and acoustic effects to put undue pressure on the player (which impacts → Ch. 38 In-Game-Advertising).
h) the presence of paid random content (e.g., loot boxes, card packs, prize wheels) should be clearly disclosed to the consumer, including an explanation of the probabilities of receiving a random item (impacting → Ch. 27 Loot Boxes).
i) only games where in-app purchases are optional can be presented as 'free' without misleading consumers (which impacts → Ch. 26 Virtual Items).
j) For online services related to video games, the Geo-Blocking Regulation rules may apply, such as those prohibiting the discriminatory blocking of access to online interfaces and re-routing without the customer's prior consent (Art. 3) as well as discrimination for reasons related to payment (Art. 5).

14 Video game content with **gambling** elements, such as addictive interface designs involving slot machines, certain loot/mystery boxes or betting are also of concern. Some Member States consider such elements to fall under gambling legislation, which may entail additional requirements going beyond the UCPD, such as licencing authorisations or banning the use of gambling elements in games altogether (impacting → Ch. 27 Loot Boxes).

15 The UCPD provides the EU Member States with title to provide enforcement mechanisms against misleading commercial practices and corrective measures, if such practice is established to have taken place. This includes administrative actions (e.g., a consumer protection authority might instigate proceedings on infringing collective consumers interests – with administrative fine liability for a percentage of a company's yearly turnover); civil law claims from consumers to cease the practice, compensation and other redress claims, claims for publication of statements, price reduction and other warranty claims (some of these claims may also be brought before by local consumer ombudsman, organizations protecting consumer rights, etc.); and/or penal law. Statute of limitations would also differ, depending on the Member State's legal regimes.

16 In terms of recent developments on unfair commercial practices (as of writing this in early 2025) towards marketing games, esp. with virtual currencies, one has to consider the **CPC-N Key Principles** on In-game Virtual Currencies,[27] and the EU Commission's publication of a final report on the Digital fairness fitness check, which may in turn materialize in the form of the **Digital Fairness Act** (DFA),[28] which is a planned legislative proposal by the European Commission.

C. DSA and dark patterns

17 Unfair commercial practices may trigger **DSA liability** – exerting undue pressure on the consumer is seldom a good idea from a legal risk perspective.

18 The DSA mainly is addressed to intermediary service providers, like online platforms, marketplaces, distribution websites, which may face liability for designing, orga-

[27] The Consumer Protection Cooperation Network's Key Principles on In-game Virtual Currencies published 21 March 2025, Ref. Ares (2025)2303808 – 21.03.2025; https://commission.europa.eu/document/download/8af13e88-6540-436c-b137-9853e7fe866a_en?filename=Key+principles+on+in-game+virtual+currencies.pdf (last accessed: 12.1.2026).

[28] See more on the report and feedback provided: https://ec.europa.eu/info/law/better-regulation/have-your-say/initiatives/13413-Digital-fairness-fitness-check-on-EU-consumer-law_en (last accessed: 12.1.2026).

nizing or operate their online interfaces in a way that deceives or manipulates the recipients of their service or in a way that otherwise materially distorts or impairs the ability of the recipients of their service to make free and informed decisions (a.k.a. **dark patterns**).

Apart from the above, the DSA regulates advertising on online platforms by information requirements on the advertising character of the content, the ad provider, and the main parameters used to determine the recipient to whom the advertisement is presented and, where applicable, about how to change those parameters. **19**

The DSA also provides a ban of personalised advertising towards minors, mandating platforms to take 'appropriate and proportionate measures' to protect minors (e.g., designing their online interfaces with the highest level of privacy, safety and security by default; with standardisation to be promoted)[29] and explaining the conditions for the use of the service to minors.[30] **20**

D. Advertising ethics

There is a substantial number of EU jurisdictions that have active **advertisement ethics** self-regulatory bodies, usually in the form of societies and trade bodies.[31] These organisations set up ad ethics codes, complaint templates or forms, procedures and adjudicating bodies for ad recipients to file complaints against ads deemed unethical. Adjudicating bodies publish their findings, and name the advertiser and describe any unethical aspect of an ad. Representation before the proceedings is usually possible. These resolutions highlight consumer sensitivities in the advertising market, especially as regards health, ecology (e.g., green claims),[32] nutrition and geopolitics. Accordingly, the advertisement ethics self-regulatory bodies' resolutions are useful to anyone responsible for advertising approvals.[33] **21**

E. Unfair competition

Unfair competition is not fully harmonised in the EU, however, there is a body of harmonisation which would apply to advertising – on misleading advertising and on comparative advertising.[34] **22**

[29] Art. 28 DSA.

[30] Art. 14(3) DSA.

[31] These include Austria, Belgium, Bulgaria, the Czech Republic, Finland, Germany, Greece, Ireland, Italy, Portugal, Slovakia, the Netherlands, Poland and the UK (although not in the EU); see list: EASA – European Advertising Standards Alliance https://www.easa-alliance.org/type-of-member/self-regulatory-organisations/.

[32] For instance, green claims may already be seen as unethical by some of these organisations. Polish-language here: Resolution of the Polish Advertising Ethics Committee of 16.10.2024: https://radareklamy.pl/uchwala-nr-zo-112-24u-z-dnia-16-pazdziernika-2024-roku-zespolu-orzekajacego-w-sprawie-o-sygn-ker-090-24/, (last accessed: 12.01.2026); see also: Kubalski, Pianka, A Guide to Ethically Responsible Advertising 2025 – SSW; https://ssw.solutions/en/a-guide-to-ethically-responsible-advertising-2025/, last accessed 12.1.2026).

[33] See also: Maz Poynter, Sky News 4.03.2025: 'Incredibly disturbing': The misogynistic tropes being used in mobile games | UK News | Sky News (https://news.sky.com/story/help-the-girl-how-mobile-games-profit-from-misogynistic-tropes-13320935, last accessed: 12.1.2026).

[34] Directive 2006/114/EC of the European Parliament and of the Council of 12.12.2006 concerning misleading and comparative advertising (codified version) (text with EEA relevance).

23 **Misleading advertising** is any advertising which in any way, including its presentation:

(i) deceives or is likely to deceive the persons to whom it is addressed or whom it reaches and which, by reason of its deceptive nature,
(ii) is likely to affect their economic behaviour or which, for those reasons, injures or is likely to injure a competitor;

24 In the evaluation of misleading advertising, all its elements should be considered, in particular those concerning the information reviewed when assessing misleading practices as well as the risk assessment. i.e., if any of the information communicated explicitly to a consumer is found to be false, and that could influence whether said consumer would purchase a game or not – a risk of misleading advertising as an act of unfair competition may become real.

25 Legal protection against acts of unfair competition may be afforded to competitors of an advertiser (an entrepreneur whose interest has been threatened or impaired by an act of unfair competition), or an organisation protecting entrepreneurs' interests.

26 **Puffery** is generally admissible (e.g., cutting-edge graphics) and is understood as advertising or promotional material that makes broad exaggerated or boastful statements about a product or service that are subjective (or a matter of opinion), rather than objective (something that is measurable), and that which no reasonable person would presume to be literally true.

27 **Comparative advertising** is advertising which explicitly or by implication identifies a competitor or goods or services offered by a competitor.

28 There is a list of preconditions to be met in order for comparative advertising to be admissible in the EU and not trigger unfair competition claims (see in detail Art. 4 of the 2006/114/EC Directive). Of the conditions which need highlighting are that the comparative advertising compares goods or services **meeting the same needs** or intended for the same purpose; it **objectively compares** one or more material, relevant, verifiable and representative features of those goods and services, which may include price; it does not **discredit or denigrate** the trademarks, trade names, other distinguishing marks, goods, services, activities or circumstances of a competitor;

29 Local jurisdictions may also want to regulate other actions related to advertising as acts of unfair competition, such as:

(i) advertising in breach of the provisions of law (e.g., regulations on marketing of **sensitive products**, such as tobacco, alcohol, energy drinks, medicine, etc.), good practice or **human dignity** (e.g., mocking someone's sexuality, gender, religion, etc.);
(ii) **subliminal advertising** (use of images and sounds to influence consumers' responses without their being consciously aware of it which is banned, e.g., in the Czech Republic)[35] or advertising appealing to feelings of customers through **stimulating fear** (which generally translates to advertisements not making decisions on purchasing a products without being mentally coerced e.g. Poland, somewhat Finland)[36] taking advantage of superstitions or gullibility of children;

[35] Olga Sehnalová - Question for written answer E-003522-15 to the Commission Rule 130 (S&D) Ban on subliminal advertising, E-003522/2015, European Parliament published 03.03.2015 (https://www.europarl.europa.eu/doceo/document/E-8-2015-003522_EN.html, last accessed: 12.1.2026).

[36] Hilma-Karoliina Markkanen and Sakari Salonen – Capitalising on Fear Prohibited in Marketing, AIJA Newsstand 17.03.2020 – (https://www.lexology.com/library/detail.aspx?g=a85781bd-79bf-4b64-bf6a-05745aee4515, last accessed: 12.1.2026).

(iii) statements encouraging the acquiring of goods or services which have the appearance of neutral information – to mitigate this, it is always a good idea to ascertain that an advertisement recipient is informed of the advertising nature of the message, through, e.g., disclaimers displayed on advertisements that declare that the content is an ad, or even the shorter hash-tag **#ad**;
(iv) advertising which is a material interference with the sphere of privacy, and in particular by **pestering** in public places bothersome to customers, sending goods which have not been ordered at the cost of the customer or abuse of technical means of information transfer;
(v) **dumping**;[37]
(vi) offering a **free** bonus if the bonus is of more than a small value or may be a sample (e.g., demo).

Legal protection against acts of unfair competition may be afforded to competitors 30 of an advertiser (an entrepreneur whose interest has been threatened or impaired by an act of unfair competition), or an organisation protecting entrepreneurs' interests. This may also include administrative actions (e.g., a consumer protection authority might instigate proceedings on infringing collective consumers interests – with administrative fine liability for a percentage of company's yearly turnover).

F. Practical examples

The below serves as a list of common types of inquiries an video games company 31 counsel would have to tackle and a practical way to approach these.

I. Comarketing, partnership deals

Impacting → Ch. 36. Marketing Tools and Cooperations, a crucial element of co- 32 marketing and partnership deals would be provisions related to legal title to IP (e.g., cross-licensing or even joint KV development), IP indemnities, liability and final materials' (or merely key visuals) acceptance procedures.

If the intention is to partner up with a company that deals with **sensitive products** 33 (e.g., alcohol, beer, energy drinks, tobacco products, finance, medicine), it would be reasonable to put emphasis on indemnify for any non-compliance with all local laws which would apply to the partner.

Deals with celebrities and influencers would need to follow the requirements as set 34 out in → Ch. 39. Influencer Marketing.

A broad-strokes tax sanity check is advisable, so as to exclude the risk of any unre- 35 ported income (so either license remuneration balancing or settlement provisions).

II. Trailers, TV, AV, radio, print commercials

Wanting to avoid misleading consumers is a front-and-centre aim for counsel, with 36 the marketing teams sitting on another bench thinking about the various ways to build hype for a video game (as should be supported by legal). Special attention ought to be

[37] The sale of goods or services below the manufacturing or provision costs thereof, or resale thereof below the purchase costs in order to eliminate other entrepreneurs if the aim is to obstruct market access to other entrepreneurs.

given to any statements on gameplay mechanics, graphical fidelity, appearance of actors or engaging renown veteran developers, statements on when-it's-ready or otherwise attesting to a particular state of completion (as these by themselves may contradict the nature of updates and bug-fixes being made available well after initial release or live-service games in general).

37 To this aim, trailers often use disclaimers to showcase to consumers whether a particular sequence is gameplay (final, beta or alpha), in-engine, cut-scene or animation, assets or concept art. Sometimes PC-build configuration or platform used for capture is also disclosed.[38]

38 The content of trailers, TV, AV, radio commercials would generally fall under the AVMSD regime, as implemented in local Member States' laws. Generally, broadcasters and audiovisual media service providers are regulated, but if the ad content would be found non-compliant, this may mean halting the broadcast or sharing of the marketing materials or risk of recourse in cases of claims or fines. This may mean that one has to be on the lookout for:

(a) any portrayal of use sensitive goods, such as alcohol, tobacco, energy drinks, etc.;
(b) surreptitious audiovisual commercial communication;[39]
(c) meeting requirements for sponsorship,[40] product placement[41] disclosures;
(d) any appearance of children or addressing marketing communication to children;[42]
(e) any communication violating human dignity; containing discriminatory content on the basis of race, gender, nationality, ethnic origin, religion or worldview, disability, age or sexual orientation; harming religious or political beliefs; threatening the physical, mental or moral development of minors; encourage behaviours that threaten health, safety or environmental protection.

39 Use of **live animals** in production may trigger local legal requirements on special care towards the treatment of animals on set, contracting professional caretakers, etc.

40 **Radio ads** should be reviewed diligently when making use of any traffic sounds, which may be mistaken by the ad recipient (e.g., automobile driver) to take place in the real world as the ad is aired.

41 Certain type of print ads in a situation of a partnership with a car manufacturer (e.g., OOH, newspaper or magazine ads) might trigger requirements laid on car advertising, e.g., disclaimers on emissions, efficiency, recycling, etc.

42 Generally, you would want to avoid any unwanted brands or **third-party IP**, e.g. considering acquiring synchronisation license for use of likeness, musical works, perfor-

---

[38] GTA VI second trailer is highlighted as captured with use of a base-model PS5; https://www.ign.com/articles/after-some-said-gta-6-trailer-2-looked-too-good-to-have-been-captured-on-a-base-ps5-rockstar-confirms-it-really-was-and-theres-even-gameplay-in-there.

[39] The representation in words or pictures of goods, services, the name, the trademark or the activities of a producer of goods or a provider of services in programmes when such representation is intended by the media service provider to serve as advertising and might mislead the public as to its nature.

[40] Any contribution made by public or private undertakings or natural persons not engaged in providing audiovisual media services or in the production of audiovisual works, to the financing of audiovisual media services or programmes with a view to promoting their name, trademark, image, activities or products.

[41] Audiovisual commercial communication consisting of the inclusion of or reference to a product, a service or the trademark thereof so that it is featured within a programme, in return for payment or for similar consideration.

[42] Directly calling on minors to purchase products or services; encouraging minors to put pressure on their parents or other people to buy the advertised products or services; exploiting the trust minors have in their parents, teachers and other people (think: Werther's Original grandpa-grandson ads); unjustifiably showing minors in dangerous situations.

mance rights, producer's rights, depending on the set of circumstances, acquiring IP to content made to order, clearing the ads for any third-party brands (esp. when using cityscape footage not only logotypes on buildings, but also the facades of buildings may have been applied for trademark protection).

III. Dynamic web advertisements, mass mailing, push notifications, pop-ups

Dynamic ads, which personalise ad content based on user data and real-time factors (through use of, e.g., cookies, third party cookies),[43] mass mailing, sending push notifications are generally legal as long as they respect user privacy (impacted by → Ch. 29), and comply with relevant advertising regulations, e.g., those implementing (i) the EC Directive – providing a ban on unsolicited commercial information (a.k.a. SPAM) and (ii) ePrivacy Directive and the EECCD – requiring consent for use of telecommunication terminal devices for marketing purposes. 43

IV. Competitions, lotteries, draws

Competitions drive consumer engagement. They usually have an organiser hand out a prize for performing specific tasks (listing these conditions in brief terms and conditions is standard practice). Depending on the local civil law regime, this may be formally regarded as a unilateral legal act or a bilateral agreement with a consumer. The distinction may be of particular import, as this would influence applicability of consumer laws, unfair commercial terms regulations.[44] 44

Once Ts&Cs of the competition are drafted, it would be important to align any marketing materials around the competition to avoid any inconsistencies, which might amount to esp. misleading practices, misleading advertising. 45

Scrutiny must be followed with any competition based around the idea of competitors adding friends to a community (also: social media platform group, subscriber or follower base), as this may edge on being considered a pyramid scheme under the UCPD. 46

Whenever winning of a prize would be contingent on an element of chance (draw of any kind), local rules on gambling would apply, e.g., restrictions on marketing, the need for authorisations, licenses, Ts&Cs content requirements. This may require entering into pre-launch administrative procedures with local public authorities, so additional time for securing these needs to be considered. 47

V. Price reductions, bundles, game or discount in exchange for data

Any communication on price reductions and bundles should follow the requirements set out in the Omnibus Directive, → Ch. 24 till Ch. 28). In situations where the consumer does not pay a price but provides personal data as consideration, the imple- 48

[43] A third-party cookie is a cookie that's placed on a user's device – computer, cellphone or tablet – by a website from a domain other than the one the user is visiting. Third-party cookies are also known as trackers or cross-site cookies.

[44] Council Directive 93/13/EEC of 5.4.1993 on unfair terms in consumer contracts. OJ L 95, 21.4.1993, 29–34.

menting local legislation stemming from the DCD would apply, as well as the GDPR, naturally (→ Ch. 29).

§ 38
In-Game Advertising

Bibliography: Arcelin, 'Les méandres de la publicité cachée sur Internet', Revue Lamy Droit de l'Immatériel, No. 90, février 2014, 34; Benghozi/Chantepie, Jeux vidéo: l'industrie culturelle du XXIe siècle?, Ministère de la culture – DEPS, 2017; Boyraz, 'It is not just a click: protection of in-game behaviour data as biometric data under the GDPR', Interactive Entertainment Law Review, 2024, Vol. 7, No. 1, 12; Chernikova/Branco, 'Putting Brands into Play: How Player Experiences Influence the Effectiveness of In-Game Advertising', International Journal of Advertising, Vol. 32, Issue 1, 2013, 17; Chernikova/Branco, 'Product Placement in Computer/video Games: An Analysis of the Impact on Customers Purchasing Decision', Innovative Marketing, Vol. 15, Issue 3, 2019, 2; Decaudin/Digout, E-publicité – les fondamentaux, Dunod, Paris 2011, p. 105; Declerck/Lievens/Verdoodt, '"A Special Offer for You!" – Personalisation of In-Game Commercial Practices at the Crossroads of Data Protection and Consumer Protection Regulation', European Journal of Consumer Law, 2024/1, 57; Hofman-Kohlmeyer, 'Method of Product Placement in Computer Games – Qualitative Research Amongst Polish Players', Journal of Marketing and Consumer Behaviour in Emerging Markets, 2024(1), 21; Huang/Yang, 'The Effectiveness of In-Game Advertising: The Impacts of Ad Type and Game/Ad Relevance', International Journal of Electronic Business Management, Vol. 10, No. 1, 2012, 61; Jahan, 'Quelle réglementation pour la publicité intégrée aux jeux video (in-game advertising)', Revue Lamy Droit de l'Immatériel, No. 53, octobre 2009, 52; Kröger et al., 'Surveilling the Gamers: Privacy Impacts of the Video Game Industry', Entertainment Computing, Vol. 44, January 2023, 100537; Küster Boluda/Pardo/Suemanotham, 'Product Placement in Video Games as a Marketing Strategy: An Attempt to Analysis in Disney Company', Advances in Advertising Research, Vol. 2, 2011, 12; Laperdrix et al., 'The Price to Play: a Privacy Analysis of Free and Paid Games in the Android Ecosystem', ACM Web Conference 2022, April 2022, Lyon, France; Leng, 'A Study on the Effectiveness of In-Game Advertisements', International Journal of Sport Management, Recreation & Tourism, Vol. 8, 2011, 65; Lobov, 'Advertising and VR: Regulatory Challenges Ahead', Interactive Entertainment Law Review, 2018, Vol. 1, No. 1, 52; Martí-Parreño/Bermejo-Berros/Aldá-Manzano, 'Product Placement in Video Games: The Effect of Brand Familiarity and Repetition on Consumers' Memory', Journal of Interactive Marketing, No. 38, 2017, 56; Nelson, 'Recall of Brand Placements in Computer/Video Games', Journal of Advertising Research, Vol. 42, No. 2, March/April 2002, 80; Newman/Jerome/Hazard, 'Press Start to Track?: Privacy and the new questions posed by modern videogame technology', American Intellectual Property Law Association (AIPLA) Quarterly Journal, 21.8.2014; Potter/Westberry/Palmer, 'An Overview of Video Game Biometrics Collection and Considerations for Cyberbiosecurity', Proceedings of the 20th International Conference on Cyber Warfare and Security, ICCWS 2025; Przybysz, 'Data protection in the video game sector', in Baujard/Bosmans/Dimita, Legal challenges and market dynamics in the video game sector, European Audiovisual Observatory, 2024, III, 2; Renault, 'Quand Gillette Venus célèbre toutes les beautés dans *Animal Crossing* – Décryptage d'une opération d'*in-game advertising*', Annales des Mines – Gérer & Comprendre, 2022/1, No. 147, 49; Saunders Lipson/Brain, Videogame Law – Cases, Statutes, Forms, Problems & Materials, 2nd edn, Carolina Academic Press, Durham, North Carolina 2016; Shalabi, 'Guide to Video Game Advertising: Trends, Tactics, and Opportunities for Marketers', EMarketer, 26.7.2024; Stamatoudi, Copyright and Multimedia Products – A comparative Analysis, Cambridge University Press, New York 2002; Terlutter/Capella, 'The Gamification of Advertising: Analysis and Research Directions of In-Game Advertising, Advergames, and Advertising in Social Network Games', Journal of Advertising, Vol. 42, No. 2/3, April-September 2013, 95; Williamson Smith/Sun/Mackie, 'In-Game Advertising Influential Factors: a Systematic Literature Review and meta-analysis', The Computer Games Journal, Vol. 3, Issue 2, November 2014, 102.

A. Introduction 1

B. Requirements relating to the identification and content of in-game advertisements 5
- I. Identifying in-game advertisements 6
  1. Professional Standards relating to the identification of in-game ads .. 7
  2. European and national legal provisions relating to the identification of in-game ads 12
- II. Other standards for in-game ads 13
  1. Identifying the advertiser behind in-game ads 14
  2. Regulating the content of in-game ads 15
  3. Regulating the content of in-game ads aimed at minors 17

C. Requirements for the processing of players' personal data in the case of targeted advertisements integrated in video games 18

I. Ensuring players' control over their personal data 19
1. The prohibition of deceptive interfaces and dark patterns 20
2. Players' consent to receive targeted advertising 23
3. Other obligations of the data controller 25
II. The challenges of targeted advertising in video games 26
1. Examples of issues raised by in-game advertising 27
2. Litigation concerning advertising personal data processing in video games 30

A. Introduction

1 Video games are complex creative and technological work positioning them at the crossroads of all types of creations. Their ability to blend creative content and interactivity explains why they lend themselves to innovative practices in many respects, engaging players, developers, publishers, and even third-party actors. While user-generated content in video games naturally comes to mind, other in-game innovations deserve attention, which transform old business practices into innovative and immersive experiences that raise new legal challenges. This is particularly true for advertisements and product placements where video games serve as the medium, and which can take several forms.[1] Some can be used in a game-related way, such as pre-roll videos which activate when the game starts, or reward videos, which play when the player reaches a milestone in the game. The same applies to banners and pop-ups that appear at strategic moments in the gameplay or remain contextually integrated into the game without interrupting it. This is particularly suitable for casual and hyper-casual games mostly developed for mobile devices. Thus, the most **innovative and effective** form of advertising is in-game advertising, which consists of including a product or a remark directly in the game design and/or gameplay,[2] sometimes even becoming an element of the interactive storyline.[3] The diversity of forms stems from the variety of games inspired by offline advertising practices. For example, a car racing game may display logos and banners on vehicles or alongside the tracks; a first-person shooter set in an urban environment may feature authentic advertising posters, like those seen in city centres; similarly, a brand's sound jingle can be used as a recurring element, punctuating the player's actions.

2 In-game advertising is of great interest to advertisers from this perspective. Unlike audiovisual works, which consist of a sequence of animated images whose order cannot be changed, video games are based on the interactive handling by the player of a series of content that can be freely accessed on **multiple occasions**.[4] Also, whereas an advertisement or product placement in a film could only appear occasionally, limiting its ability to capture viewers' attention, they can be seen an incalculable number of times in a video game, and even dynamically placed, depending on whether the player takes more or less time to progress through the scenario.[5] This is why this segment of advertising was very quickly invested in and has developed considerably, offering a vast variety of mediums and formats.[6] Beyond its more 'playful' dimension, this form of advertising has the advantage of not interrupting the game's flow, nor polluting its use.[7]

[1] Benghozi/Chantepie, p. 145.
[2] Terlutter/Capella, p. 95.
[3] Küster Boluda/Pardo/Suemanotham, p. 12.
[4] Stamatoudi, p. 24.
[5] Saunders Lipson/Brain, p. 672; Martí-Parreño/Bermejo-Berros/Aldá-Manzano, p. 56.
[6] Nelson, p. 80.
[7] Benghozi/Chantepie, p. 145.

The most integrated form of its advertising blends into the **game design** and the game's storyline, to the point that players may not be aware of its presence.[8] Furthermore, it can contribute to the realism of the game. As a result, players would be more receptive to it, which is why the process is widely favoured.[9] It also allows advertisers to leverage the game's interactivity to introduce new forms of engagement with their products and services, for example by integrating hyperlinks referring directly to the advertiser's site or automatically updating messages based on player data analysis. The effectiveness of integrated ads also depends on the attention the player gives to them,[10] which itself depends on their context, difficulty level of the game and external factors such as the player's age, maturity, and habits.[11] Behavioural data analysis can be highly beneficial in optimising in-game advertising, for example by personalising ads based on these factors (e.g., adapting them according to age, in-game preferences, etc.).[12]

There are **many examples** of successful ad placements in video games. One example is the 2020 campaign by Gillette Venus in the game *Animal Crossing: New Horizons*, which introduced a collection of clothing designed to reflect diverse skin tones and body types.[13] Some games have even served as platforms for multiple advertisers, such as the game *Neopets*.[14] Similarly, The Sims has featured a range of virtual objects branded with real-life companies, including *Ikea* furniture, *H&M* clothing, and even branded stores.[15] In 2024, Candy Crush has developed an in-game campaign in collaboration with *KitKat* on mobile platforms, integrating the physical product with the virtual environment by associating chocolate bar packaging with in-game benefits. Such campaigns are effective in simultaneously enhancing product sales and **boosting in-game engagement**. The revenues generated by this form of advertising are substantial and is estimated at 7.77 billion USD in the United States alone in 2024. As a result, mobile game advertising, which is particularly well-suited to this approach, represents more than 90 % of total video game ad revenue.[16] 3

While research on in-game advertising is already well documented,[17] its development naturally raises **legal questions**.[18] The playful nature of the advertising format does not exempt it from regulations designed to protect players as consumers. These come from a variety of legal, regulatory, and professional sources, at the international, European, and national levels. Firstly, consumer protection laws govern advertising messages and product placements, aiming to shield consumers from deceptive and misleading practices while ensuring advertisements are fair and identifiable. Then we find the regulatory mechanisms applicable to online platforms, which can specifically concern massively multiplayer online games. At last, these regulatory frameworks extend to personal data, which become relevant when integrated advertisements are based on the processing of such data for personalised marketing. These regulations have been designed for **real-world advertising** and must therefore be adapted to advertisements integrated into a virtual reality universe, such as video games. In the first section, we will see what the requirements are relating to the identification and content of in-game advertisements 4

---

8 Chernikova/Branco, 2019, p. 2.
9 Decaudin/Digout, p. 105.
10 Huang/Yang, p. 61; Leng, p. 65.
11 Chernikova/Branco, 2013, p. 17.
12 Terlutter/Capella, p. 101.
13 Renault, p. 49.
14 Saunders Lipson/Brain, p. 672.
15 Hofman-Kohlmeyer, p. 21.
16 Shalabi.
17 Williamson Smith/Sun/Mackie, p. 102.
18 Jahan, p. 52; Lobov, p. 52; Declerck/Lievens/Verdoodt, p. 57; Boyraz, p. 12.

that are intended to protect players as consumers (B), and then how the processing of personal data necessary for targeted advertising, which protects the privacy of players, should be carried out (C).

B. Requirements relating to the identification and content of in-game advertisements

5 The video game industry self-regulates its advertising by adhering to laws and regional guidelines. For instance, the Pan-European Game Information (PEGI) Code of Conduct requires members to include specific disclosures to protect players. Art. 11 provides developers with **guidelines** on managing game advertisements and specifically how to protect minors from seeing inappropriate advertising content. In addition, advertisements integrated into video games primarily fall under **consumer law**, in its provisions specific to advertising messages. The **DSA** (Regulation 2022/2065) and other **European regulations** may also be applicable in this context. These legal frameworks establish various requirements that advertisements must comply with. First, the advertisement must be clearly **identifiable** by the consumer, to prevent any risk of confusion with the creative content itself, which naturally raises questions in the case of in-game advertising (I). It must also meet other standards, in terms of **loyalty and honesty**, which may still be of professional or legal origin. Similarly, certain advertisements may be **prohibited** based on the products or services they promote (II).

I. Identifying in-game advertisements

6 The requirement to **identify advertising** is the subject of provisions that are both general, related to the objective of consumer protection, and specific for online communication services. Video games, whether they can be played in 'single player' or multiplayer mode, online or off-line, are therefore **no exception** to this obligation. As such, some game distribution services may be considered as platforms within the meaning of the DSA (Regulation 2022/2065), as may certain massively multiplayer online games in which users are allowed to publish content of any kind. This rule has been the subject of professional standards (1) which usefully complement positive law (2).

1. Professional Standards relating to the identification of in-game ads

7 The first is the *Advertising and Marketing Communications Code* of the International Chamber of Commerce (ICC), the 11th edition of which was published in 2024. Art. 7 states that:

> **Marketing communications, regardless of format or medium, should be easily identifiable, allowing consumers to clearly distinguish between commercial and non-commercial content. Identification disclosures should be prominent, clear, easily legible and appear in close proximity to the commercial message where they are unlikely to be overlooked by consumers.**

8 This obligation is reflected in national professional standards, such as in France, with a recommendation from the *Autorité de Régulation professionnelle de la Publicité* (ARPP),[19] and in the United Kingdom, where the *Advertising Standards Authority* (ASA) and the *Committee of Advertising Practices* (CAP) have published similar rules in the

[19] 'Identification de la publicité et des communications commerciales – Identification de l'annonceur', ARPP, July 2013.

Code of Non-broadcast Advertising and Direct & Promotional Marketing from 2010. It aims at preventing any practice that might take advantage of public confusion by **hiding or omitting** the advertising nature of a message. Failure to comply with this obligation may be detrimental to the brand image of advertisers, as consumers may no longer be able to distinguish between what is pure promotion of products or services and information on other subjects[20] or the gameplay itself.

The difficulty posed by in-game advertising lies in this **possible confusion** between advertisements and other video game content. The interest of this technique comes from its ability to be integrated into the narrative of the video game,[21] which guarantees a certain fluidity of use to the player who is not 'polluted' with ads as is the case in other media. This has prompted **clearer identification** requirements in video games. For example, Chapter C of the ICC Code relates to *Data-driven Marketing, Direct Marketing, and Digital Marketing Communications*; Art. C2 states that 'Marketing communications should be properly identified, subject descriptors should be accurate and the commercial nature of communications, as well as the identity of the marketer, should be transparent to consumers in accordance with Art. 7–8 of the General Provision'. The obligation is also taken up by the above-mentioned national authorities, whether in the United Kingdom or in France,[22] where the ARPP has specified that: 9

If the message appears in a place that advertising would normally appear in real life, its commercial nature is considered obvious. Therefore, there is no need for further identification elements. If the commercial nature is not obvious, it is recommended to add an explicit indication of the commercial nature of the message.

In addition, 'The advertising inserted in the video games should in no case hinder their **playability**, in particular by hindering access to the game's functionalities or controls, or by reducing the visibility of the elements that make it up'. 10

Therefore, it is important for game publishers and advertisers to place ads in spaces like those found in the 'physical' world. Various possibilities exist in games with a realistic game design: billboards, audiovisual or sound messages, logos on vehicles, clothing, virtual objects replicating authentic products. **The context** here would be sufficient for players to be fully aware of the advertising content. The few studies carried out in the field attest to this good understanding, despite the entertainment aspect of the medium. However, not all video games lend themselves to such implementation. This is particularly the case for those whose game design does not include any reference to places, behaviours or habits that can be associated with an advertising message, such as fantasy, medieval or science fiction games. And the requirement is not relevant with games whose gameplay and game design do not allow a **spontaneous understanding** of the advertising message. All kinds of concealment would then be possible. For instance, utilising hyperlinks within player actions could suffice. However, advertisements should be distinctly separated from gameplay and presented in conventional formats such as inserts, videos, banners, and pop-ups, inducing friction and potential disruption to the player's experience. This practice is quite common in hyper-casual games. These forms are also regulated: for instance, when advertising appears as text, the ARPP recommendation for France invites one to use a **different graphic design** from those of non-advertising messages generated by software installed on the user's device. 11

---

[20] Arcelin, p. 34.

[21] Lobov, p. 55.

[22] 'Communication publicitaire digitale', ARPP, December 2010.

2. European and national legal provisions relating to the identification of in-game ads

12 While sectorial regulators can express negative opinions about non-compliance with requirement, it is also sanctioned by provisions of positive law. Some advertising campaign may fall under the **prohibition of misleading commercial practices** within the meaning of Art. 3 of the Misleading and Comparative Advertising Directive (Directive 2006/114/EC) on misleading and comparative advertising. This article defines misleading advertisements as those that are likely to mislead consumers and affect their spending behaviour. Similarly, the Unfair Commercial Practices Directive (Directive 2005/29/EC) classifies as such practices which consist in concealing the commercial intent behind a message, unless this intent appears obvious in the light of the context (Art. 7 (2)). This also applies to the practice of promoting a product within editorial content without clearly indicating that it is promotional (Annex 1, (11)). The European Commission's guidelines have highlighted the application of provisions regarding integrated advertising on social networks, which must comply with the requirement for immediate identification.[23] Similarly, Art. 6 of the eCommerce Directive (Directive 2000/31/EC) provides that commercial communications must be clearly identifiable within information society services. This obligation has since been clarified by Art. 26 of the DSA (Regulation 2022/2065) for **providers of online platforms**, which in turn refers to professional standards and codes of conduct to specify how ads should be marked and identified in online platforms that have yet to be published. This reference concerns both marking devices (Art. 44) and the content of advertisements (Art. 46). Finally, non-compliance with this requirement may result in criminal or civil penalties under legislation.[24]

II. Other standards for in-game ads

13 The identification of the advertising message in a game environment is merely the prerequisite for implementing **other obligations** aimed at ensuring its honesty and transparency. Other obligations relating to the content of the ads should logically apply to in-game ads. Some of these are general and aim to identify the advertiser behind the advertisement (1) and regulate its content (2). Others are more specific, aiming to regulate ads targeting certain audiences, such as children and adolescents (3).

1. Identifying the advertiser behind in-game ads

14 **Advertiser identification** is another general requirement found in various sources, some of which are limited to online gaming. This is the case with Art. 39 of the DSA (Regulation 2022/2065), which requires very large online platforms to make available to their users the **registers of advertisements** displayed within their services and content. These documents must be easily accessible via a user-friendly interface or a search engine; they must contain a certain amount of information, such as the identity of the advertiser and the person on whose behalf the advertisement is displayed or who paid for

---

[23] Guidance on the interpretation and application of Directive 2005/29/EC of the European Parliament and of the Council concerning unfair business-to-consumer commercial practices in the internal market, OJ,2021 C 526, 01, § 4.2.5.

[24] In France: Art. L 121-3, L 121-4, L 122-8 et L 132-26 du Code de la consommation; in the United Kingdom: Section 6 and § 11 of Schedule 1 of the *Consumer Protection from Unfair Trading Regulations* 2008, reproduced in Section 227 and § 12 of Schedule 20 of the *Digital Markets, Competition and Consumers Act* 2024.

its publication, the content of the advertisement (product, brand or service concerned), the period of distribution, the types of targeted recipients and the parameters used for this purpose, as well as the number of recipients actually reached. That requirement is reinforced by Art. 26 of the DSA (Regulation 2022/2065), which reiterates the same information for each specific advertisement presented to individual recipient. Although no video games are currently classified as very large online platforms, these specific obligations clearly indicate the legislator's intent to better protect consumers against **misleading and hidden advertising**. It is anticipated that such requirements will become the standard for all online services in the future. Beyond advertising transparency, the goal here is to detect more quickly any illegal or misleading practices, which could manipulate audiences. The European Commission recently noted the failure of the social network TikTok to comply with this obligation, as part of formal proceedings initiated in 2024.[25] Beyond the platforms, the obligation to identify advertisers naturally appears in professional standards adopted both at the international level, in the ICC Code (Art. 8 and C2), and at the national level, the ARPP in France[26] and the ASA in the United Kingdom[27] having included it into their own guidelines.

2. Regulating the content of in-game ads

In-game ads must comply with several general requirements, set out in professional standards and sometimes in legal provisions. While not an exhaustive list, the following rules are noteworthy. The ICC Code (Artt. 3, 4 and 5) relates to the requirements of **decency, honesty, and truthfulness** of advertising messages. An advertisement must not violate human dignity, serve as a vehicle for hate speech, or challenge the moral standards of the countries where it is displayed. Moreover, it cannot take advantage of consumers inexperience, nor seek to manipulate them, including through subliminal techniques, nor should it be disseminated in a repetitive and harassing manner. Additionally, regarding the goods and services they promote, messages must feature authentic and verified elements, without resorting to omissions, allegations or exaggerations that could mislead consumers. These general requirements are naturally included in national professional standards, as the sector's bodies can issue public opinions on their non-compliance or facilitate mediation. Non-compliance with these requirements can be deemed **misleading practices**, contingent on their severity, and may result in legal consequences, especially concerning discriminatory communications. Complying with these standards is not necessarily easy for ads integrated into video games due to the format of the edited content and the immersive experience offered to players, and we can only give a few general examples here. **15**

Thus, moral standards may vary from one country to another. This is the case, for example, with the sensitivity to certain symbols or **political and religious messages**, which advertisers might be tempted to leverage. This would be all the easier for them because the playful environment of a video game allows a certain margin of imagination. In the case of massively multiplayer online games deployed in several countries with different sensitivities, one may wonder how this requirement could be respected, except by simplifying the advertising message to the extreme. Similarly, the gameplay and game design of some games could lend themselves perfectly to ads featuring visual or **16**

[25] 'Commission preliminarily finds TikTok's ad repository in breach of the Digital Services Act', Press Release, 15.5.2025.

[26] 'Identification de la publicité et des communications commerciales – Identification de l'annonceur', ARPP, July 2013.

[27] Rule 3.5 of the Code of Non-broadcast Advertising and Direct & Promotional Marketing.

psychological violence. We think, for example, of first-person shooters or survival horror games. Is the requirement of respect for human dignity still relevant in such a context? Of course, the gaming context explains why consumers may feel a certain distance from what they consider to be fictional. While video games can push creative content boundaries that is developed in-game, this flexibility does not extend to advertising. There is a **clear distinction** between creative expression and advertising communication within the same medium. Consequently, the ads must be considered as authentic and not fictional on a legal basis. The key consideration is to determine the extent to which fiction, if any, could be incorporated into advertising messages. Lastly, in-game ads could allow advertisers to take more easily advantage of the player's interactions. Here again, the use of hyperlinks has led to various practices, such as forcing players to watch ads to unlock certain features, gain extra lives or rewards, or even to speed up progress from one level to another. Hyper-casual games, which rely heavily on advertising funding, are already conducive to such methods. If ads are clearly identified, their content must not unduly **exploit players' behaviour** to encourage them to make a purchase. This issue is particularly relevant for vulnerable consumers, especially minors.

3. Regulating the content of in-game ads aimed at minors

17 Advertising aimed at children and teenagers is subject to specific precautions in professional standards, given the importance of protecting the moral and psychological well-being of minors, who are particularly vulnerable due to their lack of maturity. Art. 20 of the ICC Code states that advertisements 'should not **exploit the natural credulity** of children or the lack of experience of teens and should not strain their sense of loyalty'. This prohibition extends into national occupational standards, which may be more specific. In France, the ARPP Code prohibits advertisements that promote 'illicit, aggressive, dangerous or antisocial' behaviour or that exploit 'the inexperience and credulity of children and teenagers'. Some ads are classified as aggressive practices under consumer law, such as those which are intended to 'directly encourage children to buy or to persuade their parents or other adults to buy from them the product being advertised' (Art. L 121–7 of the Consumer Code). An identical prohibition exists in the United Kingdom in the *Digital Markets, Competition and Consumers Act* 2024 (schedule 20 § 30). Professional bodies are particularly vigilant on this issue and have intervened in cases related to video game advertising, some of which implying in-game ads. For example, in France, the *Jury de Déontologie Publicitaire* (JDP) considered **aggressive** the advertisement of a car racing video game where one of the protagonists, presented as 'kind', is thanked with a punch after having stated that 'the main thing is not to win but to make friends'.[28] In the United Kingdom, the ASA mediated two cases involving video games for children that contained messages urging them to **join a paid program** in order to access additional content and features.[29] In addition, professional standards remind advertisers of the need to comply with legal restrictions on certain **prohibited and controlled products**, such as tobacco, alcohol, or medications, which may be general or adapted to different media or audiences from one country to another. Video games can still pose difficulties in this area. For instance, advertising cigarettes on the sidelines of a car racing game could be possible as such practice is common in real-world competitions. However, it will be governed by the aforementioned obligations, the PEGI Code of Conduct, and the game rating itself. These difficulties extend to targeted advertising, which is based on the processing of players' personal data.

---

[28] Avis JDP No. 70/10, 22.9.2010.

[29] ASA Rulings on Mind Candy Ltd t/a Moshi Monsters and 55 Pixels Ltd t/a Bin Weevils, 26.8.2015.

C. Requirements for the processing of players' personal data in the case of targeted advertisements integrated in video games

Advertising plays a key role in funding many free to play games that consumer can download and start using free of charge. This form of funding is expanding across the entire industry, especially with the provision of **games as a service** deployed over the medium to long term, which involves an increasing amount of personal data.[30] Some games are offered for free but rely heavily on advertising, with hyper-casual games being a prime example.[31] Therefore, it is essential to consider in-game advertising in the context of regulations that protect **privacy** and players' personal data. In this respect, the European Audiovisual Observatory recently drew the attention of national regulators and legislators to these issues.[32] In context, the DSA (Regulation 2022/2065) imposes compliance with a certain number of obligations that are supposed to guarantee users a certain level of **information and control** over their data; the specific obligations of the GDPR (Regulation 2016/679) then apply to the processing itself (I). In-game advertising is subject to these obligations, although their implementation may present some difficulties (II). 18

I. Ensuring players' control over their personal data

Ensuring that players have full control over their personal data first requires allowing them to **configure** the use of a service in the most convenient way possible (1), then obtaining their **consent** to receive targeted advertising (2). Beyond that, the data controller must still comply with **several obligations** (3). 19

1. The prohibition of deceptive interfaces and dark patterns

The term 'dark pattern' refers to a form of malicious nudging embedded in digital interface design. Some dark patterns may be data-driven and personalised, tailoring manipulative tactics to individual users. However, the term 'dark pattern' does not have a legal definition under the Unfair Commercial Practices Directive (UCPD) – Directive 2005/29/EC. The UCPD applies to any unfair commercial practice that either materially distorts or is likely to distort the economic behaviour of the average or vulnerable consumer (Art. 5) or constitutes a misleading (Artt. 6–7) or aggressive practice (Artt. 8–9). Under Art. 5, traders are required to ensure that the design of their digital interfaces does not distort consumers' transactional decisions. Annex I of the UCPD provides a non-exhaustive list of practices considered unfair, some of which align with common dark patterns. These could lead to enforcement actions, including against video game publishers, particularly in relation to in-game advertising. For example: creating **false urgency** by claiming a product is only available for a very limited time or under special conditions (No. 7); falsely describing a product as 'free' when there are **hidden costs** (No. 20); and repeatedly **interrupting** the user during normal gameplay to pressure them into making a purchase or accepting an offer, which may constitute persistent and unwanted solicitation (No. 26). In addition, Art. 25 of the DSA (Regulation 2022/2065) prohibits online platform providers from designing and operating **deceptive interfaces** 20

[30] Newman/Jerome/Hazard, p. 7; Kröger et al., 100537; Declerck/Lievens/Verdoodt, p. 62; Potter/Westberry/Palmer, p. 404.
[31] Laperdrix et al.
[32] Przybysz, p. 2.

that could manipulate users or hinder their ability to make free and informed decisions. These techniques, which rely on nudging, have been criticised for their potential to influence consumer choices regarding digital content and services, leading to costly decisions.

21 Both the UCPD and the DSA specify that this prohibition does not extend to practices already covered by the GDPR (Regulation 2016/679). In other words, the prohibition of misleading interfaces only covers aspects that are **external** to the processing of personal data. However, this first level of decision can already have an essential impact for the user. Art. 25 of the DSA (Regulation 2022/2065) states that the European Commission may issue guidelines to clarify the scope of the prohibition by outlining examples of deceptive practices, such as: putting forward certain choices to the detriment of others; requesting an action repeatedly, even though it has already been performed by the user; making the opt-out process more complicated than the opt-in process. The aim, of course, is to prevent users from **being 'locked in'** to a service where various forms of intrusive data processing can be deployed. Additionally, Art. 26 of the DSA (Regulation 2022/2065) requires online platform providers to make available to users the information and settings used to determine the recipient of an advertisement and the means enabling to modify these parameters. Such interfaces and information will therefore have to be integrated in one way or another into video games that personalise content and services, including in-game advertising.

22 In 2024, the European Commission conducted a review of the Consumer Directives through the Digital Fairness Fitness Check of EU consumer law. This review identifies dark patterns as a significant concern in the digital environment, defining them as 'unfair commercial practices deployed through the structure, design, or functionalities of digital interfaces or system architecture that can **influence consumers** to make decisions they would not have taken otherwise'. The report also highlights the use of dark patterns in video games and signals the need to update the Consumer Directives to further restrict such practices, including those related to in-game advertising.

2. Players' consent to receive targeted advertising

23 The GDPR (Regulation 2016/679) establishes the most substantial obligations regarding the processing of personal data. These aim to ensure **transparency and fairness** while preventing any risk of harm to vulnerable people, such as children and teenagers.[33] Without being exhaustive, we can recall the main obligations imposed on data controllers as well as the rights granted to individuals concerning advertising-related data processing. The jurisprudence of the *Court of Justice of the European Union* (CJEU) has established that such processing can only be based on the consent of service users.[34] Moreover, the European Data protection Board (EDPB) has since clarified the scope of this requirement with regard to social networks, stating that consent can only be considered **free and informed**, as required under Art. 7 of the GDPR (Regulation 2016/679), if the free offer with targeted advertising is offered **alternatively** to two others: one free with contextual advertising, and one paid without any advertising.[35] This explains why Facebook has since rolled out a paid offer, although it was finally deemed insufficient by

[33] Declerck/Lievens/Verdoodt, p. 65.

[34] CJEU, 4.7.2023 – case C-252/21, ECLI:EU:C:2023:537 – *Meta Platforms Inc. et al. v Bundeskartellamt*; Communication Commerce Electronique, December 2023, p. 50, note Martial-Braz; Revue Européenne des Médias et du numérique, No. 68, winter 2023–2024, p. 22, obs. Mouron.

[35] Opinion 08/2024 of the European Data Protection Board of 17.4.2024 on valid consent in the context of consent or payment models implemented by large online platforms, Revue Européenne des Médias et du numérique, No. 71, autumn 2024, p. 11, obs. Mouron.

the *European Commission* under the DMA (Regulation 2022/1925), fining Meta 200 million EUR.[36] The necessity of obtaining users' consent also applies in the context of profiling, which is likely to have significant legal effects concerning them within the meaning of Art. 22 of the DSA (Regulation 2022/2065). It is discussed by the doctrine that failure to comply with legal provisions on advertising, such as those discussed in Part I, could be considered to have such effects, if it influences consumers' actions.[37] Although, the EDPB Guidelines on Automated individual decision-making and Profiling, which were originally adopted by the Art. 29 Working Party (WP29) and later endorsed by the European Data Protection Board (EDPB), provide detailed interpretations of Art. 22 of the GDPR, including what constitutes a 'decision producing legal or similarly significant effects'. They clarify that such effects include decisions that affect someone's **legal rights** (e.g., denial of social benefits, employment decisions), or have an equivalent impact. This could be the case of targeted advertising that leads to discriminatory outcomes or exclusion from opportunities. The CJEU has gone even further in protecting consumers' moral interests regarding advertising, ruling that advertisements for online gambling and games could have harmful effects on health, particularly concerning addiction risks.[38] Additionally, the DSA (Regulation 2022/2065) prohibits online platform providers from profiling their users on the basis of sensitive data for advertising purposes (Art. 26) or when users are minors (Art. 28).

Beyond that, the data controller must allow individuals to exercise the rights granted 24
to them, in particular the **right to object** and the **right to erasure**, as well as the possibility to **withdraw** consent depending on the processing purpose. Furthermore, consent must be obtained whenever cookies and other tracking technologies are installed on the consumer's device. The ePrivacy Directive (Directive 2009/136/EC) makes this a general principle, which is supported by the provisions of the GDPR (Regulation 2016/679). This is where the prohibition of misleading interfaces becomes essential in terms of personal data. Processing based on consent cannot incorporate this consent into the acceptance of contractual terms related to the subject matter of the contract for the provision of digital services or content. In this regard, it should be recalled that Google had been sanctioned in France by the *Commission Nationale de l'Informatique et des Libertés* (CNIL), which considered that its user interface for configuring data processing was **discouraging and overly complicated** due to the number of menus and actions required.[39] Publishers must therefore ensure that interface design allows players to configure the use of their data in a clear and readable way, without confusion with the game's own functional interfaces. Players must be properly informed of any data processing and must provide their unequivocal consent to it.

3. Other obligations of the data controller

Correspondingly, it is important for the data controller to comply with the standards 25
set by the GDPR (Regulation 2016/679). Prior information must therefore be made available to users, indicating, among other things, the **identity of the controller**, the

[36] European Commission, 'Commission finds Apple and Meta in breach of the Digital Markets Act', Press Release (23.4.2025).

[37] Declerck/Lievens/Verdoodt, p. 72 and p. 75.

[38] CJEU, 4.10.2024 – case C-621/22, ECLI:EU:C:2024:858 – *Koninklijke Nederlandse Lawn Tennisbond v Autoriteit Persoonsgegevens*; Revue Européenne des Médias et du numérique, No. 72, winter 2024–2025, p. 17, obs. Mouron.

[39] Délibération de la formation restreinte No. SAN – 2019–001 du 21.1.2019 prononçant une sanction pécuniaire à l'encontre de la société Google LLC, Revue Européenne des Médias et du numérique, No. 50–51, spring-summer 2019, p. 18, obs. Mouron.

purposes of the processing, the types of data used, the duration of the processing and any transferees of the data. This information obligation can be correlated with provisions in other regulations, particularly consumer law, aiming to eliminate any informational asymmetry between players and video game publishers and distributors.[40] The data controller must also comply with several obligations, including the **minimisation** of the amount of data processed or compliance with the principle of privacy by design, which ensures that products or services are designed in such a way as to respect users' privacy. As noted by the CJEU,[41] data controllers must not collect sensitive data except in the cases outlined in Art. 9 of the GDPR (Regulation 2016/679), which must be interpreted restrictively. Similarly, such data cannot be inferred from other processing activities. However, in the context of online targeted advertising, data can be shared amongst the different actors of the Ad Tech sector, with advertiser, agencies, Ad networks, demand-side platforms (DSPs), supply-side platforms (SSPs), which all may process personal data to serve ads. In the event they are identified as data controller, these provisions must be respected and made accessible to consumers when it involves the processing of personal data intended for more targeted player engagement.

II. The challenges of targeted advertising in video games

26 The application of GDPR (Regulation 2016/679) obligations faces challenges specific to the operation of games, because they seem **poorly compatible** with video games ergonomics. The examination of a few issues relating to the most essential requirements clearly illustrates this (1) although litigation remains limited for the moment (2).

1. Examples of issues raised by in-game advertising

27 This is the case, for example, with the determination of legal bases for processing. Indeed, the same data may be processed **for various purposes**, some of which, such as the proper functioning of the games, are necessary and legitimate, while others, such as targeted advertising, are only optional and pose potential risk for players' privacy.[42] Therefore, the controllers could rely on the contractual necessity basis outlined in Art. 6 of the GDPR (Regulation 2016/679), in the sense that the use of advertisements integrated into the game design is part of the normal use of the game. However, this statement can be contested, as targeted advertising embedded in a game is not an essential element of the gameplay, which the core service offered to consumers.

28 Under the ePrivacy directive, consent is required to install cookies or other trackers into the end-user device. In addition, the collection of data for a purpose other than the provision of the service, such as targeted advertising, would also require prior consent from the users. It is also crucial to uphold the principles governing data processing, in particular proportionality, and considering the players' **reasonable expectations**. The data collected should be strictly limited to that provided by the players or produced using the game. If the data were to be enriched from third-party sources or cross-referenced, then appropriate information and proper consent shall be obtained prior to this additional data processing. One of the risks to the player would be that sensitive data would be processed by inference despite the player's lack of consent. Similar risks may arise when conducting profiling with the data collected. While profiling may be neces-

[40] Declerck/Lievens/Verdoodt, p. 70 and p. 76.

[41] CJEU, 4.10.2024 – case C-446/21, ECLI:EU:C:2024:834 – *Maximilian Schrems v Meta Platfoms Ireland Ltd*; Revue Européenne des Médias et du numérique, No. 72, winter 2024–2025, p. 12, obs. Mouron.

[42] Kröger et al., p. 2.

sary for the normal use of the game,[43] and therefore falling under contractual necessity, it would in fact be important to distinguish the purposes pursued by the processing of the same dataset that requires one to **obtain consent separately**. Targeted advertising, whether it is integrated into game design or not, falls clearly into this category.

Another concern involves the communication of information to players and the options available for them to withdraw their **consent during gameplay**, without introducing frictions that might hinder the gaming experience. The *European Audiovisual Observatory* report highlights the solution adopted by some publishers, aiming to comply with the regulations, and who integrate the information, the processing settings, and related notifications directly into the **game design** in a simplified form. In other words, if players may initially configure their settings before starting a game, they retain the possibility of adjusting data processing during gameplay itself. If this technique blurs the distinction between reality and fiction, it can enhance players' responsibility, as long as the control of their data is well integrated into the operation and development of the game. 29

2. Litigation concerning advertising personal data processing in video games

Similar issues have already been brought before the regulatory authorities and the courts. In France, the publisher Voodoo was fined three million euros by the CNIL for failing to duly inform players of the installation of **tracking technologies** on their phones and for not obtaining consent in accordance with the ePrivacy Directive (Directive 2009/136/EC) and the GDPR (Regulation 2016/679). At least, this information was partly concealed and presented in a way that was not very explicit to the players. The facts are simple to understand. When a consumer installs a Voodoo game *via* the Apple App Store, a first prompt (the ATT – App Tracking Transparency) informs them about tracking and ad personalisation options based on the allocation of an IDFA (*IDentifiers for Advertisers*). This identifier allows data aggregation, correlation, and collection across all the applications installed on the same device. At this point, the consumer can refuse tracking, the said identifier being replaced by a sequence of zeros. Once this first step has been completed, a second Voodoo-specific prompt is surfaced, indicating that the user will not be subject to any advertising tracking based on the aforementioned identifier but that other types of data may be collected in order to offer 'non-personalised ads based on the user's browsing habits'. These ads continue to be processed *via* another identifier, the IDFV (*IDentifiers for Vendors*), which performs the same function as the IDFA, but only for data relating to a publisher's own applications and games. In other words, data processing for advertising purposes remains effective, but it is simply less extensive; the CNIL highlighted **the paradox** of qualifying as 'non-personalised' ads based on browsing habits. However, while users can refuse tracking *via* the IDFA, or set their phones to do so, Voodoo's interface does not provide a way to express consent or refuse tracking *via* the IDFV. In these circumstances, the regulator considered that players cannot reasonably expect that their data will be subject to such processing, even by a single data controller, the absence of this mechanism constitutes a breach of the requirement to obtain prior consent. This decision has been confirmed by the French supreme administrative council.[44] 30

[43] Boyraz, p. 15 and p. 22.
[44] Conseil d'État, 10e et 9e chambres réunies, 14.5.2024, No. 472221.

§ 39
Influencer Marketing

A. 'Influencer marketing': what is it all about? 5
B. Regulatory framework for influencer marketing activities 14
I. Most relevant European regulations 15
II. A patchwork of national regulatory and co-regulatory requirements 25
C. Key requirements and practical implications for game publishers 31
I. Transparency and disclosure of commercial intents 31
II. Content-related obligations and applicable prohibitions 39
III. Minor protection obligations 42
D. Conclusion 48

1 Over the past decade, influencers have become an essential part of modern marketing in the European Union and worldwide, especially within the video game sector. In the last five to six years, their role has expanded considerably, with game publishers and brands increasingly relying on them to promote new releases, engage with gaming communities, and shape player perceptions.

2 Influencer marketing has revolutionised marketing campaigns making it essential to pay particular attention to how they are perceived by consumers. Historically, game developers and publishers, like most other sectors, relied largely on traditional advertising. With the advent of digital platforms like YouTube and Twitch, and the strong relationships build between influencers and their audience, influencers are now able to shape public opinion and drive the decisions of consumers, especially the youngest ones such as children or teenagers.[1]

3 For video game publishers wishing to integrate influencers into their marketing strategy, it is therefore essential to understand (**A.**) the concept of influencer marketing, and (**B.**) the regulations applicable at EU level as well as any specific regulations at local level, in order to (**C.**) identify the requirements to be taken into account and their practical implications.

4 From the outset, it is important to clarify that, to date, there is **no specific legislation** governing 'influencer marketing' at EU level. However, this does not mean that influencers operate in a 'legal vacuum'. While there is no dedicated regulatory framework, several existing legal instruments apply to their activities, including consumer protection laws, unfair commercial practices regulations, etc. In addition, various guidance documents (such as the 'Good Practice Guide on Online Advertising' published by the OECD)[2] and industry codes of conduct (notably the 'Advertising and Marketing Communications Code', revised in 2018, from the International chamber of commerce),[3]

[1] For instance, a joint survey conducted in France, Germany, the United Kingdom, Australia, and the United States, highlighted that 80 % of young consumers purchased products directly via the link provided via the influencer promotion and 88 % of surveyed consumers stated that they were at least inspired by the post. It is also reported that young consumers between 15 to 24 are more inclined to buy a sponsored product. In Belgium, it is estimated that 85 % of young people follow at least one influencer and a quarter of young people mentioned that they have bought at least one product from an influencer in the last three months. Michaelsen, et. al., 'The impact of influencers on advertising and consumer protection in the Single Market', (2022), Publication for the committee on Internal Market and Consumer Protection (IMCO), Policy Department for Economic, Scientific and Quality of Life Policies, European Parliament, Luxembourg, PE 703.350.

[2] OECD, 'Good practice guide on online advertising: Protecting consumers in e-commerce', (2019) OECD Digital Economy Papers, No. 279, OECD Publishing, Paris.

[3] ICC, 'Advertising and Marketing Communications Code', <https://iccwbo.org/business-solutions/the-icc-advertising-and-marketing-communications-code/>.

along with recommendations from regulatory authorities (in particular, the 'Best Practice Recommendation on Influencer Marketing' from the European Advertising Standards Alliance),[4] have been adopted at international level with the aim to complement and clarify the existing legal framework. From the point of view of regulators, members of the International Consumer Protection and Enforcement Network (ICPEN), which is a membership organisation consisting of consumer protection law enforcement authorities from all over the world, also developed guidelines for digital influencers in 2016 to provide influencers and bloggers with general guidance for trustworthy advertising, online reviews and endorsements that respects the interests of consumers.[5]

A. 'Influencer marketing': what is it all about?

The first step for video game publishers wishing to integrate influencers into their marketing strategy is to determine whether the marketing operation envisaged involves calling on the services of an influencer, which can take **many different forms**. 5

From an operational point of view, game companies may partner up with influencers to create paid promotional content or collaborate with them in other forms (e.g., involve them in live events, game tournaments, giveaways, etc.). These influencers may be vertically focused on games (sometimes on specific game titles) or have a broader, more general, audience. In the video game industry, influencers fall into **several categories**, ranging from professional gamers to game streamers, who entertain live audiences through interactive broadcasts, as well as game critics and vlogger gamers. Video game influencers often create most of their game content organically, because of their genuine passion for games, and build a dedicated audience of gamers over time. 6

As regards the legal definition of the notion of '**influencing**', it should be noted that EU law does not yet provide one. However, it is possible to refer to several sources to try to define this notion. 7

According to the UCPD guidelines, 'an influencer is generally described as a natural person or virtual entity who has a greater than average reach in a relevant platform'.[6] 8

Also, one can cite the definition adopted by the Council of the European Union: 'Influencers are online content creators who post content on social media or video-sharing platforms through which they impact society, public opinion and the personal views of their audience, often showcased through their authenticity-based relationship with their audience. Influencers often have a commercial intent and engage with commercial actors through different business models for monetisation purposes. Influencers can also engage in off-line activities, such as patronage, meet-and-greets and product lines'.[7] 9

Finally, a European Parliament study on the impact of influencers on advertising and consumer protection in the Single Market (the 'IMCO study') defines an influencer as 'a content creator with a commercial intent, who builds trust and authenticity-based relationships with their audience (mainly on social media platforms) and engages online with commercial actors through different business models for monetisation purposes'.[8] This study identifies four key elements defining influencers: 10

---

[4] ESEA, 'Best Practice Recommendation on Influencer Marketing Guidance', (May 2023).

[5] ICPEN, 'Guidelines for digital influencers' (June 2016).

[6] European Commission, 'Guidance on the interpretation and application of Directive 2005/29/EC', (29.12.2021), C/2021/9320, OJ C 526.

[7] Council of the European Union, 'Council conclusions on support for influencers as online content creators', (May 2024), 9301/24.

[8] Michaelsen, et. al., 'The impact of influencers on advertising and consumer protection in the Single Market', (2022), Publication for the committee on Internal Market and Consumer Protection (IMCO),

- **Content creation**: the service provided by influencers to other users.
- **Commercial intent**: driven by direct revenue from brands (monetary and non-monetary), audience engagement revenue, or platform compensation.
- **Monetisation**: revenue generation through different business models.
- **Trust and authenticity**: source of influence related to the parasocial trust relationship established with the audience.

11 Trust and authenticity emerge as distinguishing features that differentiate influencers from other marketing actors. These characteristics increase influencer credibility and demonstrate significant impact on consumer attitudes and behavioural intentions, thereby strengthening brand preferences and purchasing behaviour.[9]

12 At national level it must be noted that some countries have a definition by law of the concept of 'influencer' while others have a definition contained in guidelines, recommendations, codes of conduct or other types of guidance documents.[10]

13 For example, both **France**[11] and **Spain**[12] define the concept of an influencer in specific regulations. Although the Spanish definition is wider, since included in its General Law on Audiovisual Communication (LGCA), these definitions share some similarities. Both introduce the concept of engaging in content to communicate through electronic means for commercial purposes. Besides, such person qualifies as an 'influencer' or a 'user of special relevance' notably when they address a public audience and exercise their influence over them.

B. Regulatory framework for influencer marketing activities

14 The second step for video game publishers wishing to integrate influencers into their marketing strategy is to understand the regulations applying to influencers and to make sure that influencers involved in the operation contemplated by the game publisher comply with those.

Policy Department for Economic, Scientific and Quality of Life Policies, European Parliament, Luxembourg, PE 703.350.

[9] Michaelsen, et. al., 'The impact of influencers on advertising and consumer protection in the Single Market', (2022), Publication for the committee on Internal Market and Consumer Protection (IMCO), Policy Department for Economic, Scientific and Quality of Life Policies, European Parliament, Luxembourg, PE 703.350.

[10] European Audiovisual Observatory, 'National rules applicable to influencers', Strasbourg, 2024.

[11] In France, Art. 1 of Law No. 2023–451 of 9.6.2023 defines an influencer as a 'Natural or legal persons who, for a fee, mobilise their celebrity among their audience to communicate to the public, by electronic means, content aimed at promoting, directly or indirectly, goods, services or any cause, are engaging in the activity of commercial influence'.

[12] The notion of 'influencer' is included in the wider concept of 'users of special relevance' defined in Art. 94 of Law No. 13/2022 of 7.7.2022, the General Law on Audiovisual Communication (LGCA), as users of video-sharing platforms simultaneously meeting the following specific requirements: 'a) The service provided entails an economic activity for which its owner obtains significant income derived from his activity in video sharing services through the platform; b) The user of special relevance is the editorial manager of the audiovisual content made available to the public in his service; c) The service provided is intended for a significant part of the general public and may have a clear impact on them; d) The function of the service is to inform, entertain or educate and the main objective of the service is the distribution of audiovisual content; e) The service is offered through electronic communications networks and is established in Spain in accordance with Art. 3(2)'.

I. Most relevant European regulations

There is **no specific legislation** at the EU level in place governing influencer marketing. However, horizontal legislation on consumer protection and commercial communications regulations applies. The European Union has indeed developed a regulatory framework aimed at protecting consumers and preventing deceptive advertising. Influencers in the video game sector must therefore navigate multiple regulations that govern the way they promote products. **15**

In particular, the **existing consumer law framework** remains fully applicable to influencer marketing practices if they meet the definition of 'trader' as established in Art. 2(b) **Unfair Commercial Practices Directive (UCPD)**. The Influencer Legal Hub[13] summarises the criteria for an influencer to meet the definition of the UCPD, as follows: **16**

- generating revenue through content monetisation;
- engaging in commercial practices towards consumers (including communication around advertising or selling goods or products aimed at an audience which includes consumers); and
- acting as a professional (in connection with his/her trade, business, craft or profession).[14]

In this regard, the UCPD is the most relevant EU tool with regard to the issue of misleading advertising in influencer practices. Under this regulation, as for any kind of marketing, the failure to declare the commercial element in an influencer's content or practice in a clear and appropriate manner could amount to a misleading practice under provisions of Art. 6 (misleading actions) and Art. 7 UCPD (misleading omissions). Any promotion of the products or services of a brand in a post that earns its influencer revenues or other types of benefits **must be disclosed as an advertising activity**. The European Commission Guidance on the interpretation and application of the UCPD adopted on 17.12.2021 ('the UCPD guidelines'),[15] which contains a specific section dedicated to 'influencer marketing', states that the adequacy of the disclosure should be assessed taking into account 'the medium in which the marketing takes place, including the context, placement, timing, duration, language, target audience and other aspects' and 'the disclosure must be sufficiently salient to adequately inform the average or vulnerable consumer that receives the content'. In addition, the UCPD guidelines underline that the **17**

---

[13] 'National rules applicable to influencers', Strasbourg, 2024, p.59: 'Many NRAs are still in the process of assessing how they should regulate influencers, or are in the process of developing the technical means to do so. Those NRAs may not be enforcing or not fully enforcing rules applicable to influencers as AVMS providers at the time of writing (or only engaging in the monitoring of their activities).'

[14] In the *Kamenova* case, the ECJ had the opportunity to clarify the criteria to be qualified as a 'trader' under Art. 2 of UCPD (Dir. 2005/29/CE). In order to do so, the courts will have to consider 'whether the sale on the online platform was carried out in an organised manner, whether that sale was intended to generate profit, whether the seller had technical information and expertise relating to the products which she offered for sale which the consumer did not necessarily have, with the result that she was placed in a more advantageous position than the consumer, whether the seller had a legal status which enabled her to engage in commercial activities and to what extent the online sale was connected to the seller's commercial or professional activity, whether the seller was subject to VAT, whether the seller, acting on behalf of a particular trader or on her own behalf or through another person acting in her name and on her behalf, received remuneration or an incentive; whether the seller purchased new or second-hand goods in order to resell them, thus making that a regular, frequent and/or simultaneous activity in comparison with her usual commercial or business activity, whether the goods for sale were all of the same type or of the same value, and, in particular, whether the offer was concentrated on a small number of goods.' ECJ 4.10.2018, – case C-105/17, ECLI:EU:C:2018:808, para.38 – *Kamenova*.

[15] European Commission, 'Guidance on the interpretation and application of Directive 2005/29/EC', (29.12.2021), C/2021/9320, OJ C 526.

commercial intent is considered to be present whenever an influencer receives any form of consideration for the endorsement (discounts, partnership arrangements, free products, etc.). As a consequence, the presence of a contract and monetary payment is not necessary to trigger the application, as confirmed by the European Court of Justice in its *Peek & Cloppenburg* decision.[16]

18 In addition to Artt. 6 and 7, that apply in all cases of influencer marketing, point No. 11 of Annex I (which lists commercial practices that are considered unfair in all circumstances, e.g., without the need to demonstrate any causality) **prohibits practices which do not make it clear that a trader has paid** for the promotion of a product in editorial content. The lack of adequate disclosure by the influencer concerned also increases the risk of breaching point No. 22 of Annex I, which prohibits falsely representing oneself as a consumer.

19 Moreover, given that the relationship that the influencer builds with its audience is often based on trust and a personal connection, their behaviour could in some cases amount to an **aggressive commercial practice** through the use of undue influence, prohibited by Artt. 8 and 9 UCPD. This is particularly relevant when the main target audience of an influencer includes vulnerable consumers, such as children and young people. It can also be particularly relevant when promoting video games with controversial features such as loot boxes or other specific in-game purchases (→ chapter 26).

20 In addition, the UCDP contains a number of provisions ensuring that vulnerable consumers and minors are not exposed to **harmful or deceptive marketing practices**. Influencers promoting products must ensure that their promotional content is truthful, not misleading, and does not exploit consumers' and minors' vulnerabilities.[17] Influencers must thus ensure that their promotions do not exploit minors' inexperience, especially when advertising products such as toys, games, or digital services that may be harmful or inappropriate. Additionally, Annex I (which lists commercial practices that are considered unfair in all circumstances, e.g., without the need to demonstrate any causality) of the directive explicitly prohibits influencers from making any direct exhortations to children to buy products.

21 Beyond consumer protection regulations, transparency obligations are also enshrined in various other EU legislative instruments. Notably, the **Audiovisual Media Services Directive (AVMSD)** (2018/1808/EU) concerning the provision of audiovisual media services is also of particular interest. By extending the regulation originally applicable to linear services only (regular TV broadcasting) under the 2010 Audiovisual Media Services Directive to non-linear services (to include on-demand audiovisual media services), influencers offering audiovisual content and meeting the criteria to be considered audiovisual media service providers need to comply with **specific transparency requirements** on audiovisual commercial communications provided for in Art. 9 and 10 of AVMSD.

22 The AVMSD also ensures that **vulnerable consumers, especially minors, are safeguarded** in an evolving digital media landscape. In particular, the Directive prohibits content inciting violence, hatred, or discrimination based on race, religion, gender, etc., and requires video-sharing platforms to adopt policies against illegal and harmful con-

[16] ECJ 2.9.2021 – Case C-371/20, ECLI:EU:C:2021:674 – *Peek & Cloppenburg*.

[17] Art. 5(3) of the UCDP: 'Commercial practices which are likely to materially distort the economic behaviour only of a clearly identifiable group of consumers who are particularly vulnerable to the practice or the underlying product because of their mental or physical infirmity, age or credulity in a way which the trader could reasonably be expected to foresee, shall be assessed from the perspective of the average member of that group. This is without prejudice to the common and legitimate advertising practice of making exaggerated statements or statements which are not meant to be taken literally'.

tent. Art. 9 of the AVMSD also stipulates core principles applying to commercial communications in order to protect minors. In this regard, minors must be protected from content that could impair their physical, mental, or moral development. This means that influencers must ensure they do not directly encourage minors to buy or hire a product or service by exploiting their inexperience or credulity. The AVMSD also sets clear rules regarding the content of advertisements targeted at children, including prohibiting ads for harmful products such as tobacco, alcohol, and unhealthy foods.

Similarly, the **e-Commerce Directive** (2000/31/EC)[18] and the **Digital Services Act (DSA)** (Reg. 2022/2065/EU), which entered into application across the EU for all online platforms on 17.02.2024, also require all influencers in the EU to **disclose their commercial partnership** as well as the brands for which this communication is made. **23**

It is also worth noting that one of the key objectives of the DSA is to **protect persons in vulnerable situations and minors** from harmful content and manipulation on digital platforms. The DSA thus introduces new requirements for digital platforms, many of which directly impact influencers. In particular, platforms are required to take stronger measures to address harmful content, which can include influencer content. Influencers who are subject to algorithmic promotion (e.g., promoted posts or videos) must ensure transparency in how their content is targeted, especially if minors are in the audience. Influencers must also comply with rules on the clear identification of commercial content, ensuring that advertising is distinguishable from entertainment or editorial content. **24**

II. A patchwork of national regulatory and co-regulatory requirements

On December 2024, according to a note of the European Audiovisual Observatory,[19] only two countries of the EU-27 (along with Norway, Switzerland and the UK) had adopted specific **national laws** for influencers: France and Spain. While others may have since enacted such specific regulation, the grand majority had however already published guidance for influencers.[20] **25**

A first example is the **French Law** No. 2023–451, modified by Ordinance No. 2024–978, which clearly defines the concept of 'influencer' and aims to support the influencer in its practice to assure clear contractualisation of its contracts along with brands and agencies (Art. 8) and to protect the activities of minor influencers (Art. 2). The law also aims to protect the consumer by instituting several rules on publicity specifically applicable to influencer marketing, for example related to transparency (Art. 5 of Law No. 2023–451), prohibition of promoting certain products and services (Artt. 3 and 4 of Law No. 2023–451). **26**

Another example is **Spain**, where influencers, defined as 'users of special relevance', are regulated through their activity of AVMS providers.[21] As such, Art. 94 of Law No. 13/2022 reiterates their obligation to register in the State Register of Audiovisual Communication Service Providers and affirms that they must comply with general obli- **27**

[18] According to Art. 6 of the e-Commerce Directive, 'commercial communication shall be clearly identifiable as such' as well 'the natural or legal person on whose behalf that commercial communication is made'.

[19] European Audiovisual Observatory, 'National rules applicable to influencers', Strasbourg, 2024.

[20] Except Austria, Switzerland and Luxemburg.

[21] European Audiovisual Observatory, 'National rules applicable to influencers', Strasbourg, 2024, p. 118.

gations applied to AVMS providers.[22] It also encourages associations and representatives to adopt codes of conduct to accompany them in complying with such obligations.

28 In addition, there are a number of rules stemming from **co-regulation initiatives**.

29 EASA has published **best practice recommendations** on influence marketing, providing sector-specific guidance on disclosure practices and compliance standards.[23] These recommendations emphasise the importance of clear and prominent disclosure of commercial relationships.[24]

30 Also, various Member States have developed **self-regulatory codes and guidelines**. For example, one can cite:

- Germany: Media authorities have issued guidance on advertising identification in online media.[25]
- The Netherlands: The Advertising Code for social media and influencer marketing provides detailed standards.[26]
- Belgium: The Belgian Advertising Council has issued recommendations for online influencers.[27]

C. Key requirements and practical implications for game publishers

I. Transparency and disclosure of commercial intents

31 While it is clear from EU law that influencers must inform and display to consumers commercial communications that are integrated into their user generated content in a clear and transparent manner (be it videos, photos, audios, posts, etc.), the application of these rules in real-life scenarios raises some **practical challenges** and questions about their scope and enforcement.

32 One of the main issues is **how** these disclosure obligations should be made (label, wording used, etc.), depending on the platform used or the type of content shared. In this regard, national regulations provide useful practical guidance, addressing some of the uncertainties in the broader EU legal framework. This is notably the case of the **French law**[28] which establishes clear requirements for influencers on how to disclose commercial intent. In particular, the French law provides that any content featuring a commercial communication (whether sponsored or paid) must include the mention 'Publicité' (Advertisement) or 'Collaboration commerciale' (Commercial Collaboration)

---

[22] As specified by Royal Decree No. 444/2024 of 30.4.2024 on users of special relevance of video-sharing platforms.

[23] European Advertising Standards Alliance, 'EASA Best Practice Recommendation on Influencer Marketing Guidance', 2023 <https://www.easa-alliance.org/publications/best-practice-recommendation-on-influencer-marketing-guidance_v2023/>.

[24] Michaelsen, et. al., 2022, (no. 2) 73–78.

[25] Die Medienanstalten, 'Leitfaden Werbekennzeichnung bei Online-Medien' (2021), <https://www.die-medienanstalten.de/service/merkblaetter-und-leitfaeden/leitfaden-werbekennzeichnung-bei-online-medien/>.

[26] Stichting Reclame Code, 'Reclamecode Social Media & Influencer Marketing' (2019), <https://www.reclamecode.nl/engels/dutch-advertising-code/special-advertising-codes/#advertising-code-for-social-media---influencer-marketing--rsm>.

[27] Belgian Advertising Council, 'Recommendations for Online Influencers' (2018) <https://www.jep.be/sites/default/files/rule_reccommendation/recommandations_du_conseil_de_la_publicite_influenceurs_en_ligne_fr.pdf>.

[28] Law 2023–451 of 9.6.2023 'visant à encadrer l'influence commerciale et à lutter contre les dérives des influenceurs sur les réseaux sociaux' aimed at regulating commercial influence and combating the abuses of influencers on social networks, amended by Ordinance No. 2024–978 of 6.11.2024.

in a clear, readable, and immediately identifiable manner. Similarly, under **German law**, the labelling of a post as advertising must be very apparent. The German courts clarified that sponsored posts must include a statement in German such as '*Werbung*' (promotion) or '*Anzeige*' (advertisement) at the beginning of the post or video; however, courts have ruled that the labels '#sponsored by' or '#ad' are not sufficient.[29] Some countries such as **Italy**, on the other hand, consider the English wording 'advertising' to be sufficient.[30] National guidance may also consider platform tools that label content automatically – using language such as 'paid partnership' or 'branded content' – to be sufficient.[31]

Another question is **how much** disclosure is needed and in which contexts influencers should be transparent. Influencers often play a game because they genuinely enjoy it, irrespective of whether they received it for free from the developer. They may keep creating content about that game for months, sometimes years, because they're passionate about it, and so is their audience. Do these influencers need to disclose that the game was a gift every time they create new content? The answer may differ based on the jurisdiction. 33

While not being an EU Member State anymore, the **UK** is a good example of a relatively strict jurisdiction. In the UK, influencers are required 'to make clear in any content where [they] feature or refer to the brand, that it's advertising. This is the case even when the brand doesn't know if or what [they]'re creating'. Additionally, influencers 'are expected to disclose throughout any ongoing relationship and in relevant content for a period of 12 months after'.[32] This seems to suggest that disclosure obligations would keep applying for a very long time after an influencer is gifted with the game, even if they keep playing it just because they like it. 34

To complicate things, it is more and more common for companies to set up creator programs to incentivise content creation and 'pamper' their community of players. These programs may offer content creators (big and small) various non-pecuniary benefits, such as free in-game content or early access to new releases. While disclosure may be technically necessary, it seems unreasonable to require it for **minor benefits** such as low value cosmetic in-game items (e.g.,skins) that are gifted to a large number of content creators, including both 'real' influencers and smaller 'amateur' creators. 35

In other cases, joining creator programs may entitle creators to pecuniary benefits, but those **benefits may be uncertain**. For instance, influencers may receive a certain payment only if their content reaches a certain number of views. In this case, it seems reasonable to require disclosure to the extent that the creator had an expectation to reach those views and collect the payment, irrespective of whether they were already part of the creator program or intended to join it in the future at the time of content creation. 36

Finally, the EU framework leaves open the question on **when** and **how often** such disclosure requirements should take place to ensure timely information to consumers. In 37

---

[29] Berlin Appellate Court, 10.112017, #sponsoredbypanteneprov and #ad.

[30] IAP, 'Regolamento Digital Chart', 30.10.2024.

[31] This is the case, for instance, in the UK. CMA, 'Content creators and social media endorsements – Hidden ads: Being clear with your audience', Updated 3.11.2022.

[32] 'Influencers' guide to making clear that ads are ads' (ASA & CAP 23.3.2023). Note that US guidance from the Federal Trade Commission (FTC) contains a more specific reference to video games but does not clearly indicate what would be a reasonable disclosure duration: 'How long it would be reasonable for you to make disclosures really depends on the expectations of your fans. After some period of time, it probably wouldn't matter to them that you got the game for free. If you're choosing to play a game a year after you got it for free, it probably means you truly like it. The analysis would likely be different if, instead of a $60 video game, you got a free $50,000 car and continued to post about it over the life of the car'.

France, the recently adopted legislation on influencers requires that each photo or video containing a product placement must contain an explicit mention during the entirety of the sponsored part, (i.e., embedded, and not just in captions or descriptions).[33]

38 Another issue is that of the **frequency of disclosure**. It is not uncommon for influencers to livestream a game for hours. Sometimes, this may happen as part of a collaboration with the game company. In those cases, how often should influencers disclose their relationship with the game? Continuous disclosure could be disruptive of the stream and its enjoyment by viewers, but may be necessary to maintain transparency for viewers that join after the stream has started. Where technically possible, permanent disclosure in the content description or caption may be sufficient. Alternatively, disclosure at repeated intervals in the content itself (e.g., by voice) may be needed.[34] Some jurisdictions, such as **Italy**, may require a combination of both.[35]

II. Content-related obligations and applicable prohibitions

39 One of the key issues for influencers is not to engage in the **dissemination of harmful or inappropriate content**, or in the promotion of products or services for which **advertising would be prohibited**. In this regard, it is worth noting that some national legislations have gone further than the EU framework.

40 For example, under **French law**, influencers are forbidden to promote certain types of products and services,[36] for instance: plastic surgery and aesthetic medicine (including any action, intervention, procedure, technique and method); products, actions, procedures, techniques and methods that are presented as comparable, preferable or substitutable to therapy; financial products and services (particularly crypto assets), products containing nicotine, subscriptions to sport coaching or sport forecasts. The French law also provides specific rules regarding AI-generated or altered images: influencers must display a clear indication such as 'Retouched Image' or 'Virtual Image' when publishing visuals that have been modified or generated by AI and that depict a silhouette or a face.

41 Similarly, under **Italian law**, advertising for certain sensitive products is subject to stricter regulations. Alcohol cannot be advertised during 'programs' targeting minors and within the 15 minutes before and after said programs (Art. 13, L. 125/2001[37] and Art. 22 Codice di Autodisciplina della Comunicazione Commerciale). Additionally, In Italy tobacco and gambling advertising is entirely banned (Art. 1, L. 165/1962[38] and

[33] Law 2023–451 of 9.6.2023 'visant à encadrer l'influence commerciale et à lutter contre les dérives des influenceurs sur les réseaux sociaux' aimed at regulating commercial influence and combating the abuses of influencers on social networks, amended by Ordinance No. 2024–978 of 6.11.2024.

[34] This is, for instance, the FTC's guidance in the US: 'Since viewers can start watching at any time, they could easily miss a disclosure at the beginning of the stream or at any other single point in the stream. If there are multiple, periodic disclosures throughout the stream, people are more likely to see them no matter when they tune in. To be on the safe side, you could have a continuous, clear and conspicuous disclosure appear throughout the entire stream. We also advise that you add a disclosure to any description of the stream before potential viewers click through to it.' FTC, 'FTC's Endorsement Guides: "What People Are Asking"', (2023).

[35] IAP, 'Regolamento Digital Chart', 30.10.2024, Sect. 1.1.C, providing that disclosure should be made 'as the first written information in the video description, and as a written warning superimposed in the initial scenes. In streaming videos, these warnings must also be repeated during the broadcast.' [our translation].

[36] Law 2023–451 of 9.6.2023 'visant à encadrer l'influence commerciale et à lutter contre les dérives des influenceurs sur les réseaux sociaux' aimed at regulating commercial influence and combating the abuses of influencers on social networks, amended by Ordinance No. 2024–978 of 6.11.2024.

[37] Legge quadro in materia di alcol e di problemi alcolcorrelati.

[38] Divieto della propaganda pubblicitaria di prodotti da fumo.

Art. 9 (1), D.L. 87/2018[39]) and, in recent years, the Italian consumer authority investigated the alleged covert advertising of heated tobacco by a number of influencers.[40]

III. Minor protection obligations

Additionally, influencers must take account of minors and may be subject to specific restrictions in this respect. 42

For example, **French law** introduces specific protections for minors, both as influencers[41] and as influenced individuals. With regard to minors as consumers, French law imposes strict regulations on certain promotions. For example, the promotion of sports betting websites is only allowed on platforms that target individuals over 18, with a mandatory disclaimer stating that the site is prohibited for minors.[42] According to the SREN Law,[43] the same restrictions apply to JONUM (*'Jeux à Objets Numériques Monétisables'*), which includes games based on blockchain-based assets, such as non-fungible tokens (NFTs). These measures seek to protect young audiences from the risks associated with gambling and speculative digital assets. 43

Another challenge faced by influencers who create content for young audiences – or whose content is accessible to minors – is **defining and implementing best practices** to ensure that minors are adequately protected. To address this issue, several codes of conduct and guidelines have emerged at the national level to complement existing laws. 44

In **France**, the ARPP – a key regulatory body in France overseeing advertising practices, including influencer marketing – has issued **specific guidelines to ensure that advertisements featuring children or targeting them** adhere to principles of responsibility, transparency, and protection. In particular, the ARPP underlines that 45

- When advertising targets children, it must be clear and distinguishable from entertainment content, ensuring they understand when they are being exposed to a commercial message.
- Advertisements should promote positive values, such as responsible consumption and respectful social interactions.
- Additionally, the Pan European Game Information (PEGI) classification, established by software publishers within the framework of the Interactive Software Federation of Europe, must be clearly visible in advertisements. This requirement ensures that age- appropriate gaming content is properly labelled and that parents and young consumers are informed about content suitability.

In **Italy**, the communications authority (AGCOM) recently issued specific guidelines for influencers requiring, among other things, that influencers should not share content whish is violent, hateful, discriminating or against human dignity nor 'content that is severely harmful to the physical, psychological, or moral development of minors'. Addi- 46

[39] Decreto Dignità.

[40] AGCM, decision no. 29837 (Bulletin no. 41 of 18.10.2021).

[41] Law no. 2020–1266 of 19.10.2020 'visant à encadrer l'exploitation commerciale de l'image d'enfants de moins de seize ans sur les plateformes en ligne' (to regulate the commercial use of images of children under the age of sixteen on online platforms) that regulates the commercial use of images of children under 16 on online platforms, ensuring stricter control over their participation in online advertising to protect their rights and well-being.

[42] Law 2023–451 of 9.6.2023 'visant à encadrer l'influence commerciale et à lutter contre les dérives des influenceurs sur les réseaux sociaux' aimed at regulating commercial influence and combating the abuses of influencers on social networks, amended by Ordinance No. 2024–978 of 6.11.2024.

[43] Law No. 2023–566 of 7.7.2023 'visant à instaurer une majorité numérique et à lutter contre la haine en ligne' (aimed at establishing a digital majority and combatting online hate speech).

tionally, 'when uploading content, influencers must use, where available, the functionalities provided by the video-sharing platform to indicate that the content contains potentially harmful material for minors'.[44] Special self-regulation rules also apply for advertising (including by influencers) that is either intended for, our could potentially reach, children or adolescents. Said advertising should not, in particular, induce minors to violate generally accepted behavioural norms, engage in dangerous actions, think that not possessing the product being advertised implies inferiority, or that parents are failing in their duties, or adopt an unhealthy lifestyle (Art. 11 Codice di Autodisciplina della Comunicazione Commerciale).

47 With regard to minors, it is also important to note that game companies that are **PEGI** signatories should also comply with a number of general principles, including in relation to influencer marketing as applicable (Art. 11 of the PEGI Code of Conduct), namely:

i. All advertisements shall accurately reflect both the nature and content of the video game product publicised and the rating associated with it. Advertisements should not mislead consumers as to the video game product's true character.
ii Advertisements shall not use the PEGI age rating for other purposes than informing consumers about the age suitability of a game.
iii. All advertisements shall be created with a sense of responsibility towards the public.
iv. No advertisement should contain content that is likely to cause serious or widespread offence to the average consumer targeted.
v. Signatories shall not specifically target advertising for video game products rated 16 or 18 to consumers for whom the product is not rated as appropriate.
vi. Signatories shall ensure that ancillary or separate products that are being sold or promoted in association with a core video game product contain content that is appropriate for the audience for which the core product is intended.
vii. Signatories shall not enter into promotion of video game products rated 16 or 18 with another company's brands, products, or events, if it is reasonable to believe that such company's products, brands or events will reach consumers for whom the video game product is not rated as appropriate.
viii. Signatories shall inform the public by means of a general statement of the existence of sponsorship(s) and/or the existence of product placement(s) associated with any video game product. Use of a trademark or brand solely to provide authenticity to the video game product environment shall not be held to constitute either product placement or sponsorship provided that those with a right to use such mark or brand do not receive payment in exchange for such use.

D. Conclusion

48 The regulatory landscape governing influencer marketing continues to evolve rapidly, with significant implications for video game publishers utilising these promotional strategies. The movement towards enhancer transparency requirements, site-specific restrictions, and strengthened enforcement mechanisms necessitates proactive compliance strategies capable of adapting to ongoing regulatory development.

[44] AGCOM, 'Linee-guida volte a garantire il rispetto delle disposizioni del Testo unico da parte degli influencer e istituzione di un apposito Tavolo tecnico', Resolution No. 7/24/CONS, 2024 (Guidelines aimed at ensuring compliance with the provisions of the Consolidated Law by influencers and establishment of a special technical table).

D. Conclusion

For video games publishers, the key strategic imperative involves developing governance frameworks that balance promotional effectiveness with regulatory compliance. Recent legislative developments in France for example, and ongoing enforcement actions demonstrate the increasing regulatory scrutiny of influencer marketing practices. **49**

Publishers must develop expertise in these specialised areas while maintaining awareness of broader consumer protection developments. **50**

§ 40
Guidelines and Licences for Let's-Plays

Bibliography: Bullinger/Czychowski, 'Digital Content: Work and/or software? – Ein Gedankenspiel am Beispiel von Computerspielen', GRUR 2011, 19; Dolling, Die Games-Verwertungsgesellschaft – Chance oder Pflicht für den eSport?, SpoPrax 2023, 388; Dreyer/Kotthoff/Hentsch, Heidelberger Kommentar Urheberrecht, 5th edn 2025; Franz, 'Ist "Virtual Reality" eine neue Nutzungsart? – Zur zukünftigen Verwertung von Computerspielen', ZUM 2017, 207; Furch, Guidelines und Lizenzen für Let's Plays, in Hentsch/Falk (eds), Handbuch Games und Recht, § 30, 511; Haar, Kreatives Jura für eine kreative Branche, MMR Supplement 8/2021, 1; Hentsch, 'The very first collecting society for games', Interactive Entertainment Law Review 6 (2), 66–72; Hentsch, 'Eine eigene Verwertungsgesellschaft für die Games-Branche', MMR 2023, 28; Hentsch, 'Piraterie in der Games-Branche', MMR Supplement 8/2019, 3; Hentsch, 'Games Industry Law Summit', MMR 2021, 837; Nordemann/Steinbrecher, 'Die neue Clearingstelle Urheberrecht im Internet (CUII) – Urheberrechtliche und verfassungsrechtliche Voraussetzungen der Selbstregulierung von Sperransprüchen in Deutschland', MMR 2021, 189; Pukas/Waiblinger, 'Games im "Age of UrhDaG"', MMR 2023, 628; Rodewald, 'Let's Play und Streaming', in Zimmermann/Falk (eds), Handbuch Gameskultur, 2020, 151; Schmid, 'Richtlinien und Guidelines für Let's Plays, 'Urheberrecht und UrhDaG', MMR 2023, 638; Terhaag/Schwarz, Influencer-Marketing. Rechtshandbuch, 2021; Wandtke/Bullinger, Kommentar zum Urheberrecht, 5th edn 2019.

A. Introduction 1
B. Definition 7
C. Legal categorisation and relevant legal issues 11
I. IP rights 11
II. Relevant content or elements for Let's Play videos 17
1. Story or fable 19
2. Game design 20
3. Music and sound 21
4. Game as whole 22
III. Production and distribution of Let's Plays 25
1. Production 27
2. Publication/Dissemination 36
IV. Consent/permissions 41
1. Toleration 42
2. Platforms and collective rights management 47
D. Typical rules for content guidelines 50
I. Subject of the guidelines or licences 50
II. Commercial use 52
III. Content and behaviour-related regulations 58
IV. Limitations for specific assets 61
V. Revocation and changes to guidelines and licences 63

A. Introduction*

1 In the year 2025 YouTube is celebrating its 20th birthday. Other streaming platforms meanwhile joined the business and are growing steadily. **Gaming video content, especially so-called Let's Play Videos** have been the core content on YouTube and was the main application for Twitch for a long time. The German 20th anniversary documentation of YouTube has a strong focus on gaming content creators showcasing the importance of gaming content for the whole video streaming industry.

2 Well-known international Let's Players can boast subscriber and follower numbers that many a star from the film and music industry could only dream of. The Let's Player 'PewDiePie' reaches **110 million subscribers** with his channel on YouTube alone. The

* We want to thank Kai Florian Furch for his support and allowing us to use parts of his article from the German handbook 'Games und Recht'.

currently most successful Let's Player on Twitch, 'Ninja', reaches 23.8 million followers with his channel. But national Let's Players can also boast follower and subscriber numbers in the millions. The most successful German speaking Let's Player, Erik Range aka 'Gronkh', runs a YouTube channel with 5 million subscribers and a Twitch channel with 1.7 million followers. This makes his YouTube channel one of the most subscribed YouTube channels in Germany across all genres.[1]

This makes **Let's Plays** equally interesting for the audience, development studios and publishers of video games and, of course, for the Let's Players themselves. Game-related entertainment, media presence and marketing as well as monetary interests play an equally significant role here. 3

One special feature is that the **technical threshold** for creating your own Let's Plays is now **generally very low**. An enormous number of video content is created on a daily level by non-professional and non-commercial content creators on a private level. Gaming content is recorded, stored, commented and published today on huge level and mostly by non-commercial creators. 4

Developer studios, publishers and console manufacturers have also responded to the popularity of Let's Plays and are increasingly enabling the **recording (capturing) and sharing of gaming experiences** directly in the game even offering interfaces to streaming platforms adding options of interactions of viewers with the content creators. 5

As a result, the number of people creating their own **streaming channels** is still growing steadily and the line between private, commercial or professional Let's Plays is sometimes blurred. 6

B. Definition

From a legal perspective, Let's Plays are interesting because they naturally contain pre-existing elements that are protected by copyright or neighbouring rights (ancillary copyright) with the respective game.[2] 7

Let's Plays are **video productions** in which one or more people (creators) film themselves **playing a game,** i.e., record and comment on their own interaction with the game and gameplay. Captures can be taken on PC or through an interface from any device. The files are saved and stored on internal or external hard drives and in some cases also on smartphones and tablets, but never on consoles. These videos or edited versions are **broadcasted live (livestream)** and/or recorded and **then made available as video-on-demand** on the usual platforms for gaming video content, i.e., in particular the Amazon subsidiary Twitch, the Google subsidiary YouTube Gaming and Facebook Gaming. 8

Let's Plays are usually presented in such a way that you can experience the game – be it a match or a game, sequences determined by the player, e.g., a special challenge or a fight – on the one hand and listen to the player's commentary on the other. As a rule, a video of the player himself (via facecam) is also **integrated** into the presentation. The gameplay is often creatively dramatised by the Let's Player and accompanied by entertaining or explanatory commentary. 9

The combination of the **presentation of the gameplay and the commentary** characterises a Let's Play.[3] Unlike a tutorial or a pure game solution (e.g., walkthrough), the 10

[1] Number of subscribers (YouTube) and followers (Twitch) as of 20.3.2025.

[2] See McGreevy, § 13 on EU copyright in and for games.

[3] Overview on the most popular use cases: Hentsch, 'Eine eigene Verwertungsgesellschaft für die Games-Branche', MMR 2023, 28, 29.

personality, explanations and narratives as well as the individual gaming experiences of the content creator are particularly important in a Let's Play. In the case of live-streams, the content creator often responds to comments and questions from their followers. In many cases even published videos are commented in new videos as a so-called reacts.

C. Legal categorisation and relevant legal issues

I. IP rights

11 The basis for creating any gaming content is on the one hand the game itself and on the other hand the action and comments of the content creator. As previously written, the **game is ultimately the stage or playing field** for the Let's Player's own narrative. However, it must be taken into account that the core of the content of any gaming video is the game itself.

12 In summary, computer and video games are categorised as **so-called complex works.**[4] This is based on the fact that a game consists of **many different elements** that are protected by copyright and neighbouring rights: These include the story or narrative, design elements, music, sound and the underlying code. Lacking any clear categorization in any of the copyright related directives of the past the protection of video games under copyright is still subject to an ongoing legal discussion.

13 As a result, the so-called **Nintendo judgement of the ECJ**, which resolves the classification issue by assuming a 'hybrid work', is primarily used as a guidance when it comes to determining the protection of video games.[5] Games are **complex objects which are not only computer programmes** (software) but also include graphic and sound components which, even if they are encoded in a computer game language, have their own creative value which is not limited to this encoding. All such components of video games are in itself protected under copyright and form together a separate work which is protected under copyright, not unlike a film.

14 In practice, the German Federal Court of Justice (BGH)[6] differentiates between the **individual components of the game** and explicitly mentions so-called game data, i.e., texts, graphics, music, models and film sequences. The BGH assumes that each of the aforementioned components could be **protected by copyright in its own right** 'or participate in the **originality of the overall work** and enjoy copyright protection together with it'.

15 In practice, the Let's Player can assume that the **publisher of the game has obtained all required rights** to the individual components and the game as a whole prior to publication. These are usually the copyright utilisation and exploitation rights for regular distribution, i.e., the right to reproduce (Art. 2 of the 2001/29/EC), to distribute (Art. 4 of the 2011/29/EC) and the right to make available to the public (Art. 3 of the 2011/29/EC). In particular for game titles that are suitable for tournaments and esports, the **right to perform** (under German law Sec. 19 (4) UrhG) and the **broadcasting right** or the right to broadcast on television (Art. 4 of the 2011/29/EC) may also be relevant. In individual cases, it may be that rights for individual components, e.g., pre-existing music, have not been granted to the publisher for the purposes of broadcasting and performance. Particularly if pre-existing music from relevant music catalogues or music bound to an ex-

[4] See McGreevy, § 13 on EU copyright in and for games.
[5] CJEU, 23.1.2014 – case C-355/12, GRUR 2014, 255.
[6] BGH, 6.10.2016 – I ZR 25/15, GRUR 2017, 266.

ploitation company is included in the game, this may result in restrictions for the publisher.[7]

16 As a rule, however, the publisher holds all rights of use and exploitation through a precautionary comprehensive grant of rights from the game developer.

II. Relevant content or elements for Let's Play videos

17 As described above, all relevant rights of use and exploitation generally lie with the publisher. This means that the publisher holds the rights 'to the stage' that the Let's Player wants to play on.

18 Aside from the protection as a computer program video games are **protected by a multitude of rights** depending on the individual parts of the video game used. The following copyrighted elements are generally used in the production and distribution of a Let's Play, which is why the respective rights concerned are of interest:

1. Story or fable

19 The story or plot, i.e., the **underlying plot and storylines**, including the plot of individual quests and missions together with briefings and fables in sandbox games and also the resulting often **complex character worlds and character fables** (i.e., in addition to appearance, which is more likely to be assigned to game design) and their background story and relationships to each other, are protected by copyright, in Germany in accordance with Sec. 2 (1) no. 1 UrhG.[8]

2. Game design

20 Game design components are all **graphically or visually designed elements** of the game, i.e., in particular characters, avatars, objects such as equipment, virtual buildings and their furnishings, flora, fauna, vehicles and other objects in the virtual game world. As a rule, these are protected by copyright as works of fine arts and applied arts, provided that the level of creativity relevant to protectability and at least a certain aesthetic content are present.

3. Music and sound

21 **Music and soundscapes** are often an essential part of a successful game. Considering that a player is not only immersed in the tonal worlds of a game more often, but usually also for longer, it is obvious that a good soundscape, especially good score music, is no less important for the atmosphere, perhaps even more important in individual cases than in a feature film or series. Musical works are protected, in Germany under Sec. 2 (1) no. 2 UrhG. The performers or singers and musicians are also protected as performing artists. The producer of the sound or music recording is also protected under Art. 2 of the 2001/29/EC and in many jurisdictions even as owner of an ancillary right. However, this is usually arranged by the publishers themselves, so that this right often arises directly with the publisher.

---

[7] See Boisneault on music in games, § 16; with regard to esports titles, see also Hilgert, in Maties (ed), Stichwortkommentar eSport-Recht, 2023, 146 ff.

[8] In particular on fable case law BGH, 29.04.1999 – I ZR 65/96, GRUR 1999, 984 (987) – Laras Tochter; OLG München, 7.12.1998 – 29 U 3350/98, NJW-RR 2000, 268 (269), which is also applicable to computer games. In more detail: Bullinger/Czychowski GRUR 2011, 19 with further references.

4. Game as whole

22 The video game as a whole is also recognised as a **film work**. This means that not only the increasingly epic cutscenes or in-game video sequences can be subordinated to the film work. Think not only of the cutscenes and sequences with real actors, which were first realised in a groundbreaking way over 30 years ago in Wing Commander 3 with Mark Hamill as a classic film star, but also of the now often epic digital cutscenes, e.g., for World of Warcraft, which would often also be suitable for cinema.

23 Rather, the **audiovisual game sequences or game representations in a video game** can themselves are protected as a film work.[9] This means that games are generally subject to the same protection like any movie production. The **game developer or publisher** – depending on the individual circumstance – generally assumes the **role of the film producer** who is under German law protected by his own ancillary copyright. If, in individual cases, the audiovisual design of a game is so simple that the level of creation is questionable, the animations it contains can still be protected by the neighbouring right of motion picture protection, in Germany pursuant to Sec. 95 UrhG.

24 In essence, it is precisely this element, i.e., the **audiovisual representation of the game**, that is most obviously affected by the production and distribution of Let's Plays. After all, the audiovisual presentation is the stage and projection surface for the playful and narrative performance of the content creator.

III. Production and distribution of Let's Plays

25 As explained above under C.I., computer games and their individual components are therefore generally protected by copyright and ancillary rights, whereby the rights of use and exploitation usually lie with the publisher.

26 As summarised above, the **producer or player infringes these rights** when producing and distributing a Let's Play. A distinction must be made here between the production and distribution in the context of the production of a Let's Play.

1. Production

27 Two aspects must be taken into account when producing a Let's Play: (i) The rights set out above under → para. C.II., in particular the associated reproduction rights, generally lie with the publisher. (ii) For copyrights and ancillary rights, exercising such right of use without proper authorisation is **generally prohibited by law**, unless an explicit legal exception applies.

28 With regard to the right of reproduction and with regard to the rights to the game as a film work, which are particularly relevant in the case of Let's Plays, the **exclusive reproduction right** is affected.

29 Not only the completely identical reproduction counts as a reproduction, but also the setting of a work in a modified form is to be regarded as a reproduction.[10]

30 Since Let's Plays of linear or semi-linear games usually involve the underlying game and its mechanics and processes being played unchanged and only a commentary, which can be quite creative in individual cases, is added, this is generally considered to be a **(largely) identical reproduction**.

31 This also applies as a necessary technical intermediate step when streaming directly and exclusively live. Even without creating a permanent copy of the recording, which is

---

[9] Wandtke et al. UrhG Vor § 88 mn. 61.

[10] Loewenheim, Handbuch des Urheberrechts, 3rd edn 2021, § 20 mn. 5 with further references.

then to be published on the platform via on-demand (video-on-demand), the **recording temporarily stored** on the streaming server **constitutes a reproduction.**

However, if this Let's Play is only recorded in order to serve the private use of the content creator, e.g., to show it to friends, this reproduction is usually subject to the exception to private copying pursuant to Art. 5 (2) (b) of 2001/29/EC or as transformed into German law under Sec. 53 (1) sent. 1, Sec. 94 (4). According to this, '**individual reproductions of a work by a natural person for private use** on any medium, provided that they do not serve either direct or indirect commercial purposes' are permitted. In return, the authors of computer games, including Let's Plays, are entitled to **remuneration for private copies.**[11] 32

Such remuneration is not payable directly by the content creators but is **payable by the producer of data storage devices** which are technically able to be used in the reproduction of works protected under copyright, e.g., hard drives, USB sticks etc. The remuneration is collected by collecting societies. Since September 2025 there is in Germany the very first collecting society collecting such remuneration for the producers of video games, the VHG ('**Verwertungsgesellschaft für die Hersteller von Games**'). VHG just obtained a permission by the German authorities to collect such remuneration for the private copying of video games on behalf of the producers of video games.[12] The VHG is based on an initiative of the German game association ('game – Verband der deutschen Games-Branche'). The registration process has already started and a large number of German and international video game producers have signed up.[13] 33

Since most players do not create their Let's Plays for profit or commercially, the creation of even private Let's Plays is in general permitted by law. 34

Since professional and **commercial purposes** (whether directly or indirectly) **already exclude private use** per se,[14] professional content creators or games influencers and media companies that produce Let's Plays cannot invoke the copyright exception of Sec. 53 UrhG and therefore the production of Let's Play videos without the grant of rights or consent of the rights holder, i.e., usually the publisher, constitutes an infringement of their rights. 35

2. Publication/Dissemination

If a Let's Play video has been produced and is to be published, this also infringes on the rights of the rights holder, usually the publisher. 36

The standard case for this is that the content creator makes the produced video available on one of the common platforms or on his homepage. This non-physical act of distribution is **subject to the right of making available to the public** pursuant to Art. 3 of the 2001/29/EC if the video is made available exclusively on-demand, i.e., on demand and thus 'in such a way that it is accessible to members of the public from places and at times of their choice' 37

If the video is made available exclusively or at least also live, i.e., **broadcast linearly**, either because the Let's Play is actually broadcast on television, but also if this is done on the internet, the broadcasting right is also affected. While the broadcasting right itself is not originating from EU directives it still is accepted under EU legislation and jurisdiction and often referred to. Since a linear performance of a work is not made available to the public in such a way that it is accessible to members of the public from 38

[11] Hentsch MMR 2018, 351 (353).
[12] https://www.dpma.de/english/services/public_relations/press_releases/25september2025/index.html.
[13] See Hentsch, Interactive Entertainment Law Review 6 (2), 66–72.
[14] Dreier/Schulze/Dreier, UrhG § 53 mn. 7, 10.

places and at times of their choice, the live stream on the internet does **not constitute making available to the public.**[15]

39 In connection with the publication, whether as a live stream or on demand, it can be argued in individual cases that the respective Let's Play also has a journalistic, editorial background and in this context the use of the game in the Let's Play could fall under the protective rights barrier of the **right to quote**. In this case, reproduction (i.e., production) as well as distribution and communication to the public would not infringe on the publisher's rights.

40 However, the use of the game in a Let's Play does not generally only **exceed the permissible scope** (to be narrowly defined) for a quotation. Playing the game also does not fulfil a purely evidential purpose for the statements and theses of the player. The Let's Play video is based on and adorns itself with precisely this game content as an end in itself.

IV. Consent/permissions

41 As elaborated under C.I., the **consent of the rights holder** is therefore strictly speaking required for both making the Let's Play available to the public and live streaming. Normally, such consent is granted individually or as part of a license agreement. However, such individual agreements between content creators and publishers would create **an unreasonable effort on both sides** and therefore publisher's who also have a vital interest that their games are being played by content creators as part of their product marketing, have gone a different way in order to provide at least some legal certainty for content creators.

1. Toleration

42 In practice, it has therefore become common practice for publishers to either tacitly, sometimes explicitly, tolerate or alternatively formulate authorisations. If the publisher wants to actively shape a regulation, this is usually done in the form of **guidelines** or by embedding it in the **terms of use or 'licences'** for the game.[16] These actively support the use of games for Let's Plays, but do not create an explicit agreement with obligations for both parties.

43 This means that usually such **guidelines do not constitute an actual grant of rights** under copyright. Rather the guidelines constitute a simple consent or **waiver to claim an infringement** very much like the German Federal Court of Justice stated in its decision on Google Image Search, declared that a 'simple consent' is sufficient to at least eliminate the unlawfulness of the infringement of the publisher's rights. The BGH states in general terms:

> Simple consent to copyright infringement differs from the (in rem) transfer of rights of use and permission under the law of obligations in that, although it *leads to the legality of the act as permission*, the recipient of the consent acquires neither a right in rem nor a claim under the law of obligations or any other right enforceable against the will of the rightholder[17]

---

[15] MAH GewRS/Nordemann/Czychowski § 43 mn. 404, 405.

[16] Examples of this are: Permission by Nintendo (https://www.nintendo.co.jp/networkservice_guideline/en/index.html), acquiescence by EA (https://www.ea.com/legal), 'licence' by Microsoft (https://www.xbox.com/de-de/developers/rules); a list of licences compiled by game can be found here: https://www.game.de/themen/lizenzverzeichnis-fuer-lets-plays/.

[17] BGH, 29.4.2010 – I ZR 69/08, MMR 2010, 475 mn. 34 – Google image search.

The particular advantage of this solution for the publisher as the rights holder is that it can enable and promote the use of Let's Plays, in particular to generate attention for its games, and at the same time can define specific (framework) conditions for this through reservations. This can be done **without entering into a permanent legal commitment or obligation** and allows the rights holder to revoke or adapt these regulations, i.e., the guidelines or 'licences', at any time, if expressly reserved. 44

From the content creator's perspective, it is also clear which conditions must be fulfilled in order not to unlawfully infringe on the publisher's rights. This allows content creators – regardless if commercial or private creators – an **easy review of their legal situation**. 45

Passive or silent **toleration by publishers causes more difficulties** in this context because it would then depend on the interpretation of each individual case for each game title and each publisher as to whether the publisher had to expect that the game title would be used for Let's Plays. The **lack of clear guidelines** could also cause content creators to ignore such video games as not to risk actual copyright claims. 46

2. Platforms and collective rights management

The **DSM Directive**[18] therefore stipulates that platforms must obtain permission from rights holders for the **mass use of copyright-protected works by concluding a licence agreement**, although the term 'licence agreement' was not specifically defined. The directive has in Germany been implemented with the Act on the Adaptation of Copyright Law to the Requirements of the Digital Single Market (UrhDaG), which came into force on 7.6.2020. There it was also clarified, that any permission (not just silent toleration) granted to individual uses also applies in favour of the service provider of the respective platform. 47

This implementation of the Directive therefore means that **guidelines and licences** that contain explicit permission for users are also **extended to the platform**, so that the platform does not have to strive for collective licensing. This solves the problem of the originally mass illegal use of content on social media platforms and the practice of guidelines and licences continues to be the business standard solution. 48

There is currently **no alternative collective management of rights for the games industry**. Also the VHG currently has not announced any plans to offer any licensing for their members or to request such rights. 49

D. Typical rules for content guidelines

I. Subject of the guidelines or licences

The wording, regulatory density and scope of guidelines and licences vary greatly. This applies in particular to the **form of permission (toleration, permission, licence)** itself. 50

The formulations range from the decision to 'let things take their course' (Mojang) and 'we raise no objections [...]', whereby this 'does not constitute concrete approval' (EA), to regulations that expressly grant concrete 'toleration', 'permission' or 'permission', 51

[18] Directive (EU) 2019/790 of 17.4.2019 on copyright and related rights in the digital single market (DSM Directive) (Abl. L 130,92).

to unambiguous licences.[19] An exact classification is therefore often hard or not possible at all.

II. Commercial use

52 The vast majority of guidelines and licences expressly restrict the use of games in Let's Plays to non-commercial use.

53 As a rule, however, this restriction is then opened up to **monetisation in all forms via the usual platforms** (in particular Twitch, YouTube, Facebook Gaming, Mixer, etc.) by means of an explicit exemption.

54 In individual cases, the publisher formulates a **minimum requirement** for the design of the Let's Play as a prerequisite for monetisation. Codemaster's regulations provide an example of this:[20] 'you can monetise it if you wish and you'll receive no interference from us – providing that the material you upload is largely your own content, (no simply re-uploading or posting our content)'.

55 Monetisation can also be made **dependent on mentions or links**: e.g.: 'as long as you add:' followed by credits and links to be used.[21]

56 There are also regulations stating that although monetisation is possible, access to the Let's Play is **not *behind* a paywall** as paid content and could therefore only be perceived if payment is made in advance. This is consistent because the marketing effect sought by the publisher would only take place after monetisation which is not in the publisher's interest.

57 Please also note that several publishers add restrictions and regulations regarding permission to use Let's Plays on **sponsored channels** (e.g., energy drinks, games equipment) from professional content creators. In some cases, this is not permitted. In individual cases, specific thresholds for the maximum duration of sponsorship are specified. This is intended to avoid the impression that the publisher or the game itself has an economic connection with the sponsorship or that the sponsor participates disproportionately in the reputation of the game.

III. Content and behaviour-related regulations

58 More detailed guidelines and policies contain an explicit **ban on showing or promoting hacks and cheats**. In addition, so-called inappropriate content is generally not permitted. On the one hand, this can be the execution or incitement to criminal behaviour that in the publisher's discretion is not socially appropriate or in case the content creator does not comply with existing codes of conduct.

59 In addition, there are often content-related (i.e., **no walkthroughs, key scenes**) or time-related spoiler bans, especially **for pre-release content and early unboxing videos**.

60 **Content leaked** in advance and without authorisation should generally not be used in a Let's Play, even if this is not explicitly stated in the guidelines. Under EU copyright law, this would violate the right of first publication of the author or – derived from this – the rights holder. The publication right to a copyrighted work always includes the right of the rights holder to decide 'whether' and 'how' as well as the form of publication.[22]

---

[19] Exemplary quotations from the guidelines listed in the licence directory of the German games industry association (https://www.game.de/themen/lizenzverzeichnis-fuer-lets-plays/).

[20] See https://blog.codemasters.com/codemasters-video-policy/.

[21] e.g. https://www.daedalicsupport.com/en/faq.html?open=collapse20-4.

[22] Wandtke/Bullinger/Bullinger § 12 mn. 8.

IV. Limitations for specific assets

Some publishers, such as THQ Nordic and Ubisoft, emphasise that only games as a whole, but **not assets from the game separately**, are used in videos in order to maintain control over the integrity of the game and individual elements of their franchises. THQ Nordic states: 'We're not fine with taking assets from our games (e.g., voice, music, items, artworks) and distributing those separately.'[23] Ubisoft states: 'Do not use assets from our games (e.g., voice, music, items) and do not distribute them separately.'[24] **61**

For reasons of the integrity of the game and the assets on the one hand, but also for legal reasons, the **separation of music elements is often restricted**. This may be due to the fact that either pre-existing music rights have been purchased for a game, which may not be utilised by the publisher separately from the game. If this is the case, the publisher naturally cannot actively tolerate, authorise or otherwise promote such use. On the other hand, the separation of the soundtrack or individual tracks from the game often leads to the Let's Play simply being flagged and blocked due to a content ID of the music rights holder, for example. **62**

V. Revocation and changes to guidelines and licences

As the effectiveness of guidelines and licences is **generally at the discretion of the publisher** due to the lack of an agreement, it makes sense to regularly check whether they are still valid. **63**

Many of the guidelines and licences expressly refer to this fact. Accordingly, the non-binding nature, the **revocability** and the express right to amend the guidelines, including the right to delete or remove the provisions without replacement, are clearly formulated. **64**

[23] See https://www.thqnordic.com/company/video-policy.
[24] See https://legal.ubi.com/VideoPolicy/de-DE.

§ 41
Esports

Bibliography: Ramos Gil de la Haza/Martínez Crespo, 'Comienza la partida. Punto de situación sobre determinados aspectos jurídicos de los videojuegos', 2019, Pe. i.: Revista de propiedad intelectual, No. 62, 13; Rizzi/Serao/Nowak, 'Esports in Italy: an industry ready to take off (or still in search of its regulatory soul)?' 2019 Interactive Entertainment Law Review, pp. 42–49; Shmatenko/Volkov/Ruffié-Farrugia, Esports Law and Practice, Edward Elgar Publishing, Cheltenham (UK) and Northampton (MA, USA), 2025; Rodríguez/Carrillo/Muñoz, Esports, Derecho de los Videojuegos: Aspectos Jurídicos y de Negocio, Editorial Aranzadi La Ley, Madrid, 2023; Ramos/Muñoz-Torrero, 'Intellectual Property and Esports: An Overview of the Game', 2026, World Intellectual Property Organization.

A. Introduction 1
B. Defining 'esports' 4
C. Stakeholders of the esports sector 8
I. Main stakeholders 8
II. Other stakeholders 12
D. A multi-level governance 14
E. Esports and IP 17
I. Copyright 18
II. Trademarks, patents, trade secrets, and industrial designs 27
F. A heavily contractualised sector 34
G. The professional player: employee, freelancer, athlete or artist? 39

A. Introduction

1 **Organised competitive play with video games** – usually designated by the neologism 'esports' (from 'electronic sports') – has emerged as a branch of the interactive-entertainment industry. Initially emerging in the 1980s as a form of organised play around arcade games, over the last two decades, the esports sector has evolved from the original niche communities of 'hardcore' video game players into a global network of professional organisations, event circuits, and content platforms sustained by an enthusiastic young consumer base. Esports, by their very nature, revolve around a complex framework of intellectual property rights that goes far beyond the act of playing a video game, which relates to the different stakeholders of this sector, and which determines its legal status and applicable regulatory framework.

2 The **European esports landscape** has passed through **distinct phases**. Esports began as grassroots gatherings among passionate video game enthusiasts, who organised small-scale competitions to showcase skills and foster friendly rivalries. The pioneering years at the turn of the millennium saw competitions happening mostly in LAN parties and LAN centres, and the foundation in Germany of the Cologne-based ESL that created the first supra-regional circuits, while publishers tolerated community-driven events without asserting strict IP control. In the first decade of the 2000s, the sector entered a period of growth: Online competition platforms mushroomed, and events such as ESWC in Paris demonstrated the viability of large-scale in-person tournaments. In the 2010s, *League of Legends* popularised the free-to-play MOBA model. The second half of the decade was dominated by rapid growth, increased commercialisation, and venture-capital inflows. Riot Games established a permanent studio in Berlin for its continental competition in 2015. Publishers assumed the central role, structuring the competitive ecosystems of their titles in different levels of play and territories. France saw the first

mention of esports in a law with the promulgation of the Law for a Digital Republic.[1] Finally, the period from 2020 to 2025 has been characterised by consolidation after the shock of the COVID-19 pandemic. A 2022 Resolution[2] of the European Parliament placed esports on the EU agenda. At the same time, discussions around the status of esports intensified after the celebration of the IOC's Olympic Virtual Series (2021) and Olympic Esports Week (2023) – two Olympic-brand activations out of the structure of the Games.

Nowadays, **publishers exploit esports primarily as a marketing instrument.** 3
Whether local or international, in-person or played remotely, the competitions create opportunities to attract new players, re-invigorate lapsed ones, and prolong the economic life cycle of titles. In the prevailing game-as-a-service model, constant balance patches and new content are indispensable – they keep the title relevant and sustain turnover long after its original launch. Most of this content is not necessarily linked to competitions, but esports supply an additional external narrative layer – with heroes, rivalries, and storylines – that further justifies this flow of updates and persuades the audience to engage (and spend) over the years. Therefore, esports function less as an autonomous market and more as an integrated marketing-and-licensing layer: They amplify brand value, unlock derivative income, and extend customer lifetime value within a capital-intensive creative industry.

B. Defining 'esports'

Neither the primary nor the secondary European Union legislation contain a binding 4
legal definition of 'esports'. The most authoritative point of reference is the **Resolution of the European Parliament of 10.11.2022**, approved by a large majority, in which the Parliament characterises esports as '*competitions where individuals or teams play video games – typically in front of spectators – either in-person or online, for entertainment, prizes or money*'.[3] This formulation highlights three constitutive elements: the participation of natural persons, the mediation through protected software, and the competitive determination of a winner.

Esports competitions are not spontaneous ad-hoc encounters but **structured under-** 5
takings. A private – or occasionally public – organiser selects one specific game title, fixes a tournament format and promulgates binding competition rules; teams or individual players obtain participation rights through invitation, qualification or registration. The concrete manifestations of esports are heterogeneous. They range from mass-attendance arena finals featuring globally recognised professionals to purely online weekend cups played from private homes; from amateur initiatives without monetary prizes to fully commercialised leagues financed through sponsorship, media rights and ticketing. The European Parliament deliberately leaves the degree of professionalisation and the geographical locus of play undefined in order to reflect the sector's diversity. The underlying revenue model is not specified, either – although sponsorships account for the most substantial portion of it, esports proceed benefits from other sources including media rights, merchandise sales, advertising, and, to a lesser extent, direct consumer revenue.

[1] Loi no. 2016–1321 du 7.10.2016 pour une République numérique, published in the Journal Officiel de la République Française on 8.10.2016.

[2] European Parliament. (2022). European Parliament resolution of 10.11.2022 on esports and video games (2022/2027(INI)). OJ 2022, C 161, 2–9. https://eur-lex.europa.eu/legal-content/EN/TXT/?uri=CELEX:52022IP0388.

[3] European Parliament resolution of 10.11.2022 on esports and video games. Rec. P.

6 As a matter of positive law, **esports belong to the cultural and media-industry context** rather than to the domain of sport governance. The most widely cited legal and policy definition of 'sport' comes from the Council of Europe's European Sports Charter: Sports are 'all forms of physical activity which, through casual or organised participation, are aimed at maintaining or improving physical fitness and mental well-being, forming social relationships or obtaining results in competition at all levels'.[4] The concept of physicality or meaningful bodily effort is central to understanding sports in Europe. Hence, esports rely on cognitive skills and fine motor reflexes rather than sustained physical exertion. As such, they fail the primary physicality test that sports authorities usually apply across the European Union when deciding whether an activity is a sport. Therefore, esports lack the 'not negligible physical element' that the Court of Justice has made a *sine-qua-non* for the legal concept of *sport* (C-90/16, English Bridge Union)[5] and are therefore – at least under present circumstances – excluded from the scope of Art. 165 TFEU.[6] This is also confirmed by comparative evidence that, at the time of writing, no Member State had enacted legislation fully conferring the status of a sporting discipline to esports; isolated measures – such as facilitated visa procedures or parallel tax status – constitute only partial analogies. Another decisive reason lies in the existence of exclusive intellectual-property rights: Sports (football, basketball, athletics, etc.) are part of the public domain – no one can monopolise the rules or the playing of the game. By contrast, every esports title is protected by copyright, trademarks and other IP owned or licensed by a *publisher*. Because a publisher can veto or condition any competition, esports lack the open, freely accessible character European sports law presupposes. Therefore, despite the term 'electronic sports', this nomenclature does not change the fundamental legal classification of the activity or alter its governing status under EU law, away from sports regulation.[7]

7 Moreover, competitors do not face one another in an abstract sphere called 'esports'; they participate in **institutionally framed contests** – leagues, tournaments, cups, etc. – focused on a specific videogame title whose hardware and software platforms, rules and mechanics, and creative and commercial considerations dictate the structure of its competitive ecosystem. While external observers sometimes associate esports primarily with sport-simulation video games, many of Europe's most popular and commercially successful competitions feature titles that bear no resemblance to any known sport – notably *League of Legends* and *Counter-Strike*. The sector encompasses diverse genres including strategy, action/adventure, fighting, and sports simulations, with many games incorporating elements from multiple genres. Examples of strategy games are *StarCraft* (real-time strategy or RTS), *League of Legends* (multiplayer online battle arena games or MOBA), and *Teamfight Tactics* (auto-battler). Action-oriented games are *Rainbow Six: Siege* (tactical first-person shooter), *VALORANT* (hero shooter), and *Fortnite* (battle-royale). The Fighting Game Community revolves around long-established video game franchises such as *Street Fighter* or *Tekken*. Finally, sports genre games range from respectful renditions – *EA SPORTS FC* for football or the *F1* series for racing – to hybrid

---

[4] Council of Europe, Recommendation CM/Rec(2021)5 of the Committee of Ministers to Member States on the Revised European Sports Charter, Appendix, art. 2(1) (13.10.2021).

[5] Court of Justice of the European Union (Fourth Chamber), Judgment of 26.10.2017, *The English Bridge Union Limited v Commissioners for Her Majesty's Revenue & Customs*, case C-90/16, ECLI: EU\:C:2017:814.

[6] Art. 165, Consolidated version of the Treaty on the Functioning of the European Union, OJ 2016, C 202, 120–121.

[7] This is also the opinion of Video Games Europe, as described in its 'Position on the Classification and Regulation of Esports as a Sport' <https://www.videogameseurope.eu/wp-content/uploads/2024/12/VGE-Position-Esports-and-Sport-Regulation-November-2024.pdf> (last accessed: 29.05.2025).

concepts such as the 'football with cars' title *Rocket League*. On the contrary, *extended reality* platforms and genres have not yet made a big splash in the sector.

C. Stakeholders of the esports sector

I. Main stakeholders

At the centre of every esports ecosystem is the **video game publisher**, which is usually the same company as, a subsidiary of, or contractually linked to the developer. Through exclusive rights to the video game's intellectual property assets (including software code, characters, graphics, and trademarks), publishers maintain complete control over all public exploitation of their games, encompassing competitive play and related commercial activities. The publisher's governing intensity varies along a continuum described in the literature as (i) 'highly controlled', (ii) 'controlled', and (iii) 'laissez-faire'. In the first variant the publisher organises the circuit in-house and forecloses parallel events; in the last it tolerates or licenses third-party tournaments. The chosen model determines the contractual position of all downstream actors and thereby the competitive structure of a video game. The collaborative – though still publisher-led – approach is exemplified by Riot Games, with *League of Legends* and VALORANT, where official structures coexist with licensed external tournaments, allowing limited community participation while preserving the publisher's ultimate authority. By contrast, Valve's stewardship of *Counter-Strike: Global Offensive* and *Dota 2* illustrates a markedly hands-off philosophy: Aside from sponsoring marquee 'major' events and maintaining baseline competitive standards, Valve cedes tournament organisation and commercial exploitation largely to independent stakeholders, fostering a plural, market-driven ecosystem.[8] 8

Tournament organisers (TOs) translate abstract competition into a marketable activity, including sale of media rights, sponsorship packages, or ticketing. Their authority stems directly from the publisher's intellectual property licence; without such explicit authorisation, hosting a tournament would constitute copyright infringement. In circuits run directly by the publisher, TOs are service contractors with no governing autonomy over the competition. They have the so-called 'white label' role. In licensed circuits, TOs assume residual rule-making and commercial powers, yet they remain economically dependent on sponsorship and broadcast deals that require the publisher's consent. 9

Esports **team organisations generally function as an agency** aggregating and managing playing and coaching talent, besides providing legal and performance infrastructure, and monetising the collective brand through sponsorship, merchandise and media content. Team organisations routinely take contractual assignments of their players' image rights and operate joint trademark licences with headline sponsors. 10

Players, whose status ranges from **hobbyist volunteers to salaried professionals**, supply the core competitive performance and, through streaming and social media, provide a second layer of influencer-style content monetisation. Professional players are generally employed by team organisations, whereas some players in non-team games may enjoy independent-contractor status. Their principal assets are personality and image rights. These are frequently licensed – sometimes on an exclusive basis – to 11

[8] Gian Luca Vitale, 'Publishers & Game Developers: The mighty ones within', Digital Trend Outlook 2020: Esports. PwC <https://www.pwc.de/en/technology-media-and-telecommunication/digital-trend-outlook-esport-2020/publishers-game-developers.html> (last accessed: 29.05.2025).

their team. Some players further exploit personal channels on content platforms such as Twitch or YouTube, thereby generating advertising and subscription revenue streams.

II. Other stakeholders

12 External **brands** constitute the single largest non-publisher funding source of the esports sector. Sponsorship contracts integrate logos into event broadcasts, team jerseys and, increasingly, in-game environments. Such integrations must respect the publisher's asset-usage guidelines, so the sponsor's rights package is effectively double-licensed – first from the publisher, then from the immediate counterparty. Digital content platforms (Twitch, YouTube, etc.) act as primary distributors of live and on-demand content to the public, necessitating agreements with rightsholders, primarily the publishers, to transmit the esports events. Equipment, service and technology providers, like hardware manufacturers, ISPs (Internet Service Providers), production companies, marketing agencies, anti-cheat services, data-analytics firms and payment processors furnish the technical substratum of competitions. Their ability to exploit derivative IP (e.g., data feeds, highlight clips) is contractually circumscribed by both publisher and TO.

13 **Sector associations**, including self-styled esports federations, occupy a peripheral position in the governance ecosystem, as they possess neither statutory delegations of public authority nor effective self-regulatory power. They function primarily as advocacy organisations that promote industry interests, coordinate stakeholder dialogue, and occasionally establish voluntary codes of conduct. However, these codes lack binding force without publisher endorsement. The true normative authority in esports resides exclusively in the intellectual-property prerogatives of game publishers, who either organise competitions directly or license third-party tournament operators under strict contractual conditions. This IP-centric governance model fundamentally distinguishes esports from other types of competitions, and sport in particular, where federations typically hold delegated regulatory powers from public authorities. In jurisdictions where esports associations have sought formal recognition, they have generally been limited to consultative roles rather than granted genuine regulatory competence.

D. A multi-level governance

14 Esports regulation is anchored, first, in the **internal-market provisions** of Artt. 26 and 114 TFEU (cross-border provision of digital services, online broadcasting, and consumer protection), secondly in Art. 173 TFEU (industrial policy for the creative-tech sector), and, subsidiarily, in Art. 167 TFEU (culture). Primary regulatory authority in matters of labour law, taxation or visa policy remains with the Member States; any attempt at harmonisation must satisfy the proportionality and subsidiarity criteria of Art. 5 TEU.

15 Since hard competences are absent, the Union has resorted to political guidance. The European Parliament, in its Resolution of 10.11.2022 on Esports and Video Games (2022/2027(INI)), expressly states that esports and sport constitute different sectors and urges the Commission to elaborate a long-term strategy for video games and esports, a code of conduct with publishers, and guidelines on professional players status, while deliberately refraining from proposing binding legislation. The Council Conclusions of 24.11.2023 on 'Enhancing the Cultural and Creative Dimension of the European Video-

Games Sector'[9] invite the Commission to map national support schemes and integrate video game (and, by implication, esports) policy into Creative Europe and other funding programmes. Therefore, both instruments operate as coordination devices rather than as normative acts.

16 At the national level, the regulatory landscape remains a patchwork of selective, often experimental, interventions. France continues to hold the most comprehensive bespoke framework. Artt. 101 and 102 of the Loi no. 2016–1321 pour une République numérique and the implementing Decrees 2017–871 and 2017–872, supply a legal definition of 'competitive video-game contests', prescribe age- and prize-money limits, and recognise fixed-term employment contracts for professional players. In Greece, Law 4908/2022[10] – addressing, inter alia, 'mind sports and esports' – defines 'esports' as the 'digital representation of an established sport, practised individually or in teams and administered by an already recognised sports federation'. Greece is the only Member State to introduce an expressly sports classification, albeit confined to titles that replicate an existing physical sport and operate under a pre-existing sports federation. The provision inhabits a largely hypothetical register: The structural disjunction between federation-bound regulatory competence and publisher-controlled game-IP leaves the rule with an ill-defined field of operation, rendering its normative force virtually inert. Germany follows a functional-equivalence model restricted to discrete fields. The Employment Regulation (§ 22 No 5 BeschV)[11] creates a dedicated 'esports visa', and the Racing Betting and Lottery Ordinance (§ 15 III RennwLottDV)[12] assimilates esports to sport solely for betting-tax purposes; yet federal law still lacks any overarching legal definition. The prevailing European model is still one of piecemeal legislation, functional analogies, and publisher-driven, IP-centric private governance.

E. Esports and IP

17 Esports are inconceivable **without a robust architecture of exclusive rights**. Every stage of the value chain – from coding a new game mechanic to streaming a grand-final highlight – relies on the owner's ability to license or withhold the underlying IP. Intellectual property rights such as copyrights, trademarks, patents, trade secrets, and industrial designs exist to safeguard the inventive and creative works of individuals and organisations. European Union legislation supplies the harmonised core of the regulation. Copyright, trademark and – at the margins – patent, trade-secret, and industrial design law form an interlocking grid that both enables and constrains the commercial exploitation of video game competitions.

[9] Council of the European Union. (2023). Council conclusions on enhancing the cultural and creative dimension of the European video games sector. OJ 2023, C 2023/1345, 1–7. ELI: http://data.europa.eu/eli/C/2023/1345/oj.

[10] Hellenic Republic. (2022). Law 4908/2022 'Regulation of issues regarding the organization and operation of electronic sports (esports) competitions and other provisions'. Government Gazette of the Hellenic Republic, Issue A, No. 52, 11.3.2022.

[11] Federal Republic of Germany. (2013). Ordinance on the Employment of Foreigners (Beschäftigungsverordnung – BeschV), Section 22 No. 5. Federal Law Gazette I, p. 1499, as amended by Art. 1 of the Law of 18.12.2018 (Federal Law Gazette I, p. 2644).

[12] Federal Republic of Germany. (2014). Racing Betting and Lottery Ordinance (Rennwett- und Lotteriegesetz-Durchführungsverordnung – RennwLottDV), Section 15(3). Federal Law Gazette I, p. 3662, as amended by Art. 2 of the Law of 21.6.2021 (Federal Law Gazette I p. 2065).

I. Copyright

18 Esports in the European Union (EU) are **fundamentally copyright-driven**. Every match, stream and highlight reel is mediated by rights that vest in the publisher of the game, which is the backbone of the esport sector and of the video game industry.

19 Directive 2001/29/EC[13] (the 'InfoSoc Directive') serves as the cornerstone of copyright protection in the European Union, harmonising key rights such as reproduction, distribution, and communication to the public, while safeguarding against the circumvention of technological protection measures (TPMs). Complementing this framework, Directive 2009/24/EC[14] (the 'Software Directive') specifically protects computer programs as literary works, which is also an essential element of any video game. More recently, Directive 2019/790[15] (the 'Digital Single Market Directive') modernised EU copyright law for the digital era, introducing rules for online content-sharing platforms, text-and-data mining exceptions, and enhanced protections for press publishers.

20 Under Artt. 2 and 3 of the InfoSoc Directive, esports organisers engage in acts of reproduction and communication to the public when broadcasting competitive gameplay, requiring authorisation from the publisher of the video game. Art. 2 of the InfoSoc Directive grants authors (e.g., game developers/publishers) the exclusive right to authorise or prohibit the reproduction of their works, including temporary or partial copies. During esports events, gameplay is captured, processed, and streamed, which inherently involves the reproduction of the video game's audiovisual elements (such as character models, environments, etc.) on servers, streaming platforms, or viewers' devices (e.g., buffering or caching). Even transient copies, like those stored temporarily in RAM during live broadcasts, fall under Art. 2(a), necessitating rights-holders' permission unless covered by exceptions (e.g., temporary copies under Art. 5(1)).

21 Art. 3(1) of the InfoSoc Directive, meanwhile, governs the communication to the public of copyrighted works. By streaming matches to online or present audiences, esports organisers 'communicate' the game's audiovisual expression (e.g., gameplay footage, cutscenes, or soundtracks) to a public that would not otherwise have access to the game in that specific competitive context. This requires authorisation from rightsholders, as the Court of Justice of the European Union (CJEU) has emphasised that such transmissions must be licensed unless exempted (e.g., for parody or quotation).

22 In the context of copyright law and the right of communication to the public, the CJEU interprets 'the public' as an *indeterminate number of potential recipients* extending beyond a strictly private or domestic sphere, and thus a fairly large group that is not limited to small, familiar circles, as illustrated in cases such as *SGAE v Rafael Hoteles SA*[16] and *Football Association Premier League*.[17] This interpretation is closely linked to the concept of a 'new public', whereby an additional act of communication can be said to occur if the work is directed at a segment of the public more expansive than that covered by the initial authorisation, whether through a new technical means or by reaching a

---

[13] Directive 2001/29/EC of the European Parliament and of the Council of 22.5.2001 on the harmonisation of certain aspects of copyright and related rights in the information society.

[14] Directive 2009/24/EC of the European Parliament and of the Council of 23.4.2009 on the legal protection of computer programmes.

[15] Directive (EU) 2019/790 of the European Parliament and of the Council of 17.4.2019 on copyright and related rights in the Digital Single Market and amending Directives 96/9/EC and 2001/29/EC.

[16] Judgment of the Court (Third Chamber), of 7.12.2006, *Sociedad General de Autores y Editores de España (SGAE) v Rafael Hoteles SA*, case C-306/05, ECLI:EU:C:2006:764.

[17] Judgment of the Court (Grand Chamber), of 4.10.2011, *Football Association Premier League Ltd. and Others v QC Leisure and Others* (C-403/08) and *Karen Murphy v Media Protection Services Ltd.* (C-429/08), ECLI:EU:C:2011:631.

distinctly different audience than originally contemplated. In each instance, the CJEU assesses whether the potential recipients exceed the range of those normally exempt from any licensing expectation, and whether substantive steps have been taken to ensure that the work is made available to this broader group.

The Court's broad interpretation of *public* applies here, as esports broadcasts target an indeterminate number of viewers, distinct from a private circle. Notably, video games qualify as 'complex works' (*Nintendo v PC Box*),[18] meaning their protection extends to both software (regulated by the Software Directive) and audiovisual components (protected under InfoSoc), requiring organisers to secure rights for all protected elements. This legal framework underscores that **esports organisers** must negotiate **licences** with **game publishers** or developers to lawfully reproduce and stream gameplays. For example, reproducing in-game assets (Art. 2) or broadcasting live matches on Twitch (Art. 3) could infringe copyrights if unauthorised. As described, while some publishers permit use of their video games for esports activities under broad licensing agreements, others may impose stricter terms. 23

On the other side, the copyright ownership of esports gameplays (i.e., the audiovisual output of competitive matches) depends on the interplay between the video game publisher's rights and the organiser's or players' contributions, as governed by EU copyright law. Under the **InfoSoc Directive**, the publisher (as the rightsholder of the video game) typically retains exclusive rights over the game's underlying audiovisual elements, meaning that reproducing or streaming gameplay requires the publisher's authorisation. However, additional contributions by players or organisers, such as unique commentary, overlays, or production elements added during a broadcast, including audiovisual recordings, may qualify for separate copyright protection if they meet the standard established in the copyright laws. An audiovisual recording is a fixed sequence of moving images and sounds (like a video or livestream) protected by copyright. In esports, gameplay becomes an audiovisual recording when it's streamed or saved, capturing the game's visuals (characters, maps) and sounds (music, effects), along with any added elements like commentary or camera angles. The game publisher (e.g., Riot Games for League of Legends) usually holds the main copyright because they created the game's original characters, code, and music. Organisers or players can only use or stream gameplay if the publisher allows it (via licences or contracts). However, organisers might own copyright for extra elements, like unique commentary, graphics, or the actual recordings of the gameplay, which don't override the publisher's ownership of the game itself, but, on the contrary, are dependent on them. 24

Under EU copyright law, protecting the format of a competition (e.g., rules, structure, or sequence of events) is challenging under the standard set by the CJEU in *Cofemel v G-Star Raw*.[19] The CJEU ruled that copyright protection applies only to *original works* reflecting the *author's own intellectual creation*, irrespective of aesthetic or functional purpose. Therefore, a competition format could theoretically qualify if its design involves *creative choices* that go beyond mere technical rules or generic ideas (e.g., a unique scoring system, distinctive stage designs, or narrative elements). However, most competition formats are built on functional rules (e.g., scoring criteria, match structures) or commonplace concepts (e.g., elimination brackets), which lack the originality required under *Cofemel*. The CJEU clarified that the classification of a subject matter as a 'work' 25

[18] Judgment of the Court (Fourth Chamber), of 23.1.2014, *Nintendo Co. Ltd and Others v PC Box Srl and 9Net Srl*, ECLI:EU:C:2014:25.

[19] Judgment of the Court (Third Chamber) of 12.9.2019, *Cofemel – Sociedade de Vestuário SA v G-Star Raw CV*, ECLI:EU:C:2019:721.

entails that there exist an original subject matter, in the sense of being the author's own intellectual creation (para. 29), a threshold many competition formats fail to meet.

26 While not impossible, securing copyright protection for a competition format is exceptionally difficult. Courts often view such formats as ideas, procedures, or methods excluded from protection under Art. 2 of the InfoSoc Directive, which safeguards only the *expression* of ideas, not the ideas themselves. For example, a reality TV show format might blend creative elements (e.g., unique challenges, editing styles) that could qualify as original, but standalone competition structures (e.g., tournament brackets) rarely reach this bar. Following *Cofemel*, EU law prioritises originality over functionality, hence non-artistic formats (e.g., esports tournament rules) could theoretically gain protection if they demonstrate sufficient creativity. In practice, most formats remain unprotected, forcing organisers to rely on contracts, trademarks, or unfair competition laws instead. Thus, while copyright protection for competition formats cannot be entirely ruled out, the *Cofemel* standard makes it a narrow, uncertain path.

II. Trademarks, patents, trade secrets, and industrial designs

27 Whereas copyright secures the immaterial substrate of gameplay, trademark law governs the signs that allow economic actors to differentiate their goods and services. Four main categories may be distinguished: the marks of publishers (game and franchise titles and logos), those of the tournaments and tournament organisers, the team organisations and, finally, of star players. Words, logos and other identifiers are harmonised under **Regulation (EU) 2017/1001**[20] and **Directive (EU) 2015/2436 (Trademarks Directive)**[21] In the dynamic world of esports, trademark law grants publishers and organisations a statutory monopoly known as *ius prohibendi*. Unlike traditional sports, where the essence of the game – such as 'football' or 'basketball' – exists in the public domain, esports entities retain exclusive control over their names. Titles like *League of Legends* or *Overwatch* are not merely games but legally protected brands, enabling their owners to police unauthorised tournaments, merchandise, and broadcasts. This authority stems from trademark law's foundational purposes: to identify the source of goods or services, guarantee their quality, and protect the commercial value derived from brand recognition. For instance, Riot Games can swiftly act against an unlicensed *VALORANT* tournament that misleads fans into believing it is officially endorsed, thereby safeguarding both their reputation and revenue.

28 **Trademark rights**, while essential to protecting brand identity, are inherently **territorial** and do not automatically extend worldwide. For esports stakeholders, particularly publishers, tournament organisers, and professional teams, this territorial nature necessitates careful planning to avoid gaps in protection or infringement issues. As there is no single global trademark that confers absolute coverage, securing rights involves navigating multiple systems and jurisdictions, each with its own procedural rules, language requirements, and enforcement standards. Given these constraints, many esports entities opt for registration strategies that combine a European Union trademark (EUTM) with additional national filings. An EUTM provides broad coverage, allowing rights holders to protect their mark in all current EU Member States through a single filing. However, this registration alone may not suffice where there are specific national practices or mar-

[20] Regulation (EU) 2017/1001 of the European Parliament and of the Council of 14.6.2017 on the European Union trademark.

[21] Directive (EU) 2015/2436 of the European Parliament and of the Council of 16.12.2015 to approximate the laws of the Member States relating to trademarks.

ket conditions that warrant further protection. For instance, certain countries outside the EU (such as the United Kingdom, Switzerland, or other major esports markets) may require individual registrations to ensure robust brand protection.

In terms of classes, publishers and teams frequently file under Class 9 (covering software and computer games), Class 25 (covering apparel and related items), and Class 41 (covering entertainment services, including esports events, tournaments, and streaming).[22] Such registrations capture the diverse ways in which esports brands are used, ranging from the sale of merchandise and production of software to the operation of tournaments and broadcasting of matches. By layering these core classes in different territories, esports brands can build a solid defensive wall against copycats, counterfeiters, or unauthorised merchandising. **29**

Additionally, within the framework of EU trademark law, certain uses of third-party marks, including in esports competitions, may qualify as legitimate descriptive acts, exempt from infringement claims under Art. 14(1) of the Trademarks Directive. As established by the CJEU, descriptive uses fall outside the scope of trademark exclusivity when they do not undermine the essential functions of the mark, particularly its role in guaranteeing the origin of goods or services to consumers (case C-2/00 *Hölterhoff*, para. 16).[23] For such uses to be deemed lawful, however, they must satisfy the cumulative criteria articulated in CJEU jurisprudence. First, the trademark must be employed *strictly to describe a characteristic* of the product or service at issue, such as its quality, purpose, or geographical origin (case C-228/03 *Gillette*, para. 49).[24] In the context of esports, this could encompass the depiction of an energy drink logo on a virtual athlete's jersey to authentically replicate real-world team sponsorships, provided the use is purely informational and not intended to designate commercial origin. Second, the use must adhere to *honest practices in industrial or commercial matters*, a standard further refined in *Gillette* to require that: (i) the trademark is the *only means* of providing the relevant information; (ii) the use does not imply a commercial connection between the trademark owner and the esports product; and (iii) the use does not unfairly exploit or damage the repute of the mark. Nevertheless, the line between permissible descriptive use and unlawful exploitation remains context-dependent, necessitating careful alignment with CJEU precedents to mitigate litigation risks in this complex landscape. **30**

Within the esports ecosystem, **patents** can also play an increasingly strategic role in **safeguarding technological advancements** that enhance competitive performance and viewer engagement. While traditional gameplay mechanics rarely meet the technical-character thresholds required for patentability under the European Patent Convention (EPC),[25] hardware innovations tailored to esports, such as ultra-responsive controllers, low-latency gameplay peripherals, or immersive haptic feedback systems, are frequently patented to secure market exclusivity. For instance, anti-cheat technologies, such as kernel-level detection systems used in titles like *VALORANT*, or latency-reduction algorithms for cloud-based esports platforms, are increasingly subject to patent filings. Even VR esports arenas, which rely on motion-tracking innovations, demonstrate the growing intersection of patents and competitive video gameplay. While the practical relevance of patents in esports remains narrower than copyright or trademarks, their importance is **31**

---

[22] Nice Agreement Concerning the International Classification of Goods and Services for the Purposes of the Registration of Marks, concluded at Nice on 15.6.1957, as revised and amended.

[23] Judgment of 14.5.2002, *Hölterhoff v Ulrich Freiesleben*, case C-2/00, ECLI:EU:C:2002:287.

[24] Judgment of 17.3.2005, *Gillette Company and Gillette Group Finland Oy v LA-Laboratories Oy*, case C-228/03, ECLI:EU:C:2005:177.

[25] European Patent Convention (EPC), concluded at Munich on 5.10.1973, as revised by the Act revising the EPC of 29.11.2000, OJ EPO 2001, Special edition No. 4.

rising as manufacturers seek to monopolise cutting-edge tools that confer competitive advantages, from AI-driven coaching software to real-time biometric feedback systems.

32 Alongside patents, **trade secrets** serve as a critical shield for preserving esports entities' proprietary knowledge. Under Directive (EU) 2016/943,[26] trade secret protection extends to confidential data such as proprietary matchmaking algorithms, unreleased gameplay strategies developed by professional teams, or analytics engines that predict opponent behaviour. For example, esports organisations like Team Liquid or G2 Esports guard their training methodologies and in-game tactics as trade secrets, akin to sports teams protecting playbooks. Anti-cheat developers, such as those behind *Easy Anti-Cheat*, also rely on trade secrecy to obscure the inner workings of their detection systems, preventing hackers from reverse-engineering countermeasures.

33 Finally, the visual and tactile elements central to esports' commercial appeal are fortified through **industrial design rights**, which protect the aesthetic features of products under Regulation (EC) 6/2002.[27] Gameplay peripherals, such as the sleek, ergonomic contours of a tournament-grade mouse or the RGB-lit chassis of a high-end PC, often qualify for Community design registration, granting up to 25 years of exclusivity over their distinctive appearance. Even virtual goods benefit from this protection; limited-edition weapon skins in games like *Counter-Strike 2* or *Fortnite*, though protected by copyright as artistic works, may also draw on design rights when meeting the corresponding criteria. Furthermore, UI elements tailored for esports – such as minimalist HUDs (heads-up displays) designed to minimise spectator distraction during broadcasts – can be shielded as registered designs, ensuring competitors cannot copy their layout. The synergy between industrial designs and branding is particularly evident in collaborative esports merchandise, such as jerseys featuring team logos rendered in patented holographic materials or peripherals co-branded with tournament organisers like ESL. By layering design rights with trademarks and copyrights, esports stakeholders cultivate a cohesive visual identity while deterring knockoffs in an industry where aesthetic distinction is synonymous with commercial success.

F. A heavily contractualised sector

34 After an initial stage where publishers usually didn't intervene in esports tournaments, nowadays European esports is a **heavily contractualised sector** dominated by the **intellectual-property prerogatives of video game companies**. As described above, copyright in the video game confers an exclusive legal monopoly over every reproduction and public communication. Consequently, esports competitions may only occur only with the rightsholder – almost always the publisher – has granted a licence, and every downstream relationship – whether between tournament organiser, team or player – must be negotiated against that background of exclusive rights. At the same time, private autonomy is circumscribed by mandatory layers of Union law in the fields of competition, consumer protection, data privacy, labour standards, etc.

35 Publisher control manifests itself in a dual model. Either the rightsholder stages the competition personally (the so-called 'publisher model') or it tolerates or licenses a third-party organiser (the 'third-party/provider model'). The dispositive choice depends entirely on the strategy of the publisher and may vary even within a single title among

[26] Directive (EU) 2016/943 of the European Parliament and of the Council of 8.6.2016 on the protection of undisclosed know-how and business information (trade secrets) against their unlawful acquisition, use and disclosure, OJ 2016, L 157, 1–18.

[27] Council Regulation (EC) No. 6/2002 of 12.12.2001 on Community designs. OJ 2002, L 3, 1–24.

different territories. In both models, any act of broadcasting or public display falls within the exclusive right of public communication; the organiser therefore requires a licence pursuant to Artt. 2 and 3 of the InfoSoc Directive.

Licences to tournament organisers typically address the following terms: object (title and type of competition), territorial scope, exclusivity, duration, rights granted (including copyright and trademarks), monetisation and revenue-sharing provisions, rulesets and integrity obligations, brand protection, and termination. In these contracts, publishers usually retain ownership of game-related copyrights (e.g., audiovisual assets, characters) and trademarks (e.g., logos, team names). Organisers must secure licences to publicly perform, stream, or monetise gameplay, as standard end-user licence agreements (EULAs) prohibit commercial use. For example, *Rocket League* tournaments require explicit permission to broadcast matches, ensuring compliance with Epic Games' IP policies.[28] Failure to obtain these rights risks legal action under statutes like the DMCA, as seen in disputes over unauthorised broadcasts of *StarCraft* matches.[29] **36**

Ultimately, contracts and licensing agreements heavily influence ownership. Publishers often assert control over esports gameplays through EULAs or specific licences, requiring organisers to obtain permission for tournaments and broadcasts. Absent such agreements, the publisher's copyright prevails, as gameplay (i.e., the audiovisual recording) mainly includes their protected work. Organisers, therefore, must navigate a legal landscape where publishers hold the foundational rights, while ancillary contributions (if original) may create limited, shared ownership. As described, copyright law does not merely 'influence' but structurally determines the organisation of the entire competitive ecosystem, including the contractual arrangements. **37**

On the other side, personal-data issues dominate the regulatory risk profile. Match servers, anti-cheat tools and broadcast overlays generate large volumes of telemetry that may qualify as 'personal data' whenever they can be linked to an identified or identifiable player. The organiser thus acts as a data controller and must respect the GDPR principles of purpose limitation and data minimisation. Consent is often chosen as the lawful basis, especially when minors compete; yet Art. 8 GDPR permits a child to give valid consent to an information-society service only above a nationally determined 'digital age of consent'. The Regulation sets 16 as the default but allows Member States to legislate any age between 13 and 16. Major jurisdictions have exercised that option differently – United Kingdom: 13; France: 15; Italy and Spain: 14; Germany: 16. Where a participant is below the relevant threshold, the organiser must obtain and verify parental consent before collecting or broadcasting gameplay data, and the ruleset must describe the verification method in clear, age-appropriate language. **38**

G. The professional player: employee, freelancer, athlete or artist?

The legal status of professional esports players is not fixed across Europe. Esports labour relations are governed, in principle, by the same Union-law freedoms of movement and service that frame other industries. **39**

France is one of the few countries that has regulated the relationship between esports players and teams. French law classifies top-tier competitors as fixed-term employees under Art. 102 of the 2016 Law of the Digital Republic, subject to ministerial approval of **40**

[28] Sam Anton. LeagueSpot. 'What are Gaming Tournament Licenses and Competition Guidelines?' https://leaguespot.com/blog/how-to-find-a-tournament-community-license (last accessed: 26.05.2025).

[29] Jacek Markowski. Esports Legal News. 'Intellectual Property Rights' https://esportslegal.news/esports-legal-wiki/ip/intellectual-property-rights/ (last accessed: 26.5.2025).

their employing organisation. Organisations in other territories, by contrast, may engage players through hybrid 'services and image-rights' agreements, yet the sector and authorities increasingly treat them as workers once responsibilities are dictated by the organisation – a study commissioned by the European Parliament reaches the same result for the large majority of Member States, concluding that 'an employment situation relevant to social security can typically be assumed'.[30] Contracts typically combine competitive services with commercial image-rights commitments, reflecting the hybrid role of the esports player as both competitor and an influencer/content creator. The remuneration architecture is multi-layered – a fixed salary, bounded by national minimum-wage law provides baseline security, while prize-pool participation and image rights complete the panorama. Finally, two structural features – high geographic mobility of players and the de-territorialised 'digital workplace' (remote competition) require specific considerations, but their discussion surpasses the scope of this chapter.

41 In assessing the legal status of esports players under copyright law, one of the most provocative questions is whether these players could be considered *authors* of the work they interact with. While it may appear far-fetched, this notion was in fact raised – and dismissed – in a US court, in the *Midway Manufacturing Co. v Artic International Inc.*[31] case, where the court rejected the idea that video game players could be authors of arcade gameplay sequences. The argument against such classification lies in the fundamental principles of authorship in copyright law: An author must be a natural person who makes creative choices that give rise to an original work. Esports players, while often highly skilled and capable of producing gameplay that is entertaining and unique, operate within a pre-established system of rules and environments created by developers. Their decisions, however strategic or aesthetically pleasing, are constrained by the programmed logic and graphical interface of the video game itself. Unlike traditional authors who create *ex nihilo*, gamers interact with an existing copyrighted work, one protected not only through its audiovisual components but also through its software code and gameplay mechanics. Therefore, under current legal standards and case law,[32] the players' contributions, though valuable, do not rise to the threshold of authorship as understood in copyright law.

42 Another potential legal classification for esports players may be that of *performers* or *performing artists*. The definition of a performer under national and supranational law, such as the Rome Convention and EU directives, typically includes people who 'act, sing, deliver, declaim, play in, or otherwise perform literary or artistic works'[33] in any form. Crucially, this status does not require the performance to be original or possess a certain level of artistic quality; it merely requires that the person performs a work. In this light, one could argue that players do indeed execute a protected audiovisual work – the video game – often before a public audience, either online or in live competitions. Their performance can be likened to that of a musician interpreting a score, as they interact with the game interface in real time, shaping each session with their unique timing, strategy, and reflexes. Furthermore, the complexity of the interface and the skill involved arguably surpass that required of performers of simpler musical instruments. Yet this analogy has limitations. Players are not executing the underlying software per

[30] Scholz/Nothelfer, 'Research for CULT Committee – Esports, European Parliament', Policy Department for Structural and Cohesion Policies 2022.

[31] *Midway Manufacturing Co. v Artic International, Inc.*, 704 F.2d 1009 (7th Cir. 1983).

[32] This is also consistent with the judgment of the European Court of Justice (Third Chamber) of 12.9.2019, Cofemel – *Sociedade de Vestuário SA v G-Star Raw CV*, ECLI:EU:C:2019:721.

[33] Art. 3(a) of the International Convention for the Protection of Performers, Producers of Phonograms and Broadcasting Organizations, Rome, 26.10.1961.

se but are rather manipulating visual outputs and mechanics, which themselves may not always qualify as protectable 'works'. Additionally, the primary objective of the player is typically **competitive** – scoring points, defeating opponents – rather than the communicative or expressive goal often associated with **artistic performances**. While the interpretation of 'performance' could arguably be expanded to accommodate the esports phenomenon, current legal frameworks and industry practices do not support that conclusion.

Furthermore, short-term tournament travel is ordinarily facilitated by the Schengen Visa Code (Regulation 810/2009). The visa application should characterise the visit as a **cultural or sporting performance**, and documentary evidence of professional status – invitation letter, participation contract, proof of health insurance – remains essential. For the German labour market, § 22 No. 5 Beschäftigungsverordnung introduced in March 2020 constitutes the most advanced specialised route. It authorises residence and gainful employment for players and coaches aged sixteen or older for up to ninety days per competitive season if they (1) are bound by an employment contract with a German team organisation or tournament organiser, (2) earn at least half of the annual reference income of the general pension insurance, and (3) compete in tournaments organised by an entity recognised by the Federal Ministry of the Interior. Long-term engagements, by contrast, must fit into the general migration acquis. The EU Blue Card under Directive 2021/1883, with its cumulative requirements of an academic qualification and a salary threshold of currently 43,800 EUR (or 38,688 EUR for shortage occupations), seldom accommodates professional players. National 'talent' or 'artist' permits – such as the French Passeport Talent – offer more flexible salary benchmarks. **43**

Index

Bold numbers refer to articles, normal ones to margin numbers.

Abuse **35** 2
- of dominance **35** 50 ff., 57

Account
- data **29** 9 f.
- opening **9** 44
- system **31** 29 ff.

Accounting **11** 29, 54
- reliable **11** 28 f.
- standard **10** 32, **11** 30

Acqui-hires **35** 42 ff., 48 f.

Acqui-hiring **10** 7

Acquisition **26** 9 ff., 14
- game industry **10** 9
- minority stake **10** 5
- player **6** 13
- publicly listed **10** 4

Ad
- in-game **38** 13, 16 f.
- non-personalised **38** 30
- personalising **38** 2
- targeted **36** 50

Ad-blocking software **13** 62

Adjustment
- balance **12** 83
- contract **15** 73

Adjustment clause **25** 44
- blanket **25** 43 ff.

Administrative fine **21** 23, **28** 80

Administrator PEGI **22** 39

Advertisement
- dynamic **37** 43
- in-game **38** 5 ff.

Advertising **4** 28, **17** 43, **18** 41, **22** 55, **23** 29, **32** 50, **37** 1, 22, 26, **38** 10, **39** 32
- aggressive **38** 17
- alcohol **39** 41
- bait **37** 9
- ethics **37** 2, 21
- financing **4** 4
- in-game **16** 47, **38** 1 ff., 9
- insurance **10** 36
- message **38** 13
- misleading **37** 45
- of video games **37** 4
- personalised **37** 20
- prohibited **39** 39
- rules, PEGI **22** 61 ff.
- subliminal **37** 29
- targeted **29** 17, **32** 54, **38** 17, 23 f., 26 ff.
- tobacco **39** 41
- video games **37** 4

Advertising Standards Authority (ASA) **26** 48
- rulings **26** 46 ff.

AGCM **26** 43, **28** 77

Age
- demographics **2** 31 f.
- estimation **34** 9, 12 f.
- gating **34** 9
- group, 45–64 **2** 35
- threshold **34** 40
- verification **24** 43, 47, **34** 9 ff., 13, 25, 30, 48, 51, 57, 61, 66

Age assurance **29** 40, **34** 8 ff., 29 ff., 39, 56, 65
- obligation **34** 46
- solutions **29** 42

Age classification **22** 3, 10, **29** 41, **33** 46

Agency
- marketing **36** 70
- relationship **36** 70 ff.
- video production **36** 72

Age rating **18** 47, **22** 5, 24 ff., 26, 32 ff., 43 f., 48, 60, 64, **23** 4, 10, 15, 21, 31, 34, 49, **24** 10 ff., **26** 37, **34** 3, 58

Aggressive commercial practice **24** 25, **37** 10, **39** 19

Agreement **16** 16, **31** 5
- collective bargaining **15** 37, 70
- cooperation **35** 54
- end user license **32** 29
- licensing **12** 24, 49 ff., **16** 37
- prohibited **35** 6

AI Act **4** 30, **32** 63 ff., **36** 37

Algorithmic accountability **24** 50

Algorithmic decision-making **32** 31

Ambition, creative **5** 37, **12** 21

Amount VAT **30** 17

Anti-cheat technology **41** 31 f.

Antitrust **24** 37, **35** 4, 67
- European **35** 1
- law **35** 3

Application
- bad-faith **17** 38
- decentralised **27** 48

Approval
- concrete **40** 51
- process **19** 15

App Store **6** 10, **24** 6, 17, **28** 11, **31** 14, **35** 4, 57, 59, 64

ARPP **38** 8 f., **39** 45

Article 101 Treaty on the Functioning of the European Union (Article 101 TFEU) **35** 5 ff.

Article of association **9** 17, 42, 54 ff., 57 f., **10** 37

Artificial Intelligence Act **32** 63 ff., **36** 37

Artificial intelligence (AI) **4** 24, 29 ff., **12** 52, **14** 4, 46 ff., **16** 54, **24** 38, **32** 65, **36** 35, 57 ff.
- generative **12** 11, 51
- self-learning **32** 34

– usage **32** 59
Assessment
– hierarchy **23** 41
– retroactive **30** 42
– risk **23** 25, 42
Asset
– creative **12** 48
– ownership **12** 76
Assignment **19** 63, **35** 27
– agreement **10** 25
– of rights **35** 24
Association
– consumer protection **28** 87
– trade **36** 28
Assurance
– age **29** 40, **34** 56
– financial **36** 73
– limited **21** 13
– reasonable **21** 13
Audit **11** 53
– culture **11** 51
– cycle **11** 59
– finding **11** 58
– interval **11** 52
– provision **19** 51
Authenticity **9** 14, **20** 26, **39** 11
Author **15** 5, 9, 16 f., 40, 42, 52, 60 f., 66, 72, **16** 6, 9 ff.
– name **14** 22
– remuneration **15** 71
Authorisation **9** 63, **40** 42
Authority
– designated **21** 23
– rule-making **34** 35
– supervisory **25** 26
– tax **30** 18
Authorship **13** 33, **15** 47, **16** 3, 50, **27** 15, **41** 41

Ban **28** 91
– local **20** 1
Basis **15** 72
– co-regulatory **22** 13
– legal **7** 59
– need-to-know **31** 39
Behaviour
– cheating **29** 12
– criminal **40** 58
– fraudulent **29** 46
– infringing **28** 18
– toxic **22** 4
Benefit
– non-pecuniary **39** 35
– pecuniary **39** 36
Berne Convention **13** 3, **16** 4
Betting and Gambling Act 2021 (BGA) **26** 56
Biometric data **29** 27
– identity **29** 13
– processing **34** 67
Blockchain **4** 27, **12** 28, **24** 31 ff., **27** 42, 45 f., 50, 52
Block exemption **7** 18, 23, **35** 16, 22, 26
– regulation **35** 17 ff.
Boilerplate **19** 10, 61 ff.
– provision **19** 61
Bonus
– free **37** 29
– stay-on **10** 11
Brand **10** 13, **27** 59, **36** 70, **41** 12, 27
– partnership **36** 63, 67
Budget **12** 17, 46, **17** 37
– marketing **19** 44
Business
– consideration **12** 48 ff., 73 ff.
– decision **5** 6, **20** 11
– discipline **5** 8
– Finland funding **8** 17
– foundations **5** 17 ff.
Business model **4** 4, **11** 11, 21 ff., **12** 22, 26 ff., **16** 47 ff., **18** 28 ff., **24** 2
Buy-to-play **24** 14 f.

Caching **32** 8
– exception **28** 40
Campaign
– ATL **36** 42 ff.
– marketing **19** 18
Capital
– Directive **9** 6
– increase **9** 66
– private **5** 24
– structure **9** 42
– venture **5** 23
Case law **17** 46 ff.
– CJEU **4** 14, **14** 36
CDSM Directive **33** 24
Celebrity **36** 65, **37** 34
– endorsement **36** 64 f.
Character **26** 3
– appearance **17** 28
– archetype **13** 32
– cultural **7** 56
– design **13** 25
– distinguishing **17** 13
– misleading **17** 17
Cheating **13** 4, 43 ff., **29** 46
– behaviour **29** 12
Cheat software **13** 49, 53 f., 59, 61
Child-directed monetisation **24** 18
Child pornography **33** 22
Child profiling **29** 44
Child protection **2** 31, **24** 37, **32** 59
– stricter **24** 47
Child rights **22** 47
Child Sexual Abuse and Exploitation Directive **33** 22

Child sexual abuse material (CSAM) **32** 70
Child sexual exploitation **33** 44
Chilling effect **33** 61
Choice
- in gaming **36** 4 f.
- legalform **9** 20
- of jurisdiction **28** 96
Circumvention **34** 62
- device **13** 19, **28** 34
CJEU case law **4** 14, **14** 36
Claim **36** 18
- marketing **36** 15, 17
- misleading **36** 39
- third-party **19** 56
Classification
- age **22** 10
- criteria **22** 27
- video game **13** 11 ff.
Clause **14** 50, **25** 44
- confidentiality **9** 56, **10** 12
- creative control **19** 64
- indemnification **16** 53
- key **19** 2
- subordination **9** 67
Client **32** 20
- dependency **5** 12
Cloud
- -based infrastructure **24** 38
- game streaming **35** 40
- gaming **4** 2, 25 f., **12** 29, **18** 55 f., **24** 8, 19 ff.
- gaming platform **35** 39
Code **15** 45
- adaptable **20** 14
- game **19** 24
- self-regulatory **39** 30
Code of Conduct **26** 36, **39** 12, 44, **41** 13
- PEGI **22** 11, 45 ff., 61, **26** 33, 45, **31** 26, **33** 47
Collective management **16** 3, 17, 34
- alternative **40** 49
- mandatory **16** 35
Collective management organisation (CMO) **14** 59, **16** 12, 34 ff., **28** 51
Collusion **35** 5 ff.
- anti-competitive **35** 2
Commercial **9** 45, 60, **19** 5, **39** 10, 17, 23, **40** 35, 52 ff.
- activity **19** 22
- autonomy **23** 44
- communication **39** 22
- company **14** 48
- exploitation **16** 29
Commercial practice **37** 8
- aggressive **24** 25, **37** 10, **39** 19
- misleading **37** 6
- unfair **28** 84
Committee of Advertising Practice (CAP) **9** 67, **26** 47, **36** 71, **38** 8
Communication **17** 43, **29** 14 f., **32** 13 ff.
- commercial **39** 22
- direct **32** 25
- marketing **38** 9
- public **41** 20 f.
- timely **20** 37
- Voice-over-IP **32** 14
Community **3** 17, **5** 26 ff., **12** 88 f., **18** 33, **31** 27
- active **5** 27
- building **5** 26 ff., **6** 15
- fan **31** 7
- modding **13** 45
Company
- certificate, EU **9** 13
- form, national **9** 21
Company law **9** 2, 4 ff.
- directive **9** 6
- European **9** 9
Competition **12** 21, **35** 5, **37** 44 ff.
- distortion **7** 16, 30
- economic **14** 42
- effective **35** 1
- law **13** 55, **24** 19, 48 f., **33** 70, **36** 67
- price **8** 7
Complaints Board, PEGI **22** 42
Compliance **28** 79, **36** 30, 81
- GDPR **18** 52
- strategy **39** 48
- voluntary **33** 52
Conception **12** 38
- phase **12** 39 ff.
Condition **14** 27 ff.
- release **19** 27
Confusion **17** 49
- likelihood of **17** 22
- risk of **17** 45
Consent **19** 63, **24** 43, **29** 8, 18, 25 ff., **36** 32, **38** 19, 24, **40** 41, **41** 38
- digital **34** 47
- during gameplay **38** 29
- electronic **25** 19
- express **25** 31
- parental **29** 43, **34** 47
- players' **38** 23 f.
- prior **38** 28
- simple **40** 43
Consideration **30** 5 f.
- business **12** 48 ff., 73 ff.
- legal **12** 48 ff., 73 ff., **36** 49
- organisational **20** 32 ff.
Console **2** 34, **19** 21, **31** 1, 3, 7 ff., 41, **35** 9, **36** 5
- dedicated video game **31** 4
- gaming **18** 11
- home **24** 4
Consumer **24** 25, **25** 1, 27 f., 30, 38, **28** 78, 88, **31** 2, **37** 7, 36
- rights **25** 9, **36** 20, **37** 6
- vulnerable **38** 16, **39** 19, 22
Consumer Directive **38** 22

Consumer law **28** 5, 76, 86, 90
– European Union **26** 55
Consumer protection **1** 6, **4** 20, **12** 16, 90, **24** 18, 35 f., **25** 8, **26** 33, **27** 16, **33** 33, 79, **34** 54, **36** 56, **39** 4, 15, 50
– association **28** 87
– authority **37** 30
– organisation **28** 85 ff.
Consumer Protection Cooperation Network (CPC) **28** 81
Consumer Protection from Unfair Trading Regulations **26** 46
Consumer protection law **23** 40, **27** 24
– harmonised **25** 12
Consumer Rights Directive (CRD) **4** 20, **25** 1, 7, **26** 8, 15, **36** 34
Content **18** 46 ff., **20** 20, 44, **22** 1, 26, **23** 11, 24, **24** 15, 30, 38, **27** 14, **30** 4, 36, **31** 1 ff., **32** 29 ff., **33** 5, 9 ff., 77, **34** 53, 60, **35** 70, **37** 38, **39** 10, 16, **40** 12, 17, 58 ff., **41** 11
– descriptor **18** 47, **22** 18
– digital **25** 31, **26** 20, 25
– harmful **34** 57, **39** 39
– illegal **25** 11, **33** 20 ff., 24, 56, 58, 60
– moderation **32** 27, 30 ff., **33** 51, 74
– moderation standards **24** 38
– user-generated **4** 28, **12** 27, **22** 4, 52, **28** 93
Contract **12** 69, **29** 20
– consumer **25** 1
– distance **32** 57
– exploitation **15** 4
Control
– creative **19** 14
– de facto **35** 44
– less **28** 32
– local media **20** 32
– motion **31** 9
– parental **23** 27, **34** 23, 51
– preventive **9** 18
– rights **35** 45
Cookie **29** 2, 8
– first-party **29** 28
– third-party **29** 29
Copycat game **28** 2
Copyright **4** 15, **12** 54, **13** 1, 5 ff., 28 ff., 36 ff., 41 f., 67, **16** 26, 56, **17** 48, **27** 12, **40** 7, 13, 20, 25, 27, **41** 17 ff., 24 ff., 34, 36 f.
– assignment **13** 35
– eligibility **27** 21
– EU **15** 1 ff.
– infringement **12** 94, **13** 54, **14** 2, **28** 56, 70
– license **6** 32
– limitation **4** 17
– protected work **14** 35, **28** 44
– system **14** 1
Copyright assignment policy **13** 40
Copyright contract law **15** 2 f., 43, 50 ff., 54 ff., 78
– German **15** 7 ff.
Copyright Directive **4** 19, **13** 9, 18, 51, 59, **14** 5 ff., 13, 15
Copyright law **13** 21 ff., **16** 2
– EU **40** 60
Copyright protection **13** 7, 10, 14
– independent **13** 9
Corporate Sustainability Due Diligence Directive (CSDDD) **21** 16 ff.
Corporate Sustainability Reporting Directive (CSRD) **21** 9 ff.
Counter-Racism Framework Decision (CRFD) **33** 23
Counter-Terrorism Directive (CTD) **33** 21
Country of Origin **34** 6, 54
– principle **4** 7, 18, **23** 32, **25** 26, **34** 55
Court of Justice of the European Union (CJEU) **15** 42, 44, **17** 21, **33** 30
Criminal action **28** 33
Criminal behaviour **40** 58
Criminalisation **33** 31, 78
Criminal law **28** 5, 29
Criminal offence **32** 42
Criminal penalty **28** 29
Criminal proceeding **28** 32
Criminal sentence **28** 34
Cross-border **9** 12, 34, 36, **12** 16, **16** 4, **35** 15
– aspect **9** 59 ff.
– conversion **9** 7
– e-commerce **35** 68
– exception **14** 19
– form **9** 21
Cross-Border Mergers Directive **9** 6
Crowdfunding **6** 17, 22, **9** 73, **12** 13, 20, 33, 72, **30** 6
CSAM-Regulation **32** 70
Cultural **1** 4, **3** 16, **7** 50, 56, **8** 11, 14 ff., **14** 48, **18** 19 ff., 26, **20** 1 ff., 22, 31, 40, 44
– aid **7** 20, **8** 10 ff.
– diversity **8** 14, **18** 3, 16, 27
– impact **3** 4 ff., **20** 34
– objective **7** 37, 44
– product **7** 24, 38
– test **7** 39 ff., 59, **8** 14
Currency **9** 14, **26** 14
– in-game **6** 11, **24** 13, **37** 16

Dark pattern **23** 14, **24** 39, **28** 76, **32** 53, **37** 2, 17 ff., 18, **38** 20 ff.
Data **5** 33, **21** 33 f., **23** 18, **24** 35, 37, **27** 38, **29** 2, 3, 5 ff., 12, 16, 19, 36, 49 ff., **32** 68, **34** 42, 45, **36** 53
– controller **29** 2, 32, 47, **38** 25
– personal **29** 7, 21, 47 f., **31** 32, **34** 1, **35** 61, **38** 4
– player **18** 51, **28** 100
– protection **18** 43, 50 ff., **24** 43 f., **26** 16, **31** 19, **36** 46

Data Act **4** 19, **27** 38
Deal **10** 18
- preparation **10** 10 ff.
- publishing **19** 9
- structure **10** 23 ff.
Defamation **33** 34 ff.
Default setting **34** 38
- mandatory **34** 34 ff.
Deferred tax **11** 30 ff.
- position **11** 34
Derivative work **13** 60, **16** 56, **19** 37 ff.
- unauthorised **13** 50
Design **12** 62, **27** 26 ff., 59, **28** 3, **34** 3
- age-appropriate **29** 39
- choice **34** 15
- ethical **24** 42
- game **38** 29
- law **27** 26
Developer **2** 5 f., **6** 6, **9** 25 ff., **11** 23, **12** 2, 85, **13** 45, **18** 30, 31, **19** 1, 23, 57, **31** 6, 16, 40, **40** 23
Development **5** 31, 34, **7** 46, 48, **8** 13, **12** 3, 14, 70 ff., **19** 13, 41 ff., **31** 16, **40** 3
Device
- and network data **29** 6 ff.
- data **29** 19
- smart **2** 22, 33
- TPM circumvention **13** 20
Digital consent **34** 47
- Digital age of consent **34** 44
Digital Content Directive (DCD) **24** 40, **25** 8, **26** 8, 15
Digital distribution **2** 1, 19, **5** 9, **18** 5, 13 ff., 30 ff., **21** 38, 40, **24** 6, **28** 8, **31** 15, **35** 9
Digital Fairness Act **4** 21, **26** 28 ff.
Digital Markets Act (DMA) **4** 19, **24** 39, 49, 51, **26** 46, **32** 60, **35** 2, 58 ff., **36** 33
Digital platform **12** 14, **31** 4, 11 ff., **34** 2, **39** 2
Digital service **4** 3, 13, **6** 5, **25** 32 f., 36 ff., **32** 2, **41** 14
Digital Services Act (DSA) **4** 7, 19, **23** 4, 7, 30, **24** 39, **25** 11, **29** 44, **32** 4 ff. 23, 69, **33** 10, 15, 19, 41, 60, **34** 20 ff., **36** 33, **37** 19, **39** 23 f.
Digital Single Market Directive (DSM Directive) **40** 47
Direct discrimination **35** 69
Directive **9** 4, **25** 2
- Enforcement **28** 28
- EU **27** 3
- Software **13** 53, 55
Disclosure **39** 17 f., 31 ff., 36
- continuous **39** 38
- frequency **39** 38
- influencer **39** 33
- obligation **39** 34
- practices **39** 29
- requirement **39** 37
Discrimination **22** 20, **35** 69, **37** 38
Dissemination **40** 36 ff.
- to the public **32** 17
Distribution **19** 19, **24** 21, **31** 20 f., **41** 19
- agreement **12** 78
- digital **2** 1, 19, **18** 5, 13 ff., 30, **21** 38, 40, **28** 8
- dual **35** 19
- gaming platform **18** 10 ff.
- global **20** 3
- key **16** 11, 15
- of game **7** 7
Distribution platform **19** 50
- digital **18** 32
Distribution rights **13** 64, **24** 10, **27** 34
- licensed **19** 21
Double
- anonymity **34** 66
- identity **17** 20
- indemnity **19** 59
- -materiality **21** 10
- materiality assessment **21** 15
Downloadable content (DLC) **6** 5, **18** 7, **22** 41, 57, **24** 3, 15
- paid **12** 84
Drugs **22** 20
DSA **4** 18, **23** 53, **33** 53, 55 ff., 62, **38** 5, 18
- liability **37** 17
DSM Copyright Directive **4** 17, 19, **14** 5, 16 ff., 26 f., 34 ff.
Due diligence **9** 70, **10** 4, 8 f., 15 f., 20, **21** 2, 11, 19, 21, **32** 70, **36** 63
- environmental **21** 16 f., 20
- human rights **21** 20
- legal **10** 2, 22
- obligation **32** 6, 58
Dynamic
- advertisement **37** 43
- blocking injunction **28** 47
- pricing **24** 50
- proportionality **33** 27

Early access **6** 16
- game **37** 13
- programme **12** 72
Ecodesign for Sustainable Products Regulation (ESPR) **21** 29 f., **36** 36
Economic
- behaviour **37** 23
- competition **14** 42
- development **3** 6
- law **33** 33
- operator **21** 34
- right **16** 31
- risk **7** 50
Ecosystem **16** 6 f., **18** 1
- closed **27** 39
Electronic **9** 49, **14** 29, **25** 5, 19, **27** 32, **29** 2, **30** 8, 36, 48, **32** 25, 67 f.
- service **30** 2, 22, 25

– signature, qualified **9** 47, 52
Emblem **17** 26, 52
Emissions **21** 6, 7
– carbon **21** 5
– scope 3 **21** 43
– video games **21** 4
Employee **9** 37, 71, **15** 60, **41** 39 ff.
Endangerment of minors **23** 10
Endorsement
– brand **36** 65
– celebrity **36** 64 f.
End User License Agreement (EULA) **4** 16, **12** 91, **29** 19, **32** 29, **33** 50 ff., 71 f., 79, **41** 37
Energy
– green **21** 36
– renewable **21** 43
– usage **21** 38
Energy Efficiency Directive **21** 33
Enforcement **22** 14, 65 ff., **28** 1, 3 f., 73 ff., **36** 30
– capacity **33** 48
– law **32** 42
– mechanism **37** 15
– private **21** 22
– public **21** 22
Enforcement and Modernisation Directive (EMD) **26** 8
Enforcement Committee, PEGI **26** 45
Enforcement Directive **4** 19, **28** 28, 42
Engagement **12** 85
– community **5** 30, **12** 89, **18** 33
Engine **12** 44
– proprietary **12** 34 ff.
– third-party **12** 34 ff.
Entertainment Software Self-Regulation Body (USK) **23** 1
Environmental
– art **13** 25
– due diligence **21** 16 f., 20
– footprint **21** 5 ff.
– legislation **21** 4
– reporting, general **21** 2
– sustainability **21** 42
Environment-related legislative texts **21** 1
EPrivacy Directive (ePD) **4** 19, **29** 1, 54
Equity **8** 25
– KISS agreement **9** 74
– split **5** 14
– story **10** 8
Escrow **19** 26 f.
– mechanism **16** 61
– storage agreement **10** 19
EUIPO **17** 14, 18, 25, 29
European
– company law **9** 7, 9
– reorganisation law **9** 3
– trademark **17** 19
– video game industry **2** 2, 11
European antitrust **35** 1
European Court of Human Rights (ECtHR) **33** 32, 36
European Court of Justice (ECJ) **31** 18
European Data Protection Board (EDPB) **29** 41, 48, **34** 47
European Electronic Communications Code (EECCD) **32** 14
European Union (EU) **11** 9, **24** 2
– age verification solution **34** 28
– Blue Card **41** 43
– company certificate **9** 13
– Digital Identity Wallet **9** 15, **34** 28
European Union Intellectual Protection Office (EUIPO) **17** 8
European Union Merger Regulation (EUMR) **35** 29, 32
European Union Trade Mark Regulation (EUTMR) **17** 8, **41** 28
EU-US Data Privacy Framework **29** 50
Exclusive
– license **15** 37, 39, **35** 27
– mandate **16** 38, 43
– reproduction right **40** 28
– right of public communication **41** 35
– rights **13** 6, **14** 2, 9, 40, **15** 16, 56, 76 f., **17** 4, **19** 25, 31
Exclusivity **15** 57
– provision **36** 65
– trademark **41** 30
Exemption **30** 11, **35** 70
– liability **28** 39, 64
Exhaustion **5** 13, **13** 4, 63 ff., **24** 10, **27** 36
Ex-parte **28** 20 ff.
– injunction **28** 22
Exploitation **19** 19 ff.
– authors' **15** 61
– contract **15** 4
– normal **14** 42
External
– collaboration **12** 30 f.
– contributor **16** 22
– intellectual property **12** 77
– platform **27** 44
– vendor **12** 66

Federal Office for the Enforcement of Children's Rights in Digital Services (KidD) **23** 25
Fee
– examination **22** 36
– flat **10** 16
– licence **22** 36
– licensing **12** 35
– subscription **18** 37
– unjustifiable **35** 66
Film **3** 13
– and gaming platform **23** 19
– producer **40** 23

- production **7** 27
- work **40** 22, 24 ff.

Filter **34** 19
- software **34** 18

Financial
- assurance **36** 73
- institution **29** 16
- provision **19** 40 ff.
- revenue threshold **10** 34
- risk **12** 20
- sanction **26** 36
- statement, tax **11** 46

Fine **22** 66
- administrative **21** 23, **28** 30
- significant **35** 51

Fiscal
- liability cap **19** 60
- representative **30** 43, 48

Formal investigation procedure **7** 33

Format
- competition **41** 25 f.
- machine-readable **32** 28
- tournament **41** 5

Formation
- cash **9** 28
- company **9** 18
- concealed **9** 28
- document **9** 17
- procedure, regular **9** 41 ff.

Framework
- approval **19** 14
- legal **16** 8 ff.
- regulatory **24** 1, **39** 14 ff.
- self-regulatory **33** 47

Fraud detection **29** 23

Fraud prevention **27** 41, **29** 45 ff.

Freedom
- contractual **15** 3
- creative **32** 16
- fundamental **4** 6, **33** 39
- of establishment **9** 3, 7
- of expression **14** 12, **33** 32, 79
- of speech **20** 7
- to act **33** 69 ff.

Free-to-play (F2P) **4** 4, **6** 12, **16** 47, **18** 28, 36 ff., **24** 7, 16 ff., 33, **26** 1, **36** 3

Function
- distinguishing **17** 30
- investment **17** 44
- subordinate **32** 23
- trademark **17** 42

Functionality
- additional **33** 7
- online **31** 30
- permanent **23** 41
- sharing **32** 23

Funding **5** 22 ff., **11** 42, **12** 56
- finishing **19** 41
- private **6** 19
- public **5** 24

Gambling **4** 23, **22** 20, **26** 51, **36** 55, **37** 14, 47
- law **24** 24, **26** 50 ff.
- legislation **26** 66

Gameplay **32** 19 ff.
- data **29** 11 ff.
- excessive **34** 37
- feature, core **32** 19
- mechanics **12** 62, **13** 36
- metric **29** 52
- online **33** 48

Games as a service (GaaS) **4** 26, **12** 84, **15** 47, **18** 7, 36 ff., **24** 28 ff., **41** 3

Games Rating Authority (GRA) **22** 33

General
- consumption tax **30** 35 ff.
- environmental reporting **21** 2
- exception **15** 67
- legality **7** 30
- legality principle **7** 31 ff., 36
- SME support instrument **8** 23

General Block Exemption Regulation (GBER) **7** 21 ff., 57

General Data Protection Regulation (GDPR) **4** 19, 26, **12** 95, **18** 51, **29** 1, 4, 54, **32** 53, **36** 32, 37, **41** 38

Generally Accepted Accounting Principles (GAAP), local **11** 31, 33

General-Purpose AI Code of Practice **14** 57

Generative artificial intelligence (AI) **12** 11, 51, **27** 22

Geo-blocking **24** 48, **35** 2, 67 ff.
- unjustified **35** 68

German Copyright Act (UrhG) **15** 16

German Federal Court of Justice (BGH) **4** 23, **40** 15

Ghost publishing **19** 3

Grant **8** 25, **18** 44
- development **7** 46
- R&D **8** 17

Green
- activation **21** 41
- energy **21** 36
- Game Jam **18** 63, **21** 41
- technology **21** 35 ff.
- -washing **21** 15, **37** 9

Harassment **33** 16, 34 ff.

Hard Virtual Currency **24** 26
- transaction **24** 27

Harmful content **34** 57, **39** 39

Harmonised consumer protection law **25** 12

Hate speech **33** 31 f., 38, 44

Holding company **9** 29
- asset-managing **9** 30

Hosting
- exception **28** 40

- provider **28** 54, 63 ff.
- service **32** 8 ff., 13, 15 f., 18, 36, 38 ff., **34** 20
- services provider **32** 24, **33** 4, 64

Hypercasual **12** 6
- game **28** 22, **38** 11, 16

Icon, PEGI **22** 56

Identification
- clearer **38** 9
- electronic **9** 49
- qualified electronic **9** 48

Identity
- document **34** 67
- double **17** 20
- local **18** 26
- studio **5** 10 ff.

Illegal content **25** 11, **32** 21, **33** 1, 10 ff., 14, 20 ff., 24 ff., 56, 58, 60, 65

Implementation
- EU directive **9** 53
- unique **13** 39

In-app purchase **16** 47, **18** 7, **24** 22 ff., 34, **28** 82

Inappropriate content **33** 16 f., 61, **40** 58 ff.

Incorporation
- certificate **9** 62
- digital **9** 46
- online **9** 48, 53

Indemnity **19** 10, 53 ff., 62, **37** 33
- double **19** 59
- mutual **19** 59
- unlimited **36** 72

Indie **6** 15
- developer **12** 20, **19** 23
- -friendly publisher **18** 31
- game **12** 14, **20** 16, **31** 23
- publishing **18** 32 ff.
- scene **12** 12, **18** 35
- studio **12** 8 ff., 13, 19
- team **12** 47

Information **15** 22, **32** 21, **33** 9 ff.
- barrier **31** 34 ff.
- clear and comprehensible **25** 21
- identifiable **29** 7
- material **37** 11
- obligation **15** 24, 63, 67, 69 f., **25** 22 f.
- price **25** 23
- request list **10** 19
- requirement **25** 20 ff., **37** 19
- sensitive **29** 10
- society service **25** 5
- society service provider **33** 4

Information Commissioner's Office **29** 39

InfoSoc Directive **13** 3, **16** 4, **27** 35, **28** 41, **33** 24, **41** 20 f., 24

Infringement **13** 41, **16** 56
- aiding and abetting **13** 58
- copyright **13** 54, **28** 70
- IP **28** 2
- third-party rights **19** 54
- trademark **13** 58
- unlawful **40** 45
- video game **28** 19

In-game
- ad **38** 7, 12 f., 15 ff., 16
- advertisement **38** 5 ff.
- advertising **16** 47, **38** 1 ff., 9, 27 ff.
- asset **17** 28 f.
- content **27** 2, **30** 4
- content (IGC) **26** 20
- currency **6** 11, **22** 50, **24** 13, **26** 4, 18, 23
- item **27** 45
- monetisation **22** 49 f., **24** 51
- purchase **6** 9, **22** 20, 26, **24** 27, **26** 10, **29** 22, **34** 17
- reporting tool **32** 40
- transaction **4** 4
- virtual currency **28** 84, **37** 16

In-house
- company **9** 24
- counsel **36** 9
- creation **27** 11 f.
- Legal department **31** 37

Initiative
- co-regulation **39** 28
- self-regulatory **21** 30

Injunction **13** 46, **28** 41 f., 60
- blocking **28** 35 ff., 48 f., 52
- ex parte **28** 22
- preliminary **28** 24 ff.

Innovation **1** 5, **24** 12
- business **8** 18
- data-driven **29** 54
- driver **3** 9
- game design **8** 18
- technological **1** 2, **8** 18

Input VAT **30** 21, 28

Insurance **19** 62
- advertising **10** 36
- cyber **10** 36
- key person loss **10** 36
- lottery raffles **10** 36

Integrity
- moral **33** 34 ff.
- personal **23** 13 ff., 31
- psychological **23** 14

Intellectual property (IP) **1** 6, **4** 15, **5** 38, **9** 33, **10** 1, 22, **11** 23, **12** 11, 27, 30, 76, 90, 93, **13** 5, 42, **19** 59, **27** 1, 3, 5, 10, **28** 5, **33** 38, **35** 23, **37** 4, **41** 8
- agreement **12** 55
- co-owned **12** 16
- external **12** 77
- licence **41** 9
- original **5** 3
- ownership **10** 21
- prerogatives **41** 34
- protection **12** 53 ff.
- proven **5** 22

- rights **10** 25, **16** 29, **26** 2, **27** 20, 40, **28** 3, 8, 42, 56 f., 87, **41** 1, 6
- transfer **6** 31

Intended audience **12** 41

International Age Rating Coalition (IARC) **18** 49, **23** 33, 48, 49 ff., **31** 17

Interstate Treaty on the Protection of Minors in the Media (JMStV) **23** 7, 28 ff.

Invoice **22** 50, **30** 16 f., 17, 29, 46
- VAT **30** 2, 16

IP **6** 6, **36** 14
- address blocking **28** 61
- enforcement **28** 7 ff.
- established **5** 7
- infringement **28** 2
- original **5** 11, **12** 23 ff.
- ownership **12** 32, **19** 7, 9, 23 ff.
- pledge **5** 19
- right **40** 11
- third-party **37** 42
- video game **10** 7

Item
- cosmetic **39** 35
- digital **26** 14, **27** 8 f., 55
- in-game **27** 45

Jurisdiction **13** 12, **35** 42 f.
- choice of **28** 96

Key
- clause **19** 2
- person loss insurance **10** 36
- stakeholder **12** 4, **16** 6 f.

KISS agreement
- debt **9** 74
- equity **9** 74

Label
- PEGI **22** 26
- record **16** 65

Landscape
- European political **5** 31 ff.
- gaming **18** 35
- geopolitical **20** 44
- post-Brexit **18** 61

Language
- bad **22** 28
- local **36** 56
- localisation **18** 17 ff.
- official **32** 28

Law
- competition **13** 55, **36** 67
- contract **4** 20
- enforcement **28** 99 ff., **32** 42
- EU **33** 20 ff.
- firm **36** 14
- gambling **24** 24
- marketing **36** 81
- Member State **33** 39
- national **39** 25
- private **27** 3
- sports **24** 38
- trademark **17** 9

Leadership **5** 5, 37
- alignment **5** 10 ff.
- depth **5** 40
- exhaustion **5** 13

Let's Play **14** 45, **28** 69 ff., **40** 2 ff., 25 ff., 28, 30, 34, 39 f., 44, 57, 60
- private **40** 34
- video **40** 1

Liability **27** 15, **33** 57
- cap, fiscal **19** 60
- exemption **28** 39, 64
- exposure **33** 18 ff.
- for user-generated content **34** 19
- limitation **12** 91
- strict **28** 27
- unlimited **9** 23, 40

Licence **14** 25, **16** 18, **19** 24, **26** 13, **40** 42, 44, **41** 23
- direct **16** 36, 40 ff.
- exclusive **15** 37, **35** 27
- local **22** 17
- music **16** 48, 63
- non-exclusive **35** 49
- pan-European **16** 45
- PEGI **22** 37
- PEGI age rating **22** 17
- promotional **16** 65
- synchronisation **16** 36, 65
- tournament organiser **41** 36
- unambiguous **40** 51
- video game **22** 30

License **27** 19, 33, **36** 55
- chain **15** 23
- duration, limited **27** 18
- exclusive **15** 39
- fee **22** 36
- game of chance **26** 54
- open-source **13** 37
- PEGI **22** 39
- remuneration **37** 35
- synchronisation **37** 42
- term **27** 31

Licensed
- distribution rights **19** 21
- music **16** 33
- property **12** 23 ff.
- video game **12** 24

Licensee **15** 16
- fee **15** 51
- fee, substantial **27** 18

Licensing **14** 26, **16** 20, **18** 1 ff., **19** 19 ff., **27** 15
- arrangement **12** 77
- collective **40** 48
- direct **14** 44
- fees **12** 35
- inbound **27** 12
- mechanism, suitable **14** 32
- music **36** 69

- opportunity **17** 6
- strategy **16** 32
- tripartite **16** 44

Licensing agreement **12** 24, 49 ff., **16** 37, 51, 54, **24** 19, **35** 24, **40** 41
- proper **16** 53

Limitation **14** 7, 14 ff., 34 ff., **19** 22
- copyright **4** 17
- liability **12** 91
- of liability **19** 53 ff., 60
- statute **15** 74

Litigation **11** 57
- pending **19** 55

Live
- Operations (LiveOps) **12** 38, 86
- phase **12** 80 ff., 90 ff., 96
- service **12** 27, **24** 9, 28, 29, **32** 71
- service game **2** 1

Loan **8** 25
- conditionally repayable **7** 11, 46
- interest-free **9** 68
- R&D **8** 17

Local
- licence **22** 17
- market perception **20** 43
- meaning **20** 21
- media control **20** 32
- tax legislation **11** 31
- VAT **30** 39

Loot box **4** 21, 23, **12** 92, **22** 22, 49, **24** 13, 23 f., **26** 5 ff., 8, 17, 24 ff., 32, 35, 37, 40, 41 ff., 45, 47 ff., 53 ff., 59 ff., 63 ff., 68, **28** 83, **34** 30, **37** 13 f.
- paid **26** 44

Lottery **37** 44 ff.
- raffles insurance **10** 36

Mandatory
- arbitration **28** 96
- collective management **16** 35
- default setting **34** 34 ff.
- product feature **34** 35

Manipulative
- marketing **24** 46
- practice **32** 53
- tactic **28** 89

Market **7** 48
- black **20** 2
- cinema **3** 8
- concentration **27** 49
- digital internal **25** 9
- educational **14** 31
- European **2** 16
- fragmentation **18** 3, **26** 34
- grey **20** 2
- internal **7** 19
- music **3** 8
- second-hand **2** 18 ff.
- video game **3** 8, **18** 5 ff., 65

Marketing **12** 79, **19** 16, **36** 8, 12, **40** 3
- above the line **36** 42 ff.
- agency **36** 13, 70
- below the line **36** 45 ff.
- budget **19** 44
- campaign **19** 18
- claim **36** 15 ff.
- communication **38** 9
- digital **36** 50
- direct **29** 22
- gaming **36** 20
- influence **39** 29
- influencer **37** 34, **39** 3, 14 ff., 48
- law **36** 81
- manipulative **24** 46
- material **37** 3, 45
- partnership **36** 60
- practice **39** 20
- pre-release **22** 59
- revenue **15** 49
- slogan **36** 15 ff.
- team **36** 22
- tool **36** 40 ff.
- video game **8** 15

Marketplace **6** 10
- centralised **27** 49

Market-share **35** 11, 20, 52
- combined **35** 25

Material
- breach **19** 33
- information **37** 11
- marketing **37** 3

Means
- electronic **32** 25
- technical **41** 22

Measure
- national **7** 10
- precautionary **23** 23 ff.
- technical **34** 48

Mechanism
- contract adjustment **15** 71
- enforcement **37** 15
- escrow **16** 61
- notice and action **32** 38, **33** 67
- randomised **26** 5
- redress **28** 94
- safety **29** 23

Media
- art **3** 3
- buying team **36** 44
- literacy **34** 51
- online **34** 56
- right **18** 41
- social **2** 38
- supervisory authority **23** 28

Mere conduit **32** 8
- exception **28** 40
- service **32** 13 f.

Metaverse **3** 9, **4** 27 f., **12** 28, **32** 3, **34** 53

Microtransaction **12** 92, **18** 37, **24** 7, 16, 22 ff.

Minimisation **34** 43, **38** 25
– data **34** 45
Minimum
– collection rate **21** 27
– corporate taxation **11** 17, 19
– requirement **32** 62, **40** 54
– resale price **35** 10
– taxation rules **11** 41
– tax rule **11** 19
Mini One Stop Shop (MOSS) **30** 19
Misleading
– advertising **37** 23 f., 45
– character **17** 17
– claim **36** 39
– commercial practice **37** 6, **38** 12
– consumer **37** 36
– interface **38** 21, 24
– omission **37** 11
– practice **37** 7, **38** 15
Mitigation **20** 35
– risk **23** 42, **36** 22
Mobile **36** 5
– game **1** 1, **6** 14, **12** 6, **31** 4
– game platform **31** 4
– gaming **18** 10, 12
– platform **2** 13, **35** 63
Modding **27** 13, **33** 6
– community **13** 45
Moderation
– activity **33** 62
– content **33** 74
Modification **16** 58, **25** 36 ff.
– contract **16** 27, **25** 35 ff.
Monetisation **5** 29 f., **12** 87, 92, 96, **18** 39, **24** 4, 9, 18, 21, 37, 42, **39** 9 f., 16 **40** 53 ff.
– model **6** 12, **15** 49, **24** 1, 13
– strategy **24** 5, 11, 17
Money
– laundering **9** 17
– laundering regulation **9** 75
– real-world **6** 11
Motion
– analysis **34** 12
– control **31** 9
– picture neighbouring right **40** 24
Multiplayer **29** 3
– experience **34** 2
– video game **3** 11
Music **3** 14, **16** 66 ff., **40** 21
– AI-generated **16** 53
– licence **16** 48, 63
– licensing **36** 69
– market **3** 8
– publisher **16** 11
– rights **16** 1
Musical
– authorship **16** 3
– composition **13** 26
– right **16** 8
– work **16** 7
National
– authority **28** 77 ff.
– company form **9** 21
– competition authority **35** 43
– consumer organisation **28** 88
– court **35** 28
– game industry strategy **8** 28
– guideline **39** 44
– law **39** 25
– measure **7** 10
– merger control **35** 32
– registration **17** 19
– regulation **25** 12
Necessity **7** 43 ff., 50
– contractual **38** 27
Net Neutrality Regulation **28** 59
Network, 5G **12** 29
Non-binding **19** 6
– nature **40** 64
– price recommendation **35** 12
Non-discrimination **33** 70, **34** 11, **35** 71
Non-fungible token (NFT) **4** 24, 27, **24** 31 ff., **27** 2, 41, 45, 51 ff., **39** 43
Obligation **39** 39 ff.
– age assurance **34** 46
– continuing **25** 36, 48
– contractual **33** 66 ff.
– due diligence **32** 6, 58
– imprint **25** 26
– information **15** 63, 70, **25** 23
– legal **25** 53
– main performance **25** 45
– minor protection **39** 42 ff.
– overarching **29** 33
– platform **32** 59 ff.
– pre-release **19** 11 ff.
– proactive **15** 22
– sectoral **33** 42 ff.
– stand-still **7** 17
– technical youth protection **34** 23
– territorial spending **7** 35
– to inform **15** 68
– transparency **15** 19, 27, 55, **32** 52
– video game platform provider **33** 18 ff.
Offer **25** 15 ff.
– binding **25** 16
Omnibus Directive **25** 10
One-click solution **23** 30
One Stop Shop (OSS) **30** 16, 20, 30
Online **25** 14
– advertising service **35** 59
– functionality **31** 30
– gameplay **33** 48
– gameplay environment **22** 51
– games platform **32** 66, **34** 47
– gaming **18** 2
– harm **33** 49

- incorporation **9** 48, 53
- interface **35** 71
- intermediation service **32** 61, **35** 59
- intermediation store **35** 62
- marketplace **28** 38, **32** 10
- -only game **22** 29
- persona **31** 30
- protection **32** 54 ff.
- safety **32** 2
- search engine **35** 59
- service, games-related **32** 1
- service operator **31** 24
- start-up **9** 46
- tools **36** 51 ff.
- transaction **28** 94
- withdrawal statement **25** 34

Online game **25** 6, **28** 82, **32** 12 ff., **34** 40
- UGC-driven **32** 18

Online Safety Act (OSA) **24** 39

Online Safety Code (OSC) **34** 64

Operating system **31** 8
- provider **34** 59
- youth protection mechanism **23** 30

Operator
- online service **31** 24
- system **31** 24
- video game platform **33** 40

Origin **27** 7, **31** 11
- goods **17** 42

Originality **13** 22, **27** 21, **28** 31, **41** 25 f.

Outside
- counsel **36** 9
- legal counsel **10** 16
- the European Union data transfer **29** 49 ff.
- the EU tax **30** 39

Ownership **13** 39, **20** 36, **27** 28
- asset **12** 76
- change **16** 60
- content **24** 30
- intellectual property (IP) **10** 21
- IP **12** 32, **19** 7, 9, 23 ff.
- joint **19** 24
- model, blockchain-based **24** 11
- right **12** 69
- split **16** 59 ff., 61
- structure **5** 19, **11** 52

Paid
- digital content **26** 15
- downloadable content **12** 84
- loot box **26** 44
- production service **5** 4
- random item **22** 22
- random reward mechanism **26** 34

Pan European Game Information (PEGI) **18** 46 ff., **22** 58, 60, 67, **24** 45, **33** 42, 46, **39** 45, 47

Parental
- authority **34** 44
- consent **29** 42 f., **34** 47
- privilege **23** 8
- responsibility **34** 40 f.
- tool system **29** 41

Parental control **23** 27, **24** 45, **29** 42, **34** 4, 23, 27, 39, 51, 59, **37** 13
- software **34** 58, 63
- system **31** 25 f., **34** 16 ff.
- USK-certified **23** 32

Partnership **9** 23, **36** 40 ff., 62
- brand **36** 67
- deal **37** 32 ff.
- limited by shares (KGaA) **9** 5

Patch **12** 83
- balance **12** 71, **41** 3

Payment **24** 33
- advance **16** 28
- lump sum **15** 58
- period **19** 50
- processor **30** 41
- real-world **26** 10
- schedule **12** 68
- service provider **6** 33
- term **16** 28
- threshold, de minimis **19** 51
- with data **24** 26

PEGI **18** 47, **22** 6, 13 ff., 29 ff., 33, 43, 56 ff., **23** 1, **26** 30, 35 f., 42, 50, **31** 17, **33** 48 f.
- administrator **22** 39
- advertising rules **22** 61 ff.
- age classification **29** 41
- age rating **22** 37
- age rating licence **22** 17, 45
- Agreement **22** 11, 32
- Code **22** 66
- Code of Conduct **22** 11, 45 ff., 61, **26** 33, 45, **31** 26, **33** 47
- Complaints Board **22** 42
- Council **22** 9
- descriptor **22** 28
- enforcement **26** 44 f.
- enforcement action **22** 37
- Experts Group **22** 10
- extranet **22** 38, 40
- icon **22** 56
- label **22** 26
- Labelling Rules **22** 55
- licence **22** 37, 39
- questionnaire **22** 35
- rating **18** 48, **22** 12, 21, 25, 44, 62 f.
- standards **33** 54
- system **22** 7, 18 ff., 48

PEGI Enforcement Committee (PEC) **22** 65, **26** 45

Piracy **13** 20, **28** 30

Platform-to-Business Regulation **32** 61 f.

Player **2** 28, **12** 70 ff., **15** 48, **28** 90 ff.
- acquisition **6** 13 f.
- casual **3** 2
- data **18** 51, **28** 100
- exclusion **25** 53

– -generated content **33** 5
– interaction **6** 4, **33** 2
– Let's **40** 3
– professional **28** 93, **41** 39 ff.
– toxic **33** 8, 40

Policy **32** 32
– agency **36** 26
– copyright assignment **13** 40
– priority **8** 22
– privacy **22** 53

Pornographic content provider **34** 61

Pornography **34** 60, 65

Post-launch
– phase **12** 82
– strategy **12** 85
– support **12** 86

Practice
– anti-competitive **24** 49
– deceptive **32** 53
– disclosure **39** 29
– manipulative **32** 53
– marketing **39** 20
– sustainable **18** 63
– unfair **39** 20
– unilateral **35** 68

Pre-release
– examination **22** 31 ff.
– marketing **22** 59
– obligation **19** 11 ff.

Pre-seed **6** 23
– funding **6** 21 ff.

Price **37** 12
– adjustment **25** 40 ff.
– calculation **37** 6
– competition **8** 7
– discrimination **35** 55
– expectation **10** 11
– -fixing **35** 11
– information **25** 23 f.
– minimum resale **35** 10
– modification **25** 41
– purchase **10** 12
– recommendation, non-binding **35** 12
– reduction **37** 48

Principle
– country-of-origin **4** 18, **23** 32, **25** 26
– CPC-N **37** 16
– destination **30** 7 f.
– exhaustion **13** 64
– of contractual freedom **15** 13
– of exhaustion **13** 63 ff.
– of proportionality **15** 68 f.
– once-only **9** 11
– proportionality **15** 68

Priority
– misaligned **5** 13
– policy **8** 22

Privacy **18** 50 ff., **22** 53 f., **28** 101, **34** 22, 39, **37** 4
– by design **38** 25
– concern **24** 44
– electronic communications **29** 2
– implication **34** 62
– policy **22** 53, **28** 14
– regulator **34** 65
– user **18** 52, **34** 8

Privacy notice **24** 44, **29** 18, 34 f., 53
– layered **29** 36

Private
– and family life **33** 29
– capital **5** 24
– copying **40** 32 f.
– enforcement **21** 22
– equity **6** 20
– funding **6** 19
– investment **6** 1, 17 f.
– law **27** 3
– Let's Play **40** 34
– partnership company **11** 20
– use **40** 35

Proactive
– content monitoring **34** 19
– culturalisation **20** 19

Procedure **23** 37 ff., **32** 33
– dialogic **23** 46

Process
– approval **19** 15
– creative **16** 24
– culturalisation **20** 29
– deal **10** 18
– exploration **6** 3

Processing **34** 43
– automated **29** 17, 43
– data **32** 68
– lawful **29** 30 f.
– personal data **29** 31

Product
– complementary **13** 46
– cycle **5** 9
– design **21** 28
– improvement processing **29** 24
– safety legislation, EU **24** 41

Production **12** 38, **40** 27 ff.
– phase **12** 57 ff., 75
– risk **6** 18
– video game **8** 15

Profiling **29** 17, 27, 34, 43, **38** 28
– child **29** 44

Profit **5** 42 ff.
– peak **11** 50
– shifting **11** 40

Program
– trade-in **21** 39
– youth protection **23** 27

Promotion **36** 54 ff.
– of culture **7** 37
– of game **7** 7

Property
– intellectual **12** 27, 30, 90, **27** 3

– licensed **12** 23 ff.
– tax **11** 4
Proportionality **7** 43 ff., **23** 23, **32** 56
– dynamic **33** 27
Protection **27** 28
– child **32** 59
– data **18** 43
– of minors **22** 9, **24** 45 ff.
– of minors in digital environments draft bill **26** 31
– youth **4** 18, **34** 22, 26, 57
Prototype **8** 3, **12** 44
– video game **8** 15
Provider
– electronic service **30** 8
– hosting **28** 64, 66
– information society service **33** 4
– obligations **32** 24 ff.
Provision
– anti-steering **35** 65
– boilerplate **19** 61
– exclusivity **36** 65
Publicity Directive **9** 6
Publishing
– indie **18** 34
– self-publishing **12** 13
– video game **18** 3, 27
Purchase
– in-app **16** 47
– in-game **22** 26, **26** 10, **29** 22
– price **10** 12

Questionnaire **22** 27
– PEGI **22** 35

R&D
– aid **8** 10, 17 ff.
– grant **8** 17
– loan **8** 17
– state aid **8** 3
– tax break **8** 17
Rate VAT **30** 44
Rating **23** 39
– age **18** 47, **22** 26, 60, **23** 15, 21, 31, **26** 37, **34** 3, 58
– PEGI **22** 25, 44, 62 f.
– USK **22** 44
Rating board **22** 58
– IARC **22** 44
Recording **40** 5
– temporary **40** 31
Redress **32** 41, 62
– mechanism **28** 94, **34** 33
Regional
– fund **18** 44
– pricing **24** 15
– registration **17** 9
– variation **18** 8 f.
Registration **13** 38
– design **27** 27
– strategy **17** 32 ff.
– trademark **17** 3 ff., 37
Regulation **25** 2
– broadcasting **24** 38
– ex ante **35** 58
– insider trading **10** 4
– money laundering **9** 75
– Net Neutrality **28** 59
Regulatory
– challenges, cross-cutting **24** 36 ff.
– change **36** 24 f.
– complexity **12** 20
– framework **24** 1, **39** 14 ff.
– landscape **5** 33
Release **31** 17 ff.
– condition **19** 27
– date **31** 5
Reporting **34** 51
– mechanism, grievance **22** 52
– period **19** 48
– tool, in-game **32** 40
Reproduction **40** 31, **41** 19
– identical **40** 29
Requirement **39** 3
– labeling **23** 20, 36
– minimum **32** 62, **40** 54
– novelty **27** 27
Research and development **5** 32, **11** 43, **12** 18
– activity **11** 44
– aid **8** 8
Resources **20** 42
– limited **18** 33
– state **7** 14
Responsibility **5** 16, **19** 58
– parental **34** 40
– platform **31** 24 ff.
Restriction **40** 62
– pricing **35** 10 ff.
– transfer **27** 40
Return, VAT **30** 18
Revenue **15** 73, **36** 62
– app **2** 26
– marketing **15** 49
– -sharing **12** 28, 36, 50, **16** 49
– software **2** 26
– stream **18** 28 ff., 42
Revenue share **15** 58, **18** 29, **19** 49
– day-zero **19** 46
Review
– hierarchy **23** 17
– preventive **9** 17
Rights **40** 18 ff.
– already-created **9** 28
– ancillary **40** 27
– child **22** 47
– distribution **13** 64, **24** 10
– erasure **38** 24

- exclusive **13** 6, **14** 40, **15** 16, 56, 76, **17** 4, **19** 25

Rights reservation **14** 46 ff., 53 ff., 58, 59
- asset-based **14** 60
- source-based **14** 60

Right to Repair Regulation **21** 31 f.

Risk **6** 1, **20** 33, **29** 40, **36** 49, 80
- appetite **12** 21
- Atlas **23** 3
- -based approach **32** 63
- cultural **20** 40
- dimension **23** 43

Rome I Regulation **25** 12

Royalty **16** 33, **19** 52
- advance **6** 32

Safe harbour **23** 47, **34** 19, **35** 17, 25
- principle **28** 40
- threshold **35** 20

Sale of Goods Directive (EU) **25** 9

Sales
- tax **11** 4
- territory **35** 13

Sanction **22** 67, **25** 52 f., **28** 30, **35** 51
- financial **26** 36

Scope **21** 7
- growth **12** 74
- of protection **17** 10, 40 ff.

Search engine **28** 53
- very large online **32** 11

Sector
- association **41** 13
- contractualised **41** 34 ff.

Self
- -billing **30** 29
- -declaration **22** 24, **34** 9, 14 f., 32, 45 f., 67
- -developed software **11** 32
- -learning AI **32** 34
- -publishing **2** 19, **6** 32 f., **8** 6, **12** 13, 32 f., **24** 9, **31** 23

Self-regulation **22** 5 f., **26** 55, **33** 62
- body, voluntary **23** 6
- regulated **23** 28

Self-regulatory
- body **23** 26, 47, **37** 21
- code **39** 30
- content rating system **22** 1
- framework **33** 47
- initiative **21** 30

Seller **10** 3
- remote **30** 36, 38

Share
- company **11** 20
- market **35** 20
- revenue **15** 58

Shareholders' Rights Directive **9** 6

Single Member Company Directive **9** 6

Slogan **17** 15, 30, **36** 18
- marketing **36** 15, 17

Small and medium-sized enterprise (SME) **5** 32, **7** 49, **8** 22, **9** 26
- aid **8** 10, 20 ff.
- friendly **8** 29
- risk-taking **8** 21
- support **5** 34, **8** 21

Small Investor Protection Act **9** 73

Social media **2** 38, **12** 20, **20** 4

Social media platform **36** 48, **37** 46, **40** 48
- traditional **28** 45

Societas Europaea (SE) **9** 3, 8, 34 ff.

Software **13** 24
- ad-blocking **13** 62
- ecosystem **2** 9
- esports **41** 29
- parental control **34** 58, 63
- piracy **31** 18
- protected **41** 4

Software Directive **4** 19, 22, **13** 9, 18, 44, 48 ff., 53, 55, **27** 35, **41** 23

Solution
- game-specific **27** 43
- technical **28** 62
- third-party **12** 37

Source **14** 30
- verified **34** 10

Source code **13** 56, **19** 12
- software **13** 6
- storage **10** 19

Specific
- enforcement action **34** 55
- guidance **34** 26 ff.
- process **20** 35

Speech
- free **33** 68
- hate **33** 31 f.

Stakeholder **12** 61 ff., **16** 46
- confidence **12** 43
- consultations **22** 7
- key **12** 4, **16** 6 f.
- notification **36** 27
- video game **28** 67

Standard
- accounting **11** 30
- content moderation **24** 38

Startup **6** 20, **7** 49
- online **9** 46

State aid **7** 1 ff., 8 ff., 19 ff., 26 ff., 57 f.
- criteria **8** 14
- framework **8** 4 ff., 19
- measure **7** 51
- R&D **8** 3
- regulation **8** 30

State Treaty on Youth Protection in the Media **34** 59

Steam **6** 6, 10, 15, **12** 20, 78, **24** 6, **27** 37, **28** 86, **31** 11, **33** 3, 6, **36** 48
Strategy
- BIK+ **34** 25
- compliance **39** 48
- localisation **18** 3
- monetisation **24** 11, 17
- national game industry **8** 28
Streaming **28** 69 ff., **40** 6, **41** 21
- unauthorised **28** 70
Streaming platform **28** 38, 45, **40** 5
- video game **14** 54
Strict liability **28** 27
- regime **28** 28
Studio **7** 6
- AA **12** 9
- AAA **12** 2, 9
- game **1** 4
- hybrid **5** 5
- identity **5** 10 ff.
Subscription **4** 4, **6** 9, **12** 26, **24** 5, 8, 19 ff.
- feature **24** 34
- fee **18** 37
Subscription service **6** 10, **16** 47
- multi-game **35** 38
Support **5** 43
- customer **12** 88
- government **18** 43 ff.
- post-release **12** 80
- public **8** 6, 26
- SME **5** 34, **8** 21
- structures **5** 25
- technical **19** 18
Sustainability **18** 62 ff.
- environmental **21** 42
- law **36** 36
Sustainable Finance Disclosure Regulation (SFDR) **21** 14
Synchronisation **16** 37
- license **16** 19, 36, 65, **37** 42
- right **16** 13, 64
System
- age-rating **24** 10
- age verification **24** 43
- complaint-handling **32** 33
- IARC **23** 21
- operator **31** 24
Targeted advertising **29** 17, **32** 54, **36** 50, **38** 17, 23 f., 26 ff.
Tax **11** 1 f., 4, 59
- administration **30** 38
- advantage **10** 23
- advice **9** 28
- authority **30** 18, 27
- benefit **7** 12
- deductibility **11** 37 ff.
- deduction **7** 13
- evasion **11** 58
- financial statement **11** 46
- -free funding **11** 45
- incentive **18** 44
- outside the EU **30** 39
Tax break **8** 25, **11** 42 ff.
- R&D **8** 17
Tax credit **7** 12, 56
Tax liability **30** 40 f.
- historical **30** 42
Technology Transfer Block Exemption Regulation (TTBER) **35** 23 ff.
Termination **19** 34, 36, **25** 46 ff.
- at will **33** 71
- button **25** 51
- early **16** 27
- ordinary **25** 49
Terms and conditions **25** 18, 35, **32** 27 ff., **34** 51
Terms of Service **12** 91, **14** 55, **27** 5
Terms of Use **33** 72 ff., 79
Territory **16** 34 ff., **17** 8 f., **19** 28 ff.
- exclusive **35** 14
Terrorist content **33** 63 f.
Terrorist Content Online Regulation (Regulation 2021/784) **4** 19
Terrorist organisation **23** 12
Test **12** 65
- balancing **29** 21
- cultural **7** 40 f., 59, **8** 14
- impairment **10** 26
- proportionality **7** 53
- three-step **14** 10, 39 ff.
Third-party
- business **31** 36 ff.
- claim **19** 56
- content **33** 5 ff., 54
- contributor **16** 26
- cookie **29** 29
- data **29** 5, 16 f.
- IP **27** 17 ff., **37** 42
- tool **36** 52
- unregistered **32** 40
- verification, trusted **34** 28
Threshold **30** 41
- age **34** 15, 40
- safe harbour **35** 20
Title **13** 31
- distinctive **17** 33
- video game **17** 24 f.
Toleration **40** 42 ff., 51
- passive **40** 46
Toxic behaviour **22** 4, **31** 27
Toxicity **20** 6
Toxic player **33** 8, 19, 40
Tracking technology **38** 30
Transfer
- intellectual property **6** 31
- of ownership **27** 32

– restriction **27** 40
Translation, direct **18** 18
Translator **20** 10
Transparency **24** 18, **25** 4, 10, 52, **28** 102, **29** 4, 33 ff., **32** 50 ff., **34** 39, **39** 26, 31 ff.
– obligation **15** 18 ff., 27, 55, **32** 52
– report **32** 36 f.
– requirement, specific **39** 21
– rule **15** 25
Treaty on the Functioning of the European Union (TFEU) **8** 2
Trusted
– advisor **36** 75, 79
– flagger **32** 48, **33** 59, 67
– third-party verification **34** 28
Trusted Platform Module (TPM) **13** 54, **28** 57
Twitch **16** 63, **28** 71, **36** 48, **40** 2, 8, 53
Two-factor authentication (2FA) **31** 33

UCPD **4** 21, **37** 11, 46, **39** 17
– blacklist **37** 10
– Guidance **26** 11 f., 27, **37** 13
– guideline **39** 8
UK **2** 12, **9** 61, **39** 34
– -based publisher **18** 60
– cases **13** 61
– Games Fund **18** 45
Unauthorised
– access **29** 47
– copy **31** 20
– derivative work **13** 50
– login attempts **31** 33
– sampling **16** 57
– streaming **28** 70
UN Committee on the Rights of the Child **29** 44
UN Convention on the Rights of the Child **23** 3
Underage user **34** 16
Unfair
– commercial practice **28** 84, 89, **34** 17, **37** 2, 5 ff.
– competition **13** 57, **17** 35, **37** 2, 22 ff., 28, 30
– contract terms directive **25** 4, 41, 42, 43, **26** 8
– practice **39** 20
Unfair Commercial Practices Directive (UCPD) **24** 18, 40, **25** 6, **26** 8, 23, 41 ff., **36** 34, **37** 5, 15, **39** 16
United Nations Convention on the Rights of the Child **29** 37
United Nations Guiding Principles on Business and Human Rights (UNGPs) **21** 21
Unterhaltungssoftware Selbstkontrolle (USK) **18** 49
Use
– commercial **40** 52 ff.
– descriptive **41** 30
– educational **14** 4
– excessive **34** 37
– genuine **17** 37
– incidental **17** 51
– non-commercial **40** 52
User
– consent tick box **24** 27
– content **33** 77
– -friendliness **32** 39
– -friendly refund policy **24** 41
– -generated content **4** 28, **12** 27, 93, **16** 66 ff., **22** 4, 52, **27** 13 ff., 15, **28** 92 f., **32** 3, 16 ff., 17, 22, **33** 6
– of special relevance **39** 13
– privacy **18** 52, **34** 8
– tracking **32** 44
User-base **31** 21
– large **31** 15
USK **22** 16, **23** 2, 6, 9, 21, 26, 28, 33 ff., 40, 43 f., 51, 53, **26** 33, 37 ff.
– age rating **26** 39
– -certified parental control **23** 32
– rating **22** 44

Value Added Tax (VAT) **11** 7, 9, **30** 1, 12, 34
Valve **13** 65, **28** 86, **41** 8
VAT **11** 14, 24, **30** 13 ff., 23, 27, 33
– EU **30** 15
– invoice **30** 2, 16
VAT rate **30** 11 f., 44
– EU **30** 47
– standard **30** 47
VAT return **30** 18
– simplified **30** 19
Vertical Block Exemption Regulation (VBER) **35** 18 ff.
Very Large Online Platform (VLOP) **32** 11, 24, 36, 43 f., 57, **34** 21, **38** 14
Violence **18** 21, **22** 20, **23** 12
– content **34** 60
– gratuitous **34** 65
– video game **22** 2
Virtual
– assistant **35** 59
– domiciliary right **25** 53
– goods **24** 30, **26** 58
– object **27** 54, 56
– reality **1** 3, **18** 57
Virtual currency **28** 89
– in-game **28** 84
Virtual property **27** 2
Voluntary
– ADR **15** 36
– agreement **28** 59
– alternative dispute resolution **15** 75
– code of conduct **41** 13
– compliance **33** 52
– self-regulation body **23** 6
Voucher
– multi-purpose **30** 14 f.

– single-purpose **30** 14 f.

Waiver **25** 33, **40** 43

Warranty **9** 68, **19** 8, 10, 53 ff.
– technical **19** 55

Waste Electrical and Electronic Equipment (WEEE) **21** 28

Waste Electronic and Electric Equipment Directive (WEEED) **21** 25 ff.

WIPO Copyright Treaty **13** 19

Withdrawal **25** 28 ff.
– button **25** 34
– consumer **25** 30
– function **25** 34
– right **25** 7
– right of **25** 33
– waiver **24** 27

Withholding tax **10** 31, **11** 8, **19** 52

Work-for-hire **13** 35 ff., **16** 30, **27** 25

World Intellectual Property Organization (WIPO) **10** 39

Youth protection **4** 18, **33** 28 ff., **34** 5, 22, 24, 26, 57
– mechanism, operating system **23** 30
– programme **23** 27, **34** 18
– requirement, non-harmonised **34** 52 ff.
– system **34** 50
– technical **34** 6
– tool **32** 55

Youth Protection Act (JuSchG) **23** 3, 7, 9 ff., **26** 38